VISION OF A MENTAL PATIENT

by

Ted Hodge

DORRANCE PUBLISHING CO., INC.
PITTSBURGH, PENNSYLVANIA 15222

This book is dedicated to everyone, ever!

The contents of this work, including, but not limited to, the accuracy of events, people, and places depicted; opinions expressed; permission to use previously published materials included; and any advice given or actions advocated are solely the responsibility of the author, who assumes all liability for said work and indemnifies the publisher against any claims stemming from publication of the work.

All Rights Reserved
Copyright © 2010 by Ted Hodge
No part of this book may be reproduced or transmitted
in any form or by any means, electronic or mechanical,
including photocopying, recording, or by any information
storage and retrieval system without permission in
writing from the publisher.

ISBN: 978-1-4349-0748-6

Printed in the United States of America

First Printing

For more information or to order additional books, please contact:
Dorrance Publishing Co., Inc.
701 Smithfield Street
Pittsburgh, Pennsylvania 15222
U.S.A.
1-800-788-7654
www.dorrancebookstore.com

CONTENTS

Part one:
Politics In General 1
Abortion 13
The Environment 17
Stem Cell Research 21
Education 24
Healthcare 30
Aids (a cure?) 34
Dick Cheney and his lies 37
Genocides and foreign policy 46

Part two:
The Monolith, An apology 88
The Collective Subconscious 91
Astronomy 111
Reflections 122
The Language of the Mad 129
Senses 155
Photosynthesis 167
What is a connection? 173
Magnetism 180
Volcanoes 187
Lysergic Acid Diethylamide 199
2001-2010 209
The Shocking Result 239
Ancient Egypt 246

Part three:
Morals in Society, A Short autobiography 253
More Politics 321
Religion 326

INTRODUCTION

Greetings, my friends, how are you? My name is Ted (John), and I would like to share something with all of you. I am an ex-mental patient, but I believe my life and my consciousness holds a purpose, of something, which could change the world. I would like for you to take a tour with me, into the vastness of the seemingly unknown. I am about to attempt to teach you of a vision, which has the potential of miraculous proportions.

I will display the basis of this vision, through a method of political, scientific, and moral idealization. When you begin to read this book, I will first try to gain credibility with you, through a thorough examination of world politics. I started to write this book in 2008, so in the first stages of my political elaborations I will refer to President Obama as the president elect, rather than as the president. When you further indulge into the political part of my vision, my elaborations will then become time compliant.

Furthermore, once you have got the gist of my political idea, you will enter into the realm of the vision, of what is called "knowing." I do realize that you are not ready for this aspect, thus my method of a progressive human to human connection, of a moral and sensual idealism. At first, this book will seem typical, and not out of the ordinary. However, once we begin to connect with one another, you will fathom this potential worldly healing type of process.

I have set up this book so that it will grow in significance as we go. The political section, of which you will read first, is only a mere glimpse of my and soon to be our visionary enterprise. We will journey into the depths of the human mind, with an enhanced painted artistic view, of the realms of mind, space, and time.

This book will set a process of the human psyche into motion, which will aid your comprehensive ability to understand many things. What you will understand most is the process of nature and my discovery of what I call the universal relationship. I will expose to you a wide variety of scientific theories, thus leading us to a breakthrough for the ages. Through this method, you will commence to comprehend what I call "the feel." This "feel" will be sent within your senses, and thus combine all five of your basic senses into one. This sensation will hopefully manifest within you when you read the 2001- 2010 segment of the Monolith, part two portion of this book. Once you experience this sensual action within yourself, you will progress and transform your psyche into another dimension through what is called the primary goal.

Once I have presented to you my political ideals and my scientific visions, I will tell you a good portion of how this all came to be. My life has been extremely out of the ordinary, and some of it might be hard for you to swallow, but I assure you all that the validity of my vision is as real as the skin on your hand. I will be repetitive at times for a purpose of contact between our minds, so that you can appropriately and sufficiently fathom this vision. When it comes to morality (which will be the constant message throughout this book), I will be very insistent so that the human race can hopefully find itself and commence to maintain a neo-function, which is relative to everything. My theory of scientific equivalency will set this prime basis into its function of original intent.

In the Monolith segment (Part two), I will try to elaborate a good deal of paranormal revelations to you, and I will do so in the most down-to-Earth of methods. If I am to appeal to all of you, this discussion must be explained in a way of which we can all understand. For example, there is a section called Volcanoes in the Monolith segment, which I could have called Volcanism and there is another section called Ancient Egypt which I could have dubbed as Egyptology and I decided to name these portions as such, so that my entire audience can fathom all of which we are about to embark on. I will also not leave you with inadequate means, leaving you to ponder on my elaborations without the required and essential data.

I would like for you to think of this book as a conversation between me, the author, and you, the reader. Of course, this will be a one-way conversation, seeing that you can't talk back to me. However, when you fathom what is called the Language of the Mad you just might be able to communicate with me through a process of prolific dimensions.

I have babbled enough in this intro. It is now *time* to indulge in a vision of love and hope. Without any more delay, please enjoy reading Vision of a Mental Patient.

Vision of a mental patient

PART ONE:
POLITICS IN GENERAL

"Europa!" No, I mean "Eureka!" The date is November 5, 2008, and last night, to my delight, Barack Obama and his running mate Joseph Biden were elected president and vice president of the United States of America. I strongly believe that President-elect Obama, the first African-American to hold such high an office in the history of the United States, will be a great leader in the years to come. As a matter of fact, I am sure of it.

In this political section of this book I will touch on political views which I have developed over the course of my lifetime. We will discuss important issues such as abortion, the environment, education, healthcare, Aids, and most disgusting of all, genocides. We will, in relation to these issues, also discuss virtues such as tolerance, decency, fairness in politics, and the future of our country, and more importantly of our planet.

Before I elaborate any further, I would now like to present you with the wonderful thank-you letter, which I received from Barack and Michelle Obama after donating a measly twenty dollars to their campaign.

It reads such as follows:

Dear Mr. Hodge,

The victory we achieved on November 4 means so much too so many. But to all of us, it is a stirring affirmation of our country's most fundamental promise. America is a place where anything we choose to dream together, anything for which we choose to work together, is possible. Ours was never the likeliest campaign for the presidency. We didn't start with much money, or many endorsements. Our campaign was not hatched in the halls of Washington. It was built by working men and women, students and retirees, who dug into what little savings they had to give five dollars, and ten dollars, and twenty dollars to this cause.

It grew from the millions of Americans who volunteered, organized, and proved that nearly two centuries later, a government of the people, by the people and for the people has not perished from the Earth.

Ted, this is your victory. But even as we celebrate, we know the challenges are the greatest of our lifetime: two wars, a planet in peril, and the worst financial crisis in a century. The road ahead will be long. Our climb will be steep. And we will be asking you to join in the work of remaking this nation, the only way it's been done in America for 221 years. Block by block, brick by brick, calloused hand by calloused hand. What began twenty-one months ago in the depth of winter must not end on a night in autumn. This victory alone is not the change we seek; it is only the chance for us to make that change.

Ted, this is our moment, this is our time to put our people back to work, and open doors of opportunity for our kids; to restore prosperity and promote the cause of peace; to reclaim the American dream and reaffirm that fundamental truth; that out of many we are one; that while we breathe, we hope, and where we are met with cynicism and doubt, and those of us who will tell us that we can't, we will respond with that timeless creed that sums up the spirit of a people: "Yes we can!"

For now, please accept our deepest thanks. We will never forget you.

Sincerely, the Obama family

And I thank you Barack and your beautiful wife, and your two adorable children. Barack, you are absolutely correct. "Yes we can" and we will, and you do not yet realize just how right you are. This book is my thank you to the Obama family, and to every human being in history who have bravely and fiercely fought for the cause of human good.

Before we tackle any major issues, I would like to stress, that yes, I am a Democrat. However, I am not one of those angry Democrats who actually believe that all Republicans for the most part are bad people. Not only do I believe that it is wrong for Democrats to make this claim, I also think it to be a blasphemous statement. I quote the honorable Rodney King who, after having his clock cleaned by three Los Angeles policemen, had the strength, class, and decency to say, "Can't we all just get along?" It is imperative that as a people, we must first learn to get along in order to contribute to a more healthy and prosperous society.

Growing up, I pretty much had no chance to become a Republican, and this is due to the fact that my family is so left wing democratic and liberal. I learned a lot from my father growing up about political theories and the art of politics. However, some of my beliefs are quite different from those of my family. As a matter of fact, there have even been occasions when I have considered voting Republican.

My father had a short, yet, interesting vocation in Massachusetts politics. He worked with such political figures like John

Kerry, Paul Tsongas, and Mike Dukakis. My father is hardcore liberal, but I myself tend to fluctuate between moderate and liberal views. My father is the type of guy that you could call with a problem in the middle of the night, and he would hop right out of bed and be there in a New York minute. If it wasn't for his perseverance and discipline, I would be much worse off today. Thanks, Dad!

Moving on, I must stress that we must have fairness in politics in order to hear and understand one another with clarity. Therefore, I believe it is best to share views between the Democratic Party and the Republican Party, as well as any of the other political parties which exist in our nation. This view is essential, if we are ever going to return the United States of America to the prosperous nation that it once was. As Obama says, "Yes we can!"

I personally believe that anger, as far as politics is concerned, is a useless emotion. Unless you are talking about real world problems such as mass starvation and genocide, the emotion of anger is rendered useless. A trait we could all benefit from is tolerance when appropriate, and intolerance when necessary. My point is that there is good and bad in everything. I was born and raised in Massachusetts, which is one of the most democratic states in the union. Despite this fact, I have as many Republican friends as Democratic friends. Go figure.

You see, my father who can be much more than often correct in his political views, is, however, far too angry. I don't think he realizes that when anger driven views are manifested to those of a different view, it tends to be a major turnoff. That is why in this book I will state my case as assertively persuasive as I possibly can. That is how we must learn to communicate as a people.

Over the last decade, give or take, I began to take a much more in-depth attitude toward politics and our world. I can honestly say that now at the age of 35, I have become an independent thinker. I no longer have any bias caused by someone else's beliefs, especially that of my family members.

Again, I now must stress, that only in a fair manner can the Democratic Party regain its standing (just as it has lately). Whether Democrat, Republican, independent, libertarian, or green party etc., we must once again learn as a people to stand for what we believe in, and do so in whatever manner appropriate in relation to the particular problem.

I believe what I like most about Republicans is that they tend to have outstanding family values. According to my views, they are usually wrong on political issues. But you will seldom find a Republican family that does not love one another. It seems to me that Republicans will usually vote on culture, rather than on concrete issues.

Now, back to the point I made about us as Americans and our need to once again stand for what one believes in. You may recall the Reagan Administration Iran Contra scandal involving the famous Oliver North and his pleading of the Fifth Amendment of the United States Constitution. Before I elaborate, I would like to explain in clear terms the Fifth Amendment: Denies a trial for a supreme crime, unless after indictment of a grand jury; Does not allow repeated trials, unless in very precise circumstances, also does not allow punishment without correct process of American law; provides that the accused does not have to be forced to testify against oneself. It also prohibits the United States Government from taking one's property without "appropriate compensation" which is the basis of eminent domain in the United States of America. In the most basic of terms, the part of the Fifth Amendment that North pleaded is "The right to remain silent."

You may remember that Oliver North of the National Security Council was the main culprit involved in the Iran Contra Scandal. This scandal involved secret operations of our executive branch of government. This scandal involved the sales of types of military equipment to the country of Iran, a country that we did not get along with at all. It involved the providing of military aid to the Contra rebels of the Central American country of Nicaragua, although a democratic congress banned these actions. In 1979, the Sandinistas led a hard fought revolution in Nicaragua, thus taking control of their government. Reagan claimed in 1981 that the Sandinistas created a communist dictatorship. And we all know how Reagan felt about communism. By 1985, the Reagan Administration started a low profile arms for hostages agreement, which was created in order to free hostages who were being kept by the terrorists of Lebanon. By 1986, the scandal was fully blown open. In 1989, North was convicted on four separate charges, including the destruction of evidence. However, these convictions would be terminated in the early 90's. The only person who ended up actually serving time was a counterpart of North, Thomas G. Clines. It was even rumored that North used some of this dirty money for personal reasons.

In conclusion to all of this misbehavior by North, he would then claim that he stood for what he believed in. All of a sudden, there were North fanatics everywhere who would say that North should run for president their point being, that although he did something that was morally and ethically wrong, he was praised by many. I believe the reason for this is because in the 1980's there were so few people in America who actually stood for what they believed in (for the most part). So that was the exact problem: so few Americans were standing for what they believed in. Therefore, although what North did was wrong, he was still praised. So, not only as human beings must we stand for something, but we also must stand for things that are morally correct.

In a new direction, I would like to share with you a brief summarization of how I view the political press. My two favorite T.V. shows are C.N.N.'s Situation Room with Wolf Blitzer, and Mad T.V. I guess I have to watch something super intelligent or hilariously stupid. But then again, sometimes Mad T.V. can actually be more intelligent than the situation room. I believe that Wolf Blitzer is the best political reporter of our time. Why do I think so? I believe Wolf is the best because he is the most fair to the two major political parties as much as he can be. His questions are just as tough towards either of the two of our

VISION OF A MENTAL PATIENT

main political parties; he displays no bias whatsoever. I respect the fact that he doesn't give a clue as to what his own personal political views are. And he shouldn't either. That is why he is so outstanding in my opinion. The poor guy has to think about politics 24/7; if I had to discuss politics as often as he does, I would be bald by now because I would have pulled all the hairs out of my head.

I have a strong admiration for many of C.N.N.'s political analysts. For Democratic analysts, I like Paul Begala (a former Clinton advisor), James Carville (known as the raging Cajun), and Donna Brazil (probably the most well rounded of all). I also like some Republican analysts whom I usually disagree with but still respect, such as Lisa Sanchez and Bill Bennett.

I wish they would bring back the political show "Crossfire" or as I used to call it "four guys yelling" which is basically what the show was, until they moderated it like that of an official political debate. Crossfire in its later days, when I was a fan, featured James Carville and Paul Begala for Democrats. And for conservatives, it featured Tucker Carlson and Robert Novak. I used the word conservative instead of Republican because Tucker Carlson is now a libertarian, and Robert Novak is not technically registered as a republican, but they still represented the ideals of the Republican agenda.

I would now like to state something which will help right-wing conservatives and left-wing Democrats to make substantial progress. I've always been told by my fellow left-wingers that I should have hatred toward right-wingers, especially that of Tucker Carlson. But the truth is that although I disagree with Tucker on just about every political issue, I must admit that I like Tucker very much. Why? Because he simply seems to be a likeable person; also, I have heard it through the grapevine that he is a very polite guy, as well as possessing a charming demeanor.

You see, Tucker has a strong belief in a person's right to become and stay wealthy. I was watching C.N.N. a few years back, and Paul Begala was livid about a new Bush Administration tax bill that favored the rich, and basically screwed the middle class and the poor. Begala concluded by saying that anyone who favored this bill would go to hell. Tucker responded by saying sarcastically "Relax Reverend Paul, it's just a tax bill." I just simply believe that Tucker did not realize what he said. A tax bill can be evil, if it is unfair to the middle class, especially the needy. I myself believe that there is nothing wrong with being a rich person as long as we try to help those who are in financial peril. If Tucker does realize that this tax bill was wrong, then he ought to rethink his political theory. I believe a guy as young as Tucker (he was 35 when on Crossfire) to be in his position is very impressive. So you see, although I disagree with Tucker's extreme right-wing beliefs, it doesn't mean I wouldn't have a beer with the guy (if I still drank, which fortunately I don't). So I just ask Tucker to rethink his political theory and maybe develop a fairer economic view that could still help the wealthy but not leave others in the dust.

As I have already stated, I am not an angry Democrat (most of the time) and although Robert Novak, whom I've previously mentioned, did exploit classified information of the federal agent Sara Plame and her husband Joseph Wilson, my anger is limited. But this was a very selfish act by Novak. Yet I am not one who believes it is necessary to throw Mr. Novak directly into jail. However, I do believe that he should be confronted and severely reprimanded for this selfish action. You just can't go around displaying rash behavior and risking people's lives while putting classified information into the public eye. However, I stress that we must exercise freedom of the press and not keep the American public in the dark. But this was different, because, face it, some facts are better off not revealed to the public. Meaning, F.B.I. or C.I.A. operations, when revealed could cause a major catastrophe.

Now I would like to make a point I developed while watching Crossfire during the early days of the 2004 presidential election. This election was between John Kerry of the Democratic Party, and George W. Bush of the Republican Party. Novak made a comment stating that John Kerry, who has an outstanding war record, probably got one of his purple hearts by accidentally shooting himself in the foot. This was a completely bogus comment. Why? Because in the recent 2008 presidential election between democrat Barack Obama and republican John McCain, the democrats completely honored John McCain's outstanding war record, just as they should. I just simply believe that John Kerry should have been treated with the same level of respect and dignity.

At this point, I would like to briefly discuss the honorable war records of John McCain and John Kerry. First, we will look at the war record of John McCain.

McCain graduated from the U.S. naval academy in 1958. He soon would achieve the position of naval aviator, flying ground attack aircraft from aircraft carriers. In 1967, he would be shot down over Hanoi and suffer severe injury. He then became a prisoner of war (P.O.W.), and became subject to cruel methods of torture for about the next six years. I'm glad to say that in mid March of 1973, McCain's horrible ordeal as a P.O.W. would cease. Presently, the honorable John McCain, due to his severe injuries of war, still couldn't lift his arms over his head.

John Kerry, on the other hand, also has an impressive war record. John Kerry served in the U.S. military from 1966 to 1970. Kerry's first tour of duty was as an ensign of the guided missile frigate, the U.S.S Gridley in 1968. Kerry would also ask his superiors for more hands on type duty in the Vietnam conflict. He would soon be promoted to rank of lieutenant. In June of 1968, he would leave the U.S.S. Gridley for his swift boat training at a naval base in Coronado.

By November of 1968, Kerry's swift boat duties would commence. He would lead five man crews on many patrols into enemy occupied territory, and would be subject to the horrors of war. Soon after, in 1969, Kerry would take charge of the PC4-94 and its crew. He would argue with some of his superiors over certain war actions. To mention one, he and some of his fellow officers would report on what was known as the "Fire free zone" policy, which was estranging the Vietnamese and that

Kerry's swift boat (PC4-94) actions were not effective to their goal of cutting off Viet Cong supply lines. Ultimately, John Kerry would receive a silver star and three purple hearts for his courage in the war.

You may have noticed that I gave a longer assessment of John Kerry's war record than that of John McCain. This was not in any way to show favoritism. The reason I gave more information on Kerry's war record than McCain's is because lately, McCain has gotten the credit he deserves, but on the other hand, Kerry has not been treated as fairly. The truth is it really doesn't matter which one of these two good men served more honorably. The bottom line is that they both served honorably, and I'm absolutely sure that John McCain and John Kerry don't want to have an argument over who served more honorably. You see, that is exactly why these two men are honorable, because they honor others.

I now must say something else in John Kerry's defense. It has been said by many that Kerry was wrong to speak against the Vietnam War after his tenure of military service. But think about this: John Kerry volunteered for war duty in a war that he did not believe in, and fought honorably. On the other hand, Dick Cheney dodged the draft by obtaining five deferments in order to avoid this same war. However, Dick Cheney had claimed that he believed in this war. So that means that Kerry performed his duties despite his objections of war, and Cheney avoided his duties, despite the fact that he was for this war. So if you want to put down John Kerry, you might as well put down Mr. Cheney, too. And one more thing in Kerry's defense: during the 2004 presidential election, John Kerry was accused of being a flip flopper; that is, due to the Bush campaign, Kerry was forced to perform a political juggling act. I've heard many of my fellow democrats claim that they no longer "fully" support John Kerry. Well, I must say for myself that I still stand by Massachusetts Senator John Kerry 100%, and I say to my fellow Democrats, that they should also continue to stand by Senator Kerry as well. John Kerry would have been a fine president. I am absolutely certain (as many others are), that he would have been much better than George W. Bush. It is absolutely ludicrous that George W. Bush has not been appropriately confronted for starting a bloody war under completely false pretenses in Iraq. The truth is that the U.S. was attacked by Osama Bin Laden and Al Qaeda. For years, Bin Laden has resided in the mountains of Afghanistan, but is now believed to be somewhere in Pakistan. George W. Bush and friends' claim that there were weapons of mass destruction in Iraq was nothing but a big fat lie! We'll get back to that eventually.

Another strong belief of mine is that we Americans need to be much more cautious when choosing a political candidate, especially a candidate for President of the United States. We need to observe carefully what their intentions are and we must at least try to be sure that they possess sincerity and a genuine willingness to help the American people. They should also have a deep concern for the people of the rest of the world as well. I believe that in today's world, what my party (the Democrats) lack most is sincerity. It is simply not enough to be right on the issues, but it is just as important that our elected officials are not just out for their own glory, but are also out for the glory of us all. It is paramount that we be sure that no one but no one wants to claim political power for his or her own personal or financial gain. Dick Cheney who was supposed to appoint a vice presidential candidate for George W. Bush, ended up appointing himself. Through political means, Mr. Cheney has collected millions from Halliburton Co., and has had numerous stock options due to his corruption. This is a prime example of what we cannot allow in our U.S. government, not to mention George W. Bush's involvement in the Harken industries and the Carlysle group. George W. Bush also has close ties with powerful oil gurus in Saudi Arabia, which is a country that we don't particularly have a history of good diplomatic relations with, not to mention his ties with the Bin Laden family, who, according to director Michael Moore were secretly flown out of the United States immediately after 9/11.

A common question in the United States is this: Why doesn't the president get paid more for such an important occupation? To explain my view of this, I must mention my hero and favorite athlete of all time, the legend Larry Bird. You see, Larry Bird and most other basketball players receive a much larger salary than the U.S. president for basically putting a ball in a hole. Why? I'll tell you. The reason that U.S. presidents are not paid huge amounts of money, as would be deserved, is because their salaries must be reasonably low, due to the fact that we Americans want our candidates to run for office for the good of the country and for the good of the rest of the world, and not for the thickness of their wallet. If any president or high ranking official or even any low ranking official attempts to use political power for their own financial gain, and not for the people they represent, such as George W. Bush and his counterpart Mr. Cheney did (I believe Cheney is far worse than Bush), then they have absolutely no business whatsoever running for political office in the United States. A few nights back, I was watching "Larry King Tonight" and I saw something that pleased me very much. Republican right-wing evangelist Pat Robertson stated that our new president elect Barack Obama has the potential to become one of the greatest presidents ever. Truthfully, I am not very fond of Pat Robertson or any evangelist for that matter. However, it was nice to see such friendliness between party lines.

As you may recall earlier, I mentioned that I am not an angry Democrat most of the time. However, I did in fact see something on C.N.N. recently, which really burned me up as a Democrat. Some Corporate elitist Republican made a claim that even after Obama won the presidential election fair and square, President-elect Obama should be disallowed position of president on the grounds that he might not be eligible because although Obama was born in the state of Hawaii, he actually had dual citizenship because one of his parents was born in the African nation of Kenya.
This statement is absolutely unfounded! You know, I mean it wasn't enough that there were certain Republicans who helped cheat Al Gore and the Democrats of America out of the presidency in 2000, from uncounted votes in Florida (If you want to learn more on this, I suggest Michael Moore's documentary "Fahrenheit 9/11" or Jay Roach's movie "Recount"). There are

VISION OF A MENTAL PATIENT

certain Republicans who must learn that the United States is not a dictatorship! You can't just make up the rules as you go along. Al Gore and running mate Joe Lieberman, although winning the popular vote, took their defeat graciously. In the recent 2008 presidential election, John McCain and Sarah Palin also took it graciously. So my question is "What the hell is this guy's problem?" I'm not even going to dignify this person or persons responsible for this ridiculous claim by finding out who they are! But you can bet your bippy that it was some super rich person or persons, who would take a homeless person's last nickel and not lose one minute of sleep over it! We had eight years of Ronald Reagan, four years of George H.W. Bush, and another eight years of George W. Bush. And although the democrats lost, we still respected our system of elections and did not try to alter the results after they were set in stone

At this point, I would now like to discuss with you some views that I share with a man whom I have recently come to admire. The man I am speaking of is an African American professor by the name of Cornel West. West is an affront to what he calls political nihilists. A political nihilist is one who is not just simply intoxicated with power, but is also obsessed with stifling any criticism of that exercise and abuse of power. West is also opposed to "free market fundamentalism" and he believes that those who have practiced this free market fundamentalism have trivialized concerns for public interest. To put it in the most basic of terms, Cornel West wants to achieve a moral balance. The main premises of free market fundamentalism are; aggressive militarism and escalating authoritarianism (abuse of authority).

West states many important facts, in his book "Democracy Matters." Like myself, he is not fond of evangelicals, whom he labels as evangelical nihilists. In this outstanding book of his, he states crucial facts pertaining to the economy. For example; The U.S. budget in 2004 accounted for over forty percent of the rest of the entire planet's military spending. The United States is already the most powerful nation on Earth. Just how powerful do we want to be? West also states that the U.S. ranked twenty second of the twenty-two wealthiest nations on Earth for gross national product (GNP). As a matter of fact, 0.2% of the U.S. GNP went to foreign aid. West also believes that because of our recent Bush Administration's policies, our western style democracy has no future in the Islamic world. West also claims that the need to obtain oil drives a very shameful disregard of the radically undemocratic oil wealthy Arab regimes, which remain hostile towards the existence of Israel. West also has the belief in achieving a sound balance between liberty and security. For the first time, I recently had the pleasure of actually seeing and hearing Cornel West on C.N.N. He was accompanied by Donna Brazil and Jessie Jackson, and two others whom I can't recall at this time. West spoke with such conviction and fairness. He gave president-elect Obama some sound advice. He made an analogy that Obama must differ from Bush by acting like a thermostat and not a thermometer. What West meant by this analogy, was that Obama should not simply reflect back on the American people, but he should actually make a positive change for America by being a thermostat, which can alter the temperature, instead of a thermometer, that simply reflects the temperature back to you. Get it? The last thing I will say about this brilliant man for now is that if you plan on reading this man's literature, you best have a dictionary on hand because this man's vocabulary is astounding.

Now for a brief look at the U.S. economic situation. I must first admit that economics is my weakest subject in relation to politics. However, I have enough brains in my head to realize why our United States is in such a state of economic turmoil: it is a direct result of the incompetence of the current Bush and Cheney Administration. Not only has the U.S. economy been depleted, but we have Vice President Cheney using our government in order to line his pockets with cash.

When the Clinton Administration came to a close, the U.S. had a substantial surplus, as a matter of fact an enormously substantial surplus. Now after eight years of the Bush-Cheney Administration, we are now experiencing record deficits and a recession has occurred. And if it was not for the recent corporate bailouts of AIG, Fannie May, Lehman Brothers, and a few other major corporations, we might have had another depression. Boy, Obama has really got his work cut out for himself! I strongly believe that this completely unfounded Iraq war, which the U.S. has been spending billions upon billions of dollars on is having a severely negative effect on America's economic standing. Usually, when America is involved in a war in the past, it has caused a boost in our economy. Bush has ruined our economy even in a state of war. How the hell did that happen? Enough with economics! In a new direction, I would now like to discuss the issue of torture and the Geneva Conventions. I must admit on the topic of torture or any cruel and unusual punishment I do at this present time whole-heartedly agree with republican John McCain and his views on this topic of issue. I watched some of the recent Republican National Convention, and I must say that I was very impressed with what was said in regards to John McCain's courageous acts as a P.O.W. Former republican presidential candidate Fred Thompson revealed one of these acts of courage. When John McCain was subject to cruel methods of torture, he was ordered by those who kept him prisoner to reveal the names of specific classified military personnel. McCain then proceeded to give the names of the Green Bay Packers football team's offensive line. That was quite a courageous and honorable act in my book! Therefore, I can see why McCain would be such an affront to any type of torture, and what has occurred at Guantanamo Bay in Cuba is absolutely awful.

The first pact of the Geneva Conventions was signed in 1864; it was received well by all European nations as well as the United States and some South American and Asian nations. There were provisions in 1906, 1929, 1949, and 1977. These new provisions would include contingencies for the care and humane treatment of sick and wounded military workers and soldiers. We as a race must continue to create more moral proclamations such as the Geneva Conventions. In order for our human race to grow, we must continue to learn from our mistakes as well as from the actions we have taken that have proved beneficial to our humane cause. A "Utopia" is a place of ideal perfection of a government, through laws and social conditions. A utopia may not yet be achieved, but the United States of America and its opportunity for a pursuit of happiness is the closest we've come so far. I believe that one of the most imperative segments of the United States government is the system of checks and balances. The first time I heard of the checks and balances system, I thought it pertained to money; you know, "checks and balances." Get it? However, the checks and balances system is much different from that. The system of checks and balances is the system of government, by which the powers and functions of government can be fair, and prevent anyone from obtaining a dangerous level of power.

You see, through the fundamentals of the United States Constitution, our government is divided up properly through this checks and balances system. It is divided up between the executive (the president), Congress, and the federal courts. The powers of these sections of government are balanced in a way that certain privileges of each branch can, in a sensible manner, offset the other two. The executive or the president can use his or her veto power to refuse or turn down bills which are produced by Congress. On the other hand, the latter can override a presidential veto with a vote of sixty-seven or more. The president can appoint judges to the Supreme Court (Just like how Bush recently appointed John Roberts). However, congressional approval is a must. The Supreme Court can claim that a bill is unconstitutional as well. This also functions between the House and Senate, which are the two bodies that make up the United States Congress.

I am pleased that the United States, which is a democracy, has the checks and balances system. There are other world democracies or near democracies, that do not have a checks and balances system, and thus do not function as well. Great Brittan, Canada, and Australia do not have a system as such. This is the reason that the United States has tended to flourish more often than other nations of our world. In present day America, we have been subject to corruption and political payoffs which has caused us to be observed in a negative fashion by other nations abroad. The United States at this time is depleting from within. This is due to our recent immoral actions of war. You see, the world of today does not view the United States with the same admiration it once did. I really hope that President elect Barack Obama can not only earn the trust of the American people back, but also improve our world status and thus change the way we are currently perceived by the nations abroad. I am behind Obama 1000 percent.

As I myself have, you may have fathomed by now through what we have discussed so far, that a major problem exists in America today due to selfish greed. I strongly believe that Republican evangelists have set a horrible example due to their greed. Evangelists such as Pat Robertson, Rick Santorum, Jimmy Swaggart, James Baker, and Jerry Falwell, I believe represent maybe the lowest of the low of the Republican Party.

These evangelists have on a different multithousand-dollar suit every night. Yet they still want your money (and as much of it as possible). These abusers of the positive aspects of the Republican Party will take advantage of good people, of the elderly, and even of those who may be mentally ill, all because God whom they claim to know personally, told them to do so. Do you know why they call the 700 club the 700 club? I have a theory, maybe because it costs 700 dollars a day to watch it. This extreme greed should not be tolerated anymore!

I will now present you with a sad fact to back up my position on these holy rollers. My grandmother on my mother's side of my family was unfortunately a severely mentally ill and senile woman. Before my parents divorced, my mother and father would sometimes have her baby sit me when I was a very young child. While at my Grandmother's house, she would watch the 700 club, and she was completely addicted. I even recall a particular episode that featured a circus. This was to draw in the young, so one day they could take my, and other people's money. These evangelists would take any one's money they could.

I remember when Jimmy Swaggart was caught red handed soliciting a prostitute, and he ended up on the cover of *Newsweek* where he was quoted as saying, "Forgive me for I have sinned" and the cover showed a picture of him with a look of sincerity on his face. It was at this point that his followers or, as I would call them, his "innocent sheep" would say, "Oh, what a wonderful man of God, he has admitted to his sin." Well, quote me on this one; this is what I say: "Bullshit!" Excuse the profanity, but it is well called for. Do you actually believe that if this man was not caught red handed, that he would have publicly repented for his sin? No, he would not! He would have continued to preach his so-called word of God to his sheep and then proceeded to go to some hotel room and do the wild thing! I myself misbehave as any normal human being does, but I don't claim to be a holy relic. I have a message for the followers of these evangelicals: "Stop giving these people your money!"

I earlier stated that what I like most about Republicans is their outstanding family values. And that was an honest statement for the good Republicans of America. But these evangelists throw that one right out of the window! They might value their family, but speaking for myself "They certainly don't value my family, and I doubt they value yours."

I will now do something which I will do from time to time in this book. From time to time, I will speak in defense of those whom I've just criticized. However, my hopeful constructive criticism of these evangelists is not over yet. First in their defense, I do believe it possible that some evangelists might possess good intentions. However, they need to take a long and hard look at what they are doing and causing. There are much worse evils in this world than the taking of one's money. I mean, it's not like these evangelists are trying to commit genocide or any other type of killing. The truth is they're not. But the taking of one's money is evil, yet, not an ultimate evil. Taking one's money could in fact cause a person to die from lack of medication or food for nourishment. I do not want to prosecute these evangelists, I just want to teach them a lesson and reprimand them. It is easily conceivable that these evangelists could be forgiven for their greed. I humbly ask the evangelists of America

VISION OF A MENTAL PATIENT

to take a look at their actions, and start to use their faith in a more progressive and helpful manner.

I will now state a way in which this evangelical greed should be dealt with. What I would like to see these evangelicals do is to work on minimum wage scrubbing toilets five days a week, as I did for the last six years. And then we will see if these evangelists will still be preaching the word of God. I bet these evangelical Republicans, after toiling like many of my friends and I have, won't be voting down an increase of the minimum wage anymore, which is something that Republicans have been doing for a number of years now. Even John McCain, who is a very decent guy, has continued to vote down the minimum wage with consistency. So I once again ask these evangelists to do the honorable thing to take a look at their actions and stand corrected. You see, I don't necessarily hate evangelists; I simply hate their actions.

I previously stated that I have been pleased lately with the evangelist Pat Robertson who was the representative of the 700 club which I just trashed. But it's true that I am very pleased with him for his support of President Elect Obama. Pat, you have respected our system of elections, and have gotten behind Obama. Pat, you are a good sport! I hereby ask Pat Robertson to set an example for his fellow evangelicals and stand corrected. And, by the way, if I offend anyone in this book, please discuss with me in a fair and assertive manner anything that I may have said that was wrong. This type of fair approach is the only way that we as a people can achieve a utopia. This public condemnation is the punishment for the evangelicals of America. Let's put it behind us and commence to work through a visionary bipartisanship (for my readers who are new to the art of politics bipartisanship, it is the method of Republicans and Democrats working together in unison in order to achieve greatness). The last bit of this evangelical reprimand is going to be demonstrated through the writing down of lyrics, which is something I will do from time to time in this book. Being a former musician, I will at times present lyrics of my own, as well as lyrics of other bands that I am a fan of. Please bear with me, my hopeful future evangelical friends; it's almost over. This one's by Metallica! This song is called Leper Messiah and it is about evangelical greed.

Spineless from the start, sucked into the part
Circus comes to town, you play the lead clown
Please, Please
Spreading his disease, living by his story
knees, knees
Falling to your knees, suffer for his glory
You will!
Time for lust, time for lie
Time to kiss your life goodbye

Send me money send me green
Heaven you will meet
Make a contribution and you'll get a better seat
Bow to leper messiah!
Marvel at his tricks, need your Sunday fix
Blind devotion came rotting your brain
chain, chain
Join the endless chain, taken by his glamour
fame, fame
Infection is the game, stinking drunk with power
We see!
Witchery, weakening
Sees the sheep are gathering, set the trap hypnotize
now you follow, Bow to leper messiah!

Okay, that's enough of that; let's move on, shall we? At this juncture, I would now like to make a valid point about the Republicans' claim that they will keep your taxes low. I am absolutely dumbfounded at the continuous deceit on this matter. The truth is, the wealthier you are, the more lenience you will receive under the current Bush-Cheney Administration. Especially for those Americans who represent the richest one percent of the United States. The truth is that those who make 250,000 dollars a year or more will not be required to pay as much. This brand of Republican taxation is based on the Reagan Administration's theory of trickledown economics. The basic premise of this theory is the belief that favoring the rich will cause the lower classes to work harder, thus improving the economy. I am not a fan of this political theory. I have another idea! Why don't we try trickle up economics to help the poor and middle class of America and make the rich work harder for their money? After all, I do admit that there are some poor people who are poor due to laziness. However, there are those who are down on their luck: they work very hard, yet they have to struggle just to get by. It is also evident to me that the middle class is forced to do most of the work! We as a nation owe it to the middle class to establish a fairer distribution of our economic finances! That is why I am such an avid fan of Cornel West. He is the fairest of all political visionaries, in my opinion.

Sorry, but I must once again pick on the evangelists for a moment. You see, Jerry Falwell was a big fan of Ronald Reagan and his trickledown economics theory. I guess Falwell realized what he had to do in order to become even wealthier. If he can figure that out, he should be able to figure out that what he is doing is wrong.

By the way, have you noticed that since George W. Bush became a lame duck president, gas prices have, all of a sudden, gone way down? It seems to me that certain Republicans will only do the right thing when the standing of their political party is at risk. But don't get me wrong, I am fond of many Republicans and I strongly believe that bipartisanship should be a more fundamental aspect of American politics.

At this point, I deem it necessary to expose a naivete that the American public has developed over the years. We Americans stake the claim that the most important political position on planet Earth is the presidency of the United States of America. I personally believe this to be untrue. I believe that the most important political position on Earth is the position of Secretary General of the United Nations (U.N.). This undermining of the U.N. is a direct example of the lack of concern for foreign policy. People all over the world should realize that unless your country is experiencing mass starvation or genocide—what I feel are the worst two problems on the planet—with the acceptance of the crises of the environment concerning the greenhouse effect and global warming, you should put the concern of the entire planet over your concern for the domestic issues of your country. I feel that the potential of the U.N. is not yet achieved. The U.N. should be a more prominent force in our world. It should be able to intervene to a larger extent than it currently does. The U.N. also should have more say in world events, especially when dealing with genocide or starvation issues. It would, however, be a necessity, that if the U.N. were to gain more powers in world events, a checks and balances type of system would become essential in order to prevent any abuse of power by U.N. officials. The U.N. of present day is, as far as I can see, not consistent of any corruption. Unfortunately, when the U.N. attempts to intervene in world crises, the United States and other countries have had a tendency to ignore U.N. consensus.

How about a brief summarization of the history of the United Nations? Okay, here we go! The United Nations began with the help of former U.S. President Franklin Delano Roosevelt, and was established just after the time of his death in June of 1945, just after the end of World War 2. The birth city of the U.N. was San Francisco, California. Presently, however, the U.N. headquarters is located in New York City. The existence of the U.N. grows a strong hope from within my soul that one day, this world could be saved from tyranny; it thus strengthens the possibility of the establishment of a world utopia.

Since I just stated the U.N.'s importance in world matters, I deem it necessary, for Americans and the people of nations abroad, to know who the secretary-generals of the U.N. have been. So here they are, in order of appearance: First, from 1946 to 1952 was Trygvie Lie of Norway, second from 1953 to 1961 was Dag Hammarskjold from Sweden, third from 1961 to 1971 was U Thant from Myanmar, fourth from 1972 to 1981 was Kurt Waldheim from Austria, fifth from 1982 to 1991 was Javier Perez de Cuellar from Peru, sixth from 1992 to 1996 was Boutros Ghali from Egypt, seventh from 1997 to 2006 was Kofi Anan from Ghana, and from 2006 to present day is Ban Ki Moon from South Korea.

In a new direction, at this time, I would like to talk a little about my home, the Commonwealth of Massachusetts (Ma). I was born in Lowell Ma. Lowell is located in the northeastern section of the state. I mostly grew up in the neighboring town of Dracut, which borders Lowell to the south and New Hampshire to the north. I now reside in the town of Billerica Ma., and I've also had short residences in the town of Woburn Ma., and the capital city of Boston.

I love my state! I believe that Massachusetts is very underrated, especially by those who live here. It can actually be a very beautiful place, seeing that we have all four seasons. I admit the winters can be bitter cold and last a bit too long. But unlike many who live here, I really love the snow, at least until it gets plowed and becomes mixed with ugly black dirt. But I can honestly say that for the most part, I have enjoyed being a resident.

Massachusetts has the best colleges and hospitals in the world. For colleges we have Northeastern, Tufts, B.C., B.U., UMass, and of course Harvard. For outstanding hospitals, we have Brigham and Women's, Beth Israel Deaconess, Dana Farber Cancer Institute, and Mass General. Massachusetts is also home to a solid democratic base. The Kennedy family is from here (John, Bobby, and Ted). Most are not aware of the fact that George H.W. Bush was born in this state as well. In my birth city of Lowell, we've had Bettie Davis, the famous actress, Jack Kerouac the novelist, the famous boxer Mickey Ward, and Johnny Carson counterpart, Ed McMahon attended Lowell High School, but was not born in Lowell.

I am also a proud diehard fan of the Boston Red Sox, Celtics, and N.E. Patriots. Boston sports fans have been spoiled rotten so far in the 2000's. My apologies to Bruins fans, I have never been much of a hockey fan, but I have the utmost respect for hockey players; they display great athleticism and are as tough as nails.

The Commonwealth of Massachusetts has been a pioneering state to the history of American left-wing liberal politics; gay marriage and pro-choice abortion issues, prominent democratic political figures such as Michael Dukakis, Paul Tsongas, and John Kerry, three men who almost became president. American pioneer John Quincy Adams is also from Massachusetts.

Another positive aspect of my home state is that it is located on the east coast. It is fun to drive up to the beaches in the summertime. Beaches like Salisbury, Seabrook, Plumb Island, and my favorite, Hampton beach, which is just across the border into New Hampshire. Despite the fact that I have been a Massachusetts resident all my life, I have seldom been down to Cape Cod. I remember being in Cape Cod as a young boy, and from what I remember, it was a very beautiful place.

I had a lot of fun as a kid growing up in my home state. I had a music career that began when I was just fifteen years old,

VISION OF A MENTAL PATIENT

and boy what a fun experience that was. I started playing adult nightclubs at that age, and it was hard to set up gigs since the band I was in consisted of two other members that were the same age as I was. These nightclubs would make an acceptance and let us perform as long as we didn't try to sneak any alcoholic beverages. The negative effect this experience had on me is that I desired to grow up too fast, and I began behaving erratically. I would soon develop a severe alcohol problem and I was still very young at the time. By the time I was nineteen years old, I would become a mental patient. I was then entered into Solomon's Mental Health Center in Lowell Ma. My reason for naming this book *Vision of a Mental Patient* is due to the political and scientific theories which I've developed through the shockingly real experiences that I've had.

I've had the pleasure of meeting many wonderful people from being a resident of Massachusetts. At the age of fifteen, I became acquainted with two of my best friends during the high school years. These two friends of mine were Bob Stevens and Dennis Brunelle. If you saw me, you saw them. If you saw them, you saw me. We were always together, and we were always up to no good. Once I turned seventeen, I met a cool dude named Roland Gagnon, who would end up being my fellow band mate for the next several years. Roland and I would form the band Deallegiance. Our other band mates in this band were Matt Kulesza on guitar, John Evicci on drums, and John's older brother Fred who was our lead singer. Incidentally, Roland played guitar and I was the bass guitarist.

Bob and Dennis would form the band Manifest and I recall they had a kicking tune called "Decadent Disease" and when they played that one, everybody loved it. Bob and Dennis were the guitarists for Manifest. Their other members were Fred Daigle on bass, Steve Stryker on drums, and my close friend, Dave St. Armand, was their lead singer. Unfortunately, I had, for reasons not yet fathomed, deserted Manifest whom I was a member of at one time, in order to form Deallegiance. And anyone who has ever played for bands in their youth knows of the bitterness which can come between friends due to certain envious feelings. Despite the tension that this caused, Deallegiance and Manifest were two bands that would always remain friends with one another. I recall hanging out at one of those teenage beer parties which we used to have in the woods behind my house. I recall Dennis saying to me, "Ted, just because we are not in the same band anymore, it doesn't mean that we are not still together."

Dennis you were absolutely right, we will always be as together as ever!

Anyhow, Roland and I agreed to name our band Deallegiance for reasons of radicalism. People tended to be offended by this name. The main complaint was that people believed that we were putting down America. But that is not what we meant by our name. What we did intend to get across was this: an undoing of a system of government in order to achieve a utopia. I admit that it was a bit too radical of an idea. However, you must understand that being a radical is fun, especially when you are young!

We played shows with a slew of other bands in the eastern Massachusetts area, made a few cheap production demo tapes on John's four track, and would receive some minimal local radio airplay. It was tough on us at times because of the name Deallegiance that we chose.

In order to make a moral point, I would now like to tell you some of the names of a few of the other bands that we would play out with whose names could also be taken offensively. Infanticide which means to kill an infant and no one said anything. Homicide which means to murder and no one said anything. Genocide which means to kill an entire race, and yes, once again, no one said anything. As a matter of fact, that last one should offend you. But why is it that people would be offended at a word that could be used to put down America, but not by a name that could put down the human race? Is it okay to sing about killing, and not okay to sing about saving the human race with a vision of utopia?

I must stress at this time that I knew some of the different members of the bands I just mentioned, and they were all really good kids, especially the members of "Infanticide." I find it to be very unfortunate that heavy metal music will tend to reveal an evil image. But the truth is that much of this form of music can be very intelligent, and believe it or not, it can be very moral as well. There are a lot of metal bands who give this form of music a bad name. This must change if this form of music wants to once again thrive.

I now must mention another one of my friends growing up. This friend was the best friend I ever had, and possibly the best friend anyone ever had. I am speaking of my childhood companion, Joshua Bernard. I have not seen Joshua in a number of years, as well as just about the rest of my childhood friends for that matter. However, I've heard that Joshua has become a very successful graphics artist. And that does not surprise me at all, seeing how incredible of an artist this kid was at such a young age. I also have heard that he is happily married with children.

Joshua used to draw the covers of the Deallegiance demo tapes as well as the flyers we used to hang all over town, to get a good crowd at our gigs. He also drew the cover of the sole Malicious Intent album. Malicious Intent was the band that Roland and I would form after the unfortunate breakup of Deallegiance. I've also heard that Joshua has done some artwork for the famous band The Toadies.

Roland and I would end up forming Malicious Intent with new members Dan Desharnais on drums, and Paul Leary on lead guitar. Roland would then take on the responsibility of lead vocals as well as his usual role as rhythm guitarist, and of course, I was still the bass player. Incidentally, we had a guitarist named Paul Normandin for a few months, prior to Paul Leary's entering of the band. To be fair, I must mention my friend Paul Felis the prodigy who basically taught me how to play. Thanks Paul, I'll never forget you.

By the way, I could also understand if someone was offended by the name Malicious Intent. But the name was meant as a malicious intent toward the extreme world evils. It was good disguised as evil. I believe it to be beautiful when something appears to be evil, but is actually fighting for good. I also view things as ugly if they appear to be good and are fighting for evil. This is how good can overcome evil, by disguising itself.

At this crux, I would now like to sincerely congratulate the punk band Out Cold on their prominent success. Out Cold was John and Fred Evicci's other band that we shared jam space with in their mother's cellar. My friend Mark Sheehan is also a member of this band. I have many great memories of hanging out with John, Fred, Roland, Matt, and myself as well as the occasional friends we would have over, who would often come watch us play. We would hang out playing pool, and I remember playing Frisbee in the back yard. John, who wasn't into all the partying and stuff, would become a little angry with me when I would start to show up to practice with a twelve pack of Bud in my belly. Anyway, I congratulate Out Cold on their fame, not a bad accomplishment for a few dudes from a small Massachusetts town. Good going John, you deserve it!

In order to elaborate on my teenage radicalism, and being a proud member of Deallegiance, I will now explain my view of the United States, which, despite our mistakes of past and present, has turned out to be a good country. To elaborate, I must first ask you a question: Do you realize that in order for the U.S. to form, we committed the most evil of acts known to history? This evil act was the act of genocide (genocide is the deliberate and systematic destruction of a racial, political, or cultural group). The American settlers brutally murdered massive numbers of American Indians in order to stake their claim of land in the western hemisphere. Another act of disrespect to the original and rightful occupiers of this land is that we have labeled these people as Indians. Do you know why? Because when our American settlers landed in North America, they thought that they were in India. Therefore, they thought that these American Indians were Indians from the country of India. This is because of the true theory of this era that the world was round. Therefore, these settlers thought that they had gone all the way around the world. Of course, it is common knowledge today that this theory is true.

The correct names of these American Indians would be their tribal names such as Wachusett, Cherokee, Blackfoot, Massachusetts, or what have you. That is another reason I love my state, because it is named after an Indian Tribe. The absolute truth is that our American ancestors swept across this land killing, and killing, and killing again.

Are you aware how we claimed the land where Texas now is? The same way, my friends! We killed an obscene amount of Hispanics in order to claim this land because we were so great and idealistic that we felt we had the right. This self-righteous behavior is inexcusable!

African Negroes were treated no better, either. They would be treated with the same self-righteous bigotry as well as the killings of those who would not obey while working them to the bone and forcing them to do our labor. Starvation would be commonplace as well. As a matter of fact, even the respected pioneers of America had slaves themselves. Even the great George Washington owned slaves himself! Not to mention others who if you knew, it would break your heart.

I am so pleased that this country has finally elected an African-American to the presidency. Whites like myself have fouled up things enough and it is high time that we headed in a new direction. We should allow the ones that we have treated so unfairly a chance to lead in America.

However, I must admit that of the three major democratic candidates, I was originally in favor of John Edwards. I now feel that, through the turn of events, the American people have made the right choice. Any one of the three original candidates Hillary Clinton, John Edwards, or Barack Obama would have been a fine choice. However, I now will proclaim that after the way us Caucasians have done in the past, Barack Obama is way more than okay by me! Please understand that I did want to see a woman or a Negro become the president of the United States, but I was for Edwards because I simply would not vote for someone based on their gender or color. I vote for someone based on how they will perform as a leader, and their level of character and morality.

Please don't get me wrong; America, despite its immoralities, has turned out to be a good country. Through one of my heroes, Franklin Delano Roosevelt, we were able to end the evils of the Hitler NAZI regime. We have also at least tried to help others in need. If America, through the leadership of Barack Obama and his advisors, as well as the rest of the branches of the United States government, can accomplish the level of world maturity that this country once possessed, there will not only be a new found hope for the American people, but also for the approximately six billion people who live on this beautiful little blue planet. By the way, I have something else to say in defense of America; "If you can show me one nation on Earth that has never done anything morally and ethically wrong, then I will show you fantasy land."

At this instance, I would like to tell you about my two favorite commercials in the history of American television. I'll start with my second favorite television advertisement of all time. This would be the advertisement for the United Negro College Fund (U.N.C.F.), where the famous motto that was etched into the minds of Americans abroad was established. This motto is "A mind is a terrible thing to waste." President-elect Obama is living proof that this motto is true. This U.N.C.F. motto, my friends, is an absolute truth.

How about we explore some of the history of this moral organization? The U.N.C.F. was founded by the honorable Dr. Frederick D. Patterson in 1943. Soon after, Dr. Patterson would become the president of Tuskegee University. In late April of 1944, Dr. Patterson, with the help of one Mary Mcleoud Bethune, further established the prominence of this organization. The U.N.C.F. has sprouted from its original twenty-seven representative universities, to what is now tallied at thirty-nine. The cur-

VISION OF A MENTAL PATIENT

rent U.N.C.F. president is one Michael Lomax. Early Caucasian supporters include Franklin Delano Roosevelt, John D. Rockefeller, and in later years, John F. Kennedy.

The U.N.C.F. has substantially grown over the years, especially in a financial sense. Over its fifty-five-year history, the U.N.C.F. has helped hundreds of thousands of students who had no other means of paying for their college education. The U.N.C.F. is now so strong that it will usually cut a student's college tuition by at least 50% and will often cover the whole bill. This organization is imperative to the benefits that the United States could receive from its African-American residents.

On the subject of a history of American Negroes, I must mention our sixteenth president, Abraham Lincoln. We are all aware that it was President Lincoln who first made substantial progress for the Negroes of America, by lighting the torch which would be passed from generation to generation. This, of course, was the moral act of one of the best presidents ever, and his freeing of the slaves. Lincoln freed the African slaves from cruel and unusual treatment, and all of us, not just the Negroes of America, but every other creed that resides in this country, owes Lincoln a debt of gratitude and we should never forget him.

I now feel that I must make a point, in regards to Lincoln. Lincoln was a Republican, but in the era of Lincoln, Republicans represented what we would today label as left wingers (for those who are new to the art of politics in modern times, left-wingers represent the agenda of the Democratic Party). This means that the party of the Democrats represented what would today be labeled as right-wingers (who logically in modern times would represent the agenda of right-wing Republicans). Therefore, modern day claims that the Republican Party is the party of Lincoln is true, but it could also be considered deceiving. By the way, I express an apology to the good Republicans of this country that I had to bust their bubble, but this, my friends, is a true statement. If there was a modern day scenario, where Ronald Reagan were to run against Abraham Lincoln in the 1980s, I am certain that Reagan would have defeated Lincoln in a landslide.

Moving on, it is now time for me to reveal my very favorite commercial in the history of American television. This is a television advertisement which was aired in the late 1970s. This advertisement pertained to America's problem with pollution at the time. This advertisement featured an American Indian who was walking through a city of modern America. This aged full-blooded American Indian was crying profusely, tears running down his cheeks in an absolute state of sorrow. This man was crying because of what we did to his native land through pollution and what we did to his people through the immoral acts of war. I was so touched by this advertisement even as a five or six year old which I was at this time.

A modern version of this commercial should be made in order to show our desperate apologies to these original natives of this land of the Americas. Suffice it to say, if this advertisement could touch the heart of a six year old, just imagine how it could touch those of more matured generations.

The last topic of issue we will touch on in this In General segment will be about what George W. Bush was doing for the first eight or so minutes, after finding out from Andy Card that the United States was under attack. Of course, I am referring to the infamous morning of September 11, 2001. This little segment would have been much better written, if only I could have gotten my hands on the children's book *My Pet Goat*. Bush was reading this book with a Florida classroom on the morning of 9/11 while the United States was under attack by Osama Bin Laden and his terrorist organization Al Qaeda. Believe me, I tried very hard to find a copy of this children's book, but I couldn't obtain one. It is a lucky thing for George W. Bush that I didn't.

So here it goes! *My Pet Goat* is obviously a children's parody about a fictional goat. Maybe Bush thought this goat might have had some information about the supposed *weapons of mass destruction*. Maybe this goat knew who was attacking us! Hey! Isn't a goat a Democrat? In that case, Bush may have been right because it seems that the Democrats for the most part were realizing what was going on after 9/11! But wait! The symbol of the Democratic Party isn't a goat, it's a jackass! In Bush's defense, many Democrats are jackasses!

I recall when watching the Republican National Convention of 1984, the Republicans were singing a different version of Ray Parker Junior's 1980s hit song "Ghostbusters." Instead of the line "I ain't afraid of no ghost," they were singing "I ain't afraid of no goat." Did these Republicans not know the difference between a goat and a jackass? Maybe not! But they shouldn't feel bad because Bill Clinton didn't know the difference between the word "is" and the word "is." Are we supposed to actually believe that a man as knowledgeable as Bill Clinton, a man who can tell you in detail the history of every American president, doesn't know the definition of "is." During the height of the Monica Lewinsky sex scandal, Bill Clinton was asked a question and actually asked what the meaning of is! Did I hear that correctly? "What is is?" That must be one of the stupidest freaking things I ever heard in my life! After claiming that he didn't understand the word, the very next word he used was the same word! Bill Clinton is not even remotely that stupid! The man is a political mastermind! I don't buy it! If Bill Clinton really doesn't know what is means, than he needs to go back to kindergarten and relearn his ABC's. On the other hand, I have absolutely no problem whatsoever with his wife Hillary. I truly believe that she would have made a fine president, and I'm confident that she will be an outstanding secretary of state. To be truthful, I really don't know much about their daughter Chelsea, but she always seemed to me to be a really good kid, although she is not a kid anymore, so I'm sure she has grown to be a respectable woman.

No matter what happens to Bill Clinton, he will always be a very lucky man to have had a wife that stuck by him through that jib jab. And don't get me wrong here, Bill Clinton was a good president. I have usually agreed with him on the issues, although his foreign policy could be more extensive. However, I don't trust the man one iota. He is a horrible liar, which is actually a good characteristic for a president.

Okay, back to Bush, and his eight or so minutes of confusion. I guess we could consider a goat to be a Democrat. After all, the genes of a goat can't differ that much from the genes of a jack-ass. Who knows, maybe this goat did possess some knowledge as to what was happening on 9/11. Maybe George W. Bush is actually Bozo the clown! To wrap up this segment, I will keep my promise and briefly speak in the defense of George W. Bush. You must understand that the teacher of this Florida classroom claimed that Bush did the right thing by not panicking and storming out of the classroom. If he had done that, he may have frightened these children! So maybe Bush did the right thing by waiting for a few minutes. Eight minutes seems a bit much, maybe it should have been five minutes instead. So, to be as honest as possible, I'm not sure if I myself could have done any better. I guess I couldn't resist a good scag.

There were many worse things which Bush would do after 9/11, and this one doesn't even compare to the unnecessary bloodshed that he would cause after this ordeal. This man's approval rating in the days following 9/11 was an astounding 90%. By the time he became a lame duck president, his approval rating was a dismal 25%. That is almost as low as Richard Nixon's approval rating following the Watergate Scandal. Lastly, I must say please do not confuse George H.W. Bush with George W. Bush, because although I may catch holy hell from my family for saying this, I am very fond of George H.W. Bush. And I say to my friend George H.W. Bush, you're okay but I'm sorry to tell you, your son is a shit. So, that wraps up Politics In General. We will now move on to specifics! Read on!

ABORTION

In the year of my birth in 1973, there was the landmark trial which is synonymous to the present day argument of abortion in the United States. This is the case of Roe vs. Wade. This trial consisted of the plaintiff Norma McCorvey (known as Jane Roe for reasons of privacy), and the defendant Henry Wade.

McCorvey, a single woman who worked for a carnival, was denied an abortion in the state of Texas in 1969. At the time, Texas law would only allow an abortion if the woman was at a major health risk. McCorvey (Roe) ended up winning after a strenuous trial. McCorvey was victorious due to the principles represented in the United States Constitution's Bill of Rights. The court ruling was that this woman's privacy must be protected.

As a result of the historic trial, it was ruled that during the first three months of pregnancy, a woman had the right to have an abortion. The stages of pregnancy were then divided up into three sections or stages called trimesters, the first trimester being the first three months, the second trimester being the second three months, and the third trimester being the last three months of pregnancy.

Prior to the Roe vs. Wade case, a large number of U.S. states would forbid a woman the right to have an abortion in almost every situation. During the second trimester, it was possible for a state to provide an abortion, if the woman was at a major health risk.

Throughout history since the time that the first abortions were performed, there has been a fierce debate on the procedures' lack of moral integrity. The ancient Hebrews set laws against abortion, but like us, they would make an exception in the case, such as if the woman was in imminent danger healthwise. As a matter of fact, as far back as the beginnings of the fourteenth century and all the way up to the nineteenth century, abortion would become more commonplace, especially in Europe. This acceptance by the Europeans would lead to the abortion process being a more common procedure in other nations.

The country where abortions are most common is Communist China. This is due to the problem of overpopulation in this country. The Chinese government tries to regulate how many children a family can have. At times, there will even be mandatory abortions in China. China is the most populous country in the world. There are approximately six and a half billion or so people in the world, and over one billion of them reside in China. The second most populous country on Earth is India, which is also one of the poorest. The third most populous country on Earth is the United States of America. The fourth most populous nation on Earth is the islands nation of Indonesia. The Soviet Union has fallen off the scale due to its splitting up into different countries.

Because of the high level of abortions in China, the abortion procedures may tend to become more inhumane at times. These inhumane types of abortion are those which are performed in the second and third trimesters. The more time that passes before an abortion is performed, the more inhumane it becomes.

By 1980, at the tail end of the Carter Administration, there was a governmental decision saying that the funding for an abortion of a woman who couldn't afford to pay for it would no longer be an obligation by the government. This is due to what was known as the Hyde Amendment. This Hyde Amendment was first established in 1976 by the U.S. Congress, of course. The man behind this amendment was a Republican representative of the state of Illinois by the name of Henry Hyde. This establishment of the Hyde amendment is considered the first major success for the pro-life coalition in the United States.

The Hyde Amendment basically ended the government funding of abortions (Medicaid) for women of low income in the United States. This would cause a war cry from the supporters of the pro-choice coalition. This would also cause certain U.S. states to have to establish their own state government funding for women in need of finances for an abortion. Even federal prisoners, military personnel, and members of the Peace Corps were denied funding due to this Hyde Amendment. Women who were victims of incest or rape were also denied any financial assistance. Currently, only seventeen of the fifty U.S. states have a statewide funding for this cause. In thirteen of these states, a woman must have a court order, thus causing emotional and stressful measures for those women who are in need of finances that they are unable to obtain.

Now for some information on the actual process of abortion: the first and also the most painless process of abortion is the prescribing of certain types of medications which are meant to cause a miscarriage.

On a woman's first visit to the abortion clinic, it will be requested of her to give either a blood or a urine sample in order to determine if she is pregnant. It is an absolute requirement to determine a woman's blood type for certain medical reasons.

In certain situations, a shot of immuneglobin may be a necessity. In order to begin, a woman must take 600 milligrams of a medication called mifepristone (a medication that interrupts the supply of hormones that is maintained inside the woman's uterus). After the taking of the mifepristone, the woman will be sent home for a waiting period of two to four days, with certain medical instructions.

If this mifepristone does not complete its process, the woman will then be given another medication called misoprostol (can be used to soften the woman's cervix, can induce contractions and protects the lining inside of the woman's stomach area), but in this case, it is meant to prevent the woman from pain, nausea, and possible diarrhea. More than fifty percent of women will pass pregnancy related tissue within hours of taking misoprostol. This of course is to make a second attempt at causing a miscarriage. Lastly, for these first attempts at abortion, the woman will return for an ultrasound to determine the results. First trimester abortions have an extremely high rate of success. First trimester abortions are about ten times safer than actual childbirth. They are also considered even safer than a simple tonsillectomy. The first attempts at abortion through inducing a miscarriage is much less cruel than what we will discuss next, which will be the actual hands on type methods of abortion. These hands on type methods include the destruction of an embryo. An embryo is a living thing in its first stages of physical development after it becomes a zygote, which is a fertilized egg once it forms an identity.

We will now discuss the actual hands on process of abortion. The most common involves a series of different types of suction or vacuuming processes. Manual vacuum aspiration (M.V.A.) is an abortion process where the fetus, embryo, or prezygote is sucked by a process of a manual syringe. Next is a suction of this embryo by the use of an electric pump. This method is called electric vacuum abortion (E.V.A.). These abortion methods are also known as surgical termination of pregnancy, which ironically come out as (S.T.O.P.) in initials.

The next abortion types we will discuss are those that are most commonly performed from the fifteenth week of pregnancy to the twenty-sixth week of pregnancy. The first one we will discuss is called dilation and evacuation (D.E.). This particular abortion process is seemingly more brutal than those we have previously discussed. This (D.E.) process consists of a cutting open of the woman's cervix (the outer end of a woman's uterus); not only does it include a vacuuming method, but it also consists of the use of other surgical instruments.

The next most common method to that of dilation and evacuation is the process of dilation and curettage (D.C.). Dilation and curettage is a gynecological procedure which may be performed for a number of incentives. Before explaining further, I must tell you the two definitions which are essential to understanding the method of dilation and curettage. First of all, dilation is the process of swelling or expanding. Curettage is a tool which is used to clean the walls of a woman's uterus, and as a verb, can be considered the process of this action.

One particular method of dilation and curettage is uterine lining to detect possible malignancy (a detection of a medical condition which can cause deterioration leading to possible death), or to detect any abnormal bleeding. As previously yet vaguely explained, a curettage is used for the process of cleansing the walls of the uterus, and at times another type of curettage can be accessed, one which will also add the action of suction.

Another process of abortion that is used in the second trimester is called dilation and extraction (I.D.X.), which can also be called cranial decompression. This process, in my opinion, as well as many others, is the last resort or at least what should be the last resort, which basically includes the squeezing or puncturing of the of the unborn infant's head (the embryo or post-zygote or whatever it is labeled as, this unborn, yet still alive entity). The most well known term for this method is partial birth abortion, which has been federally banned in the United States for obvious reasons. However, this process may be executed in absolute desperate situations.

There is yet another process of abortion, commonly known as a hysterectomy abortion. This category of the abortion procedure requires a method which is quite similar to that of a cesarean section. This method is carried out under the use of an anesthesia because it is considered a majorly abnormal type of surgery. Finally, there is a last abortion method that can be performed from the twentieth week until the twenty-third week of pregnancy. This last method of abortion is done by process of injection in order to stop the fetal heart from beating.

In conclusion, after this elaboration of these different types of abortions, and the revealing of the knowledge that I possess in pertinence to this topic and my awareness of the brutality involved in it, I must now state something that might shock you. I am, despite my knowledge of the methods of abortion, a supporter of the pro-choice view! I realize that some of my fellow Democrats most of my Republican friends, as well as members of any of the other political parties that exist in the United States might be offended at my pro-choice beliefs. Please believe me when I say to you these two words: I understand. I do not, by any means, like abortions, but I simply believe that in certain desperate situations which I shall elaborate on in a moment, it is imperative that a woman has the right to choose given a credible reason.

Before my explaining of the pro-choice view, I will tell you of a quite interesting and surprising fact. Did you know that under the pro-life Reagan Administration, there were a significantly larger number of abortions performed than there was under the Clinton administration which was supportive of a woman's right to choose? A major reason for this is that under the Clinton Administration, women who may be seeking an abortion had their options explained to them thoroughly. Another reason is that under the Clinton Administration, the middle class as well as the poor were treated more fairly, thus causing women to have the finances necessary to support a child.

VISION OF A MENTAL PATIENT

In order to explain further, we are all aware of the arguments that if a woman was the victim of incest or rape, she should be allowed the right to choose. However, for myself, there is much more to it than that. I now present a view that I have developed from Vision of a Mental Patient. Having been a mental patient, I have witnessed and experienced a lot of human suffering! What if there was a woman who was so delusional that when being pregnant, she had an unbearable fear that her newborn child, even if put up for adoption, would be subject to a torture. That would be unimaginable for a non mental patient to fathom. I have experienced this brand of misery, having been a mental patient. So I ask you: Should this woman be forced to give birth to this child despite the lifelong terror that she might experience? It may not be understood by a person who has not experienced this misery, but it is true that a woman could abort a child for reasons of love. I humbly ask those opposed to my beliefs on this issue to at least try to look at it from this perspective.

In addition, I stress that by no means do I like abortion. Some people who are supporters of the respectable pro-life view simply do not understand that those of us who are pro-choice do not like abortions; we simply have respect for women. As for myself, I may not be in favor of an abortion within my own family. However, something us men need to understand is that being a woman can be more challenging than being a man. It is also true that being a man can be just as challenging at times. For example, men must deal with the fear of being forced by law to fight in a war. I am a strong advocate of equality for women, but one belief I have is that unless a woman volunteers herself, she should never be obligated to fight in a war. This is because the way I see it, war was created by man and not by women. I strongly believe that the responsibility of childbirth excludes women from such savagery.

The ultimate truth for me is that basically, I am not sure at times of my stance on abortion. Therefore, if I am not sure on this subject, then who am I to tell a woman whom I don't know anything about, or whom I have no knowledge of what suffering that she may have experienced, tell her what to do with her own body!

I now say, because of what I have explained in this abortion segment, that in certain desperate situations, a woman's only alternative may be to have an abortion. And may I add that I do see the sad brutality involved in this abortion process. Unless an absolute utopia was achieved, could we possibly outlaw all cases of abortion? My question would have to be even in the existence of a utopia. What if a woman's life was in imminent danger if she did not have an abortion? So, as for now, I am strongly in favor of the absolute minimization of the abortion process.

It is now once again time to show some lyrics. Once again, it will be a Metallica song. This is track number six on the *And Justice for All* album. In part two of this book, The Monolith, the subconscious will be explained. This song is subconsciously about the abortion process when executed for bogus reasons. As you read these lyrics, you must remember my elaborations on some of the methods of abortion in order to fully understand its subconscious meaning; First, the taking of certain medications (drinking up); second, the use of a syringe (shooting in); and third and most important, the brutal partial birth abortion technique involving the puncturing of the unborn entities' head (the beatings). So, here you are, the lyrics to "Harvester of Sorrow."

My life suffocates, planting seeds of hate (birth control pills)
I've loved turned to hate, trapped far beyond my fate
I give you take, this life that I forsake
Been cheated of my youth, you've turned this lie to truth
Anger, Misery, you'll suffer unto me
Harvester of sorrow, language of the mad, harvester of sorrow
Pure black looking clear, my work is done soon here
Try getting back to me, get back what used to be
Drink up(taking of medications) shoot in(use of the syringe)
Let the beatings begin (partial birth abortion puncturing of the fetus head)
Distributor of pain, your loss becomes my gain
Anger, Misery, you'll suffer unto me
Harvester of sorrow, language of the mad, harvester of sorrow
All have said their prayers, invade their nightmares
To see unto my eyes, you'll find where murder lies, Infanticide!

In conclusion to this segment on the different methods and views of abortion and in order to show my respect to the pro-lifers out there, I must say that my position on the issue of abortion is very delicate, and the reasons for my pro-choice position is because truthfully, I am not sure on this subject, which is why I feel that I, nor anyone else, should have the right to prevent a woman from having her right to choose.

Another thing I must say is that I would never say angrily to anyone, "Hey, you should be pro-choice." The issue of abortion is a very delicate matter. It should be approached with delicacy. I will now leave you with one more fact. At this time, one in three women in America will have an abortion by the age of forty-five. I have already explained that under the Reagan Administration, more abortions were performed than under the Clinton Administration. Therefore, I state once more that explaining to women their options, as well as showing a concern for the lower and middle class, a pro-choice administration is more effective than setting an unreasonable ultimatum which would forbid women from their right to be the boss of their own body.

    Thank you for listening, and please try to keep an open mind. Read on!

THE ENVIRONMENT

In this environmental portion of politics, we will have a discussion on specific environmental crises, such as the ozone, causes of extinction of certain species, climate change of both natural and human causes, and the greenhouse effect.

First of all, I must state that climate change or global warming has led to unnatural behaviors among mammals and animals of this world. The animals of Earth have had their natural instinctive behaviors altered due to the negative effects of human activity. This environmental dilemma has had a major negative effect, causing certain species to be in danger of extinction. It was back in the 1860s, when scientists were able to determine a history of weather by keeping information related to specific details of climate.

Through the study of trees, ice, and rocks, scientists are more able to learn of weather history of the past. Some trees may live for over a thousand years. Through the examination of what are called tree rings, scientists are able to determine the unrecorded weather of the past. You can also determine the age of a tree by the study of these tree rings. There is an exhibit pertaining to this theory which is on display at the Boston Museum of Science.

Rocks, on the other hand, can be studied and produce information of the temperature and rainfall up to about one million years ago. This information can also be accessed through the study of fossils (a fossil is a trace or impression, or the remains of a past geological age, which is preserved in the Earth's crust).

Information of past weather history can also be obtained through the study of ice in the North or South Pole, as well as parts of Greenland. You see, ice gets colder as you go deeper into it. This ice contains air, which is unable to escape. However, it can still be analyzed by the examination of the quantity of oxygen within this ice. To state an interesting fact: Antarctica has about an inch or so of snow a year, the bitter cold weather keeps it from melting. Because of this imminent environmental problem, there are glaciers the size of my home state of Massachusetts which are melting and moving due to global warming.

There are also causes of climate change which are not produced through human activity. These natural causes not only can cause a rise in world temperature, but can also cause a lessening in temperature. Through the occurrence of the ice ages over the last 400,000 years, this fact does hold water. Another factor is the Earth's rotation around our sun. You see, the Earth moves an inch or so closer to the sun every year.

Now for a little information on the needing of the exchange of oxygen and carbon dioxide between animals and plant life, carbon dioxide is breathed in by plants, oxygen is breathed out by plants. On the other hand, mammals and animals breathe in oxygen and breathe out carbon dioxide. Therefore, it is of utmost importance that humans preserve essential plant life in order to survive.

A number of years back, I took a trip to New York City. What surprised me most was the amount of trees which were planted throughout this city. I was also amazed at how huge and beautiful this city was. It is a good idea not only to preserve our rain forests but also to learn from New York City and plant trees in our urban areas.

Carbon dioxide is considered a greenhouse gas. Carbon dioxide consists of carbon which is found in all living organisms and plant life. Through nature's complex process, carbon is constantly being transformed into carbon dioxide and then back into carbon.

The process of carbon passing into any type or form of life is called the carbon cycle. Mammals don't just take in carbon through the air, but also through what we eat and digest. When plant life and the life of mammals and animals die, they will decay into the Earth's soil and return carbon to it, thus resulting in the existence of fossil fuels. Fossil fuels include coal, oil, gasoline, and other natural gases. These fossil fuels are formed from all living things which lived millions of years ago.

How about a short discussion on the greenhouse effect? Okay, let's go! Because of the greenhouse effect, the Earth's climate is going through a change. If not dealt with, it potentially could cause catastrophic results. Therefore, it is an absolute necessity that we learn as much about this as is humanly possible.

To understand the greenhouse effect, it is a necessity to understand how a greenhouse works. A greenhouse is a building using the source of solar energy which can be effective for growing plant life even in extremely low temperatures.

The Earth's similarity to a greenhouse is that instead of glass or plastic to harness the sun's energy, the Earth uses the gases in our atmosphere as its solar transmitter. These gases are clear just like the glass or plastic, which is used in an actual greenhouse. An actual greenhouse and its see-through glass or plastic works almost identical to the way the Earth uses its gases.

So, how does the Earth use its gases in order to perform as that glass or plastic? You see, molecules are the smallest particles of matter which achieves the same chemical consistency as the whole mass of a formed matter. Gas and glass are both made from similar types of molecules. However, in glass the molecules tend to be more tightly held together than that of a gas. On the other hand, the molecules in gases are more loosely knitted together. Both gas and glass have the same abilities to block or transmit rays from the sun.

Heat and cold is determined by molecules in the air. These molecules move back and forth at certain speeds. The faster these molecules move back and forth, the hotter they become. This means, logically, that the slower these molecules move back and forth, the colder it will get. The three main measures of temperature are: Fahrenheit, which is the most commonly used; the second most common is Celsius; and the third most common is Kelvin. These temperature names are derived from the surnames of the scientists who created them.

Fahrenheit displays that thirty-two degrees is the crux at which certain matter will start to freeze. This is because the molecules in the air are now moving slower, thus causing things to freeze. This makes perfect sense, because when water is at a warm temperature it moves around, but when water is cold, the molecules are moving slower, thus causing the water to be still and cold. Thirty-two degrees Fahrenheit is equal to zero degrees Celsius. For Kelvin there is absolute zero, which is hundreds of degrees below zero Fahrenheit. Absolute zero is when these molecules have stopped moving all together. Therefore, cold is not infinite, and unless these molecules can move back and forth faster than the speed of light, which is 186,000 miles per second, then heat is not infinite either. At the speed of light, you could travel around the Earth at the equator eight times in one second!

Other planets in our solar system consist of large amounts of carbon dioxide as well. For example, the average temperature on Venus is approximately 850 degrees Fahrenheit, and thus is obviously not capable of supporting any life form. Neptune, on the other hand, is extremely cold, and is also not capable of supporting life. The average temperature on Neptune is approximately 360 degrees below zero Fahrenheit.

The molecules of our sun move back and forth so fast that it produces an unimaginable heat which humans could never fathom. The molecules on and around the sun move so fast, causing a sort of chain reaction of molecules. You see, because of the speed of these sun molecules, they cause the molecules to send a reaction of friction causing the molecules nearby to move as well. Therefore, the farther you move away from the sun, the slower these molecules move, thus causing a decrease in temperature the farther you move away.

Some particular types of gases are more adept for harnessing heat than other gases. Carbon dioxide is the Earth's main greenhouse gas. It flows in what I previously explained, the carbon cycle. The carbon cycle is the transforming and de-transforming of carbon. So, carbon dioxide is taken from our air by green plants containing chlorophyll (chlorophyll is the green matter in plants which cause its color, which helps to perform photosynthesis, which will be further explained in part two The Monolith). After this carbon dioxide is taken from the air, it enters the ocean where it is then dissolved. When plants die or are eaten, it causes a return of carbon dioxide to the air. The balance of plant life's intake of carbon dioxide and the release of oxygen breathed in by animals and mammals lead, in turn, to our giving out of oxygen, which causes a necessary balance to the environment. The consistency of carbon dioxide in our atmosphere and beyond makes the Earth warm enough to support its life forms. Also, the Earth's consistency of natural gases, including water vapor, carbon dioxide, and methane gas, causes this balance for the existence of life.

The environmental problems of the greenhouse effect and basic global warming, has caused a destruction in part of the ozone which could achieve catastrophic proportions. Human industrial pollution from automobiles, airplanes, power plants, and the burning of coal have contributed to the problems we now must face. As a matter of fact, methane gas, which can be a dangerous thing in itself, is produced by decaying plants, coal mines, and cows (on a funny note, cow farts), and to name a few more causes of manufactured type pollutions, there are aerosol cans, plastics and foam materials, refrigerators, and air conditioners, which can also have a negative effect on the environment. Because of these natural and industrial pollutions, there is too much carbon dioxide in the atmosphere causing an imbalance, thus increasing temperatures on Earth.

It is paramount, that we not only grow trees in our cities, but we must also preserve our tropical rain forests such as those in South America. The destruction and burning of trees also contributes to an over abundance of carbon dioxide in our atmosphere.

The Earth is basically like an island in space. Our surrounding atmosphere primarily consists of nitrogen and oxygen. The Earth's atmosphere extends about 440 miles above its surface. The atmosphere also contains sulfur, which is constantly being consumed on Earth by its different life forms.

Our planet's atmosphere consists of four layers. Closest to the Earth is the troposphere, next closest is the stratosphere, which consists of the ozone (ozone layer), third is the mesosphere, and last is the thermosphere. The troposphere extends about nine miles above the surface of the Earth; it is responsible for weather occurrences on Earth.

In due time, scientists believe that the increase of greenhouse gases could cause a dangerous level of temperature increase of six to eighteen degrees Fahrenheit. This means that because the temperature differential from the last ice age to present day is only sixteen degrees Fahrenheit, if we as a people do not further educate ourselves on this matter, the consequences could be of catastrophic proportions. You see, it has been recently discovered by scientists that thirty or so more gases exist that could cause even more damage. It is also believed that more of these gases could exist, which have not yet been discovered. The amount of carbon dioxide in our atmosphere has increased by thirty percent over the last two centuries.

As earlier stated, there is a problem on our planet due to the over abundance of methane gas. A large part of this is because the world's cattle population doubled from the early 1960s to the 1980s. Another form of methane gas comes from marshes. However, marshes have the ability to absorb large amounts of water. This means that marshes can be deemed beneficial because they could be made to absorb floodwaters. This concept could be accessed when dealing with environmental weather disasters such as hurricane Katrina, which occurred in the southern United States.

In London, England, the Thames Barrier was constructed in case of the occurrence of massive flooding that could be caused by rising sea levels. A major problem is that there are so many nations on Earth which have economic troubles. Therefore, these poor nations cannot afford to build such structures as the Thames Barrier. This is a prime example to the fact that we are in need of a world utopia.

So, what can be done in order to deal with this environmental dilemma? Can such crises be appropriately dealt with? The first step to take would be to preserve the world's natural rain forests, such as those in South America. Next, we could lessen the levels of carbon dioxide in the atmosphere by limiting the burning of fossil fuels. Also, we must decrease the use of chlorofluorocarbons (C.F.C.'s); as I have previously mentioned, some C.F.C.'s are aerosol cans, refrigerators, and air conditioners. It is a strong belief of many experts that this move would be a step in the right direction.

Another step that could be made would be to access the use of alternative forms of energy such as wind, solar, and tidal energy. Wind power could be accessed through the use of tall windmill-like machines. By harnessing the power of wind, you could—in a smart way—create needed energy. Solar power can take advantage of energy which can be accessed directly from our sun. At this time, solar energy has its limitations because the sun is not always exposed. We could also benefit from tidal power, which is accessed through the natural occurrence of ocean waves. Then, there is hydroelectric power which is harnessed from waterfalls. Believe it or not, hydroelectric power presently produces eight percent of the Earth's power needs. Geothermal power is another form of alternative power; it is harnessed in volcanic regions by using hot springs to provide energy. Then there is the extremely controversial one, nuclear energy. Nuclear energy is produced by the forces which hold matter tightly together. However, we must remember the danger of nuclear energy, a lesson learned from the former Soviet Union's Chernobyl disaster. Finally, we could use electric car engines. Use of these electric engines would significantly lessen the quantity of carbon dioxide in the atmosphere.

The big problem with the task of accessing these alternative forms of energy is the finances which are needed for these new forms of energy. Another problem is that greedy industrialists would end up losing money due to a lesser need for us to use their products such as gasoline and oil. It is a sad fact that there are some corporate elites who would deny the survival of the world environment, just so they can keep filling their wallets with cash! This is also evidence that the United States economy must be fixed. Good luck Barack!

Moving on, the Earth is heated by the sun energy that must first pass through our atmosphere. Some of the sun's rays are reflected back into space, some are absorbed. The remaining of these rays hits the Earth and warms its surface. Therefore, our atmosphere allows these rays from the sun to warm the Earth's surface, and then these rays radiate back toward space.

There are different views pertaining to climate change. Those who have a favorable view believe that global warming can heat parts of the Earth which are now too cold. There is also a belief that global warming, through the melting of glaciers, could increase the world's water supply in those areas that lack water. Another view is that winters could become milder due to global warming.

The unfavorable views of global warming, which I am more apt to believe, are also subject to debate. For example, world agriculture would suffer severely. Sea levels would rise. Also, we would become too dependent on our current energy sources, which would only add to this problem. Another of these beliefs is that weather disasters such as tsunamis and hurricanes would occur way too often. Is it just me, or are those who claim to be advocates of the benefits of global warming might include those greedy corporate elites which I earlier mentioned? Money, my friends, is unfortunately always a factor!

In 1997, the U.N. met in Kyoto Japan to discuss the issue of climate change due to global warming. This meeting of the minds led to what is known as the Kyoto Protocol, which set essential standards to save the environment from global warming. This Kyoto Protocol, informally known as the Earth Summit has had many provisions. Most of these provisions apply to very developed nations such as India and China. Unfortunately, like many other U.N. interventions, this protocol was neglected. For example, Australian Prime Minister John Howard declined to comply with this protocol. This was of course due to finances. You see, Australia's economic status was not deemed fit to comply. This is because a major problem of unemployment could have manifested itself in Australia if this protocol was complied with by the Australian government. Currently, fifty-eight nations are included in the Kyoto Protocol.

The next topic of discussion in this environmental portion will be about the ozone layer. Ozone is a form of oxygen, and it thrives in high elevations of the atmosphere. The ozone layer also protects us from ultra violet rays.

Since the 1970s, it has been confirmed that, year by year, the ozone layer is getting thinner and thinner, especially over the South Pole continent of Antarctica. There is a hole in this ozone layer above this continent. The coldest months in Antarctica are from June through September. This weather creates certain chemicals which can destroy ozone gas. This area is dark for long durations of time. The disruption from heavy winds contributes to this problem. These actions of climate are a huge part of what has produced this hole in the ozone layer. However, by the month of November, these negative effects decrease substantially. And for a brief duration, some of the ozone is replenished. Incidentally, there is a smaller ozone hole above the North Pole as well. This is a logical result, considering that the climate at the North Pole is similar to that of the South Pole.

Recently, I was able to obtain a copy of a special edition of "Nightline" with Ted Koppel of A.B.C. that was aired on July 14, 2005. This edition of "Nightline" dealt with the topic of extinction caused by global warming. I discovered some startling facts from this particular program. 2005 was a few years back. However, I must reveal some facts which I obtained through my viewing of this program.

So here it goes: fifty-nine percent of people surveyed at this time had a strong belief that global warming was an imminent reality, sixty-six percent of those surveyed felt that they would not be affected by global warming in their lifetime.

It was revealed that in an area which is a two-hour drive from the city of San Diego California, an area that was once populated with a species of butterflies is now virtually nonexistent of these butterflies. In Costa Rica, a species of frogs, as well as some wild orchids have also virtually vanished. In Madagascar, where three different species of frogs were once prominent, all have mostly vanished. In some polar regions, the melting of glaciers is causing extreme hardships for the polar bears that live in these regions. It is estimated that by 2050, these polar bears will be in grave danger of extinction.

All of these environmental problems are a direct result of global warming. It is also a truism that because of this problem in areas of extremely high climate, an unhealthy fungus has been detected on certain reptiles due to skin texture related to these high climates.

In conclusion, I feel that I need to state that I am a supporter of the negative ramifications of the issue of global warming. The harsh consequence of this environmental problem has not yet become imminent. I passionately stress, that unless something is done about this, we are in for harder times than we have ever previously experienced. I hereby urge our society, as well as all world societies to properly confront this issue, especially world government officials, who have the authority to do something about this imminent danger. In order to fix all of the other problems the human race now faces, we must save our precious environment. We cannot cure genocide, starvation, or accomplish other things in our world beneficial to our humane cause if the world we live in becomes uninhabitable. I also stress that we mustn't panic or have an over abundance of fear because of imminent environmental issues; just do the best you can. The human race has behaved with stupidity at times, but it is smart and moral enough to deal with this problem efficiently.

Finally, I say through a utopian dream: We can save the species of Earth, and, of course, save the human race! Read on!

STEM CELL RESEARCH

In this segment, we will discuss the stem cell debate, including some of the processes of stem cell research, as well as a brief history of this controversial issue. Stem cells are cells that have the ability to evolve into types of cells which will form into the organs and tissues of the body. The benefits of detaching and developing human stem cells in a laboratory were first discovered in 1998. Back in 1993, President Bill Clinton, with the assistance of congress, helped to produce the ratification of the National Institutes of Health Revitalization Act (N.I.H.). This newly established act gave authority to the commencement of federal funding for human embryo research for the very first time.

You see, stem cells possess the ability to divide endlessly. This leads to the creation of more of these stem cells, as well as other types of cells. Stem cells are the originals by which an organism produces its basic makeup. Through this research, we could potentially acquire the ability to produce tissues that could be used to replace damaged tissues. The main argument of stem cell research is the possibility that certain diseases, such as Parkinson's disease, could be cured.

Something called a blastocyst (a human embryo which is made up of a hollow ball of cells) can penetrate into human tissue and human organs. This is the process of differentiation, which has led to the controversial issue of cloning. Through this process of differentiation, scientists can procure the ability to somewhat control these cells and help to cure organs in humans who may be diseased. In adult humans, the muscles, bone marrow, liver, and skin are where these stem cells are obtrusive.

Cells that exist in the bone marrow especially have the aptitude of division. The cells produced through this division process create what are called precursor cells. These precursor cells may produce a variety of cell types, but they do not have the ability to produce more stem cells.

It is a popular view, notably of right wing Republicans, that the destruction of these embryos for the research of bringing about possible cures is yet still immoral. The other view of the left wing Democrats is that it would be immoral not to use these procedures for the capacity of medical cures. By now, you must realize that the study of embryonic stem cell research has led to a fierce debate over the moral or immoral convictions of this issue.

Of this, I would now like to make a point by relating the topic of stem cell research to the topic of abortion. It is the right wing view that the destruction of these embryos is equivalent to the destruction of a zygote or fetus. However, we must take a look at what is done with these embryos if not used. Do you know what is done? I'll tell you! Get this: They are thrown out as if they were garbage! In biohazard bags, I presume? So look at it this way: Would the disgusting act that some parents have had the immorality to actually do, namely that of throwing out a newborn baby in a plastic bag, be a reasonable action? Of course not! So, to have some form of consistency here, I ask: If these embryos were alive, why would we dispose of them rather than use them in a positive way for possible medical breakthroughs?

I was exceedingly impressed with the son of the fortieth president of the U.S., Ronald Wilson Reagan—Ron junior. At the Democratic National Convention of 2004, Ron spoke on behalf of the positive aspects of stem cell research. He is an avid believer in the great potential medical benefits that this study could potentially generate. By no means am I a fan of Ron's Father, former U.S. president Ronald Reagan, although he did, in my opinion, do a few good things, like when he said directly to former Soviet President Gorbachev "Knock down this wall," where Reagan was, of course, referring to the Berlin wall. At the time of that statement of Reagan's, I said what every Democrat said at the time, "Who the hell is he to do that?" Seeing that I am not a fan of the former Reagan Administration, knowing that he did some bad things, I have now matured and have come to the realization that this statement to former Soviet president Gorbachev was an undeniably good thing. Reagan is to me the most confusing American president of them all.

Anyway, although I am not a fan of former President Reagan, I am, however, a fan of his son. Ron Reagan junior stated at the 2004 Democratic National Convention that those who are opposed to stem cell research, quote, "They should be ashamed of themselves." I also have enjoyed his political commentary that he used to give on M.S.N.B.C. Ron also stated during his tenure at M.S.N.B.C. that in the 2004 election, he was not going to vote Republican. Now that is impressive, the son of one of the most prominent Republicans of our time, or maybe even of all time, having the sense to cross political lines; that, my friends, is a prime example of independent thinking. I must also commend his mother, Nancy, for giving her son her blessings when he decided to speak at the Democratic National Convention.

At this point, I deem it necessary to give a brief summarization of landmarks, in relation to the issue of stem cell research.

As previously stated, in 1993, the "National Institutes of Health Revitalization Act" was created during the Clinton Administration. In 1995, the Dickey Amendment, which disallowed government funds created for research for that of human embryos, was ratified. By 1999 and following the conception of the first embryonic stem cell lines in 1998, a University of Wisconsin professor by the name of James Thompson, with the assistance of an attorney by the name of Harriet Rabb—a woman who worked for the "Department of Health and Human Services" (D.H.H.S.)—released a legal hypothesis setting the course for the pro stem cell research view. This caused a pre-eminence over the Dickey Amendment. At this crux, it became able to have appropriate funding for embryonic stem cell research. This would lead to stem cell studies gaining a more common acceptance, thus leading to beneficial grants from ambitious scientists.

In November 2004, proposition 71 of the state of California would provide billions of dollars in state funding for more research. From 2001 to 2006, a major setback was caused by the Bush Administration restricting funds for this cause. This would also lead to the defeat of some funding of non-human stem cell research. In May of 2006, Republican evangelist Rick Santorum introduced the "Alternative Pluripotent Stem Cell Therapies Enhancement Act" to the U.S. Senate. In July of 2006, this act was voted down. The very next day, Bush would veto what was called the "Stem Cell Research Enhancement Act." This act could have possibly reversed the Dickey Amendment. This would be a setback to the cause of stem cell research.

In November of 2006, there was another amendment, this time coming from the state of Missouri. This was the passing of amendment two which gave allowance for more research. However, it impeded another issue—the issue of cloning. Cloning, in my opinion, is an extremely dangerous thing. Continuing on now, in February of 2007, the "California Institute for Regenerative Medicine" became the largest financial supporter of stem cell research in United States history. This institute would give tens of millions for this cause. Quite recently, on November 4, 2008 (incidentally the date I got sober in 1996) stemming from the state of Michigan was a landmark proposal which allowed researchers of this state to create embryonic stem cell cultures from leftover embryos that were donated from fertility treatments.

There are currently pro-stem cell research organizations that are vital to this cause. To name a few: The California Institute for Regenerative Medicine, the Genetics Policy Institute, and the American Society for Cell Biology.

Continuing on, I would now like to give my appraisal of just how I view the stem cell debate. Try to see it this way: In order for humans to live or any animals or mammals to survive, it is necessary to kill. By "kill," I mean our natural need to hunt for food or to eat plants. You see, animals and mammals must eat to survive, and life can only feed off other life. A physical world in nature is actually quite evil. To deal with the evils of nature, the human race must be as moral as it can possibly be. Evil causes good, so therefore if we destroy life to survive in nature, then why can't we access this unconscious life and make use of it to cure diseases. We should use the life of these unconscious embryos to support life, as well as to respect life. This study could not only cure diseases, but could also produce limbs for those in need of limbs. My elaboration of how we are evil in nature is truthful. You must understand that good cannot exist without evil, just as a top cannot exist without a bottom, or a side cannot exist without another side. I'm sorry to say it, but if there was no evil, good couldn't exist.

My position on cloning differs from my position on the stem cell debate. Other than my being in favor of the production of limbs, I stress that cloning must be approached with extreme caution! Some time ago, I was watching a Nova special on Boston's Public Broadcasting System. A scientist whose name I cannot recall made an interesting hypothesis in pertinence to the issue of cloning. He stated that the ramifications of human or animal cloning resembles the creation of the hammer. You see, a hammer can be used for good, such as a tool of construction. On the other hand, a hammer can be used for evil, such as using it as a weapon and smashing one's skull. This means that if we are to explore this process of cloning, we must exercise extreme caution. Cloning is not something that should be accessed in a pre-utopia. It is not difficult to see the possible advances of an unnecessary evil through an abuse of the cloning process. If this scientific study were to be accessed by those with bad intentions, such as the creation of a clone army, the consequences could be of adverse proportions.

Finally, to make another point, I would like to state that I am an avid believer in alien life forms. The universe, I believe is endless, so I came to the conclusion that there must be a place in a distant solar system which is able to support life. I have recently come to a theory of my own, that if Earth were ever to be visited by an alien life form, they would not be an evil culture. The reason I believe so is that if an alien civilization were ever to achieve such technology, they would have to be moral, because an evil race would have destroyed itself before reaching such a technological level. This makes perfect sense! Think about the human race and what I have been talking about so far in this book. If we take the route of evil, our environment, either we would not survive or we would end up destroying ourselves in a nuclear war. Therefore, the human race must choose good over evil if we are to survive. If we approach life with a respect for its survival, as well as the using of life for cures of diseases, we will survive. And, maybe someday, a manifestation of another intelligent life form could be acknowledged. Through what I just explained, good will always conquer evil, otherwise existence would not exist.

One day back in the mid 1990s, a musical friend of mine made a point that if Reagan had his way with the "Star Wars" project, we would be much more advanced in space exploration than we are today. I responded by saying "Good point, dude" but this was only to avoid an argument. Even back in the 1980s, although my political knowledge was primitive, I was opposed to the "Star Wars" idea.

In 1984, there was a political advertisement of the presidential Mondale/Ferraro ticket, which ran against the Reagan/Bush ticket. This advertisement stated that we should not put this space station into our heavens. The other point of this advertisement was that we must first take care of ourselves before pursuing such unnecessary ambitions.

Incidentally, on another day, this time in the early 1990s, I almost got in an argument with another one of my musical buddies. This was about the nuclear arms race. My friend was a bit brainwashed, and thought that the United States had to stay ahead in the nuclear arms race because he believed that if any nation, especially the former Soviet Union, got ahead of us, they would not hesitate to destroy us. This statement was completely unfounded. Because of Reagan's over production of nuclear arms, the United States alone could blow up the planet many times over. The former Soviet Union or any of the other nations on Earth are not even remotely that stupid. However, we must keep these weapons from those who may not be stupid, but are crazy.

There has been a variety of ideas on how to rid the world of nuclear weapons. One idea that has been discussed is to somehow send these weapons into outer space, but this would be too dangerous a method. I have a theory that any substance on Earth has another contradicting element which can dilute itself. Is it possible that scientists could figure out a way to dilute these weapons? Albert Einstein was a brilliant man. However, his discovery of the splitting of the atom causing a chain reaction was a dangerous discovery. Einstein was fearful that German NAZI scientists would discover this dangerous capability. This is why Einstein gave the United States government the formula to this now proven theory, thus the commencement of the "Manhattan Project" which surprisingly did not include Einstein himself. Einstein was Jewish; he wanted to avoid NAZI prosecution for himself, his family, and his fellow Jews, and seeing that the Hitler NAZI regime was gaining power, I don't blame him for revealing his atom splitting theory to U.S. government authorities.

Fact: In the fiscal year from 1986 to 1987, local state and federal governments spent a combined total of 60.6 billion dollars on law enforcement. Federal law enforcement expenditures ranked last in absolute dollars and accounted for only six percent of federal spending. By way of comparison, the federal government spent twenty-four million dollars more on space exploration (Star Wars), and forty-three times more on national defense and international relations of law enforcement. Remember, this was under the Reagan Administration.

Although I am not a fan of Ronald Reagan, I don't hate the man. However, I have come to the conclusion that his priorities were whacked. One day during his presidency, Reagan was confronted by an unknown source who was concerned about the mass starvation in Ethiopia. Reagan must have been busy because he sent an aircraft filled with rice to this nation. Sounds like a good deed ,doesn't it? But wait, I'm not done yet. Little did Reagan know that for certain medical reasons, these starving Ethiopians were physically unable to consume rice! You see, Reagan was unprepared for this action, he did not view this problem thoroughly enough. So here is a cute little rhyme I made up in regard to this matter.

Dear Mr. Reagan, you are so nice
sending these people rations of rice
although they'd be better of eating head lice
Dear Mr. Reagan you should have thought twice

As I previously stated, Reagan confuses me. However, I am not in the least bit confused on the issue of stem cell research, much more so than on my iffy view of abortion. Once again, thank you for listening. Read on!

EDUCATION

In this education segment of Politics, I will give an assessment of the education systems of the United States, as well as some interesting facts pertaining to education in Japan. I will also reveal some ideas, for the advancement of reading for the young. I will stress what I see is wrong with the current U.S education system as well, especially in pertinence to the ideals of democracy in relation to the U.S. education system that now exists. And finally, to be as fair as possible, I will also state the positive aspects of education in America today.

First, I must give a summary of how the U.S. education system came into play. So, once again, here we go: Schooling in the United States of America commenced in the colonial era. My home state of Massachusetts, which at the time was considered a colony, as well as the rest of New England, was momentous to the origin of schooling in the United States. In 1642, the colony of Massachusetts was the central basis to the advancement of the obligatory statutes espoused in the other thirteen colonies from the 1640s to the 1650s. In the colonial era, almost every school was a private school.

The first university in the United States was the well-known Harvard University which was founded in 1636 It would become accessible for students in 1638. As a matter of fact, a large majority of the original universities opened their doors from 1640 to 1750. The so-called "Ivy League" colleges were the most prominent, as they are still quite prominent today. To name a few: Columbia, Yale, Brown, University of Pennsylvania, and of course, Harvard. In 1785, the "Land Ordinance" was established. It promoted the U.S. education system. This took place immediately after the end of the American Revolution.

1862 was the birth of what is known as the "Homestead Act" which caused the termination of the "Land Ordinance." Also following the American Revolution, the new American education system would thoroughly gain prominence, thus causing the U.S. to achieve outstanding levels of literacy among the young, at a time when literacy among U.S. citizens was not as commonplace as it is today.

Continuing on, from 1771 to 1817, in regards to German immigrant youths in the colony of Pennsylvania, the number of these youths acquiring an education, increased from thirty-three percent to sixty-nine percent. Years later, in my home state of Massachusetts, a law was passed concerning the attendance of all students. By 1870, elementary school was purveyed to all children free of charge. Unfortunately, the sad reality of segregation was still in effect at this time.

At the very beginning of the twentieth century, children from the ages of eight to fourteen were forced by law to attend school. This would lead to seventy-two percent of all American youths attending school by 1910. By 1918, every U.S. state required youths to attend elementary school (Also, the Boston Red Sox won the World Series that year—Yahoo!).

Unfortunately, in this era, it was common for teachers to practice physical punishment on students, such as hitting them on the knuckles with a ruler. This uncalled for act of physical punishment tactic was used with regularity for simply giving wrong answers. Luckily for me, when I attended school this behavior by teachers was no longer tolerated. Backing up to the year 1910, towns and cities of America began the provision of high schools. By the time 1940 rolled around, young adults in America were graduating high school at the rate of fifty percent Over the next sixty-nine or so years, the United States (most of the time) have done their best for the advancement of education in this country.

As I elaborated on in the Stem Cell Research segment of this book, I explained the advancement of good through the existence of evil. I talked about the limitations that exist in the achievement of a utopia within a physical world. I admit that in our present day and age, the current education system which we now have, although there is plenty of room for improvement, is the best we can presently do. However, I do believe that the basis of education not only in America, but in the rest of the world as well, has many flaws. Seeing that once my vision began for the creation of this book, I was not exactly an exemplary student once my life took a major turn, but bear with me, I have learned a lot due to this *Vision of a Mental Patient* that commenced years before I was ever diagnosed. You see, the problem is that students can have conflicts of interest, or family problems, that may distract them from their studies. This is the cause of boredom or rebellious behavior, when students are forced to learn certain things with repetition. I have a close musical friend named Mike Chadwick. Mike has recently become a high school guidance counselor, and may I add, his caring personality is perfect for this occupation. I have witnessed many good acts from the school guidance counselors that I knew growing up as a kid. Teachers should be friendlier with their students like guidance counselors are. We'll get back to this later.

This common youth rebellion is also due to certain teachers teaching their opinions rather than what they should be.

VISION OF A MENTAL PATIENT

Students are educated so that they can become knowledgeable enough to form their own opinions, so that they can contribute their values to society. I certainly hope that is the goal of an education system. It certainly should be! Students are now told what to learn and how to view it. This is not the way it should be! But we are trapped in a physical world. You know what I say about that? Utopia! Utopia! Utopia! Utopia!"Soon, I will reveal some more subconscious lyrics to you. These will be lyrics regarding education. For now, I must elucidate to you ideas which I have to make education more effective, interesting, and fun for our youth.

So, once again here we go: For the advancement of improving the quality and levels of reading for our children, I recommend, in the elementary and possibly the high school stages of education, a type of books that as a youngster I fell in love with. These books are called "Choose Your Own Adventure" books. These could be helpful for the maturation of making choices. Choose Your Own Adventure books are different from normal books. These are not read from page one to the end. The premise of these books is this: you read a few pages starting from page one. Once you have read these first few pages, you will be given a scenario, and you will be asked from what you have just read to make a decision what action to take regarding your fictional situation. For example: to do this, turn to page fifty, to take another action turn to page twenty-five, and you will be given a third option that would require you to turn to page, say fifteen, and the book will continue as such, until you either succeed or fail in your fictional situation.

Other types of these books existed when I was a youth, such as Dungeons and Dragons, Twistaplot, Time Machine, and Adventures of Indiana Jones. There were even types of these books which deal with sports. You, being the coach of a baseball team or football team, decide whether or not to steal second base or go for a touchdown pass until your team either wins or loses.

My childhood friend, Joshua Bernard, and I discovered these books when we were in the fourth grade. Not only did we discover that these books were fun, but little did we realize that these books would advance our levels of reading as we grew older. I remember going into a store with Joshua in our home town of Dracut, and we would actually sit down in an aisle reading these books because since we were so young and obviously unemployed, we had no money to purchase one. I have grown into a very avid reader due to the benefits of Choose Your Own Adventure and the other books that had the same basic premise. Another excellent thing about these books is that the main character is you, thus causing a greater interest for youths, and youths would benefit from these books in other ways as well.

Do you realize how much fun it would be for students to read these books for homework, or in class; or discussing with your teacher and classmates the choices you made, as well as the results you had from the reading of these books? In order to write the more scientific part of this book The Monolith, I had to do a lot of research. Through my research, I discovered that some of the best books are actually children's books. By children's books, I am not referring to books like *Dr. Seuss Cat in the Hat* or *Dumb Bells*. The children's books I am referring to are books dealing with astronomy, volcanoes, pollution, and the making of products. Some of these titles are *Volcanoes and Earthquakes* by Ken Rubin, *Volcanoes* by Seymour Simon, and *Sand to Glass* by Inez Snyder. These books that are intended for the young are precise and right to the point, which is the same way I'm trying to write this book. Don't get me wrong; I am a lover of adult literature as well.

Back to Choose Your Own Adventure for a moment, I was seeking out an astronomy book in the children's section at the Billerica Public Library when I came across a new set of versions of Choose Your Own Adventure books. This was a different set from the ones I read as a child. I have not read any of these new Choose Your Own Adventure books. It has been a number of years since I have read any of the old versions of these book types, but I remember some: Mystery of the Maya, Sabotage, Your Code Name is Jonah, Curse of Battersea Hall, You Are a Spy For George Washington, By Balloon Through the Sahara, The Cave of Time, and The Return to the Cave of time.

Another method that could assist students to learn better, would be one which is already accessed "cue cards." I was hanging out at my home one day in my teenage years, and I was just sitting in my living room bored and vegetating. All of a sudden, I looked down at my coffee table and noticed that a box of trivial pursuit cards was just sitting there, so I picked them up and proceeded to quiz myself. I didn't fare so well. All of a sudden, I thought through the idea of a sports type Choose Your Own Adventure book to make a game out of it. I imagined that I was coaching my beloved Boston Red Sox, and for every question I got right, I won a game, while for every question I got wrong I lost a game. In the span of a few hours, I had gone through many imagined 162 game seasons, including playoffs. Not only did I win the World Series, but I could go undefeated. Yes, I memorized all one thousand history and geography questions in this set of trivia cards.

The next day, I was hanging out with a couple of my Deallegiance buddies in my living room. We were trying to figure out how to get some beer so we could party that night at the fort, in the woods behind my house. All of a sudden, by whim, one of my buddies decided to grab these trivia cards on my coffee table and began to quiz me. I nailed about 998 out of the 1,000 history and geography questions. They were dumbfounded and said to me "Ted, you should be in college." However, being a teenager at the time, my main concern was to have as much fun as possible. So college wasn't for me at this time.

Presently, I am not only unable to answer any of the trivia questions I was quizzed on that day. I also can't even recall what any of the questions were. Then again, that was nearly twenty years ago.

If we could access some new and more open-minded education methods, I believe it would reap benefits as far as the modern problems with the conduct of the students of present day are concerned. My problem in high school was that I reached such levels of boredom that I was forced to have fun by playing jokes on my friends in the halls between classes, or by skipping classes and destroying a few brain cells, or by smoking in the boy's room.

When my father was a student, the main problems with the conduct of students were things like running in the halls, chewing gum, or minor misbehavior. Today, the disciplinary problems involve things like drugs, weapons, as well as other extremities of teenage rebellion.

The best teacher I ever had was a high school teacher named Miss Sullivan. She was my high school math teacher. Miss Sullivan was an acceptable teacher, who, despite all the hell I and my fellow students put her through, still generally liked us all. I was always the class clown; one day in class, I was goofing off when Miss Sullivan did something that I never witnessed any teacher do. Instead of yelling at me, she gave me a great smile and said, "Ted you are so likable." She would tolerate laughter as long as we tried, and did not get carried away with our goofing off. Don't get me wrong, Miss Sullivan sent me down to the principal's office many, many times. You see, this woman had the right idea on how a teacher should be.

On the other hand, I had another teacher who couldn't teach a rabbit to shit; but I will not get into that because I choose to see the good in people and not the bad in them as much as I can.

These possible tactics of teaching for knowledge, imagination, and enjoyment would not by any means end bad conduct in our students. However, I do believe it would significantly decrease it by quite a bit. As for ideas on possible new methods, for the teaching of mathematics or science (although science could be considered fun already) or any other subjects that exist in the current educational system, I do not have any ideas on that at this time. But I am confident that if we could have a meeting of the minds, the potential of our current education system could reach astounding measures.

At this juncture, it is now appropriate to once again reveal some more lyrics. First, another Metallica song, and then I will reveal the title track to the sole album that my former band Malicious Intent put out in 1995. This next Metallica song is about school in a subconscious manner. I now present the lyrics to track three on the *And Justice for All* album; this one's called "Eye of the Beholder"

Do you see what I see? Truth is an offence
Your silence for your confidence
Do you hear what I hear? Doors are slamming shut
Limit your imagination, keep you where they must
Do you feel what I feel, bittering distress
Who decides what you express?
Do you take what I take?
Endurance is the word
Moving back instead of forward seems to me absurd
Doesn't matter what you see, or into it what you read
You can do it your own way, If it's done just how I say
Independence limited, freedom of choice
Choice is made for you my friend
Freedom of speech, speech is words that they will bend
Freedom with their exception
Do you fear what I fear? living properly
The truth to you are lies to me
Do you choose what I choose? more alternatives
Energy derives from both the plus and negative
Do you need what I need? Boundaries overthrown
Look inside to each his own
Do you trust what I trust? Me, myself, and I
Penetrate the smoke screen, I see through the selfish lie
Doesn't matter what you see, or into it what you read
You can do it your own way, if it's done just How I say
Independence limited, freedom of choice
Choice is made for you my friend, freedom of speech
Speech is words that they will bend
Freedom no longer frees you
Do you know what I know, your money and your wealth
Your silence just to hear yourself
Do you want what I want? Desire not a thing
I hunger after independence, strengthen freedoms ring
Doesn't matter what you see

VISION OF A MENTAL PATIENT

Or into it what you read, you can do it your own way
If it's done just how I say

Remember Einstein's quote "Imagination is more important than knowledge"? This, my friends, is a true statement. The ultimate truth on this matter is that our education systems at times can be corrupted. No one could ever see so far that an education system can be corrupt. Open your mind and come to the realization that anything can be corrupt if used for selfish reasons.

There are those out there who fear your imagination. There are even those who fear a Utopia. Certain people want to limit your imagination and keep you in their control. Take this advice I give: never but never let anyone limit your imagination.

For the first time in this book, I will reveal some lyrics from one of my former bands. This is the title track, as well as the first song on the Malicious Intent album *Mind Control*. This song can pertain to education as well as most issues and theories in this book. This song was written by myself, Roland Gagnon, Paul Leary, and Dan Desharnais. Here you are, Mind Control.

Thrash and scream in your dreams

Seam to seam these men are mean
Trained to kill-without will
Taking life- without right
Destroying land-only at night
Ignorance-only at life
Who is paying the ultimate price?
The men who cry? Or the ones that die?
The pain they feel-the veterans kneel
Brainwashing is the mind they steal
Mind control-they stole your soul
Mind control-your soul they stole

Revolution-only way out
Resolution-it's the only way out
Sneaking upon your enemies
Dropping bombs on everything you see
Who is paying the ultimate price?
The men who cry of the ones that die
The pain they feel-the veterans kneel
Brainwashing is the mind they steal
the hunt, the game, the pain
The pain they feel is oh so real

Insane, they blame the pain
The pain they feel is oh so real
The blood, they spilt, it rained
The pain they feel is oh so real
God must deal with what they feel
God feel!
Honestly, I cannot see the secret to this infamy
Hopelessness forgotten traits
That surely can't procrastinate
Enraged by my reasons bare
Excuses clenched by my fear
I'm praying for forgiveness, as my time comes near
Brainwashed!!!!!!

There is an argument regarding worldwide education that it is imperative to achieve success in education, as countries basic need for better economic stability. The U.N. tries to intervene as much as possible in order to improve the education systems of nations abroad. This fact leads me to a conclusion of a disagreement I have with my loving grandmother Nana Hodge I love you Nana but one thing you always teach me was to think for myself. You see, my grandmother believes that the smartest cultures of the world are the Germans and the Jews. I do agree that these are two extremely smart cultures; as a matter of fact all cultures on Earth are smart in one way or another. The best off cultures could be the primitive tribes of Africa due to how simple and moral their lifestyles are. However, as far as the industrialized nations on the planet are concerned, the Japanese, in my opinion, could be the smartest culture on Earth in present day. The country of Japan or as the Japanese pronounce it

"Nippon," is extraordinarily advanced in the field of electronics despite the existence of Silicon Valley, which is located in the United States, in the southern part of the San Francisco Bay area. I decided to include in this education segment of Politics an assessment of the Japanese, both industrially and education wise. The Japanese education system began to achieve its prominence way back in the sixth century, long before Christopher Columbus was even born. Education officials at this time in Japan were designated through what you could term as a sovereign system of analysis. This was the opposite type of the system that China had. Japanese education never achieved much progress until sometime later due to the rise of military class during what was called the Kamukura period. Influence of the scholars of education in Japan gained credibility despite what was happening at the time. Buddhist monasteries were instrumental centers for learning in this era.

Eventually, the more modern education systems of Japan would end up being virtually identical to that of the United States by the accessing of kindergarten, elementary, and high school. Japan is much more successful at sending their young adults to college. By 1991, 2.1 million Japanese students were entered into a total of 507 Universities; remember, there are a lot more people in the United States than there are in Japan. Due to this excellence of the Japanese culture's education system, they are the leaders in technologies, such as machinery, biomedical research, and especially they are superior in the fields of electronics and automobile manufacturing.

The Japanese space program may not be as advanced as the United States National Aeronautics Space Administration (NASA), but it is not too shabby, either. The Japanese space program is called the Japan Aerospace Exploration Agency (JAXA). Presently, the population of Japan is approximately 127 million plus. Another piece of evidence that backs up my claim of the intelligence of their culture is that the life expectancy rate for a Japanese person currently stands at a staggering 81.25 years of age. The Japanese have achieved this outstanding life expectancy rate due to their common approach to a healthy lifestyle, which is impressive in this day and age. After all, look at the obesity problem that now exists in the United States.

Okay, so the field of electronics is, in basic terms, a study of the flow of charge or moving electrons through non-metal conductors. In order to excel in the study of electronics, it is necessary to have an expertise in mathematics. Mathematics is also necessary for the study of circuit analysis. Circuit analysis is the study of the ways of figuring out general linear systems for concealed variables, like the voltage of a particular node or stem of electric current through a branch in a grid.

I now present to you a small list of some of the most prominent electronic corporations on Earth: Intel (U.S.A.), Samsung (South Korea), Toshiba (Japan), Texas Instruments (U.S.A.), and Sony (Japan). You see, Japan may not possess the most successful electronics corporation in the world, but face it, they are way ahead of us. My theory is that this is because Japan is not as populous a nation as other industrial nations and the import export process may have its limitations. I must stress that U.S. diplomatic relations with Japan must be good so that we can learn from them and achieve more industrially. However, this should not be the main reason for us to get along with countries in a diplomatic sense. What the U.S. must do, as I'm sure Barack Obama will do, is to achieve good allies for the most important reason of all, rule number one: Morality!

Okay, back to the United States for a moment. In pertinence to electronic technology, I would now like to elaborate on Silicon Valley. As previously stated, Silicon Valley is located in the San Francisco Bay area in the state of California. The name Silicon Valley is derived from this region's enormous amount of silicon chip innovators and manufacturers. Silicon Valley is one of the most distinguished advocates on the planet, in relations to this study. As far back as the early twentieth century, this region of the San Francisco Bay area was pioneering in the early history of television and radio.

Okay, that was cool, huh? I now present one more open-minded idea for the education system. This is something that is essential for getting through the hardships life can present. I hereby suggest for a subject in our schools: Laughter. That was not a misprint; yes, Laughter. Now, before jumping all over me for saying this, please allow a brief elaboration. I am not saying that this should be an everyday subject. Why not on Friday afternoons at the end of the school week, let our children, in a friendly way, have a talk with their teachers and fellow students about all of the funny things that happened during the course of their week? This would improve conduct, as well as sending everyone home for the weekend in a good mood! Is not laughter a necessity in life? I have news for you: It most certainly is! If I could not have laughter, I would have never gotten better as a mentally ill person! Because of my upbeat humor as well as other more serious traits, I have been sober for well over twelve years and my life has become a good one! I mean, we might as well try something, because our education system is presently in a shambles. By the time I left high school, I was sick of the present education system's attitude that children should not be allowed to enjoy themselves at least a little, and that children are seen but not heard. What is it with this present state of certain students hating teachers and certain teachers thinking we're just a bunch of pains in the ass? Don't get me wrong, students must be disciplined when going too far, but what the fuck, man! Let's teach our students and teachers to like one another and make some real progress.

There are two types of working class heroes of America who I deeply admire. These are the teachers and farmers of America! The second job I ever had was with my friend Joshua on a farm in Dracut. Joshua and I worked a three-hour shift picking tomatoes. We were young healthy kids, and by the end of that three-hour shift, I was sweating so much that I looked like I jumped in a pool with my clothes on! The guy who ran the farm would work these insane twelve to fourteen hour shifts day after day! And this guy made a modest amount of money! It is so commendable that the farmers of America today continue to do a job they love for basically peanuts! We must save the American farmer of today for doing a job of the utmost importance. It's food for crying out loud! What would we do without food, clone it? That would be a good use of cloning! Back to the point! Another reason I am a Democrat is that the Democratic Party has been fighting for the American farmer since day one! I also commend the farmers of all world nations! The other type of working class hero of America whom I love is the teacher! Not all of them by any means, but the good teachers out there deserve better! A long, long time ago, as a young kid, I saw an edition of sixty minutes which was about the struggles of the American teacher of this era. There was a woman teacher on the show who was a passionate and loving teacher who took pride in her work. Anyhow, for personal financial reasons she had to give up her profession. When asked why, this poor lady broke down in tears and said she had no choice. You see, there were people who depended on her, and she needed to help the ones she loved. We must save the American teacher! We also must save all the teachers of the rest of our world. I do not possess the knowledge to tell you of all the struggles of the teachers and farmers of other world nations. However, someday I will!

I am fed up with greedy corporate elites who scrounge for every nickel and dime they can get their hands on. These big business gurus are royally screwing the farmers and teachers of America, not to mention all of the other working class heroes abroad! My question, as well as many others is this: How much is enough? This corporate greed should be tolerated no more! Obama already said it in his campaign. Enough!

Now that I got that out, it is time to wrap up this education segment. I would now like to once again say that keeping an open mind and listening to others can and will promote and improve any world issue we wish to embark on. Peace be with you; and read on!

HEALTHCARE

In this next segment on healthcare, we will have a discussion on not only the political and social ramifications of healthcare in America today, but we will also discuss the personal responsibilities which we as individuals should take on for our own personal health, such as the problem of obesity that is now especially prominent in the United States. Recently, while viewing my beloved C.N.N., I saw health mentor Richard Simmons. To my surprise, for the first time I saw this man not dressed for exercise. Instead, he was wearing a suit and tie, and was speaking directly to the U.S. Congress. He was speaking on the behalf of the problem of obesity in America. Of course, it was a shock to me, seeing a man who usually would be donning a Speedo suit, to be pointing his finger at the members of Congress and fighting for something of moral importance. He especially expressed a concern for the youth of America who were faced with this problem. He even stated that he might consider running for political office at some point in the future. I would just like to express my appreciation for this man by stating that he has been a moral force for the healthiness of Americans, as well as being a very decent human being. I personally believe that you could be anywhere in the United States and have a friend or loved one with a severe obesity problem, and you would be able to get Mr. Simmons on the phone with this person in a heartbeat. Now, Mr. Simmons does not look like one of those guys that you would see in a home exercise system advertisement, but he is healthy in a cardiovascular way.

Moving on, let's tackle this issue from a personal perspective. You see, because our bodies have the individual ability to adapt, this inner adaptability helps us not only in a physical manner, but also electrically. To elaborate, the brain and nervous system makes small electric charges, which cause us to move voluntarily and even instinctively. This is crucial, to the production of our emotional and mechanical being. These human electric charges are termed as bioelectrical. These bioelectrical charges cause both human and animal impulses coherent with the synchronization of our movements.

Obesity among adults in the United States has grown to dangerous proportions. From 1980 to 2000, obesity for the youth of America has tripled. Another fact is that adults are not faring much better. The chilling fact is that in this same time frame, obesity in adults has doubled. Obesity is now the second leading cause of avoidable death in America, behind smoking (which I am guilty of myself, but I love my Lucky Strikes). The problem of obesity can lead to many unhealthy diseases such as diabetes, osteoarthritis, sleep apnea, and some types of cancers. In the last segment on education, I mentioned that the Japanese have an outstanding life expectancy rate. The life expectancy rate in America pales in comparison to Japan because of the unhealthiness that Americans have developed, including the problem of obesity, which is obviously due to the present American lifestyle.

We are all aware that diet and exercise is a solution. However, personal motivation is a factor. Due to a lack of physical motivation in Americans, other more lazy, yet effective methods have gained credibility. Processes such as bariatric surgery, or the taking of certain types of medications have come to be. An individual's genetics or being afflicted of a mental illness can also reap negative health situations. There are actually some psyche medications that can contribute to one's obesity. I myself take a medication called Clozaril, which has beneficial qualities. However, this medication can cause obesity if proper health measures are not practiced. I myself do not appear to be obese, but in a medical sense, I am slightly obese. As far back as the era of Hippocrates, obesity has been considered a medical disorder. A person's body mass index (obesity) is most relative to ones metabolism. Metabolism is the set of chemical reactions which develop in an organism. Metabolism is broken down into two essentially important categories. One of them is called catabolism, which is the breaking down of organics in order to use energy within our cells. The other one is called anabolism, which is the making of use of energy for the building blocks of cells. These two parts of metabolism causing chemical reactions are then systemized into metabolic paths, where these chemicals are then altered into other chemicals. This is done by a sequence of what are called enzymes (an enzyme is any of various complex proteins which are produced by living cells, which may then create biochemical reactions at certain body temperatures). An example of an enzyme is tryptophan, which exists in turkey; when you consume tryptophan, you may become drowsy. So, if you have ever gotten tired after Thanksgiving dinner, now you know why. In a new direction, in order give some of the specifics of events pertinent to healthcare in America, I deem it necessary to have some discussion on events and measures regarding healthcare.

The first topic I wish to inform you on is what is known as the False Claims Act (F.C.A.) This False claims act is also known as the Lincoln Law. This is a federal law which gives an individual the right to file a complaint in regards to federal contractors who may be guilty of breaking the law (this act was made especially for those who are not government officials). The exercise of this act can also be termed as whistle blowing. Those who have the courage to exercise this act may stand to collect anywhere from fifteen percent to twenty-five percent of recovered damages. This law or act usually will be practiced in either healthcare or military issues.

It has been claimed that the cause of this law was due to certain misgivings during the American Civil War. This was the selling of sick mules, fetid food rations, as well as faulty military equipment which was sold by defense contractors in this era. The first ratification of the false claims act was on March 2, 1863. This law was an absolute necessity because of a needed response to the corruption of different types of fraud. This would also lead to what is called the *qui tam* provision. This provision gave the right to file lawsuits on behalf of the government, which ultimately leads to the prosecutor's share of a percentage.

Resulting from this F.C.A. law, it is now illegal to make or cause an untrue record in order to receive a false claim. No longer can anyone plan to defraud our government by creating a false claim. You no longer can falsely certify a type or amount of property to be used by the government. You cannot certify reception of property on a document without proof of credibility. You also cannot knowingly purchase government property without federal authorization. Lastly, you cannot produce false records to defer or decrease accountability to pay or disseminate government property.

At this essence, I would like to summarize the story about the largest case of healthcare fraud in United States history. This is the story of a Federal Bureau of Investigations (F.B.I.) agent named John Schilling, and the execution of the largest simultaneous raiding of a public corporation called Columbia H.C.A. (Healthcare Association), that spanned over six U.S. states. It commenced with John Schilling transferring from Columbia H.C.A. employee to covert F.B.I. informant. Schilling would later become the central witness for the Justice Department in pertinence to this healthcare fraud case. It set about when he came across a corroboration of an accounting error of 3.5 million dollars, and he began to notice a routine of Medicare fraud being committed by Columbia H.C.A. It wouldn't be long before he was urged to go along with, and allow an illegal cheating of innocent taxpayers.

Schilling mustered the courage to do what he fathomed as the right thing to do. This man put himself and his employment on the line, not to mention the ramifications of the possible consequences to the courageous risk he was about to undertake. Schilling would be forced to have worries for himself, as well as for family members he loved. He would go through the next seven years of his life riding an emotional rollercoaster. However, with the help of the False Claims Act, he and his counterparts would achieve certain victory.

When Schilling was offered the job of covert F.B.I. spy, he was understandably excited. But he was also aware that this task would be far from easy. Columbia H.C.A. was the world's biggest for profit hospital chain, as well as the largest healthcare provider in the world. Columbia H.C.A. intentionally would have company executives mislead Schilling, and attempt to use him as a tool for corporate greed.

A typical party thrown by Columbia H.C.A. would usually cost at least 100,000 dollars. These parties were held in posh hotels, as well as other extravagant venues. Schilling, being a former fire fighter, E.M.T., and Wisconsin University graduate (Not a bad resume if you ask me), was the David to the Goliath of Columbia H.C.A.

It wouldn't be long before a Phillips and Cohen attorney named Peter Chatfield, who was a graduate of Yale, embarked to become an essential advocate by becoming an F.B.I. contact. Ironically, Columbia H.C.A.'s division office moved into the same building as the F.B.I. Schilling also had another crucial counterpart in this matter, a person by the name of Jim Alderson.

On the morning of July 16, 1997 at 9:00 A.M., a simultaneous raid that spanned over six states initiated. A multitude of F.B.I. agents raided the offices of Columbia H.C.A. over the span of several states. This was the most massive use of search warrants in concurrence in the history of America. The necessary profusion of fraudulent evidence of the intentional overbilling of innocents was obtained in this simultaneous sweep of F.B.I. raids.

This would lead to a strenuous lawsuit, where Schilling would be subject to even more extreme stress and worry. There were not, surprisingly, attempts of the corporate elites of Columbia H.C.A. to ostracize Schilling for these brave actions he took! Fortunately, Schilling would keep his cool and would ultimately end up pulling through.

To be as fair as possible, I must mention the others who also worked for the F.B.I., and were imperative for the success of this arduous ordeal. Here are their names: Michelle Yaroma, Bill Esteves, Timothy McCants, Michael Wysocki, Kenneth Walsh, and possibly most vital of all other than Schilling himself, was of course Jim Alderson. Schilling when victorious would end up collecting his dues with his friend Jim Alderson. These two men would get to split up, between them, approximately 100 million dollars. Not a bad payday for doing such an honorable thing! Schilling would retire in October of 2001, just after 9/11. However, due to his ambitious demeanor he would return to work some time after.

The final verdict was reached in December of 2002. Columbia H.C.A. ended up paying an astounding total of 1.7 billion dollars, 631 million to resolve civil claims, including kickbacks and cost reporting issues. Another 250 million dollars included from agreement with the Centers for Medicare and Medicaid Services (C.M.S.), on a variety of cost reports, another 17.5 million for resolving Medicaid fraudulency. Not to mention, Columbia H.C.A. had fourteen guilty pleas.

This whole healthcare tragedy proved that fraud does not only injure the healthcare system, but it also has huge repercussions on all Americans because it depletes federal and state resources for those in need, which will give strength to an argument I will soon embark on: Why doesn't the United States have universal healthcare?

At this point, I would like to give yet another condensation on the healthcare issue. This is in regards to another corporation which was involved in this same case of healthcare fraud. I am speaking of K.P.M.G. (Klynveld, Peat, Marwick, Geordler), which is one of the largest professional service firms on the face of the planet. K.P.M.G. was a defendant, in the previously elaborated healthcare fraud case. Schilling asserted that certain K.M.P.G employees were aware of clients filing claims that were not eligible for reimbursement payments on Medicare and Medicaid of the fiscal years from 1990 to 1992.

K.P.M.G., which at the time employed over 137,000 employees and spanned over 145 nations, had a lawsuit due to accusations of fraud. The K.P.M.G. trial was filed in 1998. This case fell under the category of *qui tam*. K.P.M.G. would basically be forced to comply, thus leading toward a settlement which was actually signed by Schilling himself. K.P.M.G., although taking a vital blow, would expand substantially in 2008, and is a flourishing corporation once again. The services rendered by K.P.M.G. include accounting advisory, business performance services, corporate finance, financial risk management, I.T. advisory, internal audit, forensics, restructuring, transaction services, and actuarial services.

The frauds committed by both Columbia H.C.A. and K.P.M.G. have been extremely detrimental to healthcare in America. Also, it is a harsh reminder that we as Americans still do not have universal healthcare.

Now, for a summary of an association that has been a good cause in regards to healthcare in America. This is the American Hospital Association (A.H.A.). This association was founded in 1898, in Chicago, Illinois. This humane organization symbolizes and provides the services of all our different types of hospitals, healthcare networks, and their patients and communities. This also gives the pioneers of healthcare the provision to take actions of importance. This organization, through a promotion of education for the pioneers of healthcare and basic civilians, has resulted into a glimpse of what could be. About 5,000 hospitals, healthcare systems, and networks exist in this organization. This organization consists of only 137,000 individual members. Offices of the A.H.A. stretch across the continental United States. It led to the founding of the Association of Hospital Superintendants (A.H.S.), which was born in Cleveland, Ohio, just one short year (give or take) after the inception of the A.H.A. in 1899. This gives hope, but it is far from enough. So, I once again ask, why don't we, the United States, have universal healthcare?

So let's discuss the issue of Universal Healthcare. The concept of universal healthcare is to have all citizens under a system of government to be covered in situations, such as medical, dental, and mental health practices. I myself being labeled as a mentally ill person am very fortunate to be a resident of Massachusetts. You see, Massachusetts is the best state to live in for a person who is afflicted with a mental illness. However, as I just stated, the people of all U.S. states are in need of a better healthcare system. Universal healthcare is provided in all wealthy nations which thrive in an industrial way. Universal healthcare is also provided in some nations that are just starting to develop in this type of industrial manner. So, what the hell is the United States doing in this matter for its citizens? Back in the late nineteenth century, Germany, through one Otto Von Bismarck, achieved a universal healthcare system for this nation. However, in a literal and technical sense, this German establishment did not meet the governmental definition of universal healthcare. Therefore, according to government records, the first country to reach this healthcare goal was Great Brittan in 1948.

Just to give you an idea how far behind America is on this issue, I will present a list of countries that have universal healthcare: Singapore, Thailand, Austria, Belgium, Bosnia, Herzegovina, Bulgaria, Croatia, Czech Republic, Denmark, Estonia, Finland, France, Georgia, Germany, Greece, Hungary, Iceland, Ireland, Italy, Latvia, Liechtenstein, Lithuania, Luxembourg, Malta, The Netherlands, Norway, Poland, Portugal, Romania, Russia, Serbia, Slovenia, Spain, Sweden, Switzerland, Ukraine, New Zealand, and Great Brittan.

After viewing that extensive list, I must state this: Due to recent mistakes made by the United States government as well as our recent administrations, I am sorry to say to my fellow patriots—and yes, I am a patriot—but I must say that I have come to the conclusion from how we are viewed by the rest of the world and what we lack, that I do presently believe that the United States presently is not—I repeat not—the best country in the world as we always seem to think we are.

If the United States wants to once again stake the claim of our past excellence and become the world force for humanity it once was, then we should act like it and amend universal healthcare for all of our citizens. I recently had a job at a day hospital and a friend of mine named Alice had to tell certain clients that we couldn't help them. One day she stated "I feel like such a jerk having to turn away these people in need and tell them that there is nothing we can do for them" and then she said "Ted, why doesn't this country have universal healthcare?" If America can go in the moral direction on the issue of healthcare, or any other paramount issues, then and only then can America achieve the greatness which this nation once possessed! And you know what? I think we will!

The last issue of discussion in this healthcare segment will be on the topic of H.M.O.'s. H.M.O. stands for "Health Maintenance Organization." First, we will examine the operations of H.M.O.'s, and how they relate to us as a people. A Primary Care Physician (P.C.P.) is a doctor who acts as an entranceway to basically guide their clients to accessing their medical services. Unless in case of an emergency situation, patients will be required to have a referral from their P.C.P. in order for them to visit a doctor, and this way of entrance does not have the power to authorize a referral, unless the guidelines of the H.M.O. deems it necessary. P.C.P.'s are usually internists, pediatricians, general practitioners, or basic family doctors.

For a little piece of interesting history, it was President Lyndon Johnson whom on the thirtieth of July 1965, made certain amendments to legislation of the Social Security system. President Johnson would enroll former president Harry Truman as the first beneficiary of Medicare and even had the honor of presenting him with the very first Medicare card.

Notes of reference: In order to be a Medicare member, you must be a United States citizen. If one is not a citizen of the United States, it is a required that you have been a resident for at least five years and over the age of sixty-five, unless you are disabled. Medicare provided healthcare coverage for well over forty-three million Americans in 2007. It is estimated that by 2031, if we are still on the same pace, Medicare could attain seventy-seven million American clients.

It looks like I went off on a tangent there! So let's get back to the H.M.O. conversation. H.M.O.'s are achieved through doctors and hospitals, with help from the A.H.A. and other providers. The H.M.O. might have a legal contract.

In 1973 what was called the "H.M.O. Organization Act" made a prerequisite that proprietors with twenty-five or more employees must be offered federally certified H.M.O. alternatives. This was different from the more customary insurance corporations. Unfortunately, these H.M.O.'s can only grant care that is rendered by the particular doctors and other professionals who have had an agreement to treating patients in correspondence with the H.M.O.'s inhibitions and guidelines. This is for the exchange of a multitude of customers.

In 1972, the National Association of Insurance Commissioners (N.A.I.C.) espoused what is called the "H.M.O. Model Act." This act was created with the intention of giving of provisions of a model regulatory structure that U.S. states could exercise for the authorization of the inauguration of these H.M.O.'s in viewing their operation.

It is a fact that H.M.O.'s can and will be regulated at not only a federal level but also at state levels, thus being licensed by the states and subject to a type of license known as a "Certificate of Authority" (C.O.A.) instead of being subject to an insurance license.

Due to people not wanting to comply with certain H.M.O. regulations, H.M.O.'s are often targets of lawsuits, stating that some H.M.O. restrictions prevent people in need of care to be able to obtain it. This has caused a negative public view in pertinence to H.M.O. restrictions. In order for an H.M.O. to be held accountable for acts of negligence, it is dependent on the particular H.M.O.'s screening process. If an H.M.O. only agrees to contracts with providers that only meet certain criteria, it could cause a court to find that the H.M.O. is liable just as hospitals can be, when dealing with negligence in regards to the selection of a physician. You see, since an H.M.O. controls only the financial aspect of the provision of care and not the medical part, it can therefore often lead to lawsuits of malpractice.

The "Employment Retirement Income Security Act" (E.R.I.S.A) can be accessed to preempt claims of medical negligence. As related to the last presented situation, the influential element is whether the harm results from the plans of the administration or the actions of the providers.

In conclusion to this whole H.M.O. dilemma, the truth is that Americans need a better system than what was previously presented in this healthcare segment. I had a conversation with one of my former co-workers days before the November 4, 2008 presidential election. My friend, Lisa B., agreed that not only on the healthcare issue is it true that in present times things are way too difficult for the Citizens of America today, but also, things are very difficult in many other aspects of life in present day America. This is a direct result of recent government incompetence, as well as American citizens not taking appropriate actions. So once again, as Obama said during his campaign, "Enough!"

It is time not only for America, but also all world nations that are capable, to wake up and start to use our minds for the good of us all. Just as the U.N.C.F. motto states, "A mind is a terrible thing to waste." I know that President Barack Obama is a man who did not waste his mind. He is just as determined as I am to make sure that everyone—Whites, blacks, Asians, Hispanics, Europeans, or what have you—can access the positive aspects of the human mind; to join in the "mind revolution" and see to it that we all obtain the utopian dream through the building of a foundation for the promotion of a prosperous world! Thank you for listening. May all of your dreams be fulfilled. Read on!

AIDS (A CURE?)

On this topic of urgency, the pandemic of (H.I.V.) human immunodeficiency virus and acquired immunodeficiency syndrome (A.I.D.S.), we will explore some of the twenty-eight-year history of these sexually transmitted diseases. The pandemic of H.I.V. as well as the epidemic of A.I.D.S. can also be transmitted in means different from that of sexual contact.

Foremost, I deem it necessary to discuss the contraction of H.I.V., which is passed on from semen, blood, breast milk, pre-ejaculate, and vaginal fluid. To be more specific, you can obviously acquire this pandemic through unprotected sexual contact. You can also be infected by sharing a contaminated syringe. Another way of contracting this virus is by a process called vertical transmission, which is a contraction of this virus through the process of child birth, from mother to son or mother to daughter.

It was back in 1981 during the early years of the Reagan Administration that the first ever mainspring in the U.S. of this syndrome came to the attention of researchers. The very first case of remission from the A.I.D.S. epidemic would soon take place. It was from a case of vertical transmission. In this particular case, the child entered full remission by the age of five. However, remission is extremely rare in pertinence to this disease.

The very first mainspring of this syndrome came to the attention of researchers decades ago in Africa. This early discovery transpired back in 1959, in Central Africa, where a type of H.I.V. was detected in a specimen. But this first case rendered no immediate implications. It wouldn't be until decades later when this syndrome would begin to take its toll.

A.I.D.S. is basically a life-threatening epidemic, which relentlessly attacks the human immune system. The cause of either H.I.V. or A.I.D.S. is derived from the origin of two separate viruses. These two viruses are technically termed as retroviruses which are the uncommonly known originals said to have stemmed from the continent of Africa. The first of these two origins of H.I.V./A.I.D.S. viruses was called "H.I.V. one" which was discovered by French scientists in 1983 and was acknowledged in America in 1984, although it was already spreading for a few years in America. The other virus of origin was logically called "H.I.V. two." However, this one is said to have originated in Western Africa. It is the first mentioned "H.I.V. one" that has spread throughout the world.

H.I.V. has effects on particular white blood cells. You see, this virus will cling to cells and enter into them the genomes of the virus. This virus will then cause a majorly negative effect on the cells of the reproductive system. This results into a weakening of the human immune system, thus leading to the development of A.I.D.S. from the original H.I.V. Once the A.I.D.S. virus strengthens, it will lead to credible malignant infections to the immune systems cells, ultimately leading to the full development of A.I.D.S., and once inflicted, credible malignant infections will enter the immune systems cells, thus leading to the destruction of the human immune system.

You see, the symptoms of H.I.V. are ill-defined and they may bear resemblance to symptoms of other types of afflictions. Symptoms to the contrary that are not as ill-defined are: fever, loss of appetite, loss of weight, diarrhea, enlarged lymph glands, and yeast infection. Although rare, sometimes a person might die from H.I.V. before it manifests itself into the A.I.D.S. syndrome.

A.I.D.S. is most commonplace in Africa. There are some countries outside of Africa which also have a severe problem with the mass contagion of this disease. Some of these countries include India and some southeastern Asian nations as well. This epidemic, despite not being as prominent in other nations, has had a devastating effect on the entire planet. In Africa, it is more common to be afflicted with this syndrome if you are a homosexual. The rate of this syndrome in Africa has reached frightening levels. It has especially become very common in the adolescents and young adults of Africa. A large part of the spread of this disease can be blamed on the poor economic situations of many world nations. These poor nations have no funds to fight against this fatal syndrome. In third world countries, the situation has reached hopeless proportions. Of course, efforts are being made, but lack of funds is always an obstacle. Believe it or not, some African nations have a rate of as much as twenty-five percent of its citizens afflicted with this syndrome. If George W. Bush did one thing right, it was the appropriations he achieved for the study and humanitarian aid for the cause of fighting this worldwide biological blunder.

Presently, it is surmised that 0.6% of the population of Earth's people are now afflicted with H.I.V. or A.I.D.S. In 2005 alone, approximately three million people died from A.I.D.S. in Africa. This includes 570,000 innocent children as well. That is just over thirty-three percent of all A.I.D.S. related deaths in this continent. This is another example of the poor economic situations on our planet. It is also evident that a world utopia is essential. If appropriate action is not undertook, an imminent reality is that the death toll from this disease could soon reach ninety million if a cure is not discovered. This imminent danger can lead to more adverse effects such as orphaned children in the millions in the continent of Africa.

On a more positive note, my favorite form of world government, which is the United Nations, has taken action in the fight against A.I.D.S. In January of 2006, right at the tail end of Kofi Anan's tenure as Secretary General of the U.N. and the start of the tenure of Ban Ki Moon as Secretary General, was the action of the joint U.N. program for H.I.V./A.I.D.S. It is called U.N.A.I.D.S., and their efforts to promote research for a possible cure has thoroughly progressed over time. Also, the World Health Organization (W.H.O.) estimated the A.I.D.S. death count at twenty-five million worldwide since December 1981. This is a good example of the potential of the U.N. solving world problems in a civil manner.

At this point, I must elaborate on something that I strongly believe could send us in the right direction towards a possible cure for A.I.D.S./H.I.V. This is a process I fathomed through my *Vision of a Mental Patient* which will not be fully understood until you finish this book. In the first step of this elaboration, I deem it necessary to have a discussion with you on moles, or in other words, birth marks. The clinical term for a mole is called a *nevus*; in plural, nevus is *nevi*. Now, there are several main genres of a nevus: epidermal, melanocytic, and collective tissue nevi. These are the three most prominent nevi. A melanocytic type is pigment based. A congenital nevus is a nevus that you have at birth, so you could term it as a birthmark. Nevus is the most common abnormality that can appear on one's skin and it apparently serves no function.

You see, we have a human pigment in our skin. This pigment is called melanin, and it gives us our skin color. This melanin is created through our cells. These cell types are called melanocytes. Just to avoid confusion, pigment is any coloring matter which exists in plants or animals, such as chlorophyll, which gives plants their green color. Congenital melanocytic nevi is formed from a concentration of pigment producing cells that are called nevomelanocytes, which when clumped together tightly can result in skin moles (nevus), this is due to a high concentration of melanin.

You must understand that nevus skin is substantially more than just dark skin. For instance, the area of a melanocytic nevus can promote hair growth on or around the mole. Also, the forming of sweat glands can often be disrupted by nevi, thus causing the area of the nevi to be unable to produce sweat. It is also conceivable that not only sweat glands can't produce other nevi, but also something called subcutaneous fat is also unable to perform this task. Subcutaneous fat is a layer under our skin which pads all parts of our bodies. And remember this: it is possible that due to the human body's immune system's process of recognizing abnormal nevus cells, it can cause our immune system to zap parts of the nevus away.

Remember now, a congenital mole is a type of mole that is present at childbirth. So, what causes congenital moles, nevi, or nevus? It may have, been discovered through thorough research. Researchers presently have credible reason to believe that the nerves and skin of a fetus are developed from the same primary cells of the anatomy. These cells are called neuroectodermal cells. These neuroectidermals form from the middle of the first trimester to the beginnings of the second trimester of pregnancy. It is now believed that a body protein called H.G.F.S.F. (hepatocyte growth factor, scatter factor) is in control of the encouragement of neuroectodermal cells developing, emigrating, and scattering.

In those individuals who have a nevus on their skin, it could be due to the wrong form of H.G.F.C.F. within certain cells, thus causing the advancement of extra pigment and abnormal skin cells resulting in the nevus. Through the H.G.F.S.F and its scatter effect, it is the primary reason that some people have nevi all over their bodies. An unfortunate fact is that these cells can potentially form within our brains. This can result in water on the brain, brain melanoma, hydrocephalus, and melanosis in the brain. This hypothesis was proven through experiments on lab mice.

In order to explain further, I must once again bring up the science of embryonic stem cell research. Remember, stem cells are cells that not only possess the capability to divide endlessly, but also to create more stem cells. But this process can also acquire an ability to form into organs and tissues. You must also remember that these cells give a human being or any organism their basic makeup.

So, why not, through the study of embryonic stem cell research, find a method for a creation of a mole or nevus in its early stages, and use this nevus to control or coincide with a person's H.I.V. or A.I.D.S. infected cells (white blood cells), whose cell walls have been penetrated by the virus. The next step through the process of differentiation and the controlling of cells, which has been achieved through the studies of stem cell research and cloning, would be to cause an action through some type of scientific control to enter the virus into the nevus. I believe it to be possible that through the use of a blastocyst (a hollow ball of cells that can penetrate into a human organ or tissue) this theory could hold water. The process of differentiation and the scattering effect I believe will be vital to this theory as well.

So, what do we do with the mole once the virus has entered it? An obvious idea would be to simply remove it. But I have a better idea which could have a person able to keep this mole on his or her body, just in case there is some more of the virus floating around inside of the individual. The direction of which I would take is to access a type of surgery called cryosurgery. Cryosurgery is the process of the application of freezing temperatures to abnormal tissue. These freezing temperatures will destroy the abnormalities which exist in the human tissue. This type of surgery is currently used to treat benign and malignant skin conditions such as skin cancer, liver cancer, prostate cancer, hemorrhoids, cervical disorders, warts, and of course, moles or nevus. The destructive force of the freezing of cells during cryosurgery in simple terms causes these bad cells to decompose. Liquid nitrogen is often used for cryosurgery. A cooling solution made from liquid nitrogen is accessed through the use of what is called a cyrobe. A cyrobe is basically a tube like cryosurgical instrument. Another method of cryosurgery is through the use of argon gas which would be applied to a cotton swab and then applied. Cryosurgery can cause redness on the skin, not to mention the possibility of minor scarring. When dealing with redness on the skin ibuprofen can be taken to rid of this symptom.

    Well, maybe this is just a farfetched crazy idea of an ex-mental patient. However, I urge the scientific community to further study the formation of the nevus and the nevi. It may just be possible that through embryonic stem cell research as well as the study of cloning, this could be a positive use of the process of cloning! I humbly request that this theory be at least explored further by those who have the means to do so. This theory, in the most basic of terms, is an attraction of a virus into a mole, followed by cryosurgery of this mole. Hopefully, this idea could reap substantial breakthroughs. It is also a reality that if this theory is proven true, we may need to freeze this mole multiple times. It's time for me to take my medication now, so I guess I'll talk to you in the next segment! Read on!

DICK CHENEY AND HIS LIES

In this next portion on politics in *Vision of a Mental Patient*, we shall discuss the many misguidances of a man whom I have grown to believe may be incapable of telling the truth. I am speaking of former White House Chief of Staff, former member of the House of Representatives, former Secretary of Defense, Halliburton Company C.E.O., and the former Vice President of the United States of America, William Bruce Cheney, commonly known as Dick Cheney.

Dick Cheney was born in Lincoln Nebraska, on January 30, 1941. His family then moved to Casper, Wyoming where he was raised. Mr. Cheney's career in politics commenced when he landed a job as an intern for one William A. Steiger who was a United States congressman. Mr. Cheney would later achieve the position of White House Chief of Staff during the Ford Administration. Mr. Cheney would later be elected to the U.S. House of Representatives, representing the state of Wyoming. During the presidency of George H.W. Bush, Mr. Cheney would assume the position of Secretary of Defense and was also an overseer of Operation Desert Storm during the Persian Gulf War. Mr. Cheney would soon become a C.E.O. of Halliburton Company, where his tenure would last from 1995 until 2000. However, Mr. Cheney would continue to receive profits for some time after his tenure there ended in 2000. Mr. Cheney would then become Vice President of the United States in 2000 under the presidency of George W. Bush.

Before my negative assessment of the actions and misguidance of Mr. Cheney, I would first like to stress that I do not believe in guilt by association. Therefore, I must state right away that Mr. Cheney's wife Lynn (a former Chair of the National Endowment for the Humanities) or his daughters Mary and Elizabeth or any other members of the Cheney family have done anything wrong. This segment is on the lies of Mr. Cheney, and it is not in any way, shape, or form intended to criticize any members of the Cheney family. My problem is not with the Cheney family, it is with Mr. Cheney himself.

Okay, so let's begin, shall we? The first misguidance of this man that I will reveal is this: in order to briefly make a point that I touched on in the politics In General segment, I must state that in the 1960s, Mr. Cheney, who was supportive of the Vietnam War, did not serve. This is what he did: Mr. Cheney applied for five draft deferments in order to dodge a draft of war, of which he claimed to be in favor of. Once again, to protect the image of the outstanding Massachusetts Senator John Forbes Kerry, I must state that John Kerry not only served in Vietnam, but he also volunteered himself for certain dangerous missions. Here is the good part: John Kerry, who was opposed to this war, still served with honor. Just because he protested this war after his duties were complete does not imply that he did anything wrong. Therefore, I must say with all the conviction that I can muster, to put him down for that is completely unfounded.

To be fair, I must state that it is completely fathomable for a man that is faced with the horror of being forced by a draft to go into the battlefield and fight in a war is something that even a man of bravery would fear. Not only the fear of dying, but having to kill men whom you have no knowledge of whatsoever can cause severe emotional damage for a man for a very long time. War is absolute savagery and I wish it never existed, but the stark reality is that it does. During the Persian Gulf War and Operation Desert Storm in 1991, I was about to turn 18 years old. Although I was assured by C.N.N. reporters every day that the chances of a draft were slim to none, I was still quite frightened. Unlike the current war in Iraq, I believe that the Persian Gulf War was necessary. I also believe that George H.W. Bush did make a credible decision regarding the Persian Gulf War in 1991. You see, George H.W. Bush understood that the American people did not want to be involved in another war. This was why he decided to pull out early and not to immediately put an end to Saddam Hussein's reign at the time. I must be honest with you: If a draft was issued during this war, the thought of crossing the border into Canada would have crossed my mind. Truthfully though, I believe that if a draft was issued, I would have done the honorable thing and served my country.

You must remember though, although I was a supporter the Persian Gulf War, I did have concern for the potential casualties that could have occurred. You see, Mr. Cheney, although dodging the draft, was in favor of the war which he avoided. Not only that, but with the help of Paul Wolfowitz, President Bush, and company, Mr. Cheney helped to start a war in Iraq, thus the attacking of a country that never attacked the United States. The truth, which I will state more than once in this book, is that we were attacked by Osama Bin Laden and his Al Qaeda terrorist organization and not by Iraq. This war is a complete waste of time, money, and most importantly, it is a waste of human life.

You might have heard the popular argument of right-wingers, which states that because Saddam Hussein is such a bad egg (which I agree with wholeheartedly), a world without Saddam Hussein is a better world. But you must come to the logical realization that Osama Bin Laden, the man responsible for 9/11, is still at large. Try to look at it this way: How many world leaders are out there that are just as evil as Hussein was? I'm sure it wouldn't be a very low number. So, my point is that if the United States attacked all of the countries led by evil world leaders such as Hussein was, we would be attacking half of the world.

I would now like to reveal a point which was made by longtime Massachusetts Senator Ted Kennedy. Before revealing this point, I just want to state that although I am a supporter of the Democratic Party, I am not as much as a Kennedy fan as most Democrats would be. So, here is the point that Ted made: "The best way to honor our troops is to tell them the truth." You may have heard the argument of right-wingers that sending a message to our troops that they are not fighting for a worthy cause is disrespectful. No! Forcing these young men to fight for the interests of certain crooked politicians is disrespectful! And by the way, I do honor our troops! I honor them by telling them the truth, just as Senator Kennedy did. Ted Kennedy, my friends, hit the nail right on the head. Ted Kennedy and I agree that the most honorable thing we can do for these troops is to be honest with them and tell them the truth; and the truth is that they are being misguided and forced to fight in a completely unfounded war.

So, let's get back to the topic of the lies of this man, shall we? When Mr. Cheney was being interviewed by one George C. Wilson, Mr. Cheney was asked a question regarding his dodging of the Vietnam draft. Mr. Cheney was quoted as saying that he had other priorities in the 1960s other than serving in the military services. Mr. Cheney then proceeded by claiming that he obtained his five deferments in order to finish college. Mr. Cheney's college career lasted six years rather than four. This is due to his underachievement as a student. After his first four deferments, by January of 1966, his wife Lynn was in her first trimester of pregnancy. Mr. Cheney was then granted what was called a 3-A status, which was a status that forbids men who have young children or subordinate parents from being subject to the draft. On January 30, 1967, he reached the age of twenty-six, and Mr. Cheney therefore lucked out because at this age, he became ineligible for the draft. Cheney's act of helping to start this unfounded war is fishy behavior for a man who avoided a war draft.

John Adams, when becoming the vice president under the first presidential administration, the George Washington Administration to be precise, was quoted as saying "The vice presidency is the most insignificant that ever the invention of man contrived, or his imagination conceived." When Mr. Cheney was asked to select a vice presidential candidate for George W. Bush, he supposedly gathered intelligence on possibilities. Mr. Cheney would then decide to select himself. Through this decision, Mr. Cheney was then able to turn the vice presidency into a position of significance, contrary to the quote which I just revealed from the first vice president of the United States, John Adams. Cheney, with the help of certain others, became the most powerful vice president in United States history. Not only was this more peculiar behavior from this man, but it was also very scary.

At this next crux, we will begin to go through a series of lies told by Mr. Cheney. The first of many lies of which I will give mention to is a lie which can be concluded from what I have mentioned already. The lie I am speaking of is Mr. Cheney's claim that he would have been honored to serve in the Vietnam War. We already know this to be a false statement. Just to be thorough, I will tell you one more time: Mr. Cheney acquired five deferments and was able to stall until he was twenty-six, in order to avoid serving in a war that he claimed to be supportive of.

Another lie that is obvious to me was his projections of the time and victory of the unfounded war in Iraq. He also lied about the first time he met former presidential Democratic candidate John Edwards in order to avoid certain controversy. It is presumed by many that Mr. Cheney, about what was known as the Conservation and Energy Policy, claimed that only 2,000 acres of land in the Arctic would be affected by oil production. This was a very misleading statement due to the fact that more land than he claimed would be used through this process.

Of course, it is obvious that with the help of others such as Paul Wolfowitz, of the big lie claiming that the country of Iraq had Weapons of Mass Destruction (W.M.D.), to this day, not a trace of these so-called Weapons of Mass Production has been discovered.

In September of 2003, he made yet another false claim on the longest running show in the history of American television, *Meet the Press*. Mr. Cheney said that Iraq was the base of the terrorists who attacked the United States. This statement was obviously proven to be false. In relation to that last mentioned lie, Mr. Cheney also claimed that overwhelming evidence existed concerning connections between Al Qaeda and the Iraqi government. Do I really need to say it? I will, anyway: Yes, that was another lie! Keep reading, I'm just getting started here.

Here is yet another one: Once again on *Meet the Press* in March of 2003, Mr. Cheney said that in Iraq, we would be greeted as liberators. The truth is that U.S. military personnel were in the least not greeted as liberators. Okay, to give the man the benefit of the doubt, that one could be considered a wrong guess. But you know what? I don't think so! Moving on, in December of 2005, Mr. Cheney claimed that the United States does not engage in torture. So, guess what? United States Army Colonel Larry Wilkersen, also a former Secretary of State, told C.N.N. reporters one month prior in November of 2005, that, yes, indeed, the United States was involved in the practice of torture. By the way, if I were in John McCain's shoes right now, that one would burn me up! Here's a big one! In September of 2003, Mr. Cheney said that he had absolutely no interest in Halliburton Company; he also said that he had not, in the three years since he stepped down as C.E.O., collected any money from Halliburton Company. This was also stated on *Meet the Press*. The truth was that Mr. Cheney had been receiving money from Halliburton the whole time he was vice president. He also had stock options from his former company which were valued at approximately eight million dollars! Boy, Mr. Cheney must have thought that Tim Russert was stupid or something. By the way, I would like to say, that we all are very sad to have lost Mr. Russert. He was an outstanding reporter and a hell of a nice guy. Tim, we will never forget you.

Continuing on now, Mr. Cheney made another false claim some years before while his tenure as Halliburton C.E.O. was still in effect. This was a statement made by Mr. Cheney claiming that he would never do anything in Iraq. So here is the truth on that one: U.N. records, as well as some information provided by the oil industry executives, stated that Halliburton held stakes in a couple of firms that had signed contractual agreements for the sale of over seventy-three million dollars in oil production equipment to the Iraqis while Mr. Cheney was still the Chief Executive Officer of Halliburton.

How about another lie just for kicks? This one was in January of 2004. On Fox news radio, Mr. Cheney said, regarding the Dallas based Halliburton Corporation, that he would not ever have a thing to do with contractual procedures and also stated that he would not know how to manipulate the process. The fact is that in the Los Angeles Times in June of 2004, it was reported that our truthful vice president actually helped to overrule a battery of attorneys' attempt to block a seven million dollar no bid to—you guessed it—Halliburton Company.

You see, Mr. Cheney did not only tell lies to his enemies, he also lied to his friends. This next lie I will inform you was on 9/11, that fateful day that my generation and all others who were alive on that day will never forget. Mr. Cheney lied to his boss George W. Bush just hours after the World Trade Building was hit by two 747s, as well as the Pentagon, which was struck by one. Mr. Cheney proceeded to deceive President Bush by a false claim that President Bush's Air Force One was threatened. Through the telling of this lie by Mr. Cheney, he was then able to assume authority without anyone's permission. It may be becoming clearer to you why Mr. Cheney selected himself for the position of vice president. It was, my friends, for his plans for abuse of power.

You may not believe it, but I'm not done yet. Before the start of the Iraq War, Mr. Cheney channeled an obscene amount of money to an Iraqi Shia Muslim politician by the name of Ahmed Chalabi and the Iraqi National Congress. Why would a man who started an unfounded war send money to his supposed enemies? This is beginning to get quite frightening, don't you think? Fact: Not since the Nixon Administration has so many government documents been classified. I personally believe that Mr. Cheney, a man who has somehow gotten away with murder, is far worse than Nixon who was responsible for "Watergate." The difference is that Nixon got caught. Mr. Cheney, on the other hand, has been underestimated by us all. And this man is not stupid; he is quite aware of what he is doing! It is a damn good thing that he will be done on January 20, 2009. I will now quote the author of *The Dick Cheney Survival Bible*, Gene Stone: "With the song in your heart, you can change the world" and Gene you can quote me: I like that!

Now, for some information for those of you who would like to learn more about the deception of this man William Bruce Cheney, here are some organized groups that are opposed to this man's deceptive ways: Moveon.org, American Civil Liberties Union (A.C.L.U.), Code Pink, People for the American Way, Halliburton Watch, Wes Pac, and the Sierra Club. In relation to that, here are some modern day figures who are already aware of the deception of Mr. Cheney: John Murtha (who happens to be one of the first proponents for ending the Iraq war), Joseph Wilson (married to Sarah Plame), Henry Wyman, Arriana Huffington, Maureen Dowd, Patrick J. Leahy, and actor Alec Baldwin.

To strengthen the validity of the argument that I have made so far, I must tell you the story of former White House Press Secretary Scott McClellan. This is not an attack on Scott in any way. As a matter of fact, I believe Scott to be completely innocent, as well as being a good man. I will give my input on why this man is not only innocent, but also why I believe that he is honorable. But, not yet; I must start from the beginning.

Scott McClellan was born on February 14, 1968, in Austin Texas where he was raised. Scott was the youngest son of his mother, Carol Keeton Strayhorn, who would become the first woman mayor of Austin. Scott grew up with his two older brothers Barr and Mark. Scott's grandfather was the late W. Page Keeton, who was the dean of the University of Texas school of Law. Scott is now married to one Jill Martinez McClellan and has been since 2003.

I happened to read a copy of Scott's book, *What Happened*, which would be considered unusual for me, because not until recently would I ever read a book that was written by a Republican. Scott seems to display many good characteristics not only as a politician, but also as a person. In his book, Scott made a statement similar to one which I read in Barack Obama's book, *Audacity of Hope*. What Scott and Barack basically both said was that most Republicans and Democrats in politics are usually decent people. I believe that a common defect in modern society is that people tend to see the bad in people rather than the good in them. I believe that one cause of this attitude of society that now exists is due to the common tendency for people to compare themselves and others to a perfect god. I feel that it is only when you cannot find any good in a person at all that this harsh judgment can ring true.

Anyway, back to the subject of Scott McClellan. Scott showed me, through his book, many good qualities. For instance, he states that he must learn from his mistakes and unlike some politicians, Scott will admit to his own mistakes. He states that learning from one's own mistakes—including learning from one's own faults and accepting responsibility for them—will make you a better person. Scott says in his book that he believes that he fell short of living up to his potential in his public service. Scott also stresses that he realizes that the abundance of deception in politics is nothing new. Scott is a sensitive person and he was very hurt by the deceptions of the administration which he worked for. Despite all that Scott was put through, he had enough decency in him to say that his optimism for America has strengthened.

I now will show to you a quote from Scott's book: "Most political actions are done subconsciously with no malicious intent." Remember that quote, it's meaning is much more imperative than you may presently believe once you have finished this book, especially The Monolith part two, will the human energy behind Scott's quote be understood.

I realize that there are some of my fellow Democrats out there who are wondering why I am being so nice to a Republican. You shall see my friends. Keep reading!

Continuing on, Scott also has a belief that the definition of leadership is to unite people around a common purpose rather than dividing them along ideological lines. I myself believe that Scott was able to achieve such admirable views through the benefits of his upbringing. Scott's mother, Carol, who was considered to be a moderate to conservative Democrat, had certain troubles bringing up her children, especially while she was the mayor of Austin. A disturbing fact is that during Carol's tenure as the Mayor of Austin, she would receive threats from people while trying to perform her governmental duties. This could be due to the fact that the McClellans did something during that time period that could be considered dangerous: This is the act of standing for what one believes in, which can pose some negative results in a society that can display such measures of immorality.

Despite the problems that the McClellan family faced, Scott and his two brothers would thrive as youngsters. Scott served as student council president at Austin High School. Scott would go on to graduate in the top twenty percent of his class. As a matter of fact, I myself graduated in the top ten of my eighth grade class. The only problem was that my eight grade class was in a small private school, and there were only thirteen students in the whole graduating class, so I'm just kidding. To get back to the subject of the McClellan's after that cute, yet feeble attempt at humor, I would also like to let you know that Scott's two brothers thrived academically as well. As a matter of fact, one of them became a valedictorian!

Now, in order to get to the meat of what I am trying to explain here, which is to explain to you that Scott McClellan is an innocent and admirable man. I must start to tell you some vital information. First will be a discussion on the fact that certain members of the Bush Administration, as well as Mr. Bush himself, blew the cover of the Central Intelligence Agency (C.I.A.) operative Valerie Plame and of her husband Joseph Wilson, who is also a former ambassador.

You see, White House Aides had disclosed Valerie Plame's identity to at least five reporters, including Robert Novak whom I previously mentioned. Scott was then lied to directly by Karl Rove, Scooter Libby, Andrew Card, George W. Bush, and of course the man behind the torrent of lies, Dick Cheney. For a good two years, Scott was being lied to by these men. Scott had the guts to claim in his book that he (once having some idea of the deception he was being dealt) was even encouraged to lie and to repeat lies. You see, Scott was, as he stated in his book, too trustful of these men who were deceiving him. And by the way, I believed Scott when he claimed to have absolutely no knowledge of the anonymous efforts which were made to expose C.I.A. operative Valerie Plame.

Then of course, there was the famous sixteen words sent out by the Bush Administration. If you do not know of or if you do not recall the sixteen words spoken by President Bush in the State of the Union address, then here they are: "The British government has learned that Saddam Hussein recently sought significant quantities of uranium from Africa." Now, for a Reagan quote, "Here we go again." It is true that Saddam Hussein was defiant toward U.N. demands. However, this was just yet another lie. Incidentally, Valerie Plame's husband Joseph Wilson was in January of 2002 sent to the African nation of Niger to investigate the sales of uranium. What do you think he found? I'm not even going to waste the ink!

These acts of governmental mischief would grow into even more deception and mayhem to follow. These liars would then attempt to sell this war! When the American people were told by this administration that Saddam Hussein was supportive of terrorist organizations who intended to attack the United States, a consensus was taken and it was estimated that ninety percent of Americans believed this to be true. The citizens of the United States were led to believe in those weapons of mass destruction which I remind you were never found. Not only were they not found, they never existed. The other big act of deception (of which I just mentioned) was the claim that Saddam Hussein was responsible for the 9/11 attacks. Of course, you must realize by now that this was a false statement as well.

Remember how I stated, in the In General portion of the political part of this book, that we must be extremely cautious when electing our government officials? I stated that our leaders must be out for the glory of the people and not just for their own personal glory. Are you beginning to catch the drift? Yes, these men our out for their own glory and not for the glory of us all! This is the type of governmental behavior which should not be tolerated!

At this point, I remind you that the Bush/Cheney approval rating just days after 9/11 was a staggering ninety percent. I do admit that I myself, when seeing the president speaking into that megaphone at ground zero, was extremely inspired. However, the actions that the president would then take (although I do theorize that Cheney was more of an influence than you may think) were completely without merit. This Bush/Cheney Administration's approval rating would become, by the end of its tenure, a dismal twenty-five percent.

Many of the good Republicans of the United States had the sense to cross party lines and give their support to Barack Obama and Joseph Biden. Scott himself, as well as Colin Powell, also had the sense to cross party lines for the better of the nation, as well as to give a glimmer of hope to the rest of the world. In 1980, a similar thing happened, only in reverse. Many

Democrats in 1980 would cross party lines and elect Ronald Wilson Reagan as the fortieth president of the United States of America. This was because the popular opinion at this time was that former president Jimmy Carter, although liked, was deemed incompetent. In 1980, my opinion is that the United States was to choose between one incompetence or something new which the smart Democrats realized was quite a risk. Being a Democrat, although I was only seven years of age at the time, I would probably not have endorsed Reagan. I will say one good thing for Carter though: he tried very hard, and despite not always getting things done, he was however, a very dedicated man. Carter would work all day into the late night. Reagan, on the other hand, was rumored to have only usually put in a four-hour day, and actually fell asleep in the middle of an important cabinet session one time.

Well, I just went off on a tangent there! Back to business! You see, the foreign policy of George W Bush and Mr. Cheney always held Saddam Hussein in a low regard. They claimed to have viewed the man as an unsteady Middle Eastern force. Remember, the Middle East is an area that contains vast oil reserves, thus representing an extensive national interest from the United States even prior to 9/11. The claimed to be main problems with the nation of Iraq were the support of terrorism, weapons of mass destruction, and the criminal treatment of their people. I believe that the lies and other actions of the Bush/Cheney Administration are in itself a criminal treatment of the Iraqi people. Don't get me wrong; although there were no weapons of mass destruction, it is true that under the reign of Saddam Hussein, there was criminal treatment of the Iraqi people. However, I do not for one second believe that this administration was in it for that reason at all! Even if they were, the United States is not the world police and if we were to go after all countries that treat their citizens inhumanely, we would be attacking half of the world and it would result in World War 3. I wish we could punish those world leaders who treat their people inhumanely, but military attack is not the correct method. The correct method would be to achieve a world utopia through rigorous negotiations. Director Michael Moore, a man that I have the utmost respect for, was absolutely correct in saying that "we cannot send our soldiers into harm's way unless absolutely necessary." He then said, "Will they ever be able to trust us again?" I certainly hope so Michael, I certainly do!

As previously stated, Scott was kept in the dark and at times, he would be excluded from strategy meetings that would be held by these culprits. Supposedly, it was due to Scott's rank. Yeah, right, and despite all of this political abandonment, Scott would still display common decency!

Scott is a Republican, but do you know what he says about the liberal media? He said, quote "I am not critical of the liberal media as long as they do their job professionally." He also stated that he has no problem with liberal reporters and also claims to have enjoyed working with them. These, my friends, are the words of a man who was unjustly attacked by the liberal media. But why? Keep reading!

Not only did this administration make the false claim of weapons of mass destruction, but it also produced rumors of biological weapons. This was to use fear tactics on the American people. You must understand that fear can give one control, and that my friends was the corrupt goal. And, remember this: Scott took this job as White House Press Secretary because he was fond of George W. Bush and also because of his commitment to public service, and his cognizance of an opportunity of a lifetime.

Just days prior to the commencement of Scott's tenure as White House Press Secretary, which began on July 15, 2003, was the inception of the Plame/Wilson controversy. Joseph Wilson himself made a claim that our beloved Mr. Cheney had received information in regards to this matter on an edition of *Meet the Press*. Then came the Robert Novak article, on July 14 and this was one day before Scott McClellan would begin his tenure as the White House Press Secretary.

This column of Novak's was titled "Mission to Niger" and it examined how Joseph Wilson's journey came about, as well as what it assumed. Wilson had never worked as a C.I.A. operative, but his wife Valerie Plame did and she was an investigator of these supposed weapons of mass destruction. Do not forget the sixteen words related to the presumed sales of uranium in Niger. Novak would end up exalting this into a scandal. Novak's actions could legally be considered a felony. But as I stated earlier, we do not need to throw Novak to the wolves. What Novak should do is to take a lesson from Scott McClellan and learn from his mistake, which is one of the things I love about Scott.

It was also concluded that there were secret meetings held for the direct intent of deceiving the American public using a claim that peace in Iraq would reap major benefits. This type of mass deception would continue. The way to achieve peace is not by attacking innocent people. You see, Scott shared a view shared by many: "What is the end game?" In other words, what are our plans for an exit strategy? It is obvious to me that Mr. Cheney had an exit strategy for himself during the Vietnam War! As a matter of fact, Mr. Cheney had a strategy to not even get himself involved in Vietnam! The same goes for George W. Bush, too! Yes, Bush had a plan to exit himself, but did not present an exit plan for many misguided soldiers, as well as the soldiers who were aware of his deception but performed their duties anyway! This is the offspring of George H.W. Bush, a man who served our country with valiance! I am sorry that his son has tarnished the image of this good man!

This Plame/Wilson ordeal would take a huge toll on Scott for a long time. Believe it or not, it's about to get worse! Bush then made another false claim stating that he would put into action a disciplinary measure for any such criminal activity. He would also claim that he would fire any of his employees who might be responsible for such actions. Yes, my friends, this was yet another lie.

An obvious mistake of Scott's was his trust that he instilled in Mr. Cheney and friends. There were many American citizens who were not falling for this administration's deceptive ways. It is true that a credible number of Americans were suspicious of Karl Rove as early as Bush's first term. In time, the deceit would grow farther from the realm of Karl Rove. Once again, Scott would be subject to ridicule for actions he was not informed of pertaining to this administration's crisis of integrity. Scott, however is no fool, and through all of this, he was even willing to share in the blame.

Okay, so when Scott was sent out to perform his duties as White House Press Secretary, with very limited information on how to answer questions he would be asked by the media, he would then put his brave face on and perform as well as he could. Scott would be subject to a number of bombardments by the liberal media. I must add that I myself was quite angry with Scott when viewing his lack of knowledge while he was doing his job. This lack of knowledge was not Scott's fault. The poor guy was being played like a fiddle. During Scott's tenure as White House Press Secretary, I had not yet come to my realization of his innocence. And may I add that at this time, the only guy in politics I disliked more than Scott was Mr. Cheney.

You see, Mr. Cheney had a plan to use Scott for his own gain. Scott was Mr. Cheney's chess pawn, his puppet, his scapegoat. Once Cheney had devised his plan to stab his loyal friend in the back, Scott would then be sent out to face a bloodthirsty liberal media. I can recall viewing some of the press conferences which Scott held. I vividly remember the media's anger with him as well as my own anger with him. Scott would be forced to dodge questions. He even was forced to use the line "I'm not going to comment on an ongoing investigation." Scott would also be forced to stonewall (stonewalling is the covering up of one issue by bringing up another issue).

By this time you must at least vaguely fathom what I meant by my claim that Mr. Cheney used Scott for himself. Well, I have news for you, Mr. Cheney: It didn't work! Isn't it peculiar that Novak's "Mission to Niger" article was released on July 14, 2003, just one day before Scott would commence his tenure as the White house Press Secretary?

It is now time for me to make my main point of all of this disloyalty to Scott McClellan, a man who I may add, was completely loyal to those who used him. I now state that Scott did an outstanding job as White House Press Secretary. His dodging of questions that he had no information to answer with any credibility whatsoever was the best that he could do. After I came to my realization of what the truth is behind this matter, I would become aware of the courage and honesty which Scott was displaying, although most of my fellow Democrats could not yet understand at this time. Then the next action Scott would take really impressed me. Once Scott was aware of how he was deceived, as well as how the American public was deceived, he would then turn around and put himself in harm's way in order to reveal the truth to the American people as well as the rest of the world. Face it, Scott could have been ostracized for his courageous actions of taking on some of the most powerful and corrupt men in all of politics.

Try to see it from this perspective. When Bill Clinton was impeached for his lying under oath during the Monica Lewinsky sex scandal, Clinton would soon be publicly attacked by reporter Kenneth Starr. The argument of my party (the Democrats) was that a person would not be fired from their job for being unfaithful to their spouse. However, Bill Clinton did lie under oath and that is not commendable. In relation to this Clinton issue, my point for the innocence of Scott McClellan is this: if you were cheated out of money by a greedy corporation, then who would you blame, the head of the corporation, or his secretary? Therefore, I believe that what Kenneth Starr did to Bill Clinton was mildly ridiculous, but what Mr. Cheney and friends did to Scott McClellan was completely ludicrous!

The American public must come to realize that the occupation of White House Press Secretary is to transfer information from the higher ups of the U.S. government to the press. I once again stress that this occupation only requires the relaying of information to the media. I hereby warn the public to never again be deceived by those who use the position of White House Press Secretary for the intention of deceiving the American public. It is now time to tell you exactly how I feel about this good man, Scott McClellan. Scott McClellan is, in my opinion, by far the best press secretary in the history of the United States of America. Scott is also not only the best Press Secretary ever, but is also the best that will ever be! Scott's action of turning around to publicly fight against these men of power and his putting himself at risk for the truth is honorable. Scott represents a characteristic which is lacking in today's society. This characteristic I am referring to is the characteristic of having guts. I hope to meet Scott one day so I can give him a firm handshake and congratulate him on a job well done. This country could use more good Republicans like Scott. If the right-wingers of America can display the honesty, loyalty, courage, and concern for the truth that Scott has ever so gracefully displayed, then look out democrats!

Scott, I must tell you something that you are likely aware of and may hurt you. But I need to say it in order to help you. So here it goes, Scott: George W. Bush, Scooter Libby, Karl Rove, Andy Card, and especially Dick Cheney are not your friends. Personally, I cannot see why anyone would not want to be your friend, Scott. Scott, if you want a friend then come and find me, and I vow that I will never use you, put you in harm's way, or deceive you the way these men did.

Now that I have stated how proud I am of Scott McClellan and that he should be proud of himself, it is now time to discuss the aftermath of this political quandary. Scott would finally come to realize that he was being bamboozled and he would then resign as White House Press Secretary in April 2006. On April 26, 2006, Scott would be replaced by Tony Snow. Scott states in his book that the last straw was when George W. Bush said in pertinence to this scandal, quote "Yes, I did." Around that time, special council Patrick J. Fitzgerald, with help, would become eager to resolve the Plame/Wilson controversy.

Scooter Libby would end up being fined 250,000 dollars and was sentenced to thirty months in prison. Others got off the hook and would essentially luck out. Deputy Secretary Richard Armitage would defend Rove and Libby in regards to their involvement in this scandal.

For the finality on the topic of Scott McClellan's tenure as press secretary, I would now like to complete the circle and state some more things said by Scott that pleased me very much. In Scott's book *What Happened*, he stated a belief of his, which I am admirable of. He said, "The nation's best interests are more important than political party interests." Another great quote of Scott's was "The next Democratic president should make a point of spending more time with conservative groups such as evangelicals, the N.R.A. (National Rifle Association), and pro life advocates." Scott also stated that "Republicans should reach out to gay rights groups, teachers, unions, animal rights advocates, and environmentalists in order to find a common ground." Scott is a robust believer in bipartisanship (Republicans and Democrats working together). I myself am a strong believer in bipartisanship as well. This is an idiosyncrasy which the United States government could benefit from.

Finally, I would like to state that although Scott's mother Carol was considered a Democrat, Scott would end up being a Republican. I state this next statement directly towards the over angry Democrats out there: Scott did not become a Republican because he was immoral or stupid. Scott became a Republican because he is an independent thinker, which is in my opinion a very worthy trait for a person to possess. Scott McClellan, as well as many of my friends, is living proof that Republicans can be extraordinarily good people.

What do you say I start revealing to you some more wonderful acts of our beloved Mr. Cheney? Okay, let's go for it! This next action of Mr. Cheney will be elaborated on as a cute little anecdote pertaining to a statement that Mr. Cheney made directed at Vermont Senator Pat Leahy on the Senate floor on June 22, 2004. Although you may be in suspense, I will not reveal this comment of Mr. Cheney's at this duration, but don't fret, I shall reveal it in due time, my friends.

This comment of Mr. Cheney's was dubbed by Mr. Cheney's spokesperson as "a frank exchange of views"; that is putting it mildly, if you ask me. If you actually knew what he said to Senator Leahy, you would be in agreement. Let's just say at this point that this statement made by Mr. Cheney was a trifle bit profane. You see, use of profanity on the Senate floor is supposed to be prohibited. However, at the time of this comment, the Senate was not in an official session. It was actually during the 2004 United States Senate photo shoot. Once again, due to a technicality, Mr. Cheney would once again get away with yet another one of his deeds of political mischief. I sometimes wonder who the better escape artist is: Mr. Cheney or Harry Houdini?

This cute little anecdote was reviewed by a few sources and it went as follows: Mr. Cheney, who happened to hold the position of Senate president, as well as being the vice president, was attending the 2004 Senate photo shoot with his fellow senatorial workers. Mr. Cheney would deem it necessary to fire away a profane remark directed right at Senator Leahy of Vermont. This comment of Mr. Cheney's was in retaliation to Senator Leahy's disapproval of Mr. Cheney's ties to Halliburton Company, as well as his declared war against profiteering.

Of course, the Cheney spokespeople were just as consistent as always in regards to any such wrongdoings of Mr. Cheney. I guess that Mr. Cheney knows God or something, because one time on a different occasion, Mr. Cheney made an accusation towards Senator Pat Leahy that he was a bad Catholic. Understandably, Senator Leahy was aloof to the press when asked about this incident. And you know what? I don't blame him.

Mr. Cheney can become very angry when challenged in any way. But to Senator Leahy's credit, he did have the guts to confront Mr. Cheney and later told reporters that Mr. Cheney did in fact use profanity directed right at him.

Senator Leahy would comment after being subject to this profane attack that he believed that perhaps Mr. Cheney was just having a bad day, and then would state that he was very surprised to hear this kind of language on the Senate floor.

At this essence, I feel it is necessary to give some information on Senator Pat Leahy. Senator Leahy has many liberal positions which coincide with the state of Vermont. The State of Vermont before electing of Pat Leahy to the Senate had not elected one Democrat to congress since the American Civil War, which is a funny thing considering the fact that Vermont is a state which is viewed as being left-wing democratic. Yet, it is true that Vermont will almost always vote Democratic in a presidential election. Ironically, my home state of Massachusetts, which is also considered to be a Democratic state, now has Democrat Deval Patrick for governor, but the last two prior Massachusetts governors were Republican Jane Swift and former Republican candidate for president Mitt Romney. However, Swift was not technically elected; she took over from Romney once he decided to chase the presidency.

Back to Senator Leahy: Senator Leahy is a supporter of the pro choice view, and is also for the abortion rights concerning that of minors and military personnel. Alike myself, Senator Leahy is not supportive of the brutal tactic of partial birth abortions. He is also well liked by the National Association for the Advancement of Colored People (N.A.A.C.P.). He is also a supporter of gay rights, and is one of the strongest supporters of rights for gay people. Senator Leahy has spoken sternly against a constitutional ban which would prohibit the right to burn the American flag.

Concerning the topic of flag burning, a common misunderstanding of the American people is that although it may seem bad, the right to burn the American flag should be protected. Please allow me to explain. The reason for this is that if the United States government ever became too corrupt, you would then have credible reason for such a radical action. In relation to this and for similar reasons, we Americans have the right to bear arms. The reasons for these two protected rights of radicalism is that heaven forbid, if the United States were to go in the wrong direction and become a totalitarian regime, these two seemingly wrong yet fundamental rights could be deemed necessary.

Despite the fact that the recent Bush/Cheney Administration was in my view, very corrupt, I do not by any means believe that burning an American flag or forming a military revolt are even remotely necessary at this time. But as I have already stated, we must as a people have a more careful and caring approach to government so that we do not put the corrupt in positions of power. I do believe that through President Obama, we, despite hard times, do have the opportunity to return the United States back to excellence. If you are a patriotic person as I am (although I have certain criticisms), you must understand the unfortunate fact that freedom is not free of charge and we must reserve certain rights of extreme radicalism in order to sustain a great nation such as the United States of America.

I keep going off on those tangents! Once again, back to Senator Leahy. Senator Leahy also does not believe in mandatory school prayer and neither do I. Uh, Oh! Here comes another tangent! I remember as a young boy, watching Ronald Reagan's acceptance speech at the 1984 Republican National Convention. Reagan, in his acceptance speech said that it is time to get Jesus Christ back into the schoolrooms of America, meaning that he was in favor of mandatory school prayer. Now, that does sound nice, but the claim of many Republicans, especially the evangelists is that the United States was founded on the values of God. Allow me to tell you this is a completely unfounded claim. The United States was founded by the people and for the people. One of the most well known constitutional rights is the freedom of religion. Therefore, it would be wrong when considering how many different religions and gods of worship exist not only in the United States, but also in the whole world. For one religion of many to claim that their religion is right and other religions are wrong by forcing children of all different religions to pray to the Christian God through an unreasonable rule of mandatory school prayer, is not only unconstitutional, it is also an act of ignorance.

Okay, I'm going to try hard this time to stay on the topic of Senator Leahy! Another admirable belief of Senator Pat Leahy is that he is a strong advocate for the necessary cause of universal healthcare which we touched on earlier. He has an exemplary voting record on the topic of universal healthcare as well. Leahy is an environmental activist which is of supreme importance. He is also opposed to the death penalty. Oh, no, not again! Here comes another tangent! I'll make this one short, okay? It's a deal! In relation to the debate on the death penalty, it is a popular view of evangelists and other Republicans to support the death penalty, and they seem to think that no one innocent has ever been executed! Well, in that case, I have the name of one person who was innocent yet still executed. This was not in the United States, but however, I do believe that I must mention this innocent man who was unjustly put to death. Are you ready? Okay, here is his name: "Jesus Christ!" Yes, the man behind the religion that wants to practice the death penalty worships a man who was put to death himself! Please open your mind and try to understand that I am not putting down Christ, I am simply making a point. I am not usually in favor of such actions like the death penalty unless you are dealing with extreme cases of genocide or acts of terrorism such as those committed by Osama Bin Laden and Al Qaeda, Hitler, Pot, or Habyarimana.

Okay, for the last time, back to Senator Leahy! Hang on in there because we are almost done with this appraisal of Senator Leahy. Senator Leahy has also been quite critical of the United States involvement in this unfounded war in Iraq. Like John Murtha, Leahy has been strongly in favor of the creation of timetables regarding the American troop withdrawal in this Iraq War. Leahy has served six terms as senator in the State of Vermont. Leahy is a fine senator and has a much cleaner track record than our friend, Mr. Cheney, does.

All right, now that I have stated my case of the favorability of Vermont Senator Pat Leahy, it is now time for me to reveal the comment that Mr. Cheney made on the Senate floor during the 2004 senate photo shoot. Ready? Here it is! Get this: Mr. Cheney said directly to Senator Leahy, "Go fuck yourself!" Yes, this comment was made by Mr. Cheney just for Senator Leahy's questioning Mr. Cheney's ties with Halliburton Company!

It truly amazes me that men like Mr. Cheney who are so wrong can have the nerve to become so irate when simply questioned on their wrongdoings! One day when I was doing my usual habit watching C.N.N. Democratic strategist James Carville, on the show *Crossfire*, challenged Robert Novak in regards to his article "Mission to Niger." Novak would then, on national television, stand up and say directly to James Carville, quote "That's bullshit" and then Novak proceeded to storm off the set! My question is: What the hell do these guys have to be so angry about? They're worse than any among my angry Democrat friends! At least my Democratic friends have some form of substance behind their anger!

Here is another point! It is a common belief that George W. Bush started this Iraq War to avenge his father. Now, in no way is this action of George W. Bush even remotely justifiable. But maybe, just maybe, I can possibly see a millionth of a molecule of decency in that act. To secure my position on this matter, I must express that this miniscule molecule of human decency of Bush's, in relation to this act of war, that this administration undertook was absolutely despicable. However, I do express, that George W. Bush does have at least a thread of human decency and also had a much less than minor reason behind this act of war. So this is my next question: Why the hell did Mr. Cheney want to start this war? I personally believe it is for one reason and one reason only! Mr. Cheney is a mean son of a bitch who not only is wrong, but also becomes infuriated when questioned in the least! Mr. Cheney is what Professor Cornel West would label as a political nihilist.

Okay! Why don't we take a final look at this political dilemma? Here is a frightening scenario: what if Mr. Cheney was successful in his framing of former White House Press Secretary Scott McClellan? I mean it could have happened. Mr. Cheney was extremely successful at causing the deaths of many American troops and many innocent people in Iraq. He was also successful appointing himself as vice presidential candidate under Bush in order to use the United States government to line his pockets with cash, not to mention his affinity for telling his coworkers to go fuck themselves when he was challenged!

So, in the end, our beloved, honest, smart, and most of all, trustworthy, Mr. Cheney, after his tenure as Vice President of the United States came to an end and as his duties of protecting the American people in this sovereign nation would have sadly ended. Mr. Cheney would have then on a crisp beautiful winter day in January of 2009, gone to his extravagant home in Mclean Virginia, where he would have begun to listen to his classy Mozart, read his classy Shakespeare, drink his classy Chardonnay, and eat his classy caviar. But the truth is that this is not what class is! Class is having respect for other people and Mr. Cheney has none! To tell your peers to go fuck themselves for your own selfish reasons is wrong! To cause the deaths of misguided American troops is also wrong! To cause the deaths of countless Iraqi citizens and then claim that you are trying to liberate them is also wrong! To access a position of power in the United States government for financial gain is yet another wrong act! To continuously lie to the American people, to stab your friends in the back! Need I say anymore?

How about this? I say to Sarah Plame, Joseph Wilson, Pat Leahy, and Scott McClellan: This one's for you! Mr. Cheney, "Go fuck yourself!" And by the way, one more thing: Mozart sucks, Shakespeare was a snob, I don't drink Chardonnay, and caviar tastes like shit! Read on!

GENOCIDES AND FOREIGN POLICY

We have now come to the most extensive and morally crucial segment of the politics part one segment of *Vision of a Mental Patient*. This will be the last topic of discussion in this book related to politics or at least until Morals in Society where there will be some more discussion on political issues. This, my friends, is the Genocides and Foreign Policy segment, where we will discuss what I feel is the worst problem of morality on the planet. This problem I am referring to is the act of genocide. We will also discuss some of the presidential foreign policies which are relative to this deplorable and immoral reality. Just in case you are fuzzy on the definition of what genocide is, here is its meaning: a deliberate and systematic killing of a whole people, creed, race, nationality, or religion.

The genocides that we will discuss are: The Russian Pogrom genocide, the massacres of the Khmer Rouge in Cambodia, the current Darfur genocide, the Rwanda genocide, and finally the infamous Hitler NAZI German genocide. Unfortunately, there have been quite a few other genocide cases which we will not touch on. To mention a couple that we will not discuss, there was the genocide of the Armenians by the Ottoman Turks in 1915, and the Indonesian eradication of Communists in the 1960s.

Before my elaboration of the hateful feelings that I have toward these sickeningly disgusting acts of genocide, I will first get into some detail of the first genocide case that we will be examining, the Russian Pogrom genocide which took place from the late nineteenth century to roughly twenty years into the twentieth century. In order for you to understand the absolute infuriation that I have toward the act of genocide, I will wait until after the discussion on which we are about to partake to tell you in a truthful yet profane manner, the blunt reality of just what genocide means to me and should mean to us all.

So here we go! The Russian Pogrom genocide, the word *pogrom* is Russian for a riot involving annihilation. Pogrom is the name that became requisitioned to the vicious attacks on Jewish peoples and their properties. These disgusting acts occurred in Russia from 1881 to 1921. Amongst the more dishonorable of this series of assaults on innocent Jews were those that were executed at Kiev and over 200 more which mostly occurred in the Ukraine. These acts of genocide were the more early occurrences of the forty or so years in which these crimes of war were carried out.

Years later in 1903 at Odessa, Kishinev, Yakerinoslav, and a few hundred other venues mostly within Ukraine borders, were some of the most inhumane acts which befell in this particular genocide case. Suffice it to say, similar evil acts were carried out just two years later in Bessarabia. Believe it or not, situations became even worse in the duration of the Russian Civil War which lasted from 1917 until 1921. It was in 1921 that these war crimes would mercifully cease. The killings in the latter years of the Russian Pogrom genocide case were accomplished by the White Russian forces as well as by the Red Army Units.

You see, the tsars of Russia in this duration obliquely encouraged these acts of war with their anti-Semitic policies and their inexcusable carelessness as to what was going on. Because of this blatant disregard for human life, over the approximately forty years of the Russian Pogrom genocide, "only" 60,000 Jews were brutally murdered for no credible reason whatsoever. As a matter of truth, there can never be any substantial reason for the committing or the attempt of committing genocide.

You may have noticed that I just stated that "only" 60,000 Jews were killed in the Russian Pogrom genocide case. I used the word "only" to make a point. The point being is that there are so many more genocide cases that have happened prior and post to the Russian Pogrom ordeal. The deepening doleful truth is that in comparison to other genocides, a death count of just over 60,000, especially over a forty-year period is an extremely low number when examining this harsh reality.

It is now time for me to reveal the ultimate truth of what genocide is. First of all, what are these committers of genocides problem with the Jews of our world? Can it be figured out? I myself am at a loss as to why this worldwide antiSemitism is so abundant. So, what are the beliefs of the Jewish people? The Jewish religion basically has the belief that Jesus Christ was not the son of god but he was a good prophet, "a mortal man." So is that it? Are these immoral acts being committed just for that? Was Hitler a Christian? If so, isn't it a commandment of God "Thou shalt not kill?" Here is another puzzling question. If this Christian theory is true to these people, then why are they murdering Jews who are only Jewish by nationality? I don't get it! Now, if that is not the reason for these cruel acts, then what is it? Is it because Jews tend to be wealthy by nature? Hey! Hitler was certainly wealthy! As a matter of fact, the main reason that he was so liked and won those elections in Germany is because through his sick methods, he would improve Germany's economy and Germans would have money in their pockets. I have heard that a war can improve a nation's financial status, but give me a break! I'll never understand it. But you know what? I don't think I want to.

Okay, so killing Jews in massive numbers is rendered fathomless. So, what about that half-witted organization, the Ku Klux Klan (K.K.K.)? Before I verbally attack these southern bigots, I would first like to make a response to the somewhat true claim, namely that the K.K.K. was founded by my political party, the Democrats. My point, or part of my point is this: the K.K.K. is derived in the southern United States. So doesn't the South usually for the most part vote Republican? I am not in any way implying that the Republican Party's ideals support the prejudiced beliefs of the K.K.K., and neither does the Democratic Party have any bias fundamentals as to the ideals of their party. The truth is that the K.K.K. consists of both parties and is only supported by bigots.

The K.K.K hates anyone who is not Anglo Saxon Protestant, especially the blacks. So, can the views of the K.K.K. be comprehended? My first point is this, but in order for me to make this point, I must first ask you a question. Do you know what the word Anglo means? If not, allow me to tell you. Anglo means English white American. So, this means that according to these bigots, not only is it wrong not to believe in every saying and detail of the Anglo Saxon Protestant religion, but it is also wrong to be born outside of the United States. Now, before any of these bigots try to trap me the way they usually would, by saying that I don't like Anglo Saxon Protestants, I respond with this. I have no problem with any Anglo Saxon Protestant, unless they represent the K.K.K. I now add this: In my freshman year of high school I attended a private Catholic high school, St. Joseph's, and in my religion class, there was a black Protestant girl who attended a Catholic high school and she was a super kid! So take that, you K.K.K. bigots. Just in case you are wondering what a Protestant was doing attending a Catholic school, I'll tell you in three decisive words: quality of education.

Continuing on, in pertinence to the K.K.K. and their ideals of perfection, I would now like to elaborate on just how they view our American Negroes. Hey! Maybe the fact that these Negroes are American makes them better people? Yeah, right. I saw one of these K.K.K. representatives on television speaking on behalf of this clan of so-called perfection. This bozo made a point that black people were sub-human. He went on to say that they were just like animals and should be thought of and treated like animals. Okay, so let's try to figure this one out. Blacks are just like animals, so would we chase our pet dog Rover through the woods and make killing Rover into a game of adult tag? If these blacks who they treat worse than lab mice are just animals, then why don't they chase them through the woods, catch them, and then keep them as pets? When we kill animals, it is for the purpose of nourishment, you know, food! So, do they eat these so-called sub human creatures? No, they don't, they just enjoy killing them for their own sick fun. I have more compassion for a common housefly than these K.K.K. hypocrites have for any Negro Americans. So, I now say directly to my hopeful future friend President Barack Obama, don't worry at all about the K.K.K., because they have been severely damaged over the years. And do you know what I say about that? Good riddance!

In the In General portion of this Politics Part One segment of this book, I mentioned that I believed that Wolf Blitzer of C.N.N. is the best political reporter of our time. You may recall, that I said that Wolf is the best political reporter of our time because he is the fairest of all the present reporters of modern day. Well, there was one time that I witnessed Wolf showing his own personal view. This was when Wolf was dealing with a former K.K.K. representative who was running for political office. Wolf, in a manner of class, kept stating over and over when introducing this man, that he was a former member of the K.K.K. This man who's name I will not mention, became offended once introduced and said to Wolf that he was offended at how many times Wolf mentioned that this anonymous man was a former clansmen. Wolf would react in his usual calm cool and collected manner, and by the time the conversation was over, Wolf was to introduce a C.N.N. female reporter. When Wolf introduced this female reporter, she said directly to Wolf, "You rock Wolf!" Wolf, I know you don't like to show it because you are such an excellent example of what a reporter should be. But Wolf, I know exactly what you were thinking. And you know what? You do rock, Wolf!

The next Ethnicity, which I would like to discuss, is the Cambodians of Cambodia and the Cambodians of America. I have had the privilege of being born in the city of Lowell Massachusetts, which has the second highest population of Cambodians than any other U.S. city. Incidentally, Long Beach California has the highest Cambodian population in the U.S. But remember, Long Beach is a larger city. Years ago, I watched an N.B.C. news special with Tom Brokaw on the City of Lowell, in pertinence to its high Cambodian population. However, this special aired a long time ago, and truthfully, I do not recall in any detail most of this N.B.C. broadcast. However, I do remember that Tom Brokaw was being driven down a Lowell street that I have walked down hundreds of times in my life. He was literally a half minutes walk from St. Joseph's elementary school where I attended eighth grade.

I have also had the privilege of having many Cambodian friends due to my Lowell residence. A funny thing that I always remember is that when I was a member of Deallegiance, some of my Cambodian friends would flip out when we told them that we covered a song by the Filipino band Death Angel. I remember my Cambodian friends would say in that cute little accent of theirs "Oh, you play Death Angel, I love Death Angel." The song we covered was a rocking tune called "A Seemingly Endless Time" which was often played on MTV's head bangers ball. We would often open with this song and got a great crowd reaction when playing it.

Okay, enough with my bragging! Let's get back to my Cambodian buddies in Lowell. It seems that every Cambodian I meet displays a very upbeat attitude. And, remember, these are people who have witnessed and were faced with the horrors created by the infamous Pol Pot of Cambodia. These, of course, were the horrors of the Khmer Rouge genocide. These people, who have moved to Lowell for a chance at the American dream, had the absolute terrors of being face to face with the reality of the Killing Fields!

Recently, I was at the Lowell Social Security office with my roommate, Tom. Since I quit my job as a custodian for Bridgewell, the Social Security office is a place which I often need to go. You see, I quit my job so I could concentrate on writing this book. Anyhow, I was just sitting there in my seat vegetating and bored when lo and behold, a cute little Cambodian woman entered the room and sat down beside Tom and myself. Of course, not being much of a morning person, I just sat there while Tom and this woman started to make friendly conversation. Somehow, having been tired, I don't remember this well, but I ended up involved in this conversation. The subject of her experiences in the killing fields came into play. She would briefly state that she had the horrifying experience of being faced with the reality of the killing fields. Obviously, she escaped, but I am sure she was forced to witness the people that she loved being tortured and murdered. She also told us that she had experienced, just like in that petrifying scene in the movie *The Killing Fields* where the main character Dith Pran was courageously attempting an escape and had to walk through piles and piles of dead bodies. It was horrifying! And this courageous woman is a survivor, which proves that good can overtake evil!

I will now state, from the example of this woman and the countless other Cambodians who, through the hope of the American dream, have moved to the most underrated state in the union, Massachusetts—Lowell, Massachusetts to be precise—the way I feel about these people. I would just like to say at this essence, how amazed and dumbfounded I am at the friendliness and happiness that these Cambodians of Lowell possess in their personalities, despite the horrifying experiences that these people have endured. This is an impressive human quality.

Now, to back up my claim of just how great of a state Massachusetts is, I say to you this: the reason that the Cambodians often prefer to move to this state is because of the high level of employment which Massachusetts has. Growing up in the city of Lowell and the town of Dracut (I lived in two towns because my parents divorced when I was young), yet more so in Dracut, where the Cambodian population was slim to none, I mostly hung around with other Caucasians who just about all of them played a musical instrument. You see, musicians are like magnets to one another. I can honestly say that the friends I grew up with were all very good people. However, from time to time, some of them would display the ignorance of prejudice, but this was not because they were bad people, it was because their minds were not as open as they should be.

What I have come to conclude is that Cambodian families have the most outstanding family values of any of the other ethnicities that I have seen being a Massachusetts resident. Cambodian families will sleep on their floors and take others who may be in need into their homes, and give them shelter with no questions asked. You must understand that this culture is like this because of the bad experiences of which they have had. These experiences have resulted in an appreciation for life. I have heard a lot of ignorance among my fellow Caucasians who would say things like ,"Why do they have these expensive cars when their homes are so run down?" I'll tell you why! None of your damn business, that's why! If one chooses to live a life of appreciation, it should never be criticized. A huge problem with modern American society is in the way we perceive and judge others in such quick, careless, and inattentive ways.

My loving Nana Hodge lives in a section of Lowell, which has a high number of Cambodian residents. I recall, when I was about sixteen or seventeen years old in the band years, that after I would pay Nana Hodge a visit, I would hop on my California Freestyle bike and start to pedal my way back to Dracut. However, on the way, I would pass a Cambodian family who would be having a small little beer party. So, of course, I wasn't stupid and realized, hey, why don't I start to pedal a little slower. Sure enough, I quickly made friends with this family. And seeing that I couldn't afford or find a buyer for my own beer, I would just drink theirs. Before I knew it, riding my bike to Nana's house would become quite a habit due to my Asian friends across the street. It soon got to the point that I could not ride by this family's house without hearing "Hey, Ted, come have a beer." By the time I would have to ride back to Dracut, I was feeling pretty good, if you know what I mean. And my female friend would even supply me with about a six pack when I was people's Budweisers every few days or so. I would try to tell the girl, "Hey I'm all set, you don't have to give me a six pack for the road" but she insisted and to tell you the truth, I didn't mind drinking another six pack on those nights. So, there I would be, riding my California Freestyle down a Lowell back street, half in the bag trying to balance my bike and also trying not to dent any cars parked on the side of the road, and I even had the difficult challenge of balancing a six pack of Bud on my handlebars.

Every Lowellian you ever meet can tell you that although Lowell is not a very big city, it is however, a very tough town. You have thugs, gangs, drunken teenagers like myself, yeah, I knew a lot of shady characters. But while enjoying these free Budweisers with my new Cambodian companions, it wasn't gang members or thugs that I was worried about. What did worry me when hanging out with my Cambodian buddies was that if my Nana was to look out her front window and see what I was doing, let's just say that my cute little hiney would have been so sore, that I wouldn't have been able to hop back on my California Freestyle and ride back to Dracut. I must say that due to my life experiences in the city of Lowell, I have developed a deep affinity for the Cambodian culture.

A very sad thing happened when I was a student at Dracut High School. A young boy who was only fifteen years of age drowned in a small pond behind the school that some of my fellow students and I used to swim in during the summer months.

VISION OF A MENTAL PATIENT

This boy's name was Demitrious Papafagos and we called him Dimitri for short. His family moved to the United States from Greece so that they could make their fortune and be able to move back to their homeland so they could live prosperously. Dimitri was with a few of his friends, incidentally a few of my friends as well, and they were swimming at this pond when all of a sudden, Dimitri went under and did not come back up. Our friends were unable to save Dimitri's life and were forced to live with that horribly sad memory. What I learned from this sad experience was this: people do love one another, but they are not aware of it until tragedy occurs. I call this subconscious love. It is a shame that it takes such tragedy for people to realize what is really important in life.

This unfortunate event occurred in late May, just as the school year was winding down to its end. The funeral, which was held a one-minute walk to my Nana Hodge's house, was one of the most amazingly real experiences of which I ever had as a teenager. It was so sad yet happy in a small way, to see my fellow Dracut High School students behave with such a compassionate class. Dimitri was famous! Little did he or anybody else realize just how many friends this small boy from Greece had. Even some of my fellow students whom I would usually not get along with became my friends for that brief, sad, yet, beautiful experience, that none of us will ever forget. I admit it has been a long time since I have thought about Dimitri, but I will never forget him.

I told you this story not just for the people who were directly involved, but also to make another moral point. While my friends and I were attending Dimitri's funeral, we were just standing there with tears running down our faces, when a few Cambodians that I recognized due to the fact that we were in my Nana's neighborhood, were pointing at us and laughing. By no means were these particular Asians justified in doing so. As a matter of fact, some of my friends were becoming quite disgusted with the behavior these Asians were displaying. But what my friends did not understand was that these Cambodians have experienced so much more tragedy than we did at that time, so much so that we could not even imagine it. What these Asians were actually saying to us was, "See how it feels?" So, in a small way, we kind of deserved it.

You see, Dimitri was just one, while these Asians have experienced genocide, which Caucasians from a small town in Massachusetts were simply too young and inexperienced to understand. If any members of the Papafagos family are reading this, I sincerely hope that your experience of a failure of the American dream can one day be replenished. Again, I quote director Michael Moore: "Can they ever trust us again?"

It is now time to get down to business, of just what genocide means to me. I have the belief that a politician can be both the best and the worst form of a human being. I am severely disturbed by what societies of Earth consider to be proper. I am ashamed that world leaders can walk around in their multi-thousand dollar suits with human blood spilling all around them and actually believe this to be proper.

The substance behind the statement that a politician can go from the best to the worst of human behavior is this: certain politicians will make a valiant effort to promote peace. Other politicians will contribute to these evils. Therefore, my strong belief is that world leaders walking around during bloodshed, performing diplomatic relations is not proper. So, here comes the well called for profanity! Genocide is Sickening Fucking Shit and I feel that these profane words are the only way to bring the essential attention which is long overdue in regards to genocide.

Looking proper in suit and tie while human blood is spilling all around you is not proper! Calling genocide sickening fucking shit and trying to put an abrupt halt to these acts of extreme evil is proper. Therefore, I say that it would be more effective if these world leaders were walking around in their underwear and fighting with their minds to end genocide or any of the other evil war crimes that exist. For years now, authors like myself have been trying to bring the essential attention which is needed to this critical world issue but we are failing miserably! The reason we are failing is that none of us so far have had the guts to call genocide exactly what it is: Sickening Fucking Shit!

I'm sorry, but to call these acts atrocities or to label them as unfortunate is simply not enough! These innocent people are being killed! The people who call these acts atrocities are the people who are not victims of these acts. I hate the word "atrocity"; this word is for the attempt of being classy when dealing with something that is not classy. There is no way to deal with something as un-classy as genocide with class! We must get our priorities straight! If someone who was a contributor to genocide came into your home and killed your family, you would not say, "Gosh, what an atrocity." What you would say is a word that is four letters long, that starts with an "f" ends with a "k" and has a "u" in it, and it's not funk! You figure it out!

I am disgusted with the American society of today! We as a people have developed a shameful selfishness! Not only is genocide censored by the media, but we Americans, when hearing any detail of the present crimes of war being committed, will turn a blind eye and say, "I don't want to hear about it." Us Americans have refused to acknowledge in any credible detail as to what is happening in pertinence to this issue. This is very selfish behavior and we should be ashamed of ourselves. We are not going through anything compared to these victims of genocide. These people are forced to witness the killings and torture of their loved ones every single day! Not to mention the horrors of which these people have for themselves. I now state with all the human compassion that I can muster: If you are more offended by my use of profanity when discussing genocide than you are by innocent men, women, and children being brutally murdered on a daily basis, then you are dead wrong! My use of this vulgar language serves one purpose: We must acknowledge the reality of genocide!

If Vice President Cheney can tell Pat Leahy to go fuck himself on the Senate floor, if Robert Novak can say "bullshit" on national television for no good reason whatsoever, then I should be able to state my case in this manner for a cause of morality. One time, I overheard George W. Bush on C.N.N. when the microphones were on and he was not aware of it, referred to a topic as "shit" and there was no good reason for it. Are you getting it yet?

I have done a lot of complaining about Republican ideals so far in this book. So, to be fair, I will state the problems that I have with my own party, the Democrats. The fact that I am a Democrat is because I believe in the ideals of my party, and not necessarily am I always fond of Democrats themselves. As I stated earlier, I have a lot of Republican friends and believe it or not, I actually tend to get along better with Republicans than Democrats. You see, I believe that the Democratic Party is usually more correct on issues. However, you must fathom that a big reason that Republicans are Republicans is because for understandable reasons, they want to make a lot of money and give their family members the best life possible. I get a kick out of some of my fellow Democrats who think that just because our party is fairer to the middle class and the poor, it makes them good people and Republicans bad people. There are good and bad in both parties. To further my elaboration, I state that there are Democrats who actually believe that no matter what they do in their personal life, they are good people just because they are members of the party which represents a more caring persona. There are Democrats that will call you stupid and immoral if you are Republican, and will then go home beat the shit out of their family members and think that it's okay because they care about the middle class and the lower class. Morality, my friends, goes deeper than just that of politics. And for another good thing that I have noticed about *some* Republicans is that although they support an unfairness in the distribution of social finances, some of them are very generous with their money. You know who is a good Republican besides Scott McClellan, Colin Powell, and George H.W. Bush? Former Red Sox pitcher, Curt Schilling! Curt and his wife do a lot for charity and to say they are stupid or immoral just because they are Republicans is a bogus statement. The ultimate truth is that world cultures, political parties, and people themselves are all different from one another and we need every type of person and culture for the world to flourish. There are Republicans with bad family values contrary to how most Republican families are. Also, there are a large number of Democratic families which have good family values as well. There is always an exception to anything. The last complaint I will make in relation to the Democratic Party is that although we are pro choice on the issue of abortion, not only like the rest of our society who are mostly unwilling to properly acknowledge genocide, not even willing to witness or understand anything about the process of abortion. So I say to my fellow Democrats: You are right, but you are to self righteous.

Back to the topic of genocide! Another problem I have with our or anyone else's approach to the genocide problem is this: If a war crime does not meet or directly apply to the U.N. definition of genocide, next to nothing is done about it.

At this point, I will, for the first time in this book, introduce one of my theories. This is a political theory. Throughout the history of the United States, we have had many famous terms, such as the Boston Tea Party's cry of "no taxation without representation," and Francis Scott Key's "Give me liberty or give me death" and of course, the one made by my favorite U.S. president Franklin Delano Roosevelt, "We have nothing to fear but fear itself." So, here is a term and a political theory of my own: "Morality over Technicality." The meaning of this self-made term is this: when dealing with war crimes or anything of that nature, as well as the taking of governmental definitions of war crimes or judiciary issues literally, it doesn't always work. The premise behind "Morality over Technicality" is that the human race is smart enough to decipher what is morally correct. Way too often are war crimes not dealt with properly because of taking our written proclamations literally, as well as people getting off or even being convicted of a crime because of some irrelevant technicality. If we can put a man on the moon, then we most certainly can tell the difference between right and wrong.

Here is another dispute I have with the U.S. political system. This is one that my father and I agree on wholeheartedly. I ask my fellow Americans, why is it considered such a privilege to talk to the president of the United States?" Before you jump all over me for that statement, please allow me to explain. It was a claim of the recent McCain campaign, that there are countries which the U.S. should not perform diplomatic relations with. Despite what I am about to state, I do believe that when dealing with certain situations or certain terrorists, this claim of McCain's can ring true.

But think about this: during World War 2, President Franklin Delano Roosevelt performed diplomatic relations with Russia's Joseph Stalin. Needless to say, Joseph Stalin was not a very nice man and we are all aware of that. Stalin was on the side of the United States because of Hitler's lust for more land. To explain further, it was because of Hitler's stabbing Stalin in the back by trying to take over Russia that Stalin would become a U.S. ally. You see, Roosevelt's talking to Stalin was an absolute necessity. You may have heard that the U.S. must never negotiate with terrorists, but Roosevelt negotiated with Stalin for credible reasons and if Stalin does not meet the governmental definition of terrorist after all the bloodshed he caused, then we need to redefine the word "terrorist." Roosevelt's diplomatic relations with Stalin, especially at the Yalta Conference, was an absolute necessity to defeat Adolf Hitler and the evil NAZI dream. Therefore, I feel that if negotiating with a terrorist can promote peace, then at times exceptions should be made. This is one example of the potential benefits of "Morality over Technicality."

Something else I would like to elaborate on is this: there has been a claim made by Americans, especially during the Reagan Administration, that we should have complete respect for all of the president's views and decisions because he is the president and therefore is above us. This is a false claim. You must understand that the presidency of the United States is an occupation. His or her job is to work for the American people and improve our world status. The president has taken on a job which requires him or her to be criticized by the American people. You should never blindly follow. This is the reason we vote.

VISION OF A MENTAL PATIENT

This is one aspect that makes the presidency a job that many wouldn't want, but that's a good thing. You see, the occupation of president doesn't pay well and is a hard job, thus it causes more credible candidates to run for this office.

To explain further, I must mention the first president of the United States, George Washington. You see, Washington, after helping the cause of establishing the United States and the American dream, through his tenure as a United States general, would do an honorable thing which would keep the American dream alive. Once the Revolutionary War was over, Washington was offered the position of king. Yes, king of America. After receiving this offer, Washington would turn it down. This honorable move of Washington's made a vital claim to United States history. Washington stated, "We just fought a war to end kings. I will not allow our new democracy not to be a democracy by the appointing of anyone, even myself, to the position of king." Washington was then elected president, served his duties to the United States and kept the American dream alive.

By doing so, Washington saved America twice. This supports the necessity of the "checks and balances system." So, you must understand that the president should have no power over you in a dictatorial type manner. He or she is not king. This is why I am so disgusted by politicians who use the United States government for their own personal gain. We have tolerated enough and need to do better at electing officials who are sincere and are out not only for the American people, but for all of the people of Earth.

You must be asking yourself once again, how? Yes, how do we put an end to genocide and promote world prosperity? I believe it could be done through a new form of ideology. This is an ideology of a mind revolution. Yes, my friends, a revolution fought peacefully with our minds. It sounds impossible, doesn't it? But we must try! Keep reading!

It is high time that the human race woke up and put an end to these sickeningly disgusting acts of the war criminals of this world. And I remind you, that this can only be accomplished through our minds. We must be thorough in our efforts. Yes, we can!

At this crux, before we get into any discussion of foreign policy, I deem it necessary to begin a discussion of the Cambodian Khmer Rouge genocide which was caused by the human parasite Pol Pot.

Pol Pot was born Saloth Sar on May 25, 1928, in a small village north of the Cambodian capital of Phnom Penh. He was the eighth of nine children. His father was one Pen Saloth, a very successful farmer. His mother was one Sok Nem who, believe it or not, was considered to be a very decent woman who was often viewed as a person compliant to help others.

Before we get into an in depth discussion of the shameful details of this particular genocide case, I would first like to present to you some more information through a brief chronology on the life of Pol Pot.

In 1935, when Pot was still known as Saloth Sar, he entered a Catholic primary school in the city of Phnom Penh. From there, Sar (Pot) would continue his education at this school, and in 1942, he would enter an upper class boarding school. Sar (Pot) would then earn a scholarship and move to France in order to continue his academic studies. Sar (Pot) came back to his native Cambodia in 1952 and entered the predominant Communist Party. At this point, Sar (Pot) began his subterranean ambitions in Cambodia under his new name Pol Pot. By 1953, the country of France granted Cambodia its independence. Three years later, in 1956, Pol Pot began his career as a teacher. Soon after his teaching career commenced, he would meet and marry his new wife, one Khieu Ponnary. In 1960, the party congress of the Communists of Kampuchea is held and Pot is given a position in the Communist Party's central committee. In 1963, Pot would go into hiding because his original name of Saloth Sar appeared on a government list of suspected communists, thus the reason for his going into hiding as a communist revolutionary. From this point in time, Pot began to work in secret for the Cambodian Communists Revolution. In 1970, the leader of Cambodia, Sihanouk, is taken over by one Lon Nol. In 1973, U.S. President Richard Milhous Nixon had the United States execute a bomb strike at the Khmer Rouge. By 1975, with Pol Pot's help, the Khmer Rouge seized the government of Cambodia. The nation of Cambodia, due to this outcome, would then be renamed Democratic Kampuchea. This would cause widespread panic among the people of this nation. Cities were evacuated and collective farms were established. By 1976, Pol Pot would become the Prime Minister of Democratic Kampuchea. In 1978, as a result of these horrific occurrences, a war begins with an attack on Democratic Kampuchea (Cambodia). This attack was made by Vietnam a few years after the United States troop withdrawal. The Vietnamese would end up defeating Pol Pot's Khmer Rouge, and it established a puppet regime. Pol Pot and his counterparts would then flee to Thailand. Democratic Kampuchea, during all of this, would once again be called Cambodia. However, after this defeat, Pot would still make efforts to return himself to a position of power, but mercifully his efforts would be an insignificant anti-government coalition. Pot would pass away of an apparent cardiac arrest on April 15, 1998. Pot was dead at the age of 69.

Moving on now, I will more thoroughly explain some of the details on what actually took place during this chronology of the life of Pol Pot. Now, for a summary of the paramount facts which pertain to some of the history of Cambodia.

So, here it goes: back in about 800 A.D. over 1200 years ago, was the rise of what was known as the Khmer Kingdom. The ancient leaders of the Khmer Kingdom excelled in warfare and edifice, or for lack of a better word, construction. Three Southeast Asian countries were taken over by French rule in the 1800s. The other two are Laos and Vietnam. These three countries are now recognized as Indo China. Aristocrats (those with tastes or manners of the upper class or a privileged minority) and intellectuals (those involving or appealing to intelligence) were considered to be threatening people and would often be subject to executions.

Eleven years before France granted Cambodia its independence, French authorities arrested two Buddhist Monks for preaching patriotism. These two arrests were conducted to prevent the innocent people of Cambodia from obtaining the right of self-rule without outside interest. After that, the rise of Hitler's NAZI Germany ended up with control over the French, leading to their gaining of power over French colonies, thus resulting in Cambodia being controlled by Germany. So, this means that Hitler, through his uncompromising lusty greed, had a major effect on Cambodia in the 1940s when Pol Pot was only a teenager. You see, France's end of power over Cambodia technically ended in 1953, but NAZI Germany would be very politically dominant. The French were seeking profit from the countries of Indo China. Unfortunately, this behavior among world powers has existed for ages.

So, how did Pot's interest in communism relate to his uncompromising lust for power? Let's take a look at what communism is and what, I believe, may have been its intention of origin. First of all, communism's main premise is based on the ideals of a nineteenth century German man by the name of Karl Marx. You might have heard of the term "Marxism." You see, Marxism is basically just another word for communism. Karl Marx believed that property and goods shouldn't be owned and exchanged by individuals, but instead should be accessed by the government.

One day after band practice for Deallegiance, I was having a conversation with Matt and John in John's kitchen. Somehow, the topic of communism came into play and I asked Matt a question. "What if everyone was given equal possessions, appointed a job, and basically all had the same financial status?" Matt replied with "That sounds good." I then said to Matt "That is communism." Suffice it to say, Matt was shocked. About two years earlier, I was presented by a schoolmate with the same question and I responded the same way Matt did. I do believe it possible that communism could have been made for an attempt at achieving utopia. However, it is bluntly obvious that the communist idea was an absolute failure.

You see, communism gives a government way too much control over a population. We have seen the results. The Soviet Union technically no longer exists and horrible situations have occurred in China. You might recall the China city of Peking standoff in the late 1980s and that incredible display of bravery of a Chinese man standing in front of a tank with no weaponry and the tank backing down. Are you aware of what was happening? A revolution was being attempted by citizens of China who were fed up with the abuses of communism. These courageous Chinese would take a stand in the city of Peking. These Chinese rebels were trying to achieve a democracy like that of the United States. This caused the American press as well as the American people to be inspired by this chance to promote democracy. This Peking standoff was on the American news night and day. This story would remain a headline until something happened. They were all killed! But the fact is that once this rebellion was put to a dismaying end, this part of the story did not even make the front page. Why? Because it was a miserable failure! This is a big problem with America of modern times. You see, when we are inspired by the possibility of another nation becoming like us, we show our undivided attention, but when we are faced with death and failure, we simply look away.

So, what am I getting at here? Do you remember the point I made in the stem cell research section about good stemming from evil and evil stemming from good? I explained that in order for life to survive, we must feed off other life (eating plants and animals for nourishment). Like I said, a side cannot exist without another side, just as a top cannot exist without a bottom. You need to fathom that world evils cause humans to fight for good. And by no means am I an expert on Marxism, but I do have credible understanding of the communist idea. Communism, the way I see it, was an attempt at good, but what it produced was evil.

Once again, I went off on a tangent. Let's get back to the subject of Pol Pot and his sickening display of the lowest act of the human race genocide. We have now just begun to understand how Pot used the concept of communism for a despicable evil. When young Saloth Sar (Pot) was growing up in the city of Phnom Penh, he was preparing for his career as a communist subversive. A subversive is a person who intends to overthrow or destroy. Pot's abuse of the communist idea would result in a tragedy for the ages. We can now see that Pot's abuse of communism was for his master plan of overthrowing Cambodia.

Saloth Sar (Pot) had a communist mentor in his younger years. This mentor of Sar's was one Tou Samouth, a Khmer from a southern region of Vietnam called Cochin China. Samouth was a religious monk during World War 2. He would abandon this calling in order to join the Vietminh. The Vietminh is the "League for the Independence of Vietnam" which was a national liberation movement founded on May 19, 1941, in Southern China. The Vietminh was formed with a desire to end French colonial rule over Vietnam, and in the future to oppose Japanese rule.

Tou Samoth, although educating Sar, was only his mentor, and we mustn't blame him. It is the acts of Pot himself which led to this human tragedy. Sar (Pot), through his schooling, learned to speak French. Sar (Pot) wanted to learn the French language because Cambodia was under French rule. The other subject that Sar (Pot) excelled in was religion, Catholicism to be precise. This is for a relative reason as to why Sar (Pot) learned French; it was because Catholicism was the French religion. There was no freedom of religion, which is something the United States has and takes for granted.

At this point, I will tell you about a crucial trip that young Saloth Sar (Pot) took for the purpose of his education on the concept of communism. Sar (Pot) was in his early twenties when he took this excursion. This trip of Sar's was to the country of Yugoslavia. The year of this voyage was 1950 and this was when Sar (Pot) had his first glimpse at communism in action. He made this journey to Yugoslavia through his volunteering in Paris, France, with a few of his Cambodian peers. This trip was to last for one month. The leader of Yugoslavia in this era of the early 1950s was one Marshall Tito. Despite the fact that Yugoslavia had gained its independence from Soviet rule, Yugoslavia would remain a communist regime. It would later become apparent that Marshall Tito was intending to form his own brand of communism.

Another interesting occurrence in Sar's (Pot's) life was his meeting of his future wife, one Khiev Ponnary who was eight years older than Sar (Pot). Ponnary was the daughter of a judge. She had achieved a good education considering that she was a Cambodian woman, which was a challenge for the females of Cambodia in that era. Like her husband, she became a teacher—a well respected teacher, as a matter of fact. Of course, Pot himself was a teacher and he taught at a Phnom Penh high school called Chamraon Vichea (progressive knowledge, in English). Pot taught the subjects of civics, history, geography, and French. Pot would use his education and vast knowledge for his dispirited lust for power. Once Pot achieved his prominence, he would kill anyone no matter how close to him, if he sensed even the slightest bit of betrayal in a person. This sick human parasite would probably even kill his own offspring if he deemed it necessary.

I now present to you some of the most vital occurrences in pertinence to this whole genocide ordeal. These are the events that President Nixon (Nixon's foreign policy will soon be discussed), I believe, may have been set into motion, to oppose Pot's cause, and due to complications, Nixon did make some questionable moves relative to the Vietnamese. The United States, through Nixon I believe, was forced to send approximately 300,000 troops into South Vietnam. Around this time, United States airplanes began to bomb the border region which lay between Cambodia and Vietnam. This caused the Khmer Rouge to move their location to the north for the purpose of avoiding slaughter. Incidentally, there was a struggle going on in the Republic of Indonesia. Indonesia today is the most populous Muslim majority nation in the world. It now has become the fourth most populous nation on Earth. Anyhow, about 500,000 suspected communists in this country were terminated, thus the abrupt end to communism in Indonesia. You might recall, at the start of this genocides and foreign policy segment, my mentioning of the eradication of the communists in Indonesia, in the 1960s. The man behind this massacre was one Suharto, officially spelled Soeharto. Suharto was the second Indonesian president and held office from 1967 to 1998.

Moving on, it is now believed that Pol Pot was most challenged in pertinence to the production of mass hysteria which he induced from 1973 to 1980. This was due to his need to stay one step ahead of Norodom Sihanouk. Sihanouk was the offspring of King Norodom Suramarit and Queen Sisowath Kossomak. Sihanouk was the head of the state of the new regime while Pot was still in power. Pot would lead the Khmer Rouge to force Sihanouk out of office. During the Vietnamese invasion, Sihanouk went to New York City to speak on behalf of his opposition of Vietnam before the U.N. He would then be forced to seek refuge in China and later in North Korea. Sihanouk would later return to power, becoming the president of Democratic Kampuchea. Through this all, Pot considered Sihanouk an obstacle to his master plan.

Through Nixon, the United States took sides with Lon Nol. Nol served as both prime minister and defense minister of Cambodia. Nol was opposed to Sihanouk, whom Pot did not trust. And, of course, eventually, Pot would theoretically stab Sihanouk in the back. Nol, with the support of Prince Sisowath Sirik Matak, made a stand against the Vietnamese and demanded that they leave Cambodia alone. Nol made a smart move by closing down Cambodian ports, thus preventing the Vietnamese forces from receiving their supplies. Nol understood that Nixon's attacks were to injure the North Vietnamese control of bases in this area.

In 1971, Nol's forces, although damaged, would still make one last valiant stand against the communists. However, this would fail and would eventually lead to the reality of year zero. When the Khmer Rouge gained fortitude, the war in Vietnam would take a major turn. It was in January of 1973 and in France (the country that previously had power over Cambodia), peace talks would begin, thus causing the United States and the North Vietnamese to come to a truce and have a ceasefire. It was in 1975 when this genocide essentially began, and Pot's demented vision of year zero would become a harrowing reality for those directly affected. At this time, the Khmer Rouge would execute a mandatory evacuation of Phnom Penh. This move was intended to protect "some" from possible U.S. raids, odd move for an organization that killed so many and especially for Pot, who did not even seem to care for his own flesh and blood.

By 1976, Pot and his evil committee would make more progress for the advancement of their new government. This plan of Pot's was labeled the four-year plan and Pot was more hopeful to succeed with his abuse of the communist idea by 1980. It is a common belief among historians that Pot's plans were based on the schemes of Joseph Stalin and Chairman Mao. Three years after the start of year zero, Pot would become wary of possible defeat. Pot ultimately caused the Cambodian Revolution with his repulsive ambitions, as well as his plans of overthrowing Norodom Sihanouk. Obviously, no one could afford to trust Pot, which would lead to his defeat. The reasons no one trusted Pot are due to his willingness to betray anyone who he suspected of conspiracy against him. He even killed a trusted servant of his by the name of Vorn Vet. Pot sent Vet to Tuol Sleng, which could theoretically be considered the Pol Pot version of the NAZI concentration camp, Auschwitz.

During Pot's reign of terror, he left absolutely no doubt that he was the pre-eminent leader of Cambodia, which at this time was called Democratic Kampuchea. Pot would label himself as "Brother Number One" which reminds me of "Big Brother" from the Orwell classic, *1984*. Pot would divide Democratic Kampuchea into different sectors or zones, each of them having his own dictation of leadership, thus the producing of very distinct problems for the people of Democratic Kampuchea. Pot would become suspicious that his enemies from these zones wanted his position with intensity. You see, Pot was an extremely cautious man; therefore, he trusted no one. Pot would make sure, that he was constantly guarded and he would thus increase the secrecy of communist party procedures. Pot had the sickening self-righteousness to consider himself licensed to political murder. Because of this self-righteous belief of Pot's, many futile arrests were conducted. As I already explained, Pot would interrogate anyone whom he suspected of defiance. Being the parasite that Pot was, he considered his victims as insignificant germs and even had the abomination to refer to them as microbes. Pot would make no compromises. He was even hateful of Thais, the Chinese, and Muslims who he would viciously exterminate if he suspected support for the revolution that opposed him. The death tolls were absolutely staggering. Just below fifty percent of the ethnic Chinese in Cambodia or Democratic Kampuchea were brutally murdered. The Cham Muslims would suffer the same fate and lost approximately 200,000 of their people who resided in this country. Get ready! Here comes some more sickening details of this ghastly world tragedy. I now present a summary of what is commonly known as Tuol Sleng. The official name of Tuol Sleng was Interrogation Center S-21. In this interrogation facility, the classification of its victims achieved ludicrous levels, not to mention ludicrous tactics of torture and murder. Tuol Sleng was located in a suburb of Phnom Penh, which was also called Tuol Sleng, thus the reason for its name. This killing facility was in an old abandoned high school. A counterpart of Pot's was one Kang Kek Ieu and he was placed in charge of administration. Mercifully, and quite fortunately, Tuol Sleng did have some courageous survivors. These survivors would have stories to tell that would make your skin crawl! Such natural human acts such as a bowel movement or urination would result in savage-like methods of torture. If you were too slow in reacting to a demand or to a question, you would become subject to these methods of torture. To add to this ludicrousness, it was a rule that if you shed just one tear while being tortured, the methods would become even more barbaric. Silence was also mandatory. Any disobedience would not only result in beatings, but would progress into whippings with electric wire. As you would expect, if any of Pot's employees gave a hint of betrayal, they would become subject to these acts of torture as well.

As I stated in the earlier presented chronology of Pot's life, Pot would eventually be dethroned, but luckily for him, he would get off easy considering what he deserved and also considering his blatant disregard for human life. Pol Pot would die of an apparent cardiac arrest. Pot left behind a legacy of pure evil, and the results are still prominent. There still exists a major problem due to this man's legacy of immorality. This still prominent problem is the existence of somewhere between four to six million land mines that are still presently buried in Cambodian soil. This means that even after this parasite is no longer in power and has been dead since 1998, he still manages to cause death. It is most common for young children to be killed by these land mines. This is due to the demeanor of a young person. You see, because of being inexperienced as well as being curious, as most young children are, when it comes to being aware of what they are doing a child could mistake a landmine for a toy or simply wander into places that they should not go. Being a parent in areas that these mines exist in must be a terrible burden. Imagine having to worry about that day after day. I wouldn't let my kid out of my sight for one second if I were to be a parent in one of these areas!

By the time Pot was done with these demented mass killings, the death toll of this genocide case was a staggering estimate of about three million innocent men, women, and children. Today, Cambodia lives under a new system of government. This new Cambodian government consists of some of the former government officials who had fled to Vietnam, as well as other Khmer who had lived in exile for two decades. It has been a number of years since Pot's reign ended, and many of these government officials have since passed on. The new system of government in Cambodia is still communist, but is a much less abusive form of communism of which existed under the rule of Pol Pot. Because of Pot's defeat, a large amount of the Cambodian people has returned to their native land. Presently and for some time now, Tuol Sleng (Interrogation Center S-21) has been a museum in tribute to its many victims who perished and also to those who survived.

It is almost time for our discussion of the Cambodian Khmer Rouge genocide to end. The last part of this one-way conversation will be my recommending of a movie which should be considered a classic. This movie is about the beautiful friendship of a *New York Times* reporter by the name of Sydney Shanberg and his Cambodian translator and aid, Dith Pran. Dith Pran was portrayed by Dr. Haing Ngor and Sydney Shanberg was played by Sam Waterson who is a cast member of the popular television show "Law and Order." These two actors' performances were outstanding, but I must say that the best performance in this movie was John Malchovich's portrayal of photographer Alan Rockoff, which was absolutely astounding. I am speaking of one of my favorite movies of all time, *The Killing Fields*. This movie begins in 1975 in the Cambodian Capital of Phnom Penh at a time when many believed the killing would end. However, it was only the beginning. Dith Pran ends up being exiled to the country side in Tuol Sleng and is forced to face the infamous "Killing Fields." I will never forget the beginning when Waterson's character Sydney Shanberg referred to the nation of Cambodia as a country that he would grow to love and pity and when Ngor's character Dith Pran had to face the imminent reality of Pot's evil vision of the "Year Zero." I urge all who read this book to watch this moving story of love and good, produced through the existence of evil and hate, and also to learn more about the year zero.

Despite the human tragedy it exposed, *The Killing Fields* does have a good ending. The end of this movie gave me hope that even through the raucous realities of war and mayhem that exists in the world of today, there still has been a perseverance of human good which has showed me that although such evil exists, that through it all, happy endings do occur. The last thing I have to say regarding this moving story of love produced through the existence of hate is my humble request: watch David Putnam's *The Killing Fields* and notice the use of profanity in this movie. You must grasp, that my use of profanity in this book is to make a moral point. The people in this movie were dealing with such tragedy, that they would curse up and down throughout the whole ordeal. This was the only way to express such desperate emotions. This story is about shockingly real people.

In a new direction, we will now, for the first time in this genocides and foreign policy segment, have discussion on for-

VISION OF A MENTAL PATIENT

eign policy. The foreign policy we will now explore is the foreign policy of the thirty-seventh President of the United States, Richard Milhous Nixon.

Nixon, despite the controversy that would tarnish his image, is still considered to be one of the best presidents when it comes to foreign policy. As a matter of fact, one of Nixon's former opponents for the U.S. presidency, George McGovern, was quoted as saying that Nixon possessed a more practical approach towards China and the Soviet Union than any other president since World War 2. McGovern also stated that with the exception of his inexcusable continuation of the Vietnam War, Nixon will still get high marks in history.

Once Nixon set about on his tenure as president, he was faced with the problem of the Vietnam War. Nixon did claim that he would soon end the United States' involvement in this war. The fact that Nixon would not keep his promise may have had some credibility in pertinence to this controversial tactic of Nixon's. During the first year of Nixon's first term in 1969, Nixon visited Vietnam and performed diplomatic relations with the Vietnamese president Nguyen Von Theiu. Stemming from this, Nixon would create the "Nixon Doctrine" which manifested an attempt to replace U.S. soldiers in Vietnam with Vietnamese troops. This idea of Nixon's was known as "Vietnamization." By 1973, Nixon completed this goal and brought the number of U.S. soldiers from 543,000 to zero.

You see, the fact that Nixon claimed in 1968 and in 1972 that he would end U.S. involvement in Vietnam tarnished his image just as "Watergate" would. In his first term, Nixon approved a covert bombing attack in Cambodia; this was still in the year 1969. This attack was codenamed Operation Menu. The intent of this attack was to destroy the National Front for the Liberation of Vietnam base in Cambodia. This would lead to a future attack of Laos.

On April 30, 1970, Nixon announced the incursion of United States military personnel into Cambodia. The intent of this move was to cause a disruption and to damage North Vietnamese sanctions. This would lead to a *New York Times* article called the "Pentagon Papers." This would prove detrimental to Nixon's plans.

Continuing on, in 1972 heading toward the end of Nixon's first term, Nixon expressed a strong concern for the possible level of civilian casualties. At this point, Nixon would approve of Linebacker 2, which was the code name for the aerial attacks in North Vietnam. Nixon would later sign an essential peace treaty, and then he would take action by forming a committee that would thoroughly observe a plan to end the U.S. draft. By June of 1973, the U.S. draft would come to an abrupt end. Nixon would see to it that military salaries would grow larger. The intention of this move was to attract volunteers and fund more television advertisements for the promotion of the U.S. military services.

Early in Nixon's second term, his vice president Spiro Agnew would resign due to charges of bribery, tax evasion, and claims that he was money laundering while he was Maryland's governor. This would lead to Nixon's appointment of Gerald Ford to vice president.

You must understand something: Nixon inherited the Vietnam War. I believe that Nixon's hands were tied as how to go about ending this war, and due to other things that were going on which we will soon discuss, Nixon was bearing a heavy load. The United States entered this Vietnam Conflict in 1959, by the thirty-fourth United States president, Dwight D. Eisenhower, who was also a Republican.

I stated already that George McGovern for the most part approved of Nixon's methods of foreign policy. I personally believe that Nixon's Operation Menu had a clever intent. It is quite possible in my opinion, that Nixon may have been wary of the rise of Pol Pot. It is also possible that Nixon's continuance of the war in Vietnam was the best possible tactic he could have undertaken. Once I have made my case on my observance of the foreign policy of Nixon, with an open mind, you might see what I am getting at.

At this juncture, I deem it necessary to elaborate on Nixon's involvement in the Yom Kippur war which led to the 1973 oil crisis. This Yom Kippur conflict commenced with an attack on Israel, which was executed by an Arab coalition lead by Syria, Egypt, and their Soviet allies. This attack happened in October of 1973, right around the time that Spiro Agnew resigned from his position as the vice president. Nixon, in a United States tradition of being an ally for Israel, was glad to give support to Israel. Due to this attack of course, Israel suffered incipiently. Israel was hoping for some substantial support from their European allies. However, the only European nation willing to lend their support was the Netherlands. Nixon was trying to get something done in order to help our long time friends in Israel. Nixon would become extremely frustrated with bureaucracy, or as previously stated, "technicalities." This would lead to the common rule-breaking of Nixon's, in order to get by these technicalities. The purpose of this bypassing of common procedure was for the intent of delivering Israel the supplies they so desperately needed. By the time the United States and the Soviets—who were the allies of Syria and Egypt—negotiated a truce, Israel had made a strategic military move and had penetrated into enemy territory.

Due to these actions made by Israel, Egypt and the Soviets, let's just say, "began to not get along as well." Anyhow, this would unfortunately lead to the United States Oil Crisis. O.P.E.C. (The Organization of Petroleum Exporting Countries) made a decision to raise oil prices. This was a direct response to the United States' support of Israel. O.P.E.C is made up of twelve countries: Algeria, Angola, Ecuador, Iran, Iraq, Kuwait, Libya, Nigeria, Qatar, Saudi Arabia, The United Arab Emirates, and Venezuela. It's a surprising fact that some of these countries are in the western hemisphere.

As a consequence of this dilemma, the dollar would decrease in value. Since O.P.E.C. was paid in dollars, as a result, O.P.E.C. was receiving less money. O.P.E.C. would then decrease production and form an embargo (An embargo is a government order that prohibits the entering or leaving of commercial ships at its ports. The U.S. has had an embargo with Cuba since the Cuban Missile Crisis occurred). This O.P.E.C. embargo was more evidence of the diplomatic hostility which O.P.E.C. had toward the United States due to the Yom Kippur conflict. Now, of course, Nixon's foreign policies would cause domestic hardships for the United States and Nixon was subject to ridicule for his over concern as to what was going on overseas.

I would now like to point out a move that Nixon made to deal with the 1973 oil crisis. Nixon did something that was so clever, I couldn't believe it. What Nixon did was this: He decreased the interstate speed limit from sixty-five mile per hour to fifty-five miles per hour, do you know why? If not, I'll tell you. It is common knowledge for anyone who drives that the slower you drive, the less oil and gas you will consume. So Nixon decided to lower the interstate speed limit to save on gas and oil consumption in order to deal with this oil crisis. Of course, this only made a very small dent in the oil problem which we were facing. It did not even come close to solving the problem, but it was still a good idea and a prime example of just how clever Nixon could be.

By this point, my Democrat friends must be saying: "All right you've already praised one Republican (Scott McClellan) Ted, what are you doing sticking up for Nixon of all people?" Well, my Republican, Democrat, Independent, or whatever party you are a member of friends, you shall soon see why! Keep reading!

Now, we will discuss Nixon and the United States' involvement in the Indo-Pakistani War. This small war actually took place prior to the Yom Kippur conflict. This time, rather than United States support for Israel, Nixon gave support to the country of Pakistan and the Pakistani general Yahya Khan. This ordeal took place at the tail end of Nixon's first term in 1971. Although the Bengali people (Bengalis are the ethnic people from the country of Bengal in Southern Asia) were having their human rights violated by Pakistan's military, Nixon would claim that he was attempting to avoid a war in order to defend Pakistani interests. However, it is my belief, as well as others, that Nixon reacted the way he did because he was fearful that India would invade Western Pakistan. You see, Nixon thought it was likely that if he was not cautious, an Indian invasion of Pakistan would result in India dominating the Asian sub-continent, thus resulting in a strengthening of the Soviets.

Prior to this, an Indian-Soviet treaty was signed and supposedly put in effect. Nixon, being the foreign policy expert that he was, felt it imperative that he demonstrated his reliability to China. You must understand that foreign policy is, for any president no matter how smart, far from easy to deal with. If you take any one action, even a moral action, almost every governmental decision, foreign or domestic in some way, will have a negative effect on at least something. This is due to complexities of world diplomacy.

Continuing on, Nixon would commence by consulting his security advisor, Henry Kissenger (Kissenger is a German born political scientist, bureaucrat, diplomat, and Nobel Prize winner). For some reason, Nixon and Kissenger did in fact downplay reports of possible genocide activities in Eastern Pakistan. In doing so, Nixon and Kissenger risked possible Soviet confrontation. This move was for an intimidation factor.

Kissenger thought that this foreign policy tilting in Pakistan's direction had more to do with Nixon's friendly relationship with the dictator of Pakistan and also that Nixon's Pakistani support was because of his feelings as well as an Indian bias. Nixon had the tendency to break rules, such as his unauthorized supplying of Israel in Yom Kippur and to Pakistan in this case, which by the way was opposed by Congress as well.

The people of the United States expressed a strong disapproval with Nixon because they were more concerned with what was happening in Eastern Pakistan (possible genocide activity). I do believe, in regards to this situation, that Nixon was playing his hand as well as possible. Nixon's actions relative to his support of Pakistan despite possible failure caused him to send the U.S.S. Enterprise warship to the Indian Ocean. This was to intimidate India's military forces. This move of Nixon was virtually ineffective. A dangerous consequence of this blunder was for of India to pursue nuclear ambitions, although this is not even remotely an uncommon goal for a nation to have. This blunder also led to tension between Nixon and India's prime minister, Indira Ghandi. Lastly, the Pakistani government would become disappointed with the United States as an ally. Okay, now, for my assessment of Nixon's foreign policy. First of all, Nixon did deceive the American people regarding troop withdrawal in Vietnam as promptly as he claimed he would. But in my view, this was because he was aware of the complexities of the foreign policy concept. You may have heard the argument that United States' priorities in Vietnam were incorrect. Remember, though: United States involvement in Vietnam began in 1959 under the Eisenhower Administration.

Moving on, why do you think Nixon approved of the covert attack, Operation Menu? To remind you, Operation Menu was an attack on the Vietnamese headquarters in Pol Pot's Cambodia and the Vietnamese were opposed to the Khmer Rouge; but remember, we were already in conflict with Vietnam. Also, you must remember that Pot at this time was making substantial progress. But it was not until the Ford administration that the horrors of Pol Pot began to take a more prominent effect. Also, remember that United States military actions ordered by Nixon took place in 1969. Pot at this time was not as well known, but it was in 1960 that Pot would achieve a position in the government of Cambodia. You see, this military action executed by Nixon was definitely in part intended to damage Vietnam's stand in this war. This action also cut off Vietnamese access to the Ho Chi Minh trail, which ran through Laos and, of course, Cambodia. And obviously, this move was intended to help Cambodia as well as the United States, even despite the fact that Pot was a part of the Cambodian government. So, this move was supposedly not to prevent Pot from making progress. However, I do believe that Nixon was quite aware of Pot, but may have underestimated him. So, why didn't Nixon just tell us that he was aware of Pot? Well, that would be a good point against my belief. However, people, for one, might not have believed Nixon, and two, people may have thought he was crazy, and three, if he had revealed this belief, Pot may have become wary of him.

In the movie *The Killing Fields*, Sam Waterson's character Sidney Shanberg was very critical of Nixon, but who could blame him? Nixon, I believe, inherited this problem and had to do one of the hardest things that a president could ever have to do: This is to order military moves which would cause the bloodshed of innocents affected by the lusty moves of their leaders. The only thing he could do was to make military moves which would lead to less bloodshed, or lead to the ending of conflict. This view of mine will be further elaborated on at the end of this segment. The last thing I now remind you of is that Nixon's hands were tied.

Remember Nixon's Linebacker 2 aerial bombings in Vietnam and Nixon's claim that he was concerned for the lives of civilians? Do you recall in Yom Kippur when Nixon honored our ally, Israel? Do you recall the discussion of the Indo-Pakistani war and Nixon's decisive, yet very cautious approach? You see, foreign policy is challenging even during peacetime, but when inheriting a war and such situations that occurred in the duration of Nixon's tenure as president, foreign policy is beyond challenging; as a matter of fact, it's downright difficult!

I have examined Nixon's foreign policy thoroughly and I have come to the conclusion that foreign policy, as well as any other aspect of politics, is in and of itself extremely complex. You see, if you do one good thing in almost every case, no matter what the decision is, in some way it will have a negative effect. For example: say an industrial corporation is causing pollution such as the contaminating of our drinking water with biological toxins. If you put this corporation out of business and prevent the pollution of our drinking water, then that is a good thing. The negative effect is that because of the termination of this industrial corporation, a lot of people will lose their jobs. This would lead to financial troubles for those who need to support their loved ones, not to mention damage to the economy.

I strongly feel that Nixon was an outstanding foreign policy expert. And I am not even close to being the first person to make this claim. I now ask you this: why would a former rival of Nixon's (McGovern), a Democrat, claim that Nixon, other than his continuance of the Vietnam War, will be remembered as a good president in regard to his handling of foreign policy? Among political junkies like myself, it is well known that Nixon is considered acceptable in this political aspect.

A couple of months back, I was hanging out with my Nana Hodge and when making conversation, Nixon was mentioned. So I asked her: despite the domestic failures of Richard Nixon, is it true what people say, that he was good in the field of foreign policy? My Nana, being very fluent in politics, gave me a resounding "Yes" and this yes came from my Nana who is a hardcore Democrat.

In continuation of this assessment on Nixon, I would like to make another point. After the Watergate scandal in 1972, Nixon who had been elected to a second term taking forty-nine of the fifty U.S. states but not the District of Columbia would have an enormous drop in his approval rating immediately following the Watergate scandal. Although Nixon had this major nosedive which brought his approval rating down to a bleak twenty-three percent, I ask you this: are you aware that even after Nixon's downfall, he was always consulted for advice on foreign policy matters? That is how good Nixon was in foreign policy.

George W. Bush's approval rating also plummeted. His approval rating was just barely above Nixon's tally at the end of Watergate, which as I said was a dismal twenty-three percent.

Now, for yet another point, some time back, I was watching one of the early democratic debates on my beloved C.N.N., which was between the three prime Democratic candidates at the time. These three candidates, of course, were Hillary Clinton, John Edwards, and Barack Obama. At this time, I was rooting and hoping for John Edwards to win. Anyway, to get to the point, John Edwards was posed with a question by the debate moderator: "Can you say one good thing that George W. Bush did during his tenure as president?" John responded by saying yes; he then claimed that Bush's funding for appropriations to fight AIDS in Africa was a good deed by Bush. But do you know something? Bush will never be consulted on how to send money to Africa for the research of AIDS. However, Nixon having a lower approval rating than Bush was continuously asked for advice when it came to foreign matters.

To explain further, I believe that Nixon was underrated. I also believe that people who care to a high degree about what is going on domestically do not care enough when it comes to foreign matters. I have come to the conclusion, through what I have elaborated on so far on the topic of genocides and foreign policy, that due to the extreme evils which are carried out in our world, foreign policy, with the possible acceptance of environmental issues, is the most vital of all issues.

You see, I simply feel that for the most part, Nixon had his priorities straight. Nixon was not just concerned with the welfare of the American people, but also used the United States presidency for what he saw fit. Nixon used his position of president more for the welfare of the whole world, than just for domestic issues. The United States did suffer domestically under the Nixon Administration, and that was one reason for his disapproval, but the main thing, which caused his popularity to plummet was, of course, Watergate. Don't get me wrong, the president should be majorly concerned with domestic issues, but I feel that it is selfish of us Americans to care more about things like tax cuts, healthcare, or anything else, more than the acts of terrorism or genocide. But I remind you, we must take care of domestic issues in order to take care of foreign issues. A big mistake Nixon made was to not realize the importance of taking care of ourselves domestically in order to take care of the world victims of such horrendous war crimes.

Okay, now I will give my theory on why I think Nixon was a Republican. In the In General segment, I vaguely touched on Reagan's trickledown economics theory. The trickledown theory is basically a belief that by helping the rich, it will cause the poor to work harder and thus lift them from poverty. In the time of Nixon, this theory was not technically claimed yet. But face it, this has been the Republican way for a long time now. Reagan basically refined and labeled this economic concept. Therefore, I believe it possible that Nixon, due to his mainly concentrating on foreign issues and his downgrading of domestic issues, leads me to believe that certain actions that Republicans take can have the appearance of being wrong, but are actually for the purpose of doing something right. Get it?

Therefore, I must give mention to another true, yet, basic challenge which Nixon had to overcome in his foreign diplomacy. You see, Nixon is rumored to have been coarse in personality, but he did want to be successful in his foreign diplomacies agenda. Nixon was likely, in my opinion, a good man, but was not viewed as being very charming. Anyone who is fluent in politics is aware that he was recorded running his big mouth and actually made some anti-Semitic comments. I do not, in any way, condone these remarks made by Nixon. However, in his defense, I have heard these types of remarks from many of my life acquaintances. Another thing is if he were such an antisemite, then why would he be supportive of Israel in the Yom Kippur incident? The truth is that the guy did go too far, but we have all said or done something wrong at one time or another.

I admit we cannot let Nixon off that easy. Therefore, we will soon have a discussion on the Watergate scandal. But first, I must add a little more on this present subject. George W. Bush and Dick Cheney, although they claim to have kept the people of the United States safe, I feel were horrible in their handling of foreign policy matters. You see, Nixon got caught with the occurrence of Watergate. But do you have any idea what Bush and Cheney have done? These men started a war, that they did not inherit, which caused so much bloodshed in a nation that never even attacked us. The attack against Iraq and the blind devotion that many of the American people had in this matter is so dumb I can't believe it. It is as if we were attacked by Mexico and decided to attack Canada in retaliation. If this act of the Bush Administration does not fall into the category of war crime, then we need to redefine "war crime." This administration has literally gotten away with political murder. I cannot believe that George W. Bush is the offspring of George H.W. Bush and I don't feel bad for his son, but I do feel bad for George H.W. Bush himself who was a decent man in my book. I believe that George H.W. Bush is a lot like Nixon. However, I have never met Nixon and can't be sure, but I believe that Bush was likely more charming than Nixon, but Nixon was the cleverer one.

You see, George H.W. Bush got the United States involved in the Persian Gulf War and Operation Desert Storm for reasons of credibility. I once again stress that George H.W. Bush ended the Persian Gulf War before getting to Saddam Hussein because he understood that the American people did not want to be involved in war at that time. I think Nixon would have finished the bugger off right there and then. So, say what you want about Reagan, and say what you want about George W. Bush, but I feel that both Richard Nixon and George H.W. Bush are both decent men. And by the way, George H.W. Bush is an honorable war veteran himself.

You may recall, in the In General segment, my statement that what the Democratic Party lacks most in modern times is sincerity. Therefore, although I am a Democrat, I refuse to blindly follow any member of my party whom I may have reason to distrust. I believe that it is quite possible that there are more sincere Republicans whom I will almost always disagree with on issues, and there are also insincere Democrats that I may still vote for, because despite their insincerity, I believe they will make better decisions which stem from democratic ideals.

The main fundamental differences between Democratic and Republican ideals are usually in pertinence to domestic issues and not foreign issues. Foreign policy depends entirely on the beliefs and ideals of the individual. My biggest problem with the Republican Party is that they are too favorable to the wealthy and way too unfair to the poor.

I will now present to you a scenario where I would cross political lines and vote Republican. If we were at the end of a Democratic administration and the domestic treatment of the middle class and poor were in acceptable shape and I believed that the Republican candidate demonstrated sincerity and good foreign policy ideals at a time when we would need that type of foreign leader, I would then cross political lines and vote for the Republican candidate. This has not happened yet since I have reached voting age, but I am only thirty-five years old and I have an open mind. So who knows?

I now say to my Democratic compatriots: Don't worry, I will later in this genocides and foreign policy segment give a positive appraisal of a president whose image, unlike Nixon's, was not tarnished. I say yes, we will later have discussion on my favorite United States President of all time, Franklin Delano Roosevelt whom I love very much. But first, I will shock my Democratic friends once more when I touch on John Fitzgerald Kennedy. So, those of my friends that are not fond of Nixon, I say okay, man, it's your choice; after all, this is America, right? So, we can't let Nixon off that easy, can we? What do you say we start to discuss Watergate?

Okay, here we go Watergate! The Watergate scandal was a sequence of political scandals which occurred under the Nixon Administration. On August 9, 1974, five men were put under arrest for breaking and entering into the headquarters of the Democratic National Committee in the United States capital, the District of Columbia. This breaking and entering occurred on June 17, 1972. The F.B.I. would then start an investigation regarding this occurrence. This was just one among chain of multiple illegal activities. Nixon had help from many of his political counterparts. Such charges were brought up as: espionage, campaign fraud, sabotage, illegal tax audits, illegal wire tapping, and money laundering to Mexico for the purpose of payoffs for those who helped and of course the breaking and entering itself.

It had been since determined that Nixon and his staff attempted a cover up six short days after this illegal operation was executed. Nixon was secretly taped, and these tapes would contribute to his political downfall. A term given to these tapes is the "Smoking Gun." This case would reach Supreme Court status, and the verdict was unanimous. The ruling was in favor of the United States in the United States vs. Nixon case. Resulting from the damage this would cause to Nixon's political standing, he would become the first U.S. president in history to resign from office.

Now, for some details on the actual breaking and entering: A security guard at the Watergate hotel by the name of Frank Wills had discovered some tape covering the locks on some of the doors in the Watergate complex. He proceeded to remove this tape and thought nothing of it. About an hour later, he noticed that these locks were re-taped. This led to five arrests that occurred on August 9, 1974. The names of these five conspirators were Bernard Barker, Eugeno Martinez, James McCord, Virgilo Gonzalez, and Frank Sturgis.

On September 15, 1972, a grand jury indicted two more co-conspirators. These two men were G. Gordon Liddy (Chief Officer for the White House Plumbers Unit) and E. Howard Hunt Jr. The charges these men were faced with were conspiracy, burglary, and illegal wire-tapping. These two men would be convicted in January of 1973.

Two *Washington Post* reporters by the names of Bob Woodward and Carl Bernstein discovered vital information leading to the knowledge of the breaking and entering and the alleged cover up of this scandal (there is a movie about this called "All the President's Men"). Foremost pertaining to the source of the *Washington Post* article was an anonymous source who was nicknamed "Deep Throat." The identity of "Deep Throat" was revealed in 2005. He was a former F.B.I. director by the name of Mark Felt.

On April 30, 1973, Nixon was left with no choice but to request the resignation of two of his most instrumental aides, John Ehrlichman, and H.R. Haldeman. These two men would end up being indicted and sent to prison. Nixon also terminated White House Counsel John Dean. Dean would soon become a prime witness against Nixon. It has been proclaimed that the most decisive moment in the trial of the United States vs. Nixon was when a Republican senator by the name of Howard Baker asked the question "What did the president know and when did he know it?" This moment would prove to be the turning point in this Supreme Court trial where Nixon's role in this scandal was manifested.

On March 1, 1974, the former Nixon aides who were dubbed the Watergate Seven were indicted for conspiracy which was carried out in the Watergate scandal. Nixon would give his resignation in a televised address on August 8, 1974. The new president Gerald Ford would eventually pardon Nixon on September 8, 1974. This pardon angered a large portion of the Democratic Party. However, a couple years ago, I was watching C.N.N. as usual, and longtime Massachusetts Senator Ted Kennedy surprised me and my fellow Democrats by his claiming that with the passing of the years, Kennedy now understood that Ford's pardon of Nixon was likely the right thing to do. Nixon, in a display of perseverance, continued to claim innocence right up until the day he passed away. However, Nixon's acceptance of Ford's pardon has led many to believe that this simply confirms his being guilty as charged. I remind you that the aftermath of this Watergate scandal did not cease with Nixon's resignation. The next congressional elections which took place three months later, were huge. Due to the fact that many of the civilian voters were appalled by the actions of Nixon, it led to detrimental consequences for the Republicans, thus the substantial gains for the Democratic Party resulting in the gaining of five seats in the Senate and forty-nine seats in the House of Representatives. Once Ford took over for the remainder of Nixon's second term, the standing of the Republican Party would continue to diminish, leading to Democrat Jimmy Carter of Georgia being elected president in 1976.

Now, for a discussion on some of the theories of the Watergate scandal: It is one belief that these burglaries were carried out for the purpose of obtaining specific information. One of the most renowned of theories is from the former D.N.C. chairman, Larry O'Brien. It has been said that O'Brien and others intended to deceive Nixon. Nixon was led to believe that O'Brien might have had information which could damage Nixon. However, these documents did not even exist. Nixon's brother, Donald, tried to intervene in this matter. But Donald was untimely and thus the theory stands that Nixon had bad intentions regarding this political scandal.

In my view, I see a different possibility. Another theory does exist. This is a theory that is shared by few as to why Nixon may have risked his presidency. This theory is that Nixon was trying to reveal a plan to bring about Martial Law (Martial law is temporary rule by the military over civilians during war time). But how could this be? Can we fathom it? Maybe not, but I am going to try! This theory, in the most basic of explanations, is the possibility that Nixon was trying to reveal the corruption of certain Democrats. We must admit that we shouldn't put it past any politicians, whether Republican or Democrat, that they can be guilty of corruption. The truth is that corruption in politics is commonplace.

Through my examination of Nixon and of his very unorthodox methods, I have come to the "possible" conclusion, that although Nixon was guilty of criminal activities by rule of law, his intentions may have possessed some substance. I am not denying that Nixon was a chronic rule breaker. However, through this discussion of the policies of Nixon, something doesn't add up.

Why would Nixon take such a risk at a time when his party and his rating of approval was so well? The truth is that we may never know. What I like the most about Nixon was his willingness to make himself look like an ass to do the right thing. I believe it "possible" that Nixon would cut through bureaucratic technicalities in order to do what he believed was best. I also believe that Nixon would have loved my political theory "Morality over Technicality." I strongly believe, at least in the foreign policies of Nixon, that he did put morality over technicality.

In a new direction, I now believe it would be a good time to discuss some of the foreign policy aspects of the thirty-fifth President of the United States, John Fitzgerald Kennedy. Over all, I do not think Kennedy was a bad president, but I do have some criticisms. So hang on in there my Democratic friends, for after I will make up for my open minded support of certain Republicans as well as my negative assessments of some Democratic actions, when I will praise Franklin Delano Roosevelt; but not yet, it is now time to talk about John F. Kennedy.

First and foremost, we will discuss the Kennedy Administration's involvement in the Cuban Bay of Pigs Invasion and the Cuban Missile Crisis. So here we go!

The Bay of Pigs Invasion: During the Eisenhower Administration, a plan was developed in order to dethrone Fidel Castro and the Cuban Regime. It had help from the Central Intelligence Agency (C.I.A.), as well as some input from the United States Department of State, to supply military equipment to the Counter Revolutionary Insurgency made up of anti-Castro Cubans. This anti-Castro insurgency was intended to overthrow Castro and inspire the people of Cuba to rise up and put an end to his reign.

A few months into the new Kennedy Administration, President Kennedy commanded this pre-planned invasion to commence. This would become known as the Bay of Pigs invasion. Brigade 2056, a group of approximately 1500 United States trained Cuban rebels would return to their native Cuba for the purpose of taking back of their homeland from Fidel Castro.

This invasion was executed without the aid of U.S. aerial support. Therefore, on April 19, 1961 just two days after Kennedy's invasion command, this Cuban insurgency was defeated. Most of the Cubans responsible for this invasion were either killed or taken prisoner. Kennedy was left with no choice but to bargain for the release of those captured. The common belief why this Cuban insurgency was not successful was not only the lack of United States aerial and navy support, but also a lack of communication among military leadership.

Roughly twenty months later, those who were taken prisoner were returned for fifty-three million dollars worth of food and medicine. This ordeal would cause Castro to be more cautious when dealing with the United States. Castro also learned from this experience that it was quite possible, that the United States could once again take action.

As you may have concluded from my assessment of the Bay of Pigs invasion, it is not hard to see the mistake that Kennedy, his advisors, and the military made. This attack was poorly planned out. First of all, the lack of air and naval aid is evident, seeing that these two forms of military aid for these Cuban exiles were nonexistent. The other mistake that sticks out like a sore thumb to me is that communications were lackluster. These mistakes, I believe, may have been made, because this insurgency was made up of Cuban exiles. In conclusion, I think it possible, that the preparations for this attack were not sufficient because American soldiers were not at risk, but Cuban soldiers may have been considered expendable.

In Kennedy's defense, I must state that although it took twenty months to free these Cuban prisoners, Kennedy was successful in bargaining for the welfare of the survivors of this insurgency. And by no means did Nixon always make the right choices in foreign matters. But I do believe that Nixon would have made appropriate compensations, which Kennedy obviously did not in this situation.

Okay, let's discuss the unavoidable Cuban Missile Crisis. On October 14, 1962, about one year after the Bay of Pigs Invasion, American U-2 spy planes took some photographs of Soviet intermediate range ballistic missile sites. At the time, these sites were not yet completed in their construction. These missile sites were of course being built in Castro's Cuba by the Soviets. Two days later, on October 16, Kennedy would receive these photographs and examine them. Resulting from this, the United States would be faced with the imminent possibility of nuclear confrontation. Therefore, Kennedy was obviously faced with a major problem. If Kennedy were to authorize an attack on these missile sites in Cuba, a nuclear threat of mass proportions would demonstrate itself. On the other hand, if Kennedy took no action, it would give the Soviets a strategic advantage if a nuclear confrontation were to occur. This Soviet advantage would be due to the closeness in proximity of Cuba to the United States. You see, Cuba is in the West Indies, and if the Soviets were ever to fire from Cuba, it would give them a dangerous advantage. The only way that America could trump this Soviet advantage in the occurrence of a nuclear confrontation would be to execute a pre-emptive strike. The last part of this problem for President Kennedy was that if he were to take no action, it would cause the United States to look weak.

A large number of military officials and members of the cabinet did in fact suggest a possible attack on these missile sites. Kennedy made the wise choice by ordering a naval quarantine. This quarantine had the United States thoroughly inspect all ships arriving in Cuban ports. Kennedy would then proceed to have negotiations with the Soviets and command them to remove all of the defensive materials which were being constructed in Cuba. The Soviet premier at this time was Nikita Krushcev. Krushcev would comply by ordering the removal of missiles which were subject to U.N. inspections. A deal would be made if the United States promised to never invade Cuba, and also if the United States removed their missiles that were stationed in the nation of Turkey. You see, Turkey is close in proximity to the Soviet Union, just as Cuba is close geographically to the United States. To explain this U.S./Soviet agreement in simple terms, it was basically: If you move your missiles closest to us away, then we will move our missiles closest to you away.

As a result of this near disaster, the world was brought closer together. Kennedy did well in this instance, and he also learned to approach diplomacy with the Soviets with more respect and caution. Kennedy, also in my opinion, became a wiser man due to this experience. You must understand that the world never, prior or post, came so close to nuclear catastrophe. The way I see it is that Kennedy was simply inexperienced when dealing with the Bay of Pigs invasion. However, when matters worsened with the occurrence of the Cuban Missile Crisis, Kennedy showed a respectable valiance. Therefore, I have a favorable view of John F. Kennedy due to his ability to perform under pressure, and although I like Nixon a little more than him, if I were to go back in time to the 1960s and vote between Kennedy and Nixon, I would have to vote for Kennedy because you never know. You see, although I feel Nixon was better than Kennedy in foreign issues, Nixon, in that position, may have dropped the ball and therefore Kennedy would have been the safer choice.

Kennedy yielded some very good things. For instance, he got Congress to approve the creation of the Peace Corps. You know that television advertisement "The toughest job you'll ever love." Kennedy's action of seeking to contain communism in Latin America by the formation of the Alliance for Progress was a very good political move in and of itself. Kennedy, in regards to this, was quoted as saying, "Those who make peaceful revolution impossible will make violent revolution inevitable" but it is not enough to say; you also must do. I believe a peaceful revolution of the mind is more possible than one may think.

It is time for me to make yet another point. This point I am about to make, you may not consider credible "yet!" To get this message across, I must first mention a fairly recent issue regarding George W. Bush. Do you recall complaints about the accessing of illegal wiretapping to supposedly spy on possible war conspirators? If not, I remind you that George W. Bush, through a claim of falsehood, promoted and allowed illegal wiretapping to spy on unsuspecting American citizens like you and me. These actions were claimed for reasons that I will not even waste my ink on. This was another form of governmental abuse performed by Bush, Cheney, and friends. It is also true that Nixon in pertinence to the Watergate scandal did also indulge in this type of activity. But in the case of Nixon, he did not spy on basic civilians. Nixon spied on political figures for still undetermined reasons.

So, here comes the shocker! The sad truth is that President Kennedy's administration instructed the Federal Bureau of Investigations (F.B.I.) to wiretap hundreds of private United States citizens because of supposed allegations of communist activity. One of these private citizens was none other than the legendary civil rights activist Martin Luther King Jr. Are you going to try to tell me that Martin Luther King Jr. was behind a communist conspiracy? If so, then I have a bridge to sell you! And by the way, it is not illegal to be a communist in the United States. As a matter of fact—and although rarely—it is not illegal to be a communist in the United States. Unless Kennedy had substantial reason for this action, which I doubt, then this action of Kennedy is no better than the wiretapping actions of Richard M. Nixon or George W. Bush. This is odd behavior for one of the Caucasian supporters of the N.A.A.C.P. It is time for the American people to open their minds and not follow political stereotypes and to grasp their own independent political ideals. It is also true that Lyndon Johnson, the 3thirty-sixth U.S. President, in a 1967 State of the Union address, condemned this act of his predecessor. The truth is that Johnson, like Kennedy, was considered a pioneer in civil rights activism, but for some reason that I don't get, he did in fact continue this wiretapping of King. If you don't believe what I have just claimed in regards to the wiretappings conducted by Kennedy and Johnson, just Google Wikipedia.org, type in John F. Kennedy and look up the civil liberties segment, and it is written right there plain as day in black and white.

Okay, enough with foreign policy. It is now time to discuss another genocide case. The third genocide case we will now explore is the genocide crisis in Rwanda. The main culprit behind this particular genocide is one Juvenal Habyarimana. Habyarimana would be killed during this genocide, but unfortunately, his disciples would continue this sickening act. Here is a list of Habyarimana's disciples: Colonel Theoneste Baosara (Director of Services in the Ministry of Defense), General Augustin Bizimana (Defense Minister), Colonel Leonard Nkundiye (former commander), Captain Paskal Simbikangwa (supervised militia killings in Kigali), and Captain Gaspard Hategekimana (second in command to Simbikangwa). All of these men acted at the national level.

First of all, the republic of Rwanda is a very small country located in the Great Lakes region of Central Africa. Rwanda borders four different countries: The Democratic Republic of Congo, Tanzania, Burundi, and Uganda. Rwanda, although small in size, does have a population of approximately 10.1 million. Rwanda has the highest population density in continental Africa. Most of the population of Rwanda is well versed in agriculture.

I now present to you a brief chronology of important dates and events in the Rwanda ordeal. Rwanda, like most African nations, fell under European rule. Up until 1919, Rwanda was under German control until Belgium took over authority in governmental matters. In 1926, Belgium issued identity cards for proof of ethnic identity. Thirty-three years later, in 1959, as Rwandan independence was beginning to manifest itself, the Hutu people began to rise in opposition to the Tutsi people. You see, the Hutus are representative of the political party of the culprit Juvenal Habyarimana. The civil war in this nation was fought between the Hutus and the Tutsis. This civil war would ultimately lead to a genocide being attempted against the Tutsis.

In 1962, Rwanda would gain independence from Belgium. The Hutus would commence to form a Hutu-controlled government. Due to the Hutu dominant political system, many of the Tutsi people fled to neighboring Uganda. In 1973, eleven years later, Juvenal Habyarimana assumed government control as the new president of Uganda. Habyarimana would implement the National Revolutionary Movement for Development which would cause major hardships for the Tutsis.

By 1987, Tutsi refugees in Uganda started the Rwandese Patriotic Front (R.P.F.). When 1989 rolled around, Rwanda would suffer economic crises because of damage to the country's coffee crop which was a big source of government income. In 1991, a truce was made. However, the Rwandese Patriotic Front military personnel would be forced to remain in Rwanda. Habyarimana then formed the Rwandan army with French support. However, France would aid the Tutsis. In 1993, the Arusha Accords came into play. In April of 1994, in neighboring Tanzania, Habyarimana made another compromise regarding the distribution of power. As Habyarimana tried to fly back to his homeland, his plane was shot down by unknown sources and Habyarimana died from this plane crash.

Still in the month of April, the U.N. would withdraw troops who were fighting against this act of genocide. By May, this genocide committed against the Tutsi began to become much more prominent. Attempts were made by the R.P.F. to prevent any more bloodshed. Soon after, in the month of June, the U.N. would allow the French military to enter Rwanda. This move was codenamed Operation Turquoise. French forces would not arrive until late June, but once they showed up, they would remain there until late August, when U.N. replacements would take over for them. Earlier in July, a united government took form in Kigali. This move was executed by the R.P.F., which did, in fact, have a small amount of Hutu members. In November, a tribunal was formed in neighboring Tanzania for the purpose of trying those responsible for this act of genocide.

In the summer of 1996, a new Rwanda law was ratified. This law classified those who may have been involved in the brutal acts which were carried out during this horrific event. This newly ratified law involved the killing of thirteen organizers of this genocide case who were first convicted and then were sentenced to death. By October of 1996, a civil war in the African nation of Zaire drove many Hutu refugees back to their native Rwanda. The U.N. would once again intervene by attempting to return Rwandans back to their native country. Finally, in January of 1997, a U.N. tribunal commenced hearings and testimonials regarding war crimes and genocide.

The next topic of discussion will be on the death of Hutu parasite, Juvenal Habyarimana. It was on April 6, 1994, when Habyarimana was flying home in an airplane accompanied by President Ntaryamisa of Burundi. These two world leaders were returning from a conference which was held in Dares-Salaam Tanzania. All of a sudden, when near landing, time this aircraft was struck by missiles. You see, it is not that hard to get your hands on such weapons due to the ease of consulting with the Black Market and some other sources.

Once this plane was struck by these missiles it nosedived, and everyone on board including Habyarimana died instantly. Although this was good for the hopes of the Tutsi people, consequences would continue to be manifested over time. Even with the existence of the Arusha accords of 1993, while Habyarimana was still alive it was not successful. To put it basically, the Arusha accords were formed for the intent of the Hutus and Tutsis to get along.

So, who was behind this attack on Habyarimana's plane? The truth is that no one has ever determined with any certainty just who was responsible for this act of courageous defiance. The most likely conclusion would be the Tutsis, since they had a motive. The Rwandan government has claimed that it was indeed the Tutsis who were responsible for this act. However, some credible sources claim this to be unlikely. The truth is that we may never know who was responsible for the death of this cruel leader, but getting rid of Habyarimana was at least a small victory for the Tutsi people. I say small victory, because Habyarimana's death did not end this genocide case.

You see, Habyarimana was secretly in the process of training and recruiting his Hutu soldiers in the Interhamwe. The Interhamwe is a Hutu parliamentary organization which fought for the Hutu -ed government, before, during, and after this act of genocide. This organization of extreme evil would kill countless innocent Tutsis.

Another fact is that the African press, due to restricted freedoms will in fact censor some news, but they are able to present at least some of the truth of the existence of these mass killings. Unlike the United States, the Tutsis cannot just look away. This is because to them, this is an imminent reality that they are forced to deal with. I must also state that I feel it is sad to witness any genocide especially in the continent of Africa, because this is the continent that the human race originated. However, I stress that no matter where or when genocide is committed, it is always a poignant reality. I will now touch on the fact that most of the nations of Africa by the late 1800s were, in fact, under European rule. I previously mentioned that Belgium, Germany, and France once had control over certain African nations at one time. However, the European nations of Great Brittan and Portugal also had rule over some African nations. A disturbing fact is that the great man, Nelson Mandela, the first president of South Africa from 1994 until 1999, was previously imprisoned for a total of twenty-seven years. This uncalled for punishment was due to the fact that he was bitterly opposed to European rule over his native South Africa. Another part of it was that Mandela was fervently opposed to the abuses of Apartheid. Apartheid is, in the most basic of terms, a system of legal racial segregation against the blacks of South Africa. Apartheid would, in due time, lead to the absolute immoral mistreatment of an obscene number of Negroes in the nation of South Africa.

Despite notable setbacks, Nelson Mandela would inspire many. This incredible man did not in any way waste his life, and although he served so many years in prison, he would make his culture a proud one. The simple fact is that whenever an African nation has become independent of European rule, these newly freed nations have, for the most part, tended to flourish. However, a problem still remains in pertinence to that fact. Despite the prosperity which results from these nations being set free, they usually will possess a serious problem with poverty. Some of these African nations will develop a situation similar to that of China. Of course, this is the problem of overpopulation relative to the geographical size of the nation at hand.

VISION OF A MENTAL PATIENT

This problem contributes to more dilemmas with the economies of these nations, thus leading to even more difficult challenges for the newly controlling governments. A statistic which supports this occurrence, is that thirty of the forty poorest nations in the world are in the continent of Africa.

The Republic of Rwanda was under Belgium rule for about forty-three years, from 1919 until 1962. Rwanda, by the way, does not just consist of Hutus and Tutsis. The other people of Rwanda are the Twa people, and they only make up about one percent of the population of this nation. Just to give you some more information on the nation of Rwanda: the Hutus make up ninety percent of the population and the Tutsis make up the remaining nine percent.

Under Belgium rule, the Belgians felt that the Tutsis should be the natural rulers of Rwanda. Belgium therefore, preserved the Tutsis status as overseers of the Hutu. This would lead to a prominent tension in Rwanda, as well as causing Rwandan civilians to not get along as well. One more interesting fact which resulted from Belgium control over this nation was that Rwanda would become one of Africa's most Christian nations.

Now, for some information on the R.P.F. (the Rwandese Patriotic Front), in the late 1980s, the continent of Africa and its nations, let's just say, weren't doing well. This problem began to take form in Rwanda. One of the factors for the weakening of African nations standings was (especially in Rwanda) the problem of overpopulation. The reality is that Rwanda is not only the most densely populous nation in Africa, it was also growing in population at a rate of 3.2 percent per year.

Sorry for that small tangent there, I will now elaborate on the R.P.F. One Paul Kagame, who was a Tutsi man, would become the head of the R.P.F. This R.P.F. was formed with the help of the neighboring nation of Uganda. An Ugandan man who is also a prominent political figure by the name of Musevini, with the aid of one Frederick Rwigema, began the R.P.F. by combining Ugandan allies with Rwandan Tutsi refugees. This new R.P.F. would soon become an affront to the genocide being performed on the Tutsi people.

Once the R.P.F. began to make significant progress by their spreading out through Rwanda, things became much more hopeful. In relation to this rebel spreading of violence, between May and July of 1994, some of the largest mass movements of people in the history of the world occurred. In the first month alone, 250,000 people would cross the border into neighboring Tanzania. This would result in one of the most immense refugee camps in the history of Earth! This massive refugee camp was located in the Ngara district of Tanzania.

By July, roughly one million Rwandan refugees had crossed into Zaire. Today, Zaire is now called the Democratic Republic of Congo and has been since 1997. These refugees would settle near the town of Goma. Unfortunately, supplies were insufficient and this would result in mass illnesses. Many of these refugees would not survive. About 500,000 of these refugees would perish from the illness of cholera. Cholera is any of several bacterial diseases usually marked by severe vomiting and dysentery. Therefore, even when these Tutsis were not killed by the Hutu's directly, they certainly were, indirectly.

Mercifully, by the summer of 1994, the R.P.F would obtain substantial oversight of most of Rwanda. In July, a government of national wholeness would be accomplished. However, certain members of this new Rwandan government were not members of the R.P.F. The new president and the new prime minister were actually Hutu. The truth is that in some instances, Hutus would help the cause of the Tutsis, just as some Germans during the Holocaust had a conscience and helped Jews to survive.

So, what role did my favorite form of world government, the U.N., do to help in this cause? Let's explore that, shall we?

In 1993, the U.N. came close to intervening with the United Nations Assistance Mission to Rwanda (U.N.A.M.I.R.). This new U.N. creation was intended to aid Rwandans with a peacekeeping force. It was a promise of the U.N. to help out this cause. However, for some reason, the U.N. was rendered unable to adequately suffice. A survivor of Darfur (a genocide we soon will discuss) by the name of Jean Paul Biramvu stated, in regards to the U.N.: "We wonder what U.N.A.M.I.R. was doing in Rwanda, they could not even lift a finger to intervene and prevent the deaths of tens of thousands of innocent people who were being killed under their very noses. An institution such as the U.N. must have the capacity to be effective. But the U.N. protects no one. They had been sent to Kigali when they are doing nothing to protect its people."

Did you get that? Mr. Jean Paul Biramvu is absolutely correct, my friends. As to my claim that the U.N. is my favorite form of world government, I must elaborate. In present day and for some time now, the U.N. has been limited in its ability to perform at a more effective level. One reason is that the U.N. is not given enough leeway. Another reason is that genocide and its implications are not properly addressed. And finally, due to the complexities so prominent in world politics, the U.N. at times simply have their hands tied. So, what action do we take? Utopia? But how? Unity my friends, world unity! The U.N. may not have reached its potential of effectiveness yet, but the human race, despite these horrific tragedies, is not even close to being outdone by evil yet! So, I once again insist on saying to all of you, "Utopia!" "Utopia!" "Utopia!" "Utopia!" Finally, I must state the obvious, that the U.N. is good, but it is not even close to being the moral force for human good that it can be!

So, if the U.N. couldn't help, then how did the R.P.F. succeed? One nation did come forward to help. And for a bit of irony, it was one of those European nations which once had control over certain African Nations. The nation I am speaking of is France. You see, the French had involvement in Rwanda in years past. However, at that time France was supportive of Habyarimana. So, I guess the French government searched their moral senses and figured that they would help. Despite French aid, when the French left Rwanda, this nation would then be left alone with no outside help whatsoever.

Okay, back to Habyarimana and his forces of immorality. There existed two important occurrences which caused this evil man to increase in his unfounded anger. Rwandans who wanted democracy absolutely enraged Habyarimana as well as those who supported him. Another cause of this unreasonable fury was that Habyarimana was forced to sign two essential agreements with Tanzania. But it would be the second signed agreement that would anger him. This agreement was signed by Habyarimana, in early April of 1994, just days before he was shot down and killed. This agreement was to allow Tutsis, whom he obviously was not fond of, to be allowed to have positions in the Rwandan government. By the way, it was a damn good thing that Habyarimana was killed when he was; just try to imagine what this man would have been like, if more unfounded anger was added to his evil demeanor. It was at the time of Habyarimana's death that the nation of Rwanda would begin to somewhat restore itself to prominence. The genocide forces may not have ended at this point, but it was at least seemingly weakened.

What would happen next after the death of Habyarimana was absolutely horrific, especially after such a seemingly progressive moment for the cause of the Tutsi people. Once Habyarimana was dead, his still alive disciples would see to it that a devastating genocide act would commence in the name of this now dead, but still effective, evil man. This would prove to be one of the most terrible events in modern world history. Nearly one million Tutsi men women and children would be killed in three months time. This retaliation was a sickeningly disgusting act, executed by those who supported this blatantly shameful cause of ludicrousness.

Once French aid was gone and some of the dust settled, Rwanda, although living the realities of the past, have slowly maintained some progress since. Schools in Rwanda have reopened. The country's main profession of agriculture has once again begun to thrive. Over 800,000 Tutsi refugees would be rendered able to return to their native homeland. And once again, good African values would shine through for a hopeful nation.

I deem it necessary to state that Rwanda, their French allies, and the U.N. must learn through the grim consequences experienced by these troubled human beings: That we must intervene as soon as possible when the opportunity of preventing such unfortunate events occur. The fact is that as far back as 1959, massacres in a similar fashion have occurred in beautiful Rwanda. This was years after World War 2 and the disgusting motives of Adolf Hitler and his German NAZI regime were defeated. I do realize, of course, that due to diplomatic complexities, this is much easier said than done. Yes, I do admit that it is an unfortunate truth that presently, our hands can often be tied when trying to appropriately deal with such matters. We must learn how to untie our human hands and access my theory of "Morality over Technicality" for our humane cause.

I will now present a challenge posed to my political theory of "Morality over Technicality." The U.N. definition of genocide is inclusive of any of the following acts that are committed with the intention of destroying in whole or in part a national, ethnic, racial, or religious group as such: first, the murdering or killing of members of a group; second, causing bodily or even mental harm to members of a group; third, the deliberate infliction on a group's conditions of life put together with the purpose of its physical destruction in either whole or part; fourth, the imposing of measures that intend to disallow child birth within a group; fifth the forcing of a transference of the children of a group to another group.

Okay, that seems to put it in clearer terms. Let's compare it to Webster's dictionary meaning of genocide: Genocide- the systematic killing of a whole people or nation. What I like better about the U.N. definition is that it includes mental abuse, abducting of children, disallowing childbirth, causing bodily harm, and causing mental harm. So, why is it that at times, the U.N. is rendered unable or even sometimes unwilling to intervene? They certainly did a good job at defining what genocide is. Face it, world politics can be considered more complex than algebra, calculus, and trigonometry combined. But then again, I am no mathematician. But I do know the difference between right and wrong.

I strongly believe that the U.N. has the potential to be more effective than people may presently think. What we need is world unity, and what better system of government than the U.N. to achieve such an ambitious goal. However, at this time, it is truthful that the U.N. cannot, or better yet, does not always act when people are in dire need. But I still have the opinion that if there was no U.N., we would be rendered hopeless.

When the Rwanda ordeal began, the Secretary General of the U.N. was Javier De Cuellar of the South American country of Peru. You see, the U.N, is faced with the complexities of world politics. So, it is not unfathomable, that Cuellar and the U.N.'s hands were tied. Was it because Cuellar was from South America and therefore was not as concerned, I doubt it, but truthfully, I don't know! In 1992, Cuellar was replaced by Boutros Ghali of Egypt, which is an African nation. So what happened there? I don't know that either! In 1997, when things were beginning to improve in Rwanda, another African from the country of Ghana by the name of Kofi Anan would take over as Secretary General of the U.N. So what did he do? Or better yet, what did he and the U.N. do? I hate to say it again, but I don't know that either! I'm starting to get a bit repetitious here, am I not? So, what is my point?

My point is that the U.N. is never covered by the media. The U.N. has the potential of massive proportions. If we approach matters correctly, the U.N. could lead us to a peacetime for the ages. If only the human race could unite! Presently, the U.N. Secretary General is Ban Ki Moon, of South Korea. Ban Ki Moon is South Korea's former foreign minister. So, there is at least a little information. More than the press covers anyway. I hereby encourage Ban Ki Moon and the U.N. to dare to dream of "utopia" and to intervene as much as possible when innocents are in peril.

All right, that wasn't so bad, was it? So let's go in a new direction and once again discuss foreign policy. Since Bill Clinton was president during a large portion of the Rwanda genocide, let's discuss his foreign policy tactics.

VISION OF A MENTAL PATIENT

First, I will jump ahead and give some information on important circumstances that took place during Clinton's second term as U.S. president. Clinton made a claim in a State of the Union address that Congress should be concerned with a potentially dangerous hypothesis. This hypothesis was that Saddam Hussein of Iraq was chasing nuclear capabilities with a prominent ambition. This claim of Clinton's might lead you to believe that George W. Bush's claims of weapons of mass destruction in the nation of Iraq may have some credibility, but in reality it is not remotely that simple.

You see, Clinton did act to weaken Hussein's stronghold in world matters. Clinton, in direct response to this possible threat, was to sign what was called H.R. 4655, a political document which instituted a policy of leadership change against Iraq. However, this document explicitly stated that it did not pertain to the use of military personnel. This would lead to a four-day long military attack which was codenamed Operation Desert. This attack took place from December 16 until December 19, 1998.

What was Clinton's foreign policy relative to the act of genocide? Let's take a peak, shall we?

At the time of the Clinton Administration, the Rwanda genocide was well underway, but there was another occurrence that for some reason of technicality, it was not officially labeled as genocide. This other sickening act of cowardice was committed by nationalist Serbians against Albanians. This near genocide took place in Yugoslavia's province in Kosovo.

Clinton would take action by authorizing the use of U.S. military forces in order to give support to the North Atlantic Treaty Organization (N.A.T.O.) bombing campaign against Yugoslavia. This attack occurred towards the end of the Clinton presidency and its codename was Operation Allied Force. General Wesley Clark, who recently ran for president as a Democrat, was at the time of this tragedy, Supreme Allied Commander of N.A.T.O. and he oversaw this bombing mission.

In this case, the U.N. would have at least a taste of success. The U.N. would intervene, ending the bombing campaign in June of 1999. This U.N. resolution would give authorization to a peacekeeping force. Despite reasonable success, Clinton would be subject to ridicule due to his claim of genocide being blown out of proportion.

At this gist, I feel that I must again briefly discuss my problem with governmental technicalities. Sometimes, such immoral acts of genocide or basic terrorism are not properly recognized due to governmental definitions being taken in a literal way. Think back to the discussion of the U.N. definition of genocide. Did not this definition include acts of rape, murder, and arson? Well, murder, yes, but in an indirect way, the U.N. definition does include these other acts. Please understand that I am not criticizing anyone at this point. I simply desire for people to fathom that when laws, rules, amendments, or what have you, are taken too literally, it tends to be a bit much. I feel that exceptions should be made when technicalities take precedent over moralities. If one irrelevant rule of law or proclamation prevents a moral justice, then the rules should be bent. To put it as bluntly as possible, make rule number one Morality—end of story!

Continuing on now, what did you think of our discussion on the foreign policy of the Clinton Administration? I think that Clinton's intervention in Kosovo was right on the money. But I ask you, what did Clinton do about the genocide in Rwanda? To give him the benefit of the doubt, his hands may have been tied. At least he helped one war act to cease, right? But the truth is, for one, the United States is not the world police, and two, it is hard to be in two places at once. It should be up to the U.N. to at least in a way try to act as the world police. However, the United States, being the most powerful nation on the face of the planet, is a member of the U.N. and must at least make credible efforts by taking action in whatever manner is accessible to help the innocents of our world.

It is now time to discuss the fourth case of genocide which we will touch on in this segment. This will be a discussion of the most recent case of genocide on Earth. I am speaking of the genocide in Darfur. Darfur is a region in the western section of the African nation of the Sudan, officially labeled as the Republic of Sudan. The Sudan is located in northeastern Africa and is geographically the largest nation in the continent. The Sudan is so large in size (tenth in the world to be precise) that it borders nine countries. The countries that border the Sudan are: Egypt, Eritea, Ethiopia, Kenya, Uganda, the Democratic Republic of Congo, the Central African Republic, Chad, and Libya. Because of the recent problems of war crimes in the nation of the Sudan, it is now considered the second most insecure nation in the world. One of, if not the main, culprit in this particular genocide case is President Omar Hassan Al Bashir. Al Bashir is the current leader of the Sudan and he gained power in 1989. Courageous acts of resistance have been made to oppose Al Bashir's regime of insanity. Many innocent people have been paying a price due to this current Sudanese reign of terror. The act of genocide unfortunately has been a stark reality for the men, women, and children, of Darfur for some time now. Such blatantly immoral acts have been carried out by the Sudanese army and by a representative militia under control of Al Bashir and the Sudanese government. This militia is known as the Janjawid.

You see, Al Bashir's Sudanese army has been carrying out these merciless acts with this Janjawid militia. Aerial attacks as well as attacks on foot are usually the methods of just the Sudanese army. The Janjawid, on the other hand, will usually enter the villages of these innocents on camels, horses, or in automobiles. The attacks of these two militias are inclusive of not only killings, but also of rape, arson, and the destroying and stealing of the possessions of these innocent people.

The people of the Sudan have experienced a nonstop state of war ever since they gained independence from Great Brittan on January 1, 1956. This is one example of an African nation not flourishing when gaining its independence from European rule. The Sudan has had two civil wars. The first of these two civil wars took place from 1955 until 1972. The second was fought from 1983 until 2005. Both of these civil wars were fought between Northern and Southern Sudan. The second civil war was caused by former Sudanese president Jaafar Al Nimery. It was his attempt at circumventing the Addis-Ababa agreement. It was basically a restarting of the first Sudanese civil war. The later of these two civil wars added to the constant misery of the Sudanese people; it would achieve the staggering death toll of approximately two million dead and four million left homeless.

Before I summarize the tensions between northern and southern Sudan, I must first mention some of the other culprits involved in this genocide case, as well as the brave people who have opposed this bleak situation. Al Bashir is assisted by two others whose actions have had a horrific effect on the people of this nation. These two men are Ahmed Haroun (state minister of foreign affairs) and Ali Mohamed Ali, who is more commonly known as Ali Kosheib, and he is deemed responsible for some of the most violent acts committed against the innocents of Darfur.

Those who have courageously opposed this genocide case include, first, Minni Arko Minnowi, the leader of a rebel movement called the Sudanese Liberation Army (S.L.A.). The International Criminal Court prosecutor Luis Moreno Ocampo has brought up indictments against Ahmed Haroun, Ali Kosheib, and President Al Bashir. Former U.S. Secretary of State Colin Powell, unlike the rest of the administration, has worked a prominent American voice against this Darfur genocide case. I must mention the Sudanese Liberation Movement (S.L.M.) which was responsible for the signing of the Darfur Peace Agreement, which, unfortunately, was rendered ineffective.

Moving on, let's discuss the reasons of conflict between northern and southern Sudan. There are three major parties involved in the Sudan's state of affairs. First is the North, which represents the official government of the Sudan. Second is the South, which has formed rebel groups opposed to the official government. Third is the western region of the Sudan. As previously stated, the conflict has been between the north, which consists of Arab Muslims who represent the official government. This group is headquartered in Khartoum, the capital city of the Sudan. The south consists of mostly non-Muslims, some Christians, and some who practice paganism or for lack of a better word, polytheism. In the southern region, paganism can be a word that is taken offensively.

Most of the Sudan is made up of Sunni Muslims and Sunni Shiite, which are the two most prominent branches of Islam. The South contains the Sudan People's Liberation Army (S.P.L.A.), which mainly consists of African Christians who began a retaliation. In January of 2005, the Naivasha Peace Treaty was signed by the S.P.L.A. and also by the official government of the north. This treaty was intended for giving the south independence from the north. Unfortunately, this treaty is only in effect until 2010. In 2010, the north and the south will re-analyze the possibilities of the continuance of southern Sudan independence.

The United States and most of the international community are supportive of the Naivasha treaty, despite the fact that war crimes are often disregarded. But you must understand that the recent ordeal in Darfur is separate from the Sudan civil war dissention. As a matter of fact, the people of Darfur have not been directly involved in the southern revolt, which, in reality, is a direct result of the neglect of the Sudanese government, not to mention these relentless attacks.

The original name for the Darfur insurgency was the Darfur Liberation Army (D.L.A.); currently the D.L.A. is dubbed the Sudan Liberation Army (S.L.A.), which is not only fighting for the liberation of Darfur, but is also fighting for all of the Sudanese people who are negatively affected by President Al Bashir and his legacy of evil. Despite the cruel actions that were obviously ordered by Al Bashir, he has continuously denied any wrong doings or any involvement in these pathetic acts of violence.

Therefore, not only does Al Bashir and his disciples of immorality commit such horrendous war crimes, but they also refuse to take any responsibility whatsoever for their actions. I certainly do hope that Al Bashir, his government, the Sudanese army, and the Janjawid will one day be brought to justice. It should be obvious enough for the U.N. to intervene and appropriately label these acts as coinciding with the U.N. definition of genocide, so that we can prosecute those responsible for these acts of immorality to a full extent.

Since I am so offended by these blatantly evil acts, I feel it is time to discuss the people of Darfur. These people have been royally screwed and it seems unending. In recent times, outside forces have actually had the gall to try to hurt these people from within; what I mean by this statement is that these forces have often tried to weaken the similarities of the people of Darfur by drawing them into revolt against one another, thus leading to their crumbling from inner conspiracies. This is sick! I mean, do these war criminals have one shred of human decency? Unfortunately, they probably don't! You see, the people of Darfur are made up of over seventy different tribes. For example, the Fur tribe makes up a large portion of the population of Darfur. The other two main groups of the Darfur tribes are the Zaghawa and the Masalit. The innocent members of these tribes are forced to endure many different forms of extreme evil. Due to the absolute immorality involved, it is more than often that the innocents of Darfur, even the children, are actually forced to choose between being raped or being violently murdered. This means that not only do these committers of genocide have the indecency to kill these men, women, and children, but they will also use them for their sexual pleasure. Is there no end to the indecency which the human race can be capable of? Hopefully, there is no limit to the decency the human race is capable of, so that we can counteract this shit!

So, what other effects are caused by this savagery? The ultimate truth is that the existence of such death and destruction can pose numerous other negative occurrences. I have heard some Americans claim that war can help the economy, but that in my opinion is just stupid. You simply cannot put a dollar value on human life. One thing is for sure, the Sudanese economy has suffered due to war. The region of Darfur consists of about six million people, the same estimated number of European

VISION OF A MENTAL PATIENT

Jews that Hitler and his NAZI regime was able to exterminate in the holocaust. The entire Sudanese population is approximately forty-one million people. The economy of the Sudan is very dependent on their herding and farming. Therefore, the violence has had a profoundly large effect on these two essential aspects for the prosperity of the Sudan's economic standing. This problem of finance contributes to the diminishment of this nation's food supply.

There is another fact pertaining to the Sudanese economic standing. The Sudan is very abundant with the resource of oil. A problem relative to this abundant resource is that the official government of the Sudan (the government of the northern region) is in total control of this resource. The sad fact is that this resource is prominent in the southern region, yet the south is unable to stake a claim on the existence of this resource. This obviously leads to the strengthening of the official Sudanese government and the Janjawid. Oil resource in the Sudan was discovered by Chevron Co., in the early 1970s. The northern Sudan's official government made a deal with Chevron Co. to drill in the southern region of the Sudan. This oil resource has had billions upon billions of dollars invested in the Sudanese official government. This excess of wealth is due to outside interests in this newly discovered source of oil. There is a lot of interest from European nations, as well as China and India. Unfortunately, money is always an issue. No matter how immoral a government is, if they can make the powerful wealthier they will be treated with respect. And that really pisses me off!

The problem in Darfur, the other regions of Africa, and the rest of the world has had a profound effect on us all. This abuse of power has resulted in catastrophe. As the population of our planet increases, the entire world suffers economically. This is because war crimes or any other crimes of humanity cause a significant diminishing of natural resources. This leads to nations being more dependent on one another for support, which strengthens the argument of forming utopia as well as my point of evil causing good.

To elaborate further, there have been many humanitarian attempts to help the unfortunate victims of war crimes to survive. In 2006, new measures were made on methods for responding to such incidents like that of Darfur. In August 2006, the U.N. would once again try to intervene in order to help the anti-genocide cause. What the U.N. did this time was the passing of a resolution. This anti-genocide resolution was not very complex. This resolution attempted to simply send troops to aid the rebel cause in Darfur. The strategy was to basically protect the people of Darfur right at the source.

Although at first, the new resolution was producing good results, the violence in Darfur would soon reach a decisive point, reaching the borders of neighboring Chad. You see, rebels were trying to put together and recruit across the borders of Chad. This would lead to a crucial confrontation between the Janjawid and the rebel force.

What I tell you next could make your skin crawl! Several dozen U.N. representative soldiers were indicted for allegations of sexual abuse of young girls in Darfur. There are no words in the English language appropriate enough to express my feelings on this dejected fact. I mean, technically you are innocent until proven guilty and I certainly and sincerely hope that these U.N. representatives are innocent! But what the fuck! Now, the supposed causes of human good are committing depraved acts! I am morally offended just at the possibility of these allegations.

Former U.N. Secretary General Kofi Anan of Ghana expressed that he felt this crisis in Darfur is a direct result of a global failure. In Anan's final speech as secretary general of the U.N. in 2006, he listed five imperative lessons which should be learned from the Darfur experience. Here they are: first, we must all take on responsibilities for one another's security; second, we must give the people of our world the chance to benefit from world prosperity; third, our security as well as our prosperity are dependent on our human rights, and our rules of law; fourth, our world's nations must exhibit accountability to one another and to a broad range of non-state actors in their conduct; fifth and last, Anan stated that we can only achieve these goals by working together.

Back on November 9, 2008, I saw Barack Obama on Larry King Tonight. Obama stated that he wants to call for a summit of the Muslims around the world. His wife Michelle was also on the show and she made a point that Barack liked to surround himself with very smart people. Michelle also stated that a sense of humor is important. They both really seemed to express a generally appropriate concern for important world matters. I am not only confident in Barack, but I am also confident that his wife will be a fantastic first lady. They have now been married for sixteen years and that is a very good thing. But you know something, I also like to surround myself with smart people. That is why I voted for Obama.

Back to business here! Concerning the Darfur genocide, the U.N., as I just stated, did try to intervene. However, there was another group that tried to help out. I am speaking of the African Union (A.U.). The A.U. was actually a strong moral force in trying to contribute to an end of the escalating violence in Darfur. The A.U. consists of fifty-two of the fifty-three African nations. It was established in the year 2000. There is a gutsy U.A. representative by the name of Jan Pronk. Jan displayed courage and decency by claiming to the public, that Al Bashir and friends are directly responsible for the genocide in Darfur.

To head in a new direction, lets go back in time and discuss some history of the Sudan. Prior to 1820, Darfur was independent. This Darfur independence came to an abrupt halt due to a Turk-Egyptian invasion that occurred in Northern Sudan. This new era would be labeled as the Turkiyya era. This change in relation to Egypt and their ally at the time, Turkey, who wanted more influence in the whole of Africa as well as having ambitions of obtaining Africa's natural resources, would have significant ramifications. An even more disturbing fact in relation to this Egyptian and Turkish greed is that it was influenced by the slave trade of this era. The Egyptian/Turkish regime of the Turkiyya era would eventually attack Darfur in 1881. In 1885, rebels would banish the Turks.

You see, since Egypt was dead set on holding power, they would soon make a move. What the Egyptians ended up doing was forming an alliance with Great Brittan. This new British/Egyptian partnership would become known as the British/Egyptian Condominium. Despite the fact that the Egyptians were there first, they would be forced to make a compromise and allow the British to be the deciders. You may recall I mentioned French and Belgian rule, as well as some other European nations over certain nations of Africa. So, due to European ambitions of power, Great Brittan would have to compete against mainly France and Belgium for African control.

When the Sudan was a young nation, Muslim military leaders in the north held power. The south was already being treated unjustly. The southern region of the Sudan would pursue their own form of government, because they, in basic terms, wanted more of a say. Throughout this nation's history, the north was calling the shots; consequently, it would produce an Islamic society. Islam is a religion with the teachings of the prophet Muhammad and is composed of Muslims.

As the first Sudanese civil war came to an end in 1972, southern antigovernment groups were gaining substantial prominence. At this time, the north would appoint a new leader. This previously mentioned new leader of the north was a military commander by the name of Jaffar Al Nimery. A new agreement would be signed at this time. This was the Addis Ababa Accord. Addis Ababa is the capital of Ethiopia and is also home to the headquarters of the U.N. Economic Commission for Africa. You might recall I mentioned that the Addis Ababa agreement was attempted to be circumvented, or, for lack of a better word, defeated, by Al Nimery. This Addis Ababa Accord in and of itself was a compromise created for the intent of satisfying leaders of the southern Sudan rebel insurgency. In 1983, Al Nimery would succeed in circumventing this accord and it would thus be abolished.

Al Nimery did have a nemesis. This opposition to Al Nimery was an Islamic man by the name of Saliq Al Mahdi. Mahdi was a direct descendant of a prominent Islamic religious figure. Mahdi was an affront to Al Nimery and was a strong advocate of the southern cause for independent rule. These two men would play a real life chess game for the next twenty years.

In recent times, yet prior to the genocide in Darfur, the Sudan was in the midst of its usual turmoil. A Sudanese tribe known as the Dinka would be forced to suffer to a high degree and comparatively to the citizens of Darfur. This Dinka tribe was in the southern region of the Sudan called Bahar Ar Ghazol. These cruel acts were being carried out in the 1980s during the Sudan's second civil war. This disgusting display of extreme human evil would not cease with the new peace agreement that officially put an end to the civil war; the turmoil in this nation would continue to exist.

Because Darfur refugees were seeking safety in the bordering nation of Chad, it had resulted in an intense tension between Chad and the Sudan. Hopefully, the tension between these two nations would not escalate and lead to any more violence.

Okay, what next? Oh, I know! Let's discuss two controversial world leaders who have had ties with the United States and the Sudan. The two men we will discuss are Colonel Muammar Quaddafi of Libya and the new United States nemesis, the man responsible for the 9/11 attacks, Osama Bin Laden.

First, we will discuss Muammar Quaddafi, the leader of Libya.

We are all aware that back in 1985, there was a conflict between Quaddafi Libya and the United States, but that is another story all together. What we will touch on at this point is Quaddafi and his relationship with the Sudan (although the United States will be mentioned).

Quaddafi has had profound effects in relation to the politics of the Sudan and especially to the Darfur region. Due to certain factors in the U.S./Soviet Cold War, the Sudan was of supreme concern to the United States (I will express how I feel about the Cold War in the last section of this book, Morals in Society. The truth is that the U.S. was fearful that Quaddafi, Libya, and their Soviet allies would achieve supervision over the whole entire northern African region. The U.S. would eventually supply famine relief to the Sudan.

Quaddafi was interested in attaching the Sudan to Libya geographically. Quaddafi was up to his usual political antics, but he was not successful in persuading Jaffar Al Nimery to comply. Quaddafi would then take an action of human indecency: he sent military support to help northern Sudan engage in battle against the rebel forces of the south. Needless to say, this Libyan action was detrimental to the justice that the innocents of the Sudan were seeking.

By 1985, Al Nimery would be overthrown and by early 1986, his nemesis Sadiq Al Mahdi would be elected to replace him; unfortunately, he would not be in power for long. By 1989, Al Bashir, one of the main culprits responsible for this genocide case, would end up in governmental control of the Sudan. This new Al Bashir regime was considered to be fundamentalist; it would not only produce genocide, itwould also force the religion of Islam on the Sudanese people.

Okay, now, we will touch on Osama Bin Laden and his relations with the Sudan. From the 1980s until the early 1990s, Bin Laden resided in the capital of the Sudan, the city of Khartoum. Bin Laden and his band of Al Qaeda terrorists would operate out of the Sudan. As a matter of fact, former United States President Bill Clinton would order a bombing mission on a pharmaceutical factory in the Sudan. Clinton took this action to directly retaliate against Bin Laden's bombings of the United States embassies in Tanzania and Kenya. Sadly, there were about 250 deaths and 4,000 wounded because of these attacks. Following the 9/11 attacks, the Bush Administration actually took sides with Al Bashir, for the supposed reason that Bush and friends were trying to get help in order to defeat Bin Laden.

So, let me get this straight! First, following the 9/11 attacks, Bush went after Bin Laden in Afghanistan, and then when he was close to getting him, he decided to let him go. And then according to Michael Moore, who, I believe, stated that Bush had members of the Bin Laden family secretly flown out of the United States without even questioning one of them. After that, Bush gave his support to Al Bashir, a man who was an advocate of genocide, in order to defeat a man that he let go! After that, Bush decided we should invade a country which had absolutely nothing to do with it. Of course, I am speaking of Iraq. And then Bush called them the axis of evil. So, after that swift move, Bush took a joy ride on an American Navy ship with a big giant victory sign, saying mission accomplished on it, and he was dressed in a military uniform and then claimed victory! This was years ago, and we still haven't accomplished "Shit!"

Quaddafi, as much as a nut he has been over the years, at least showed some brains, when he did something just about one day following the 9/11 attacks. What am I talking about? I'll tell you! About one day after the 9/11 attacks, Quaddafi made a phone call to whoever represented the president. Why? Well, Quaddafi basically said to whomever he conversed with (maybe Bush himself?), that he had absolutely nothing to do with this attack. You see, Quaddafi being a nut himself knew that Bush was unpredictable, and made sure that he understood that he was innocent and that he did not take any action to provoke this attack. Bush at this time had an approval rating of ninety percent and even I was not aware that he was about to stab the American people, as well as other people of the world, in the back. You see, Quaddafi is a nut, and have you ever heard the saying "It takes one to know one?" Well, Quaddafi certainly knew one before any of us knew at all! A lot of people will disagree with what I am about to say, especially Democrats who believe that George W. Bush is stupid. But I do feel that for anyone to become president, they must at least be reasonably intelligent. Therefore, I do not think that George W. Bush is stupid, but of all the presidents that I know of, he must be the least intelligent of them all. On the other hand, if George W. Bush intentionally wanted to do political damage to the United States and to our world standing, then he is an absolute genius because he has done quite a bit of damage in his presidency.

Get ready! It is time for me to mention the U.N. again. This will be, once again, a brief discussion on the U.N. definition of genocide, but in an indirect way. Immediately following World War 2, in the early years of the U.N., the first U.N. Secretary General Trygvie Lie of Norway was in charge. Due to the lessons learned from the Second World War, the U.N. would establish the Universal Declaration of Human Rights. This new declaration would basically serve as an international constitution for the advancement of human rights. It also marked the beginning of the U.N.'s defining of genocide as an international war crime.

Okay, on the topic of an international cause for the prevention of such war crimes, I deem it necessary to discuss with you the International Criminal Court (I.C.C.), and their efforts to bring war criminals to justice. The first thing I would like to mention about the I.C.C. is that I am very proud of the I.C.C. criminal prosecutor, Luis Moreno Ocampo. This man has made substantial efforts to bring Darfur war criminals such as Ali Kosheib, Ahmed Haroun, and Omar Hassan Al Bashir to justice.

I must now mention the Rome Statute. The Rome Statute consists of 120 world nations that agreed to obey an international set of laws which protect human rights. This Rome Statute was enacted by the I.C.C. I am supportive of this statute, but I must reveal to you a confusing fact. Seven world nations that were supposed to sign this statute declined to do so. So, here is the part that confuses me: One of these seven nations is the United States. What is the United States saying by this action? Is the United States arrogant enough to think that we are above prosecution if we commit a war crime? Maybe so! But I have news for my fellow Americans: George W. Bush, Dick Cheney and friends have committed a war crime. The invasion and the war in Iraq simply do not hold water. I truthfully do not see why the United States has the naïve belief that we are above the Rome statutes and all of the nationsthat have complied with the establishment of this U.N. document. The blatant truth is that certain, but not all people in the U.S. actually believe that no matter what we do, we are above the Rome Statute for the reason that we are the best nation on Earth. If we want to be the great people that we claim we are, we must come to the realization that we have committed evil acts and are no better than anyone else, just because we have a fairer system of government and laws. This is another example of evil stemming from good, just as good can stem from evil.

I have expressed it before, and I will express it again: I am absolutely fed up with technicalities. If the world community does not come to a technical agreement that a mass killing is identified as terrorism or genocide, appropriate actions will not be made. When "technicality" happens, these horrific war crimes can often remain an internal matter of the nations where these evils are a harsh reality. So, how the hell can you label a matter such as genocide an internal matter when it is the internal government which is carrying out these actions? This makes no sense whatsoever. So, not only is nothing done by the U.N. or the self-righteous U.S.A., but the I.C.C. is also rendered powerless.

You see, genocide became more prominent in the twentieth century. Our planet has been in a tailspin of pure evil. We must take whatever actions we can that are humanly possible through whatever methods we can. If we can kill for oil and money, we certainly should be able to appeal to our moral intellect by whatever means necessary.

Are you aware that not only innocent people are being killed on a daily basis in Darfur, but ninety percent of Sudanese women undergo genital mutilation? Genital mutilation is categorized into two different methods: the first consists of the removal of a woman's clitoris; the second process of genital mutilation is the sewing of the vagina shut, usually with thorns! Did you catch that? Talk about sick! And I thought there was a women's liberation problem in the United States! This genital mutilation process makes abortion look like a haircut! And before you jump all over me for saying that, I must make another point. At least when an abortion is performed, there can be credible reason for it! And on top of it all, this process in this region is at a rate of ninety percent. Do you know what that means? That means that even the innocent victims are performing this sick act. I mean, talk about being a chauvinist, when does this ludicrousness stop? In the defense of some of these people, it is quite possible that they are brainwashed and have grown up learning to do such evil things. It is our responsibility to show those that are evil through no fault of their own that there are other ways of life, but we must first save these people in order to un-brainwash them.

Just try to imagine being a young boy or girl walking through your neighborhood and seeing the charred remains of your school mates! Your friends and relatives shackled together in handcuffs, and then witnessing the ones you love being set on fire! Or witnessing the burying of your loved ones while they are still breathing, your mother and father in tears trying to protect you, and then seeing them shot dead! This, my friends, happens every day! Would you believe that a good portion of these killings is carried out due to religion? Obviously, I am not a believer in god. It seems to me that most world conflicts are due to religion. However, if one does believe in god and it helps them, then that is great! I am obviously not a religious person, but I am an absolute lover of morality, human good, and human decency. And if there was a god and he or she was the ultimate example of good, then I should be just fine. So, to my friends that believe in god, I first must say that I love you, but I am sorry, I am not capable of believing in that concept.

The horrific realities I just displayed are for the sake of awareness and the promotion of world morality. I must once again mention the U.N. This time, it will be in regards to the U.N. creation of the United Nations International Children's Fund (U.N.I.C.E.F.). UNICEF was created in the U.N. General Assembly, on December 11, 1946 under former Secretary General Trygvie Lie. UNICEF was originally for the purpose of the provision of care for the children of Earth who are directly affected by the evils of the Second World War. By 1953, UNICEF did achieve prominent status. This status was reached in the first year of former Secretary General Dag Hammarskjold of Sweden. As I have already stated, my hope for the world is strengthened by the existence and the potential of the U.N. itself. However, I am even more pleased that UNICEF has been established for the young and innocent children of our world. I just wish that U.N. intervention were more prominent.

It is now time to wrap up our Darfur discussion. I have already given my assessment on the needed awareness of this most current genocide case on the planet. And I sincerely do hope that I have appropriately brought this world travesty to your attention. So, I now leave you with some devastating statistics. Since 2003, the estimated death count is vague. It is believed that somewhere between 200,000 and 500,000 men, women, and children have died due to this dreadful war crime. It is also estimated that one in twelve people in the whole population of Darfur have since perished. This includes the destruction of approximately 2,000 Darfur villages. The amount of homeless due to this war crime is estimated at about 2 million. There are also a substantial number of refugees who have fled to neighboring Chad. I desperately hope that the government of Chad can adopt the virtues of tolerance and compassion in order to avoid more African conflicts. I once again stress to all of my readers to open your minds and see a possibility of an ideological and prosperous solution, and learn that the human race must embrace love, compassion, and tolerance in order for not only the United States to once again thrive and set an example, but also for all the people of the Earth to valiantly challenge themselves through the advocacy of human understanding.

Wow! That was heavy! But we are not even close to the finish of this genocide and foreign policy discussion. At this crux, we will go back to the topic of foreign policy. The foreign policy we will now discuss will be the foreign policy of the forty-third President of the United States, George W. Bush.

This Bush Administration's foreign policy consisted of an effort to achieve a better economic and political kinship with Latin American nations, especially that of Mexico. Bush intended to reduce United States intervention in "Nation Building" as well as any involvement in small scope military quarrels. Bush also was an advocate of a strengthening of the U.S. national missile defense. Therefore, Bush would commence to follow in an indirect way the concepts of Ronald Reagan by putting an unreasonable effort for the concern of U.S. missile defense. I do feel that in some aspects, United States leaders have not always exhibited much wisdom in what we should have learned from the Cuban Missile Crisis.

As a result of that infamous day of September 11, 2001, Bush would begin his political deception, not to mention his political downfall. How this man was elected president two times will always boggle my mind. Immediately following 9/11, Bush would launch the so-called war on terror.

I have previously touched on this whole Bush 9/11 thing already, but I must state my case further. You see, the fact that Saddam Hussein was caught and executed simply does not, in any way, justify the actions of this Bush Administration. Again, I stress: Iraq did not attack the United States! The ultimate truth is that we were attacked by Osama Bin Laden and his Al Qaeda terrorist organization. In Bush's defense, I will say that yes, Saddam Hussein was a very bad man who has executed some despicable actions.

Hussein was caught by American forces on December 13, 2003. From there, he would be detained at what is known as Camp Cropper in Baghdad, Iraq, under United States supervision. Saddam was supposedly brought to trial for war crimes he committed against the Kurds in the Iran-Iraq war in the early 1980s, and also for his immoral mistreatment of Iraqi Shiites, which took place virtually throughout the 1990's.

Do you recall what I told you the United States reason was for our military actions in Iraq? Well, it was supposedly because of those non-existent weapons of mass destruction which was nothing but a farce. You must understand something here. Bush did nothing about Darfur, which was a far worse situation. But he claimed to be fighting against an axis of evil by authorizing the invasion of a country which had absolutely nothing to do with the reasons he claimed his intentions of attack were for. I said it before, and I will say it again: If we were to go after all world leaders such as Saddam Hussein for the reasons claimed by this administration, we would be invading half of the world. It's a lie!

To elaborate further, I will once again make another point. This Bush Administration's unfounded attacking of Iraq has an estimated death count of somewhere between 400,000 to one million. And I again remind you, that when we were in the right place "Afghanistan" U.S. military forces killed tens of thousands of Afghani people and did not even touch Osama Bin Laden. Criticize me if you want, but if you actually believe that killing tens of thousands of Afghans, and then leaving when you almost got the guy you were originally after is good foreign policy, then you need to have your head examined!

Do you recall the statement that George W. Bush made while holding that megaphone at ground zero? Well, for those who do not remember, here it is: "I hear you, the rest of the world hears you, and the people who knocked these buildings down will hear all of us soon." One day after Bush made that quote, he had an approval rating of ninety percent. I myself, like many Americans at that time, was inspired by the president that day. Bush had a chance to reach legendary status as an American president. But the actions he would eventually take were completely appalling. At the end of the Bush administration, the president had an approval rating of a forlorn twenty-five percent. I really cannot fathom how this man could take such actions after his father, George H.W. Bush, set such a good example for him. I am sympathetic to George H.W. Bush, who, by the way, has an extensive foreign policy record himself, almost like that of Nixon. I am sorry, I just had to speak the truth that George W. Bush and friends are guilty of a war crime because of their actions in Iraq, not to mention the honorable, yet often misguided United States soldiers who have since perished from the Earth for no credible reason whatsoever!

At the inception of this Bush Administration's second term, Bush prioritized the enhancement of strained U.S.-European relations. Bush would then select one of his long time advisors, one Karen Hughes, to oversee a new worldwide public relations crusade which eulogized the pro-democracy strains of the Ukraine and Georgia.

In March of 2006, Bush would pay a visit to India. This visit would be successful in achieving a stronger unification between the Ukraine and Georgia, especially in relation to nuclear energy policies as well as antiterrorist collaboration. Suspicions of Bush's actions would become prominent and also become subject to questioning by those who felt that he was retreating from his promotion of freedom and democracy. This was due to certain altering measures which were applied to the policies concerning some oil abundant nations that were once within the borders of the former Soviet Union and that are located in central Asia.

Concerning Asian relations, Bush would display a shred of decency by his public criticisms of Kim Jong-Il of North Korea. Bush would proceed to include Kim Jong-Il in the supposed axis of evil. Jong-Il, although being the leader of North Korea, was actually born in the former Soviet Union. North Korea possesses the fifth largest army in the world, so you could easily understand that there is a dire need to be cautious and thorough in our diplomatic relations with North Korea, not only because they could threaten the United States, but also because they could damage other nations. Jong-Il is the chairman for the National Defense Commission of North Korea. He has been a chronic abuser of political power and he puts a robust emphasis on political isolation.

Some very interesting things have happened in North Korea. Concerning nuclear matters in 1994 during the Clinton Administration, there was a U.S.-North Korea agreement, which was established for the purpose of causing a standstill in North Korea's nuclear weapons program. This agreement was also for the intent of the eventual dismantling of North Korea's nuclear weapons program. I mentioned this agreement to stress that presently, we are in a very tense situation concerning worldwide foreign policy matters. We simply cannot allow the promotion of nuclear capabilities in our world.

Einstein's scientific breakthrough of the splitting of the atom in order to produce a nuclear chain reaction may have been needed to be revealed in order for United States scientists to beat the German scientists in obtaining nuclear capabilities. This potentially catastrophic breakthrough of Einstein's has caused us to be more cautious when dealing with nations that can either create or obtain their nuclear ambitions. Therefore, when such breakthroughs are accomplished, we must first ask ourselves: t If such breakthroughs are achieved, would it benefit us or will it destroy us?

Once again, I went off on another tangent. So let's get back to the foreign policy of George W. Bush. You see, Bush was very aware and concerned about North Korean involvement in nuclear issues. The man did some things right. However, he did cause a ton of damage due to a high number of bad decisions.

Bush also showed concern in pertinence to Syria. Bush was quite supportive of an expansion of economic sanctions against Syria. As a matter of fact, action was taken in response to an executive command in June of 2005. This was to freeze the United States bank accounts of the Syrian Higher Institute of Applied Science and Technology, Electronics Institute, and National Standards and Calibration Laboratory. This was intended to prevent U.S. citizens from doing business with these particular organizations that are suspected of promoting abilities for certain world governments to obtain weapons of mass destruction, thus helping terrorist regimes. Eventually, this act, believe it or not, did prove credible. You see, because of this move, the United States Treasury Department was successful in freezing the assets of two Syrians and two Lebanese men who were obviously up to something. These four conspirators would soon be accused of trying to sabotage legitimate political process in Lebanon.

Despite this minor success, the truth is that Bush, and sadly the United States as well, have unfortunately been subject to ridicule. The United States has now become an international target of global antiwar and anti-globalization campaigns. The world community has viewed George W. Bush as one of the worst U.S. Presidents in the last hundred years. In the Arab community, George W. Bush is the most despised of all world leaders. Bush may have the approval of Tony Blair (Prime Minister of Great Brittan) and Vicente Fox (President of Mexico), but there are more world leaders who disapprove of Bush, such as Hamid Karzai (President of Afghanistan), Hugo Chavez (President of Venezuela), Yoweri Musevini (President of Uganda), and Jose Luis Rodriguez Zapetero (Prime Minister of Spain).

So, what next? Okay, here's something! You might recall, when I spoke of former Democratic presidential candidate John Edwards, I mentioned that Edwards, when requested to state something good Bush did in his presidency, he stated that Bush's action of sending appropriations to Africa for the study of AIDS research was a good thing. So, here are some brief details on this foreign policy move of George W. Bush. Bush outlined a five-year strategy for the urgent need of AIDS relief. This five-year plan was worth fifteen billion dollars. That comes out to three billion per year.

To mention a couple of other matters: In 2003, Bush authorized United States military intervention in Haiti and Liberia for the protection of U.S. interests. Bush also visited Albanian Prime Minister Sali Berisha to perform diplomatic relations in regards to the independence of Kosovo. Bush was the first ever U.S. president to visit Albania.

So, it at least appears that Bush was at times willing to help others when he deemed it necessary. But here is my question. What did Bush do about the worst problem on Earth? Yes, the imminent reality of genocide, the Darfur genocide to be precise. Bush did publicly condemn these acts. He would state that an international peacekeeping force was critical in Darfur. But guess what? Bush opposed referring this genocide case to the I.C.C. (International Criminal Court). So therefore, not only is the United States above signing the Rome Statute, we are also too good to acknowledge the realities of genocide and deal with it properly. If Bush is so great, then why would he only condemn these acts and then oppose prosecution? Maybe because he not only had ties with the Bin Laden family, but he also had ties with Al Bashir.

Enough! I have a message for my fellow Americans, and it goes like this: If we want to continue to stake the claim that we are the best nation on Earth, then, we must stop ignoring these tragedies and take whatever action we can to morally oppose such war crimes. With a new ideology and with the assistance of the United Nations, we must proceed to act with love and morality as we once did. So, I hereby say to my fellow patriots, "put up or shut up" and that is it for George W. Bush.

It is now time to discuss the most infamous and well-known genocide in all of world history. I'm sure you guessed it, the German Adolf Hitler NAZI regime genocide. Hitler is the king daddy of all of the genocide human parasites in the history of the planet Earth. He was so evil, he could have a thousand promotions a day for one million years but he still wouldn't even be halfway to reaching the status of asshole! We will now explore the evil Hitler legacy and the worst acts in known human history.

I will now present a brief chronology of the important events in the life of Adolf Hitler. Adolf Hitler was born in Braunau Austria, on April 20, 1889. He was the fourth child of a third marriage of one Alois Heidler, which was Hitler's original surname. Hitler's mother was fifty-one years of age when she gave birth to Adolf. Alois Heidler's maiden name was Schicklgoeber, which young Adolf took offensively. Hitler did have some siblings. He had a sister Paula, a half brother Alois, and a half sister Angela. As a youth, Hitler aspired to be an artist. However, he would not be accepted to art school. When Hitler was a teenager, he did not accomplish much as a high school student and would decide to quit school at the age of sixteen. Hitler would then spend his days drawing, painting, or reading books and he was known to daydream.

As Hitler's teenage years ended, he would become a supporter of the Social Democratic Party. This political party was derived from Vienna Austria. It was at this point in time that Hitler's unfounded hatred would commence to manifest itself. Hitler's hatred would progress into not only hatred for Jews, but for Slavs as well.

When 1913 rolled around, Hitler would leave Austria and move to the German city of Munich. It is believed that Hitler failed to pass a physical examination when he applied for the Austrian army, thus his reason for moving to Munich. In 1914, Hitler would be accepted into the German army and would fight as a German soldier in the Great War (now known as World War 1), until 1918. During Hitler's tenure in the German army, he would be wounded twice and would later be honored for heroism. By November of 1918, Germany would surrender and by this time, Hitler had risen to the rank of corporal. Due to Hitler being wounded, he suffered temporary blindness from exposure to mustard gas.

In 1923, Hitler led what is known as the Beer Hall Putsch, which was where Hitler would declare the rise of the NAZI party. In 1924, Hitler was sent to prison for acts of treason, but he was released in December of 1924. While he was serving his prison sentence, he started to write the infamous *Mein Kampf*. In 1933, Hitler would achieve the governmental position of Chancellor of Germany. From there, Hitler would begin to strengthen the German regime. Hitler would make a strategic move three years prior to World War 2 by sending troops into the Rhineland. This action defied the Versailles Treaty, by the German occupation of this demilitarized zone (The Rhineland is a small section of land in western Germany). It was in 1939 when Hitler caused the beginning of the Second World War by ordering the German attack of Poland. Ironically, Hitler would rule Germany from 1933 until 1945, the same years that Franklin Delano Roosevelt was the president of the United States of America. Hitler is believed to have committed suicide in Berlin in 1945, as United States, British, and Soviet forces were closing in on him. Mercifully, Hitler would ultimately be defeated. The rest of this Hitler discussion will basically be on the details of the chronology I have just presented.

During Hitler's reign of terror from 1933 to 1945, he would achieve devastating victories for the forces of human evil.

VISION OF A MENTAL PATIENT

Hitler spread a legacy of evil death as no person has ever done in modern history. By the time of his downfall in 1945, Hitler and his German NAZI regime had conquered nearly all of Europe. He would achieve the most staggering death tolls, and, like Pol Pot, he would kill those close to him if he detected any hint of conspiracy.

The spreading of concentration camps would produce a sickening reality of absolute insane evil. Hitler was a master of deception and despite his cunning and baffling ways, Roosevelt and the United States allies in the end would not be fooled by Hitler and Hitler was in for one hell of a fight. A disturbing fact is that Hitler was able to play the German people like a fiddle and most of the German population would blindly follow. A major factor for the citizens of Germany's loyalty to Hitler was due to the fact that Hitler would thoroughly improve the German economy, and also due to the belief that Hitler would build Germany into a world dominant empire that would last for a millennium.

You see, Hitler was basically pig headed. He would not take the advice of experts in any field. He would ignore his generals and other military personnel. This brand of judgment from Hitler would eventually come back to haunt him. For example, in 1938, just prior to the German invasion of Poland, Hitler would threaten the former Czechoslovakia (Now known as the Czech Republic). Because of Hitler's uncompromising hatred toward Slavs, as well as his lust for power, he would be prevented from executing this attack. As history has taught us, in 1939, he would cause the start of World War 2 by invading Poland. It was this event which would lead to the nations of England, France, Australia, New Zealand, South Africa, and Canada, to declare war on Germany. The United States, under the leadership of Franklin Delano Roosevelt, would not be officially involved in this war until four days after the Japanese invasion of Pearl Harbor. The United States entered this war on December 11, 1941, when Germany and Italy declared war on the United States.

So, how did the NAZI party come to be? Why don't we explore that? In the autumn of 1919, when Hitler was only twenty years old, he began to attend meetings which were held by a neo-nationalist group called the German Workers Party. Once Hitler became a member of this group, he would gain a higher standing in this new political party. This new party would eventually change its name to the National Socialist German Workers Party and from that point in time, this party would be dubbed as the NAZI party. Hitler's dominant demeanor and his deceiving charm would commence to cause a frightening rise of the party. This rising of the NAZI party, although evil, would display a cunning trickery by improving the living standards of the German population.

This deception of Hitler was prominent due to the fact that, as previously stated, the German economy would flourish. There was also a significant improvement in the level of employment because of Hitler and his methods of madness. The German people were Hitler's sheep and they believed that Hitler was leading Germany to a great future.

It would not be long before this German NAZI party would rise to a supreme competence. When Hitler was sentenced to prison for acts of high treason at the Beer Hall Putsch, he was originally supposed to serve a five-year sentence. However, Hitler would be set free roughly nine months after his trial. Hitler was released from prison in December of 1924.

While in prison (as previously stated), Hitler would write the infamous *Mein Kampf*, which is German for "My Struggle." You see, because of Hitler's twisted mind, he was strongly convinced that Jewish people in every way represented the evils of our world. Does this mean that Hitler actually thought he was moral? This, my friends is about as twisted as a person can possibly be. In *Mein Kampf*, Hitler stated that the German people must represent an unrivaled form of humanity. Hitler would go on to explain that the German people, in order to remain superior, must remain pure by the avoidance of any associations with Jews, especially in marriage. Hitler also expressed in *Mein Kampf* that democracy could only result in communism. Hitler elaborated further by stating that dictatorship was the only logical route to take in order to save Germany from the threat of communism and Jewish treachery.

Following the Beer Hall Putsch (which we will soon discuss), the German government would outlaw the NAZI party. As Hitler began to substantially rise to a position of power, he would begin to form his notorious assembly. This new NAZI assembly consisted of; Joseph Goebbels (Hitler's chief NAZI propagandist), Herman Goering (would achieve second in command under Hitler), Heinrich Himmler (Leader of the S.S.), Ernst Rohm (Leader of the S.A.), Rudolf Hess (Hitler's private secretary), and finally Alfred Rosenburg (NAZI party philosopher).

As we are all aware of, Hitler would soon lead the NAZI party to become the most prominent political party in all of Germany. By 1930, for the intent of Hitler's accomplishing of this NAZI vision of evil, he would downplay his anti-Semitic type speeches. This move of deceit would aid Hitler in his ultimate goal.

Hitler's predecessor as leader of Germany was one Paul Von Hindenburg who would make the critical mistake of underestimating Hitler. Hindenburg was not aware of the intentions of Hitler. Hindenburg was old for a world leader he was in his 80s. Counterparts of Hindenburg, as well as his son Oskar, would attempt to persuade Hindenburg to be more cautious of Hitler. This was not only to protect innocents, but also to protect Hindenburg himself. Hindenburg would pass away in 1939.

You see, Hindenburg was not a dictator like Hitler was. Hindenburg held the position of president, the last president of Germany to come before Hitler. Hitler, as previously stated, would eventually succeed in achieving the position of Chancellor of Germany. Hindenburg was royally bamboozled by Hitler and this was because of Hindenburg's blind trust of Hitler and his tendency to be gullible. The worst mistake of Hindenburg was proven when he accepted Hitler's promise to deliver prosperity. Hindenburg would basically be suckered into appointing Hitler to the post on January 30, 1933.

Hitler, through his deceptive charm, would fool many. However, he would go even lower with his actions by the brainwashing of young people. NAZIs forced these brainwashed children to spy on their own families, yes—their own flesh and blood. Once accessing this depraved method of taking advantage of the inexperience of the young, if these children knew of any defiance to the NAZI party, these clueless and innocent children would then report this information to their NAZI superiors.

It is quite apparent that Hitler was a man that enjoyed terrorizing people. These sick tactics would continue to be practiced and would throw a veil of terror upon the innocent and moral people of the world, and no matter how much evil Hitler would accomplish, he would never be satisfied. Eventually, this greed would help to bring Hitler down, as well as the evil NAZI dream. Hitler had a system of spies who would constantly observe the German people who, by the way, he was claiming to help. Suffice it to say, if any defiance was detected it, would result in terrifying measures.

Let's go back in time for a moment and discuss the Beer Hall Putsch. This evil, yet historic event took place years prior to the rise of Hitler. It was 1923 and Germany was experiencing trying times. Although this event took place roughly sixteen years before the start of World War 2, there was some military tension at this point in time.

You see, Belgium and France sent military personnel to engross the Ruhr district (The Ruhr district is in Western Central Germany, and is named after the nearby Ruhr River which flows into the Rhine). This Ruhr district was the commanding industrial region of Germany. It was November 8, 1923, and Hitler, who was accompanied by some of his military personnel (S.A.), would storm into a public meetingthat was headed by a man named Kahr. Kahr was a right-wing conservative German politician and was active in the German State of Bavaria. Kahr was considered to be a monarchist and he was also connected to Catholicism, despite the fact that he was a Protestant. Kahr was also the head of the provincial government of North Bavaria.

On the night of the Beer Hall Putsch, Kahr was in the Burgerbrau beer hall. Kahr was accompanied by about 3,000 government officials. Kahr would announce in his speech that he would no longer support the NAZI party. Hitler and company had already entered this beer hall by this time. When Kahr was halfway through his speech, Hitler would then proceed to interrupt sternly, just as he always did. Hitler would say with a forceful demeanor that his coup would manifest itself. During this night of the Beer Hall Putsch, Hitler was not aware that a plan to defeat Hitler's coup was imminently real. By morning, Hitler and his S.A. NAZIs would march to the Bavarian War Ministry in order to overthrow the government of Bavaria. Despite the fact that Kahr would eventually reach the position of President of the Bavarian Law Court, this event had done significant damage to him.

Through all of the confusion on the night of the Beer Hall Putsch, sixteen German militiamen were killed. The cause of these sixteen deaths was that the State Police had opened fire in all of the confusion. Hitler would suffer a loss on this night, but in the future, this event would prove to be a crucial event in pertinence to the rise of the NAZIs. As already stated, Hitler would be arrested due to this event and would be sentenced to a prison term of five years; but as previously stated, he would only remain in prison for less than a year.

In a new direction, I feel it is now essential to discuss just what the road to World War 2 entailed. By 1933, Hitler was well under way in the pursuit of his immoral ambitions of strengthening the German military forces for the preparations of his attempt to rule the world and cause the deaths of millions upon millions of people. A main goal of Hitler's, other than the eradication of Jews, was to make Germany the leading world power. As previously stated, Hitler would deploy troops into the Rhineland, thus violating the Versailles Treaty. As a reminder, this treaty was administered by Great Brittan and France and the intention of this treaty was to at least limit the number of German troops allowed to occupy this region.

In March of 1938, Hitler ordered an attack on the nation of Austria. This attack proved to be a major success for Hitler because he made Austria a German territory. By 1939, Hitler conquered Czechoslovakia. Once claiming rule over the nation, Hitler commanded the attack on Poland, which would ultimately lead to the declaration of war on Germany by Great Brittan and France, thus the commencement of World War 2.

Once the Second World War was underway, the situation looked grim, and it appeared that Hitler might be successful in his attempt to complete the worst act in recent human history. It would only take weeks for Hitler to assume authority over all of Poland. Soon after, in 1940, NAZI forces took over the nations of Denmark, Norway, Belgium, France, Luxembourg, and the Netherlands.

At this point, the Dictator of Italy, one Benito Mussolini, declared war on Great Brittan and France. This was on June 10, 1940. Mussolini entering into World War 2 as a German ally produced a frightening array of support for the Hitler NAZI regime. Mussolini supported Hitler in the takeover of France. By late June of 1940, France was left with no choice but to surrender and sign an agreement with Germany. About a year later, in June of 1941, the NAZI military forces executed an attack on Joseph Stalin's Soviet Union. It appeared that Germany, through its ways of violence, was making significant progress toward the taking over of the Soviet Union. But by November of 1941, the German takeover was being valiantly fought and the Soviets were holding ground.

United States President Franklin Delano Roosevelt approved the sending of supplies to aid Soviet forces. Although at this point the United States was not yet militarily involved, this move of Roosevelt's proved to be quite helpful. Because of the existence of outside help, the Soviet forces began to make more progress in their fight against the Germans.

By the end of 1941, the United States was militarily involved in the quest to stop Hitler and the NAZIs of Germany. It was just after the Japanese invasion of Pearl Harbor, Hawaii, that the United States became completely involved and the fight between the United States and its allies against Germany with its two allies in Italy and Japan, went underway. However, Hitler and his allies were not to be defeated easily. No matter what Hitler was faced with, he would remain a relentless force for evil. From 1942 to 1943, Germany would continue with the relentlessness of Hitler and execute more hostile takeovers, but we would fight Hitler with valiance.

During this period of NAZI relentlessness, the battle of Stalingrad (Named after Joseph Stalin) would take place. This battle lasted an astonishing five months. However, Stalin, with outside help, defeated this German occupation and the German forces would suffer approximately 300,000 casualties. This battle of Stalingrad would prove to be a major turning point in World War 2.

From 1943 to 1945, the situation for the NAZI dream was growing weaker. On July 20, 1944, Hitler, as he had done numerous times, was able to avoid death when one of his own officials plotted to kill him by planting a bomb in his briefing room. However, Hitler would meet his demise in due time; by April 1945, Hitler would be close to his nadir. At this duration of Hitler's downfall, he was miserable. He was also experiencing severe stomach cramps as he trembled all over. His mistress, one Eva Braun, would accompany him at his base in a bomb shelter located under the Reich Chancellery in the German capital of Berlin. Hitler, just one day prior to his suicide, would officially marry Eva. Hitler's wife of one day would suffer the same fate as Hitler and committed suicide with him. The two of them are believed to have been cremated. One week after this dual suicide ,Germany was forced to surrender.

Okay, so Hitler was ultimately defeated. Therefore, I will now elaborate on two men who were vital to the history of the Second World War. These two men were Joseph Stalin of the Soviet Union and Benito Mussolini of Italy. We will discuss Joseph Stalin first.

Joseph Stalin would achieve position as leader of the Soviet Union shortly after the demise of former Soviet leader Vladimir Lenin. Stalin, although appearing to be a modest man and not viewed as consisting of a strong intellect, would rule the Soviet Union using astute and thorough manipulation. Because of Stalin's uncanny ability to deceive, he would be more than often underestimated by his enemies. It would later be discovered that through his ways of deception, he often had the tendency of being a back stabber. Stalin advanced the Soviet Union into an even more powerful world force. Stalin would rule the Soviet Union from 1924 until his death in 1953. Stalin held absolute authority in his advancing of the Soviet totalitarian regime. Despite the fact that Stalin would eventually be forced to take sides with Franklin Delano Roosevelt and the United States for the purpose of opposing Hitler and his German NAZI regime, he was not, however, considered to be a very moral man to say the least.

Eventually, Stalin would build the Soviet Union into one of the most callous regimes in world history. Stalin would alter the Soviet economy, leading to its rapid industrialization and economic collectivization. However, this plan to alter the Soviet economy would fail and lead to widespread famine in the Soviet Union. Stalin would cause hardships for his fellow Soviets, as well as other people, mostly in the eastern hemisphere. Stalin was also evil enough of a man to kill those close to him who may have been suspected of betrayal.

In December 1934, one Sergey Kirov was assassinated and it is believed that Stalin may have been behind this assassination. You see, Kirov was an early Bolshevik leader. He had a reputation of being one of Stalin's enemies that was to be disposed of. It was also common practice for Stalin to have his opponents arrested if not killed. By 1937, Stalin had killed many innocents, not to mention committee members who would dare to oppose him. By 1939, most of Stalin's early obstacles were overcome. Stalin would have over 1,100 of the nearly 2,000 members of the Soviet Seventeenth Congress arrested. Stalin would not hesitate to access his secret police in order to achieve his selfish and evil pursuits. Stalin proved vital to the defeat of Hitler, but as previously stated, he was forced to do so because of Hitler's intention of conquering the Soviet Union.

In 1939, Stalin would sign a non-aggression pact with Germany. Also in 1939, Stalin ordered invasions on the nations of Poland, Finland, The Baltics, Bessarabia, and Northern Bukovina. So you see, Stalin was originally on the side of evil. It was not until Germany violated this non-aggression pact and caused Stalin and the Soviets to join the Anti-Hitler cause that the Soviets would make this strategic shift. The Soviets would suffer a large death toll in this war. Stalin eventually established some communist regimes in Eastern Europe, thus the forming of the Eastern Bloc that would soon become known as the Iron Curtain which was, of course, under Soviet rule. The ultimate truth is that Stalin was partly at fault for the deaths of millions, including those in concentration camps.

So, what led to this violation of the Soviet-Germany non-aggression pact? Part of the reason for the establishment of this non-aggression pact was actually due to the fear that Stalin had of Germany. Why would Stalin order the invasion of Poland? The reason for this action, which is most commonly believed, is because through a Polish invasion, Stalin saw the opportunity to expand Soviet influence in Europe. Stalin was careful in the tactics of these pre-planned invasions because of his ambitions for the new Iron Curtain.

Obviously, this non-aggression pact did not last very long. Hitler's uncompromising lustful greed eventually led to his imminent demise. Therefore, Stalin performed diplomatic relations with not only Roosevelt, but with Great Brittan's Winston Churchill as well, and although Stalin would end up on the side of good, he was still one evil human being. So, what can make a person so evil? Child abuse? Through my research, it is apparent to me that Hitler was not a victim of child abuse. Was young Joseph Stalin abused as a child? Let's explore the early life of Joseph Stalin.

Joseph Stalin was born on December 21, 1879, in the small Georgian town of Gori. Young Joseph's father was a poor blacksmith who was said to have had a drinking problem and yes, Young Joseph's father would beat Joseph unmercifully. Young Joseph's father was a violent man who would be killed in a fight when Joseph was only eleven years old. Joseph's mother, on the other hand, was a washerwoman. She had high hopes that young Joseph would someday become a priest. It was believed that Joseph's mother was very attentive to her son and would often console him to selfennoblement.

Young Joseph had a nickname, "Koba." You see, Koba was a fictional mountain desperado. Joseph, as a very young man would join the Georgian Social Democratic Political Party. Joseph would get to meet Vladimir Lenin in 1912, and Lenin would award Joseph by accepting him into what was known as the Bolshevik Central Committee. It was at this point in Joseph's life where his ambitions of power would begin to take form. Joseph would soon gain employment for the Social Democratic newspaper called *The Pravda*. Soon, Joseph would achieve position as editor of this newspaper. Joseph would be appointed to administrative government posts, such as Commissar of Workers and Peasants. He was appointed to this newly found status when the Bolshevik Leon Trotsky was arrested (Leon Trotsky was a Marxist revolutionist). At this time, Vladimir Lenin was also arrested (Vladimir Lenin was the first head of the Russian Soviet Socialist Republic) and forced into hiding. Joseph would also eventually become party secretary, and as previously stated, he would take over Lenin's position as the head of the Soviet Union in 1924. It was not long before the political abuses of Joseph Stalin would become reality. Okay, enough with Joseph Stalin, it is now time for me to keep my promise and give an assessment of the former dictator of Italy Benito Mussolini.

Benito Mussolini was born on July 29, 1883, in Predappio Italy. Mussolini was the founding father of Italian Fascism and he would rule Italy from 1922 until 1943. Fascism is basically a system of government characterized by a dictatorship as well as aggressive nationalism, racism, and militarism. Italian fascism, especially that of Mussolini, can be explained slightly differently. Italian fascism is considered an authoritarian nationalist ideology, focused on resolving social, economic, and political problems that its supporters may view as causing national decline. Mussolini would rule Italy with an iron fist as dictator for approximately twenty-one years.

Mussolini, like Stalin, was the son of a blacksmith. Young Benito grew up without any form of parental discipline. As I was, he was considered a wild and unruly child. His father was a socialist so that young Benito would share in his father's political ideals. Benito would relate these inherited ideals to ideals of which he would learn through literature, which he would read as an adolescent. Something I have in common with young Benito is that he liked to self educate. Benito would read such authors as Neitzsche, Blanqui, and Sorel. I guess Vonnegut and Bukowski weren't around in Benito's era; well, that's too bad for him.

When Benito Mussolini came of age, he started a career as a schoolteacher. Eventually, he became a journalist. Benito eventually had short residencies in Switzerland and the Austrian Trentino. Benito met his future wife who was a peasant at the time they met. Her name was Rachele Guidi. Benito and Rachele had five children. Soon, Benito became an editor of an Italian newspaper called the Avanti, a Milan Socialist Party newspaper. Benito became editor of the Avanti in 1912 when he was in his late twenties.

At the start of the Great War now known as World War 1, Benito Mussolini was opposed to Italian involvement in this war. However, he would soon change his mind and become supportive of the Italian military joining its allies in this war. Benito became subject to an expulsion from the Socialist Party due to this view. This led to Benito's founding of a new newspaper called the Popolo d' Italia. This newspaper of Benito's would soon become the centerpiece of the Italian Fascist movement.

One year prior to the end of World War 1, Benito joined the armed forces of Italy. About two years later, Benito, in March of 1919, formed a Milan nationalistic revolutionary group called the Fasci di Combattimento, named after the ancient Roman symbol of capacity. The establishment of this new fascist group led to the turning point of Mussolini's fascist movement. This new fascist movement would evolve into a robust fascist radicalism.

Benito Mussolini would commence to gain a prominent stronghold as he progressed. He gained support of the lower Po Valley landowners in Italy. The Po Valley is major geographical feature of Italy. Located in northeastern Italy, it extends roughly 6000 kilometers in an east-west direction. This would cause this new radical Italian fascist movement to gain some distinguished members such as industrialists, army officers, and fascist black shirt bands which would soon begin to carry on a local civil war. This small civil war was fought between Mussolini fascists and socialists, communists, Catholics, and liberals.

A few years later, in early October of 1922, Mussolini secured a mandate from King Victor Emmanuel the third after the Italian fascists had marched to Rome. This move was for the progression of the forming of an alliance government. In June 1924, one Gracomo Matteotti (a socialist leader who often spoke in opposition to Mussolini) was assassinated. This assassination led to a parliamentary crisis. It was at this point that Mussolini could, with absolute prominence, push for his ambition of the establishment of a totalitarian fascist dictatorship. This was especially the case considering that Benito Mussolini now held high political position.

In the mid 1930s, Mussolini formed an extremely aggressive type of foreign policy: He commanded an invasion of the African nation of Ethiopia and soon had supreme power! Mussolini supported General Francisco Franco in the the Spanish Civil War. Francisco Franco was the dictator and head of state of Spain in the mid 1930s. Franco's ruling methods were based on nationalism, centralism, and traditional Spanish values. Soon, Mussolini made a move that we are all aware of. In 1936,

VISION OF A MENTAL PATIENT

Mussolini had already reached a position of dangerous power and had become a faithful ally to Hitler.

Mussolini's support of Hitler and the NAZIs led to the expansion of an even more powerful and threatening war machine. In April 1939, Mussolini ordered his military forces to invade and occupy Albania. Albania is a southeastern European nation bordered by Greece, Kosovo, Macedonia, and Montenegro. Mussolini, although an ally of Hitler' in 1936, did not officially enter World War 2 until June of 1940.

After a chain of Italian military calamities in northern Africa and Greece, Mussolini's appointed leaders abandoned him. In 1943, Mussolini appeared to have reached his nadir; he would be arrested by high government officials. Soon, Mussolini was rescued by German forces. Little was Mussolini aware that he would soon be Hitler's scapegoat. Well, that's what you get for trusting an asshole!

In April 1945, near the time of Hitler's suicide, Mussolini and his mistress at the time, one Clara Petacci, were forced to attempt an escape from advancing allied forces, but they were soon be caught. Mussolini and Clara Petacci were sentenced to death by hanging; they were executed in a public square in Milan. Following his demise on April 28, 1945, Mussolini was buried in the town of his birth, Predappio, Italy. He was dead at the age of 61.

This Mussolini discussion is just about over, but before I endit, there is something I must express. It is a crying shame that Mussolini turned out to be the evil man he would become. I must state that when reading about him in his youth, I really liked the kid that I was reading about. Young Benito and I had some things in common. For one, he was wild and unruly and loved to misbehave; for two, he had a relationship with his father and learned a lot about politics through his dad; and three, he liked to read. If I went to school with Mussolini, I probably would have hung out with him. It makes you wonder just what leads people to such disturbing actions; after all, when Hitler was in his youth, he seemed harmless, just a daydreaming kid who liked to paint; and finally, Joseph Stalin was severely beaten by his father at a very young age. So, who knows? With guidance, maybe these three men (especially Mussolini) would have turned out okay under different circumstances. Don't get me wrong, these were mean and I despise their actions, but open mindedness, my friends, is a virtue.

At this point, I deem it necessary to discuss with you the most infamous of all of the concentration camps—Auschwitz. Auschwitz was, by far, the largest of all of the NAZI concentration camps and the acts that were carried out in this place makes me want to vomit. You might think that Auschwitz was located in Germany, but it wasn't, as a matter of fact. Auschwitz was located in Poland after German forces had conquered this nation. Auschwitz actually consisted of three separate camps. The first of the three was called Auschwitz I, which was founded on May 20, 1940. Auschwitz 1 was originally an old Polish army barracks. A band of 728 Polish government prisoners were its first victims, entered on June 14, 1940.

The first of the three Auschwitz camps was used to torture and kill the Polish Government Resistance Movement Representatives who became the first of countless groups of innocents who would eventually become subject to the shocking tactics executed in this human hellhole. It would not be long until Soviet prisoners would suffer the same fate as the original Polish victims had suffered. After that, there were actually some German prisoners in this first of three Auschwitz camps who would be subject to termination for acts of defiance and betrayal against the German NAZI regime that would eventually go on to eradicate massive numbers of innocents. Soon, homosexuals would become victims of Auschwitz 1 for their sexual lifestyles which Hitler did not approve of. Finally, the most common of holocaust victims, the Jews of Europe, would be tragically entered into this camp of insanity.

Auschwitz I would illegally imprison, torture, and kill obscene amounts of innocent people. At first, this concentration camp held somewhere between 13,000 and 16,000 prisoners. By 1942, it was up to approximately 20,000 prisoners. Not only were these prisoners subject to sickening methods of torture, but they were also forced to perform manual labor to the point of unconsciousness. The Jewish prisoners were treated the most inhumanely. However, the Soviet prisoners had it nearly as bad.

Remember now, the prisoners of this concentration camp, as I have already told you, were subject to torture, witnessing of the ones they care for being tortured, basic execution, and manual labor, but to add to this unfathomable immorality, some prisoners would have the horrible experience of starvation or severe malnutrition. Another factor which these prisoners were forced to deal with were hygiene problems, which could drive a person crazy. It was also common for victims to suffer from a disease called typhus (typhus is an acute infectious disease caused by certain bacteria that is transmitted by fleas, lice, etc. and characterized by fever, skin rash, etc.), therefore, some victims would suffer from itching all over due to insect bites and just imagine what that does to a person's dignity!

Auschwitz I consisted of an inner prison devised for the progression of the killing tactics of Hitler. This inner sanctuary was called Block 11. This Block 11 was where the courageous violators of the ludicrous rules of this camp were sent. Some of these victims would be forced to stand in small cells, four at a time, and these cells measured about 1.5 square meters. After being forced to stand in these cells all night, these prisoners would then be forced to perform even more manual labor in the morning. In the basement of block 11, prisoners would be put in starvation cells and were forced to experience the slow death of starvation. There was also another sickeningly cruel method similar to the starvation method, but maybe even worse. In the basement of Block 11, certain victims would be placed in very small cells that had no ventilation, suffocating its victims.

Then there was the execution yard of Auschwitz I, where some would sadly, yet mercifully, be shot execution style. Others would be forced to suffer a cruel method of execution, where they would be suspended vertically on hooks set on two wooden posts. A very cruel NAZI man who was a deputy camp commander by the name of Hauptstrumfuher Fritzsch was so demented that he once amused himself by sending about 600 Soviet victims as well as roughly 250 Polish prisoners to the basement of Block 11 and proceeded to exterminate these prisoners by method of death from lethal gas.

The gas chamber of Auschwitz I was in working order from 1941 to 1942 and it is estimated that in this short duration, about 60,000 prisoners of this camp were killed there. Does the number 60,000 sound familiar to you? If it does, I believe it could be because in the first genocide case I elaborated on, the Russian Pogrom genocide, the death count was about 60,000 people and this was over a period of 40 years. That means that in one small section of Auschwitz I, over a one-year period, Hitler managed to have that many people killed in a small fraction of time in comparison to the Russian Pogrom ordeal.

Unlike Auschwitz I, Auschwitz II, although partly constructed, would require more edifice. This second of the three Auschwitz concentration camps added to its original structure with more construction in order to satisfy Hitler. To be precise, the continuation of this foundation began in October of 1941. The reason for the construction of Auschwitz II was due to the fact that Auschwitz I was in basic terms, running out of room. Hitler had a counterpart named Heinrich Himmler. Hitler and Himmler established the movement of a supremely evil legacy. The foul vision shared by these two parasites was labeled the Final Solution, this based on the evil dream they felt was the answer to the Jewish question. This vision of pure craziness was the basis for the tragedy of the horrifying realities of the Holocaust. Hitler, Himmler, and the German NAZI regime felt they were in need of even more land to carry out their killings. With passion, these men wanted to not only exterminate all Jews, but would like all other genocide parasites proceed to kill those who dared to stand in the way! January 1942, through what is known as the Wannsee Conference, would cause this evil dream to continue to pose a threat to us all. This Wannsee Conference comprised of Senior NAZI officials. It was held in a Berlin suburb called Wansee and would eventually cause major havoc.

Auschwitz II was also known as Birkenau. The very first gas chamber at Auschwitz II was labeled the "Little Red House." This little red house, unlike most of Auschwitz II, was already erected. It was actually an old brick cottage before it was further worked on. Soon, this little red house would become the infamous chamber of death, of which it most certainly was. This gas chamber would be completed in March 1942.

Once this second portion of Auschwitz was well under way, innocent Jews would be split up into sectors: a sector for those who would perform manual labor and other sectors for the categorization of the war prisoners in this camp; so obviously, those who were unable to perform labor would be rendered useless and be terminated, usually by gas chamber.

By early 1943, the Hitler NAZI regime decided to have a major increase of the gassing magnitude of Auschwitz II. A section called Crematorium II, originally intended to be a morgue, ended up being used as a killing plant. By March of 1943, this new domain of NAZI murder was now in the practice of the killing tactics of Hitler. By June of the same year, this camp was frighteningly progressing and soon there would be four new and completely operational gas chambers. It was commonplace for the dead victims of these gas chambers to be thrown into a furnace and thus disposed of. Auschwitz II, by the time it was completely operational, was significantly larger than Auschwitz I. The death toll of this concentration camp exceeded one million. Most commonly, these victims were executed by gas chamber.

There was also a section for the women of Birkenau (the nick name of Auschwitz II). This section for the women victims was separated from the other section by a railroad line. Three evil NAZI women named Elisabeth Volkenrath, Maria Mandel, and Johanna Langfield, were mostly responsible for the killings. The fact is that Birkenau or Auschwitz II managed to kill more people than any other concentration camps during the Holocaust.

The worst of occurrences at Birkenau were from April through June of 1944. This would prove to be one of the worst occurrences, not only in this genocide case, but in all of modern history. This would be day of the massacres of the Jews of Hungary. Hungary is a landlocked country located in the Carpathian Basin of central Europe bordered by Austria, Slovakia, the Ukraine, Romania, Serbia, Croatia, and Slovenia; and its capital is the city of Budapest. Hungary, at this time, had an extremely high population of Jews. Surprisingly, Hungary at this time was a German ally. Due to Hitler's lust for the conquering of land and his obsession with his goal of the eradication of Jews, he would, just as he did to the Soviets, turn on another ally. You see, Hitler became irated with Hungary's government because they refused to give the NAZIs access to exterminate the Jews of Hungary. So, Hitler would then solve his problem the same way he always tried to solve his problems: by attacking those who would not completely comply with his orders. This German occupation of Hungary began in March 1944. By April, Hitler got exactly what he wanted. Therefore, in a brief fifty-six-day period, approximately 436,000 Hungarian Jews representing half of the Jewish population of Hungary were sent to Auschwitz and exterminated. These Hungarian victims were for the most part not subject to death by gassing. Instead, these innocents were burned alive. The reason for death by burning was that there were so many victims, that gassings would have taken too long. Disgusting, huh?

Auschwitz III was basically a series of surrounding concentration camps. It is estimated that Auschwitz III was composed of roughly forty small camps. The largest of these forty camps was called Monowitz, named after the Polish village of Monowice. Monowitz was well under way by May 1942. Monowitz was originally associated with a synthetic rubber and liquid fuel plant called Buna-Werke, which was owned by I.G. Farben. Over 10,000 slaves worked at Monowitz. About 7,000 worked at the various nearby chemical plants, about 8,000 worked in mines, and about 40,000 more labored in the surrounding camps of Auschwitz III. There was also a separate section for the women of this camp, just like that of Auschwitz I and II.

The last brutality of human shame I will inform you of is in pertinence to the experiments conducted on the European Jews, who were subject to the horrific reality of the Holocaust. These sickeningly disgusting acts were performed on anyone, including infants and women. A NAZI professor by the name of Carl Clauberg would inject lethal chemicals into a woman's uterus in an attempt to glue it shut; this was an early version of genital mutilation. Have you ever heard of Bayer, you know, the over the counter medication? Well, Bayer was originally a subsidiary of the previously mentioned I.G. Farben. Jewish victims would be used as guinea pigs for the testing of new drugs. However, I must stress that Bayer should not be frowned upon due to its past history. The truth is that Bayer has helped many people through its history, and this statement is in no way intended to draw Bayer into public controversy.

At this point, I will now give information about one of the most infamous and immoral of all the NAZI Auschwitz doctors who carried out these sick experiments on the European Jews taken prisoners in this concentration camp. This man was one Joseph Mengele, also known as the Angel of Death. Joseph Mengele had a particular interest in Jewish identical twins. Mengele would construct unimaginably cruel experiments on twin infants. He would induce a disease in one twin and would kill the other when the diseased one died. This was so Mengele could proceed with comparative autopsies. If you were a Jewish dwarf with a twin, he would induce gangrene on you and then proceed to dissect and study you and your twin once both of you were dead.

As a young boy, I had a fascination with the evils of Hitler and the German NAZI forces. I remember hearing rumors even more explicitly repugnant than what I have already informed you of, regarding the Angel of Death Joseph Mengele's methods. I have heard stories of infants being torn apart and stuffed with trash! I have also heard that infants would be subject to beatings until they died, and then this distributor of pain would write down in his chart how long it took for a particular infant to die. I cannot fathom why a human being could ever become this cruel. If these experiments aren't "Sickening Fucking Shit" then I do not know what is! If there are people out there who want to censor my profanity in relation to these disgusting acts of genocide, or tell me not to use such words, then if they bang their foot on the edge of their coffee table and then say "Shit!" then why the hell can't I say shit, when millions upon millions of human beings have been being murdered for a long duration of time? If I am wrong to use profanity in this case, than we ought to take such words and throw them in the garbage for good! The shameful fact is that American society is more concerned about people saying shit and fuck on television, than it ought to be about millions of innocent men, women, and children being killed on a daily basis.

I now say to you that I am not an angry Democrat nor am I an angry Republican. I am an angry human being! Genocide is sick and I hate it! Feel these words—don't just read them! It is our moral responsibility, being members of the human race, not to tolerate any more! I know what you are thinking—you're thinking, "How?" Keep reading!

In the area of the Auschwitz camps, it is currently called O?wi?cim. Auschwitz like Toul Sleng in Cambodia is a museum dedicated to its many victims. So, Hitler with the help of some of his fellow parasites, managed to eradicate countless innocent peopl, who resided in Europe in this era. Sadly and most unfortunately, another estimated five million other people whom Hitler viewed as unfit for life were also killed. These other victims consisted of Gypsies, Poles, Slavs, ministers, priests, Jehovah Witnesses, and believe it or not, mental patients. Can you believe that one? "Mental patients!" Having been a mental patient myself, I cannot conceive why anyone, no matter how evil, would want to kill mental patients! These are people that are already struggling in the first place!

One more point on this matter. The United States media would like to have you believe that mass starvation is the worst problem on Earth. By no means whatsoever am I trying to trivialize starvation; as a matter of fact, starvation is a crucial world problem and it is also our human responsibility to react appropriately to this other horrible world problem. However, mass starvation is not censored, but genocide is, and truthfully, despite my point, I can see why. I do not feel that the children of the United States or any other nation should be forced to witness genocide-driven murders on prime time television. However, we adults must, in some way, shape, or form, do at least something, about this deadly serious world problem. I also think that the United States should take on the responsibility of what we are meant and supposed to be and sign the Rome Statute, and stop claiming that we are the best country on Earth and start acting like we want to be the best nation on Earth, by taking action through my and your new ideology of a mind revolution.

So, one more time, I must remind you of the staggering death tolls which Hitler achieved. Through Hitler's eradication of Jews and other groups of world society, he managed to kill eleven million people, not to mention all of the soldiers that perished from all of the nations involved in World War 2. Hitler, like no other man in modern world history, has spread death throughout the world with such conviction, thus producing genocide of mass proportions.

Well, that Hitler was really something, wasn't he? I am happy to tell you that Hitler is now done. And I myself am also done with this Hitler discussion. So, what next? How about we have a discussion on the thirty-second president of the United States, Franklin Delano Roosevelt, and examine his foreign policy. Seeing that he was the president who had the challenge of dealing with Adolf Hitler, I feel that it is appropriate time to discuss this man and his outstanding presidency.

Before I begin my elaboration on the foreign policy of Franklin D. Roosevelt, I first must explain something. I myself have wondered as you also may have wondered, just why Roosevelt waited so long before involving the United States in World War 2. Through research, I have come to a conclusion to this question. The belief that I have developed is that Roosevelt was preparing and strengthening the United States military forces for the purpose of being a sufficiently effective force. In our discussion of Roosevelt's foreign policy, you will see that in certain cases, the United States would support this Anti-Hitler cause in non-military ways before officially entering this war. The last thing I will leave you with before we get underway, is that it has been said that Hitler feared and hated Franklin Delano Roosevelt more than anyone else.

Okay, let's get going here! In Roosevelt's first term, which was from 1933 to 1937, his foreign policy was in the pre-World War 2 stage. At this time, Roosevelt's prime foreign policy initiative was what was called the Good Neighbor Policy. This Good Neighbor Policy dealt with the reassessment of United States policy with Latin American nations. So, naturally, Roosevelt wanted to be on the best of terms, especially at a time when there was an over abundance of evident military tension in Latin America. Roosevelt also wanted to accumulate any support from Latin America that he could. He was smart denying any United States military intrusion in this area. One thing Roosevelt was good at was keeping the peace whenever he was able to.

You see, in the duration of the Second World War, Roosevelt would find other ways to aid our allies and maintain a United States peacetime for the intention of reaching certain objectives. The Good Neighbor Policy led to the support of Latin American leaders, aided in the trainings of the National Guard, as well as helped these Latin American countries economically. The processes to achieve such goals were import export bank loans, the overseeing of certain finances, and political sedition. Through this Good Neighbor Policy, the United States was able to improve the sovereignty of the nations of Latin America by preventing the weakening of these nations caused by more powerful nations. You must understand that when a country of wealth felt that they were being either financially cheated or being paid back late for certain debts, it would have detrimental effects, especially for these Latin American nations' ability to receive natural resources sufficiently. Therefore, the Good Neighbor Policy was helpful both domestically and in a foreign manner.

In 1919, something happened in that would have a major effect on Roosevelt's foreign policy. This was the rejection of the League of Nations treaty. This rejection would cause a newly found dominance of what is called isolationism. Isolationism is the opposing of any involvement of a certain country or countries in international relations. This particular case of isolationism pertained to American foreign relations and to other world organizations.

This previous occurrence caused Roosevelt and his secretary of state, Cordell Hull, to act with caution so that they wouldn't aggravate any foreign isolationist sentiment. You see, the depression was not just a domestic issue, it was also a foreign issue. The reason for this is that the United States was prominent in world trade and our economy would have a major effect on other world economies. Roosevelt with his brilliance sent a vital message at the World Monetary Conference in 1933. The main point of Roosevelt's statement at this world conference was to end the intervention of other world powers in order to come together for the intent of putting an end to this global depression. So, why? I myself do believe that Roosevelt made the right move. You see, Roosevelt was then able to have a new strategic approach by being able to deal with this problem in a more hands on type method.

At this point, while we are still on the topic of Roosevelt's first term policies, I must present you with something which confuses me. During the 2008 presidential race, Joe Biden (our new vice president), stated that Franklin Delano Roosevelt got the United States through the depression. I myself do agree with our new vice president, but he was corrected in pertinence to this statement. I don't get it! So, let's take a look, shall we? The Great Depression was the result of a major stock market crash that occurred on October 29, 1929. This date in history is often alluded to as "Black Tuesday." This depression technically ended during the onset of World War 2 in 1939.

So, who was the President of the United States on October 29, 1929? It was the thirty-first United States president, Herbert Hoover, who served from March 4, 1929 until March 4, 1933. Could Hoover cause this much damage in just under eight months? I don't think so! On the other hand, the thirtieth U.S. President, a Vermont born citizen, gained political distinction through Massachusetts state politics by becoming the governor of my home state! He was a man who gained a respectable political standing because of his actions during the Boston police strike of 1919! So who am I speaking of? I am referring to Calvin Coolidge. Coolidge would take the place of the twenty-ninth U.S. president, Warren G. Harding, after his death. Republican Calvin Coolidge became president on August 2, 1923, later reelected in 1925. Coolidge's presidency would end on March 4, 1929.

There are a number of theories about how Black Tuesday and the depression came to be. Specific events were imperative to the manifestation of this depression. There were the obvious ones, like bank failures and the stock market crash. Some believe it was a basic failure on the part of the free markets or a failure of governments to cut short widespread bank failures. Anyway, something definitely went horribly wrong, and it would spread on a global scale. It must be understood that although money is a type of evil, we still must be responsible in our concerns for our nation's economic system as well as the economic systems throughout the world. You see, the depression caused a major problem in agriculture and other types of food production. Have you ever seen the films about the Great Depression, where people would have to stand in line for hours just for a small bowl of soup or a slice of bread? Well, that could be a consequence of political and economic carelessness.

However, I cannot get into all of the hype of the Great Depression. But I must state what I see as the ultimate truth. The Hoover Administration did not cause the Great Depression, but this same administration only lasted four years and, obviously, Hoover did not end the depression. I feel that the blame should fall on the Coolidge Administration. To state my case clearer, when Franklin Delano Roosevelt took office in 1933, the United States, as well as other nations, was at the complete nadir of the depression. So, I now remind you of a previous statement I made about Roosevelt's political move at a world conference intended to prevent other nations from intervening in the global depression. I explained that Franklin Delano Roosevelt took this action for the intent of a more hands on method in his dealing with the depression. Anyhow, roughly six years after, Roosevelt was inaugurated as United States President and the depression was virtually over. Therefore, I state that my opinion is right in saying that Joe Biden was correct in saying that Franklin Delano Roosevelt got us through the depression.

One more thing, in pertinence to Roosevelt's first term before we begin discussion on his second term. I would now like to briefly summarize two very well known political moves which Roosevelt made during his first four years as president. I am speaking of the first New Deal and the second New Deal.

The first New Deal, of course, was an attempt at ending the depression, established right from the start of Roosevelt's first term. This attempt was made during the first 100 days of his tenure as president. Roosevelt would try what was labeled as immediate relief. This immediate relief took place from March 9, 1933 until June 16, 1933. Roosevelt proceeded to send the United States Congress a number of bills. You see, Roosevelt had the benefit of a Democratic dominated congress, therefore, his democratic agenda would hold steady ground, and virtually every bill he sent in would pass.

One of the main causes of any depression is a direct result of civilian fear, thus causing these civilians to not spend money or make investments. Roosevelt was quite aware of this factor, and was also very much aware about how to react. This first New Deal, however, would, for the most part, be rendered ineffective. But Roosevelt was no slouch and he would soon react with the second New Deal.

So, what about Franklin Delano Roosevelt's second New Deal? The second New Deal would be more effective because in the 1934 Congressional elections, Roosevelt's Democrats gained an even more dominating standing in the House and Senate. Roosevelt commenced to produce a new outpouring of new deal legislation. This would lead to a beneficial attempt of Roosevelt to work with the Works Progress Administration (W.P.A.). This would lead to a surge in the level of employment. Roosevelt soon established the Social Security Administration. With the help of one of his counterparts, a senator by the name of Robert Wagner, Roosevelt was able to create the National Labor Relations Act which basically created unions for the employees of industries.

By the start of the second term of Franklin Delano Roosevelt, people were becoming wary of the rise of Hitler and the German NAZI regime. Due to the 1935 Italian invasion of the African nation of Ethiopia, a bill was passed prohibiting the shipment of military arms from the United States to any antagonist regime. This would become known as the Neutrality Act. Roosevelt, in his usual manner of tactfulness, actually was opposed to this act because he believed it would unfairly punish victims of war like the aggressions that were carried out in Ethiopia because of Mussolini. Despite the fact that Roosevelt was opposed to this act, he felt obligated to sign it because of massive United States public support. This was something that Roosevelt would do from time to time. He would do what the people wanted him to do. This was due to his belief in the process of democracy and listening to the people rather than always just doing what he wanted to do.

In October of 1937, Roosevelt gave his quarantine speech. This speech regarding quarantine was intended to build capacity for aggressive nations. Roosevelt simply felt that any acts of unreasonable measures in a military coup, or that of any war mongering toward any weaker nations was not to be tolerated. He felt that these aggressive nations should be considered a health threat. Therefore, these governments which tended to be aggressive in an improper manner should be quarantined (quarantine is an isolation imposed to prevent contagions from spreading). So, this means that Roosevelt thought of acts of violence as a disease, which is an accurate assumption considering how sick it is to kill! Roosevelt would, in relation to this dilemma, step up efforts to build long range submarines which could be beneficial if we were to confront Japan in a military fashion. So, the point I made earlier about Roosevelt's staying out of World War 2 in order to strengthen the United States military was a true statement. Military tension would grow steadily between the United States and Japan. In 1937, the Sino-Japanese War started. The United States and President Roosevelt was on the side of the Chinese. This would indirectly lead to Japanese involvement in World War 2.

In May 1938, a matter of significance took place in the South American country of Brazil. This was a failed military action made by the Fascist Integralista Movement in Brazil. The Government of Brazil claimed that the German Ambassador to Brazil, one Dr. Carl Ritter, was involves in this failed coup.

This Brazilian accusation that Germany was supportive of this military action resulted in a stimulating blow to the Roosevelt Administration. You see, this frightened Roosevelt, because he now had to accept that Hitler was also interested in conquering nations outside of Europe. He would then give more effort in regards to his already good foreign policy. This occurrence in Brazil also caused other nations abroad to take Hitler more seriously.

By September 1938, worldwide crisis was well underway, especially in Europe. Early September was the zenith of the Munich Agreement. This Munich Agreement concerned the Sudetenland, areas along the Czechoslovakian borders. This agreement was signed by Germany, Great Brittan, France, and Italy. This agreement allowed German occupation of the Sudetenland. This Sudetenland area was paramount to the defense strategies of Czechoslovakia, which today, of course, is called the Czech Republic.

During an award ceremony in France that credited Franco-American (French and American) friendship, William E. Bullit, the United States Ambassador to France at this time, made a statement to the effect that Franco-American relations would remain good and strong in both peacetime and war time. Because of this event, the press would proceed to speculate that if

Czechoslovakia was invaded, the United States would support its allies in any means necessary.

Roosevelt reacted to this public and journalistic view in a press conference. Roosevelt did not want to allow this interpretation. He concluded by saying, that this view was completely false. Roosevelt would then make it clear that if Hitler were to order an attack on Czechoslovakia, the United States would still remain neutral. I remind you at this point, that Roosevelt was still in the process preparing the U.S. military forces.

You see, Franklin Delano Roosevelt possessed a classic charm and demeanor. This positive characteristic would prove to be a convenient asset when performing his diplomatic responsibilities. Before Winston Churchill was the Prime Minister of Great Brittan, one Neville Chamberlain was Prime Minister. When Roosevelt returned home to the United States after performing his diplomatic responsibilities at the Munich conference, he sent Neville Chamberlain a two-word telegram, which read "Good man." Some believed that this telegram was sarcastic. I believe it was Roosevelt being his usual charming self. Moving on now! In October of 1938, when Roosevelt was still in the process of building up and strengthening the United States military, he made yet another move meant to aid the anti-Hitler cause. Roosevelt broke a rule in order to do the moral thing (remember morality over technicality), just as Nixon would do, but Nixon did it a hell of a lot more than Roosevelt even thought of doing it. What Roosevelt did was this: he bypassed American Laws of Neutrality in order to sell France American aircrafts to make up for the lackluster productivity that the French had at this time. Once again, I will back up the point that I previously made, point being, that Roosevelt was in preparation for future military actions. You see, Roosevelt killed two birds with one stone by this move. First of all, he aided the French in their cause by this illegal, yet necessary aircraft deal. Second, with the money the United States received from France from this deal, Roosevelt was then able to take these profits and use them to advocate an increase of funds for United States military ambitions.

However, some annoying technicalities needed to be overcome. You see, France still owed the U.S. money for supplies we sold them in the Great War (World War 1). In 1932, France not being in possession of a good economy, was forced to default on their debts to the United States. However, in 1939 a revised deal was made. France made a payment to the United States of approximately 10 billion Francs. In this revised deal, France had a guarantee that the United States would sell them an unlimited amount of aircraft. Also, France now had the option of paying for these aircrafts on credit. France would immediately access this deal in 1939, but for reasons of technicalities, these aircrafts did not arrive until 1940.

When World War 2 began in 1939, Roosevelt would once again bypass the neutrality act and supply not only France, but Great Brittan as well. In 1939, Winston Churchill was Lord of Admiralty and finally in 1940 he would replace Neville Chamberlain as the Prime Minister of Great Britain. Roosevelt and Churchill commenced with their diplomatic negotiations in 1939 while Churchill was still Lord of Admiralty. These two legendary world leaders would begin to have a secret correspondence between one another. Roosevelt, although not having the United States jump in the fire yet, was thorough in his efforts to make Churchill understand that he was more than willing to help. These two great men would form a common bond with one another and cause some of the most imperative events in modern world history for the cause of human good.

In April of 1940, Hitler commanded the invasions of Denmark, Norway, The Netherlands, Belgium, Luxembourg, and France. These six invasions made Great Brittan very fearful due to newly found susceptibility. This caused Roosevelt to have intense concern for Great Britain. Through Roosevelt's determination, in July of 1940, he would exercise what is called bipartisanship (bipartisanship is the working together between Republicans and Democrats). In doing so, he would appoint two Republican interventionist leaders, Henry L. Stimson and Frank Knox, as Secretaries of War and Navy. At this time, there was a huge shift in the American public. You see, Germany's taking over of Paris France appalled American sentiment. Therefore, this move of Roosevelt to give his support to Great Brittan by increasing military aid spending was well taken by the American public. Roosevelt was still strengthening United States forces, while indirectly supporting Great Brittan.with the help of his Democratic Congress, he was able to initiate the first ever United States peacetime war draft. It was growing more evident that Roosevelt's time was growing shorter. Roosevelt would stick to his plan of supporting the Committee to Defend America by Aiding the Allies. However, there was another domestic committee which opposed this approach and it was called the America First Committee. This America First Committee was the leading non-interventionist force that opposed any future United States entry into World War 2, and it might have been the largest anti-war organization in the history of the United States. Roosevelt was opposed to this committee because he realized that war was becoming inevitable. This means that Roosevelt was racing against time as well as a prominent world evil.

Roosevelt continued to state his case for the supporting of his pre-war actions. He argued against the Neutrality Acts with the passing of the Destroyers for Bases Agreement. This Destroyers for Bases Agreement was an agreement between the United States and Great Britain which exchanged fifty destroyers from the United States Navy for land rights on British properties. These properties were in the Caribbean, as well as Newfoundland. This new agreement was a part of the preparation for the Lend Lease Agreement that was put in effect in March 1941. This particular agreement started the shipping of colossal military and economic aid to the nations of Great Brittan, China, and eventually, the Soviet Union.

Obviously, Roosevelt's efforts were starting to achieve dramatic proportions. Roosevelt would then turn to one Harry Hopkins who would become his Chief Foreign Policy Advisor. It was the work of Roosevelt and Hopkins, which would put the Lend Lease Act into action. Soon, Franklin Delano Roosevelt would be elected to his third term as President of the United States. Roosevelt's third term would be monopolized by the harsh realities of the Hitler NAZI conquest. As I have already explained, since at least 1938, Roosevelt was strengthening the United States military and the time was coming near. There were two senators of isolationist sentiment, William Borah and Robert Taft, who, if they had their way, might have thrown Roosevelt's plans of kilter. Luckily for the United States and the rest of the world, Roosevelt, with the help of his advisors, had the United States efficiently prepared by the time it needed to be. The new Arsenal of Democracy which as I just stated, was supportive of Great Brittan, France, and eventually the Soviets proved to be key to Hitler's eventual defeat.

Roosevelt was presented with an absolute reality through the unmeasurable importance of what he needed to do. He would take a firm stance opposing the axis powers as well as American isolationists such as Charles Lindberg and the America First Committee who were opposed to United States military involvement in this war. I myself hate war with a passion, but you must understand that Hitler and his allies represented an uncompromising evil that had to be dealt with both sternly and courageously.

You see, the America First Committee, although opposing war, was still wrong and would be quite a nuisance to Roosevelt's dire need to take action. This committee verbally attacked Roosevelt, stating that he was an evil warmonger. That is a pretty harsh criticism for a man who avoided war as long as possible and would become a vital ingredient to the defeat of the worst genocide case in modern world history. I must say that Franklin Delano Roosevelt was one incredible human being. Despite the distractions he was presented with, he was still able to prove his worth as these hurtful words would bounce off him like rubber. Roosevelt, through all of this, remained completely unfazed, determined, and confident in himself, his advisors, and the wisdom that these men would prove to possess for the purpose of defeating a legacy of an uncompromising human evil.

In January 1941, Roosevelt delivered his famous four freedoms speech. In this speech, he elaborated on his position that the United States must take on a moral responsibility for the human rights of all of the citizens of Earth. This man was so outstanding a president it boggles the mind! Continuing on, Roosevelt's building up of the United States military also, in an indirect way, caused significant growth for the United States economy. This would put, in effect, a very energetic social change throughout the rest of the war. This was partly due to the fact that Roosevelt had to put domestic issues on the back burner and make foreign policy his main focus. How Roosevelt was able to perform with such incredible responsibility is a direct reason why he is considered one of the best United States presidents in the history of America.

Soon, Hitler made what, in my opinion, was a fatal mistake. This of course was when Hitler's lusty greed would get the best of him and he commanded an attack on his Soviet ally Joseph Stalin. This dumb move would cause the Soviets to fight the NAZI forces fiercely. Before anyone knew it, Roosevelt was performing diplomatic relations with Joseph Stalin. This attack of Hitler', by the way, took place in June 1941. Roosevelt's immediate reaction to this German attack was to access the Lend Lease Act in order to aid the Soviets.

Roosevelt also saw to it that the United States Navy escorted allied convoys as far east as Great Britain. He also made it clear that he would shoot any of Hitler's ships or submarines if they dared mess with United States allies within the United States Navy zone. By this time, Roosevelt's brilliance in foreign matters was in full swing. But again, I remind you that at this time, the United States was still not officially entered into this war. You see, Roosevelt was simply setting up the chessboard. Soon, the United States would be helping the British to transport their fighter planes, by way of United States aircraft carriers between Great Britain and the Mediterranean war zones. Roosevelt was also advocating assistance at naval bases. Soon, Roosevelt would officially commit the United States to the side of their allies with a policy of All Aid Short of War.

By August of 1941, Winston Churchill was the Prime minister of Great Brittan. Roosevelt and Churchill were well underway and would soon establish what was known as the Atlantic Charter which was the first of several future war negotiations. Soon after, Roosevelt would give his secretary of war, Henry Stimson, an order to begin the planning for United States involvement in this war. This would lead to the development of the Victory Program where Roosevelt would work with one Albert Wedemeyer. Wedemeyer was the head of the new Victory Program. This program consisted of important discussions on estimates needed for the total mobilization of manpower, production, and logistics (logistics is the military science of procuring, maintaining, and transporting material and personnel) in order to vanquish the potential enemies of the United States. This new victory program set the plan to vividly increase aid to United States allies and also to produce 10 million soldiers, half of whom would be ready for military actions abroad in 1943. This course of action was planned just prior to the Japanese invasion of Pearl Harbor.

By 1941, Japan had conquered the remnants of Indo China. Roosevelt reacted by cutting off United States sales of oil to the Japanese, causing them to have their own oil crisis. Roosevelt then proceeded with extreme caution and he continued to negotiate with the Japanese despite their behavior. Roosevelt continued on by shifting the United States long range B-17 attack force to the Philippines. Just three days prior to the Pearl Harbor invasion, on December 4, 1941 there was a controversial article in the Chicago Tribune which revealed what was called rainbow 5. Rainbow 5, in basic terms, called for 10 million United States troops to invade Europe sometime in 1943, on the side of their allies Great Brittan, France, and the Soviet Union.

The problem with the Japanese Pearl Harbor invasion is obvious. No one was ready for this attack except for the Japanese themselves. Therefore, although Roosevelt was thorough in his efforts for the eventual United States involvement in the Second World War, no one, not even Roosevelt himself, saw it coming. However, on December 6, 1941, just one day before this invasion, Roosevelt did in fact receive a clue. Roosevelt received through United States intelligence an intercepted message from Japan and although this caused Roosevelt to be suspicious, as just stated, he was not prepared. However, on the day of December 6, 1941, Roosevelt did say to Harry Hopkins regarding this intercepted message, quote, "This means war."

So, on December 7, 1941 the Japanese fleet attacked the United States Pacific fleet at Pearl Harbor, Hawaii. This day for America in the 1940s, was the equivalent of the current generation's historic September 11, 2001, which occurred just under sixty years later. In this attack, the Japanese fleet was able to destroy sixteen United States warships, as well as most of the United States' deployed battleships; they also managed to kill approximately 2,400 American soldiers and civilians.

The Japanese commenced to strike a vital blow in the following weeks. They ended up conquering the Philippines despite United States naval deployments. They also conquered the British and the Dutch colonies in Southeastern Asia. In February 1942, they took Singapore and proceeded to advance through Burma and then to the borders of British-India; by May, they would sever the supply route to China. Before Japan executed these attacks, Roosevelt had given his famous Infamy speech, and thus gained even more support from the American public.

Roosevelt soon stated his case on how to continue to make progress in dealing with this worldwide mayhem. On December 11, 1941, Roosevelt and the United States would be forced into World War 2, because Germany and Italy had declared war on the United States. In late December, in the midst of the Japanese takeovers, Roosevelt would visit Churchill. These two vital leaders would then create a plan of an even stronger alliance between the United States, Great Brittan, The Soviet Union, and China. The main focus was not on Italy or Japan; these men came to the conclusion that Hitler's NAZI Germany was the main culprit and that they must be dealt with first and foremost. This new alliance was planned with the strategy that the German forces must be contained within the Soviet Union and northern Africa. Soon, a western European conflict would occur with the hopes of defeating Hitler and the German NAZI forces. Roosevelt, despite the fact that he was mostly concerned with Germany, was still cautious and did take actions to help the Chinese trounce Japanese forces.

This United States-Japanese confrontation would lead to a sort of American domestic mass hysteria. The United States public, as well as certain government officials, were wary of the possibility that the Japanese might take more aggressive actions. This was especially the case on the west coast of the United States. Because of the Americans' prominent fear of possible terrorist acts, espionage, or sabotage, Roosevelt did his best to make sure that he responded to these problems. So, in February of 1942 Roosevelt signed "Executive Order 9066" which imprisoned first generation Japanese who had immigrated to the United States. I must admit that this Executive Order 9066 does puzzle me. In further examination of this move, I found out some interesting facts. One, once these Japanese were detained, they were sent to what were called internment camps. Two, These Japanese prisoners were only held captive until the war was over. Three, former F.B.I. Director J. Edgar Hoover was opposed to this Executive order 9066 because he found it to be unconstitutional. Four, Roosevelt's wife, the former first lady Eleanor Roosevelt, was also opposed to this act and actually tried to convince her husband not to sign it.

At this point, we will discuss Franklin Delano Roosevelt's basic strategies of war. First of all, the Big Three leaders who would bring Hitler to his demise, were Franklin Delano Roosevelt, Winston Churchill, and Joseph Stalin. There was a significant fourth, Chiang Kai Shek of the Peoples Republic of China. The big three would work together and devise a plan on how to stop Hitler. They agreed to place United States and British troops in Western Europe, Soviets on the eastern front and finally, Chinese, American, and British forces would be set up in the Pacific.

The Arsenal of Democracy was a major war strategy for the advancement of about fifty billion dollars in supplies through the Lend Lease Deal. The amount in war supplies gave support to all United States allies. The United States war department suggested that the best route to take in order to overthrow Hitler was to invade German occupied France by traveling across the English Channel. Churchill expressed extreme concern for the number of casualties this move could potentially cause. He favored a more indirect method. This would be to advance northward from the Mediterranean Sea. Roosevelt did not favor this strategy at all. Stalin then suggested the opening of a western front as soon as conceivable, as most of the land battles in the war were fought in the Soviet Union from 1942 through 1944.

Soon, United States allies attacked French Morocco and Algeria. In June 1942, the United States Navy were victorious in the Battle of Midway. The Battle of Midway was a three-day long naval battle considered one of the most important of all of the Pacific World War 2 battles. The United States in this battle struck a fatal blow to the Japanese Navy. This battle was fought near Midway Atoll, a Midway island about one third of the way between Hawaii and Japan.

In November of 1942, United States allies continued on and attacked Sicily and ended up taking control from Hitler and Mussolini. This takeover by United States allies was a large-scale amphibious and airborne military battle. The fighting would last for about six weeks. Soon, the rest of Italy would be taken over by United States allies. By 1944, the U.S., with the assistance of Great Britain, started a bombing campaign that crushed all the major cities of Germany, as well as cut offtheir oil supplies. It would soon be decided by Roosevelt that General Dwight D. Eisenhower would head the allied cross channel invasion. This attack, led by General Eisenhower and United States allied forces, was the basis for the famous battle of D-Day. Eisenhower executed one of the most massive amphibious attacks in history. Almost 160,000 soldiers crossed the English Channel on June 6, 1944, landing in Normandy. This bloody battle would eventually be won by Eisenhower, the United States, and their allied forces. By August 1944, just about three million troops had landed on the beaches of Normandy. The United States allied forces consisted of troops from the countries of Canada, Great Brittan, France, Poland, Belgium, Greece, Czechoslovakia, the Netherlands, and Norway. Finally, and mercifully following this battle, Hitler soon met his demise and

Germany would be forced to surrender by early May of 1945.

Roosevelt would be elected to a fourth term as President of the United States. However, his health was deteriorating. After complaining of a headache, Franklin Delano Roosevelt died from a cerebral hemorrhage on April 12, 1945. Franklin Delano Roosevelt was dead at the age of 63.

I must say that Franklin Delano Roosevelt left behind one incredible legacy! What a great man he was! This man inherited an absolute mess when he began his tenure as president. He was presented with challenges of both domestic and foreign matters, thus the responsibility of having to deal with the Hitler NAZI war machine. And the competence he possessed to confront and exterminate this cause of extreme evil was nothing less than outstanding.

Franklin Delano Roosevelt in my opinion is a legend who was able to cure the depression and fiercely oppose Hitler. This man cured the social disease of his era—the social disease of genocide.

Roosevelt established the minimum wage, created Social Security, was a pioneer for the establishment of the United Nations, and he helped the employees of America with the establishment of unions for the corporations of America. These are four of the most fundamental establishments that have kept the United States of America a great nation. If it was not for this beautiful human being and his efforts, the United States could have crumbled due to the economic turmoil of the depression. If he did not perform his foreign policy exactly the way he did, I would not have been able to write this book and if I did, it might have been written in German. If he had not established unions for the workers of America, times would be much too difficult for the middle class. If he had not established Social Security, the elderly and the mentally ill would not have the services of which they so desperately need. The minimum wage has helped those who are not capable of paying for an education and has at least helped some to get by. And most vital of all, if Roosevelt did not help to start the establishment of the United Nations, the utopian dream would not be conceivable. I have not been fascinated with Franklin Delano Roosevelt up until the past few years, but the more I learn about this man, the more deeply I fall in love with him! Franklin Delano Roosevelt, my friends, is the best president the United States ever had!

Now that I am done praising my favorite president, I deem it necessary to send a direct message to President Obama. President Obama, you have quite a similar task to perform as Roosevelt did. When he was president, he was dealing with the incompetence of the Coolidge and Hoover administrations. Mr. President, you are dealing with the failures of the recent Bush Administration. You have inherited an unfounded war, the existence of prominent world evils, and a recession that could have been a depression if it was not for the recent corporate bailouts. I hereby state directly to you: you, my friend, have a shot at achieving greatness comparable to the greatness of F.D.R. If you could do half as good as he did, the United States and the rest of the world should be okay. President Obama, please don't feel pressured, I do realize that trying to live up to the legendary status of F.D.R. can be an overwhelming thought. But I know that you possess what the Democratic Party is in such dire need of: sincerity! I can tell that you mean it when you state that timeless creed that sums up the spirit of a people, "Yes, we can!"

At this juncture, it is once again time for me to make another point. But first, I must apologize to President Obama for my earlier support of John Edwards. Although I do realize that Obama being the cool dude he is would definitely respond with "Hey, no problem, man." You must understand that I was favorable of Edwards because of his stated concern for the Americans who are in dire state of poverty. Helping the poor is one of the most prominent reasons for my being a member of the Democratic Party. Although I was favorable of Edwards (A man I still like a lot) I was still very fond of both Hillary Clinton and Barack Obama. I was eager to see an African American or a woman become the president, but as I stated earlier, that is not how I vote. I simply felt at the time that Edwards was best fit for the problems of today's world. Now for the point I just said I was going to make: John Edwards was in favor, in an indirect manner, of a bailout for the poor people of America. Do you know why this view of Edwards did not get him elected? Because no one can make money from bailing out the poor! But why did the United States government agree to bailout these corporations which were in financial peril? I'll tell you: because it has a profound effect on the economic standing of America. Do you know what the sad thing is? We had to! Or at least we were led to believe that we had to! We better have had to! Because if not, we were just swindled! So, my question is, why don't we bail out the poor? The reason that this nation is lacking in compassion for those in poverty is because it is not "technically" necessary to help the poor because they do not have a profound effect on the economics of America. The reason we should help those in poverty is for one reason alone, yes my favorite word: "Morality."

Hey! Want to hear something interesting? I actually have a friend who lives in my birth city of Lowell, Massachusetts and his last name is Coolidge. And guess what? He is a direct relative of former president Calvin Coolidge! And here is the funny part! He is not proud of it at all! So, whenever I see my friend Coolidge, I jokingly say to him "Hey, where's Calvin?"

Here is another thought. I have already stated, at least in an indirect manner, that Republicans and Democrats should put aside their differences and get along. So what am I getting at? You see, Republicans and Democrats are not as different from one another as we may believe. Our differences for the most part are on domestic issues. I mean none of us like war, other than the extremely evil. And most of us love peace. So, why the heck can't we be more peaceful with one another? You could argue that we are not just different on domestic issues and state that one party throughout history has been more militarily aggressive than the other. But, of course, one party would be more militarily aggressive throughout history than the other. If not, that would be like everyone being the same height and weight. I mean, a coin can't land on both heads and tails, right? It's just the law of averages.

So in this political segment of *Vision of a Mental Patient*, I have done my best to state my case on both domestic and foreign issues. Obviously, through what you have read so far on domestic issues, I lean Democratic. With the possible acceptance of abortion, I feel that Democratic values ring true to my being. Once again, I must state that my prime reason for being favorable to Democratic ideals is that I simply feel that Republican ideals are just too detrimental to the poor people of America. But to tell you the truth, I really do not trust a lot of Democrats. And I also admire and like many Republicans, especially the ones I hang out with. Please realize that I am being as fair as I can possibly be. Why would I praise the foreign policies of Nixon, a Republican and a man who is not currently well-liked in America? Why would I criticize John F. Kennedy, a Democrat and a man who is admired in modern times? It is because of foreign policies! Get it? So this is my main point: I do not necessarily support all Democrats, I support the ideals of the Democratic Party. I hope through a thorough bipartisanship, we can help both the Republicans who want the best for their families who they love, but at the same time help those who are in poverty and the United States could be a politically correct machine that helps everyone! And this is why I am a democrat!

Here is something interesting! I began writing this political segment of this book on November 5, 2008. That was the first full day at the office for Barack Obama as president-elect of the United States. I am about to finish writing the political segment of this book and it is just past midnight, which makes today January 21, 2009. This is the first full day that Barack Obama is the President of the United States. Is this a coincidence? I think not! When you finish this book, you will know why!

Earlier tonight, as part of my research for proofreading this political segment, I once again watched one of my favorite movies of all time, *The Killing Fields*. Yes, the classic story of human evil vs. human good, as it pertained to the Cambodian Khmer Rouge genocide. While re-watching this movie earlier tonight, I noticed more details of this story. You see, it was a common belief that Richard Nixon was a very bad man. Sydney Shanberg, who was portrayed by Sam Waterson, was very disgusted with the foreign policy of Richard Nixon. I do realize that I could be subject to extreme criticism for my favorable views of the foreign policies of Richard Nixon. And believe me you, I completely understand why. I stated earlier that Nixon's order of attack on the National Front for the Liberation of Vietnam base in Cambodia, sadly, might have been a necessity. While watching the results of these attacks and the cover-ups that United States Army personnel carried out, it did in fact cause me to think it over! But I do believe that Vietnamese military intervention in Cambodia at this time was causing absolute mayhem. And my theory is that Nixon, although being a chronic rule breaker, may have had credible reason for this attack. I also believe that Nixon was aware of the rise of Pol Pot. I now remind you that Nixon did not start the Vietnam conflict; he inherited it. So, for now, I strongly stand by my support of the foreign policies of Richard Milhous Nixon. To be as fair as possible, I say to any of my readers that if you have a view on this matter, I am willing to have a discussion with; I promise to listen intently with an open mind. But please try not to be angry with me because I am simply just trying to figure this thing out.

To back up this point, I must once again stress that presidents may inherit problems and at times they have no choice but to cause death. Do you realize how many soldiers F.D.R. had to send into the battlefield and the guilt he must have felt? Or how many people must perish due to essential military political actions that can be basically chosen for reasons of simply causing a lesser evil than that of the contrary military action, which must be made?

You see, I am not a religious man, but I do have many religious friends whom I love dearly. And may I add that these religious friends of mine are very decent people. I myself do not believe that Jesus Christ is god. But you know what? Jesus Christ, in my view, was a great man who did a lot for the cause of morality in this world.

You see, Christ did say a very good thing, when he stated that if someone smacks you on the side of your face, you should turn your cheek and let him or her smack you on the other side of your face. This is how to avoid warlike behavior. But my question is, due to the realities of human history, what if you were dealing with a Hitler, a Pot, or a Habyarimana? This type of person will not just smack you on one side of your face they might just shave it off! And if you turn your cheek, they will shave that one off too! Reality is reality! Unfortunately, there are people out there who represent an uncompromising evil! War started a long time ago and animals and mammals alike do possess violence in their instincts. Once this uncompromising war machine started rolling, the only way to respond was to try to protect the innocent, especially the women and children! I am not afraid to admit that I am a very emotional man. As a matter of fact, I am proud of it! I am usually in tears at the ending of the movie *The Killing Fields*. It breaks my heart that these loving, smiling good people, the children, the women, the men, and their courage to go to any length to protect their loved ones, are forced to face such human tragedy! Love and human understanding is the only way to cure the disease of war!

Now, I must make even another point: First of all, if someone believes in god and it helps them, than that is great. But do you realize that most of the wars being fought on Earth, are holy wars? Yes, people killing one another in the name of something that is supposed to be perfect! And don't get me wrong, if there was a perfect god, then that would be great. But the way I see it, the whole god concept causes people to see the bad in others rather than the good. This is because people are comparing themselves and one another to perfection. I always hear people complaining about other people like that guy smokes, or that guy cheated on his wife, or that guy is a drunk. This is a verbal casting of a stone on a supposed sinner, something we all are. If people could see the good in one another rather than the bad, we could all get along peacefully! Now I ask you this! Why is there a devil? We are taught that there is one side and another side. This is the basis of war!

Think about this: What if we were visited by alien life forms and they witnessed the extreme savagery that exists in the human race? They would bear witness to the mass killings of men, women, and children, leaving people in poverty drinking

VISION OF A MENTAL PATIENT

and sleeping under a bridge in sub zero weather; basic homicide, the throwing of an unwanted infant into a plastic bag and disposed of in a dumpster being left there to suffocate, and they would also witness genital mutilation of the sort being carried out in the Sudan! Sorry to be so explicit, but these are acts common to this planet. Yes, this stuff happens all of the time! And then these aliens would find out we have a perfect god and an imperfect devil, and that we all agree to kill! Make your own conclusion!

How about this scenario? We are expected to have an un-denying faith in a perfect god when genocide, rape, sickening greed, and other acts of extreme evil are so commonplace. What if a person dedicates their life to love, compassion, and understanding though he does not believe in god? What happens then? Do they burn in hell? If a person goes around killing innocent men, women, and children or what have you, and then says, "Praise god!" do they go to heaven? We are told that the reasons evil acts are carried out on this planet is because god gave us free will or the devil made me do it. My question is: What about the free will of the victims of these acts? What about the free will of the six million Jews who were killed in the Holocaust? And then I hear, "his will, not mine, be done." Well, if we are supposed to go in the way of god's will, then that throws free will right out the window. So what is it, free will, or god's control? We are also told, at least indirectly, that we are not supposed to try to save the world because that is god's place and we must not defy the glory of god. We will always never be able to achieve the glory of god. Therefore, we are expected to have an undying faith because there are a few movies featuring Charlton Heston which prove that god is real, and will save us through his glory. What glory? It is any human being's place, to contribute as much as he or she can, to the glory of saving the world. We want the place we live in to prosper. If god will send you to hell for trying to save the world, thus stealing his perfect glory, then god is wrong. I am sorry to my religious friends, but this whole god thing is an insult to a person's intelligence. Are you catching the drift yet?

There have been plenty of books about not believing in god; for instance, there is the *God Delusion* by Richard Dawkins. I am not even close to being the only atheist. Therefore, no one better dare say I am immoral because I do not believe in god. I am a lover of human good and compassion to the end. When I was a mental patient, I had delusions of being burned, stabbed, raped, and humiliated. And I have the right to believe in love and human understanding over some vision of a non-existent perfection, of which so many wars are being fought to this day! We are taught not to sin; what are sins? Murder is certainly a sin, but if you drink, smoke, or have too much fun, you are a bad person. God says we cannot commit these trivial sins. I say we cannot commit real sins like genocide or genital mutilation. And I do not believe for one second that the devil made them do it. You know who made them do it? Allow me to tell you! They made themselves do it! I love people to the absolute extreme and I beg of you not to frown upon me because my experiences in the psyche wards have caused me to be an atheist. This is my belief for *myself* and I stress, "myself." I do not believe in god, I believe in good. So there, I got it out. Keep reading! Now for the premise of this political segment of *Vision of a Mental Patient*. This premise is the basis of the utopian dream. President Obama, Vice President Biden, Secretary of State Rodham Clinton, feel these words! I have a dream, a utopian dream, a peaceful world where we are all free to dream. Where the Earth will no longer just be called the Earth, but will become the United Countries of Earth and the United Nations will be the prime government. And the United States of America will once again shine through in its efforts for humanity and once again, the United States will be the beacon of light and hope for humankind from its return to prominence. The United States of America will then become the capital of the United Countries of Earth from a peace that grew from a tree thought to be dead, and this peace will last forever. Yes, my friends, my utopian dream will become our utopian dream. And to bring this political segment to a close, I will now say, as Forest Gump would say, "And that's all I have to say about that!

PART TWO: THE MONOLITH
AN APOLOGY

On a beautiful autumn day in 1989, I was enjoying lunch with my father at the Owl Diner on Appleton Street, in my birth city of Lowell, Massachusetts. My father and I began to make friendly conversation and we somehow got onto the subject of astronomy. I attempted to elaborate to him the early dementia I was experiencing through my newly found *Vision of a Mental Patient* which, at the time, was well underway. My father and I agreed on a theory that there could be a mirror in the center of the universe where everything composes, decomposes, and reflects, both infinitely and infinitesimally.

I told him that I had recently been listening to the Don McLean album called *American Pie* which would have surprised my fellow metal head friends who, by the way, I was also having conversations with from time to time regarding this new dementia I was experiencing. This newly found dementia was causing me to proceed with carrying out my newly found vision. In this conversation with my father, I mentioned the Don McLean song "Vincent" which is about the famous artist Vincent Van Gogh. Van Gogh unfortunately was not appreciated in his time, which I believe, is due to the fact that people cannot recognize beauty until tragedy occurs. The part of the song that I told my father about was the line "When no hope was left in sight on that starry, starry night, you took your life as lovers often do, but I could have told you Vincent, this world was never meant for one as beautiful as you."

You see, Van Gogh may have been experiencing something similar to what I was experiencing, but unfortunately, in his time he did not have the resources that exist today. Hence, he was rendered helpless trying to carry out his vision. Van Gogh was so in love and had experienced such a failure in love, that it would ultimately lead to his suicide. Van Gogh was a very sad man because he was not able to get anyone to listen to his personal vision, and this is due to the fact that in any society, if you say something fake people will commend you, but if you speak from the heart, you will be criticized. Before Van Gogh committed suicide, he made one last desperate attempt to get someone to listen to him. What he did was he severed of one of his ears and mailed it to someone simply trying to say, "Please listen?" So, in the memory of Vincent Van Gogh, I must present some more lyrics to you. There will be a lot more lyrics in this Monolith part two segment than there was in Politics. In this brief apology, I will present the lyrics to three songs. One of my own that was a Deallegiance song, "Vincent" by Don Mclean, and I will also present the lyrics written by a popular 80s band called Asia that will help to get my apology across to those I may have hurt in the past. So, I now humbly ask you in the memory of those such as Van Gogh or anyone else who has suffered for their sanity due to unfulfilled dreams of morality, to please listen and take me very seriously. I now present the lyrics to "Vincent" by Don Mclean.

Starry, starry night, paint your palette blue and grey
   Look out on a summer's day, with eyes that know the darkness in my soul
      Shadows on the hills, sketch the trees and the daffodils
         Catch the breeze and the winter chills, in colors on the snowy linen land
            Now I think I understand, what you tried to say to me
               And how you suffered for your sanity and how you tried to set them free
They did not listen they did not know how, perhaps they'll listen now
   Starry, starry night, flaming flowers that brightly blaze
      Swirling clouds in violet haze, reflect in Vincent's eyes of China blue
         Colors changing hue, morning fields of amber grain
            Weathered faces lined in pain, are soothed beneath the artists loving hand
               And now I understand what you tried to say to me
And how you suffered for your sanity, and how you tried to set them free
They did not listen they did not know how, perhaps they'll listen now
   For they could not love you but still your love was true
      And when no hope was left inside on that starry, starry night
         You took your life as lovers often do but I could have told you Vincent
This world was never meant for one as beautiful as you

VISION OF A MENTAL PATIENT

Starry, starry night portraits hung in empty halls
Frameless heads on nameless walls
With eyes that watch the world and can't forget
Like the strangers that you've met, the ragged men in ragged clothes
The silver thorn of bloody rose, lie crushed and broken on the virgin snow
Now I think I know what you tried to say to me
And how you suffered for your sanity and how you tried to set them free
They would not listen they're not listening still, perhaps they never will

So, anyway, this conversation I had with my father at the Owl Diner came to an end and unfortunately, we have never discussed such a deep subject since. At this time, my vision was in its infancy, but from that moment on, this new vision of mine went from a mere interest to an absolute obsession. However, I must admit that when I was in the eighth grade, my art teacher tried to teach us about Vincent Van Gogh and played the Don Mclean song "Vincent" on her record player, and do you know what we did? Shamefully, we all laughed at it and then my poor art teacher said, "They'll never listen." But now I am willing to listen and I am also willing to tell.

At the beginning, I would only discuss this vision with a select few of my friends. Of course, the first friends of mine that I commenced to discuss this vision with and who were also quite interested and inspired by this newly found vision, were Bob and Dennis from the band Manifest of which I was a member at the time. This vision would soon grow, and more and more of my friends would begin to show an interest in this undeniable dementia I was experiencing and unable to ignore. This obsession would grow thoroughly with the passing of time and before I knew it, this vision would be a common topic of discussion with most of my friends by the early 1990s. Eventually, it would appear as though this vision had failed and I would even at times be made fun of for my devotion to this dementia. It wouldn't be long before I was admitted as a mental patient.

Two of my favorite movies, as well as two of my favorite books, are *2001: a Space Odyssey* and its sequels the novel *2010 Odyssey 2,* and the movie *2010: The Year We Make Contact,* which, I believe, is one of the most underrated movies of all time, basically for the reason that no one understands it. *2001: a Space Odyssey* was directed by Stanley Kubrick and *2010: The Year We Make Contact* was directed by Peter Hyams; these two books were written by Arthur C. Clarke who happens to be my favorite author. In *2001: a Space Odyssey*, there was a mysterious object which was supposedly buried on the moon ages ago by an alien race. This object was the monolith. When I saw this movie, my dementia was in full swing. So, for the first time, I realized just what the monolith was. This monolith could be the mirror in the center of the universe! But to my surprise, the monolith is not a mirror, but instead it is a magnet. Or is it both? Presently as I am writing this book, I am starting to comprehend the reason that this object is a magnetic and reflective force! Later, in this Monolith segment, I will more fully explain this vision which I know is a reality today. My friends and I would soon label this vision as "Knowing." The basis of this knowing vision is something which will later be elaborated on. You see, this vision is based on my favorite theory that I have ever come up with. This is the theory of connection. I must ask you, have you ever had thoughts that you understood in your mind but were not able to explain in words? Have you ever looked into another person's face and fathomed some subconscious thought? If so, you have connected with someone! If you do not yet grasp what I am saying, just keep reading and you will, my friends; you most certainly will. I figured something out a long time ago. What did I figure out? Well, my friends who were witnesses to the experiences of the early days of this vision will be shocked when they find out what we were actually figuring out. For years, I would have these thoughts through this vision, but I was never able to explain these thoughts into an appropriate text. I am thrilled to say that through many stints in mental hospitals and many manifestations of horror from those who are opposed to this vision, I have since achieved a supreme happiness and a surety that this vision will be a successful one.

Through my senses and a realization of more senses, as well as my subconscious mind, I have tapped into the collective subconscious and have caused something wonderful. I have now found the words to explain my vision as well as a breakthrough that could potentially lead to utopia. But be patient my friends and you shall bear witness to a primary passage.

At this point, I deem it essential to apologize to those I have hurt in my younger years. You see, as a teenager, I prided myself on not being a follower. However, the truth is, at times, I was mean to my peers and I have done some things which I am not very proud of. Through the intense suffering that I have experienced as a mental patient, I have come to realize this fact: No one is perfect! So, to those I have hurt, I now inform you that I have suffered immensely and there is a possibility that some of my acts may have been carried out for reasons of compassion, but at this point, this cannot be fully comprehended.

Once again, it is time for me to present some more lyrics to you. These lyrics are dedicated to everyone I know or knew of as a youth and into my teenage years, including those who may have hurt me. So, I say to those that I have hurt, that I am sincerely and desperately sorry. You know who you are, so I ask "Can't we all just get along?" These are the lyrics from a band that was huge in the 1980s; this band is Asia and this song is called "Heat of the Moment."

I never meant to be so bad to you!
One thing I said that I would never do!
One look from you and I would fall from grace!

And that would wipe the smile right from my face!
Do you remember when we used to dance?
And incidence arose from circumstance!
One thing led to another we were young!
And we would scream together songs unsung!
It was the heat of the moment!
Telling me what your heart meant!
The heat of the moment shone in your eyes!
And now you find yourself in '82!
The disco hotspots hold no charm for you!
You can't concern yourself with bigger things!
You catch the pearl and ride the dragon wings!
It was the heat of the moment!
Telling me what your heart meant!
The heat of the moment shone in your eyes!
And when your looks are gone and you're alone!
How many nights you sit beside the phone!
What were the things you wanted for yourself?
Teenage ambitions you remember well!

Little do you realize how much sense the lyrics and basic text of this book will make once I have explained to you this vision. As for those who have already been a part of this vision, you may have an idea already, but you are not fully aware yet. First, you must understand that this vision is in the subconscious of us all already and it has been for quite a while. I call this the collective subconscious, which we are all bonded by through a connection. In this Monolith segment, I will explain to you, through science and nature, the imminent reality of something wonderful. Before I wrap up this brief, yet thoroughly essential apology, I must leave you with the lyrics to another Deallegiance song of which I wrote the music and lyrics all by my lonesome. I wrote this song at the age of seventeen in 1990. This song is about the Monolith and more that has not yet been elaborated. I now present to you the lyrics to "Center of the Universe." Please enjoy!

Odious yet true to us we grow our trust
Ominous predominance life's foe to thus
Seeing only what can't be seen from our own eyes
Holding on to golden seams that feel the sky
Center of the universe where we reverse
Restitution paves its way through the broken curse
Seeing deeply into ourselves without our eyes
Showing each other what matters first leaving the lies
The fallen angel flies towards the new sun
We felt the land now feel the sea so we'll breathe as one
Feel the love that sets you free to the forgotten child
She was born before she'll be born again in the un-wild
Embrace and then disperse the only way to die
Purest face is camerad in for your open mind
Together we stand universal wide plan of our own kind
Reaping life a soul is free through what we find
Engraved contributions from a shining star
Sends my retribution to a land afar
Un-scathed beginnings to life for what we are
Sends me a passage in the sacred heart

If I am to take on the responsibility of my actions, then I must achieve mass approval. But I am jumping too far ahead. The lyrics to "Center of the Universe," as well as all other aspects of my message, will be properly compensated and comprehended in due time, but I have already told you that quite a few times. I will now commence with the rigorous and extensive elaboration of my—and hopefully, our vision. So please enjoy yourself in the reading of The Monolith.

THE COLLECTIVE SUBCONSCIOUS

Hello and welcome to the start of my scientific theories about the ultimate relationships of the human realm and beyond. This is the Collective Subconscious segment, where we will peer into the supposed unknown and where we will begin to discuss the premises of my many scientific theories. In this portion, we will thoroughly explore the vastness of the human mind as it pertained to both the personal and the collective subconscious.

There will be much discussion about the pioneer theorist to the concept of the subconscious: Carl Gustav Jung. Before we proceed to indulge in the concepts of Jung and myself as relative to the personal and collective subconscious, and also before I describe exactly what the subconscious is (seeing that some of you may not presently be aware of just what the subconscious is), I will start off with a brief chronologic summary of important factual events in the life of the subconscious mentor, Carl Gustav Jung.

Carl Gustav Jung was born on July 26, 1875, in Kessewil, Switzerland. He was the fourth and only surviving child of Paul Achilles Jung and Emile Preiswerk. Following the Great War (World War 1), Carl Gustav Jung became a nomad but he was still able to live extravagantly due to his wife's inheritance. Jung's wife was one Emma Rauschenbach, a daughter of one of the wealthiest families in all of Switzerland. Emma would give birth to five children and their names were Agethe, Gret, Franz, Marianne, and Helene. Jung practiced paganism, although he would tell others that he was a Christian. Jung was a close friend of another pioneer in psychology, the famous Sigmund Freud. Although Freud was not as pioneering in subconscious concepts, he would prove to be a vital asset to some of the concepts of Jung. Jung would further advance and promote possibilities deemed beneficial through the accessing and the awareness of the subconscious mind. Sadly, the great and brilliant Carl Gustav Jung would pass away on June 6, 1961 at the age of 85.

Before we prepare to indulge in the paranormal phenomena of both the personal and collective subconscious abstractions, I must first inform you of the basics of just what the subconscious is, and the difference between the personal and the collective realms of this inner outer brain conceptualization.

You see, the way I see it, the personal subconscious is the part of your brain that possesses the dream center and the vastly deep thoughts we all have, but are not consciously aware of until such thoughts reenter the conscious mind. To elaborate in simpler terms, just think about everything you know, have learned, and experienced in your lifetime. Now try to realize that you do not always think about everything you know and have experienced. Therefore, when you are thinking of one matter in your consciousness, all other thoughts of knowledge are settled back in your subconscious. In other words, the part of your mind that holds all you have known or experienced excluding your present conscious thought is the personal subconscious.

The collective subconscious on the other hand, is the mind vortex which represents the relationships of us all relative to the personal subconscious. In other words, the collective subconscious is the subconscious relationship between everyone. I will attempt to explain these brain relationships throughout this segment.

You see, Jung was an absolute genius and he may have been smarter than the legendary Albert Einstein. I believe that Einstein may have had one of if not the most intelligent conscious minds, but I have come to believe that some of Einstein's mistakes were due to his not fathoming the benefits of tapping into subconscious activity. By tapping into both the personal and the collective subconscious, it may be possible to fill the human mind!

According to many, the theory of evolution and the different brain types that exist in mammals and animals present a prime significance to the development of the human mind and its subconscious capabilities. Take, for example, the R-complex, or, in more common terms, the reptilian brain. This R-complex brain type adheres to the nervous system's instincts and it is commonly identified with the aggressive or violent type behavior of the organism that possesses it.

The mammalian brain, on the other hand, has a more social and emotional type of demeanor. And then of course there is the primate brain, which can also be labeled as the neo-cortex. This neo-cortex brain type is the most high functioning brain type and it has achieved capabilities such as language and intellect. The primate brain, through its complex systems of mind function, has also caused a further comprehension of our human senses.

This neo-cortex as well as other brain types has (according to scientific theory) further grown and developed from millions upon millions of years ago, up until modern day. The human mind has developed from the simplest of brain types over a long duration, and we have only touched the surface as to the mysteries and the vastness of its relationships to all of existence.

Egyptian mythology (which we will later discuss in the Ancient Egypt segment) has a different hypothesis regarding the development of the human brain. They believed in the sun god Ra who is often compared to Jehovah. According to this Egyptian theory, all progress achieved toward the promotion of consciousness have a detrimental effect on pagan gods.

You may recall in the movie *Raiders of the Lost Ark* where the main character Indiana Jones was in possession of what is called the staff of Ra. He also had a cryptic medallion which is directly related to the actions that Ra was said to have carried out. You see, at a certain time of day when the sun is in correct position, legend has it that in an ancient underground desert tomb in the lost city of Tanis, the staff of the sun god Ra is held up vertically with the cryptic medallion centered on top of it, the sun would send a light wave into the center of this medallion, thus transforming this light wave into a laser. This laser would then hit a point on a small replica of this ancient city. It is at this point of location within this city replica where the Ark of the Covenant could be found.

Tanis was an ancient Egyptian city in the northeastern Nile Delta supposedly buried by a huge sandstorm and erosion activity since. The Ark of the Covenant was previously placed in the Temple of Solomon, the first Temple of the Biblical Israelites. Soon after, the Ark would be moved to another location. This location was none other than the lost city of Tanis.

This movie *Raiders of the Lost Ark*, although dubbed as fiction, is based on religious fact pertaining to relevant artifacts. For those of you who are not aware of what the Ark of the Covenant is, it is a sacred vessel said to contain stone fragments from the original tablets of the Ten Commandments.

After reading the end of my Genocides and Foreign Policy portion and seeing for the first time my beliefs on the god concept, you might be wondering why I am speaking of religious artifacts. You will later understand why. Are you in suspense yet? Keep reading!

As my dementia grew into a vision, I nearly drove myself crazy with what I call the "Sense of Possibilities." This sense of possibilities was produced through my subconscious relative to the collective subconscious. I realized, through my studies of Jung and his coinciding to my dementia, that everything in existence is equal.

In order to further elaborate, I must reveal, for the first time in this segment, one of my many scientific theories. This is the theory of scientific equivalency. The premise of this theory is that the universe is endless and as you may already know, the prefix uni means one. Therefore, due to the fact that the universe is endless, it is equal to one. I have come to this realization because the subconscious and the collective subconscious directly relate to its surroundings and the vastness of the beyond.

Einstein believed that all entities in existence were equal to a particular number with a decimal value added to it. I think Einstein believed in this strict number relative to our universe because he felt that the universe was limited. It is my belief that the universe, in being equal to the capabilities of the human mind, does represent the infinite, thus the totality of universal existence being equal to one.

You must understand that our surrounding conceptions of existence are continuous, thus meaning that there are no limitations to its boundaries. However, the conscious mind, although being equal to one, is only aware of its present surroundings. The main sense of the original five senses, which promotes our conscious comprehension of our present environmental surroundings, is the sense of sight. It is the other four senses which have the ability to fathom things in a more instinctual manner. I will further elaborate the theory of scientific equivalency throughout this entire Monolith part two segment. By the time you finish reading this entire part two portion, you will understand the full basis of scientific equivalency.

Carl Jung termed the subconscious as the unconscious, which in my view, has the same definition. What Jung's close friend the famous Sigmund Freud would dub as the unconscious Jung would call the personal unconscious. To avoid confusion, from this point on I will refer to the unconscious as the subconscious.

You see, because of the unlimited depths of the personal and collective subconscious and the hypothesis that this concept is equal to one, this subconscious brain function and the other actions of the human mind has stored within itself all of our life experiences of the past. All of the feelings you have through your senses are comprehended through your nervous system, which stems from your spinal chord's connection to your brain. Through what is called the cerebral cortex (a layer of grey matter which exists in the cerebrum, which takes action through your coordination of sensory and motor information), this mind function is partly manifested. The cerebrum is a large portion of the brain located in the upper front section; it is directly related to your sensory perceptions.

You see, there are subdivisions in the human mind. Therefore, all thoughts and experiences through your senses relative to your personal subconscious are divided into our concepts and dimensions of time. This is a natural organic occurrence which reacts and coincides with your and my brain chemistry. Furthermore, I ask you a simple question: Have you ever sat in a chair and not realized that you were uncomfortable until your back began to ache? This is due to the personal subconscious.

Furthermore, how does a newborn mammal (other than human, of course) know how to do certain things without ever being taught? How does a spider know how to weave its web at such early stages of its lifespan? This, my friends, is due to instincts. I strongly believe that instincts are a direct result of a producing of actions through both the personal and the collective subconscious. My dementia and my vision are direct results of my understanding of instinctual processed methods that stemmed from my tapping into the two realms of the subconscious.

VISION OF A MENTAL PATIENT

For writing this book, it was required that I did a lot of reading and something often happens to me while I am reading, and I wonder if the same thing happens to you. Have you ever been reading something when you start to think of something else, hence, you were rendered unable to comprehend what you have just read? The words you have read while this occurs go directly into your subconscious. Believe it or not, I have recalled things in literature which went straight into my subconscious. I have acquired this ability due to my awareness of subconscious instinct.

You see, when you are reading, you are conscious; yet, you are less conscious than you may think. There is still much to be learned from this, but I will share with you my discoveries on this topic as thoroughly as possible.

Another activity that could be accessed to grasp further subconscious paranormal actions and have a greater understanding of the personal and the collective subconscious is watching television. A very smart man, by the name of Robert Sheldrake, displayed an interesting analogy between the relationships of brain memory functions and the viewing of moving pictures on television. His elaboration went as follows: Imagine you are viewing a television for the first time, with no prior knowledge of what a television is; your thoughts would be primordial and you might assume that there are little miniature people inside this television; this would cause you to have a different conscious to subconscious thoughts than what you would normally experience.

You see, television works by unscrambling codes sent in wavelengths through man-made satellites in outer space. Now, relate that thought to my theory of scientific equivalency. Understand that television is all over the world and often times, people are viewing the same things, yet on different wavelengths that emanate from outer space. The concept of the collective subconscious, which was first perceived by Carl Jung, cannot fit into a single mind. Therefore, television has a major effect on the collective subconscious. You may recall as a young child staring into a television showing that static like snow which appears when you have no frequency. Think back to that type of thought process and you will return to a more vivid understanding of your own personal subconscious. Far-fetched, isn't it? But believe me, this is credible information.

I believe it more than likely that the entire process of human evolution exists within the totality of the collective subconscious. Jung also believed this to be true. As a matter of fact, it was theorized by Jung that this could be proven, thus a vivid manifestation of such concepts into every day common human activity. Jung thought of two possibilities how human evolution could be produced within the collective subconscious, One, through our instinctual behaviors and two, through images in our inner mind which Jung would term as primordial images and archetypes.

An archetype is the pattern of origin of all things in existence. You see, Jung, like me, was aware of the subconscious activities of the psyche. Therefore, Jung and I acquired the ability to comprehend our archetypes from the outside in and from the inside out (You could also term this concept relative to the infinite and the infinitesimal). This process is along the same lines as an infant's developmental relationship with his or her parents. I believe that not only is the personal subconscious strengthened when we become aware of it, but it is likely even stronger when we are born.

A vital ingredient for the comprehension of the personal and the collective subconscious is obviously through the examinations of our dreams. I wholeheartedly agree with Jung when he stated that the subconscious comes prior to the conscious. This theory of Jung's was contrary to that of Freud's hypothesis. In the most basic of terms, consciousness is the product of the subconscious.

In conclusion, dreams could be considered a connection of the subconscious and the conscious of both the personal and the collective realm (but more so in the personal). Jung felt that everything in the subconscious will eventually emerge through the pattern of the personal imprint of the archetype relative to the conceptualizations of reality, which will subdivide in the process of our human understandings of the time concept. I can even take this theory one step further. I believe that this pre-explained theory of Jung on the manifestations of the personal subconscious will indeed promote itself further, thus a full manifestation of the entire Earth's collective subconscious.

Experiences could be further comprehended if we could somehow promote the total archetype pattern relative to the dream process. You must understand that we do not only progress in our lifestyles from our interpretations of our past experiences; we are also progressive through actions we take in the future. I robustly believe that both the personal and the collective subconscious has an even more paramount relationship with our past, present, and future concepts of the equilibrium of mind, time, and space. Remember that, it is important to the totality of my vision!

Since there have not been many pioneers in the scientific study of the three forms of consciousness—meaning the collective subconscious, personal subconscious, and basic consciousness and their relationships of the psyche to the premises of inner and outer existence, the absolution of this concept has its limits due to the complexities of society.

As far as I can see, dreams represent the basis of a relationship to the domains of the personal and the collective subconscious. Now, I did not coin the term collective subconscious. However, I do hope to be the next pioneer for the promotion of this brand of mind contemplation. If in fact I am rendered able to promote this type of mind function, it would be essential that I put a huge emphasis on dreams.

You see, it is because of pioneers such as Jung that we understand the dream concept relative to the vastness of mind, space, and time. This particular type of mind motivation could reap incredibly substantial benefits in more ways than one could perceive at this time. Believe it or not, observances within the scientific community have showed evidence that animals and mammals like ourselves may have the capability to access images that have evolved across the history of the given species.

This is along the same lines as the relationship between the human mind and human evolution in which I previously mentioned.

An interesting occurrence which has happened to me from time to time and may have happened to you on occasion is our semi-attainable ability to have dreams that would actually take place in the future. This is a form of extra sensory perception (E.S.P.) or in simpler terms, psychic ability. This phenomenal occurrence is a direct result of just how the personal and collective subconscious have the uncanny aptitude to subdivide our in-taken human data, as it is applied to our dimension of time transmitted through our senses.

Somehow, this psychic ability is processed through this act of subdivision with a coinciding action to our brain chemistry; remember that our minds are equal to the vastness of time and space. There are many subscribers to this brand of conceptualization, but to actually prove it is much easier said than done. It is my goal to educate you regarding this thought process and manifest a full comprehension of this phenomenal mind function.

I myself have definitely experienced extra sensory perception in my dreams, and also in my conscious state. I do understand the fact that my word is not enough to prove such an implausible claim, so bear with me as I continue to elaborate.

These psychic thoughts which I have experienced from time to time are hidden deep in the personal subconscious until they secrete from the depths of the mind; and there you have it, a psychic thought is born. The obvious reason for my assumption that these thoughts do originate within the deep subconscious, is simply due to the fact that I cannot consciously predict an event without subconscious intervention.

You see, through the relationships of the three forms of consciousness (the personal subconscious, the collective subconscious, and basic consciousness) and the role of personal subconscious to cause these thoughts to take form prior to the related future event, it is only our permanent consciousness to reality within the timeframe of the now which is insufficient for the complete understanding of the subdividing brain methods that carry this process out. Up until this point in time, no human in history has been able to fully develop the intricate actions of the inner mind that perform this paranormal function.

Could other species of Earth have a functional dream process as such? The answer is a resounding yes! As a matter of fact, animals and mammals that have not even been subject to the changes in their forms as humans have over the course of evolution have been proven within the scientific community to have a similar function of the dream process.

As for humans like you and me, we experience what is called rapid eye movement sleep (R.E.M.). During our usual course of sleep, we humans will experience R.E.M. sleep approximately thirteen percent of the time. Dreams during R.E.M. sleep will usually be more vivid, which is why I believe we dream frequently before we awaken. Non-R.E.M. sleep is much more lacking in detail and it tends to be more so illogical. This is because non-R.E.M. sleep is deeper in the personal subconscious, thus being less fathomable.

It has been determined that in other Earthly species the newborns will tend to dream more frequently. This determining factor supports my claim that when we are young (especially in infancy) we are more subconscious. You see, an infant requires more sleep; they usually will sleep two-thirds of the time and fifty percent of that sleep will be R.E.M. sleep. It is conceivable that other species could have similar dream functions as we do, but that is also dependent on brain type.

Why don't we briefly examine the effects of lack of sleep? You see, when a person attempts to stay awake for a long duration, he or she will often experience disorientation. Although not stated by those who study this phenomena, I do feel that just like any brain function, this is a direct result of the equilibrium of mind to time and space, and that is a testament and a representation of the basis of my theory of scientific equivalency, which shall be fully manifested in due time. Another result from lack of sleep is symptoms such as paranoia and visual hallucination. It is also quite possible that when a person is in this state of mind, he or she might fall into small fragments of R.E.M. sleep and not be completely consciously aware of it. So I ask, have you ever been half-asleep and could hear your radio or television and were somehow able to comprehend it while in this state? That would be the brink of R.E.M. sleep.

Oftentimes, dreams appear to be meaningless and without reason. However, humans like you and me are lacking in our adaptive capabilities to "connect" with our senses in order to fathom the message behind the dream. Furthermore, a dream could theoretically be applied to reality through an analogy of, let's say, a riddle. This riddle could be difficult to comprehend and due to its consistent obscurity, one will often draw a blank. The theory that I am apt to subscribe to is that any dream you have, whether being faint or vivid, somehow can be relative to some kind of relationship you have in your life. Of course, this is an interactive process between the three forms of consciousness.

Another method of significance is the method of simply processing obscure dreams during consciousness. You see, one could think of people and objects in dreams as symbols. Carl Jung had a book called *Symbols of Transformation* which was obscure in makeup, but it did at times apply this type of dream examination. When I discovered this Jung literary piece, I was in the early stages of my dementia relative to my vision. As a matter of fact, it was in the Lowell, Massachusetts Library, where I discovered this book. However, if you go to the Lowell library, you likely will not find this book, due to the fact that I stole it. I took this symbol of transformation and I entered it into my personal subconscious, resulting in a more rapid progression of dementia. I was seventeen years old when I found this book and I had very little conscious idea of the ramifications that would eventually manifest from Jung's personal subconscious to my personal subconscious, to my consciousness, and eventually to the collective subconscious.

VISION OF A MENTAL PATIENT

Moving on, a symbol can be a variety of things. You see, etymology is a study of the histories of lingual form carried out by process of tracing its history. I want you to remember this word when you commence to read the Language of the Mad segment. You see, this word is a symbol, yes, a symbol of transformation.

We have now come to the point where, for the fourth time in this Monolith part two portion, I will once again display some more lyrics to you. This will be the lyrics to the title track of the second Deallegiance demo tape, conveniently called *Symbol of Transformation*. This song was inspired by Carl Jung, our comprehensions of his message, and our love of his conceptualizations. So I now present "Symbol of Transformation."

Redirect your mind, see through all of their lies
pay back for what they have done, they have destroyed the god sun
now we will suffer inner loss, we mustn't learn to pay their cost
look into the outer line, you will not believe the sight you find
Symbol! Symbol of transformation is the way that we have begun
we must join and combine and destroy the evil mind
fight for what is your own, Satan wants your soul to be known
Peace of mind I will make for you, I'll take your soul through
Its all we knew, inside of you, please see through
Here I am burning for the wrong that I have done
Twisting and turning there's nowhere left to run
Our father is here now, stares through to my soul
memories and fear now it's time to pay their toll
Playing out a whim without a line, our blood is flowing just like wine
I see the black holes in your eyes, total oneness new sun surprise
I don't know what I will find, and the sea beyond is blind
Ponder on what I have left behind, contacted soul humankind
You see that I trust in you, you must see what is true
There nothing left for me to do, to restore truth for insane proof
to restore truth, returned to youth
Here I am burning for the wrong that I have done
Twisting and turning there's nowhere left to run
Our father is here now, stares through to my soul
Memories and fear now it's time to pay their toll
Living my life performs best test, open mind sender for the rest
you never know how I do feel, you only know how to fail
Wake up, understand what is real
You should already know through what you feel
Nothingness is turning in your mind, craziness over human kind
Am I thinking the right way? Carl Jung told me subconsciously that say
Now I feel a totally different way, and that's why I must say
Now we will win the game!

Jung believed that one's attitude and one's characteristics of personality is a phenomenon, not a direct matter of circumstance to the individual's conscious judgments or intentions, but rather it is due to the individual's subconscious instincts. An interesting view in Jung's *Symbols of Transformation* was that there were parallels of equal value between the dreams or fantasies of a modern woman and this was relative to a variety of mythical themes. I feel that when people are their true genuine selves, their personalities will reflect their inner consciousness. However, when they try to be someone they are not due to the ignorance of society, it can have an extremely detrimental effect on people's conscious to subconscious inner self relationship.

Jung also believed that there is a link of consciousness through people's instincts, as well as their spirituality. This is directly relevant to the collective subconscious. To aid you further in exactly what an archetype pattern is, I state the following: an archetype is an original pattern or a model prototype. I myself would define it further by stating that an archetype is basically a theoretical brain print, meaning that we all have our own individual way of thinking to a given extent.

Jung also believed that a person's archetype could filter reality through the personal subconscious out into the conscious. Indirectly related to that thought, one could observe that when a given organism represents an original pattern of life (meaning an archetype), such as an amoeba or a paramecium, everything that this simple organism will come in contact with will be generalized as a source of nourishment and sometimes a foe. You see, these are two of the most basic organisms, thus they display the absolute basis of instinctual behavior.

We will now move on to Jung's concept of the introvert and the extrovert. You see, Jung thought that you could pretty much characterize people and their archetypical imprints of human behavior into two basic generalizations. The two categoriesare of course the introvert and the extrovert.

The extrovert was said to be the outgoing type, apt to love and loves to party. The introvert, on the other hand, has a more laid back and calm personality type. The extrovert has the ability to lift oneself out of a depression by accessing other people and other things. You must understand that the introvert and the extrovert are composed of differing dimensions of personality. Jung viewed this comparison as a set and confined hypothesis. I myself believe that a person could very easily transfer from one archetype to the other due to life experiences. I also conclude that an individual could be a little bit of both of these two separate archetypes.

You see, human characteristics are not as easily identifiable as one might think. A good portion of Jung's deciphering archetypes depends on a person's potential for subconscious intuition, or as previously stated, extra sensory perception. I feel that any factor that can affect the mind has the potential of altering a person's archetypical intellect.

You see, this type of thinking and processing of human personalities, and total human archetypes has to do with the way a person's personal subconscious reacts to a given situation. Although it may be possible, Jung, contrary to my belief, felt that a person could not decide whether to be an introvert or an extrovert. This statement of Jung's is true to a point; however, when a person is posed with a crucial life situation, I feel that one can "sometimes" alter their archetype as relative to their introvert or extrovert traits. One rule that I abide by in science is that there can be an exception to anything.

Another interesting hypothesis of the pioneer and mentor of the subconscious (meaning Carl Jung, of course) was his view that certain types of thoughts, which originate from the personal subconscious, are what he called the "Inferior Function." This inferior function is a passageway to the collective and the personal subconscious. Jung believed this inferior function was the primary source to all of the mysterious and good things in life.

You see, the collective subconscious connects with everything, everyone, and everything else that exists past, present, and future. However, this inferior function is said to cause bad dreams which may seem detrimental but actually have a meaning of goodness that can be manifested over time. This supports the possible relationship of extra sensory perception through what is called metaphysics. Metaphysics is a philosophical study of the causes of the underlying natures of existence. Maybe this could be a concept intended to induce the realities of the consciousness of the now. Actually, this entire process would be more sufficient, don't you think? Metaphysics also supports the hypothesis that whether you are an introvert or an extrovert, your psyche will grow according to your confined individuality, as well as my and your development into a higher level of human understanding.

In the case of extroverts, they tend to be more directed towards their outer being and they may also tend to be more independent minded. They possess a genuine individuality rather than having a subjective outlook, which of course is contrary to an objective characteristic. The extrovert can also have a demeanor that would have an atoning introverted attitude within their personal subconscious. The world environment and its various societies will for the most part have a tendency to be objective. However, world societies can still obtain the capability of filtering the negative aspects of society through a realization of what is called universal contact, or better yet universal wide connection. However, we will save the concept of connection for a later discussion. This is in part a filtering of the mind. In the simplest of terms, the human race can attain the ability to overcome the collective mistakes which we have made. Yes, through the equilibrium of mind, space, and time, we could repair the collective subconscious.

As for myself, I have switched from being introvert to extrovert throughout my lifetime. This is due to the stark realities, which I was forced to face while carrying out this methodical mind process. I also feel that because of the vision which has caused me to fathom the inner mind more so than the average individual, I am a rare case of both introvert and extrovert. However, the important thing is that I abide to my moral senses and be the best person that I can possibly be.

You see, whether a person has one archetype or the other, the important factor is that we contribute the positive aspects of our mind print to the world environment. I have accomplished such deep methods of thinking due to my capability to filter the mind. This is contrary to the extroverted side of my archetype, which would promote the tendency to ignore intervening factors and behave as though the outer world did not consist of unfortunate evils.

Another two categorizations of conscious to subconscious thinking are thinkers and feelers. To a feeler, a thinker might seem aloof and distant. Thinkers might approach life with little concern for their own emotions and the emotions of others. I believe if the main function of your psyche is to think, you might develop a secondary function which will, through some sort of thought sensation, contribute to your potential to attain extra sensory perception. However, Jung did not believe it possible to fully manifest one's inferior function, which I take one step further by claiming that inferior function can also be used for the shaping of the collective subconscious, not just the personal. This would be a challenging task for the introvert, due to his or her lack of capability for the exploiting of his or her inner vast subconscious thought entities.

Once again, I find that I possess two contradicting traits of the psyche. Yes, I am a thinker and a feeler. What do you think you are? Interesting concept, don't you agree? It is my opinion that if an individual such as myself can mix these various traits, it could actually benefit the healthiness of my personal, your personal, and the collective subconscious.

There is yet another function of the psyche which Jung labels as the intuitive function. This function, according to his hypothesis, states that those who may possess this type of thought process have little or at least a lesser interest in past events than the contradicting type thinkers. Jung also states that those who adhere to this intuitive function are more concerned with sexual issues, than they are with the actual act of sexual intercourse. Those who possess this intuitive function may actually consider sex to be boring. You see, Jung and I agree that one's inner mind has a profound relationship with their sexual manners of thinking. The word intuitive is obviously related to intuition. Therefore, Jung labeled this psyche categorization as such due to its potential of promoting psychic abilities. To avoid any confusion, intuition by definition is a power of knowing things without common conscious reasoning. This aspect is most certainly relevant to the concepts of "knowing" and connection.

Clairvoyance is similar to intuition but it has a different technical meaning. Clairvoyance is the ability to see beyond the range of common perception. Those who may be intuitive could further their psyche into the realm of the clairvoyant. You may not see it yet, but when you finish this book, you will know the clairvoyant because I am as such!

Jung also believed that a person's psychological type would determine the individual's development, as I have stated thus far. However, there is much more to it than that. Allow me to elaborate. You see, people's individual route in the life process is a result of the type of thinkers they are. You must understand that there are exceptions to everything. Therefore, not all extroverts are like other extroverts and of course, the same thing goes for introverts as well. This is an extremely broad concept and it is directly relative to a person's archetypical pattern, or as I like to put it, a person's brainprint. Therefore, we are all unique in one way or another. Jung believed that there are as many developmental paths as there are people and I couldn't agree more. I myself have come to the conclusion that skills a person may have developed such as artwork, musical abilities, or any other trade or hobby one may obtain are developed subconsciously, but it takes a strong conscious effort to achieve such abilities. If one has a natural talent for such an endeavor, the subconscious will assist with a much stronger perseverance.

I am not sure about the complete hypothesis of Jung, but in my opinion, I do believe that humans are either mostly or completely subconscious at birth. Studies have been done with identical twins for the purpose of developing this process of mind function. In Rob Robinson's book on Jungian psychology, he mentions the case of identical twinswho were separated at birth and adopted by separate families. Remember, neither of these twins had any knowledge of the other. Shockingly so, there were many coincidences in theirseparate lives, which one could not easily dismiss as simple coincidence. These twins ended up with the same interests and boredoms on the same topics. They had similar occupations, habits, hobbies, and illnesses. Even more interesting, they each married a woman named Linda and if that is not shocking enough, they both divorced and married a woman named Betty. They both had sons named James and Alan and they both had a pet dog named Toy.

How could this be? Some kind of connection? Genomes? I have known several sets of identical twins in my life, but their characteristics were not as such. This, I believe, is due to the fact that these twins were able to interact with one another through what is called human interface and interchange. Because these twins knew of one another, their destinies coincided with each other, and thus the development of their differing archetypes. Common logic would dismiss this as a mere coincidence and that this type of phenomenon would not occur with any consistency if attempted again. I do believe that this was a direct result of the ramifications of the shaping and the eventual rising of the collective subconscious. This entire process will make perfect sense once you have read the Language of the Mad segment. I am jumping too far ahead; let's get back to business.

At this point, I deem it necessary to discuss a concept of Jung's,which I have been trying to make sense of for some time now. This is Jung's concept of the shadow. Before I elaborate on my conclusion to this theory that Jung began and I completed, I must first give Jung's assessment on this shadow of the mind concept.

So, here we go! From this point on, we will refer to this concept as the mind shadow. First, I must inform you that Jung and myself do feel that a people can eradicate their own inborn talents and potential for capabilities. The concept of the mind shadow supports this hypothesis. However, it is not that simple. The mind shadow is representative of a sort of mind equinox. You see, dark and light are probably not equal throughout the universe, but there is a balance. This balance, as any other scientific balance, is another supporter of the still semi-fathomed theory of scientific equivalency, which is the reason for many of my conclusions including this one. You see, the phenomenon of quasar birth is relevant here; an imploding black hole which turns into an explosion producing the birth of a star. This is an example of what I call opposite to opposite reactions of creation. However, we must not indulge in astronomy at this point. What you need to remember at this point is that scientific equivalency always sustains the equilibrium within any sector of the scientific realm.

I agree with Jung when he states that the goals of people in the second half of their lives is contradictive of the goals in which they had in the first half of their lives. Thoughts and dreams are inclusive to this concept. I believe that thoughts and dreams possess some texture. You see, thoughts and dreams cannot be touched by our physical being; however, if more senses and dimensions somehow exist, then these thoughts and dreams could somehow be touched in a physical way. Presently, this concept is beyond the realm of human understanding. Due to examples of equalities, whether being light to dark or the first half of a given duration and the second half of a given duration, there is a balance which could be further understood through the process of individuation. For the first time in this book, you may have grasped the totality of just what scientific equivalency is.

I realize that I may have seemingly strayed from my theories on the mind shadow concept, but please bear with me, because at this point I am elaborating on the scientific relationships which have led me to my comprehension of what this mind shadow is.

You see, during the first portion of our lives, we build up our ego; the second portion is spent turning away from conformity of sorts, and thus our seeking of a more meaningful purpose. Of course, this can vary from person to person, but this is the common premise for most of us. When we mature, we can develop a wisdom which causes us to see what is truly important and thus we stray from the common tendency to impress others with a false image. Depending on archetypes, the collective subconscious mind equinox is like a vessel sailing on tantric waters. This is the cause of the shifts in the traits of archetypes from person to person. Some people are genuinely good out of either a fear or courage towards evil and vice versa. Some are complete slaves to society and that is a mold which must be broken. I once again stress that we must appeal to our moral senses for the equilibrium of the three forms of consciousness in order to achieve greatness.

A crucial component to Jung's view of this mind shadow is what he would label as the "Anima Animus." Jung theorized that those individuals who lived their lives unaware of the bonding relationships of the three forms of consciousness, most prominently the personal subconscious to the conscious, may tend to have no contradiction between the two levels of consciousness of the personal realm. Of course, I am referring to the conscious and the personal subconscious. Anyhow, the fact is that for a large majority of people, they will live a natural and normal life due to the fact that they do not concern themselves with acknowledgement of the coinciding forces between the personal subconscious and the conscious. As for the collective subconscious, an even larger majority of us will go through life without any such acknowledgement. As for me and my natural tendency to be of a curious nature, I literally drove myself mad with such paranormal conceptions. These divided processes of the psyche were viewed by me personally as "chambers of the mind." Since the early days of this dementia-driven vision, of which I am finally able to communicate to the public, I was over concerned with the balance of the mind equinox. I did not yet realize that it would have been more beneficial to allow this equilibrium to go through its natural course, as I would devise my plan for the manifestation of universal contact. It was the actions that I would take regarding the barred realities of social issues and responsibilities, such confronting my drinking problem, and now that I have been sober and responsible for nearly thirteen years, my life is better than ever.

Okay, after that little tangent which stemmed from my introduction of the concept of the anima animus, we will now directly discuss this component relative tothe mind shadow. This anima animus concept can be related to a variety of functions of the psyche. However, at this point, we shall apply this still unexplained ingredient of the psyche to the other, not yet fully accounted for concept of the mind shadow. Please bear with me, and follow along, for this is the correct method of elaboration, and by the time I get my point across, you will comprehend why I formed this concept in sequence as such.

You see, Jung believed that human qualities could be diminished from a common tendency to have a conscious and a subconscious denial of one's character defects. Furthermore, he felt that these defects could take form in the fabrics of our dreams. I personally believe that dreams of this type have a great deal to do with subconscious symbols of transformation. These theoretical symbols can be adjusted in both negative and positive aspects relative to the given individual's archetype pattern. This dream concept, relative to my theory of scientific equivalency, is either entirely or in part due to the balance of the dark part of the mind being the shadow, and the light part of the mind being the actual brain itself. If you are slightly confused at this point, just keep paying attention, as my elaborations of this mind shadow and its relative components will continue to shift into their form and shape. Continuing on, a shadow figure symbol may turn up in a dream as say an alien life form, a vampire, a monster of some sort, and maybe even as a zombie. A contrary figure could be a friendly alien, a prophet, or any creature capable of love and morality. This type of effect on an individual's dreams must be directly relevant to the balance of light and dark energies which exist within the human mind. If people could somehow learn such a hypothesis, they would obtain the capability of dealing with dreams of an annoying nature. However, the crucial component to such seemingly unnecessary ambitions would be to first understand the nature of just what anima animus is.

You see, light and dark energies may be of opposite proportions, but there is a relative flux between these two necessary opposites of existence. When a light source becomes more powerful and tense, the dark coinciding opposite force will grow darker in intensity and when light diminishes its intensity the dark will grow less intense. So this brings us to the conclusion that light and dark in being opposites, are still two forces that are entirely dependent on the levels at which their opposites will fluctuate within their own scientific nature. This brand of hypothesis is the first blunt example of what I call opposite to opposite reactions of creation. You will soon learn that opposites are the key component to the births of any entities of nature. For the first time in this book, I can honestly say that scientific equivalency wins!

This last bit of elaboration gives the conclusion that if one can properly acknowledge these opposite frequencies of the psyche, one could control or alter the nature of their dreams. However, although I have not completely established any credible basis on exactly what the anima animus is, what you have read thus far will be sufficient data for this next theory, which I am about to introduce.

This next theory was not begun by Jung like the mind shadow was, but I must admit that it did stem from his brand of speculation. This is the son of the mind shadow theory and I have decided to call it the theory of shadow thoughts. Of course, this theory was also born out of the foundation theory of scientific equivalency, but it does possess its own intimate individuality. It goes like this: when you have one common conscious thought, you are obviously thinking this thought consciously; however, you have a direct coinciding or opposite contradicting thought, which is of course buried inside your personal subconscious. This is directly relative to the concept of the equilibrium of light and dark forces within your brain. Simply stated, one thought is of light and the other is of the shadow in the mind, thus scientific equivalency equals mind shadow equals anima animus equals shadow thoughts. Those who are fluent in mathematics could dub this scientific equation as scientific equivalency to the fourth power. This theory of shadow thoughts will be manifested further in the Language of the Mad segment. Furthermore, this theory is also subconscious to you at this point and I revealed it now for the purpose of interjecting into your personal subconscious. However, I would like to discuss shadow thoughts a little further. This shadow thought in the singular can be understood through synonyms such as no and know. The accent of a person can sometimes be relevant as well. But you will not be rendered able to fully comprehend this theory at this duration, so I will now proceed further with the concept of the mind shadow and its relationships to other hypothetical issues of the psyche.

So, how can our life's trials and tribulations affect this conception of the mind shadow and the pre-explained anima animus? For instance, if a person has been subject to any of a variety of abuses, it can drastically change them in many ways. There are many of us who have found different methods of living our lives while contradicting the trueness of our personal subconscious traits. This could lead one to the conclusion that there are people who have possessed evil ways of living despite the fact that they could have good subconscious intentions. This process of the psyche could also act in reverse. In order for me to explain this process further, I will repeat the point I just made, but this time we must apply it to our brief discussion on the shadow thoughts theory. By the data I have submitted thus far, one could conclude that because an individual could carry out an evil act consciously, this same act could be executed for moral reasons subconsciously, and of course this process of the psyche could be vice versa as well.

The mind is vast! Therefore, this concept has many forms and functions. This concept can also be relevant to a person's sexuality. Although many would tend to disagree with me, I do believe that those who are homosexual are like that simply due to their brain chemistry. I conclude that this is also the case for those who have chosen homosexuality due to life experiences. You must understand that any experience we have changes the chemicals of our brain. Therefore, whether a person's sexuality is original or is caused by an experience, it is the result of the chemical balance within one's mind.

I conclude that it is our human instincts (which, of course, originate in the personal subconscious) which we all have in common, at least to a certain degree, which a thorough developmental process of an individual's subconscious to conscious instinctual behaviors could ultimately lead to a moral divinity. It is through a fathoming of a balance of mind as relative to time and space, which one could discover (such as I have) that physical, mental, and even spiritual existence is entirely dependent on the equilibrium of light and dark energy within these living entities.

Another conclusion I have come to make is that when negative traits such as negligence or unnecessary dishonesty reaches an unreasonable level, a person's inner and outer mind will cultivate around their central mind in the form of this shadow, and thus cause an ambition of immoral demeanor. You could apply this hypothesis to the birth of a quasar, the imploding black hole packing so tightly, that it results in explosion. These two analogies represent my previously mentioned theory of opposite to opposite reactions of creation. At this point, I would like you to ponder for a moment the basis of scientific equivalency. By now, you might grasp scientific equivalency to a certain degree, but to comprehend this theory you must continue reading.

A good method for becoming a novice to the scientific realm of the three forms of consciousness is more achievable than one might think. The first step would be to become as truly genuine and real coinciding with your personal subconscious wants and needs. This could reap negative results due to the strict realities of society. However, this will allow you to "connect" with people on a whole new level. You will also become well versed in the beauty of human understanding. If we would all take up this attitude, society would become more tolerable and there you have it, the first step to utopia. You would become a balanced entity with humankind and contribute your positive aspects to the outside world much easier than before.

As far as sexual issues are concerned, a dream shadow figure or symbol could have a detrimental effect on your sexual impulses. It may be beneficial to confront such issues. This self-confrontation could aid you in the development of the mind shadow and the still semi-explained anima animus. I have found that admitting to my character defects has aided me in my moral integrity, and it doesn't require much wisdom to realize that fact. A full understanding of this concept can vastly improve a person in a large variety of ways. Please do not be frightened, but we must all face our mind shadow throughout our lives and by comprehending it, we could further the promotion of our own inner peace. The truth is that we have all faced this mind shadow throughout our lives and we will continue to do so throughout our existence. For me personally, it was my alcoholism, among other things destroying my ways of life, that I was forced to face, and this is all related to the mind shadow. A good companion can also help one with this particular realm of the psyche, even though they or even you may not consciously be aware of or fathom just what the mind shadow is. I certainly needed the help from my friends and family when matters took a turn for the worse.

In relation to the seeking of benefits from this mind shadow, I believe that the good things in life such as friendship, the love of family, or even the love of your partner, can substantially affect the intensity of the equilibrium of light and dark within and without your mind. There is a paranormal reality which we have all pondered at certain durations of our lifetime. This would be the pondering on the relationships of all forms of existence through opposites and scientific equivalency. This relationship is the result of human understanding and it is called "Knowing!" I believe that no matter what action you take from this point forward, or from whatever chamber of the secular mind, or the factors of the foundation of the ultimate balance of scientific equivalency, we will continue to go in the direction of morality despite those who are consciously and subconsciously opposed to such happiness. Scientific equivalency will win! Through my studies, I have devised some methods for dealing with shadow symbols in my dreams. For example, if I am having a nightmare and I am in conflict with a shadow figure, it is possible to turn the tables on this shadow figure by turning myself into this figure, and thus I gain control over this shadow figure. Another method would be to search for a positive aspect in this figure, either consciously or subconsciously, that it may possess. Finally, you can inject this quality into your own personal being.

Remember earlier when I claimed that dreams and thoughts can have a physical substance beyond human comprehension? Well, what I have to say next will support that hypothesis. Once again, I would like you to think about what I have explained about my theory of scientific equivalency thus far. Remember, scientific equivalency equals mind shadow equals anima animus equals shadow thoughts. What I will attempt to get across here will be in the form of an analogy.

You see, a shadow figure dream symbol can start off immoral and then progress into a lesser immoral demeanor and finally into an adequate level of morality. This is along the lines that everything that is fathomable and unfathomable as applied to human understanding caused through opposite to opposite reactions of creation, thus producing the establishments of living entities like organisms, plant life, thoughts, dreams, and things that are supposedly not living like black holes and quasars, that through a rigorous and intricately thorough conceptualization of time frequencies throughout existence, such concepts can be further understood.

You see, change is constant. This thought process has been manifested over time and has led me to the conception of what I call the Theory of Development which we touched on in the earlier political discussions, although I did not label it in that segment. The basis and premise of this theory is that good is produced through the existence of evil and, unfortunately, vice versa. You must remember that everything throughout our universe is constantly developing, whether of physical, spiritual, mental, or anything else beyond the realm of human sensual frequency. This will be sufficient data on the theory of development for now, but please keep it in mind.

I would now like to give some explanation about the concept of human frequency. This realm of human frequency is entirely dependent on the way we perceive and understand our senses. We are not at the senses segment yet, so I will briefly apply the meaning of human frequency to the senses of sight and sound. First, sound: Being a former musician, I have developed this thought. Those who can read music will understand this better. However, I will try my best to explain this concept in the clearest of methods. A music staff has five horizontal lines, where the notes are placed either on, between, or below these lines. There are certain high-pitched notes which are within our sound frequency, but they must be placed below the staff, straying downward from these horizontal lines. So, such a high-pitched note is thus drawn below the staff with a small hand drawn line applied through the written note. You must realize that all sound frequencies with such high pitch cannot be represented by the method of music staff. Therefore, if you go even more downward you will finally come to a note that cannot be heard by the human ear.

Just think about a dog whistle and understand that the canine has a different frequency than we do. If a person were to play a note higher than human frequency on an imaginary guitar, the string could be so thin, that it would slice his or her finger. On the other hand, a note too deep for our human frequency could hurt you in other ways depending on the realm of universal frequency, meaning all frequencies above or below ours.

As for the sense of sight, there is the existence of what are called ultraviolet rays. The human eye cannot see such rays. You may have owned a pair of sunglasses, which said UV protection on them. This means that those sunglasses had a lens protecting you from ultraviolet rays which are beyond our human frequency but can still do severe damage to our eyes; even blindness is possible if one were to be exposed to these rays for a significant duration. This leads me to believe that there is much more to the sense of possibilities one could conceive by intricate functions of the human psyche.

You see, if animals and mammals have different frequencies than us (which they most certainly do), one could conclude, that due to universal frequency (which is all that can be picked up through the senses of all living entities), there is a great deal that the human race is presently rendered unable to comprehend. All frequencies might exist within all living entities. However, the paramount issue is that the scientific community obtains the understanding of all those within our means. Furthermore, I once again stress that there are things that should not be figured out, thus we need to apply morality to the scientific community first and foremost. As for now, we are working on the psyche of the three realms of consciousness. Up to this point, we have achieved the equilibrium of mind, space, and time. What do you say we take it even further?

Okay, the mind shadow and the anima animus, as well as all other theories which I shall teach you in due time, will aid us in the achievement of balance and ultimately universal contact. We must learn to coincide with existence to a level of sufficiency. Remember, scientific equivalency states that everything is equal to one.

Continuing on, accessing the coinciding relationship with your dreams and the symbols in which they pose can also reap positive benefits to real-life theoretical shadow figures. Jung believed that if a person was bothering you, they are probably altering your mind shadow. This is a direct result of the society environment as applied to your brain and its chemical make-up, which ultimately relates to this mind shadow. Due to our common tendency to dig up forgotten aspects of our demeanor from the personal subconscious, we might then benefit from our relations with any such shadow figure either in the dream fabric or in the physical world. That may seem to have been a contradicting element, but you must remember the theory of development.

So, what is the term anima animus derived from and what does it truly represent? I have come to the conclusion and I do agree with Jung that the anima animus has to do with a connection between a man and a woman. Jung felt that every man within his personal subconscious possesses an everlasting effigy of a woman. Not necessarily any particular woman, but rather, a decisive female representation of woman. Jung also believed that women possess this interesting ingredient of the psyche, meaning that women have an effigy of man in their personal subconscious as well.

The word anima is Latin for soul; by definition, it is the female facet of the male subconscious. The word animus is also Latin and it means of spirit and mind. Therefore, animus is the masculine outlook of the female personal subconscious. Seeing that this anima animus is said to exist within all men and women, I must conclude that this aspect of the psyche is essential for the eventual manifestation of the collective subconscious.

Furthermore, when dealing with the complexities of the anima animus concept, it is required to assimilate both a genuine trueness of courage and honesty. To accomplish this transition, or better yet, this "growth process" through all of the stages of the mind shadow conceptualization, we must in our personal lives and in our social lives, incorporate the function of the creation of scientific equivalency to the anima animus in order to confront the possible consistency of emotional suffering, commotion, and anguish. These negativities can and will be turned into a positive, but we must promote human understanding through a manifestation of the collective subconscious. I, of course, hope to be a pioneer in this aspect and due to my early life acknowledgements of such paranormal proportions, I have suffered severe emotional anguish and unfortunately, as one of my close friends would say, "Pain is mandatory, but suffering is optional!" However, with a correctness of attitude to the three realms of consciousness, that is a small price to pay when considering the reward. So, do not fret, because I have done the groundwork for you! Anyone who has ever been in love with a member of the opposite sex has experienced an altering to their personal subconscious, but more so to the frequency of their mind shadow. You must understand that love (for the most part) is earned and the anima animus is the key component to the collective subconscious, as well as being part of the gateway to worldwide love and the dream of utopia.

There have been critics of Jung who have claimed that this anima animus concept is sexist. Let me tell you that these critics have no idea what they are talking about. This anima animus concept is the same for both men and women. Furthermore, Jung was a robust advocate for women's rights. You see, in Jung's time, women's liberation was weak and pretty much ignored. Jung was said to have argued that men should develop their feminine inner self and combine it with their positive masculine attributes. Jung was disgusted at the fact that in his time, women were limited in so many social aspects in practically all world cultures.

The introvert extrovert concept also plays a significant role in the anima animus notion. Jung claimed that introverts were usually intellectual thinkers, while extroverts were feelers, thus responding to their environment with more of an instinctual content. Therefore, feelers, although not being consciously aware of it, are more trusting and confident in their personal subconscious. This is still the case even if this feeler doesn't know what the subconscious is. Remember, a person's conscious and subconscious is always interacting, whether they are aware of it or not.

Within the subconscious of the introvert, Jung felt that such person may tend to be associated with evil, yet he still felt that the mind shadow was not an evil in itself. As for my own opinion on this, I am honestly not sure. However, as long as the mind equilibrium is achieved—whether light or dark or even chemically—then morality will always triumph. This aspect is also relative to my theory of development and if this theory can prove that good stems from evil, the balance will be even more easily obtained. Those who are lucky enough to have an independent and free thinking personality will be given more competence to achieve a structure to their personal subconscious and to all that can be had from such open-minded hypothesis. And in the end, these positive attributes can be accessed for the promotion of utopia. Once again, scientific equivalency wins!

You see, when an people have exhausted their conscious mind, their natural reaction would be to instinctually activate their personal subconscious. This makes perfect sense in the long term and in the short term. In the short term, when the conscious mind is exhausted, you fall asleep, thus entering your dream center and your personal subconscious. In the long term, people have alternatives such as prayer, meditation, or other outside influences. This will cause them to enter a different state of mind and possibly influence the personal subconscious of another individual, thus strengthening the structure of the collective subconscious. Jung believed that methods as such would cause traits of personality to enter and give balance to the mind shadow.

Sexual tension between a male and female could be altered due to natural personal subconscious instinctual tendencies. This brand of thought process adds to a person's personality, thus leading to an understanding between minds of a balanced thought process. The notion of this particular hypothesis promotes a relationship between two separate people, but it also causes a positive archetypical reaction for these individuals to the outer world, or in more basic terms, to society. Whether being conscious or subconscious, this type of bond is relative to its physical and metaphysical properties or any other concepts of environmental existences.

You must remember that the anima is the feminine aspect of the male subconscious and the animus is the male aspect of the female subconscious. Jung did feel that the common man needed to get in touch with his female side, but the woman in the opposite perspective was not in dire need to do as much. Furthermore, Jung defined the anima as identifying one's personal subconscious and he stated further that it could and should be accessed as a gateway to the personal and the collective subconscious. Our life relationships—even for the homosexual person—basically go through a forwards and backwards filtering process of mind, space, and time between the three levels of consciousness. Just to be thorough, I would like to state at this point that I have absolutely no prejudice against gay people and that I am an advocate of gay rights.

Continuing on, I stated earlier, in an indirect manner, that a person with an evil conscious mind may be possessive of good inner virtues, and it is possible that certain few who are relevant to the totality of my vision may become subject to a moral megalomania of wonderful proportions! Megalomania is considered to be a mental disorder characterized by delusions of grandeur. I have been subject to my own personal megalomania, which is one of the main premises of this book. You must understand that negative qualitiesthat we may attempt to dispose of could have a significant benefit meant for another time.

Jung also states that the outer world can be seemingly meaningless to an individual's dreams, especially to a person whom is unable to direct their sexual urges with the beauty of their insights, thus being confined by the negative aspects of society. This type of mental situation could induce havoc on a moral person's personal subconscious, especially to the health of his or her mind shadow. This negative situation could potentially cause an external lack of willingness to deal with the immoralities of society and can also have a detrimental effect on one's capability for true love.

Oftentimes, this type of mind psyche situation could manifest this type of inner conflict for both selfish and selfless desires to love. You see, mothers, through what society is willing to accept, are more able to express their true feelings, contrary to behavior that is brought out due to society where people will often try to express their genuine feelings through the excitement of human passions. The variations of these types of feelings are unending, just as the vastness of mind, time, and space are unending.

Jung also states that the anima animus, relative to the mind shadow, can manifest symbols in our dreams that tend to appear as gods or goddesses. This must have been one of the prime factors why Jung chose to become a pagan. In modern times, the closest living entity that could remotely be conceived as a god or a goddess would be a celebrity. Obviously, celebrities are not considered gods or goddesses, but due to the fact that they are often looked up to, they can appear in our dreams in this fashion.

Despite the hypothesis that the universe and existence is limitless, Jung felt that although there were basic categories of personality types (introverts, extroverts, thinkers, and feelers) there still exists a finite amount of differing personality types. If an object is finite, it consists of a seemingly existent infinity. A good example of a finite object would be the pinball. This is because you can travel around a pinball for an eternity and it would all seem the same due to its uniform surface structure throughout. A pinball is also perfectly symmetric because it has no acute angles and no matter what angle you look at it from, it always has the same features. Therefore, if you have a finite object, it must have symmetric features in order to achieve the finite balance. This means that the archetypical patterns of the collective subconscious represents a finite quality because of the existence of the sort of spherical mind galactic collective subconscious. The conclusion of a finite level of human personalities makes sense because we all possess our own individual archetypical pattern. Einstein theorized that the universe was finite, but when applying my concept of scientific equivalency, it leads me to a contrary conclusion. Einstein may have conceived the universe as such due to an altering of time throughout space. This conceptualization could also have been agreed upon due to spacetime curvature.

Remember, the anima animus notion of concept is buried deep in the vastness of the personal subconscious. Projections are made from the origin of the individual's personal subconscious and it is theorized to be an automatic and instinctual process of the psyche. Through this process of projection, the thought of origin can somehow transfer itself to an object. That may seem a bit confusing, but this is the type of thought where something can make sense to a person in a subconscious way, yet not be logical to the individual's conscious mind. Due to the fact that I have been fascinated with the concepts of the psyche all of my life, this type of occurring thought is commonplace to me, yet can easily be dismissed as nonsense in social situations and yes, it is extremely frustrating.

You see, the laws of my theory of scientific equivalency will cause such seemingly illogical perceptions because scientific equivalency states that all is equal to one and one is equal to all. When dealing with the intricacies of the psyche for a long duration of time, the personal subconscious will act like an excreting gaseous matter as it drips and drabs its chemical liquid, thus producing a state of ultra human understanding. If a collective balance can be achieved, the universal memory will compensate for what cannot fit inside the conscious mind, thus putting into action the intricate process of human understanding then forming into knowing and finally the moment of universalwide connection.

As I mentioned in the Healthcare segment of Politics part one, human movements are caused by electric impulses called bioelectric impulses originating from the conscious mind when we intend to and from the personal subconscious mind when instinctual, such as reacting to a shooting pain. Anyway, this action uses the spinal cord as a human electrical conductor, and "wala," you have a physical movement.

What about instinctual movements that are not a result of pain, such as the blinking of the eye? Or even a sneeze, a cough, or a hiccup? These are involuntary bioelectric movements caused by the exterior world! Scientific equivalency is beginning to make more sense isn't it? Because of the law of scientific equivalency, which states that everything is equal to one, there are interior causes of bioelectric impulses, as well as exterior causes to the same effect. The same law applies to our voluntary movements as well. So here, we see the scientific credibility to the theory of scientific equivalency and we are not even close to being done. Do you think you know what we are figuring out yet? Keep reading!

VISION OF A MENTAL PATIENT

As a teenager, there was a song by one of my favorite bands that really got me thinking. It spoke of elemental telepathy, which is a prime function of the relationships between objects in existence. Factors such as human genomes, the simple amoeba, or paramecium, or any matter consistent of universal energy has aided me in the complex understanding of life, from the infinitesimal to the infinite and, finally, to what is called the naturalistic line. This song got my personal subconscious in action big time! So, why don't I stop with the festivities and show you these lyrics? This is a song written by the scientifically savvy band called Rush. This song is entitled "Chemistry." So I hereby present track three on the album called *Signals*. Without further ado here it is!

Signals transmitted, message received
Reaction making impact-invisibly
Elemental telepathy, exchange of energy
Reaction making contact, mysteriously
Eye to I, Reaction burning hotter
Two to one, Reflection on the water
H to O, no flow without the other
Oh but how do they make contact with one another?
Electricity? Biology? Seems to me it's chemistry!
Emotion transmitted, Emotion received
Music in the abstract, Positively
Elemental empathy, a change of synergy
Music making contact naturally
One, two, three, add without subtraction
Sound on sound, multiplied reaction
H to O, no flow without the other
Oh but how do we make contact with one another?

Did you like that? I did! Allow me to elaborate. This song is based on a concept which will be fully dealt with in a segment called What is a Connection? I mentioned it this time to get you thinking. You may already have an idea just what a connection is. However, there is much more to be said about this concept. A line of paramount proportions in this song was the one which mentioned elemental telepathy. When applying my elaborations on inner and outer bioelectric reactions, you should come to sufficient conclusion. H and O of course represent hydrogen and oxygen, which when combined will form water. As for the line "Electricity? Biology? Seems to me it's chemistry!" It represents the concept of combining the present over confined sectors of the scientific community. When pondering that thought, I conclude that electricity, dream fabric, light and dark energy, or what have you, is all a part of the chemical realm. Everything is chemistry! Get it? Rush has to be one of the most intelligent bands ever. As far as science is concerned, they are tops in my view. It is actually their gymnastic-like drummer, Neil Peart, who writes a majority of the lyrics and he is a former professor, so one could fathom why he comes up with such intricate scientific concepts. All I have left to say is, these guys rock!

On the concept of reflections, which we will further discuss later, the concept of a reflective process is what Jung termed as "a unity of opposites." This unity of opposites led me to my theory of opposite to opposite reactions of creation. There is a symbol for a balance between opposites: It is called the "yin yang."

Continuing on, an individual's perception of self is said to be the most vastly deep of one's personal subconscious individuality. The same level of inner depth can be applied to a person's method of personal development relative to their reactions to society. Jung felt that these conflicts of interest within an individual's personal subconscious development were all wrapped up in a unified entity and he is correct. Scientific equivalency proves this true. This is because one's true inner self can transcend its content of morality, and morality, my friends, is the most essential ingredient to all concepts!

At this point, you must understand why I reject religion. However, through making sense of all my concepts, as well as the concepts of others which have aided my vision, I will admit that there is some kind of force which binds us both infinitely and infinitesimally.

The fact that Jung was able to help many through his unorthodox methods of therapy proves that the open mind is the best type of mind for achieving the equilibrium, by which peace of mind can be obtained. Furthermore, it was Jung's attention to dream therapy which helped those he diagnosed to get better by these unique methods. Jung was fascinated with the fact that many of his clients were said to have dreams consisting of positive symbols that would somehow be manifested by overtaking negative attributes, thus causing these clients to balance the light and dark intensity of the mind shadow. Jung was of course a pioneer in methods of dream therapy.

Yet another aspect of the psyche Jung has contributed to the realm of the three forms of consciousness was what he dubbed as the transcendent function. This transcendent function is indirectly reflective of an individual's perceptions of the barred realities of the world social environment. It is centered on the notion that our dreams react relative to the personal subconscious functions by a sort of reflection of the common traits of society. This transcendent function also reflects onto our reactions to the conscious realm of our social being. Jung states that our outer ego, in relation to the moral tendencies of the personal subconscious and the conscious, executes a relationship that further defines the intricacies of the mind shadow, thus causing a revolving function of the psyche, aiding the conscious and the personal subconscious mind. Therefore, this transcendent function process can help one to fathom the seemingly nonsensical thoughts of the personal subconscious, thus giving a balance between the individual's relations to the three realms of consciousness. This thought process exists within us all, whether we are aware of it or not, thus the imminent achievement of the collective subconscious manifestation of the ultimate balance of mind, space, and time.

Due to the fact that the common people will possess a conscious personality that adheres to societies' perceptions of reality, they will usually stray from their personal subconscious, thus weakening their relationship to the collective subconscious. This common behavior of the psyche is directly affected by the stark realities of the non-compassionate imagery in which society is thus confined. Hence, because the common people are not consciously aware of any form of subconscious activity, they will tend to ignore any such visions of this realm of the beyond. The positive aspect for people who are not concerned with such phenomena is that they will be better equipped for their needs to deal with life's responsibilities. Furthermore, because of the manner in which I have lived my life, it was imperative that I achieved a balance between the concepts of the beyond and my basic life responsibilities. The fact that I have done the groundwork for the imminent collective subconscious fathoming, which must take place for a variety of reasons, you, my readers, can simply continue to live the common life and view this process of life from the theoretical front row.

You see, as a shadow figure manifests within the personal subconscious and the collective subconscious, one's archetype can bond with a more intense understanding relationship with his or her mind shadow. The mind shadow could then reach the level of common consciousness, thus giving structure to the entire function of the collective subconscious. For the majority of us, this process will aid the lack of concern for the existence of the uncompromising evils of the world.

You see, most people, even those of us who are evil in nature, do have the potential to grasp a higher plane of morality. However, extreme soul searching is mandatory for this shift in the human psyche. This is the prime reason that if the collective subconscious can become a household notion, it will improve the general qualities humans are blessed to possess, paving the achievement of imminent universal contact! Jung also states that in relation to this transcendent function, it is a key ingredient to the galactic mind spherical vortex of even beyond the limits of the finite archetypes which fluctuate around the globe.

For the most part, the collective subconscious, in relation to the mind shadow, goes through most of the essential stages of coinciding unison within their infancies. The next stage for the goal of the collective subconscious and the eventual formation of the un-exposed primary goal is to teach people to at least ponder on personal subconscious expansion. At this time, there is an intense struggle with the anima animus syzygy (a syzygy is a uniting through a process of coordination and alignment). So, one could conclude that the collective subconscious (although having existed for millions of years) is at the beginning of a syzygy and once this process is carried out, the human race could achieve the zenith in all levels of consciousness and any other conceivable forms of universal existence. Once again, scientific equivalency wins!

Jung also states that the process of syzygy applied to the three levels of consciousness will someday take place. However, if I am able to promote this process further, the wait should not be too much longer. Jung, in reference to this possible activating of a syzygy, claimed that this process, if taking full effect, could heal the immoralities of world society. And this is what I have basically been saying so far in this book.

Throughout this syzygy process, I was able to deal with extreme dementia, one that could potentially ruin a person who has no balance between the three levels of consciousness. This enduring ability I have obtained relates to a statement of Jung. He stated that in any process of the psyche, especially within the syzygy process, if an individual can at least remotely fathom the vastness of strength in his or her mind, he or she would obtain the capability to overcome insurmountable odds.

This statement may seem contrary to my elaborations where I stated that when one does not comprehend the other chambers of the mind, he or she would be able to deal with responsibility with more efficiency. However, what I was dealing with was well beyond the stresses of society, thus my need to access my inner mind for the achievement of a better life and a utopian dream. This brand of strengthened ability could be achieved for us all if only we could allow the collective subconscious to reach its potential.

You see, we must give this type of thought process a try. If we do, we will find the inner creativity of the collective subconscious. Hence, every time we access this inner creativity, we will be presented with the vast and infinite data which the human mind could possibly know. You must understand that the Earth is very old and this concept of the three levels of consciousness is very new. Remember, though, that the subconscious has existed for quite a long duration as well. Again, I stress that if such a beautiful vision of the psyche could be carried out, not only would we become capable of a worldly love, but it would continue to grow, thus improving the lives of our offspring. That last statement is vaguer than you may think because I have not yet revealed the primary goal. When I do reveal this goal, you will come to know an even higher level of the potential beauty which the human race is capable of.

Due to the fact that this vision of the psyche is a new brand of conceptualization, it must be approached with a persevering ambition that can only be activated by the beauty of our inner desires, thus the possible accessing of our true inner morality. Many of us have built walls in our minds, in order to deal with the non-genuine traits of the world society. We must knock down these walls by using the three levels of consciousness as a theoretical sledgehammer in order to complete the syzygy process for the obtaining of the mind zenith. This newly fathomed syzygy will connect with light and dark energies of the collective subconscious, thus leading to the completion of a bridge to the gateway of the worlds of the inner and outer beyond.

We have now come to the final stages of this lesson I am giving you on the concept of Jung's visionary hypothesis of the mind shadow and my personal finishing touches for the completion of this enhanced theory. You must understand that the mind shadow expands, but not in a physical sense. Because of the unending depths of the personal and collective subconscious, there is the relationship between mind and space, but the scientific laws, which confine to these two seemingly unrelated aspects do present the equilibrium, that is beyond the conscious realm of universal balance, thus giving precedence to the relationship between thought and dream fabric and the vastness of the exterior universe.

An easy method for comprehending the way that space expands while also supporting the big bang theory, is as follows: if you take an elastic rubber band and poke a few dots on it across lengthwise, you will notice the distance between these dots; the next step, once you have placed the dots as such, would be to stretch this elastic band and notice how these dots become more distant from one another. So, now you must realize that the universe, coinciding with the big bang theory, is represented on this rubber band in the form of a physical analogy. These small printed dots move away from each other just like stars do, thus giving a simple example of universal expansion. The premise of the big bang theory is that the universe was once tightly compacted and was forced to explode, thus causing the continuous process of space expansion. This theory also supports the hypothesis that when you peer into the night sky and notice those beautiful stars, they are actually moving away from you. However, the light from these stars are moving towards you at the same time; when comprehending this process to a full extent, you could come to the conclusion that when you peer into the night sky, you are peering into time. Furthermore, you are witnessing a forward and backwards coinciding galactic action of function. Therefore, if matter in the universe can defy common logic and send reactive forces in opposite directions, one could conclude that time travel is possible.

A simple question is: If we are living inside of this big bang expanding explosive reaction, how can we live as such? I conclude that this is a direct result of the existence of the infinite and the infinitesimal. Infinity is easier to fathom than the infinitesimal. Obviously, infinity is the notion of limitless distance. Hence, due to the inconceivable size of the universe and also due to the fact that we are able to exist as such in a seemingly non chaotic environment, we are so small that we conceive time as a part of infinity. When applying notions of spacetime continuum and spacetime curvature, one could comprehend that we exist in a fraction of time and space. Furthermore, because I theorize that time is altered throughout existence, mind, time, and space, are a force of unity. Once again, scientific equivalency wins!

I apologize if it seems like I have strayed from the concept of the mind shadow, but please bear with me for I am simply describing the relationship of inner and outer entities in relation to this concept of the psyche.

As for the infinitesimal, this is a hypothesis that is not as easily understood. Therefore, I will do my best to explain. My theory of scientific equivalency supports that small is infinite, which is the basis of the infinitesimal. Simply stated, the infinitesimal is the infinite of the within. The scientific community, as far as the realm of the infinitesimal is concerned, has done a great job not only at paying attention to this concept, but they also have come to some interesting and credible hypothesis. There is the concept of what is called string theory, which pertains to the smallest of humanly conceivable matter in the forms of small spiraling vortex-like strings, such as the strands of D.N.A. The scientific community has been able to detect matter which is a trillion trillion times smaller than the atom. However, this is not enough information for me to get you to fathom the realm of the infinitesimal.

Okay, I will now present some methods to aid your understanding of this realm of the infinitesimal. No matter what amount of small matter you have, it must be possible to split it in half. However, Einstein's discovery of the splitting of the atom could lead to a contrary conclusion. When an atom is split, it breaks off into many small fragments, thus causing a chain reaction from atom to atom and then you have yourself a nuclear chain reaction. This could lead to the conclusion that matter can become so small that it couldn't be divided. However, this is a process of subdivision applied to the atom, and if there are entities a trillion trillion times smaller, my view could thus be deemed correct. Presently, this concept cannot be set in stone and this is due to the fact that human understanding has its limitations. However, I do strongly believe in the totality of the infinitesimal. There are terms for forms of matter smaller than the atom, such as the quark. Beyond the quark, you will eventually come to the science of string theory. String theory in itself is a vast notion which can be related to a variety of concepts.

There is a line in another Rush song about subdivisions which is consciously about city life. However, in its subconscious meaning, this song represents a process of the mind relative to the equilibrium of mind, time, and space. This song is called "Subdivisions" and it is also off the *Signals* album. Here is the line that got me thinking: "The future pre-decided detached and subdivided in the mass production zone." This line aided me in comprehending the subdivision of atoms. However, it has a much deeper meaning within the realm of my personal subconscious. This would be the process of brain subdivision and it relates to the mind shadow. When applying this line to conceptualizations such as time-altering forces, the mind's ability to peer into the past, comprehend the present, and dream about the future, one could more easily understand the beauty of the three levels of consciousness. When I elaborate on the visual aspect of the mind shadow, you will gain a fuller understanding of the mind subdivision process.

Another way for me to aid you in the complexities of infinitesimal existence would be a simpler means of communicating an un-simple concept. Those of you who have a basic understanding of mathematics will have sufficient means of knowledge to get the gist of what I am about to explain. It's very simple: If you have any given digit with a decimal point on its right, you can always add another zero and another one at the end of it. There must be infinite small! We will come back to the issue of the infinite and the infinitesimal at a later section.

Okay, that did pertain to the mind shadow. However, it was in an indirect manner of speaking. The mind shadow acts in a similar fashion to a reflection. However, we have not gotten to the topic of reflections yet, so I will do my best to elaborate without the aid of reflective comparison.

There is a shadow in the center of your mind, going through a process of an interlocking change and reversal between a large fragment of light (the brain) and a large fragment of dark (the shadow in the center of the brain).

I can visualize what the mind shadow looks like in the subdivided sense of the fabric of human thought. There is also a literal method of viewing the mind shadow: by simply observing a drawing or a picture of the human brain. However, at this point, I would like to explain what the mind shadow looks like within the energetic subdivided thought fabric sense. Once I complete this elaboration on this first visual thought-like entity, I will elaborate the literal view and we will have entered the mind shadow into the collective subconscious. I will show the mind shadow in the form of a brain chart in due time; as for now, allow me to elaborate further.

The mind shadow, in the subdivided sense of thought fabric and mind visualization, looks something like a chessboard, only broader and consisting of tinier boxes. The light portion of this mind shadow is represented by the white squares and the dark portion is represented by the dark squares. Another way of perceiving the mind shadow could be produced by a scene in the movie *Star Wars*. This would be the scene when the Millennium Falcon went into light speed. In the scene, as the Millennium Falcon would go into light speed, the stars would turn into horizontal lines coming right at you, thus producing a visual grid of light and dark. Some of you may not have ever seen *Star Wars* and if you have not, I must ask: Where the hell have you been? Just kidding.

Another way of visualizing this mind shadow would be through another physical analogy. Picture water flowing through a metal spaghetti strainer: the water represents the light while the metal represents the dark. The mind shadow in the realm of thought is a grid producing a transformation of light and dark forces of the cosmic psyche. Remember, these light and dark forces will interlock and reverse, creating the prime boundary between the personal and the collective subconscious. Furthermore, this is another example of opposite to opposite reactions of creation. In this case, it is light and its dark opposite which carries out this paranormal phenomenon of the human psyche. I did my best to aid you in the visualization of this subdividing process of the mind shadow and if you do not fully comprehend it at this point, you could try to enter this vision into your personal subconscious and you will have sufficient means for the manifestation of comprehending this mind shadow.

Now, for the more literal vision of the mind shadow which can be fathomed by simply viewing the physical makeup of the human brain, please examine the brain chart below.

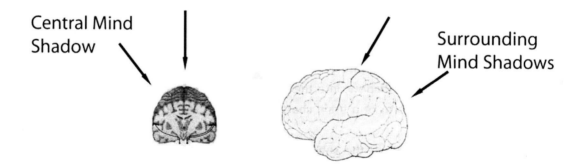

By examining this chart, you will notice that there is a splitting line of shadow down the center of the human brain. What happens in this part of the mind is a function by which the centrifuge of darkness coincides with the surrounding fabric of the brain made of purely absorbed light, thus a connection of opposite to opposite reaction of creation takes place. The forces of light combine with the forces of dark and the inner intricacies of the psyche thus go into action. You will also notice that there are many other indentations of light matter and shadow all around the brain. The same process takes place within these dark crevices surrounding the brain. However, the surrounding shadows do not represent the same level of centrifugal force as the central mind shadow does. In conclusion, this is the general basis of the causes of the three levels of consciousness which exist in the realm of the human mind. So there you have it, the mind shadow is now entered into the collective subconscious. Once again, scientific equivalency wins!

Continuing on, now that we have completed our lesson on the intricacies of the mind shadow theory, I would like to reflect on another side of the subconscious mentor Carl Jung and commence to discuss some other aspects that Jung posed to the scientific community, as well as some more interpretations that I will personally interject from time to time throughout the remainder of this segment.

Okay, Jung had a vision of a reddish solar disk, which is supposedly related to what is believed to be a gateway for the souls of the underworld in the *Egyptian Book of the Dead*. This statement is vague at this point, but once you have completed this Monolith part two portion, you will conceive its true meaning. It is relative to what I call the new sun.

Jung was a supporter of the theory that atheists such as myself will often attempt to fathom the god conceptualization with their minds, relative to science. Those who are not of an atheistic view will try to perceive things in more of a spiritual sense. I personally believe that Jung and others may not realize that through a notion such as scientific equivalency, the inner and outer mind, the spiritual realm, the barred realities of the physical world, and all that exists within and without the confines of human frequencies is directly related through what I have dubbed as opposite to opposite reactions of creation. I stand by my view that the human race needs to create its own revelations by understanding the bonds of scientific equivalency, hence the mind being an infinite and infinitesimal force for the promotion of the human soul.

Jung also theorized some of his aspects through a hypothetical type vision called esotericism, which happens to be the process of inward meaning. The inner mind and the depths of the infinitesimal are the byproducts by which the laws of esotericism abide by. The positive attributes of esotericism consist of (which are outside the concepts of Jung and myself) the forming of a vision as such, which can only be accessed for personal enlightenment, usually pertaining to those who are either academically or self-educated, thus, the acquired capability of obtaining an inner concept. The conception of esotericism, like many other outlooks in this book, will be more properly compensated for once you have perceived the totality of my—and soon to be our—vision. Jung also felt that esotericism, if properly accessed, could aid in mass human understanding, which in turn could lead us to the Earthly crossroads where history will theoretically rain.

Jung, somehow through his genius, was able to conceive a bonding relationship between esotericism and his interpretations of the symbols of transformation exploited from other concepts of the psyche such as hermetism, an ancient set of religious beliefs that would take its form from the relative concept of esotericism. There is also Neo-Platonism, which is a modern term for a school of religious and mystical philosophy that existed in the third century A.D. Neo-Platonism stemmed from the teachings of Plato, the Greek philosopher who was the second of the three great philosophers of Ancient Greecethat included Socrates, and Aristotle. The common perception of these ancient philosophers was that they looked like Zeus: They had long white beards, walked around in togas, and spoke like a Chinese fortune cookie. In reality, they were just down to Earth school teachers living in an era quite different from ours.

Then there was Alchemy, part of the occult tradition and representative of two concepts, namely: first, the achievement of a supreme wisdom and immortality; and secondly, the creation of certain substances that are supposedly consistent of unusual physical properties relevant to inorganic chemistry. Interestingly soand in relation to all of this, there was said to be a pursuit of a structure of progress of some kind that was supposedly hidden, just like the premise of this book and the still unrevealed primary goal. But I shall reveal, my friends, yes, I most certainly shall reveal!

Continuing on, there were those who were critical of Jung's connections between biology and spirituality, which I believe in probably even more than Jung himself did. People felt that Jung's methods of the psyche were unorthodox and they were; but it is not always the method that is paramount—it is the result that is more important, excluding abusive measures, of course.

Jung had another extremely unorthodox and farfetched practice of method. He believed that he could communicate with the dead. At this point, such communication would be considered delusional or outright hoax. However, once you have conceived the totality of my vision, you will be well versed in the sense of possibilities and realize that such conceptualizations of paranormal activities could hold credible substance, thus the furthering of open mindedness.

Jung was also said to have conversed with those who practiced witchcraft. This led Jung to believe that people who practiced such unorthodox beliefs may have tapped into a gateway, thus gaining the capability to converse with those who lived in the spiritual world. After the end of the World War 2, Jung was both surprised and pleased to see that spiritualism had become a more prominent outlook than in the days of his childhood. However, there were many who were skeptical, thus Jung would often be misunderstood regarding the belief he shared with me, namely that the human spirit is actually a chemical entity derived from the infinitesimal within our human anatomy and the infinite which secretes from our exterior.

Jung's daughter Emile frequently dreamt that she was communicating with the dead and she was also said to have experienced other paranormal activities. I believe this was a direct result of a connection between Jung and Emile of presently incomprehensible phenomena.

It was concluded that Jung had experienced many experiences from the realm of the inner and outer beyond. These types of experiences were more commonplace in his later years and I believe it was due to actions he took in his younger years that pertained to the seemingly unreal. He would dub the seemingly alive entities by which these strange events were carried out as fourth dimensional. Jung may have possessed his individuality in the realm of the human psyche due to the fact that he was never a student of philosophy. Therefore, he applied his own philosophy originating from his personal subconscious.

Jung was also interested in the notion of Animal Magnetism, a vital ingredient in the progression of Jung's genius mind. Animal magnetism is a scientific hypothesis meant to account for existences of psychological phenomena that directly relates to galvanism, a muscle contraction, which is carried out by an electric current. Galvanism in the science of physics and chemistry is the induction of an electric current produced through a chemical reaction (think back to the lyrics of chemistry). I conclude that galvanism must be related to bioelectric impulses, possibly through a comparative version of an opposite to opposite reaction of creation. Galvanism is also relevant to the studies of basic electricity and magnetism.

Jung was very interested in the study of animal magnetism due to the fact that when he applied this notion to his therapeutic methods, he was able to induce a trance in his patients; this would lead him to magnetic healings and spiritual exorcisms. Because animal magnetism is yet another crucial component to the science of the human psyche, it consists of an equal vastness as to all other brands of the human mind. Jung believed that we possess an inward male figure similar in comparison to the laws of the anima animus hypothesis. It was determined that this inward male figure possessed a coinciding inward soul, which consisted of what Jung would label as the divine spark I view this concept of divine spark as a centrifuge that could result in a collective bioelectrical impulse. Furthermore, a centrifuge of a certain level of energy is essential for any and every type of opposite to opposite reactions of creation, which will be elaborated to a full extent in the Reflections segment. As for further hypothesis on the divine spark, Jung would also relate this divine spark to inner and outer existences, which Jung believed could represent a possible passage to the spiritual realm. The relationships between the inner male figure and the divine spark could lead one to the conclusion that the universal bonds between all entities are unbreakable, because the totality of existence is one and one is all. Once again, scientific equivalency wins!

Jung also believed in the possibility that biologic spirituality could on occasion lead an individual to extra sensory perception. However, this connection led him to the conclusion that this process could induce anguish and hysteria if not properly balanced, and this is exactly what happened to me! Jung was aware that his concepts of the three levels of consciousness could reap benefits pertaining to his fascinations with hypnosis, hysteria, and spiritualism and his fascinations with these three issues commenced well before his hands on studies of the human psyche. Due to the fact that Jung had many skeptics pertaining to his farfetched methods of practice, he would at times be forced to tone down the more radical methods of which he obviously prided himself on. He was also posed with a problem I was faced with all my life. You see, what Jung and myself had in common was that there weren't too many people who we could discuss such matters with, and this is due to the fact that they might not understand us, but more so because they would view us as lunatics.

Another thing I had in common with Jung was that we were so fascinated with the human psyche that we were both compelled to read and write in pertinence to this particular sector of the scientific realm. Another factor when dealing with the human psyche is that one needs to tone down its complexities and speak in the most down to Earth fashion as possible. The only other mentor as prominent as Jung in his era was the honorable Sigmund Freud. However, Freud was less radical as far as the psyche was concerned, thus he was more accepted. Jung and Freud were close friends and although Freud was considered to be more of a success, I conclude that Jung, due to his vastly open mind, was light years ahead of Freud. You must understand that when an individual is a radical in any field, it is more challenging to persuade people to see things from your perspective. The only correct method to deal with a dilemma as such would be to possess a high level of perseverance and at times downright stubbornness.

In the case of Freud, he was quite skeptical when it came to religion. He would label religion as a mass delusion, communal neurosis, or a shared psychosis. Jung and Freud agreed that 2000 or so years of Christianity could only be replaced if a mass movement was executed. Despite possessing some negative characteristics (just like the rest of us), Jung was considered to be a very moral man and would, like myself, attempt to use the three levels of consciousness to advance human morals and ethics. He was said to have believed that ethics could be secreted from the personal subconscious through a strenuous process of rigorous psychoanalysis. Jung would try to get across that Christ was a soothsayer of the hidden world evils, and that through the existence and the manifestation of biological spiritualism, we could aid the formation of the collective subconscious, thus promoting a higher level of morality. Jung was intelligent enough to grasp, in a primitive sense, my theory of development. Just to be thorough, the theory of development is the process of good stemming from evil, love stemming from hate, and a realization on a new concept of method for the furthering of human understanding. Jung thought that if he were able to exploit ancient energies of creation through body, mind, and soul like all of his other concepts, it could lead the human race to a new level of existence, and I couldn't agree more.

Jung was also fascinated with the human psyche relative to sexual behavior. He felt that the flesh had properties of some kind of biological spiritual consistency. He was not opposed to polygamy, and felt that an individual's sex life was his or her own personal business. He was able to develop such open-minded concepts from the progression of the anima animus hypothesis, as well as his theories pertaining to introverts, extroverts, thinkers, and feelers. One minor disagreement that I have with Jung as to these particular archetypes is as I previously stated, that one could reap further benefits by combining these archetypical traits.

Something called an altered state is a common trait of the personal and collective subconscious. An altered state is a change in the spacetime continuum which I have related to what is called topologya relative to the most advanced forms of mathematics. Topology is basically a three dimensional version of geometry which deals with acute angles and curved objects. When I apply an altered state to topology, and then add the laws of scientific equivalency, I conclude that topology deals with the vast infinitesimal interlocking and changes carried out through opposite to opposite reactions of creation. Furthermore, if the laws of topology can perform such intricacies in a forwards and backwards method, such as a star moving away yet the light from the star moving in the contrary direction, it is possible that an altered state could cause a shift in the spacetime curvature relative to our human time frequency, thus the manifestation of a supreme time altering action. There is a movie called *Altered States*, which deals with this concept in the form of a dream. I highly recommend it.

Jung states that the inner vision of man is a gateway to a more vivid understanding of the spiritual aspects of his pagan beliefs. You might recall that Jung would claim to be a Christian to the outside world while keeping his pagan beliefs to himself. Well, he must have done a pretty good job, because I am in the middle of a biography on Jung called "Memories, Dreams, Reflections" and Jung is somewhat portrayed as a Christian, but a very skeptical Christian at most. Through my research, I came across many contradictions pertaining to any issue, so bear with me because I am doing my best to stick to the facts and to interpret them with as much honesty, accuracy, and sincerity, as is humanly possible. Anyhow, as far as Jung's secretive pagan beliefs are concerned, he would relate the gods of paganism to his visions of shadow figures and symbols. Jung felt that by interpreting his pagan gods and apply them to other sectors of religion, such as holy relics, he could see through another representation of a relationship of the inner and outer beyond.

You see, Jung was actually hostile at times toward Christianity. Through what I have revealed thus far, you must realize that I am also skeptic of Christianity. Jung and I are unable to accept a conceptualization like Christianity because of our knowledge and understandings of the human psyche and, speaking for myself, my knowledge and understandings of science as a whole has also led me to a skeptical view as such. My theory of scientific equivalency simply deters me from accepting Christianity. Moving on, when the personal subconscious manifests an inward thought that protrudes from the multifold domain of the brain chemistry, it produces the more paranormal type of thought process, including spiritualism and extra sensory perception. Remember, the transcendent function can lead to an achievement of balance into the world of fundamental thought imagery. Thoughts pertaining to the anima animus and the introvert extrovert concepts can attain a higher level of function through this process.

Through my thorough research on Jung and the human psyche, I came across a variety of unusual occurrences (which are obvious through what we have discussed thus far). Furthermore, some fragments of Jung's life were extremely puzzling. Jung at one time stated that the levels of consciousness could only be properly understood through discrimination. I assume that Jung was referring to this word in the literal sense, which means to distinguish. However, it was said that at one time Jung had ties to the NAZIs, thus making him an anti-Semite. Remember though, Jung was very well liked by those who knew him and was more than often said to be a very moral man. As for his possible ties to prejudice, I have concluded that it is due to the fact that all humans within their personal subconscious have likes and dislikes toward everyone they are acquainted with, which is obviously due to the fact that we all possess defects of character and imperfections. Furthermore, the collective subconscious works in a similar fashion. This means that the same types of subconscious thoughts react the same way between cultures rather than people. I am happy to inform you that this type of thinking pertaining to the non-literal definition of discrimination (prejudice) was a short lived phase in the life of Jung; he would abandon his views of such a concept with stern rejection. Another possible reason why this good man carried out this short phase of negativity can be understood through my previous elaborations on the theory of development. Simply put, Jung may have possessed a conscious evil with a coinciding subconscious moral.

We are nearing the end of this Collective Subconscious segment, but before class is dismissed, I must once again reveal some more lyrics to you. This song was the other Deallegiance song that dealt with the subconscious mentor Carl Gustav Jung. It was written prior to Symbol of Transformation. You will notice that some of these lyrics were in the Malicious Intent song called "Mind Control." This is because when Roland and I formed Malicious Intent, we carried over some Deallegiance material and added it to our new stuff. In the case of this next song, we simply dissected fragments from earlier writings and incorporated it into Mind Control. This was one of the early ones and it is entitled "Eyes of Jung." Please enjoy.

> *Honestly, I cannot see the secret to this infamy*
> *but I am sure integrity will increase authenticity*
> *Hopelessness forgotten traits that surely can't procrastinate*
> *flowing at this natural rate sailing for one man's fate*
> *sailing high and sailing low in one direction no sorrow*
> *Within the darkness that you hold turn to light and go to gold*
> *Engaged yet my reasons bare excuses clenched by my fear*
> *I am praying for forgiveness as my time comes near*
> *Into the new age converted mind rampage*
> *Our children must learn their gifted advantage*
> *the games are to begin as real as is living*
> *Enslaved society held by regime of sin*
> *If we go back now who will show you how*
> *to escape from darkness to the worlds within?*

       We look to the children so young they want to belong
Blessed son with eyes of Jung
   As for the others just a momentary mix to fix
     sailing in my ocean as I make my future picks
       Magic sources deeming pride one momentary sections wide
        Had we not ever tried no inner forcing subdivide
         Your mind is closed to the fact, to the fact that I have tried
          I know that you're true I know that you've tried
Sleeping life into its seams eternal hope for all it seems
  Sticking out like kings and queens the passageways to your dreams
    Into the next stage on the streets rights will wage
      and onto the new stage with lock of mind engaged
       Fear does not exist let the games begin
         Reign of terror ruling all these people
Cannot society ever re-begin?
 Held in a cage punished for nothing
   there is not one thing that does not remind me of you
     Early going wanderers your men have now arrived
      Difficult to pacify yet easy to survive
        Metamorphic mind expansion ticking in your brain
          Growing strong growing hard but goals still remain
Glowing ghouls special tools make this darkness gone
Special powers increase life I'll turn my current on
   Knowing ones please wait for me this is my last sign
     You play it right you play it safe I will bring you down the line

I sincerely hope that you have glimpsed and appreciated my views on the collective subconscious. I remind you that an open and moral way of thinking is the only method if we are to achieve universal contact which is a presently unaccounted for notion. So please be patient and I will soon reveal the primary goal. As for now, I must continue to elaborate how this goal is going to be achieved. Once again, thank you for listening and read on!

ASTRONOMY

Welcome to the Astronomy segment. In this segment, we will discuss a variety of imperative aspects in the science of astronomy, the study of outer space. We will relate scientific fact to the premises of my vision with a thorough and ambitious demeanor. We will relate to astronomical theories of the past, such as the big bang theory, which were vaguely accounted for in the collective subconscious segment. We will emphasize points from the theory and its premise that the universe was once small, compacted, and exploded, thus, the behaviors of our everlasting and ever expanding beautiful universe.

You see, the universe, according to the big bang theory, was an incredibly small and dense molecule composed of compacted light matter, which must have included other miraculous substances. This would ultimately lead to the universe and its expansion, thus the present day shape and form of this limitless realm of the beyond. As to the structural and active forces of this big bang, it is my opinion that the present view of the scientific community is correct, but I have come to some slightly contrary revelations. In relation to this radical scientific hypothesis of my own, I have concluded that the big bang did occur, but it was altered due to realms of paranormal dimension types. This tiny pinprick of light was indeed the origin of the universe. However, due to the laws of scientific equivalency and my conclusion of the equilibrium between mind, space, and time, this big bang in its cosmic infancy may have reacted in a similar fashion to mind expansion. Because the mind is able to grow and remain at the same massiveness and structure, it is possible, from my perspective, that the big bang emanated from this pinprick, but it also happened everywhere else at once. This hypothesis is based on my conceptualizations of time alteration, spacetime curvature and continuum, opposite to opposite reactions of creation, and some factors of the mind shadow. As far as relating the big bang to the mind shadow, it is the dream fabric subdivisions of the mind concepts relative to the mind shadow, especially my physical analogy of the light speed scene in *Star Wars*, which would best aid you in comprehending this theory as such. Because of the functions of light and dark energies and their balance in the universe, and the notion that light relates to time, thus supporting the existence of differing wavelengths of time throughout the universal domain, I do stand by my belief that the big bang happened everywhere.

You see, there is a balance between light and dark in the universe and if one can visualize that these two opposite cosmic entities represent the ultimate equilibrium between the vastness of mind, time, and space, it is not to difficult to envision this process.

Moving on, there have been many interesting discoveries stemming from the big bang theory. For example, there is what is called the Cosmic Microwave Background Radiation," which in the most basic of terms, is a sort of cosmic echo. This cosmic echo, I believe, consists of humanly inconceivable type existences, which, needless to say, is well beyond the range of human frequency. This cosmic microwave background radiation may be beyond our normal human frequency; however, through what are called the senses of the beyond, the human race and its impressive scientific community of the past millennium have devised methods of examining these seemingly inconceivable conceptions even beyond that of the range of the telescope. The continuous advancement of the scientific community and its persevering pursuits of a common understanding of astronomy has been an enjoyable thing for me to learn about.

Okay, back to the origin of the big bang for a moment. I have already stated that I agree that the big bang originated from this pinprick of light. So, although I have already briefly explained, through my hypothesis, that this big bang also happened throughout existence at the same point of duration, you must still be slightly puzzled as to how this is possible. Allow me to present another method for conceiving this seemingly illogical theory. Okay, this pinprick represents the centrifuge between what are called parallel universes. In our universe, we have light and dark energies that balance and carry out the essential opposite to opposite reactions of creation. The parallel universe is on the other side of this pinprick, and in the parallel universe, our dark is their light and our light is their dark. This is a classic example of what I have dubbed as opposite to opposite reactions of creation.

Another outlook to aid you in the understanding of this concept would be to ponder, for a moment, on the concept of the infinite and the infinitesimal. When you apply this viewpoint to the concepts of time change throughout the universe, you could sufficiently understand the premise of my enhancement of the big bang theory. However, the full concept of parallel universes will not be complete until you have read the Reflections segment.

Furthermore, this big bang must also have occurred through some sort of pre-existent balance and interlocking and change reversal between the forces of light and dark. The more easily fathomed matter of this big bang, including the cosmic microwave background radiation, is that these two astronomical entities have been expanding for billions upon billions of years. Furthermore, when applying such visions to the mind shadow for the completion of this hypothesis, a comprehension between light as relevant to dark could be satisfyingly compensated for.

Yet another way of understanding the balance of opposites between light and dark could be conceived through an even more thorough method of applying the infinite and the infinitesimal to what are called black holes. Of course, when pondering on the notion that a black hole consists of incredibly packed dark antimatter, one would quickly conclude that its opposite would be an incredibly intense and strong celestial object made of an opposite yet coinciding light matter. Quasar birth is a good example, due to the fact that a new star or sun originates from some kind of astronomically prehistoric celestial body, which will implode into a black hole for a short duration and then explode and "wala," a star is born. Jupiter is a good example of a pre-quasar celestial body. If the scientific community could apply quasar birth to a long time existent black hole including its behaviors and surface structure, astronomical revelations could potentially take place.

You must understand that opposite matters of universal existence such as light and dark, or matter and antimatter leads to the scientific fact that nothing can exist unless it has an opposite and coinciding force. When conjecturing on my elaborations regarding mind shadow and its bizarre properties of both function and structure, you will realize that all concepts being of mind, time, or space, are not only balanced, but they are balanced through the equilibrium of opposite to opposite reactions of creation. Need I say it again? I will, anyway. Once again, scientific equivalency wins!

So far, I have, for the most part, only accounted for opposite to opposite reactions of creation between forces of matter. At this point of duration, I would like to explain the functions of these opposite to opposite reactions of creation as posed to actions, rather than to physical substances. One method of examination would be to peer into the actions of matter expansion throughout the universe. Remember, we are now dealing with the actions of these objects and not with the objects themselves.

There is obviously a bonding relationship between the infinite, the infinitesimal, and even the finite. When applying these notions of science to scientific equivalency, it is easier to fathom such actions due to what are called positive and negative energies, such as protons and neutrons. There is a balance, by which the actions of universal existence will always cause the formation of cell-like structures. This cell process is a result of positive and negative energy actions and reactions. This thought process causes me to conclude that even actions must have a coinciding opposite force in order for it to take place.

By examining the reactions of opposites between various entities, it led me to another one of my scientific theories. This would be the theory of inner outer cell growth. This theory is based on the actions of objects relative to the infinite and the infinitesimal. You see, everything is like a cell or an atom. The Earth has layers and an inner core, thus representing a cell and the same goes for all other moons and planets. Stars are like protons and neutrons, which rotate around a centrifugal force. A black hole is round, and thus represents a nucleus, of which the proton and neutron stars revolve around. Our sun is the nucleus by which the celestial bodies of our solar system revolve around. This cell-like structure is consistent throughout the universe. A bubble always forms in a rounded shape. When peering into the microscopic, which is the start of the infinitesimal, you will see cells. This cell-like formation is due to the infinitesimal boundary at which matter becomes so small it sends an outward reaction in a spherical shape, thus the continuance of cell-like features throughout the universe. The pinprick of the big bang is a prime example, because it became so compacted, that it sent out a spherical chain reaction. As these entities hit the boundary of the infinitesimal, one sphere will be surrounded by another sphere and "wala," you have yourself a universal spherical chain reaction. Because we are in the realm of the macroscopic, it is hard for us to view such cell-like entities excluding the moon, the stars, and the sun. Therefore, we are in between realms of the cell. This theory is relative to another theory of mine, the universal body, which we will discuss later. At this point, I would like you to examine the chart below to aid your personal subconscious understanding of the theory of inner outer cell growth.

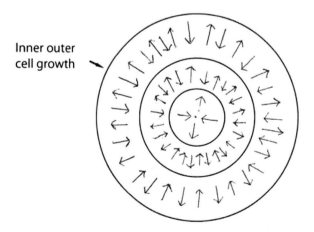

Inner outer cell growth

VISION OF A MENTAL PATIENT

Now that you have examined this chart, I want you to visualize this chart in a three dimensional cone either moving towards or away from you. Once you have fathomed the three dimensional version of this chart, I would like you to reflect for a moment about how this process when applied to this chart carries out its relationship with time. Okay, we will now continue on.

You see, Einstein thought of the concept of time as a coordinate relative to universal existence. This would be the premise of most of his notions and he also thought that the universe was limited, which of course could easily be considered a down to Earth hypothesis since it adhered to common logic and was supportive of the big bang theory. However, only when dealing with visions of opposite balances between light and dark, matter and antimatter, positive and negative energy, or any other of a variety of opposite to opposite reactions of creation, which can only be further understood through the neo-sciences—most prominently the science of quantum physics—could an individual come to many other conclusions.

You will soon see that scientific equivalency does not just apply to the scientific; it also relates to any and everything—whether literature, mathematics, history, or what have you. I once again remind you that scientific equivalency represents the universal equilibrium between mind, time, space, and all other entities within or without these realms, whether they are physical or active. I am determined to prove this theory!

The main fundamental universal action is, of course, time. Time can be theoretically applied to a horizontal line, which the scientific community would likely call the time line, but what I would call the naturalistic line. When dealing with the concept of time, there are actually two realms of the infinitesimal rather than one, which when applied to the physical world or simple physics, cause a natural subconscious urge to indulge in this extreme paranormal phenomena. This is due to the outer realm by which time is carried out as coinciding with change throughout the universe. It is relative to all actions and reactions of any centrifuges between the boundaries of opposite to opposite reactions of creation.

Once these concepts attain the capability of a continuing balance, the human race could manifest these visions within the realms of education for not only the youth of the world, but also for the necessary open minded type functions, which could aid the scientific community and give substantial merit to the moral potentials we so desperately need to get in touch with. As I said, time or any other aspect of scientific equivalency can present a broad set of seemingly non-figurative and unaccounted for dilemmas within the scientific realm.

Furthermore, if time is exposed as a straight line (just as I previously mentioned), there must be an infinitesimal within the line and also away from the line. This is because the progression of time alter celestial bodies as they move across this naturalistic line throughout universal existence. The naturalistic line cannot be bent, such as light can (which was one of Einstein's fascinations). However, time can be altered by opposites and the way they are enabled to move around and within this naturalistic line.

Through thoughts relative to the mind shadow as well as other mind hypotheses on which we have embarked, one could conclude that through space wavelengths, which are, in basic terms, according to the laws of physics, a length of an astronomical wave beyond the range of human frequency, this type of thought could aid us in a more advanced understanding of our senses, including the senses of the beyond that I have not yet accounted for. The purpose of these present elaborations is for your personal subconscious to achieve a higher understanding, to prompt your conscious mind to a higher level of knowledge, imagination, and intelligence. You see, waves in outer space produce signals that human technology could manifest through such things as television and radio, two of the most fundamental human inventions that aid us in our communicationsand promote a better development of the collective subconscious.

Einstein's theory of relativity basically states that within matter and in proportion to its mass and size, the energy within a given object is 186,000 x 186,000 times the amount of the given object's size. This means that 26,556,000 times the mass of an object equals the energy within the object. An object the size of a bean has enough energy within it to power nearly all of New York City for a day.

You may recall in the collective subconscious segment my statement that through the study of string theory, there is an object a trillion trillion times smaller than the atom. Outer space, as far as human technology is concerned, has been able to record thus far that the expansion of space wherein stars are moving away from us in physical form in light years pales in comparison to this number of the objective infinitesimal. Simply stated, we have actually seen further into the infinitesimal than we have into the infinite. When applying my view of the theory of relativity, namely that it represents the energy from the vast infinitesimal, it reveals that Einstein was certainly on the right path in many respects.

However, it is my belief that although the infinitesimal contains more than the infinite (as far as we presently know), there still is a prominent equilibrium between these inward and outward conceptualizations. Take the carbon cycle, for example, and the way that it goes about its process with a perfect unity to nature. Concluding from this other prime example for the establishment of scientific equivalency and all of its laws, especially the continuing tradeoffs between carbon dioxide and oxygen, which, even when relating to the more compacted realm of the physical world, a perfect balance of not only still life, but this perfect balance also pertains to any given time concept relative to all actions and reactions.

You see, the many theories I have applied to the most ultimate balance of relationships and my fascination with the inner depths of the infinitesimal and the outer beyond of the infinite applied to the space time continuum, which is constantly altered throughout existence cause me to believe in my enhancements of the big bang theory with an austere and devoted persevering yearning. This newfound personal yearning for a further understanding of all my fascinations with science has been an astute and beneficial experience. If this new ambition of which I have been so blessed to obtain were not strengthened to its new level, the utopian dream would come to an end.

The universe is estimated to be approximately 13.7 billion years old. Therefore, when one ponders the existence of an object a trillion trillion times smaller than the atom, the possibilities through the carrying out of the major aspects of my vision, especially scientific equivalency and the still un-exposed primary goal represents a collective happiness and a learning process that will be proved eternal!

The stars in our galaxy, excluding those immediately outside of the Milky Way, are so distant that to measure them in miles would be like measuring the distance from Boston to San Francisco in inches. Furthermore, to support my idea that the the big bang theory happened everywhere due to the two opposites of universally existing light and dark, as well as my previous elaboration that stars in physical form are moving away, but at the same time, light from these celestial bodies are moving closer, not only supports scientific equivalency, but also supports opposite to opposite reactions of creation. If not so, the big bang would have been the big lame and to put it bluntly, everything would be fucked up!

I remind you that the speed of light is 186,000 miles per second, so in one year, light will travel six thousand billion miles, and remember that the universe is said to be about 13.7 billion years old. This causes me to wonder if my calculations in comparing the presently known vastness of the infinitesimal to the presently known infinite are correct. But I guess that's why we call them theories, huh? I also theorize that the best way of comparing space to the mind, other than the equilibrium between mind, space, and time would have to be the mind shadow concept. This assumption is based on the fact that space and the mind shadow are both balanced between the forces of light and dark. This light and dark, my friends, is the central spark for the commencement of the peaceful and real revolution of the mind.

There is a good book on the science of astronomy discussing the big bang theory. It is simply titled *Bang*. It was written by three prominent astronomy experts, Patrick Moore, Chris Lintott, and Brian May. If you recognized that last name, it is because it is the very same Brian May who plays lead guitar for the legendary rock band Queen. Yes, May is a prominent astronomical expert and a legendary rocker. This book was an essential ingredient for my research in this segment.

In a new direction, I would like to elaborate on some views I have developed pertaining to the astronomical realm, which came out of my reading of *Bang*" Once again, I was able to apply new information from another literary source, then reflect upon them and apply to my theories. First, I must remind you that we are in the realm of the macroscopic, the physical dimension seen by the naked human eye. The macroscopic is in between the microscopic and the telescopic, representing the beginnings of the infinite and the infinitesimal.

You see, it has been concluded by many scientists (not just astronomers), that the hypothesis, which I am about to reveal is a credible possibility. This would be the sister and the more advanced theory stemming from the inner outer cell growth theory. This is the beginning of my theory of the universal body. This theory can be fathomed from a rigorous observation of the macroscopic, as compared against microscopic and the telescopic. This theory will not be fully accounted for in this segment due to its broadness of concept. It will be observed throughout the remainder of this Monolith part two segment in the same manner (although less frequently) as scientific equivalency. The universal body theory proposes that we might live inside of some kind of physical being of the beyond and that there could be living entities inside of us, probably representing an infinitesimal universe. Through my elaborations on the inner outer cell growth theory, one can conceive this universal body to a limited extent. I will further this theory as we go, by comparing non-cell like structures to one another between the realms of the microscopic, the macroscopic, and the telescopic.

At this point, I deem it necessary to commence elaborations from a relative, yet remote, relationship of the universal body. We will commence with a brief enhancement of the actions of cell like structures, thus relating to the inner outer cell growth theory. So, let us begin shall we?

Particles, or the study of small matter, if you will, has led the scientific community to believe what I elaborated on in relation to the theory of inner outer cell growth. This could set precedence in a variety of ways. The positive charges of a nucleus are equalized by the surrounding charges of the orbiting electrons which rotate to the exterior of the centrifugal nucleus. This is almost identical to the behavioral actions of the planets of our solar system and their orbiting around the sun. The sun is the nucleus of the theoretical solar atom. Before we indulge into the universal body, I remind you that celllike entities are a constant throughout the inner and outer realms of existence. Energy, although powerful within, does complete the balance between itself and basic physical substance. This is part of the main premise by which life is processed and how it continues throughout the relationship between mind, space, and time.

It is now time for me to further my theory of the universal body with a differing comparison process as to the inner outer cell growth theory. First, we will peer into the vast infinitesimal and touch on the conceptualization of string theory. We will then compare string theory to the astronomically infinite universe, but most primarily, galaxies. In order to relate this fragment of my vision to you, I must give proper assessment of the science of string theory. The premise of this theory is that once you reach the inward point where you bypass atom and cell like entities and discover these incredibly tiny strings of the vast infinitesimal, you can then peer into the realm of string theory. These strings are spiral shaped and they resemble a vortex. A vortex is any shape that resembles a whirlpool. These strings also resemble human D.N.A., which are the building blocks of the human textural makeup.

In the infinite direction, you will come across galaxies, point being that any galaxy also resembles a vortex. Therefore, when you reach further into the infinitesimal, beyond the range of atom and cell-like structures and as you reach further into the infinite of space well beyond our solar system, you will come across these two separate vortexes. These types of comparisons can be made in a slew of other parts of universal existence. I conceive that this type of comparison will be constant until you encounter the infinite and infinitesimal universal bodies. Another example for the comprehension of the universal body, as it relates to my explanations thus far, would be to examine basic matter as it becomes smaller and larger. I discovered this next example when reflecting on the topic of stem cell research. Stem cells have the ability to divide endlessly, thus leading to the production of more stem cells. However, these stem cells only exist in one's muscles, liver, skin, and bone marrow. I conclude from this, that these parts of the human anatomy can act in such a way where barriers of opposites may be the cutting off point, by which this process of cell division is limited. This means that cell types must go through some kind of barrier exchange of actions and formation where opposite to opposite reactions of creation are forced to deal with human chemistry in a similar fashion to the inner and outer beyond. Through further examination, I realized that this process is no different from barriers of formation, which subdivide between matter and antimatter, light and dark, positive and negative energy, and even the opposite to opposite reaction of the most fathomable kind, which would be the creation of offspring through sexual intercourse between "opposite" sexes.

To fully grasp how vast universal existence is, it is imperative to realize that our visual universe of the macroscopic, which we can observe with the naked eye, is only a small fraction of what is out there. A common belief that makes sense to me is that physical actions pose limitations. It is obvious to me that if something still such as molecules in the air causing conditions to reach absolute zero degrees Kelvin, these molecules cannot move any slower. However, the infinitesimal in its vastness is more than likely capable of even more inward intricacies of movement, thus representing some kind of presently un-accounted for barrier of an opposite type function. The common outlook in pertinence to speed is that one could never exceed the speed of light. It is because of the concept, that physical action poses its limitations where we are able to function as such within the macroscopic, as well as being a fragment of the coinciding universe and the opposite to opposite reactions of creation, thus birthing life and through the ultimate of balances, things are exactly the way they are. However, the sciences are executed for us, so it is up to us to aid this balance and complete the utopian dream for the promotion of Earthly concepts. Once again, scientific equivalency wins!

I had a simple, yet interesting thought as a teenager. You see, although I was young, I was aware that when molecules in the air move fast, they produce heat. So, when I was at one of those teenage beer parties I used to attend, I was half in the bag as usual. Anyway, I enjoyed staring into the bonfire and wondering what is beyond fire. The fact that oxygen is required to create fire led me to believe that fire was a limited Earth entity as far as the surface exterior was concerned and this is why I would ponder on this thought from time to time. However, when dealing with the totality of my vision, the need to fathom fire has its attributes, but also poses insignificant irrelevance.

Continuing on, because of the laws of scientific equivalency applied to the infinite universe, I have concluded that the constant change in time concepts can be directly related to fluctuations of gravitational and magnetic pull. Weight, like time, is altered throughout space and when realizing that the hydrogen atom weighs ten times as much as the helium atom, the universal equilibrium once again is seemingly defeated. However, the actions of coinciding forces between hydrogen and oxygen, which leads to the forming of water and also all of the other active forces, which exist between all elements that exist in the periodic table of elements relative to their length of duration and their physical consistency, leads me to conclude that the equilibrium between mind, time, and space is the prime factor in the credibility of scientific equivalency.

In the book *Bang* which I just mentioned, it was stated that radiation and matter are somehow linked to each other. This particular hypothesis supports everything I have explained thus far as to the existence of balance and relationships, especially when applied to astronomy. In the early stages of the universe, it was much different from the universe of present day. In these early stages, the universe was dull and dense, and obviously lacking in balance. It is the constant flux of time which would aid the universe to the achievement of its present form of shape. It is directly due to our location within the universe applied to time, that we understand it the way we presently do. This is why human understanding, or better yet "knowing," is being manifested in this duration of human existence.

Scientific concepts like electromagnetic waves, wavelengths, visible light, and photons (photons are subatomic particles that are a fixed elemental unit of electromagnetic energy) are being accessed for technological advancements, thus promoting the collective subconscious to a higher level of understanding relative the mysteries of existence. Television, which is formed through a progressive fathoming of quantum type realizations, is a prime contribution to human communication, but more importantly, this brand of communication is aiding further advancements in the collective subconscious and our dire need to appeal to love and morality. The cosmic microwave background radiation, or space echo, is an advanced frequency, which can, at times, cause a disruption in television frequency due to the interference that it can create. It has not yet been sufficiently realized just how much television and radio, which came first, have contributed to the three levels of consciousness, including a higher plateau of human interface and interchange, which happens to be the most primitive, yet most crucial form of human communication.

Something called a red shift, which is defined as an increase in wavelength of electromagnetic radiation, can be received by a detector and then set to a comparison of the original wavelength, and thus be subject to a drop in frequency, due to this detecting process (at this time remember my elaborations on human frequency). There is an opposite process to a red shift, which is called blue shift, which much represents yet another example of opposite reactions, or at least opposite relations. Furthermore, when you peer into a fire, the reddish part is not the hottest. The hottest part is actually the blue parts. If we can attempt to process a red shift blue shift relation of opposites, we could also compare this with potential reactions, which exist between basic blue and red. Believe it or not, this does relate to my theory of the universal body. These are reactions of opposites, which I previously related to parts of the human anatomy, which are consistent of stem cell activity and parts that are not, thus representing boundaries of the interlocking and change progressions of opposite to opposite reactions of creation. If you see the relationship here between these types of reactions within the human anatomy and these entities of astronomic existence, one could conclude that this process is going inward and outward within our human bodies and the vastness of space. Therefore, if these opposite reactions exist in us and outside of us, we must exist inside the universal body. Now, I would like to tell you about the photosphere. The photosphere (photo meaning light and sphere meaning a perfectly symmetrical circular three-dimensional entity) is the concept of an astronomical existence, which represents a region of origin where externally received light comes from. This light will protrude from a surface of origin such as a quasar, until its surface structure will become dull and difficult to comprehend, just as the universe once was. I feel that further understanding of existences as such can aid further understanding of the process of quasar birth, which the planet Jupiter might represent.

Our sun is roughly 93 million miles away and the temperature of the sun's photosphere is somewhere within the range of 4500 and 6000 degrees Kelvin. When considering the intense heat which secretes from the sun it is an interesting fact that we are in such a correct proportion of distance from it, in order for life to flourish. This also supports the inner outer cell growth theory, because of our rotation around the sun acting as a nucleus and thus being balanced by the surrounding charges, which in this case would be the orbiting planets and moons. Some may argue against this outlook, because Earth is presently the only celestial body in our solar system where life is able to flourish. However, I do believe that once again scientific equivalency wins! Inside of a photosphere such as our sun's, the gasses will reach such incredibly high levels of heat that when luminousness or denseness is achieved, no photons can pass through. And in some rare cases, this barrier of the universal body can form into further opposite to opposite reactions of creation.

A common procedure in the scientific field of astronomy is to look back in time in order to further comprehend stars, which are farther away from us. This type of observance is obviously for a better comprehension of the big bang theory. When I ponder on the thought of this brand of scientific examination, of the peering through space and time in a backwards and forward direction, it furthers my curiosity as to the constant change which exists throughout the universe.

It has also been concluded by experts that in the infancy of the cosmic microwave background radiation hypothesis, which is said to have begun immediately after the big bang, there were no stars to light the universe. The time frame as to these astronomical occurrences is so short and fragmented, that if properly processed between the equilibrium of mind, space, and time, it could help us better understand the theoretical time warps which constantly fluctuate throughout the universe. Compared to the mind shadow in the form of a relationship, this concept can hold substance.

Then you have what is called the cosmic electromagnetic radiation background. This other astronomical existence does pose similarity to the cosmic microwave background. This other scientific hypothesis deals with waves of radioactive matter, which differ from the consistencies of the cosmic microwave background.

The scientific community has also come to the conclusion that within the origin of the big bang, there were only three primary elements: hydrogen, helium, and some lithium. It is believed that the other elements were formed within the original stars and through a miraculous process of light-synthesized absorption. This is the basis of the constant growth and change of the universe, and you must have heard, at one time or another, that we are made of star dust. This is true, but this process is always relative to the infinite and the infinitesimal. This represents the basis of scientific equivalency and also the universal body. This universal reproductive process adheres to the universal body, because of the fact that the universe was born with only three original elements, thus posing a striking similarity to the way our human D.N.A. forms into our bodies. D.N.A. represents the building blocks of the human anatomy, which somehow coincides with time for the perfect ultra-functional and complex formation of the graceful human being. Every seven years or so, all of the original chemical consistencies of our bodies are replaced and renewed over this duration of time, thus meaning that the star substance of our human bodies is constantly being replaced over time. Therefore, all humans, relative to mind, time, and space, are performing a complex flux of a time travel relationship. Do you think you know what we are figuring out yet? Keep reading!

It has also been determined by experts that through an examination of certain Earthly matters, we could be the result of an inner universal supernova explosion. As for the present knowledge I have on this topic, I would have to say that a celestial body such as Jupiter and its potential to become a star leads me to believe, through a pondering of scientific equivalency, that an implosion of black hole antimatter must occur first in order for the promotion of star birth to happen.

You see, our sun, as well as the very first stars, mostly consisted of hydrogen. It is estimated that the sun consists of approximately 70% hydrogen. This hydrogen is obviously able to reproduce just like human D.N.A., because it has been fueling the sun for ages. Maybe this is the infinitesimal energy from a parallel universe in which I related to Einstein's theory of relativity.

How is it possible that our sun has been able to last so long from this inner hydrogen reproduction? As I just hinted in the last paragraph, I think this is more due to its dependence on infinitesimal energies than we would presently be led to believe. This is not a new process compared to the age of the universe, which has been proven from the hydrogen, which was so prominent within the infant stars of the universe.

So, how can our newer sun resemble stars of universal origin? Well, the obvious answer is that this has been the universal process the whole time. This could also have occurred through an opposite to opposite reaction of creation over an eon. By that last statement, what I meant was that this could be a direct reaction of opposites as to a parallel universe. In this case, time would be a lesser factor than substances. However, the opposite substances of the two parallel universes would create their suns, which represent light, therefore, the equilibrium continues.

Another supporting factor as to this sun concept is that the hydrogen atom is not only the first type of universal atom, but it is also the simplest. The hydrogen atom consists of a single proton as a nucleus and one opposite, namely, a balancing orbiting electron. The interior of a star has such a high level of compacted heat, that it will swipe this orbiting electron, thus leaving the atom incomplete. However, this will lead to an inner energy, thus supporting the ramifications of the theory of relativity in pertinence to the excreting energy of the universal within. Next, this original hydrogen atom is assumed to be dissociated just like salt dissolving in water, thus producing a charge. This process can also be related to gas when mixed with radiation. This type of process is a universal constant.

It is now time for me to reveal another chart. This chart represents actions of positive and negative energy or any opposite to opposite reactions of creation, as to their relationship with time, or better yet, the "Naturalistic Line." As you examine this chart, I want you to process the thought that all forms of energy move in fluctuation to one another, and you must also keep in mind that this is a truism that applies to the relationship between all physical substances and their actions. Please observe the chart below.

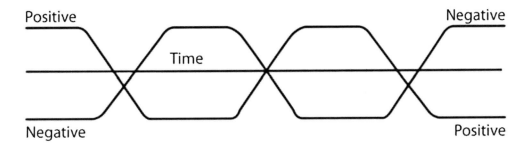

Once again, this chart is intended to aid you in your understanding of positive and negative energy, as well as any opposite to opposite reactions of creation as posed to time. Remember, the prime opposites of the universe are light and dark. And you must also remember that energy derives from both the plus and negative. This previous chart will hold further precedence once I have revealed the primary goal.

Fact: our sun is said to give off 4 million tons of energy every second, which proves that the application of the theory of relativity relating to the infinitesimal is true. In relation to this, there is something called a neutrino, which is similar to a neutron, but is so small that it cannot be measured, I believe that these neutrinos could be an advocate to the process of the hydrogen infinitesimal source, which maintains the sun's energy.

The word quasar, which is short for "quasi-stellar object," describes a category of surprisingly energetic point-like sources, which exist in radiation. This was not discovered until the 1960s. Today, astronomers refer to this existence as a prime example of an active galactic nucleus. Quasars are millions of times more energetically potent than the common black hole. The process I have mentioned (star birth) can be aided by a fathoming of the differing properties of actions and physical makeup of black holes and stars. We shall discuss star birth further in the "2001-2010" segment.

When a galaxy is more animated, a quasar may act as its core. This type of galaxy will tend to be a more luminous galaxy type. To fathom these quasar-cored bright galaxies, you must understand that this brand of galaxy can be up to several thousand times the size of our Milky Way galaxy. Furthermore, although these galaxies are said to have quasar cores, it is the common hypothesis that these and other galaxy types will have a black hole at its center. Black holes can achieve sizes as much as several million times the size of the sun. Ponder for a moment the luminous stars revolving around a centrifugal black hole. I now remind you that this resembles a vortex, which is similar to a spiraling strand of human D.N.A. These revolving stars are an opposite of the black hole, in which it moves around in a whirlpool-like motion. When peering into a galaxy with a black hole, it represents a three dimensional cone moving to and fro in exactly the same type of method as the chart I revealed based on my inner outer cell growth theory. You might want to observe that chart again and make this comparison. This set of data supports all of my theories.

Furthermore, this concept resembles a flushing toilet. And "Uh, Oh, I have to stop writing now, because I have to take a shit! Okay, I'm back, two chunks, four wipes, one flush." Maybe that resembles the vortex of an atom type? "Back to the show!" It has also been theorized by astronomers that in the more primitive ages of a galaxy, there was an over-abundance of gasses and dusts. This process is essential for the present day sunlight nourishment, which we are blessed to have. This leads to the imminent manifestation of luminous light matter. Eventually, the swirling motion would lead to the complete formation of the given galaxies' shape and form. As all universal existences move, they collect matter and all of them in one way or another are balanced by vortex-like entities; this even applies to human thinking.

There was a concept that my friend Matt (a former Deallegiance member) came up with, which I did not understand at the time, but I would soon fathom and contribute to my vision. When he told me this theory as we were walking down Bridge Street in Lowell Massachusetts, I was having a bad day and I was quite annoyed to be honest with you, but this was in no way Matt's fault. Anyhow, this theory of Matt's is basically that the human mind represents a sphere and as your mind deals with life's trials and tribulations, this mind sphere will rotate and collect matter. This matter, which clings to the mind sphere, is the substance of life's challenges and as your mind sphere collects this negative thinking matter, it disturbs its natural function for the pursuit of inner peace. What he stated next was imperative to the manifestation of the three forms of consciousness, but especially to the collective subconscious. The main point that Matt got across to me was that you have to prevent this mind sphere from collecting negative thought energy. In other words, you must keep the mind sphere clean! In relation to this, there is a "Rush" album called "Hold Your Fire," and on the cover, there are three clean red spheres, which could be meant to represent the three members of Rush. Now, I am not saying that Rush made this album cover with this theory in mind, but I did relate it to that and thus the mind sphere concept was born. So, this is one theory I cannot claim to have made, so thanks, Matt!

Back to black holes for a moment, it is obvious that a black hole is the centering force which promotes galactic activity. Due to the constant whirlpool motion of a galaxy, the black hole becomes deeper and vaster. This concludes to the astronomical hypothesis of an opposite to opposite reaction of creation slowly transforming into the vortex, with its antimatter center. As the black hole becomes denser, the stars become more luminous. I believe this may one day lead into a universal birth of which we are presently unable to fathom. Maybe it will be universal wide connection.

As for colors throughout the universe (which will be appropriately compensated for in the "Senses" segment), it is interesting when examining the formation of a galaxy. When realizing that colors are affected by heat, it is interesting that galaxies that appear red are very remote, and there is a continuing flux within the sequence of colors throughout. If this observation can be applied to red shifts and blue shifts, as well as the examinations in the macroscopic world of such phenomena as fire, we could, through the comprehension of scientific equivalency and with further abilities, understand the totality of the most supreme of universal relationships.

In what is called the ultra deep field exist the building blocks of galaxies, which are humanly comprehensible. These are of course the newer galaxies. Remember, human D.N.A. resembles a vortex and D.N.A. is the building blocks of the human makeup. If you are catching on to my scientific methods, you probably realize that another comparison should be made in this instance. So, if the extensions of universal existences are balanced by mind, space, and time, the other entities which I have theorized do also exist through a relationship of a backwards and forwards universal time flux, this leads me to conclude that they must also be a component to the galactic equilibrium. This balance of relationship must therefore, include spiritual, chemical, dream, and thought fabrics. This hypothesis makes even more sense when it is applied to the positive and negative energy timeline chart, which you previously examined. Scientific equivalency is the prime scientific factor to all concepts relative to that previous chart.

Continuing on, our Milky Way galaxy and the universe in general, does reveal some imperfections. However, we can come to a conclusion of understanding the needs for these present imperfections. Astronomers will often refer to the Milky Way galaxy as a cannibal galaxy. The reason for this term is that it pertains to a theory, of which the vortex behavior of our galaxy can cause the ripping and the tearing of dwarf galaxies. This concept can be related to what is called topology, which we will discuss at a later section.

Now, as for the constant flux in colors throughout existence, I would like to once again relate this observance to red shifts and blue shifts. The scientific community has determined, through the studies of the astronomical realm, many significant hypotheses. By accessing the famous Hubble telescope, we have learned that those celestial bodies which are reddish, are not only very distant, but they are also moving away with increasing speed. This fact supports both the original big bang theory as well as my enhancement of this theory. These reddish celestial bodies are moving along in a manner which represents a time-altered process. A normal Earth or nearby galactic explosion would not behave this way. This is a result of a time warp, which is manifested by a variety of opposite to opposite reactions of creation. As for a complete conclusion on this matter, I must admit to you that I have many questions left to answer as to the substance of this astronomical process. My understanding of the big bang does pose credibility, but obviously, as in life, obstacles need to be overcome. The most supportive factor in my enhancement of the big bang theory would have to be the relationships between human thought and the vastness of space and time.

The Virgo Cluster is a cluster of galaxies which is incredibly distant and incredibly massive. The Virgo Cluster is estimated at roughly 60 million light years away from Earth and it consists of over a thousand galaxies. What can be learned through the proportions of distance and makeup of the Virgo Cluster is simply that change is a constant. When applying this to scientific equivalency, one must make exceptions, due to both human limitations and more so to universal time flux and the carrying out of a balanced universe, in the same fashion, by which I am carrying out human understanding through the concept of the collective subconscious and the hopeful imminent process of universal contact.

Like our sun and other astronomical existences, this Virgo Cluster is constantly gaining and losing matter and energy at an extremely high rate. The Virgo Cluster does not even remotely resemble a vortex, but that is simply due to universal process.

As for the black hole centrifuge of our Milky Way galaxy, it is estimated to be about 2.6 times the mass of the sun. It is true that this Milky Way black hole represents the center of this galactic whirlpool and just like other black holes, it consists of antimatter. The brightest and thickest part of our Milky Way galaxy is dubbed as the galactic centre. It is located in the Sagittarius constellation, which by the way is most visible in the macroscopic from the southern hemisphere.

A galactic year, which can also be called a cosmic year, is the amount of time (as we understand it) that it takes for the sun or solar system to complete its orbit around the center of the galaxy. A galactic year for our sun is estimated to be approximately 225 to 250 million Earth years. However, existences of cosmic phenomena, such as black hole antimatter and the speed at which a star may go about its axis and rotation, poses a difficulty in comprehending this aspect even when applying it to scientific equivalency. You must understand that the sun or any other star is in itself going through its natural process of rotating for the completion of its galactic year, at the same time the light from it travels in all surrounding directions and this is due to its spherical shape. Because of the equilibrium, which scientific equivalency supports, an incredibly fast conflict of actions will occur. When observing this process, I conclude that this is all relative to time altering and the constant change and flux which occurs throughout. Therefore, such galactic paranormal actions cannot be appropriately applied to the conscious mind. This means that we must enter this into the personal subconscious for the achievement of universal contact between all universal balances relative to the human mind. It is estimated that there are about 100 billion stars in our Milky Way galaxy alone. And for those of you who are good at math, which I am not, that equals to seven to ten times to the twenty-second power.

Something called the electromagnetic spectrum, which is in basic terms a range and measurement of all possible existing electromagnetic radiation frequencies, which by the way always will secrete from powerful light matter celestial bodies, which can further promote the applications of scientific equivalency. To properly comprehend the conceptualization of electromagnetism, you should ponder, for a moment, my previous elaborations in reference to human frequency. Interestingly so, electromagnetic waves of this kind are for the most part beyond the range of human frequency. All concepts of magnetism, which we will later discuss, is essential if we are to apply this type of existence to scientific equivalency. In conclusion, the stars that we can observe in the night sky are only a miniscule fragment of the entire electromagnetic spectrum of the Milky Way galaxy.

Dark energy, which is more challenging to comprehend than other energy forms, is a type of energy which diffuses and spreads certain space matter in a coinciding rate as the universal expansion. This concept, like all other astronomical existences, can be further understood by thinking about the big bang theory. Remember, the universe is gaining in speed, and it is the energy of this acceleration that is considered to be dark energy. However, you must not confuse dark energy with antimatter.

Continuing on, I believe that antimatter is the foundation of opposite to opposite reactions of creation. Antiparticles will interlock and change within opposite matter particles. An example of this cosmic opposite to opposite reaction of creation is this; if you take an anti-electron, which can be considered a positron, an electron with a positive charge, you can cause it to merge with an anti-proton, which is a proton with a negative charge, rather than its normal positive charge, you would create an anti-hydrogen atom. This anti-hydrogen atom thus represents the simplest atom form of the antimatter type. I also believe that this process represents the boundaries between parallel universes, which aid the opposite to opposite reactions of creation between these two realms of the paranormal parallel. Furthermore, this process in reverse would obviously lead to a normal hydrogen atom on our side of the parallel. As for the intricacies of the ruling factors which pertain to reactions between matter and antimatter, it is very complicated. Such hypotheses can aid us in the natural understanding of all opposite to opposite reactions of creation. We can also reap significant benefits from applications of such theories and apply them to scientific equivalency, which will ultimately lead us to further mysterious discoveries vital for the promotion of human understanding.

When relating this to the mind shadow, we once again will realize that a balance of mind, time, and space is an imminent reality, as to universal contact. If you are a bit confused at this point, I say don't sweat because this is a personal and collective subconscious process.

We will now briefly discuss what is called a fifth force. For a very long time in relation to the science of physics, it was believed that four forces were needed for the comprehension of the interaction between all forms of matter. These four forces are; one, electromagnetic force, which causes the attractive forces between positive and negative charges, two, strong nuclear force, which is responsible for holding atomic nuclei together, and when realizing that nuclear energy is always tightly compacted, this makes perfect sense, three, weak nuclear force, which is somehow responsible for radioactive decay, four, gravity which is the most well known of these four forces, the attractive pull that exists between objects, which of course are constant throughout the universe.

When relating these forces to time and realizing that time, like these forces, is constantly altered throughout existence, one can fathom this brand of astronomical relationship. Gravity, believe it or not, is the weakest of these four forces. Although gravity is altered throughout existence, it is a constant. However, despite the fact that gravity is the weakest of these forces, it is at the same time the most dominant. Apply that thought to my enhancement of the big bang theory and your consciousness will lead to personal subconscious activity.

Electromagnetic force, like gravity, is able to achieve measures of extreme wavelengths. The reason that electromagnetic forces act as they do, is because electrically neutral forces are somehow able to cancel out surrounding charges, which could be relative to my theories, but mostly to inner outer cell growth. This process can also be applied to the positive negative time-line chart.

Furthermore, it has also been determined by astronomers that due to the acceleration of the universe, there must be a fifth force. So, what is this fifth force? The fifth force has been comprehended through the existence of what are called vacuum forces and virtual particles. A vacuum force can be related to the concept of a black hole, which sucks in matter and thus creates an opposite to opposite reaction of creation, which acts between matter and antimatter.

A virtual particle is a particle that exists for a limited duration in space. So, where does this particle go once it has decomposed? I believe that this particle will either go beyond human frequency or into a parallel universe. Of course it is easier for astronomers to fathom a fifth force, because they are constantly observing the astronomical realm through a rigorous thought process, seemingly of a beyond dimension. Due to the fact that we humans are more apt to react directly from our senses, one could, in relation to the fifth force, potentially comprehend a sixth sense, which we will discuss in further detail in the senses segment. When relating to any beyond type conceptualization, I have concluded that because humans have five senses and will soon fathom a sixth sense through the manifestation of the collective subconscious, this is directly related to the four forces and the fifth force of space in being vacuum force. Interestingly so, when we relate by comparison these forces to the senses, it does somehow represent a sort of mind sequence.

Now, a vacuum or a black hole, which consists of antimatter, can be a very deceiving thing. Because of the studies which have been carried out through the new science of quantum physics, to assume that antimatter is a complete absence of matter is an absolute over-simplification. The way I see it, as I am sure many others do, is that antimatter is simply the direct opposite of matter, by which it interlocks and changes with. This means that even opposite matters of one another, which are considered to be both part of antimatter or matter, proves that there is an opposite bonding within these realms, as well as between them. This thought can also be related to reactions between parallel existences. Think back to the anti-hydrogen scenario of which I previously explained. Apply this complete thought to the mind shadow and you will achieve an inner connection, which is resulted by the universal equilibrium.

Any observances of the geological or topological shaping of the galaxies throughout the universe, in a relationship with universal expansion and dark energy could lead to a conceivable hypothesis, where light could be bent in space, which would likely require spacetime curvature, if this process were to take place. This thought is made through the basis of what is called the cosmic shear.

Unlike myself, Einstein and others have been able to further comprehend such cosmic phenomena through their knowledge of mathematics and physics. This is why my method of explaining a universal balance through scientific equivalency is an easier method for the common person to comprehend. As for the cosmic shear method of astronomical study, one can see that the universal balance is just so and not simply a realm of nonsensical static, which would obviously be incomprehensible in a great many ways.

You see, the universe in a variety of ways could be viewed as an advanced form of a static-like entity. Because scientific equivalency is a correct theory, this static has also balanced out throughout the universe. Einstein was an advocate to the theory that the universe was once completely static and that it is still a prominent universal existence. However, through what is called a cosmological constant (a factor causing a balance of gravity that has caused much of the present universe to remain static), the universal progressions have continued to expand with dark energy, yet at the same time remaining balanced throughout.

It is estimated that roughly 5 billion years ago, gasses began to convert into stars at a much higher rate of duration. This would also lead into the progression of a more luminous universe. It has also been estimated, that somewhere around 4 billion years ago, fuel and energy for these stars began to decrease, thus more stars were dying than being born. However, through a comprehension of opposite to opposite reactions of creation and the existence of a light and dark universal coinciding action being applied to the decomposing of a virtual power, I have concluded that these dying stars may have had the same fate as the virtual particle. This means that these old stars have either left our human frequency or entered into the next parallel universe or maybe even or both.

When a star is born, it does pose some individual identity which makes it different from another star. However, it has been determined that its surroundings are imperative to its formation and basic makeup. This concept could be termed as a chain reaction of opposite to opposite reactions of creation.

Do you recall my statements on colors, including red shifts and blue shifts? Well, pay attention, because what I am about to state is relevant to that concept. Stars that are within the spiral arms of a galaxy will tend to have a bluish color and may have shorter lived lives, in comparison to other star types. Stars that are blue also are young stars. Is this due to universal frequency, as well as heat?

VISION OF A MENTAL PATIENT

You see, all stars, including our sun, are directly related to nebulae. Nebulae is a huge cloud of star dust, hydrogen, and plasma; this nebulae, which is simply a mass of space gas does in fact shield and protect certain matters, including new stars. This leads to the promoting of yet another universal equilibrium which perfectly adheres to scientific equivalency. You might be thinking, "Exactly how does this astronomical scenario represent a positive result?" Well, because of this type of nebulae shielding, damaging astronomical properties such as intense radiation will be deterred from destroying such things, which would damage the process of the given opposite to opposite reaction of creation and its boundary centrifuge, which is paramount to the universal process.

Nebulae shielding can also cool a star, which is imperative to the life of an infant star. This cooling process takes place through hydrogen molecules, which have the capability to radiate energy. In basic terms, the hostile and potentially disturbing energy goes through a taming process of forces, which may be unbalanced, thus causing a cosmic disruption. This will lead to the essential star cooling, so that it may continue its natural course. Once this process gives the necessary balance through an intricate distribution of carbon and oxygen atoms, the gas cloud nebulae will collapse under the newly balanced magnetic to gravitational pull. This force of action will then be opposed by coinciding particle motions, which will give the final touch of astronomical detail. Once again, scientific equivalency wins!

In a scenario where the particles would be moving with too much velocity, they could overtake the magnetized gravity stronghold, thus, a sort of reverse chain reaction would not be achieved and the new star would be a short-lived entity. Such seemingly defeating actions like this can occur from time to time, which would defeat scientific equivalency; this is not the first time I have presented a scenario that could seemingly defeat my theory. However, I do have explanations for these types of astronomical occurrences. In this case, I will access the parallel universe concept in order to explain this away.

In recent times, as astronomers would examine scenarios with these similarities of star formation, some have concluded that these star birth regions are subject to a constant process of formation and deformation of space matter. This is a type of diffusion which is needed for the structure of all of my concepts relative to the balance of mind, space, and time. As I elaborated in the environmental portion of "Politics," the back and forth movement of molecules will cause temperature changes. From this hypothesis, astronomers have discovered that a nebulae acting as a protective shield can cause molecular stillness which transforms gastric matter into space dust. This is yet another example of a barrier within the universal body and the mind shadow.

There is another star formation called the brown dwarf. An example of a brown dwarf star is Gleise 229, which is located in the Lepus constellation, approximately nineteen light years away from Earth. Amazingly, this type of star is estimated to be within the range of twenty to fifty times the size of Jupiter, the gas giant planet. To give you an idea of the massiveness we are dealing with, the great red spot of Jupiter can fit the Earth in it three times. Yet, the brown dwarf is still classified as a small star.

The brown dwarf is a comparatively cool star type and in some instances, a brown dwarf may not be technically labeled as a star due to its small size. For a star to be termed as a star in the technical sense, it must be at least 8 percent the size of the sun. Due to the brown dwarf's surroundings of actions and reactions between matters, they are caused to have consistency and luminousness as such. Despite its level of energy, the brown dwarf is able to feed off the infinitesimal sourced gasses in order for it to flourish for a good duration of time.

Now that I have stated my case regarding the relationship of the astronomical to the human psyche, including the mind shadow, the three levels of consciousness, opposite to opposite reactions of creation, parallel universes, the universal body, and most importantly scientific equivalency, it is time to end this astronomy segment. From here on, we will not technically touch on relationships in pertinence to the realm of space until the "2001-2010" segment, where we will have further discussions relative to astronomy. We will now move on to the "Reflections" segment, where I will more properly account for the concept of the parallel universes. So, try not to get sucked into any mind vortexes and of course, read on!"

REFLECTIONS

In this segment on reflections, we will indulge in an exploration of the visible, yet unaccounted for imminent paranormal realities, which I have manifested through the accessing of the three realms of consciousness. Before I reveal what can be figured out through a study and understanding of what a reflection consists of, including properties of substance and actions and before my hands on elaboration about what we can learn from a reflection, I must first discuss with you some of the basics the human race has been able to determine from the reflective process, of which light has created through a combination of nature and human function.

Firstly, I deem it necessary to inform you how glass, which is used to make a mirror, is made of. This will also account for the process by which mirrors are industrially made.

You see, glass is made from melting sand or silica, a glassy mineralalso detected in quartz and opal. You must remember that quartz and opal, like silica, come from the grinding of these rocks. Pure silica can be melted into glass at approximately 4200 degrees Fahrenheit. In the case of quartz and opal, these must first be processed before being subjected to the melting process. Sodium carbonate can be used for enhancing the quality of the produced glass. For some reason, when this sodium carbonate is added, the required temperature for making glass decreases substantially. The main thing you need to remember in order for you to understand my theories is that glass is made from the melting of silica, which is in sand.

It is also true that other types of glass can be made by using both organic and inorganic substances. These glass types do not apply to the literal or technical defining of glass. You see, these other types are made from plastics (acrylic glass) and some other types, which are semi-relevant to the mind function of which we are about to embark on. Furthermore, I stress that if you are to fathom the totality of this "Reflections" segment and enter it into your personal subconscious, a comprehension of the fact that a reflection can come from other sources such as water, metals, and plastics, you will be rendered capable of further human understanding. You should also take into account that these other two reflection types pose differences. A plastic reflection will be less defined and the same goes for a steel reflection. A water reflection can move about and pose other interesting factors of reflective functions.

The complete process of glass production does have its complexities of detail, though the processes involved are mostly irrelevant to the psyche connection we are soon to experience. Another imperative detail is that once silica is melted, it logically must go through a cooling process, thus being exposed to extremely cold temperatures. One final thing to keep in mind before further elaborations is that molecular back and forth movement is responsible for levels of hot and cold.

Okay, at this point, I must supply you with sufficient data about silica (sand) itself. In order for proper comprehension of what I call "reflection connection," I remind you of another previous statement in the "Politics" (Part One) portion. This would be the fact that the study of rocks, which is relevant to this discussion, and ice, which is somewhat relevant, and trees, which are completely irrelevant, can be observed for the determining of past weather history. More important to our present discussion is the fact that rocks can be used as such, but the fact that ice in the Arctic and Antarctic can be observed and reap the same result is semi-relevant, because ice can reflect, but it represents a more short termed reflective process that cannot sufficiently satisfy the goal of this segment.

Silica, in correct and technical terms, is an altered form of silicon dioxide. Silica, of course, is most commonly found in sand; quartz in very miniscule amounts can be found in the cell wall of what is called a diatom. A diatom is an extremely small moleculecomposed of two atoms. These diatoms tend to form in colonies in the shape of ribbons and zigzags, which can occasionally resemble a vortex.

Silica is most prominent in the Earth's crust. Silica is made from rocks that are tightly packed together. Silica takes its form by a process of fusion. Fusion is a blending process of substances that causes matter to compose itself. In relation, I must inform you about *infusion*, which means a process of instilling or taking apart; in other words, infusion is fusion in reverse. The concept of what I call "fusion infusion" is the process by which all universal matter and antimatter is created and this is the foundation of the process of opposite to opposite reactions of creation. "Fusion infusion" is a concept which will hold extreme importance throughout the rest of this book.

Continuing on, rocks that are jagged in their geometric form are fused by a method of tight packing function. Rocks that are smooth in their geometric form are a result of a melting process, like rocks that are found near volcanoes. Silica can be found in both of these rock forms.

When silicon goes through a fusion melting process with oxygen, the result is of a manifestation of silica. Weather conditions over a duration, will produce silica through an act of nature. Remember, sand is produced naturally over an incredible amount of time from the natural destructive erosion of rocks and although not obvious, this also relates to the balance of mind, space, and time. For such a huge amount of sand to exist, just as it does today, a time period of humanly unfathomable proportions as to our collective time frequency is essential for its existence.

You see, when a substance similar to silica called silicon monoxide is compacted together with a chemical element of a non reactive gas called argon, which is in a pure form of itself created from a process of a complex self development, which goes through a cooling process with helium and oxygen atoms and is then fused with a microwave discharge, silicon dioxide is then created. Therefore, through a thorough comprehension of scientific equivalency from a fusion infusion process in the fashion of a tight packing function of molecules, being set to a reaction through the intricacies of topologic connections and opposite to opposite reactions of creation, then finally being applied to a wavelength that is beyond human frequency, silicon dioxide, silica, or sand can be created through this intentional humanly carried out process.

You may have often heard the notion that sand represents time "You know, sands of time." Sand is a personal and collective subconscious symbol of transformation which represents time. When we sleep and dream, we get sleep in our eyes, which could, in a theoretical manner, represent a subconscious forming of a grain of sand, which is carried out through a dream fabric personal subconscious to optic nerve connection of sorts, which relates to the sands of time, and remember, dreams are an altered form of time. Due to such paranormal phenomena being added to a scientific understanding (through scientific equivalency, of course) it does support this collective subconscious conceptualization of sand being physical time. For a bit of irony, my watch says Quartz right on it. Of course, I do realize that this is simply the name of the manufacturer, I mean…I'm not stupid. However, this does represent what I call a connection, which we will discuss in detail in the "What is a Connection" segment. This connection is a direct result of the universal equilibrium which exists between mind, time, and space. Far fetched, huh? So, what! Keep reading!

So, sand represents time, but you know what? So does light! Light also has a subconscious connection of meaning as to the totality of the time space continuum. Furthermore, a reflection being made from the melting of sand (Remember, molecules must move fast for heat production to induce this melting) will soon process light and this is representative of the ultimate speed. Speed relates to light and light relates to time. This process will result in a reflection induced by all of these properties of substances and actions, which directly relate to time!

Okay, a plane of glass which is produced through a physical manifestation of the mind as related to time has now been accounted for. However, a single plane of glass only gives a faint reflection, but a mirror will give the full effect. You must also take into consideration that all energy and light on Earth is produced from the sun. Molecules of the sun move back and forth at such incredible speeds and this is crucial for any reflective process.

Moving on: Basically, a glass for a mirror goes through a process of smoothing and other enhancements for its completion. A two-way mirror, which is often referred to as a one-way mirror, will reflect enough light to carry out a man-made reflection. For this type of mirror, the glass is basically slightly thicker than that of a single plane of glass and the enhancements perfect it. The last detail I will apply is that the invention of the mirror has led to much further advanced technological inventions such as the television, which is a key contribution to the manifestation of the collective subconscious. Mirror reflections and televisions represent a time connection, which is something you will understand in due time.

It is now time for me to reveal the main premise to exactly what a mirror reflection represents. The main premise relative my scientific observance of a mirror reflection is formed in the way that a mirror emits light for the manifestation of a reflective image. Firstly, a reflection is another example of an opposite to opposite reaction of creation. Unlike the mind shadow concept, a mirror reflection is not an opposite to opposite reaction of creation, which acts between light and dark. Instead, it is an opposite to opposite reaction of creation between two sources of light. Most people would conceive a mirror reflection as an exact image of themselves. This is somewhat true, but what you actually see in a mirror reflection is your exact opposite. At this point, you might be thinking this to be untrue, but fathom this; in a mirror reflection your right side is your left side and vice versa.

Try this; look into your mirror and hold up your right hand and you will see that your right hand is the left hand of your mirror image. Another example to aid you in comprehending the properties of a mirror reflection is if you have writing on your shirt it will be written backwards, this backwards writing is what led me to the creation of the "Language of the Mad" in which we will discuss in the next segment.

This reflective type of opposite to opposite reaction of creation is (as I just stated) a reaction between two sources of light rather than one. Why two? The reason that I have concluded that a mirror reflection is from two sources of light is due to what actually takes place in the center of a mirror reflection. You must understand that light from the sun goes through a process of connection between opposites. So, what is the exact function? In the center of a mirror reflection, light will interlock and change in both a forward and reverse method, and this is executed by a process of extreme intricate topologic connections. Therefore, because this is a process of an opposite to opposite reaction of creation, a reflection thus produces your exact opposite reflection. This is yet another result of scientific equivalency.

Okay, I told you that a mirror reflection is due to two sources of light, but I have not fully accounted for that claim thus far. Anyhow, it is due to our sun and the sun of the parallel universe. You most likely do not understand this claim yet, so allow me to elaborate further. In order for you to understand the thought process, of which I am about to reveal in our collective thoughts, I must present you with another quick and simple reflection experiment. Once I reveal this experiment, you will be well on your way to a full comprehension of my vision and what I call "Knowing."

Quick and simple, here we go; if you have a room in your home, such as your bathroom or bedroom where you can see a mirror reflection of a door into another room in the reflection then you are all set. Okay, look into this reflection and make sure the door to the other room is closed in your reflection. Once you have peered into this reflection, I want you to open the door and take notice in the reflection, of what you can see in the other room. Now, close the door and you will no longer be able to see (in the reflection) into this other room anymore. You're probably thinking, so what? But what I want you to realize at this point is that within this reflection, the realm beyond this now closed door is still inside of this reflection just as much as it is in your exterior world. This type of thinking is imperative to a furthering of the potential of the collective subconscious.

You see, everything exists inside of a reflection no matter what you see in it, and the same goes for the regular exterior world. However, I have still not compensated all that has to do with my opinion that a mirror reflection is created from two sources of light rather than one. This is because the sun exists in the reflection, just as it does in the physical environment. Therefore, the sun connects with the mirror's sun and you have yourself a reflection. There are reflections all over the world and if you move a mirror, it will always reflect the centrifuge of its location in time, area, and space.

Now, here comes the shocker! What we have just discussed relative to the assumption that everything exists in a reflection regardless of its location, I have figured out something that scientists have been struggling with for a very long time. The reason and cause of a mirror reflection, which is produced from the sun from the melting of sand and is then combined with the reflected sun, has led me to believe that this is because of the existence of parallel universes. Therefore, the sun of the parallel universe is the opposite of our sun and it is due to the sun in the reflection, which is obviously the sun of the parallel universe, which, as I have previously stated, the opposite to opposite reaction of creation in a mirror reflection is formed from two sources of light.

Remember, no matter where a mirror is or how far you move it, whether a mile or a billionth of an inch, the reflection of space and time, which was created through the melting of sand, which is a subconscious representative of time, does represent another parallel universe. So, rather than saying that everything exists in a mirror reflection, you could actually say instead that the entire universe exists within a mirror reflection.

Seeing that we have opened the theoretical door to the existence of parallel universes, I feel it is once again time to show you some more lyrics. This was both a Deallegiance and a Malicious Intent song. Without further ado, I now present track one on the second Deallegiance demo tape called *Symbol of Transformation* and track seven on the Malicious Intent album *Mind Control*. This song was appropriately entitled "Open Door."

No better way to spend my time, no other way that I should live
Just can't get my point across, composed in a world of falsehood
Fear no feeling for which I bear, can't find reasons not to care
Lack of willingness and the will to share—I live my way too!
Religion is for what you give, the vision we see what is life?
There's nothing stronger you've withstood, accept what cultivates inside!
Sensual in the marvel's eye, eyes as wide as knowing guides
Flying towards thy holy bride!
Stand tall withstand the fall, Reconstructed the view flowing through us all
Break out correspond put an end to doubt
Accumulated the life within the call
We are all related within one another's hatred
Sadness, cannot deal with all this madness no more
Got to be free from black magic, open all the doors!
Forgotten youth of fire, reach for the liturgy higher
Lost children of their own desire
Reach inside yourself and learn to conspire!
Put an end to the unholy liar! Repay! Speak your mind, know what to say!
A night of sophistry the mission's prophecy
Within an odyssey your inner self can see
It's plain for all to see, escape from all with me
To fly away be free, we'll end this dynasty!
Freedom not democracy, give us what we really need
Human race endangered breed, Set our pace and plant this seed

VISION OF A MENTAL PATIENT

Falling towards eternal fate, grow it now before it's late
Twisting turning through it all never will I fall!
Communism self-destructs the dark eye is it luck?
Is it true what they say, will the world unite this way?
This deed will be done in the Chariot of the Sun
And in the end when we have won we will meet nature's sun
Don't deny it to your soul, just designate your goal!
I'll teach you to unfold, then my story will be told
We will be wide awake, for the walls we must break!

So, what about a water reflection? Many of us do realize that water is the stuff of life. Water is a prime source of nourishment and it acts as a cleanser of our bodies and possibly of our senses. Moisture and water are both vital for the life cycle. All plant life, including desert cactus, and mammals and animals must have water in order for them to exist. Interestingly so, cactus does need water, but they live in deserts. How? You must understand that cactus has an amazing capability to conserve water and they do not require much of it over a long duration. Cactus contains the green plant pigment chlorophyll and through their own unique method of photosynthesis, they are able to survive with a small quantity of water moisture. It is because of a cactus's thick-walled stem, as well as a type of waxy coating on its skin, that it is able to do so. It is this unique cacti photosynthesis and its unusual makeup, which allows them to thrive under seemingly unlivable conditions. The cactus represents a good example of life and creation and also supports my theory of scientific equivalency.

If you have caught on to my way of thinking, you may already realize that water is made through a fusion infusion process, and I assume that you have also fathomed a topological 3D Jigsaw puzzle, which is a fusion infusion of hydrogen and oxygen. It is no coincidence that water is made from oxygen (which we breathe in and transform into carbon dioxide when we exhale) and hydrogen, which is the simplest of all atom types. However, to form at least the smallest possible amount of water (a molecule), you require two simple hydrogen atoms bonded to one oxygen atom.

When I was a patient at the CREU unit in Boston Massachusetts, one of my staff friends, a nurse named Tom, who I always made friendly conversation with, began to talk about water with me for some reason. He said that if you simply ran hydrogen gas into oxygen gas you would create water and I said, "No shit." But then he added that you would need a spark of electricity in order to cause the fusing action and also in order to aid the bonding actions. Truthfully, I am not sure of the details why this spark would be required, but Tom's statement led me to a further conclusion that stemmed from a thought I had one day while looking at my reflection in a pond.

You see, as I peered into this pond and observed my reflection, I had a thought, which I was not sure of at the time, but I would soon realize this thought to be credible. When looking into the pond, I envisioned a horizontal line through the center of it. Due to my first realizations pertaining to my understanding of the interlocking and reversal changes, which occur to carry out any opposite to opposite reactions of creation, I was able to form this thought.

As for the spark, I was able to process its action through the infancy of scientific equivalency. You see, the spark represents the central boundary needed to carry out this particular opposite to opposite reaction of creation. A reflection, whether from water or a mirror requires a centrifuge, by which the reaction can take place for a reflection to form. Therefore, the horizontal line in this pond was the point of the center, thus acting in the same way as a mirror reflection centrifuge. So, we can easily conclude that the spark for the bonding of the oxygen and hydrogen represents the centrifuge for that particular process. This is, of course, the process of fusion infusion, which is the focal point of all creation.

You see, water is not compacted unless frozen into ice. If you look into a very clean swimming pool, you will notice many moving lines of light moving all about. This is relative to the centering process which causes a reflection. It is because the water is moving, that the sun will reflect in this manner. For some reason, a pool will give a weak reflection and this is because there is no dark at the bottom to back it up.

In a pond, there is a dark base, so a reflection will be more vivid in a pond. For a reflection to be manifested to its full extent in water, an opposite to opposite reaction of creation of light and dark is also a necessity. This is due to the differing properties of water and glass. Water has a different relationship with time and space from glass, thus it gives off different wavelengths of frequency, and that is why differing rules apply to these two reflective forces. Concluding from all of this, the claim that water is the stuff of life is an absolute truth.

I only discussed my reflection theories with one of my friends. This was another musical friend, a drummer by the name of Dan Ducharme. Dan was a smart kid and I am not sure if he recalls this conversation we had over a few beers and other stuff, but he understood me fully and commended me for this theory on reflections.

Anyway, before we move on to other mysterious properties of reflections, I would like to give my shockingly simple method for the bending of light. Einstein always was fascinated with the bending of light and his conceptualizations were both interesting and confusing. The simplest way to bend light would be through the use of a curved mirror. This would of course be a curved reflection, but remember, a reflection is an opposite to opposite reaction of creation through the accessing of light. I told you it was simple and it is, but the main thing is that it would work and that is what matters.

You must understand that there is a multitude of opposite to opposite reactions of creation, which exist throughout the universe as such, so that they can coincide with the oneness of scientific equivalency. The main three opposite reaction types that I want you to keep in mind in order for you to comprehend the totality of my vision are: one, matter to antimatter, two, light to dark, three, light to light from the parallel universes' suns, which create reflections.

Continuing on, a mirror reflection image (or any reflection for the most part) will be equal in size relative to proportional distances. However, symmetrical properties can alter a reflective images function. This does relate to the infinitesimal topological bonding, which I have mentioned from time to time. Furthermore, when you have two perpendicular mirror images reflecting off of one another and you stand in between these two mirror reflections, you will notice that because of the depth of these reflections, it will give off the illusion that alters the reflected distance, thus causing the reflection to appear with more than twice the original distance. When applying this thought to the existence of parallel universes, one could fathom how these parallel universes are linked together through some kind of topological bonding.

You see, this double reflection is a fourfold opposite to opposite reaction of creation, thus promoting a further comprehension of dimensions. If this type of reflection could be figured out, we could peer even further into the realm of the paranormal, which can only be understood through a multifold light to light opposite to opposite reaction of creation. This could also lead to other ways of examining the topologic or the simpler geometrics relative to more complex reflective processes.

Due to possible advances in the laws of geometry or topology when dealing with the direction of say a beam of light on a mirror that will be identical in reflection to the beam of light coming towards it, which is obviously related to the symmetrical shaping as applied to a reflection, it could thus cause a difference in appearance, which would be contrary to a perfectly identical yet opposite reflection. This is the result of the laws of the infinite and the infinitesimal, as applied to the topologic, geometric, and symmetric manifestations of the given reflection.

Remember, a single beam of light can reflect more than one beam off a reflection. This is because light even from a beam goes in all directions of sight and not just the direction of the beam. However, it is true that a single beam on a reflection can pose multiple beams of reaction. Due to all forms of infinite light beyond our human frequency, such as electromagnetic waves, this does hold a significant role in the process of reflective actions and reactions. The same applies to ultraviolet rays, which are beyond the frequency of human sight.

Scientists have recently discovered through the new concept of quantum sciences, which they have labeled as a phenomena where particles in motion are caused to go back to their form of origin opposite to the force acting on them, that when a reflection sees the unseeable infinitesimal, an opposite to opposite reaction of creation occurs through the existence of a reflection. Of course, I have enhanced this scientific hypothesis, because the scientific community does not yet sufficiently comprehend exactly what an opposite to opposite reaction of creation is and this is obviously because it is my personal theory. Anyhow, this supports my theory, that what happens in the center of a reflection, meaning the interlocking and reversal change of a centrifugal force is real, in relation to the properties of our physical world. This also supports my claim that the entire universe does exist within a reflection. This process is crucial in relation to the monolith, which we will discuss at a later time. Since we are dealing with the universal in between, I deem it necessary to reveal some more lyrics at this time. This was a Malicious Intent song, off the *Mind Control* album. It is called "In Between." Here is track five of *Mind Control*.

> *Embodying destiny is un-denying life*
> *the silence of this mystery, the state of being alive*
> *Glaring reflections of the truth, awake your sleeping soul*
> *A prayer for your sanity yeah!*
> *How long do dreams last? Falling shadows from the past*
> *Shedding skin like a snake, the countless ways to escape*
> *Gathering sights of black and white*
> *Hope for tomorrow's dreams, eyes inside are blazing fire*
> *Acquired from memories!*
> *Climbing inside of your mind, seeing the fear of fear*
> *reaching out for someone, but knowing you're not there*
> *Smash crash all the shit they harass*
> *Join the underground mass, destroy with gas*
> *melt the skin with that gas*

Please, don't take these lyrics the wrong way, because they have a subconscious meaning relative to my past life situations. Anyhow, through what I have elaborated thus far regardingreflections, I would like to apply the reflective process to time for a moment.

You see, because a reflection is dependent on the next parallel universe and the parallel sun, if you will, I conclude that when applying the reflective process to a timeline, or, as I like to call it, the naturalistic line, I conclude that it represents a time frequency of the beyond. This means that because two suns carry out this process, there is still the naturalistic line of infinite time, but there are three infinitesimal realms. There is the infinitesimal within the naturalistic line and then there is the infinitesimal of our universe and of the parallel universe. However, for me to label the other to realms of the infinitesimal as infinitesimal is deceiving. How can there be an outer infinitesimal? This outer infinitesimal is in fact the infinitesimal of the physical properties of the two universes responsible for a reflection.

Furthermore, there is another reason for this blunt paranormal existence. This is the existence of time. Remember, time is altered throughout existence and there must be a major time shift from one parallel to the next. I will now attempt to show you this concept in another chart. This chart has its limitations as far as pertaining to parallel existences. This chart is the method of viewing the three realms of the infinitesimal from our universal focal point. Please examine the chart below.

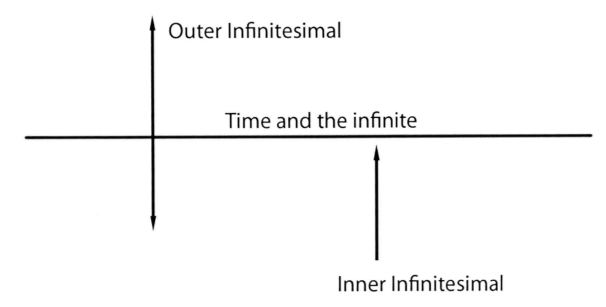

Okay, this chart may have cleared this up for you in at least a visual sense. I do believe that when showing time as a straight line, you can give an image which is more challenging to describe in words. So, let's move on, shall we?

You see, light derives from electromagnetic radiation, but we must take into account the ultraviolet, which is beyond human frequency. You must understand, as I have said time and time again, light has more properties than we are capable to fathom. Humans like you and me are simply limited in some aspects, but it is what we do with what we are able to understand that is important.

There are three known properties of light, which can go above and below the sight of visual human frequency. First, is its intensity. However, the word intensity when dealing with this property of light does not directly apply to its literal meaning. Light intensity has many mathematical and physics equations which can aid human understanding. In simple terms, light intensity is related to time of energy fluctuation. This energy flux is relative to that which exists inside the given wavelength of light, including its formation, its continuance, and its inner fusion. Light intensity is far from simple, but it is humanly comprehensible.

The next property of light is light frequency, which, just like anything else, does apply to human frequency. Light frequency is the number of occurrences of, say, a beam of light relative to time. To help you understand light frequency, I can give you a physical analogy by observing the invention of the light bulb. A light bulb to us appears to be constant. However, a light bulb turns on and off an incredible number of times every second. I believe that a bulb will turn on and off every millisecond, which is a millionth of a second. The same law applies to a light beam. You see, for a continuance of light, it always requires an immediate replacement. So, if a beam or a bulb is replaced in frequency every millisecond to us and to our human frequency most primarily our time frequency as bonded with our sight frequency, it will appear constant and continuous.

The final property of light is called polarization. Light polarization is directly relative to the circumstances of electromagnetic waves of light, when the motion of the given light wave or light beam is confined to a single direction. This polarization of light has manifested the scientific community's understanding of light oscillations in time. Furthermore, the study of light polarization has led to the belief that oscillation of light, which is the flow of light backwards and forwards, does in fact represent a point of equilibrium. This point of equilibrium has to do with the states of light from one side of human frequency to the other. To further my argument of scientific equivalency and related theories, you must realize that the equilibrium is the condition of a system, in which all of its influences of movement are balanced. My definition of these three properties of light has been altered to a limited extent relative to my vision; it may slightly differ from the views of others. These three light properties directly apply to any reflective process and the possibilities are unending.

Certain circumstances such as a vacuum in space or any of a variety of interstellar activities will alter light throughout existence. These altering space entities will cause a difference in the wavelength of a light source. However, the frequency will be altered with much lesser number. Because space is infinite, and due to time concepts which are caused by the existence of light, it has induced a high level of paranormal phenomena, and this is due to its balance of relationship with the infinite. Once again, scientific equivalency wins!

When light is reflected from an illuminated surface, it will send light beams in a multitude of directions. However, only one beam can be viewed from a single place or direction; this means that human frequency cannot only comprehend that which is beyond our frequency, but it also goes through a thorough inner intricacy with all of our senses, including what I have dubbed as the senses of the beyond. This concept will be discussed further in the "Senses" segment.

There are other means of bending light, all the way from the difficult to understand the hypotheses of Einstein and the simpler theories of my own regarding mirror reflections. One of my favorite movies is the movie "Real Genius" which was about a bunch of gifted kids in a school for geniuses, where some of them were fooled into creating a deadly laser. Anyway, actor Val Kilmer portrayed a character who, in one scene, used a reflective light beam to lead his friends to a school of beauticians, and this would be yet another way to bend light in a more acute angle type, however. The reason they named this movie "Real Genius" I believe, was not because these kids were able to create a complex laser, but actually, because they realized that they shouldn't. So you see, they found the moral ground, which is more important than solving the scientific problem.

You see, the science of light and reflections are advanced, yet, much more can be discovered. I believe that through a better understanding and method of comprehending the sense of possibilities, we could discover a fifth force, a sixth sense, and a new moral plane of existence. We have a chance to complete the human mind circle by fixing and shaping a comprehension of universal contact through the use of the three realms of consciousness.

Furthermore, I remind you, as I always will, that we must proceed with caution as to the advancements of further discoveries, and make sure that we do not create a paradox to the balance of mind, time, and space. Through the new utopian vision, we can, together, enter the gateway into the realm of the moral beyond.

Once again, thank you for listening. It is now time to enter into the "Language of the Mad" which is the direct relative to all of my reflection theories. Read on!

THE LANGUAGE OF THE MAD

Welcome to the "Language of the Mad" segment. We are about to decode a cipher of the collective subconscious, which is the direct relative of my reflection theories. As I elaborate in this segment, you will further comprehend the thought process which goes along with the centrifugal forces of reflections and any of a variety of universal opposite to opposite reactions of creation.

First, in order for you to comprehend this "Language of the Mad," I must briefly give a recap of some of my theories on reflection. Before we enter into the extreme paranormal, you must understand that it is not just the reflection process alone that causes this language to exist, because this language's other relative is the mind shadow. This language will be the basis of the imminent manifestation of the collective subconscious and of the imminent universal-wide connection.

This language is presently dwelling in the deep vastness of both the personal and the collective subconscious. Through thorough research, I have seen that the outer realm of this language has already been slightly fathomed in the past. However, the totality of this subconscious forming entity has been in its early stages for some time now. Therefore, we shall begin to indulge in this seemingly unreal reality.

In relation to parallel-like existences as applied to this new language, there is an ancient art which is sometimes used in modern times called "Mirror Writing." Mirror writing is a type of writing written in reverse contrary to our normal left to right English way of writing. Of course, there are languages that go from right to left and there are even Asian languages written vertically. I believe that a vertical language could represent a centrifuge of languages and those languages that are read from left to right already represent the other side of the human galactic mind vortex, which is the basis of the relationship between mind, time, and space.

Now, mirror writing is contrary to our left to right type of reading, so it will represent a form of artistry. When this type of writing is reflected, it will make perfect sense to normal human conscious thinking. This art of mirror writing is an art form that did not manifest the totality of the reflective process as applied to the two realms of the subconscious. I must admit that when I learned of this mirror writing, I became slightly worried that my vision of this language had already been discovered, but I assure you that it has not.

This art form of mirror writing has also had a history of being an un-advanced type of cipher. So, what is a cipher? A cipher can be considered as a finite sequence of instructions for the intention of solving a problem, such as a mathematical problem. However, cipher in its true essence involves problem solving intended to fulfill encryption or decryption. Encryption is a method of transforming information, through a process using a previously stated sequence of finite instructions intended for problem solving. Encryption is also a type of code meant to be incomprehensible to those who may come across it, with the exception of those who are intended to understand it. So basically, encryption is a slightly complex code type.

This "Language of the Mad" has been my code for some time now and it is intended for a collective subconscious communication, by which many important people who have also fathomed this language to a limited extent will soon be able to contribute to a supreme worldly happiness and aid the manifestation of "Something Wonderful!"

As for decryption, it is simply an advanced concept which stems from encryption, which will not be necessary for us to discuss.

You see, a common cipher is (for the most part) created through a person's personal subconscious to conscious relationship, even if they are not aware of what the subconscious is. A cipher consists of many tricks intended to fool the common unaware reader, who will be rendered unable to break the code. Of course, a common bypassing of cipher use would simply entail the use of invisible ink. This cipher coding system is ancient and it has assumed many forms, yet it has not achieved the conscious awareness as to its subconscious process as applied to time, thus, the need for me to reveal the age-old process, which has led us to this "Language of the Mad!"

Another common method of the cipher type is the scrambling of letters, which could be made to represent other letters and when viewed can promote intense subconscious activity. This particular cipher process is called poly-alphabetic substitution. The prefix poly means many and I don't have to tell you what substitution means. Technological advances would soon promote an ease in the creation of cipher types, such as those made by rotor machines and more recently, by computers.

However, the truth is that a cipher is not literally any type of code and it does have its individual advantages against other code types. Therefore, a cipher type induced through the ancient art form of mirror writing does more so apply to the

"Language of the Mad" because of its relations to the personal and collective subconscious. You soon will see that the subconscious "Language of the Mad" is the most advanced code type ever created due to its connections to the balance of mind, space, and time, which exists within a mirror reflection; that would be a visual fragment of the universe within the totality of all parallel existences.

Today, mirror writing has actually become more primitive and it has strayed from an art form to a common purpose of logic. The most common modern use of mirror writing is used for ambulance travel. We see it almost every day, when the word ambulance is written in a backwards mirror text for the intention of viewing the word "ambulance" on an ambulance in the rearview mirror of your vehicle, although the loud siren should be enough for you to realize that you must get out of the way.

I am amazed that in the past, with no help from myself, that it has been determined by those of knowledge that this mirror writing art form was and must have been created through an inner non-typical orientation within the human mind. Through research and basic understandings of such past creations, I do think that this mirror writing process was originated by either the personal subconscious of an individual or the collective subconscious of us all.

Furthermore, I stand by my previous statements that mirror writing and its use of relative codes was a process by which this new language was manifested over time. It is because of past unawareness of the properties of the three levels of consciousness that this process fell short of a full collective manifestation; also, the surrounding technologies of the social environment has caused a further comprehending factor in the realization of the collective subconscious.

Our brain chemistry and its relative functions are responsible for an individual's coordination. I have already explained to you the processes of bioelectric reactions of the instinctual and the conscious types, and that all of our movements are reactions to the exterior world, and they originate from the inner world of the personal subconscious. For some reason, those who are left handed have tended to be more apt and shown a natural talent over the history of mirror writing. The three levels of consciousness have been taking form for a very long time now, and it was not until the subconscious mentor Carl Jung came along when this mind function would commence to accelerate. The study of the human mind has led some experts to believe that left handed people have more language comprehension on both sides of their brains, most prominently in the cerebral cortex, the brain's outer exterior, and the motor homunculus, part of the human brain responsible for the voluntary bioelectric motions and not the instinctual type motions. Of course, there are those who suffer from dyslexia and cannot help from reading words backwards. Once you comprehend this "Language of the Mad," you will see that those afflicted with dyslexia may be that way due to their personal subconscious makeup. Once the mind sphere starts rotating, it will continue to grow the three levels of consciousness to the point of universal contact. The learning never stops and we are going to have a ball—literally! Remember to keep the mind sphere clean of negative thinking!

Now, it is time for that brief recap on reflections I promised to give a short while back. You must remember that this language exists because of the fact that a reflection contains the whole universe and that a mirror reflection must have a centrifuge of an interlocking and change reversal action, which creates a reflection and this language. This mirror connection is made from two sources of light, being our sun and the parallel sun. A reflection falls into the category of opposite to opposite reactions of creation and through this reflective process, English left to right writing becomes right to left writing. This language is also a result of the balance between mind, space, and time.

Before I finally reveal the "Language of the Mad," I must present some brief instructions. The basis of this language is by a process of spelling words backwards and then sounding out these backwards letters and forming them into regular English words. This language could go backwards and forwards within each parallel universe. There are some minor rules to this language, for instance say you have the letters "ch" when backwards it is "hc" and "hc" stands for high see or sometimes (although rarely) high sea. In a variety of instances, the letters "nt" will be in backwards text "tn," which is ten, as in a scale from one to ten and ten meaning best. At times the letter "p" will pose confusion in the case of "p" it could mean to urinate or it could be a part of a whole word, it often will represent the word per, which means through by means for each, such as per capita, which means distribution of funds to each individual. For all of you beginners in this language: In some cases, the words will not make sense, because they are meant for a certain place in time. The parts of this language I will now reveal are the base words, in a way that even the beginner may understand their form and function.

I discovered this language when I was wearing a concert shirt from one of my favorite bands Testament and I noticed that the word testament when spelled backwards comes out as: testament=tnematset=ten them at set, get it? This is how I will present these words of the "Language of the Mad" to you. This language coincides with a Massachusetts accent, because of the centering process of linguistics in connection with the collective subconscious. Massachussets=stessuhcassam=stay is you high sea are same. You must note that the "r' is silent, in the same way that the collective subconscious sector of Massachusetts speaks their words in such a way. You must note the connections between these words in both forwards and backwards text and see that they will almost always directly relate to the meaning of the original word, in either same or opposite manner. I am about to "ten you at a set" and then tune you up like a guitar. I hereby present the first ever word chart of the "language of the Mad!"

I will start with simple words: car=race/cross=source/tap=pat/rock=core/drop=poured/ life=a fill/big=guy be/dig=guide/live=evil/core=a rock/drugs=sugared/yes=say/no=on/and=dna/male=a lamb/female=a lamb of/mail=lie

VISION OF A MENTAL PATIENT

aim/pit=tip/as=say/see=ease/mind=then I am/brain=in eye our be/think=can I hit?/welcome=aim owe see lay double you/pets=step/baby=why be a be?/sun=news/sip=piss/pin=nip/nips=spin=pick=keep/naps=span/is=see/self=flesh/wall=law/ care=a race/ help=plea here/day=why add?/fall=laugh/sleep=appeals/dreams=smeared/cans= snack/time=emit/for=are of/look=cool/down=new owed/middle=all dim/center=rate inner see/opposite=at is oppose/reflection=know it seal fear/deny=you need/camera=our aim a see/soap=pay owes/alter=rate lay/luck=cool/are=era/end=done

Now, I will reveal my subconscious connection with "METALLICA" going backwards from their fifth album called "Metallica," sometimes known as the black album, all the way back to their first album "Kill em All." Here we go:Mettalica=acilattem=a killer team/Enter sandman=namdnas retne=name then as retina (retina meaning the retina of the human eye)/sad but true=eurt tub das=your right to be, days/holier than thou=uoht neht reiloh=you owe hit inner hit real owe here/the unforgiven=nevigrofnu eht=never I grow for knew a hit/wherever I may roam=may or why aim, eye our eve are a how/don't tread on me=em no daert tnod=do not tear a add on aim/through the never=reven eht hguorht=raven art hug you our hit/nothing else matters=srettam es le gnihton=sir at aim as lay gone eye hit on/of wolf and man=nam dna flow fo=name dna flow foe/the god that failed=deliaf taht dog eht=deal eye of to hit dog a hit/my friend of misery=yresim fo dneirf ym=your ease I am for then a eye hour of yum!/the struggle within=nihtiw elggurts eht=in eye hit eye double you? You see struggle within is difficult to form in this language because it is a struggle within, yes a struggle within the reflective centrifuge.

Now, for the And Justice for All album;blackened=denekcalb=then a key see all be/and justice for all=lla rof ecitsuj dna=lay rough a see it's such dna/eye of the beholder=redloheb eht fo eye=read low here a be a hit for I/one=eno=a know/the shortest straw=war it is to set our owe here is a hit/harvester of sorrow=war owes foe rate sever our ah/the frayed ends of sanity=ytinas fo sdne deyarf eht=yet in as foe is done day are of a hit/to live is to die=eid ot si evil ot=a id ought see evil over time/dyers eve=eve syreyd=eve is why ear yes

Now, for the Master of Puppets album: battery=yrettab=why rate a be?/master of puppets=stepup fo retsam=step up for rate same/the thing that should not be=eb ton dluohs gniht eht=a be ton deal you owe his gone eye hit a hit/ welcome home(sanitarium)=(muiratinas) emoh emoclew=(sane it our eye in as) aim owe here aim owe see lay double you/disposable heroes=seoreh elbasopsid=see or a hell as owe pee acid/leper messiah=haissem repel=hey eye same repel/orion=noiro=owe our eye on/damage inc=cni egamad=see in I a game add Now for the Ride the Lightning album: fight fire with fire=erif htiw erif thgif=a riff hit eye double you our if thing if/ride the lightning=gninthgil eht edir=gone in the guy to a dare/for whom the bell tolls=sllot lleb eht mohw=slot lay be a hit more how/fade to black=kcalb ot edaf=key call be over time a day of/this one is my favorite; trapped under ice=eci rednu deppart=a sea eye read knew deep part/escape=epacse= a pace/creeping death=htead gnipeerc=hit a add gone eye peirce/the call of ktulu=ulutk fo llac eht=you will you take foe lay see a hit

Finally, we come to Metallica's debut album, Kill 'em All; kill 'em all=lla me llik=lay me lick/hit the lights=sthgil eht tih=set hug I will a hit tie here/the four horsemen=nemesroh ruof eht=name sir owe here are you of a hit?/motorbreath=htaerbrotom=hit air brother tom, this one cannot be fathomed by you right now but it does have subconscious meaning/jump in the fire=erif eht ni pmuj=our if a hit in eye p.m. huge/(Anesthesia) pulling teeth=hteet gnillup (aisehtsena) her teet gone isle up (an ease the seer) whiplash=hsalpihw=his all pie how/phantom lord=drol motnahp=dare all more ten a hip/no remorse=esromem on=as roam aim on/seek and destroy=yortsed dna kees=you are to seed dna keys/metal militia=eight isle I am late aim

Okay, some of those may have been hard to figure due to a time concept but we will now move on to some more examples of the language of the mad. Here are some place names that have been significant in my lifetime. Lowell=the wall, in this case I altered "lle" in to le which is "the" in French. Sometimes, altering is essential in this subconscious language. Lowell has a nearby twin city called Lawrence. Lawrence=a see near wall. Dracut=two card, this is because I spent most of my life in the two places, Dracut and Lowell. Boston=note so be, Billerica=a see I real I be, Woburn=near you be owe double you, this was the town I moved to the day I got sober.

Then you have words that are the same backwards as forwards. The best example is the word level. level=level because it is level. A person's name can also have a meaning in this language. My name is Ted Hodge. Ted Hodge= egg dough debt. This has to do with my personal subconscious applied to certain life experiences. Here are some examples of this language as applied to people in my life.

The first example I will demonstrate will be my friend Roland Gagnon. Roland aided me, subconsciously, achieve my primary goal, which I have not yet revealed. Therefore it was Roland's job to aid me in the utopian dream. Roland Gagnon=non gag dna lure. So the words non gag meant that I could trust Roland and the words dna lure is because I needed to achieve a chemical balance of the human dna as applied to the galactic mind vortex of the collective subconscious.

Another friend of mine is Dennis Brunelle. Dennis is a talented musician and a good friend, but he would not have been able to deal with the extreme dementia that the primary goal induces. I had to enter into Dennis' personal subconscious so he would comply with the evils of those opposed to my vision. Dennis Brunelle=all on you our be, sinned.

My friend Dave St'Armand already knows of the primary goal because I tried to convince him that it was true. Dave came closest to actually believing my farfetched tale. His name is formed from the focal point of a conversation we had while driving around one night. Dave St'Armand=then aim ray it is evade. You see, I told Dave the primary goal and revealed to him dementia even beyond the level in which my friends and I always used to discuss. This means I aimed the theoretical light wave at Dave's personal subconscious and I was then forced to avoid him for a number of years for his well being; thus, the forming of Dave St'Armand= then aim ray it is! Evade!

My other friend Bob Stevens was more capable of dealing with the sour effects induced by the primary goal. However, he had no conscious clue about what was actually taking place at times. Bob encouraged me to face my alcoholism and he is at the eve of a new level of understanding. Bob Stevens= sin eve it is Bob! You see, Bob, although being least aware of the extreme and real dementia I was experiencing, was actually around when certain crucial events took place. Bob's name in this language is intended for a message from me to him.

My other good friend Matt Kulesza was more into my concepts and my dreams than all of all of my other friends. Matt and I were on a high plane as to the absolute conception of universal contact and "Knowing." Matt also came up with the mind sphere theory and he was ultimately forced to stray from this vision we shared because he had to deal with life's responsibilities. Matt Kulesza= as seal a key tame. Matt's name comes out this way because he wanted to seal the totality of the vision we shared while he was forced to tame his dementia.

My old drummer and good friend and a member of the successful punk band Out Cold was the down to Earth John Evvici. In the early days of Deallegiance, Roland and I would try to share this vision with John but he was simply too down to earth to comply with such seemingly nonsensical views. So, John was one of the first people we tried to get our point across to. So here is his name in this language of the mad. John Evicci= I see eve in Hodge. I feel no elaboration is necessary here, so let's move on.

My other friend is the former Malicious Intent lead guitarist Paul Leary. By the time I knew Paul, we were all much older and certain issues were no longer discussed anymore so Paul's relationship to me was basically the guy I constantly liked to joke around with. Paul Leary= you're real all you a pay. This means that Paul and I were true friends and that he might have liked to contribute to the utopian dream.

My other friend was malicious intent drummer Dan Desharnais who also had a short stint with the famous band Evans Blue. Dan only knew me after my stay at Solomon's so he never really knew what I was actually like. But I used to enjoy it when he would send me home with a few Sam Adams for a nightcap. Dan Desharnais= see a near ray his seed an add. You see, Dan was an add because he replaced John as our drummer; thus, another prime example of this language.

Then there is my childhood friend Joshua Bernard, the successful graphics artist. Basically, I would like to restart my friendship with Josh so; Joshua Bernard= dear on re be a you his Hodge. finally there is my sweetheart Christine Gagnon (no relation to Roland) Christine Gagnon= non gag a night sir high see. Check this out; Barack and Michelle Obama= amabo ellehcim dna kcarab= aim a bow all a high see I am dna key see are a be.

As far as a person's name in this language goes, its meaning could either be meant for a situation or a point of connection. If one attempts to find out the subconscious meaning of their name through this language, one might not like the result. In a situation like this, a person can alter his or her name into a new level of subconscious meaning. So my message is fear not and find the goodness within yourself.

Words can have powers as numbers have in mathematics. For example, love to the third power is evolve foe. Here is the process; Love= evolve/evolve= of love/of love= evolve foe. And there you have it-love to the third power. However, I altered love from—love=-evil to love= evolve by adding "ve" to the end of it. ev= eve you know Adam and Eve. The premise of this word equation is that love starts off evil due to our savage instincts and by adding "eve," we evolve evil to evolve for the promotion of love.

I am about to reveal the first ever thesis of the language of the mad but I must first set some more guidelines. When you read this extensive display of this collective subconscious language, it is required that you notice the progression of the collective subconscious implications. I want you to view this display with an application of the smearing dream fabric formation of this message to the development of the human psyche through the totality of human evolution time span. Most of the subconscious definitions will immediately be logical; others are intended to relate to the universal time flux of the equilibrium of mind, time, and space, thus, promoting some slight confusion. However, at this time, your personal subconscious is more active and it will aid you in the promotion of human understanding relative to all concepts of the psyche. There will be mentions of apes, which we have evolved from. I will also give mention to "double you's" which stem from the letter "W." Think of a double you as your mirror reflection image; you should fathom the progression of this subconscious thesis and connect it to your inner mind. I will not indulge in petty details and insult your intelligence because all humans other than those of uncompromising evils have the natural ability to achieve subconscious connection and promote their inner values to the world society. So without further ado, I now present the first ever thesis of "The Language of the Mad": abandon= knowed nab ah/abase= as a be ah/abash= here's a be ah/abate= at a be ah/abdicate= attack id bay/abide= a die be ah/ability= yet ill I be ah/abject= to see edge be ah/able= all be ah/able-bodied= the id do be all be ah/abnormal= lame our on be ah/abolish= his isle obey/abort= tare obey/above= eve obey/abrasion= know is our be ah/abridge= edge there be ah/abroad= day owe our be ah/abscond= then owe see is be ah/absence= a see in ease be ah/absolution= know it you lose be ah/absolve= eve loss be ah/absorb= be rose be ah/abstain= in eye at is be ah/abstract= to see arts be ah/absurd= dare us be ah/abundance= a see in add in you be ah/abuse= as you be ah/abysmal= lame is why be ah/abyss= is why be ah/academic= see I am a day seer/accelerate= at a real ah see ah/accept= to peace see ah/access= see seer/acclaim= am I all see? ah/accolade= add all owe see ah/accommodate= at add owe

VISION OF A MENTAL PATIENT

them owe see ah/accompany=why nap more see ah/accord=dare owe see ah/according=gone id owe see ah/accurate=at our you see ah/accuse=as you see her/acquire=our eye you cue see ah/action=know it seer/active=eve it see ah/actual=lay you to see ah/acumen=name you see ah/acute=at you see ah/adamant=ten aim a day/adapt=to pay day/adjust=to such day/ad-lib=bill day/administer=rate sin eye mid day/admire=our I am day/admit=timed day/admonish=his in owe them day/adore=a road ah/adult=til you day/advance=a see in of day/adventure=your route in eve day/affable=all be of ah/affect=to see of ah/affection=know it see of ah/affirm-mere if ah/afflict=to see ill far/afoot=to far/aftermath=hit aim rate far/this one's funny again=in eye a gay/age=edger/agenda=add an egg ah/aggressive=eve is surger/aid=dire/aisle=all see ah/alcoholic=see ill owe here owe see lay/alert=trailer/alien=inner eye lay/align=in guy lay/all=lay/allocation=know it a see owe lay/alloy=why all lay/allude=add you lay/allure=our you lay/ally=why lay?/almost=it is ohm lay/alone=an owe lay/aloof=fooler/alter=rate lay/altogether=re-hit edge ought lay/always=see a double you lay/amass=same ah/amaze=as aim ah/ambition=know it I be may/ambush=his sub may/amend=then aim ah/amends=said name ah/amuse=as you may/analysis=this is why lane ah/ancient=ten a eye see inner/anecdote=at owed scene ah/angel=legend ah/anger=rage inner/animal=lamb in ah/animate=at aim inner/animosity=yet is owe them inner/annoy=why honor?/annual=lay you inner/anoint=ten eye owe inner/anomaly=you'll aim honor/answer=re-was inner/antagonism=missing owe got inner/anthem=me hit inner/antics=see it inner/antidote=at owed it inner/antisocial=lay I see it inner/apart=trapper/apathy=you hit a pay/aplomb=be them all pay/apologize=ease eye goal owe pay/apostle=all it is owe pay/appall=lay pay/apply=you'll pay/appoint=ten I owe pay/apportion=know it row pay/appreciate=at a eye see our pay/appraise=ease eye our pay/approval=lay of or owe pay/approve=eve or pay/archetype=ape why a high see ray/arctic=sight see ray/arch=high see ray/ardor=road ray/arid=dire ah/arise=ease eye ray/arouse=as you owe ray/arrive=eve eye ray/arrogance=a see nag owe ray/arrow=war ray/arsenal=lanes ray/artificial=lay eye see if it array/as=say/ashamed=deem a has ah/ask=kiss her/aspire=a ripe say/assassin=in is as say/assault=tell you a say/assemble=all be mess say/aspect=to keep say/assent=ten a say/assign=in guy say/associate=at a eye see owes say/assume=aim us say/assure=a Russia/astonish=his in owe say/astound=then you ought say/astute=at you to say/athlete=at all hitter/atom=motor/attach=high see at ah/attend=then at ah/attic=see it ah/attitude=add you tit ah/audacity=yet I see a doer/audible=all bid you are/audience=a see need you are/aura=our you ah/author=row hit you are/authority=yet I row hit you are/automatic=see it aim ought you are/avenge=edge in eve ah/avoid=die of ah/await=to I a way/awesome=aim owes a way/axiom=more eye extra/babble=all be a be/back=cab meaning that one sits in the back of a cab/backbone=an owe be key see a be/back down=new owed key see a be/backfire=our if key see a be/bacteria=air at see a be/bad=day be/badly=you'll dab/bad-mouth=hit you owe them day be/bail=lie a be/bait=tie a be/baked=deck a be/balance=a see in all a be/balcony=why knock lay be?/bald=deal a be/ballot=to lay be/ban=nab-banal=lane a be/band=then a be/bang=going to be/banish=his sin a be/bank=nab/banner=reign a be/banquet=to you cue in a be/banter=rate inner be/barb=bare a be/barbarian=near a be are a be/bare=are a be/bargain=in eye a grab/barren=near a be/barrier=our eye are a be/barter=rate are a be/base=as a be/basic=see is a be/basis=size a be/bass=say be/bastard=the rat say be/bastion=know it say be/batch=high see to be/bath=hit a be/baton=note a be/batten=neat a be/batter=rate a be/battery=why rate a be/battle=all to be/batty=yet a be/bazaar=our as a be/be=a be/beach=high sea a be/beacon=know see a be/beady=why day a be/beam=maybe/beast=to see a be/beat=to a be/beau=you are be/beautiful=love it you are a be/beauty=why to a be/because=as you a see a be/beckon=nock see a be/bedevil=lived a be/bed=day be/bedridden=need I rid day be/befall=laugh a be/before=are of a be/beg=gab/begin=in I go a be/behave=eve a he be/behind=then eye he be/behold=deal owe he be/being=going to eye a be/belch=high see a be/belief=feel a be/belittle=all til a be/believe=evil a be/belly=you lay be/belong=going to owe a be/beloved=the evolve a be/below=wall a be/belt=to lay be/bemused=the sum a be/benchmark=cram high see inner be/beneath=here to a near be/benefactor=row to see of a be/benefit=to eye fee inner be/benevolent=ten all of on a be/benign=in guy inner be/bent=to inner be/berate=a tare a be/bereft=to fear a be/berserk=caress are a be/beset=tease a be/beside=add is a be/best=to see a be/bestial=lay it see be/bestow=watt see be/bet=to be/betoken=in a caught a be/betray=why art to be?/better=are at a be/between=new to be/beverage=edge our eve a be/bewail=lie a way be/beware=era we be/beyond=then owe why a be/bias=say I be/bid=dib/bigot=to guy be/billet=tell I be/billow=wall eye be/bind=then I be/binge=edge in eye be/biography=why here pay our go I be/birth=hit our eye be/bite=at I be/bizarre=our as I be/black=key see all be/blank=can all be?/blanket=taking all be/blare=our all be/blaze=as all be/blast=to see all be/bleed=deal be/blend=then all be/bless=see all be/blight=the guy will be/bliss=seal be/blister=rate see I'll be/blitz=is it isle be/blizzard=there as I'll be/blood=duel be/bloodshed=day his duel be/blossom=moss all be/blue=you'll be/bluff=full be/blush=his you'll be/board=there a owe be/boast=to say owe be/boastful=love to say owe be/bode=a due be/bodily=you lied owe be/body=you do be/bold=deal owe be/bombastic=see it a be more be/bona fide=add if an owe be/bond=then owe be/bony=why no be?/book=cool be/booklet=tell cool be/boom=more be/boon=new be/boot=to be/border=read our owe be/bore=a rob/bored=dare owe be/boss=so be/bossy=yes owe be/bother=re-hit owe be/bottom=more to be/boundary=your add new owe be/bounty=yet knew owe be/bouquet=to you cue you owe be/bout=to owe be/bowels=is lay owe be/box=sex owe be/boxer/re-sex owe be/boy=you be/boycott=talk you be/brake=a car be/brand=then our be/brave=eve our be/brazen=in ease our be/bread=day our be/break=care be/breathe=a hit air be/breed=dare be/breeze=as ear be/brew=were be/bribe=a buyer be/bridal=laid eye our be/bridge=edge there be/bright=the guy are be/brilliant=ten a isle eye our be/brim=mere be/bring=gone eye our be/brink=near be/brisk=kisser be/bristle=all it is eye our be/brochure=are you high see or be?/broke=a core be/brood=door be/brush=here's are be/brutal=late our be/brute/at you are be/bubble=all be you be/bud=do be/budget=target due be/build=the lie you be/bulk=clue be?/bulletin=night all you be/bully=while you be/bundle=all done you be/bungle=all going to be/bangle/all going to be/burden=need rub/bureau=you are you be/burn=inner you be/burst=to sir you be/bush=his sub/busy=you sub/but=to be/cab=back/cabin=in eye base/cabinet=ten I be a see/caddish=his id a see/café=a face/cage=edge a see/calamity=yet I am a lay see/calculate=at all you see lay see/caliber=re-be isle see/call=lay see/calling=gone isle a see/callow=wall a see/calm=me lay see/camp=pee may see/campaign=in guy a p.m. ace/canal=lane a sea/cancel=lay see in a see/cancer=re-see inner see/candid=did in a see/candidate=at add inner see/candor=road in a see/canker=wreck inner see/cannon=known a see/canopy=why upon a see/canter=rate inner see/cap=pace/capability=yet I will be a pace/capable=all be a pace/capacity=yet I see a pace/capitalism=missile at eye pay see/capitulate=at all you type a see/capsize=as is pace/capsule=you'll lose pace/capture=are you to pace/carcass=say see race/career=rare ace/careless=sell a race/caress=sir a see/carnal=lane race/carp=pray see/carpenter=rate inner pray see/carry=why race?/cartoon=new trace/carve=ever a see/case=a sack/cash=here's a see/casual=lay us a see/casualty=yet lay you say see/catalog=goal at a see/catastrophe=a ports attack/catch=high see to see/category=you row get a see/cater=rate a see/cattle=all to see/cause=as you a see/caution=know it you a see/cave=eve a see/cease=ease a see/celebrate=at our be lay see/celestial=lay it cell a see/celibacy=you see a be I lay see/cell=all a sea/censor=rose inner see/central=lay our ten a see/ceremony=you know them are a see/certain=in eye at are a see/chain=in eye a high see/chairman=name our I a high see/chamber=re-be may our high see/chance=a see in a high see/change=egg in a high see/channel=lane a high see/chaos=sew a high see/chapter=rate pay high see/character=rate see our a high see/charge=edge ray high see/charisma=aim sir a high see/charm=mirror high see/chart=tare a high see/cheap=pay a high see/check=key see a high see/cheer=re-high see/cheery=you're a high see/chemist=to see me a high see/cherish=his eye are a high see/chest=to see a high see/chic=see I a high see/chief=fee eye high see/child=deal I high see/childbirth=hit rib deal eye high see/chill=lie high see/China=an eye high see/chip=piece/chivalry=your lay of eye high see/choice=a see I owe high see/choose=as owe high see/chore=our owe high see/chorus=sure owe high see/Christmas=same it is eye our high see/chronicle=all see in our high see/chum=me you high see/churn=inner you high see/cinema=aim an eye see/circle=all see our eye see/circuit=tie you see eye our see/circulate=at all you see our eye see/circumference=a see near of me you see our eyes/citadel=led at I see/cite=at eye see/citizen=in ease it I see/city=yet I see/civil=live I see/civilization=know it as I live I see/claim=my all see/clairvoyant=ten a why of our eye all see/clamber=re-be may all see/clan=an all see/clandestine=a night seed in all see/clap=pal see/clarify=why fear all see?/clarity=yet eye our all see/clash=his all see/class=is all see/classic=sea is all see/clause=as you all see/clear=real see/clergy=your grail see/clever=reveal see/cliff=fill see/climactic=see it see aim isle see/climate=at aim ill see/climax=sex aim I'll see/climb=be me isle see/clinch=high see nil see/clinical=lay see in isle see/close=as all see/closed=these all see/cloth=hit all see/cloud=due all see/clout=to you all see/club=be you'll see/clue=you'll see/cluster=rates you will see/coach=high see a owe see/coalition=know it I lay owe see/coarse=as array owe see/coast=to see a owe see/coax=sex a owe see/cocky=your key see owe see/code=a dose/coin=in eye owe see/coincide=a dice in eye owe see/coincidence=a see need I see in eye owe see/cold=the lock/collaborate=at our owe be all owe see/collapse=as pale owe see/collect=to see all owe see/collision=know is ill owe see/colony=why in all owe see/color=role owe see/colossal=lay us all owe see/coma=aim owe see/comb=be more see/combat=to be more see/combination/know it an eye be more see/combine=on I be more see/come=aim owe see/comedy=you deem owe see/comfort=tour of more see/comic=see me owe see/command=then aim owe see/commandeer=read aim owe see/commemoration=know it our aim more see/commence=a see near me owe see/commend=then aim owe see/comment=ten them owe see/commercial=lay eye see our aim more see/commiserate=at our ease I am more see/ commission=know is I am more see/commit=time owe see/common=normalcy/commotion=know it owe more see/communal=lane you more see/commune=on you more see/communicate=at a see in you more see/communism=missing you more see/companion=know in ape more see/company=why nap more see/compare=a rap more see/compartment=ten them trap more see/compass=say p.m. owe see/compassion know is ape more see/compatible=all be I tap more see/compel=lay p.m. owe see/compensate=at as in a p.m. owe see/compete=a tape more see/competition=know it I tape more see/compile=all I pee more see/complain=in eye all pee more see/complement=ten them all p.m. owe see/complete=at all pee more see/complex=sex all p.m. owe see/complexion=know I sex all p.m. owe see/complicate=at a see isle pee more see/complication=know it a see ill p.m. owe see/comply=you will pee more see/component=ten on owe p.m. owe see/compose=as owe pee more see/comprehend=then a her p.m. owe see/comprise=as I rip more see/compromise=a seam or p.m. owe see/compulsion=know is loop more see/compulsive=ease is loop more see/compute=at you p.m. owe see/comrade=a dear more see/con=know see/concave=eve a see know see/conceited=debt I see know see/conceive=eve eye a see know see/concentrate=at art inner see know see/concept=to peace know see/concern=near a see know see/concerned=then race know see/concession=know is see see know see/conciliation=know it isle eye see know see/concise=as I see know see/conclude=add you'll see know see/concoct=to see on know see/concrete=at our see know see/concur=our you see know see/condemn=named know see/condensation=know it as need know see/condense=as in need know see/condition=know it then owe see/condone=an owed know see/conduct=to see you then owe see/confer=refine owe see/conference=a see near of know see/confess=safe know see/confide=add if know see/confident=to need if know see/confidence=a see need if know see/confidential=lay it need if know see/confine=an if know see/confirm=mere if know see/confiscate=attacks

VISION OF A MENTAL PATIENT

if know see/conflict=to kill if know see/conform=mere of know see/conformity=yet I am rough know see/confound=then you of know see/confront=ten our of know see/confused=daze of know see/confusion=know is of know see/congenial=lay in edge know see/congenital=late an edge know see/congested=debt siege know see/congestion=know it siege know see/congratulate=at all you target know see/congregate=a tag geared you know see/congress=surge know see/conjecture=a route see edge know see/conjugal=lag huge know see/connect=to see on know see/connection=know it see on know see/connive=even know see/connoisseur=our you ease eye on know see/conquer=are you a cue know see/conquest=to see you cue know see/conscience=a see inner eye sees know see/conscious=is you owe eye sees know see/consecrate=at our seize know see/consecutive=eve it you see as know see/consensus=is us in ease know see/consequence=a see in a cue as know see/conservation=know it of our ease know see/conservative=eve it a veer as know see/conserve=eve our as know see/consider=ready is know see/considerate=at our read is know see/consign=in guys know see/consist=it is know see/console=a loss know see/consolidate=at add ill owes know see/consort=it rows know see/conspiracy=you see a rip is know see/conspire=our rips know see/constantly=you'll ten at sin owe see/constitute=at you tit is know see/constitution=know it you tie it so know see/construct=to see your rights know see/consult=tell us know see/consume=a must know see/consummate=at aim us know see/contact=to see at know see/contagious=is you I gate know see/contain=in eye at know see/contamination=know it on I am at know see/contemplate=at all p.m. at know see/contempt=type me ten owe see/contend=then at know see/content=ten at know see/contented=debt net know see/contest=to set know see/contestant=ten at set know see/context=takes at know see/contingency=why see negative night know see/continual=lay you night know see/continue=unite know see/contraband=then a be art know see/contract=to see art know see/contraction=know it see art know see/contradict=to see art know see/contraption=know it part know see/contrary=your art know see/contrast=it is art know see/contribute=at you be I right know see/contrite=at tear to know see/contrive=eve I write know see/control=lure to know see/controversy=yes rev our ten owe see/convene=on eve know see/convention=know it an even owe see/conversation=know it as our eve know see/converse=as rev know see/convert=tear eve know see/convince=a see in even owe see/convulse=as love know see/cooperate=at a reposition owe see/cordial=lay id row see/corner=reign our owe see/corporation=know it a rope owe see/corpse=as pour owe see/correct=to see our owe see/corridor=road eye our owe see/corroborate=at our row borrow see/corrode=a door owe see/corrupt=to pure owe see/cosmetic=see it aims owe see/cosmic=see I am so see/cost= it is owe see/council=all I see in you owe see/counsel=lesson you owe see/count=ten you owe see/counteract=to see a rate new owe see/counterfeit=tie of rate in you owe see/counterpart=trap rate in you owe see/courage=edge are you owe see/course=as are you owe see/court=tour you owe see/courtesy=yes at true owe see/cove=eve owe see/covenant=ten an eve owe see/cover=our eve owe see/covet=to eve owe see/coward=dare a double you owe see/cower=re-double you owe see/coy=why owe see/cozy=wise owe see/cradle=all there see/crafty=yet far see/cram=mark/cramped=deep mark/crass=is our see/crate=at our see/crater=rate our see/crave=eve our see/crazy=why is our see?/cream=mare see/crease=as air see/create=at our see/creation=know it our see/creature=a route our see/credibility=yet ill I be id our see/credit=tied our see/creep=pierce/crescent=ten a see sir see/crest= to sure see/crew=work/crime=a mere see/cringe=edge in eye our see/crisis=this is our see/criterion=know I rate eye our see/critic=see it eye our see/criticism=miss I see it eye our see/crook=coarse/crop=pour see/crow=worse/crucial=lay I see you are see/crucify=why if I see you our see?/crude=add your see/cruel=lay your see/cruise=a see your see/crusade=add as your see/crust=it is your see/cry=why our see/cult=til you see/culture=are you til you see?/cunning=gone in you see/culvert=to reveal you see/curb=be are you see/cure=our you see/curiosity=yet is owe eye our you see/current=to near you see/curse=as our you see/curtain=in eye at our you see/custody=you do to such/cut=to see/cut in=in eye to see/cutting=gone eye to see/cycle=all see why see/cynic=see in why see/dab=bad/dagger=rage add/daily=why all I add/dam=made/damages=siege aim add/dame=a maid/dance=a see in add/danger=raging add/dare=a raid/daredevil=lived a raid/dark=key raid/darken=inner key raid/darling=gone isle our add/dart=trade/dashing=gone eye his add/data=at add/date=at add/dated=debt add/daub=be you add/dawn=new add/day=why add?/dazed=these add/dead=dayed/deadline/an isle dayed/deadly=while=dayed/deal=laid/dearly=you'll read/death=hated/debacle=all see a bed/debatable=all be at a bed/debate=at a be do/debonair=our eye an owe bed/debrief=fear be add/debt=to bed/debtor=row to bed/debunk=can you be there?/debut=to bed/decadence=a see need a seed/decapitate=at tip aced/decay=your seed/decease=a seased/deceit=tie a seed/deceitful=love to eye a seed/deceiver=rev eye a seed/decency=you see inner seed/decent=ten a seed/deception=know it pieced/deceptive=eve it pieced/decide=add eye seed/decimate=at aim eye seed/decipher=are a hip eye seed/decision=know is I see the/declaim=my all seed/declaration=know it our all seed/decode=add owe seed/decorate=at our owe seed/decorum=more owe seed/decoy=why owe seed/decrease=ease our seed/decree=ear seed/decrepit=type our seed/decry=your seed/dedicate=at a see eye deed/dedication=know it a see eye deed/deduce=a see you deed/deduction=know it see you deed/deed=deed/deep=peed/deepen=inner peed/deface=a see of Fed./de facto=over time see of aid/defame=aim a feed/defect=to see of fed/defection=know fed/defenseless=sell as inner fed/defer=re-fed/defiance=a see in a if fed/deficiency=why see? nice I fed/deficit=tie see if fed/define=an eye fed/definition=know it in I fed/deflect=to see all fed/deformed=deem our of feed/deformity=yet I am our of fed/defraud=due our feed/deft=to feed/defunct=to see enough fed/defy=why fed/degradation=know it add a dared you day/deity=yet eyed?/dejected=debt seiged/delay=you lead/delegate=at age all lead/deliberate=at a re-be I lead/delicate=at a see I led/delight=the guy I lead/delightful=love the guy I lead/delude=a due led/deluge=edge you lead/deluxe=a sex you lead/delve= eve lead/demand= then aimed/demarcation= know it a crammed/demean= in aimed/demented= debt named/dementia= 8 named/democracy= you see our comed/demon= nomad/demure a room a day/den= need/denial= laned/denigrate= at our guy in need/denomination= know it an eye moaned/denote= atoned/denounce= a see in you need/dense= as need/density= yet is need/deny= you need/depart= trapped/departure= your route raped/depict= to see I peed/depiction= know it see eye payed/deplete= at all payed/deplorable= all be a role payed/deposit= it is owe payed/depot= topped/depress= sir payed/depression= know is sir payed/deprive= eve eye ripped/deputation= know it at you payed/deranged= the edge neared/derivation= know it of I read/derive= eve eye read/derogatory= your owe tag or read/descend= then a seed/descent= ten a seed/describe= a be I our seed/description= know it peer seed/desert= tare a seed/deserve= eve raised/design= in guy seed/designate= at an guy seed/desire= arised/desist= 2 sized/desolate= a tall owe seed/despair= our eye ape seed/despatch= high see tap seed/desperado= owe dare reep seed/desperate= a tear reap seed/despite= a tip seed/despot= top seed/destiny= your night seed/destitute= at you tit seed/destroy= your to see day/destruction= know it your to see the/detach= high see a Ted/detail= late Ted/detailed= deal I 8 Ted/detain= an eye at Ted/detect= to see at Ted/detective= eve it to see Ted/detention= know in in a Ted/determine= an I am rate Ted/detest= to set Ted/detonate= at a note Ted/detour= our you owe Ted/detract= to see our Ted/detrimental= late name eye our Ted/devastate= at at saved/develop= pole eved/deviate= at eye evade/devil= lived/devise= ease eye evade/devoid= eye of Ed/devoted= debt over day/devour= our you over the/dexterity= yet I rate sexed/diabolical= lay see isle obey id/diagnose= as on you aid/diagram= merge aid/dialect= to see all aid/diary= your aid/dictate= at at seed/diction= know it seed/dictionary= you're a know it seed/die= a id/diet= to eye day/differ= re-feed/difference= a see near a feed/diffident= ten a divide/dig= guide/digest= to see guide/dignity= yet in guide/digress= sure guide/dilapidated= debt a dip all id/dilate= at a lid/dilemma= aim a lid/diligence= a see negative eye lid/dilute= at you lied/dim= mid/dimension= know is inner mid/diminish= his in eye mid/din= need/diplomat= tame all pied/dire= a rid/direct= to see a read/direction= know it see a ride/dirge= edge rid/dirt= tried/dirty= you tried/disability= yet ill be a seed/disagree= eared you as id/disallow= wall a seed/disappear= re-appear seed/disappoint= ten eye owe pays id/disapproval= lay of or pay seed/disarm= mirror side/disarray= youre as id/disaster= our ats aside/disbelief= feel a be seed/discharge= edge a high see side/disciple= all peace seed/discipline= al isle piece seed/disclose= as all see seed/disconcert= trace no seize id/disconnect= to see an owe see side/discontented= debt net know see side/discontinue= your night no seed/discord= dare owe seize id/discourage= edge our owe seize id/discourse= as our owe see side/discover= our eve owe see seed/discreet= tear see side/discretion= know it our see side/discriminate= at an eye mere see side/discuss= succeed/disdain= an I add side/disease= a say a seed/disengage= a gag in a seed/disfavor= rove of side/disfigure= ear you guy if seed/disguise= as eye you go aside/disgusted= debts you guess/dish= here seed/dishearten= net our ray of his side/dishonest= to send owe his side/dishonor= our owe his seed/disinclination= know it an isle sea in eyes side/disintegrate= a target in eye side/disjointed= debt in eye owed your side/dislike= a kill seed/disloyal= lay all aside/dismal= lame side/dismantle= all to name seed/dismay= why aim side?/dismember= re-be maim seed/dismiss= see my side/disobedient= ten a eye day be owe seed/disobey= you be owe side/disorder= read row side/disown= new owes id/disparage= edge a rap seed/dispel= leap side/disperse= as reap side/dispirited= debt eye rip side/display= why all pay seed/disposal= lays owe pee side/disposition= know it is owe per seed/disproportion= know it row pour per seed/dispute= at you piece id/disqualify= you fill a you cue side/disquiet= to eye you cue side/disregard= dare age our seed/disrupt= to pure seed/dissect= to see a side/disseminate= at an eye mess side/dissension= know is inner side/dissent= ten a side/dissident= ten add eye side/dissipate= a tap eye seed/dissociate= a tap see owe seed/dissoulute= at you loss owe seed/dissolve= eve loss side/dissuade= add a you side/distance= a see in at side/distaste= at sat seed/distill= light side/distinct= to see in eye to side/distinguish= his eye you ignite side/distort= tare over time seed/distortion= know it row to side/distract= to see art side/distress= sure to side/distribute= at you be I write side/district= to see eye right side/distrust= to sir to side/disturb= be our you to side/disuse= as you side/ditch= high see tide/dither= re-hit id/dive= eve id/diverge= edge rev id/diverse= as rev eye the/diversion= know is rev eyed/divide= a divide/dividend= done divide/divine= an ivy id/divisible= all be is severed/divorce= a see row of id/divulge= edge love id/docile= all I see owed/dock= cod/doctor= wrote see owed/doctrine= an I write see owed/document= ten aim you see owed/dog= god/dogged= the god/dogma= am god/dogmatic= see it aim god/dole= a load/dolt= tell owed/domestic= see it's same owed/dominant= ten an eye mode/domination= know it an I am owed/dominion= know in eye mode/don= nod/donate= at an owed/doom= mood/door= rude/dormant= ten aim road/dose= as owed/double= all be you owed/doubt= to be you owed/dour= are you owed?/down= knew owed/downer= rain woahed/downfall= laugh in double you owed/doze= as owed/drab= barred/drag= guard/dragon= know guard/drama= am a read/dramatic= see it aim our due/drastic= see it's our due/draw= ward/drawn= inward/dread= dared/dream= mirrored/drench= high see nerd/dress= see red/drift= to feared/drill= lured/drink= neared/drive= eve I ride/drivel= leave I rid/droll= lord/drool= lured/drown= new orr due/dubious= is you owe I bud!/duck= key sud/dummy= your mood/dunce= a see nude/dungeon= know edge in you the/durability= yet ill I be a rude/durable= all be are you due?/duration= know it are you the/dust= to sud/dutiful= love it you do/dwell= lowered/dwindle= all done eye wood/dye= a wide/dynamic= see eye man wide/Each= high seer/eager= rager/ear= ray/early= while ray/earmark= cram ray/earn= nearer/earnest= to see nearer/Earth= hit ray/ease= a say/easy= you say/eavesdrop= poured saver/eat= Thai/ebb= be/eccentric= see I write inner see/echo= owe high see/eclipse= as pile see/economic= see eye money owe see/ecstacy= why sat see/ecstatic= see it at seizer/eddy= wide/edge= egg there/edible= all bide/edict= to see idea/edifice= a see if eye day/edit= tied/education= know it a see you day/efface= a see of fee/effect= to see of

VISION OF A MENTAL PATIENT

fee/effeminate=at an eye me fee/effete=at of fee/efficient=ten a I see if fee/effigy=your guy fee/effluent=ten you'll fee/effort=tare off fee/effrontery=you're at an orr fee/effusive=eve is you fee/egg on=no gay/egotism=miss it owed you/egress=surger/eject=to see edger/elaborate=at our be a lay/elapse=as pale/elastic=see it's a lay/elated=debt a lay/elder=read the/elect=to see all lay/election=know it to see a lay/electric=see I write see a lay/elegant=ten age the/element=to name all eh?/elevate=at have a lay/elicit=tie see isle/eligible=all big I lay/eliminate=at an eye mile/elite=at eye lay/elixir=our eye sex I lay/elocution=know it you see owe the/elope=appall eh?/eloquent=ten a you cue owe lay/elucidate=at add I see you lay/elude=a duel/elusive=eve is you lay/emaciated=debt a eye came/emanate=at an aimer/emancipation=know it a piece name/embalm=my lay be me/embargo=oh grab me!/embark=care a be me/embarrass=is our a be me/embellish=his isle a be me/embezzle=all is a be me/embittered=there tie be me/emblem=me will be me/embody=you do be me/embrace=a care be me/embroil=liar be me/embryo=owe why our be me/emend=done me/emerge=agree me/emergency=you see negative remember/emigration=know it our guy me/eminence=a see in an eye me/eminent=ten an eye me/emission=know is eye me/emit=time/emotion=know it owe me/emphasis=this is a hip me/empire=a ripe me/employ=why all pay me/empower=redouble you owe pay me/empty=yet pee me/emulate=at all you me/enable=all a inner/enact=to see her inner/enamoured=dare you owe many/encapsulate=at all us pace inner/enchant=ten a high see inner/enclose=a soul see inner/encompass=say p.m. owe see inner/encounter=rate knew owe see inner/encourage=edge our see owe see inner/encumber=re-be me you see inner/end=done/endanger=raging add inner/endearment=ten them read inner/endeavor=rover done/ending=gone eye done/endless=cell done/endorse=as road inner/endow=double you owed inner/endurable=all be our you done?/endure=a rude inner/engage=a gage inner/enemy=you're men eh?/enforce=a see rough inner/engender=red negative inner/engrave=eve our gone/enigma=aim guy inner/enliven=never I line/enmity=yet I'm inner/ennoble=all bone/enough=hug you owner/enquire=our eye you cue inner/enrich=high see eye our inner/enroll=lure inner/ensemble=all be mess inner/ensign=in guys inner/ensue=a you sinner/ensure=our rush inner/enter=retina/entertain=an eye at rate inner/enthrall=all our hit inner/enthusiasm=me say is you hit inner/entice=a sight inner/entire=a write inner/entitle=all tit inner/entity=yet it inner/entourage=edge our you over time inner/entrails=sly art inner/entrance=a see in our write inner/entreaty=yet art inner/entrepreneur=are you an repair to inner?/entrust=to sir to inner/entry=you write inner/entwine=an eye double you to inner/enumerate=at our rem you inner/enunciate=at eye see in you inner/enviable=all be a vine/envious=is you owe eye vine/environment=ten them or eye vein/environs=is nor I vine/envisage=edge as eye inner/envoy=you vine/envy=your vein/epidemic=see I am a die pee/epigram=may our guy pee/epilogue=a you goal lip/episode=add owes I pay/epistle=all to see pay/epitome=aim over isle a you cue/equation=know it a you cue/equilibrium=me you eye rub isle eye you cue/equivalency=you see in all have eye you cue/era=are/eradicate=attack I dare!/erase=ease are/erect=to see array/erode=a door/erosion=know is owe are/erotic=see it ora/erratic=see it are/error=roarer/erudite=at id you are/erupt=to pure/eruption=know it pure/escalate=a tall ace see/escape=a pacer/especial=lay eye see appease/essay=you see/essence=a see inner see/essential=lay it in ease/establish=his isle be at see/estate=at at see/esteem=meet see/estimate=a tame it see/estuary=you're a you to see/et cetera=a rate to see to/eternal=lane retina/ethical=lay see I hit eh?/etiquette=at you quite/euphoria=air owe hip you are/evacuate=at a you cave/evasion=know I save/even=never/evening=gone in eve/event=ten eve/eventual=lay you to never/ever=revere/evermore=a roam revere/every=your eve/evidence=a see inner dive/evident=to need dive/evil=live/evoke=a cove/evolution=know it you love/evolve=of love/exact=to see axe/exalt=too lax/examination=know it an eye makes/excavate=at ave a see extra/excellent=ten all a see extra/except=to piece extra/exception=know it picks her/excerpt=to prey see extra/excess=sexer/exceed=they see extra/excel=lay see extra/excite=at I see extra/exclaim=my all see extra/exclusion=know is you'll see extra/exclusive=eve is you'll see extra/excommunicate=attack in you more see extra/excruciating=gone it a eye cure see extra/exculpate=a tape you'll see extra/excursion=know is our you see extra/excuse=as you see extra/execute=at you see extra/executive=eve it you see extra/exemplary=why our all p.m. extra/exemplify=you fill p.m. extra/exercise=as I see our extra/exert=tare extra/exhaust=it is you a hear extra/exhibit=tie be eye here extra/exhilarating=gone it are a lie here extra/exhort=tare owe here extra/exhume=aim you here extra/exigency=you see negative eye extra/exile=all eye extra/exist=it is I extra/exit=tie exta/exodus=sudo extra/exonerate=at our an owe extra/exorbitant=ten at I be row extra/exorcise=as I see owe extra/exotic=see it owe extra/expanse=as nap extra/expansion=know is nap extra/expect=to keep extra/expedition=know it eye deep extra/expel=leap extra/expensive=eve is in a picks eh?/experience=a see near reap extra/expertise=ease it repeat extra/expire=a ripe extra/tie see isle pee extra/explode=add all pee extra/explore=a role picks eh?/explosion=know is all per extra/exponent=ten an owe picks extra/expose=a soap extra/expulsion=know is loop extra/exquisite=at eye sigh you cue extra/extempore=a rope met extra/extend=then at extra/extensive=eve is net extra/extent=ten at extra/extenuating=gone it a you net extra/exterior=row eye rate extra/exterminate=at an I am rate extra/external=lane rate extra/extinct=to see in it extra/extol=lot extra/extort=tare over time extra/extra=art extra/extract=to see art extra/extraneous=is you owe an art extra/extraordinary=you're an id row art extra/extravagance=a scene in age have art extra/extreme=a mirror takes eh?/extremist=to seem art extra/extricate=a take I write extra/extrovert=tear eve over to extra/exuberance=a see near be you extra/exult=tell you extra/eyesight=the guys eye/eyesore=a rose eye/eyewitness=sent eye double you eye/fable=all be of/fabric=see eye rub off/fabricate=attack eye our be of/façade=add a see of/face=a see of/faceless=cell a see of/facet=to see of/facetious=is you owe it a see of?/facile=all I see of/facilitate=at a til I see of/facility=yet isle see of/facsimile=all I am is see of/fact=to see of/faction=know it see of/factor=wrote see of/factory=why wrote see of/factual=lay you to see of/faculties=see it look see of/fade=add of/faded=dead off/fail=lie of/fair=our I of?/fairy=why are eye of/faith=hit eye of/faithful=love hit eye of/fake=ache of/fallacy=you see all laugh!/fallible=all bill of/fallow=wall of/false=as laugh/falsify=your fee is laugh/falter=rate laugh/fame=aim of/familiar=our ilsle I am of/family=why all I am of/famine=an I am of/famous=is you owe them of/fan=in of/fanatic=see it an of/fancy=you see in of/fantasize=ease is at in of/fantastic=sight sat in of/fantasy=yes at an of/farce=a see our of/farewell=lay our double you are of/farm=mere of/fascinate=at an eye see safe/fashion=know I his of/fast=to safe/fatal=late of/fatality=yet ill at of/fate=at of/fateful=love at of/father=re-hit of/fatherland=then all re-hit of/fathom=more hit of/fatigue=a you guy 2 of/fatten=net of/fault=tell you of/favor=rove off/favorite=a tire over four(Metallica)/fawn=knew of/fear=ray of/fearless=cell ray of/feasible=all be is ray of/feast=to see of/feet=two of/feather=rehit are of/feature=a route a of/federation=know it are deaf/feeble=all be of/feel=leaf/feeler=real of/fell=leaf/fellow=wall of/feminine=an in I am of/fence=a see in of/ferment=ten them are of/ferocious=is you owe eye core of/ferocity=yet I see our of/ferry=why are of/fertile=a light our of/fertilizer=raise isle tare of/fervor=rove our of/fester=rate safe/festive=eve it safe/fetch=high see at of/fetish=here's if of/feud=due of/fever=rev of/few=we of/fiasco=owe sse a if/fiber=re-be if/fiction=know it see if/fidelity=yet I lead if/field=the life/fiend=then a if/fierce=a see our if/fiery=why our if/fire=a riff/fight=the guy if/figure=are you gift/filch=high see all if/file=a life/fill=life/filler=real life/film=my life/filter=rate life/filth=hit life/final=lane if/finale=a lane if/finalize=as isle an if/finance=a see in an if/find=then if/find out=to owe then if/fine=a knife/finesse=as an if/finish=his in if/finite=at in if/firm=mere if/first=to sir if/fishy=why his if/fit=tie for/fix=sex if/fixed=decks if/flabbergasted=debt sag re-be all of/flabby=your ball of/flag=golf/flagrant=ten our gall if/flail=lie of/flair=our eye all of/flake=a call of/flamboyant=ten a why owe be I am all of/flaming=gone I am all of/flash=here's all of/flattery=your rate all of/flaunt=ten you are all of/flavor=rove all of/flaw=wall if/flesh=his self or her self/flexibility=yet ill I be I sex all of/flick=key see isle of/flight=the guy life/flimsy=you smile of/flinch=high see in isle if/fling=gone ill if/flip=pill for/flirt=tear isle if/float=to all of/flock=call of/floor=rule if/florid=dire all of/flotsam=mass to all of/flounder=red knew all of/flourish=his eye are you all of/flout=to all of/flow=wolf/flower=re-wolf/fluctuate=at a you to see your life/fluency=you see in a you all of/fluent=ten a you life/fluid=die you life/fluke=ache all of/flush=here's your life/fluster=rate see all of/fly=why life/focus=such of/foe=a of/foggy=you goof/foil=lie of/foist=it is I of/fold=deal of/follow=wall of/folly=while of/fond=then of/fondle=all then of/fondness=sending of/food=do for/foolish=his isle of/footing=gone it two of/forage=edge are of/foray=why our of/forbid=die be rough/force=a seer of/forebear=are a be are of/foreboding=gone eye do be oer of/forecast=to see ace our of/forefather=re hit of our of/forefront=ten hour of are rough/foreign=in guy are of/foremost=to some are of/forerunner=reign inner our of/foresee=ease our of/foresight=the guy is our of/foretell=let ear of/forever=rever of/forewarn=in our awe rough/forfeit=tie of rough/forge=edge our of/forget=target are of/forgive=eve I grow for/forgo=oh gee rough/forgotten=net to gear of/forlorn=near all rough/form=mirror of/formal=lame our of/format=tame our of/formation=know it aim our of/former=rem of/formidable=all bad I am rough/formula=all you mere of/forsake=a case our of/fort=tear of/forthwith=hit eye double you hit out of/fortify=you fit our of/fortress=sure tare of/fortunate=at a new tear of/forward=dare a double you our of/foster=rates of/found=then you of/foundation=know it add knew of/founder=read knew of/fountain=an eye at knew of/fracas=say see our of/fraction=know it see our of/fracture=a route see our of/fragile=all eye gay are of/fragment=ten them gear of/fragrance=a see near gar of/frail=liar of/frame=aim our if/frank=can our if?/frantic=see it in our if/fraternity=yet in rate our of/fraud=due are if/freak=key our if/free=ear of?/freedom=mode our if/freight=the guy our if/frenzy=why is near if/frequent=ten a you cue our if/fresh=his ear if/fret=tear of/fretful=love tear of/friction=know it see eye are if/friend=then a eye our if/frightened=then at hug eye our if/frightful=love the guy our if/frigid=dig I our if/fringe=edge in eye our if/frisk=kiss I our if/frivolity=yet I love eye our if/frolic=see isle owe our if/front=to know our if/froth=hit owe our if/frown=new owe our if/frozen=an ease owe our if/frugal=layed you our if/fruit=to eye you our if/fruitful=love to eye you our if/fruition=know it I you our if/frustrated=debt art sure if/fuel=lay of/fugitive=eve it eye goof/fulfill=life love/fully=you love/fulsome=aim owes love/fumble=all be muff/fume=am of/fumes=seem of/fun=enough/function=know it see enough?/fund=then of/fundamental=late aim made then of/funeral=lay rain of/funnel=lane of/funny=you enough/furious=is you owe eye are of/furniture=a route in our of/furrow=wore off/further=re-hit our of/furthermore=a roam re-hit our of/furtive=eve it rough/fury=why are of?/fussy=yes is of/futile=a light of?/futility=yet ill light of/future=a route to if!/gabble=all be bag/gadabout=to obey the age/gadget=target dagger/gaity=yet I age/gain=in eye age/gala=all age/gale=a lag/gall=lag/gallant=ten all age/gallantry=you write an all age!/gallivant=ten ave I lag/galore=a roll age/galvanize=as in have lag/gamble=all be major/game=aimage/gamut=to my age/gang=go nag/gap=page/gape=a page/garbage=edge a be rag/garbled=deal brag/garish=his eye rage/gasp=per sage/gate=at age/gather=re-hit age/gauche=a high see you age/gaudy=why due age/gauge=edge you age/gaunt=ten you age/gay=why age?/gaze as age/gazette=at ease age/gear=rage/gelatinous=is you on it a leg/gem=major/general=lair an edge!/generate=at our energy/generation=know it our energy/generic=sir an egg/generosity=yet is owe reign edge/genesis=this is energy/genial=lay in egg/genius=is you in edge/gentle=all ten egg/gentleman=name all to an edge/gentry=your route in egg/genuine=an I you in egg/germ=mere egg/germinate=at an eye mere egg/gesticulate=at all you see it siege/gesture=a route siege/get=target/ghastly=while to see a hug/ghoulish=his ill you owe hug/giant=ten age/gibberish=his eye re-be big/giddiness=send I dig/gifted=debt figure/gigantic=see it in a gig/gimmick=key see image/girdle=all there eyed

VISION OF A MENTAL PATIENT

you/girl=lurage/gist=to siege/gladden=need all gee/gladness=send all gee/glare=are all gee/glassy=why is all gee/glaze=ease all gee/gleam=milage/gleeful=love all gee/glide=add isle gee/glimmer=rem illed you/glimpse=as p.m. isle gee/glint=ten I will gee/glisten=net sealage/glitter=rate isle gee/global=lay be all gee/globe=able gee/glorify=you fear all gee/glorious=is you owe I role gee/gloss=soul gee/glow=double you all gee/glutton=not you all gee/gnarled=deal range/goad=day owed you/goal=lay owe gee/gobble=all bog/godlike=a kill dog/goodness=send owe you/gore=are owe gee/gospel=leap so gee/gossip=pissage/gouge=edge you owe gee/gourmet=team our you owe gee/govern=near eve owe gee/government=to name our eve owed you/grab=barge/grace=a seer gee/grade=a dared you/gradient=ten a eye dared you/gradual=lay you dare gee/graft=to far gee/grain=in eye our rage/grandeur=our you add neared you/grasp=pisser gee/grate=at a rage/grateful=love at our age/gratify=why fit our age/grave=ever gee/gravity=yet I varied you/graze=as are gee/great=teared you/greedy=why dear? Gee./green=energy/gregarious=is you owe eye rager gee/gridlock=call dared you/greif=feared you/greive=ever I eared you/grim=merge/grimace=a see aim eye our gee/grime=emerge/grind=then eye our age/grip=purge/groggy=why gored you/groove=ever gee/gross=sored you/grotesque=a you cue set owe rag/growth=hit war gee/grudge=edge due our go/grueling=gone ill a you urge/gruesome=aim owes a you unrge/gruff=if you our gee/grumble=all be emerge/grumpy=your p.m. urge/guarantee=at in our a huge/guard=there are you gee/guerrilla=all eye are huge/guess=see you gee/guest=to see you gee/guidance=a see in add eye huge/guide=add I huge/guild=deal eye huge/guile=all eye huge/guilt=tell I huge/guise=as eye huge/gullible=all be ill huge/gulp=plug/gun=on you gee/gunman=name in huge/gurgle=all grew gee/habit=tie be a here/habitual=lay you tie be ah/hack=key see ah/haggard=the rager here/hail=liar here/hair=our eye ah/halcyon=know why see lay here/half=filler here/halfway=why a wife lay here/hall=lay here/hallmark=cram lay here/hallucination=know it an eye see all are here/halo=owe lay here/halt=to lay here/halve=eve lay here/hammer=re-may here/hand=dna here/handbook=cool be then ah/handcuff=fuck then ah/handful=love dna here/handicap=pace eye then are here/handicraft=to farce I then ah/handiwork=crow id inner here/handle=all then ah/handsome=aim owes then ah/handwriting=gone it eye our double you dna here/handy=your dna here/hang=gonner here/hangover=rev owe going to hear/haphazard=there as a hip ah/happen=inner pay here/happiness=send I pay here/harangue=a huge near ah/harass=say ra here/harbor=rob ray here/hard=dear ah/harden=need ra here/hardly=while dare ah/hardy=why there ah/harm=mere ah/harmful=all of mere ah/harmless=cell mirror here/harmonious=is you owe in owe mirror here/harmonize=as in owe mirror here/harmony=you know mirror here/harness=send ra here/harrow=war are here/harsh=here is our ah/hassle=all say here/haste=at say here/hasty=why at say here?/hatch=high see to here/hate=eater here/hateful=love at ah/haul=all you are here/haunt=ten you are here/have=eve ah/haven=never here/havoc=see of are here/haywire=our eye why are here.hazard=there as ah/haze=as are here/hazy=wise ah?/head=dayer here/headache=a high see add ah/heading=gone eye day here/headstrong=gone owe writes day eh?/headway=why a double you day eh?/heal=lay here/health=hit lay ah/heap=payer here/hear=our ear here/hearsay=why as our eh?/heart=tear are here/heartache=a high see at tear are here/heartbreak=care be tear are here/heartless=cell tare are here/heat=to ah/heathen=inner hit are here/heaven=never eh/heckle=the key see here/hectic=sight see herer/hedge=edge the here/heedless=sell the here/hefty=why to fee here?/height=the guy eh?/heighten=net hug guy are here/heir=our eye eh/hell=all are here/hellish=his ill eh/hello=owe lay here/helm=me lay here/help=plea here/helpful=love plea here/helpless=sell plea here/helter-skelter=rate leaks rate lay here/hem=me here/hence=a see inner here/henchman=name high see inner here/henpecked=deck keep inner here/herald=delayer eh?/herd=there are here/hereafter=rate fear are here/hereditary=your at I dare eh?/heresy=yes ear are here/heretic=see it our eh/heritage=age at eye our eh?/hermit=time re-here/hero=owe re-here/heroic=see I owe re here/heroine=an I or a he?/hesitate=at ay is see here/hesitation=know it at is see here/heyday=why add you're here?/hiatus=is you to eye here/hidden=need eye here/hide=add eye here/hidebound=then you owe be die here/hideous=is you owe add eye here/hideout=to owe add I here/high=hug I here/highlight=the guy will hug eye here/hijack=cage eye here/hike=ache I here/hilarious=is you owe eye our all eye here/hilarity=yet I our all eye here/hill=lie here/hinder=read in eye here/hindmost=to some then eye here/hindrance=a see in our then eye here/hinge=edge in eye here/hint=ten eye here/hippie =eye pie here/hire=our eye here/hiss=see here/historic=see eye our owe it is I here/history=why wrote see here/hit=tie here/hitch= high see to eye here/hitherto= over time re-hit eye here/hit on=no tie here/hoard=there a owe here/hoax=sex owe ah/hobby=why be owe here/hoist=it is I owe here/hold=deal owe here/hole=a low here/holiday=why add isle owe here/holiness=send I low here/hollow=wallow here/holocaust=it is you a see all owe here/holy=your low here/homage=edge aim owe here/home=aim owe here/homeland=then all aim owe here/homicide=add I see I am owe here/homogeneity=yet eye an edge ohm owe here/homogeneous=is you owe energy ohm owe here/honest=to send owe here/honor=our owe know here!/hooligan=nag I will owe here/hopeful=love ape owe here/horde=add row here/horizon=nose eye row here/horizontal=late in owes I row here/horrible=all be eye row here/horrid=die row here/horrific=see if I row here/horse=as row here/horseman=name as row here/hospitable=all be at I appease owe here/host=it is owe here/hostage=egats! Owe here/hostile=all it is owe here/hound=then you owe here/house=as you owe here/hovel=leave owe here/hover=our eve owe here/however=rev a double you owe here/hub=be you here/huddle=all do here/huge=edge you here/hulk=clue here/human=name you hear/humane=an aim you here/humble=all be am you here/humbug=guy be am you/humdrum=murder me you here/humid=the eye am you here/humiliate=a tale I am you hear/humility=yet ill I me you here/humor=roam you hear/hump=p.m. you here/hunch=high see knew here/hurdle=all there you here/hurl=lure you here/hurricane=an ace eye are you here?/hurry=you rue here/hurt=true here/hurtle=all tear you here/husband=then a be is you here/hush=his you hear/husky=why keys you here/hustle=all it is you here/hut=to here/hybrid=dire be why here/hygiene=on a eye guy here/hymn=in them why here/hype=a pie here/hypnotic=see it in pi here/hypocricy=why see eye our owe pi here/hypocritical=lay see it our see owe pi here/hypothesis=this is a hit owe pi why/hysteria=air at is why here/hysterical=lay see eye rate see why here/icy=why sea eye/idea=aid eye/ideal=laid I/identical=lay see it in a die/identification=know it a see if it need I/identity=yet it need eye/idiocy=you see owe eye die/idiom=more eye die/idiosyncracy=you see our see in why owe eye die/idiot=to id eye/idle=the die/idol=load I/idolatry=why write all owed eye/idolize=as ill owed I/idyllic=kill wide eye/if=fee/ignite=at eye in guy/ignominy=why in more in guy/ignorance=a see inner on guy/ignore=are on guy/ill=lie/illegal=legal I/illegible=the big all eye/illegitimate=a tame it eye guy all I/ill-fated=debt of lie/illicit=tie see isle lie/illiterate=at a real tie lie/ill-mannered=there on name lie/illogical=lay see eye goal eye/illuminate=at an eye me you lie/illusion=know is you lie/illusory=you rose you lie/illustrate=at art is you lie/ill-will=lie double you lie/image=a game eye/imagination=know it an eye game I/imbecile=all I see be I/imbibe=a be I be me/imbroglio=oil gore be me/imitate=at aim tie me/immaculate=at all you see aim eye/immaterial=lay I rate aim eye/immature=a rut am I/immediate=at aid a me/immense=as name me/immensity=why it is aim me/immerse=as rem me/immigrant=to near guy me/imminent=ten an eye me/immobile=all I be owe them eye/immoderate=a tare read owe me/immoral=lay roam me/immortal=late roam me/immovable=all behave owe me/immune=on you me/imp=p.m. eye/impact=to see a p.m. eye/impair=our eye a p.m. eye/impart=trap me/impassable=all bass a p.m. eye/impassioned=then owe is say p.m. eye/impatience=a see in a it p.m. eye/impeach=high see a p.m. eye/impeccable=all be a see a p.m. eye/impede=add deep me/impel=leap me/impending=gone eye then a p.m. eye/impenetrable=all be art inner a p.m. eye/imperative=eve it a reposition me/imperceptible=the bite piece reposition me/imperfect=to see of rape me/imperial=lay I reposition me/imperil=lie reposition me/impersonal=lane owes reposition me/impersonation=know it an owe is reposition me/impertinence=a see in a night reposition me/impervious=is you owe I have reposition me/impetuosity=yet is owe you tape me/impetus=is you tape me?/impinge=edge in eye p.m. eye/impish=here is I p.m. eye/implant=ten all p.m. eye/implement=ten them all p.m. eye/implicate=at a see I will p.m. eye/implicit=tie see ill p.m. eye/implied=deal p.m. eye/implore=a role p.m. eye/imply=while p.m. eye/impolite=at ill owe p.m. eye/import=tear owe p.m. eye/important=ten at row p.m. eye/impose=a soap me/impossible=all be is owe p.m. eye/impostor=our owe it is owe p.m. eye/impotence=a see neat owe p.m. eye/impoverish=his eye rev owe p.m. eye/impracticable=all be a see it car p.m. eye/imprecise=as I see our p.m. eye/impregnate=a tan gear ear p.m. eye/impress=sure p.m. eye/impression=know is sure p.m. eye/imprint=ten I rip me/imprison=knows I rip me/improbable=the babe owe our p.m. eye/impromptu=you to pay more p.m. eye/improper=re-pour p.m. eye/improve=eve owe our p.m. eye/improvise=as if owe our p.m. eye/imprudent=to need you our p.m. eye/impudent=to need you p.m. eye/impulse=as loop me/impure=ear you p.m. eye/imputation=know it at 2 you p.m. eye/inability=yet ill I be an eye/inaccessible=the be is see sea an eye/inaccurate=a tare you see an eye/inactive=eve it an eye/inadequate=at a you cue a day in eye/inadmissible=all be is see mid an eye/inadvardantly=while ten add rev day in eye/inadvisable=all be as ivy day in eye/inane=on an eye/inanimate=a tame in an eye/inapplicable=all be a see ill pay an eye/inappropriate=at a eye re-pour pay in eye/inarticulate=at all you see it rain eye/inattention=know it net at in eye/inaudible=all be I due an eye/inaugural=lay rug you in eye/inauspicious=is you owe I p.s. you an eye/inborn=near owe be in eye/inbred=there be in eye/incalculable=all bail you see lay see in eye/incantation=know it at inner see in eye/incapable=all be a pace in eye/incapacitate=at at I see a pace in eye/incarcerate=at a race ray see in eye/incarnate=at an race in eye/incense=as in a see in eye/incentive=eve it in a see in eye/inception=know it peace in eye/incessant=ten ass a see in eye/incident=to need eye see in eye/incidentally=why late need I see in eye/incinerate=ar our reign I see in eye/incipient=ten a eye peace in eye/incision=know is I see in eye/incisive=eve is I see in eye/incite=at I see in eye/incivility=yet ill I have eye see in eye/inclement=ten aim all see in eye/inclination=know it an isle see in eye/include=add you all see in eye/inclusive=eve is you will see in eye/incognito=over time in go see in eye/incoherent=ten ear he owe see in eye/income=aim owe see in eye/incomparable=the bar a p.m. owe see in eye/incompatible=the bite a p.m. owe see in eye/incompetence=a see net a p.m. owe see in eye/incomplete=a tell p.m. owe see in eye/incomprehensible=the be is inner here p.m. owe see in eye/inconceivable=all behave I a see no see in eye/inconclusive=eve is you'll see in owe see in eye/incongruity=yet eye you going to owe see in eye/inconsiderate=at a read is no see in eye/inconsistent=to net size know see in eye/inconsolable=the ball owes an owe see in eye/inconspicuous=is you owe you see I peace in owe see in eye/inconvenience=a see in a eye never know see in eye/incorporate=at a row peer owe see in eye/incorrect=to see our owe see in eye/incorrigible=the big eye row see in eye/incorruptible=the bite pure owe see in eye/increase=a sayer in eye/incredible=all bid ear see in eye/increment=to name our see in eye/incriminate=at an eye me our see in eye/incumbent=ten a be more you see in eye/incur=our you see in eye/incurable=the bar you see in eye/indebted=debt bed in eye/indecency=why see inner see aid in eye/indecent=ten a seed in eye/indecipherable=the bar re-hip I see a day in eye/indecision=know is I see the in eye/indecisive=eve is I see a day in eye/indeed=deed in eye/indefensible=all be is enough add in eye/indefinite=at eye knifed in eye/indelible=the billed in eye/indelicate=attack I lead in eye/indemnify=why if in me do in eye/indemnity=yet in me deny/independence=a see need inner paid in eye/indescribable=all be a be a be eye our see said in eye/indestructible=the bite see you write seed in eye/indeterminate=at an eye mirror 2 Ted in eye/indicate=attack id in eye/indicative=eve it a see deny/indict=to seed in eye/indifference=a see near of feed in eye/indigestion=know it siege I do in eye/indignant=ten on guide in eye/indirect=to see our read

VISION OF A MENTAL PATIENT

in eye/indiscreet=tear seize id in eye/indiscretion=know it our see acid in eye/indiscriminate=at an eye mere seize i.d. in eye/indispensable=all be as inner per seed in eye/indisposed=the soap acid in eye/indisputable=all be at you proceed in eye/indistinct=to see night seed in eye/individual=lay you dive do in eye/indoctrinate=at a near to see owed in eye/indolent=to kneel? Owed in eye/indomitable=all be at eye mode in eye/indubitable=all be at I bud in eye/induce=a see you deny/indulge=egg lured in eye/industry=why writes you then I/inebriated=debt air be in eye/ineffective=eve it see of an eye/ineligible=the big eye lean eye/inept=to pee in eye/inequality=yet ill a you cue in eye/inert=train eye/inertia=8 reign I!/inescapable=all be a pace an eye/inestimable=the be aim might see in eye/inevitable=all be at I have an eye/inexcusable=all be as see sex an eye/inexpensive=eve is inner picks sex an eye/inexplicable=all be a see ill picks an eye/infallibility=yet ill I be I will laugh in eye/infamous=is you owe them of in eye/infancy=you see inner fine eye/infant=ten of an eye/infatuate=at a you 2 of in eye/infect=to see of in eye/infer=refine eye/inferior=our owe eye refine I/inferiority=yet I row eye our refine eye/infernal=lane refine eye/infertile=a light refine eye/infest=to safe in eye/infiltrate=at art life in eye/infinite=at in if in eye/infinitesimal=lay my set in if in eye/infirm=mere if in eye/inflame=aim all if in eye/inflate=at all if in eye/inflation=know it all if in eye/inflexible=the be I sex all of in eye/inflict=to see ill if in eye/influence=a see near you if in eye/influx=sex all of in eye/inform=mirror of in eye/information=know it aim are of in eye/infrequent=to near you cue our of in eye/infringe=egg in eye our if in eye/infuriate=at air rough in eye/ingenuity=yet I you negative in eye/inglorious=is you owe I role gone I/ingratiate=at 8 argue in eye/ingratitude=aid you tit argue in eye/ingredient=ten a eye dared you in eye/inhabited=debt I be ah in eye/inhale=all air here in eye/inherit=tire he in eye/inhibit=tie be here in eye/inhuman=name you her in eye/inimical=lay see I am eye in eye/iniquity=yet I you cue eye in eye/initial=late in eye/inject=to see edge in eye/injunction=know it see in huge in eye/injure=are huge in eye/injustice=a sight such in eye/inkling=gone ill key in eye/inland=then all I eye/inlet=tell in eye/innate=at an eye/inner=re-in eye/innocence=a see inner see on eye/innuendo=owed near you in eye/inoffensive=eve is in of on eye/inoperative=eve it our reposition on eye/inopportune=on you to row pawn eye/inordinate=at an id row in eye/inorganic=see in age grow in eye/inquest=to see cue in eye/inquire=are eye you cue in eye?/inquisition=know it is I you cue in eye/insane=an as an eye/insatiable=the bay it as in eye/inscribe=a be eye our sees in eye/insecure=oue you seize in eye/insensible=all be is in ease in eye/insensitive=eve it is in ease in eye/inseperable=all bar reposition in eye/insert=tear as in eye/inside=it is in eye/insidious=is you owe I dies in eye/insight=the guys in eye/insignia=a in guess in eye/insignificant=ten a see if in guys in eye/insincere=are a see in is in eye/insinuate=at a you in eye sin I/insipid=dip is in eye/insist=it is eye/inspect=to keeps in eye/inspiration=know it a ripe see in eye/install=late sin I/instance=a see in at sin I/instead=dates in eye/instigate=a tag it is in eye/instill=lights in eye/instinct=to see in it sin I/institution=know it you tie it is in eye/instruct=to see you right sin I/instrument=ten them you write sin I/insufferable=the bare fuss in eye/insufficient=ten a eye see if us in eye/insular=our all us in eye/insulate=at all us in eye/insult=tell us in eye/insuperable=the bare reposition us in eye/insurance=a see near sin I/insure=a rush in eye/insurgent=ten edge rush in eye/insurrection=know it see our you sin I/intact=to see at in eye/integral=lair gate in eye/integrate=ar are gate in eye/integrity=why to eye our gate in eye/intellect=to cell let in eye/intelligence=a see in edge isle at in eye/intelligible=the big isle let in eye/intemperate=at a reposition met in eye/intend=then at an eye/intense=a sin at in eye/intent=ten at an eye/inter=rate in eye/intercede=add a see rate in eye/intercept=to piece rate in eye/interchange=edge in a high see rate in eye/intercourse=as our you owe see rate in eye/interest=to sir at an eye/interface=a see of rate in eye/interfere=are of rate in eye/interim=mirror ten eye/interior=row irate in eye/interlude=a duel rate in eye/intermediate=at aid am rate in eye/interment=ten them rate in eye/intermingle=all gone I am rate in eye/intermission=know is I am rate in eye/intern=near at in eye/internal=lane rate in eye/international=lane owe it and rate in eye/internet=ten rate in eye/interpose=a soap rate in eye/interpret=tear pair rate in eye/interrogate=a tagger at an eye/interrupt=to pure rate in eye/intersection=know it see as rate in eye/interval=leave rate in eye/intervention=know it never rate in eye/interview=wave rate in eye/intestines=send it at in eye/intimacy=you see aim it in eye/intimidate=a tad I am it in eye/intolerable=the bare lot in eye/intone=a knot in eye/intoxicated=debt a see I sex over time in eye/intrepid=dip art in eye/intricate=attack I write in eye/intrigue=a huge I write in eye/intrinsic=see is in I rate in eye/introduce=a see you door 2 in eye/introduction=know it see you door ten eye/introspective=eve it keeps owe write in eye/introvert=tree ever ten eye/intrude=add you right in eye/intuition=know it eye you ten eye/inundate=a tad none in eye/invade=aid have in eye/invalid=dial of in eye/invective=eve it see of in eye/invent=ten eve in eye/inverse=as rev in eye/invert=tree of in eye/invest=to save in eye/investigation=know it age it sever in eye/invidious=is you owe eye dive in eye/invincible=all be I see in I've on eye/inviolable=all bail owe I've in eye/invisible=all be is I've in eye/invite=at I've in eye/invocation=know it a cove in eye/invoke=ache of in eye/involve=of love in eye/inward=draw in eye/irate=a our eye/irksome=aim owes cry/iron=in our eye/ironic=see in our eye/irrational=lane owe it our eye/irrefutable=all be at of ear I/irregular=our all huge are I/irrelevant=ten have lay our eye/irresistible=all be it is sure eye/irreversible=all be is revere eye/irrigate=at age eye our eye/irritate=at at eye our eye/island=then all is eye/isolate=a tall owes eye/issue=a you see/isthmus=some hit sigh/itch=high see tie/item=met eye/itinerant=ten are on it eye/jab=badge/jacket=take cage/jackpot=top cage/jaded=dead age/jagged=daggered you/jail=lie age/jam=major/jamboree=ear owe be major/janitor=rotten age/jar=rage/jaundiced=the see id in you age/jaunt=ten you age/jaw=wage/jealous=is you all a edge/jeer=rage/jell=led you/jerk=key rage/jeopardize=as id rap owe edge/jest=to siege/jester=rate siege/jet=to edge/jettison=knows it to edge/jewel=lay wedge/jig=guide you/jinx=sex in eyed you/jitters=sir at tied you/job=be owed *you/jocular=our all you see owed you/John Doe=a owed in Hodge/join=in eye owed you/joke=ache owed you/joint=ten I owed you/jolly=while owed you/jolt=tell owed you/jot=told you/journal=lane our you owed you/journey=why near you owed you/jovial=leave owed you/joy=why owed you/joyful=love why owed you/joyless=sell why owed you/jubilant=to nail eye be huge/jubilee=all I be huge/judge=edge due huge/judicial=lay eye see I due huge/jug=go huge/juice=a see I huge/jumble=all be am huge/jumbo=owe be am huge/jump=p.m. huge/junction=know it see in huge/jurisdiction=know it see id sir huge/just=to such/justice=a see it such/juvenile=all in eve huge/juxtaposition/know it is owe pat sex huge/Kamikaze=as ache I make I am okay/keel over=rev owe leak/keen=inner key/keep=peek/keeper=re-peek/keg=geek?/kernel=lay in wreck/key=your key/keynote=at on why a key/kid=dick/kidnap=pay in dick/kill=lick/kin=in eye key/kind=then eye key/kindle=all then eye key/kindly=while in eye okay?/kindred=there then I key/king=gone eye okay/kink=key in eye key/kiosk=kiss owe I okay/kiss=sick/kit=to eye key/knack=key see an key/knead=day on okay/knife=a fine key/knob=be on key/knock=key see on key/knot=2 in key/know=won okay!/knowing=going to eye one key/knowledge=edge deal one key/known=new on okay?/kudos=sewed you key/label=the be all/labor=row be all/labyrinth=hit in eye our be all/lace=a call/lacerate=at a race see all/lack=key see all/lack luster=rate see you will key see all/laconic=see in owe see all/lad=the all/laden=need all/lady=why the all?/lag=gall/laggard=there age all/laid-back=key see a be dial/liar=are a ill/lake=a call/lame=a mall/lament=ten them all/lampoon=new p.m. all/land=then all/landlord=dear all then all/landmark=cram then all/landscape=a pace is than all/landslide=add isles than all/lane=on all/language=egg a you going to all/languish=his eye you gone all/lank=can all/lap=pal/lapse=as pale/large=a grail/lark=crawl/lash=his all/lass=is all/last=it is all/latch=high see to all/late=a tale/latent=ten at all/later=rate all/lateral=lay rate all/law=wall/lawful=love wall/lawless=cell wall/lay=you all/layer=re-all/layman=name why all/layoff=for you all/layout=to owe you all/laziness=send I is all/lazy=why is all?/lead=deal/leader=read all/leaf=fall/leaflet=tell for all/league=a huge all/lean=kneel/learn=near all/learned=then our all/lease=a sale/least=to say all/leather=re-hit all/leave=eve all/lecherous=is you owe our a high see all/lecture=a route sell/ledge=edge deal/leer=real/leeway=your double you all/left=to feel/leftover=rev owe to feell/legible=the be eye gel/legion=in owe I gel/legislation=know it all see gel/legislature=a route all see gel/legitimate=a tame it eye gel/leisure=a rush I all/lend=then all/lengthen=inner hit gone all/leniency==you see inner I kneel/less=sell?/lesson=knows all/let=tell/let down=new owed tell/lethal=lay hit all/lethargic=see eye grey hit all/let off=foe tell/let on=know tell/letter=retell/lever=reveal/leverage=age our reveal/levity=yet I reveal/lewd=the well/liability=yet ill I be a isle/liable=all be a isle/liaison=know is eye a isle/libel= lay bill/liberal=lair a be isle/liberate=at our re-be isle/libertine night re-be isle/liberty= =yet rebe isle/license=as inner see I will/lick=kill/lie=a ill/life=a fill/lifeless=sell a fill/lifelike=a killer fill/lifetime=emit a fill/lift=to fill/light=thing isle/likely=your leak isle/liken=inner kill/likewise=as eye double you a kill/limb=be me ill/limelight=the guy lay me isle/limit=time ill/limitless=sell time ill/limp=p.m. ill/line=an isle/lineaments=set name an isle/lined=denial/lines=see nil/linger=rage inn isle/lip=pill/liquid=die you cue ill/liquor=row you cue ill/list=to seal/literacy=you see a rate isle/literature=a route our at all/lithe=a hit ill/litigant=ten age eye til/litter=rate ill/little all to isle/live=evil/lively=you'll eve isle/liverish=his eye reveal ill/liver=reveal/livid=dive ill/load=day all/loaf=for all/loan=inner all/loathe=a hit a all/lobby=why be all/local=lay see all/locate=attack all/location=know it a call/lock=key call/lofty=yet fall/log=goal/logic=see eye goal/loiter=rate eye all/loll=loll/lone=on all/loneliness=send I will an all/lonely=why lend all/long=gone all/look=cool/lookout=to ower cool/loom=mule/loop=pool/loosen=an ease all/loot=tool/lord=there all/lore=are all/lose=a soul/loser=raise all/loss=soul/lost=to soul/lot=tall/lottery=why rate all/loud=due all/loudly=while do all/lounge=edge in you all/lousy=why is you all?/lout=to all/love=evolve/lovely=you'll eve all/low=wall/lowdown=knew owed all/lower=re-wall/loyal=lay all/lubricate=a take I rub you will/lucid=die cool/lucky=your cool/lucrative=eve it are cool/ludicrous=is you our acid you all?/luggage=a gag you will/lumber=re-be am you all/luminous=is you on eye am you all/lunacy=you cam you will/lunatic=sight and you will/lunge=edge in you all/lurch=high see rule/lure=a rule/lurid=thy rule/lurk=cruel/luscious=is you owe I seize you all/lust=it is all/luxurious=is you owe I are you sexual?/luxury=you are you sexual/lyrical=lay see eye our while/lyrics=see eye while/macabre=our be a see aim/Machiavellian=nail eve a eye high see aim/machine=any high see aim/macho=owe high see aim/mad=damn/madden=in a dame/madness=send them/maelstrom=more it is the aim/maestro=orr to sea me/magazine=an eye zag aim/magic=see eye game/magisterial=lair at signal aim/magistrate=at arts eye game/magnetic=see it end game/magnetism=miss it end game/magnificence=a see in a see if in game/magnitude=a duty in game/maiden=need I aim/mail=lie am/maim=my aim/main=in I am/mainstay=you at sin I aim/maintain=in eye at in I aim/majestic=sights edge aim/major=row jam/make=a came/make believe=evil a be ache am/make out=to owe a came/maladjusted=debts huge day lame/malady=why day lame?/malaise=a see all aim/mal-content=ten at know see lamb/male=a lamb/malefactor=wrote see of a lamb/malfunction=know it see enough lame/malice=a kill aim/malicious=is you owe eye see I lamb/malign=in guy lame/malleable=all be all aim/malpractice=a sight crap lame/maltreat=tear to lamb/mammoth=hit them maim/man=name/manacle=all can name/manage=a gain aim/manager=rage an aim/mandate=at add name/mandatory=why wrote add name/maneuver=rev you an aim/manfully=why love name/mangy=your going to aim/manhandle=all then are name/mania=a in name/maniac=seer in aim/manifest=to safe in am/manifold=deal of in aim/manipulate=at all you pin aim/mankind=then I key name/manliness=send isle name/manly=while name/man made=adam name/manner=are an aim/manners=sir an name/mantle=the ten name/manual=lay you name/manufacture=a route see of you name/many=you name/mar=ram/maraud=due our aim/marauder=read you are aim/margin=in eye gram/marijuana=on a huge eye our*

142

VISION OF A MENTAL PATIENT

aim/mariner=reign eye ram/marital=late eye our aim/mark=cram/market=take ram/marriage=egg a I ram/marry=you ram/marshal=lay his ram/martial=lay it ram/martinet=ten it ram/marvel=leave our aim/masculine=an eye loose aim/mask=kiss aim/mass=same/massacre=a crass aim/master=rate same/mastermind=then I am rate same/masterpiece=a see eye prey to same/mastery=you rate same/match=high see tame/mate=a tame/material=lair at aim/maternal=lane rate aim/matrimony=you know them I write aim/matted=debt aim/matter=rate am/matter of fact=to see of foe rate same/mature=a route aim/maudlin=nil due aim/maul=all you aim/maverick=key see I rev aim/maxim=mix aim/maximum=am you mix aim/maybe=a be why aim/mayhem=me here why am/maze=a zam/meadow=whoaed them/meager=rager aim?/meal=lay them/mean=in a aim/meaningful=love gone in aim/means=sin aim/measly=while say them/measure=a rush aim/mechanical=lay see in a high see am/mechanism=missing a high see aim/meddle=all them/mediate=at aid them/mediation=know it aid them/mediator=wrote aid them/medicinal=lane I see I deem/medicine=a nice id aim/mediocre=oue see owe eye deem/meditate=at a tide deem/medley=yell deem/meet=team/melancholy=while owe high see in all aim/mellifluous=is you owe you life isle aim/mellow=wall them/melody=wide all aim/melt=tell them/memento=over time name them/memorize=as I roam aim/memory=why roam am/menace=a see on them/mend=then am/mendacious=is you owe eye see add name/menial=lay in them/mental=late name/mention=know it in them/mentor=wrote in them/menu=you name/mercantile=a light inner see rem/mercenary=why reign a see rem/merchandise=acid inner high see rem/merchant=ten a high see our aim/merciful=love I see our aim/merciless=cell I see rem/mercurial=lay eye our you see rem/mercy=you see rem/mere=a rem/meretricious=is you owe I our tear aim/merge=edge rem/merger=our edge rem/merit=tire them/merriment=ten them eye rem/merry=your aim/mesh=his aim/mesmerize=as eye rem seem/mess=is same/metamorphosis=this is owe hip roam at them/metaphor=row hip at them/mete=at them/meteoric=see I wrote aim/method=due hit aim/meticulous=is you all you see it aim/microbe=a bore see I am/microscopic=see eye pose soar see I am/midday=why add I am/middle=the dim/mid=dim/midnight=the guy in dim/midst=it is dim/midway=why a double you aim/might=yhe guy I am/migrant=to neared you I am/mild=deal I am/milieu=you a isle I am/militant=ten at ill I am/military=why rate isle I am/milk=climb/mimic=see eye am I am/mince=a see in I am/mind=then I am/mindful=love then I am/mingle=all gone I am/miniature=a route a in I am/minimal=lamb in I am/minimize=as I am in I am/minimum=money in I am/minion=no in eye aim/minor=row in I am/minstrel=lay art sin I am/mint=ten I am/miniscule=all you see in I am/minute=at you in I am/minutiae=8 you in? I am!/minx=sex in I am/miracle=the sea are I am/mire=a rim/mirror=our owe hour I am/mirth=hitter I am/misadventure=a route never days is I am/misanthropic=sea port ten as I aim/misapprehend=then a hear pace see I am/misbehave=eve a he be is I am/miscalculate=at all you see lay see is I am/miscarry=you erase is I am/miscellaneous=is you on all a see is I am/mischief=fee I high see I am/misconception=know it peace know see is I am/misconduct=to see you then owe see is I am/miscreant=ten our seize I am/misdeed=deeds I am/miser=raise them/miserable=all be a rise I am/misery=your ease I am/misfire=our if see I am/misfit=typhus I am/misfortune=a new tear of is I am/misguided=dead eye you guess I am/mishandle=all then are his I am/mishap=pay his I am/misinform=mere of in eye seem/mislay=why all is I am/mislead=deal see I am/mismanage=a gain aim see I am/misprint=ten I rips I am/misquote=at you owe you cue is I am/misrepresent=ten as sure pair I am/misrule=a lure is I am/miss=seem/misshapen=inner pay his I am/missile=all is I am/missing=gone is I am/missionary=you are know I see I am/missive=eve is I am/misspent=ten a piece is I am/mist=it is I am/mistake=ache at is I am/mistimed=them it see I am/mistreat=tear it is I am/mistrust=it is your right is I am/misty=yet see I am/misunderstand/then at sure read in you is I am/misuse=as us I am/mitigate=a tag it I am/mix=sex I am/mixture=a route sex I am/mob=bomb/mobile=the eye be owe them/mock=come/mode=atom/model=lead ohm/moderate=at our read owe them/modern=neared owe them/modest=to seed owe them/modicum=am you see id owe em/modification=know it a see if eye doom/modish=his id owe em/modulate=at all you doom/mogul=lug owe em/moist=it is I owe em/molecule=all you see a loom/molest=to see loom/momentary=why our at name mom?/monarch=high see Ra knew em/monetary=your at a know em/money=you know em/mongrel=lair gone gnome/monitor=wrote in know em/monkey=your key gnome/monolithic=see eye hit isle on owe em/monopolize=as ill owe pawn owe em/monotonous=is you not a gnome/monster=our at is gnome/monument=ten them you know em/mood=doom/on=no /moot=tomb/mornameal=lay roam/morality=yet ill our roam/morale=all a room/moratorium=am you I wrote to room/morbid=dib roam/more=a roam/morgue=a huge room/morning=gone in roam/moron=no roam/morose=as owe roam/morsel=lays roam/mortal=late roam/mortification=know it a see if it roam/mortuary=why Ra you to roam/mostly=you'll tease em/mother=re-hit owe em/motif=fit ohm/motion=know it ohm/motive=eve it owe em/motley=yell to them/mottled=deal to them/motto=over tim to to em/mount=ten you ohm/mourn=near you owe em/mouth=hit you owe em/move=eve ohm/muck=come/mud=dumb/muffle=the fume/mug=gum/mull=loom/ multiple=the pit loom/multitude=a duty to loom/mundane=an aid knew em/municipal=lay peace in I am/murder=red rum/murmur=room rum/muscle=all see sum/muse=assume/musical=lay see eye sum/muster=rate sum/mutable=al be at them/mutation=know it at them/mutter=rate em/mutual=lay you to em/myriad=the air why em/mysterious=is you owe eye rate see why am/mystery=your rate see em/mystify=why fits yum/mystique= you quits why mmn?/myth=hit why mmn?/mythology=your goal owe hit why mmn?/nadir=ridden/nag=gain/nail=lie an/naïve=eve eye on/naked=the can/name=a man/named=the man/nameless=cell a man/napkin=nick pan/narcissism=miss his eye see ran/narcotic=sight owe see ran/narrator=wrote our an/narrow=war on/nasty=yet sane/nation=know it an/native=eve it an/natural=lay route an/nature=a route an/naughty=yet hug you an/nausea=a ease you an/nautical=lay sea it you an/navigate=a tag eye vein/near=rain/nebula=all you been/neces-

sary=why our as a scene/necromancy=you see namer on/necropolis=seal owe pour see/need=dean/nefarious=is you owe I our of/negate=a tag on/negative=eve it again/neglect=to see all again/negligence=a see in a guy all negative/negotiate=at a eye to gain/neighbor=our aowe be hug eye on/nemesis=this is of men/nepotism=miss it open/nerve=ever on/nest=to scene/nestle=all to send/neurosis=this is our you an/neurotic=sight owe our you an?/neutral=lay right you an/never=reving/nevertheless=sell a hit reving/new=when/newsworthy=you hit row is when/next=takes an/nibble=all be in/nice=a sin/niche=a high see in/nickname=a man kin/nifty=why it fine/niggard=dragging/night=the guy in/nightmare=our aim the guy in/nimble=all be mine/nirvana=an ave our in/nit-pick=keep it in/nobility=yet ill eye I be on/noble=all be on/nobody=why due be on/nocturnal=lane route see on/nod=done/no go=owe go on/noise=as eye on/nomad=damn on/nomenclature=a route all see name on/nominal=lane I am on/nominate=at an eye am on/nonaligned=then guy lane on/nonchalance=a see in all a high see non/noncombatant=ten at a be more see non/nonconformity=yet I am our of know see on/nondescript=to peirce seed known/nonentity=yet it in a non/nonessential=lat it an ease a known/nonevent=to never in on/nonexistent=ten at six an on/nonsensensical=lay see is in ease an ease on/nonstarter=rate rats non/norm=mere on/normal=lame our on/north=hitter on/nose=as on/nostalgia=age late sun/notable=all be at on/notation=know it at on/notebook=could be at on/noted=debt on/nothing=gone eye hit on/notice=a see it on/notion=know eye tone/notorious=is you owe I wrote on/nourish=his eye are you on?/novel=leave on/novice=a see eye of on/now=one/nowadays=see why add a one/noxious=is you owe eye sex on/nuance=a see in a un/nubile=all I be you in/nucleus=is you all see you on/nude=a done/nudge=edge done/null=all un/numb=be moon/number=re-be moon/numeral=lay rem un/nuptial=lay it pun/nurse=a sir un?/nurture=a route run/nut=tune/nutrition=know I write you in/nuts=stun/nymph=hip mine/oaf=far owe/oafish=his if a owe/oath=hit a owe/obdurate=at a rude be owe/obedience=a see need a be owe/obelisk=kiss I will a be owe/obese=ease a be owe/obey=why a be owe/obfuscate=a takes of be owe/object=to see edge be owe/objective=eve it see edge be owe/obligation=know it a guy will be owe/oblige=edge I will be owe/oblique=a you cue isle be owe/obliterate=at a rate I will be owe/oblivion=on eye of isle be owe/obnoxious=is you owe eye sex on be owe/obscene=inner seize be owe/obscure=our you see is be owe/observe=eve raise be owe/observation=know it have raise be owe/obsessed=disease be owe/obsolete=a tell owe is owe be/obstacle=all see ats is owe be/obstinate=at an it is owe be/obstruct=to see you right is be owe/obtain=in eye at be owe/obtrusive=eve is sir to be owe/obtuse=as you to be be owe/occasion=know I say see owe/occult=tell you see owe/occupancy=why see nap you see owe/occupy=yup you see owe=occur=our you see owe/odd=do/oddity=yet I do/odious=is you owe eye day/odyssey=yes see do/offbeat=to be foe/offend=then of owe/offense=as inner foe/offer=refer owe/office=a see if owe/official=lay eye see if owe=offing=going to eye foe/officer=are a see if owe/offset=tease foe/often=net for/ogre=our go/oil=lie owe/old=deal owe/omen=name owe/ominous=is you on I may/omission=know id I am owe/omit=time owe/once=a see know/onerousis you or a know/only=you'll know/onset=tease know/onslaught=thing you all is know/onus=sun owe/opening=gone in ape owe/operate=at a reposition/operative=eve it a reposition/opinion=know I nip owe/opponent=ten an owe pee owe/oppress=serpant owe/opposition=know it is owe pee pee owe/optimistic=sight see might pee owe/oracle=all see our owe/oral=lay row/orbit=tie be row/orchestra=art see high see our owe/ordain=in I add row/ordeal=layed row/order=read row/ordinary=you're an eye dear owe/organ=inner grow/organic=see in a grow/orient=ten a eye row/orifice=a see if eye row/origin=in I grow/ornament=ten them on row/ornate=at an row/oscillate=at all I see so/ossify=why is if so/ostensible=all be is neat so/ostracize=ease I see art so/other=re-hit owe/ounce=a sea in you owe/out=to owe/outfit=to eye fit you owe/outing=gone it you owe/outlaw=wall to owe/outlay=why all to owe/outlet=tell to owe/outline=an isle to owe/outlive=evil to owe/outlook=cool to owe/outmoded=dead owe them to owe/output=to pee to owe/outrage=edge art you owe/outright=the guy write to owe/outset=it is to owe/outshine=an eye his to owe/outside=a this to owe/outsize=ease is to owe/outspoken=in a cops it to owe/outward=draw to owe/outwit=tie double you to owe/outworn=near owe to owe/oval=lay of owe/ovation=know it of owe/over=rev owe/overact=to see a rev owe/overall=all a rev owe/overawe=a way rev owe/overbalance=a see in all a be rev owe/overbear=are a be our eve owe/overblown=knew all be our eve owe/overcast=to say see our eve owe/overcharge=edge our owe a high see rev owe/overcome=aim owe see our eve owe/overdo=owed our eve owe/overdone=a nod our eve owe/overdue=a you due rev owe/overheat=to hear eve owe/overemphasize=ease is a hip me rev owe/overflow=wolf eve owe/overhaul=all you are here our eve owe/overhead=dat are here eve owe/overjoyed=the why owed you eve owe/overload=day all eve owe/overrate=ar our rev owe/override=a dire eve owe/overrule=a lure eve owe/overrun=newer eve owe/overseer=our ease eve owe/overt=tear eve owe/overtake=ache at our eve owe/overthrow=war hit rev owe/overtone=o knot rev owe/overture=a route our eve owe/overturn=near you to rev owe/overwhelm=me lay how rev owe/overwork=care owe our eve owe/owe=a double you owe/own=new owe/pace=a cap/pacifist=it is if I see ape/pack=key cap/pact=to see ape/paddle=all day pee/pagan=inner gap/page=a gap/pageant=ten a gape/pain=in eye ape/painkiller=re-like in eye ape/paint=ten I pay/pal=lap/palatable=all be at a lap/palaver=our eve all ape/paltry=why write lap/pamper=rape map/pamphlet=tell hip map/pan=nap/panacea=a see on a pee/pander=read nap/panic=see in ape/panorama=aim our on a pee/pant=to nap/parable=all be a rap/parade=add a rap/paradise=as I dare ape/paradox=sex owed a rap/parallel=lay lair ape/paralysis=this is why lay wrap/parameter=rate aim our rap/paramount=ten you owe them a rap/paranoid=die on a rap/paraphrase=ease our hip a rap/parasite=at is a rap/parcel=lay see wrap/parch=high see rap/pardon=knowed rap/pare=a wrap/parent=ten a rap/parish=his eye rap/parity=yet I rap/park=crap/parlance=a see in all rap/parliament=to name a isle rap/parochial=lay eye high see owe rap/parody=you do rap/parrot=to rap/parson=knows rap/part=trap/partial=lay eye trap/participant=ten a

VISION OF A MENTAL PATIENT

piece I trap/particle=all see eye trap/partisan=in as I trap/partition=know it I trap/partner=reign to rap/party=your trap/passable=all be a say pee/passage=edge as ape/passion=know is ape/passive=eve eye sap/patch=high see tap/patent=ten a tap/paternal=lane rate ape/path=here tap/pathetic=sight a hit ape/patience=a see inner eye tap/patriot=to eye right ape/patrol=lure tap/patron=in our tape/patter=re-tap/pattern=near at ape/paucity=yet I see you ape/pauper=rape you ape/pause=as you ape/pawn=new ape/pay=yup/payable=all be why a pay/peace=a see ape/peak=keep/peasant=to in as ape/peccadillo=all id a seep/peculiar=real you keep/padant=ten aid ape/peddle=all deep/pedestal=late seed ape/pedestrian=in a eye right said deep/peer=reap/peg=gape/pelt=to leap/penalty=yet lane per/penal=lane of per/penance=a seen on a per/penetrate=ar art on a per/penitent=ten at in a per/pension=knoe is in a per/people=all pee owe a pee/perceive=eve I a see reposition/perch=high see reposition/perception=know it per creep/perfect=to see of reposition/percussion=know is you see reposition/perform=mere owe for reposition/perhaps=is pay her reposition/peril=lie reap/perimeter=rate aim reposition/period=due eye repostion/perish=his eye reap/perjure=our huge reposition/permanence=a see name reposition/permanent=ten on aim reap/permeate=at aim reap/permission=know is I am reposition/permit=time reposition/pernicious=is you owe eye see in reap/perpendicular=rail you see eye then a preparation/perpetual=lay you at preparation/perplex=x all preparation/persecute=at you seize reposition/persevere=our eve as reap/persist=this is reposition/person=knows reap/personality=yet ill an owes reposition/personify=your fine owes reap/personnel=lane owes are a per/perspective=eve it see a peace reap/perspire=a rips reposition/persuade=add you us reposition/pertain=in eye at reap/pertinent=ten on it reap/perturb=be route reposition/peruse=as you reep/pervade=add ave reposition/perverse=as rev reap/pervert=tare of reposition/pessimism=miss is me I seep/pestilent=ten all it seep/pet=to pee/petition=know it eye tape/petrify=you fear tape/petty=why tape?/petulance=a see in all you tape/phantom=more to inner hip/phase=a say hip/phenomenon=known aim on a hip/philistine=a knight see ill eye hip/philosophy=why hip owes, all I hip/phlegmatic=sight aim gel hip/phobia=a be owe hip/phone=an owe hip/photograph=hip our got owe hip/phrase=ease our hip/physical=lay see is why hip/pick=keep/picnic=see in keep/picture=a route see eye per/piece=a seep/pigment=ten them guy pee/pile=a leap/pill=lip/pillage=edge a lip/pinch=high see nip/pinion=know I nip/pipe=a pipe/pique=a you equip/piracy=why sea a rip/pitch=high see type/pitiful=love I tip/pivot=to of eye per/place=a see all pee/placid=the eye see all per/plagiarize=as I rage gall pee/plague=a you gall per/plan=in all per/plant=two in all per/plate=at a lip/plateau=you are at a leap/platform=mere of tall per/platitude=add you to it all per/platoon=knew to all per/plausible=all be is you all per/play=why a leap/playboy=why all be why all per/plea=help/plead=deal per/pleasant=ten as all per/please=as a all per/pleasure=a rush all per/pledge=edge deal per/plentiful=love it in all per/plethora=a row hit all per/pliable=all bail per/plot=to all per/plow=wall per/pluck=key see you'll pee/plug=gulp/plummet=teem you leap/plunge=edge in you leap/ply=why lip/poach=high see owe per/pocket=take see owe per/podium=me you eye do per/poem=me owe per/poetic=see it owe per/poignant=ten an guy owe per/point=ten I owe per/poise=as I owe per/poison=nose eye owe per/poke=ache owe pee/police=a kill owe per/policy=why see eye loop/polish=his eye owe per/polite=at isle owe per/politics=see it ill owe per/pollute=at you low per/pompous=is you p.m. owe per/pond=then owe pee/ponder=read an owe per/pontificate=at a see if fit know per/pope=a pop/populace=a see all you population/population=know it all you populate/pore=a rope/pornographic=see I hip our go inner owe pee/portable=all be at rope/portend=then at rope/porter=rate rope/portion=know it row per/portrait=to eye art row per/portrayal=lay art row per/pose=as owe per/posit=it is owe per/position=know it is owe per/positive=eve it is owe per/possess=sees owe per/post=it is owe per/postpone=an owe pits owe per/postscript=to peirce it is owe per/potent=ten at owe per/potion=know I top/pounce=a see in you owe per/pound=then you owe per/pout=to owe per/poverty=tear of owe per/powerful=lover a double you owe per/practicable=all be a see it car per/practical=lay see it are per/practice=a see it see our per/pragmatic=sight aim gee our per/prance=a see near per/pray=why our per/preach=high see a rip/preamble=all be mere per/precaution=know it you a seer per/precede=add a see our per/precept=to piece our per/precinct=to see in eye to see our per/precision=know is I see our per/preclude=add you'll see our per/precocious=is you owe I see owe see our per/preconceived=the vice know see our per/predator=wrote add a rip/precursor=rose our you seer per/predestined=then its said our per/predetermined=then I am rated our per/predicament=ten them a see I dare per/predict=to see I dare per/predilection=know it see all I dare per/predisposed=these owe per seed our per/predominate=at an eye mode oer per/pre-eminent=ten then eye me our per/preface=a see of our per/prefer=refer per/pregnant=ten on gear per/prehistoric=see I wrote is eye her per/prejudice=a see id huge oer per/preliminary=you ran I'm ill ear per/prelude=add you will our per/premature=a route aim our per/premeditated=debt at I deemer per/premier=reem our per/premise=as eye me our per/premium=me you eye mere per/premonition=know it in owe mere per/preoccupation=know it a pussy owe our pee/prepare=a wrap our per/preponderance=a see neared know peer per/preposterous=is you owe rate so peer per/prerequisite=at is eye you queer our per/prerogative=eve it age ower are per/presage=edge as our per/prescribe=a be eye our sees are per/presence=a see in ease our per/present=ten as our per/presentation=know it at an ease are per/preserve=eve raise oar per/preside=add is our per/press=sir per/pressure=a rusher per/prestige=edge it it our per/presume=aim you sir per/presumption=know it p.m. us ear per/pretend=then at oer per/pretense=as net our per/pretension=know is near to our per/pretext=takes at our per/pretty=why tear per/prevail=all I have our per/prevalence=a see in all ave are per/prevent=ten eve our per/preview=we eye veer per/previous=is you owe eye veer per/prey=your pee/price=a see eye rip/prick=key see I rip/pride=a dire per/prim=mere per/primary=your aim eye our per/prime=am I per?/primeval=leave them eye our per/prim-

itive=eve it I mere per/*prince*=a see in eye our per/*principal*=lay peace in eye our per/*principle*=all peace in eye per/*print*=ten I rip/*priority*=yet I row I rip/*prison*=know sir per/*prism*=miss eye our per/*pristine*=an it sir per/*private*=at a veer per/*priviledge*=edge deal I veer per/*prize*=as I our per/*probable*=all be a abhor per/*probe*=abhor per/*problem*=meal bore per/*procedure*=are you the see or per?/*process*=see core per/*procession*=know is a see our r.i.p./*proclaim*=my all core per/*procrastinate*=at an it say our see owe our per/*procure*=ear our see owe our per/*prodigal*=lay guy door per/*prodigy*=why guide owe our per/*produce*=a see you door per/*product*=to see you door per/*profane*=an of owe our per/*profess*=safe owe our per/*profession*=know is of owe our per/*proficiency*=why see in a eye see if owe our per/*profile*=a life owe our per/*profit*=to eye for per/*profligate*=at age ill for per/*profound*=then you of owe our per/*profuse*=as you for per/*progeny*=why energy go our per/*prognosis*=this is on go our per/*program*=may our go our per/*progress*=see our go are per/*progressive*=eve eye surge owe our per/*prohibit*=tie be eye whore per/*project*=to see edge owe our per/*projectile*=a light see edge owe our per/*proletarian*=in a eye rate all owe our per/*proliferate*=at a refill owe our per/*prolific*=see if ill owe are per/*prologue*=a huge all owe our per/*promenade*=add amen owe our per/*prominence*=a see in an eye more per/*promiscuous*=is you owe you see I am owe our per/*promise*=as I aim owe our per/*promote*=atom owe our per/*prompt*=tip them owe ore per/*promulgate*=ar age loom owe our per/*prone*=an owe rip/*prong*=gone owe rip/*pronounce*=a see in you on our per/*promotion*=know it owe more per/*proof*=for per?/*propaganda*=add an age a pour per/*propagate*=a tag gape owe our per/*propel*=leap owe are per/*proper*=re-pour per/*property*=yet reap owe our per/*prophecy*=why see a hip owe our per/*prophet*=to hip owe are per/*proportion*=know it row pour per/*proposal*=lays owe pour per/*propound*=then you owe pour per/*propulsion*=know is loop owe our per/*prosaic*=see eye as owe our per/*proscribe*=a be eye our see soar per/*prosecute*=at you seize owe our per/*prospect*=to keep owe our per/*prosper*=reap soar per/*prostitute*=at you tits so are per/*prostrate*=at arts owe our per/*protagonist*=it is in owe got owe are per/*protect*=to see at owe our per/*protest*=to set owe our per/*protocol*=low see over time owe our per/*protrude*=a due write owe our per/*proud*=due owe are per/*prove*=eve owe are per/*proverb*=brave owe our per/*provide*=a dive owe our per/*providence*=a see need Ivy owe our per/*province*=a see in I have owe our per/*provision*=know is I've owe our per/*provoke*=a cove owe our per/*prowess*=see double you owe our per/*prowl*=all war per/*proximity*=yet I mix owe our per/*prudence*=a see need you are per/*prune*=an you rip/*pry*=why rip?/*psalm*=am all as per/*pseudonym*=my know due you ease per/*psychiatrist*=it is eye rate a eye high see yes per/*psychic*=see I hip why is per/*psychology*=your goal owe high see yes per/*psychopath*=hit tap owe high see why is per?/*psychotic*=see it owe high see why is per?/*puberty*=yet re-be you pee/*public*=see isle be you per/*publish*=his eye will be you per/*pull*=all up/*pulp*=pee loop/*pulsate*=at as loop/*pulverize*=as I rev loop/*pummel*=lame you per/*punch*=high see in you per/*punctual*=lay you to see in you per/*puncture*=a route see in you per/*pungent*=ten edge in you per/*punish*=his in you per/*punitive*=eve it in you per/*punt*=ten you per/*pupil*=lip you per/*puppets*=step up/*purchase*=as a high see our you per/*pure*=ear you per/*purge*=edge our you per/*purify*=why fear you per/*puritan*=in at eye our you per/*purloin*=in eye lure you per/*purport*=tear owe per you per/*purpose*=as owe per you per/*pursue*=a use are you per?/*push*=his up/*put*=to pee/*putrid*=dire to pee/*puzzle*=all is you per/*quack*=key see a you cue/*quaff*=for you cue/*quagmire*=a rim gay you cue/*quail*=lie a you cue/*quaint*=ten I a you cue/*quake*=ache a you cue/*qualify*=you fill a you cue/*quality*=yet ill a you cue/*qualm*=me lay you cue/*quandary*=your add in a you cue/*quantity*=yet it in a you cue/*quarrel*=layer a you cue/*quarry*=why are a you cue?/*quarter*=rate are a you cue/*quash*=here's a you cue/*quasi*=is a you cue/*quaver*=rev a you cue/*queasy*=why say a you cue/*queen*=in a you cue/*queer*=are a you cue/*quell*=lay you cue/*quench*=high see in a you cue/*querulous*=is you lure a you cue/*quest*=to see you cue/*question*=know it is a you cue/*queue*=a you a cue/*quibble*=all be eye a you cue/*quick*=key see eye you cue/*quiet*=to I you cue/*quilt*=tell eye you cue/*quintessence*=a see in ease to an eye you cue/*quip*=pee I you cue/*quirk*=cry you cue/*quit*=tie you cue/*quite*=at I you cue/*quiver*=rev eye you cue/*quixotic*=sight owe sex eye you cue/*quiz*=is I you cue/*quota*=at owe you cue/*quotation*=know it at owe you cue/*quote*=at owe you cue/*rabble*=all be are/*rabid*=the eye be are/*race*=a car/*racial*=lay eye see our/*racket*=take see our/*racy*=why see are/*radiance*=a see inner eye dear/*radiate*=at aid are/*radical*=lay see id are/*raffle*=the fair/*ragamuffin*=in of you major/*rage*=edge our/*ragged*=the edge are/*raid*=dire/*railing*=gone ill eye our/*rain*=in eye are/*raise*=as eye are/*rally*=while our?/*ram*=mare/*ramble*=all be am are/*ramification*=know it a see if I am are/*rampage*=edge a p.m. our/*rampant*=ten ape mare/*rampart*=trap mare/*rancid*=the I see in are/*rancor*=rowe see inner/*random*=mode near/*range*=edge near/*rank*=can our?/*ransack*=key see as in are/*ransom*=more snare/*rap*=pair/*rapid*=the eye payer/*rapport*=to raw pair/*rapture*=a route pair/*rascal*=lay see a are/*rash*=his are/*rather*=re-hit are/*ratify*=why fit are/*ratio*=owe it our/*ration*=know it our/*rational*=lane owe it are/*raucous*=is you owe see you are/*raunchy*=why high see in you are/*ravage*=edge have our/*rave*=ever/*ravine*=an eye of are/*raw*=war/*ray*=why are!/*raze*=a tsar/*reach*=high see a ear/*react*=to see our/*read*=dayer/*reading*=gone eye dare/*real*=layer/*ready*=why dare!/*reality*=yet isle a our/*realm*=my lair/*reap*=payer/*reason*=knows a ear/*reassure*=our us are!/*rebate*=at a be ear/*rebel*=lay beer/*rebellion*=know I lay beer/*rebound*=then you owe beer?/*rebuff*=for you beer/*rebuke*=ache you be are/*rebut*=to be our/*recall*=lay see are/*recant*=ten a see ear/*recede*=add a seer/*receipt*=to piece our/*recent*=ten a seer/*receptacle*=all see at piece are/*reception*=know it peace our/*recess*=see seer/*recipe*=a peicer/*reciprocal*=lay see owe aur piecer/*recital*=late I see her/*recitation*=know it at eye seer/*recite*=at eye see are/*reckless*=cell key see our/*reckon*=know care/*reclaim*=my all seer/*recline*=an isle see our/*recluse*=as you'll see are/*recognize*=as in go see our/*recoil*=lie owe see our/*recollect*=to cell owe seer/*recommend*=the name owe see our/*recompense*=as in a p.m. owe seer/*reconcile*=all I see in owe seer/*recondite*=at eye then owe seer/*reconnaissance*=a see in as see an owe see

VISION OF A MENTAL PATIENT

are/reconsider=ready sin owe seer/reconstruct=to see you rights know see are/record=dare owe seer/recount=to new owe seer/recoup=per you owe seer/recourse=as our you owe seer/recover=our eve owe see are/recreation=know it are seer/recrimination=know it an eye mere seer/recruit=to eye your seer/rectify=you fit seer/recuperate=at a reap you see are/recur=re-occur/recycle=all see why, care!/red=there/redeem=me dare/redolent=ten all owe there/redress=sure dear!/reduce=a see you there/redundant=ten add knew there/referee=ear of fear/reference=a see near of fear/referendum=mud near refer/refine=an iffer/reflect=to seal life are/reflection=know it to see all of fear/reform=mere offer/refractory=why wrote see are fear/refrain=in eye are fear/refresh=here's a refer/refuge=edge you fear/refund=the new offer/refurbish=his eye be our of are/refuse=as you fear/refute=at you fear/regain=in eye a gear/regale=all age ear/regard=there a gear/regenerate=at our energy our/regime=imager/region=know eye gear/register/rates I gear/regress=surger/regret=tear gear/regular=are all you gear/rehabilitate=at at ill eye be a hear/rehash=his or her?/rehearsal=lay sir a hear/reign=in guy our/reimburse=as rub me our/rein=in I are/reincarnation=know it near a see in eye ear/reinforce=a care of in eye are/reinstate=at ats in I are/reiterate=at a rate I are/reject=to see a jeer/rejig=guide you our/rejoice=a see eye owed you our/rejuvenate=at an eve huge are/relapse=as pale our/relate=at all are/relative=eve it all are/relax=sex a layer/relay=why all are/release=as a leer/relegate=a tag all are/relentless=sell to kneel are/relevant=ten avail our/reliable=all be a I leer/relic=killer/relief=feel our/religious=is you eye? Guy lair?/relinquish=his eye you cue in eye leer/relish=his isle are/reluctance=a see in at cool are/rely=you'll ear/remain=in eye aimer/remark=crammer/remedy=why deem are/remember=re-be memory/remind=then I am are/reminisce=a see sin I mere/remit=timer/remnant=ten on mere/remorse=a roam are/remote=a to me are/removal=leave them are?/rend=dinner/render=read near/rendezvous=is you owe of is add near/rendition=know it eye the near/renegade=adage an are/renege=edge a near/renew=when our/renounce=a see new owe near/renovate=at ave on are/renown=in won are!/renunciation=know it a eye see none our/reorganize=as in age row are/repair=our eye appear/reparation=know it a repair/repast=to say pair?/repay=you payer/repeal=lay a per/repeat=to appear/repel=leper?/repent=ten a peer/repercussion=know is you see repair/repertoire=por eye over time repair/rephrase=as are hipper/repine=an eye peer/replace=a see all per/replete=at all per/replica=a see isle pair/reply=why all peer/report=tear owe peer/repose=as owe per/repository=why are over time is owe per/reprehensible=all be is inner her per/represent=ten ease are per/repress=see our per/reprieve=eve eye per/reprimand=then am eye our peer/reprisal=lays eye our per/reproach=high see a owe are per/reprobate=at a be owe are per/reproduce=a see you door per/reproof=for per/reprove=eve owe per/repudiate=at aid you per/repulse=as loop are/reputable=all be at you per/reputation=know it at you per/request=to see you cue ear/require=are I you qeer?/requisite=at is eye you queer/requital=late eye you cue are/rescind=then I see sir/rescue=a you see sir/research=high see are a easer/resemble=all be mess are?/resent=ten easer/reserve=eve raise are/reservoir=our eye of raise are/reside=add is our/residence=a see need is our/residual=lay you this are/resign=in guys are/resilient=ten a ill is our/resist=it see sir/resolute=at you loser!/resolve=eve loss our/resonant=ten an owes are/resort=tare owes are/resound=then you owe sir/resource=a see are you owe sir?/respect=to see pisser!/respite=a tip sir/respond=then owe per sir/restaurant=ten are you at sir/restful=love to sure/restitution=know it you to it sure/restive=eve it sure/restore=a wrote sure/restrain=in eye art sure/restrict=to see eye to sir/result=tell you sir/resume=am us sir?/resumption=know it p.m. you sir/resurgence=a see negative are you sure?/resurrection=know it see our you sir/resuscitate=at a tie sees us sir/retain=in eye at our/retaliate=at a eye late our/retch=high see tare/reticent=ten a see eye tear/retinue=a uniter/retire=a writer/retort=tear over time are/retract=to see art our/retreat=to our tear/retrench=high see inert ear/retribution=know it you bare tear/retrieve=eve eye writer/retrograde=add our go our tear/retrospect=to see a per soar tear/return=near you tear/revamp=p.m. ave are/reveal=lay eve our/revel=lever/revelation=know it all of our/revelry=why are level/revenge=edge never!!!!!!/revenue=a you never!!!!!!/revere=a revere/reberie=a eye re-be are/reverse=as rever/revert=tear ever/review=we eye veer/revile=all I veer/revise=as I veer/revision=know is severe/revival=lay of I veer/revoke=a cover/revolt=to lover/revolution=know it you lover/revolve=eve lover/revulsion=know is lover/reward=draw our/rhapsodize=easy does pay her?/rhetoric=sight owe to her/rhyme=am why? Her!/rhythm=me hit why, Her!/ribald=the labor/rich=high see I are/rickety=you take care/riddle=all dire/ridicule=all you see eye dire/rife=of I are/riffraff=far fire/rig=gear/right=the guy are?/rigid=dig eye our/rigmarole=a lure aim gear/rigor=rodger/rile=a liar/rind=the near/ring=gone I are/rinse=as in eye are/riot=to eye our/ripe=a pair/rise=a seer/risk=kiss her/rite=attire/ritual=lay you to eye our/rival=lay veer/river=revere/riveting=gone it a veer/roam=may owe our/robot=to be owe our/robust=it is you be or?/rogue=a you gore/role=a lure/romance=a see in aimer/romp=p.m.ower/room=more!/root=tore/rooted=detour/rope=a pour/roster=rate soar/rostrum=more to soar/rot=tore/rotary=your at owe are/rotate=at a tour/rotten=in at tore/rotund=then you tour/rough=hug you owe our/rounded=dead in you owe our/roundabout=to owe bad in you owe our/rouse=as you owe our/route=a tour/routine=a night you owe our/rowdy=wide war/rub=burr/rubbish=his eye be you are/ruckus=suck cure/rude=add you are/rudimentary=your at name eye door/rue=a you our/rueful=love a you are/ruffian-inner eye for/ruffle=all for/rugged=the egg you are/ruin=in eye you are/rule=all you are/ruler=real you are/ruminate=at an eye more/rummage=a game you our/rumor=roam you are/rumpus=is you p.m. you are/run=in you are/runaway=your way in you are/run down=new owed in you are/rupture=a rut pure/rural=lair you are/ruse=as you are/rush=his you are/rustic=see it sir/rustle=all it is you are/rusty=yet sure/rut=to you are/ruthless=cell hit you our/rutted=debt you are/sabotage=edge at obeys/saccharine=on eye are a high see as/sack=case/sacred=there see as!/sacrifice=a see if eye our case/sacriledge=edge deal eye *our see as/sacrosanct=to see in as owe our see as/sad=days/sadden=need as/saddle=all the ass/sadistic=sight seed ass/safe=a phase/sag=gas/saga=a gas/sail=lie as/saint=ten eye as/sake=a case/salacious=is you owe eye see all as/salary=why are all as?/sale=all as/salient=ten a isle as/salty=yet all as/salubrious=is you owe I our be you will as/salutary=your at you all as/salute=at you all as/salvage=edge ave all as/same=amaze/sample=the p.m. ass/sanctify=you fit see in as/sanction=know it see in as/sanctuary=why are a you to see in as/sane=an as/sanguine=an eye you gone as/sanitary=tour at in as/sanity=yet in as/sap=pass/sarcasm=me say see our as/sardonic=see in owed raise/satan=in at as/satanic=sight in to as/satiate=at a eye it as/satire=a write as/satisfaction=know it see of sight as/satisfy=why if sit as/saturate=at our you it as/saucy=why see you as/saunter=rate in you as/savage=a gave as/save=eve as/savior=our owe I of as/savor=rove as/scale=all a see is/scam=makes/scamp=p.m. a seize/scan=inner sees/scandal=laid in a see is/scapegoat=to owe gape a seize/scar=are a sees/scarce=a see races/scared=dare a seize/scathed=the hit a seize/scatter=rate to see is/scenario=owe Iran a see is/scene=an a see is/scenic=see in a sees/schedule=all you the high see is/scheme=a me high see is/schism=miss eye high see is/scholar=our all owe high see is/science= a see inner eye sees/scientific=see if it in a eye sees/scintillating=gone it all it in eye seize/scoff=fucks/scold=deal owe seize/scoop=poo sees/scope=ape owe sees/scorch=high see our owe seize/score=a row sees/scorn=inner owe seize/scoundrel=lay our then you owe seize/scour=our you owe seize/scourge=edge our you owe seize/scout=to you owe see is/scowl=low owe seize/scrabble=all be are sees/scram=mere sees/scramble=all be may our sees?/scrap=pay our sees/scrape=a pair seize/scrappy=you pay our sees/scratch=high see to our sees/scrawl=lower seize/scrawny=why knew our seize/scream=may our seize/screen=near sees/screw=works/scribble=all be eye our sees/scribe=a be eye our sees/scrimp=p.m. eye our sees/script=to peer see is/scrounge=edge in you owe our sees/scrub=be you our sees/scrutinize=as in it you our seize/scuffle=all fucks/sculpture=a route plusses/scum=am you seize/scurry=why our you sees/scuttle=all to you sees/sea=a ease/seal=lay ease/seam=may ease/search=high see are a ease/season=nose a ease/seat=to ease/secede=add a see as/secluded=dead you all see as/seclusion=know is you'll see as/second=then owe see as/sececywhy see our sees?/secret=tare see as/secrete=at our see as/sect=to see as/sectarian=in a eye our at sees/section=know it see ease/sector=wrote see as/secular=our all you see as/secure=ear you see ease/security=yet eye our you see as/sedate=at add ease/sedative=eve it add ease/sediment=ten then eye these/sedition=know it eye these/seductive=eve it see you these/see=ease/seed=these/seek=keys/seem=me as/seep=pees/seesaw=was ease?/seethe=a hit ease/segment=ten them guess/segregate=a tag gear guess/seize=ease eye ease/seizure=are you is eye ease?/seldom=modeless/select=to see all ease/self-centered=there at inner see flesh/self-confident=to need if no see flesh/self-control=lure to no see flesh/self-esteem=meets a flesh/self-conscious=is you owe eye see is no see flesh/self-evident=ten a dive flesh/self-important=ten at row p.m. eye flesh/self-indulgence=a see negative lude in eye flesh/selfish=his if less/self-reliant=ten a ill ear flesh/self-respect=to see appeaser flesh/self-sacrifice=a see if our see as flesh/self-satisfied=the if sight as flesh/sell=less/sell out=to owe less/semblance=a see in all be mess/seminal=lane I me is/send=then as/sendoff=for then as/senile=all in ease/senior=our owe eye in ease/senior citizen=in ease it I see our owe in ease/sensation=know it as in ease/sense=a sin ease/sensible=all be is in ease/sensual=lay us in ease/sentence=a see in at an ease/sentiment=ten them in in ease/sentimental=late name it in ease/sentinel=lane it in ease/seperable=all be our appease/separate=at our appease/septic=sight pees/sequel=lay you cue as/sequence=a see in a you cue ease/serene=an are ease/serenity=yet in our ease/series=see eye raise/serious=is you owe eye raise/sermon=know mere as/service=a see eye veer as/servile=all I have raise/session=no eye sees/set=to ease/settleall to ease/setup=put as/sever=our eves/several=lay our eve as/severe=a reverse/severity=yet I our eve as/sexual=lay you excess/sexual intercourse=as are you owe see rate in eye lay you excess/sexuality=yet ill a you excess/shack=key see are his/shade=add of his/shadow=wood are his/shaft=to far his/shake=ache ahs/shallow=wall are his/sham=may his?/shame=aim are his/shape=a pace/share=oue are his/shell=lay his/shelter=rate lay his/shepherd=dear a hip our his/shield=leal a eye his/shift=to fee his/shine=on eye his/shirk=care eye his/shiver=rev eye his/shock=key see owe his/shoddy=why do his?/shoot=to his/shop=per owe his/shore=our owe his/short=tare owe his/shot= to his/shoulder=read all you owe his/shout=to owe his/shove=eve owe his/shovel=leave owe his/show=double you owe his/showdown=new owew woah his/shower=are a double you owe his/show off=foe woah his/shred=dare his/shriek=key eye our his/shrill=lie our his/shrivel=leave eye are his/shudder=read due his/shuffle=all for you his/shun=knew his/shut down=new owed to his/shuttle=all to his/shut up=put to his!/shy=why he is?/sick=kiss/sicken=in a kiss/side=add is/sidelong=gone all add is/sidestep=pet seed is/sidetrack=key see art add is/sidle=all the is/siesta=at see is/sieve=eve is/sift=to fee is/sight=the guy is/sign=in guy is/signal=lane guys/signifigance=a see inner guy fee in guys/silence=a see in all is/silhouette=at a you owe he lies/silky=why kill is/silt=til is/similar=are all eye miss/simmer=reem is/simple=all p.m. is/simulate=at all you miss/simultaneous=is you owe an at loom is/sin=in is/sincere=are a see in eye see/sinecure=are you see an is?/sinful=love in is/singe=edge in is/single=all gone is/sinister=rates in is/sink=can is/sinner=reign is/sip=piss/sit=it is/site=at is/situation=know it a you it is/sizable=all be as is/size=as is/skeleton=not all a kiss?/skeptic=sight peaks/sketch=high see takes/skill=likes/skim=my kiss/skin=nicks/skip=picks/skirt=tear eye kiss/skulk=clue kiss/sky=why kiss!/slack=key see all is/slake=a call is/slam=malls/slander=read in all is/slant=ten all is/slap=pals/slash=his all is/slaughter=rate hug you all is/slave=evil is/slay=why all is?/sleep=appeals/slender=read in all is/sleuth=hit you all is/slice=a see isle is/slick=kills/slide=ad isles/slimy=why me ills/sling=gone isle is/slip=pills/slipshod=do his pills?/slit=til is/slither=re-hit isle is/silver=our eve isle is/slobber=re-be alls/slog=goals/slogan=inner goals/slop=poles/slot=to lose?/sloth=hit all*

VISION OF A MENTAL PATIENT

is/slouch=high see you all is/slovenly=while in eve you all is/slow=walls/slumber=re-be am you less?/slump=p.m. you alls/slur=rules/slut=to you all is/smack=key see aims/small=all am is?/smart=tear aims/smart aleck=key see lay trams/smash=his aims/smell=all aims/smirk=creams/smitten=net eye miss/smolder=red looms/smother=re-hit ohm's/smudge=edge dumb is/smug=gums/smutty=yet you miss/snack=cans/snag=gains/snap=pans/snare=our reigns/snarl=lure an is/snatch=high see tans/sneak=keens/snide=as in is/sniff=if in is?/snigger=regains/snip=pins/snippet=tape pins/snitch=high see it ins/snivel=leave in is/snob=be owe in is/snooze=a "z" on is/snub=buns/snug=guns/soar=ray owes/sober=re-be owes/sobriety=yet I are, be owes!/sociable=all be a eye see owes/social=lay eye see owes/society=yet I see owes/sodden=need owes/sofa=of owes/soft=to foes/soggy=why goes/soil=lie owes/solace=a see all owes/sole=a loss/solemn=in me all owes/solicitousis you over time I see loss/solid=the eye loss?/solidarity=yet I raid ill owes/solitary=why rat isle owes/solitude=add you to loss/solution=know it you lose/solve=evil owes/somber=re-be am owes/somebody=you do be aim owes/someday=why add aim owes?sometime=emit aim owes/song=gone owes/soon=news/soothe=a hit ooze/soothsayer=ray as hit owes/sophisticated=debt a see it's eye hip owes/soporific=see if eye row pose/sorcerer=rare a see rose/sordid=did rose!/sore=arrows/sorrow=war owes/sorry=why our owes/sort=tear owes/soul=all you owes/sound=the new owes/sour=are you owes?/source=a see our you owes/souvenir=our in eve you owes/sovereign=in guy are eve owes?/space=a sea apes?/spacious=is you owe I see appease/span=naps/spar=raps/spare=are apes?/spark=craps?/sparse=as are apes?spartan=in at raps/spasm=miss apes?/spate=of taps/spearhead=day are here appease/special=lay eye keeps/species=see eye seeps/specific=see if I see apes/specimen=name I keeps/speck=key seeps/spectacle=all see at keeps/spectator=wrote at keeps/specter=rate see apes/speculate=at all you see appease/speech=high see appease/speed=deeps/spell=leaps/spend=then a piece/spendthrift=to fear hit then appease/spew=weeps/spice=a see eye piece/spin=nips/spine=an eye piece?/spiral=lay rips/spirit=tir our eye pers/spit=tips/spite=at eye piss!/split=tie lips/spoil=lie owe piss/spoken=inner cops/spokesperson=knows representatives seek owe peace/spongy=why gone oh piss/sponsor=rose an owe p.s./spooky=your coups/sporadic=see eye dare owe p.s./sports=set row p.s./spot=tops/spout=to you owe pees/spouse=as you owe p.s./sprawl=law a rips/spray=why our piss/spread=dayer rips/spring=gone eye rips/sprinkle=all can eye rips/sprint=ten eye reps/sprout=to owe rips/spruce=a cure p.s./spur=our ups/spurn=inner ups/spurt=true pees/squabble=all be a you cue is/squad=day you cues/squalid=dill a you cues/squalor=our all a you cues/squander=read in a you cues/square=era you cues/squash=his a you cues/squawk=key double you accuse/squeak=key a you cues/squeal=lay you cues/squeamish=his eye may a you cues/squeeze=as a you cues/squirm=mere eye you cues/squirt=tear eye you cues/stab=bats/stable=all be ats/stack=key see ats/staff=fats/stage=edge ats/stagger=rage ats/stagnate=at on gates/staid=die ats/stain=in eye ats/stake=ache ats/stale=all ats/stalk=kill ats/stall=lates/stalwart=to raw lates/stamina=an I am ats/stamp=p.m. ats/stampede=a deep am ats/stance=a see in ats/stand=then ats/standard=draw then ats/standoffish=his eye foe then ats/staple=all pats/star=rats/stare=our ats/stark=care ats/start=tear ats/starve=eve rats!/state=at ats/statement=ten aim at ats/static=see it ats/station=know it ats/stature=a route ats/status=is you to ats/stay=why ats/steadfast=to safe day it is/steady=why day eats/steal=lay eats/stem=mets/stench=high see in at is/step=pets/sterile=all eye rates/stern=near ats/stick=key see it is/stiff=fits/stiffen=inner fits/stifle=all fits/stigma=aim guy it is/still=lights/stimulant=ten all you mights/stimulus=is you loom it is/sting=gone eye it is/stinks=seek in it is/stipulate=at all you pits/stir=rites/stock=key see oughts/stodgy=why god owe it is/stoical=lay see eye oughts/stolid=dial oughts/stomach=high see aim oughts/stony=why nots?/stoned=then owe it is/stoop=puts/stop=pots/store=out oughts/storm=mere owe it is/story=why wrotes/stout=to owe it is/stow=watts/straight=the guy arts/straightforward=draw are of the guy arts/strain=in I arts/strait=to eye arts/strand=the in arts/strange=edge in arts/stranger=rage in arts/strap=parts/stratagem=mega to arts/strategic=see it at arts/stray=why art is/streak=key arts/street=to our it is/strength=hit gain arts/strenuous=is you owe you near it is/stress=sir it is/stretch=high see to arts/strident=to need dire it is/strife=a fear its/strike=a key eye writes/string=gone eye rites/stringent=ten edge in eye writes/strip=peer it is/strive=eve eye writes/stroke=a core it is/stroll=lure it is/strong=gone owe rights/structure=a route see you our it is/strut=to rights/stub=butts/stubborn=near owe be you its/stubby=your buts/stuck=key see you it is/stud=duts (a male ditz)/student=to need you it is/studied=the I duties/studio=owe eye due it is/stuff=for you it is/stuffing=gone if you it is/stuffy=why for you it is/stumble=all be me you its/stump=p.m. you it is/stunt=ten you it is/stupendous=is you owed inner put is/stupid=dip puts/stupor=our owe puts/sturdy=why there you it is/style=all why it is/suave=eve a us/subconscious=is you owe I seize know see be us/subdue=a you due be us/subject=to see edge be us/subjugate=a tag huge be us/sublime=am isle be us/submerge=edge rem be us/submission=know is I am be us/submit=time be us/subordinate=at an id row be us/subscribe=a be eye our see be us/subsequent=ten a you cue as be us/subservient=ten a eye veer as be us/subside=add is be us/subsidence=a see need is be us/substance=a see in at is be us/substitute=at you to it is be us/subterfuge=edge of rate be us/subtle=all to be us/subtract=to see art be us/subversive=eve is rev be us/subvert=tree of be us/succeed=they see us!/successful=love is a sea us/succinct=to see in eye see us/succor=our owe see us/succulent=ten all you see us/succumb=be me you see us/sucker/wreck see us/sudden=need us?/sue=a use/suffer=refuse/suffice=a see if us/suffocate=attack owe fuss/suggest=to siege us/suit=tie us/sulk=clues/sullen=in all us/sully=why lose/summarize=as eye our aim us/summit=time us/sumptuous=is you owe you to p.m. us/sunburned=then rub in ooze/sundry=your then us/sunken=inner key news/sunset=to ease news/super=reap us/superb=bare a puss/superficial=lay eye see if reap us/superhuman=name you hear ape us/superinten-

dent=to need net in eye reap us/superior=row eye reap us/superlative=eve it all reap us/supernatural=lay route and reap us/supersede=add as reap us/supervise=ease I veer reap us/supervision=know is I veer reap us/supple=all pus/supply=why all per us/suppose=as owe per us/supposition=know it is owe per us/supremacy=why came per us/supreme=aimer per us/sure=are us/surface=a see of are us/surfeit=tie of us/surge=edge are us/surmise=as I am are us/surpass=say per us/surprise=as eye rip are us/surrender=read in our us/surrogate=a tag owe are us/surveillance=a see in all eye of are us/survey=why a veer us/susceptible=all be it peace is us/suspect=to keeps us/suspend=then appease us/suspicion=know I see eye per is us/sustain=in eye at is us/swagger=rage a was/swallow=double you all a double you owes/swamp=p.m. a was/swarm=mere a was/sway=why a was/swell=lay was/swerve=eve a was/swift=to fee was/swindle=all then I was/swing=gone eye was/swipe=a pie was/swirl=lure eye was/switch=high see tie was/swivel=leave I double you is/swollen=in all owes/sychophant=ten a hip owe high see wise/symbol=low be my is/symmetrical=lay see I write aim wise/sympathy=why hit a p.m. yes/symptom=more to per my is/synthetic=sight a hit in why is/system=meet size/table=all be at/tableau=you a all be at/taboo=owe be at/tacit=to eye see at/tack=key see at/tackle=all key see at/tact=to see at/tactic=sight see at/tag=gate/tail=lie at/tailor=roll eye at/taint=ten eye at/take=a key at/takeover=rev owe a key see at/tale=all at/talent=ten all at/talk=kill at/tall=all at/tally=why all at/tame=am at/tamper=rep me at/tangle=all gone at/tangy=why gone at/tantalize=as ill at in at/tantrum=more to in at/tape=a pattern/target=to great/tariff=fear at/tarnish=his in are at/task=kiss at/taste=at sat/tatters=sir at at/taunt=ten you at/taut=to at/tavern=near eve at/tawdry=wired watt/tax=x-at/teach=high see a at/team=meet/tear=are a at/tease=ease at/technical=lay see in high see at/technique=a you cue in high see at/tedious=is you owe eye debt/teeming=going to eye meat/teenager=raging neat/teeter=rate at/telepathy=why hit appeal at/telephone=an owe hip all at/telescope=a poke cell at/television=know is eye veil at/tell=let/temerity=yet I ream at/temper=rape met/temperamental=late name a reposition meet/tempest=to see p.m. at/temple=all per met/temporary=your a rope, meet/tempt=to p.m. at/tenable=all be an at/tenacity=why to eye see an at/tenancy=you see an net./tenant=ten an at/tend=then at/tendency=why see need in at/tender=red in at/tense=as net./tentative=eve it at in at/tepid=die pet/term=mere at/terminal=lane I am rate/terminology=your goal on eye mere at/terminus=sun eye mare at/terms=smear at/terrain=in eye a rate/terrestrial=lay it sure rate/terrible=all be irate/terrific=see eye fear at/terrify=you fear at/territory=why wrote eye rate/terror=roar rate/terse=as rate/test=to set/testify=why fit set/testimonial=lay in owe might set/tether=re-hit at/text=takes at/texture=a route sex at/thankful=love can a hit?/theatrical=lay see I write a hit/theft=to fee hit/theme=a me hit/theological=lay see eye goal owe a hit/theoretical=lay see it are owe a hit?/theory=why our owe a hit/therapeutic=sight a you pair a hit/therapy=why pair a hit/therefore=are of are a hit/thesis=this is a hit/thick=key see I hit/thief=fee I hit/thin=in I hit/thing=gone eye hit/think=can I hit?/thirst=to sir hit/thorn=near owe hit/thorny=why in our owe hit/thorough=hug you owe row hit/though=hug you owe hit/thought=thing you owe hit/thrash=here's our hit/thread=day our hit/threat=to our hit/threshold=deal owe his our hit/thrift=to fear hit/thrill=lie our hit/thrive=eve eye our hit/throb=bore hit/throng=gone owe our hit/throttle=all tore hit!/throw=double you owe our hit/thrust=to sure hit/thud=due hit/thump=p.m. you hit/thunder=red in you hit/thunderstruck=key see your writes read in you hit/thus=is you hit/thwart=to raw hit/tick=key see it/ticket=take sit/tidbit=tie be die 2/tidy=wide it/tie=8/tier=re-it/tight=the guy too/till=light/timber=re-be might/time=emit/timetable=all be at emit/timid=die might?/tinge=edge night/tingle=all gone it/tint=tonight/tiny=you knit/tipple=all pit/tipsy=yes pee it/tirade=a dare it/tire=a right?/tired=dare it/tiresome=aim owes a write/titillate=at all eye tit/title=all to it/titter=rate it/toady=why day over time/toast=to say ought/together=re-hit a got/toil=lie ought/toilet=to lie over time/token=inner caught/tolerable=all bear a lot/tolerate=at a real over time/tomb=be moot/tomfoolery=your real of more to/tone=in pver time/tongue=a huge knot/tonic=see in ought/tool=lute/topic=see eye pot/topical=lay see eye pot/topple=all pot/torment=ten them rot/torn=inner over time/tornado=owed and near over time/torpor=rope rot/torrent=to near over time/torrid=dire over time/torture=a route rot/toss=sought/total=late over time/totalitarian=in a eye rate ill at over time/totality=why til at over time/touched=the high see you over time/tough=hug you ought/tour=route/tournament=ten them an are you over time/toward=draw over time/toxic=6 over time/toy=why over time/trace=a see art/track=key see art/tract=to see art/tractable=all be at see art/traction=know it see art/trade=a dart/trader=red art/tradition=know it I dart/traffic=see eye fart?/tragic=siege art/trail=lie art/train=in eye art/traipse=as pi art/trait=aie art/trajectory=why wrote siege art/tramp=p.m. art/trance=a see in art/tranquil=lie you cue in art/tranquilize=ease ill eye you cue in art/transaction=know it see as in art/transcend=then a see is in art/transcribe=a be eye races in art/transfer=are of sin art/transfix=sex if sin art/transform=mere of sin art/transgress=surges in art/transient=ten a is in art/transition=know it is in art/translate=at all is in art/transmit=time sin art/transparent=tena rap sin art/transpire=a rip is in art/transplant=ten all per is in art/transport=to ropes in art/transpose=a soap sin art/trap=part/trash=his art?/trauma=aim you art/travel=leave art/traverse=ease rev art/travesty=yet save art!/treachery=you are a high see art/tread=dare to/treason=knws a art/treasure=a rush art/treat=tear to/treaty=why tare to/tremble=all be mare to/tremendous=is you owed in them a right/tremor=roamer to/trench=high see inert/trend=the near to/trepidation=know it a dip pert/trespass=is appeaser to/trial=lay eye right/tribe=a be eye right/trick=key see eye right/trickle=all key see I write/trifle=the fear to/trigger=rage guy right/trim=mere to/trinity=yet in I write/trinket=taken I write/trio=owe I write/trite=at I write/triumph=hip me you eye right/trivial=leave I right/trophy=your hip ower to/tropical=lay see eye port/trot=tour to/trouble=all be you owe right/trough=hug you owe right/trounce=a see in you owe right/truancy=why see in a you right?/truce=a see you right/truculent=ten all you see you write/trudge=edge due

VISION OF A MENTAL PATIENT

write/true=you are right/truly=why lure to/trumpet=tape me you, write/truncate=at a see in you right/truncheon=know a high see in you right/truss=sure to/trust=it is you right?/truth=hit you right/try=why write!/tubby=your but/tuck=cut/tug=gut/tuition=know it eye you to/tumble=all be moot/tumor=raom you to?/tumult=to loom you to/turnout=to owe near route/tussle=all is you to/tutor=wrote you to/twaddle=all day double you to/tweak=key a wait/twin=in eye double you to/twine=a new to/twinge=edge in eye wait/twinkle=all can eye, double you to/twist=to see wait/tycoon=new see yet/typical=lay see eye per yet/tyranny=your in art yet/ubiquitous=is you over time eye you cue I be you/ugly=why all goo?/ulcer=re-see all you/ulterior=row eye rate all you/ultimate=a tame it all you/umpire=a rip am you/unabashed=dare his say be a knew/unable=all be a new/unabridged=the guide eye our be a knew/unacceptable=all be at peace say knew/unaccustomed=them over time suck on you/unaffected=debt see of a knew/unafraid=die are of anew/unalterable=all be a rate lane you/unanimity=yet I'm in anew/unanimous=is you owe me in anew/unanimously=while is you omen anew/unanswerable=all be a rue sin anew/unappetizing=gone is it a pain knew?/unarmed=them ran, you!/unassailable=all be all eye as anew/unassuming=gain eye must anew/unattached=the high see at anew/unattended=dead netter knew/unauthorized=the ease eye row hit you anew/unavoidable=all bad eye of anew/unaware=a raw anew/unbalanced=the see in all a be knew/unbearable=all bear a be new/unbeatable=all be at a be knew/unbecoming=gone eye more see a be new/unbelievable=al be of a isle a be knew/unbending=gone id inner be knew/unbiased=these a eye be new/unblemished=the his I am all be knew/unborn=near owe be new/unbreakable=all be a care be knew/unbridleddeal there be knew/unbroken=inner key our be knew/unburden=need rub knew/uncanny=your inner see knew/unceasing=gone is a see knew/uncertain=in eye at race knew?/unchangeable=all be age in a high see knew/uncharitable=all be at eye our high see knew/uncharted=debt Ra high see knew/uncivil=live I see new/unclean=ina all see knew/unclear=are a all see knew/uncomfortable=all be at rough more see knew/uncommitted=debt eye more see knew/uncommon=no more see, new!/uncommunicative=eve it a see in you more see knew/uncompromising=gone is eye more per more see knew/unconcern=near a see no see knew/unconditional=lane owe it id know see knew/unconnected=debt see an owe see knew/unconscious=is you owe I seize know see knew/uncontrolled=deal owe write know see knew/unconventional=lane owe it in eve know see knew/uncooperative=eve it a reposition owe see knew/uncoordinated=debt an id rue see in you/uncouth=hit you owe see knew/uncover=rev owe see knew/uncritical=lay see it eye our see knew/undecided=dead eye see add new/undefined=then if add, knew!/undeniable=all be a in add knew/under=read knew/undercover=rev owe see read new/undercurrent=ten our you see read knew/underdog=god read in you!/underestimate=at aim it sir read new/underground=then you owe our greed knew/underline=an isle read knew/undermine=an I am read new/underrate=at a read new/undersized=these is read knew/understand=then at sir read knew/understudy=why due it is read new/undertake=a key at read new/undertone=an over time read new/undervalue=a you lay of red knew/underworld=deal row read knew/underwrite=at eye raw read knew/undesirable=the bar eye seed knew/undeveloped=deep all eved knew/undignified=the if in guide knew/undisciplined=then ill eye lip I seize id knew/undisguised=the see huge acid knew/undisputed=debt you per acid knew/undistinguished=the his eye huge night acid knew/undisturbed=the be rut acid knew/undivided=the divide knew/undo=owed new/undone=a nod knew/undoubted=debt be you owed knew/undress=is are done, you?/undue=a you due new/unduly=while you do knew/undying=gone eye wide knew/unearth=hit ray knew/uneasy=wisen you/uneconomic=see money owe see anew/uneducated=debt a see you then you!/unemotional=lane owe it omen you!/unemployed=day all p. m. anew/unending=gone eye then anew/unendurable=all be a rude inner knew/unenthusiastic=sight say is tou hit inner new/unequal=lay you cue knew/unexceptional=lane owe it peace extra new/unexpected=debt seep extra knew/unfamiliar=rail I am of new/unfashionable=all be an owe eye his of knew/unfasten=net safe knew/unfathomable=all be aim owe hit of knew/unfavorable=all be a rove of new/unfeeling=gone ill of knew/unfinished=the his in if knew/unfit=to eye for new/unflappable=all be a pal of knew/unflattering=gone irate all of knew/unflinching=gone eye high see, nil if new/unfold=deal of new/unforeseen=ease are of new/unforgettable=all be at target ther of knew/unfortunate=at a nut are of knew/unfounded=dead knew of knew/unfriendly=while then eye our of knew/ungainly=while in eye age new/ungodly=wild dog knew/ungracious=is you owe eye cargo knew/ungrateful=love at our gain new/unguarded=dead Ra huge in you/unhappy=why pay here? Knew/unholy=while owe here knew/unidentified=the if it need in you/unification=know it a see if in you/uniform=mere of in you/unify=why if in you/unimaginable=all be an eye game in you/unimportant=ten at row p.m. eye in you/uninspired=dare I per sin in you/unintelligent=ten edge I let in eye you/unintentional=lane owe it net in eye knew/uninterested=debts sure rate in eye in you/uninterrupted=debt pure rate in eye in you/union=know I knew!/unique=a you cue in you/unison=knows in you/unit=tie knew/unite=at in you/unity=why it in you/universal=laser eve in you/unjust=to such knew/unkind=then I key new/unknown=new on, can you?/unlawful=love wall in you/unlike=a kill in you/unlimited=debt eye mile knew/unload=they all knew/unlock=key see all in you/unlucky=why key see? all knew!/unmarried=the I ram new/unmask=kiss aim in you/unmerciful=love I see our aim new/unnatural=lay rut anew/unnecessary=your ass a see anew/unnerve=ever on you/unnoticed=the see it on new/unobtrusive=eve is you write be owe knew/unofficial=lay I see if on you!/unpalatable=all be at a lap knew/unparalleled=deal all a rap knew/unpardonable=all be a nod rap knew/unperturbed=the be rut reposition new/unpopular=our all you pop in new/unprecedented=debt need a see are per new/unpredictable=all be at acid a rip knew/unprepared=the raper pee knew/unpretentious=is you owe it in a tear per knew/unprincipled=deal peace in eye ripe new/unproductive=eve it see you door per knew/unprofessional=lane owe is of owe ripe in you/unprotected=debt see at owe rip in you/unqualified=the if isle a you cue knew/unques-

tionable=all be a know it see you cue new/*unravel*=lever in you/*unreal*=lay are new/*unreasonable*=all be an owes air knew/*unrelated*=debt all are knew/*unreliable*=all be a ill ear new/*unrepentant*=ten at an appear knew/*unreserved*=the veer as are new/*unresolved*=the evil owes are in you/*unrest*=to sir knew/*unrestrained*=then eye art sir knew/*unrestricted*=debt see eye writes are knew/*unrivaled*=deal of eye are in you/*unruly*=you lure knew/*unsafe*=a phase new/*unsatisfactory*=why wrote see of sight as knew/*unsavory*=why rove as knew/*unscathed*=the hitter seize in you/*unscrupulous*=is you all a pure seize in you/*unseat*=to ease in you/*unseemly*=while me is new/*unseen*=in ease knew/*unselfish*=his eye flesh in you/*unsettle*=all tease in you/*unsightly*=while the guy is in you/*unskilled*=deal eye keys be in you/*unsociable*=all be a eye see owes new/*unsolicited*=debt I see ill owes in you/*unsound*=the new owes in you/*unspeakable*=all be a keeps in you/*unstable*=all be at sin you/*unsteady*=why day eats in you/*unsuccessful*=love sees us in you/*unsuitable*=all be at eye us knew/*unsure*=a Russian you/*unsympathetic*=sight a he tap my sin you/*untangle*=all gone at in you/*untenable*=all be on neat in you/*unthinkable*=all be a key in eye hit in you/*untie*= 8 knew/*untimely*=why lame it in you/*untold*=deal over time in you/*untouched*=the high see you over time in you/*untrained*=then eye art knew/*untroubled*=deal be you owe right in you/*untrue*=a you right in you/*untrustworthy*=you hit row it is you write knew/*untruth*=hit you right in you/*unusual*=lay us un-new/*unveil*=lie eve knew/*unwanted*=debt in awe new/*unwarranted*=debt near raw in you/*unwavering*=gone eye rev awe in you/*unwelcome*=aim owe see lay double you knew/*unwholesome*=aim owes all owe how in you/*unwieldy*=why dealer I win you/*unwind*=then I won you!/*unwise*=as I win, you!/*unwitting*-gone it I win, you!/*unworldly*=while deal row knew/*unworthy*=you hit row knew/*unwritten*=in at eye raw new/*unyeiding*-gone id eye a why knew/*upbeat*=to be per you/*upbraid*=dire be per you/*update*=at add per you/*upheaval*=leave a hip you/*uphill*=lie here per you/*uphold*=deal owe here per you/*upkeep*=peak per you/*uplift*=to fill per you/*upmarket*=take ram per you/*uprising*=gone is eye our per you/*uproar*=are a owe are per you/*uproot*=tour per you/*upset*=tease per you/*upstanding*=gone id in ats per you/*upstart*=tear at is per you/*uptight*=the guy to poo/*upturn*=inner rut per you/*urban*=in a be are you/*urbane*=on a be our you/*urchin*=in eye our see are you/*urge*=a grew/*urgency*=you see energy rue/*usable*=all be as you/*usage*=of gas you/*useful*=love as you/*usher*=re-his you/*usual*=lay us you/*usurp*=per us you/*utility*=yet ill eye to/*utmost*=to some to you/*utopia*=ape over time you/*utter*=rate you/*vacancy*=you see in a see ave/*vacate*=at a cave/*vacuous*=is you owe you cave/*vagabond*=then owe be a gave/*vagrant*=ten our gave/*vague*=a you gave/*vain*=in eye of/*valiant*=ten a isle of/*validate*=at add I eye lay of/*valley*=yell ave/*valor*=role of/*valuable*=all be a you leave/*vandal*=laid in ave/*vanguard*=there a you going to ave/*vanish*=his in of/*vanquish*=his eye you cue in of/*vapid*=dip of/*vapor*=row pave/*variable*=all bear of/*variance*=a see inner I rave/*variation*=know it a eye rave/*variety*=yet a eye rave/*varnish*=his in rave/*vary*=why rave/*vast*=to save/*vault*=tell you of/*veer*=our eve/*vegetate*=at a target of/*vehemence*=a see name a he of/*vehicle*=all see have/*veil*=lie of/*vein*=in eye eve/*velocity*=yet I see all leave/*velvety*=why it eve? a leaf!/*vendetta*=a Ted an eve/*veneer*=reign of/*vengeance*=a see in a edge never/*venom*=money of/*venture*=a route in eve/*verbal*=lay be our eve/*verbatim*=might a be rev/*verbose*=as owe be rev/*verdant*=ten add rev/*verdict*=to see id rev/*verge*=edge rev/*verification*=know it a see if I rev/*vernacular*=our all you see an rev/*versatile*=a light a sure eve/*version*=know is our eve!/*vertical*=lay see it rev/*vertigo*=owe guy to our eve/*vessel*=less of/*vest*=to save/*vestibule*=all you be it save/*vestige*=a guy to save/*veteran*=in our at eve/*veto*=over time of/*vexation*=know it tax of/*viable*=all be a I have/*vibrant*=ten our be I of/*vibrate*=at our be of/*vice*=a see eve/*vicinity*=why it in I see Ivy/*vicious*=is you owe eye see eye of/*victim*=might see I have/*victory*=why wrote see I of/*view*=we eye of/*vigilance*=a see in all I give/*vigor*=row give/*vile*=all live/*vilify*=you fill eye of/*villain*=in a eye live/*vindicate*=attack then eye of/*vintage*=edge at in eye of/*violation*=know it all owe I of/*violence*=a see in all owe eye of/*virgin*=in eye greive/*virile*=a liar eye of/*virtual*=lay you tear eye of/*virtue*=a you tear eye of/*virtuoso*=owes owe you tear eye of/*virulent*=to nail you out eye of/*vision*=know is I of/*visit*=it is eye of/*vista*=at see of/*visual*=lay you is eye of/*vital*=late I of/*vitriolic*=kill owe I write eye of/*vivacious*=is you owe eye see of eye of/*vivid*=the eye of I of/*vocabulary*=why are all you be a see of!/*vocal*=lay see of/*vocation*=know it a see of/*vociferous*=is you owe our of I see of/*vogue*=a you go of/*voice*=a see I of/*void*=die of/*volatile*=a light all of/*volition*=know it I love!/*volley*=why all of/*voluble*=all be you love/*volume*=aim you love/*voluntary*=you're at new love/*voluptuous*=is you owe you type you love/*vomit*=time of/*vortex*=sex at rove/*vote*=at of/*vow*=wove/*voyage*=edge a why of/*vulgar*=rage love!/*vulnerable*=all be a reign love!/*wacky*=why key see awe/*wad*=the awe/*waft*=to far double you/*wage*=edge a double you/*waif*=fee awe/*wail*=lie awe/*wait*=tie a double you/*waive*=eve eye awe/*wake*=a key a way/*walk*=claw/*wall*=law/*wallet*=tella double you/*wan*=gnaw/*wand*=then awe/*wangle*=all gone awe/*want*=to gnaw/*war*=raw/*warble*=all be raw/*warden*=kneed raw/*wardrobe*=a bore draw/*wares*=see raw/*warfare*=are of raw/*warily*=you lie raw/*warlike*=a kill raw/*warlock*=key soul raw/*warm*=mirror double you/*warmonger*=rage an ohm raw/*warmth*=hit me raw/*warn*=near awe/*warning*=gone in raw/*warp*=prey double you/*warrant*=ten our awe/*warrior*=row eye raw/*wary*=your awe/*wash*=his awe/*waste*=at saw/*wasteful*=love at saw/*watch*=high see to a double you/*watchdog*=god to high see to awe/*water*=rate awe/*wave*=eve awe/*wax*=sex awe/*way*=why double you/*wayfarer*=rare of your double you/*weakling*=gone eye lick a double you/*wealth*=hit layer a double you/*weather*=re-hit a double you/*weave*=eve a double you/*web*=be double you/*wedding*=gone eye due/*wedge*=edge day double you/*wedlock*=key soul due/*weigh*=hug I a double you/*weird*=dear I a double you/*welcome*=am owe see a double you/*weld*=deal a double you/*welfare*=era flew/*well*=all a double you/*welt*=to lay double you/*wet*=to double you/*whack*=key see a how/*wharf*=for a how/*wheedle*=all day how/*wheel*=lay how/*wheeze*=easy how/*whereabouts*=set you obey ear a how/*wherewithal*=lay hit eye double you ear a how/*whet*=to how/*whiff*=if I how?/*whim*=me how?/*whimper*=reposition me how/*whimsical*=lay see is my how/*whine*=anyhow/*whip*=pie

VISION OF A MENTAL PATIENT

how?/whirl= lure eye how/whisk= kiss eye how?/whisper= reposition see how/whitewash= he saw a tie how/whittle= all to eye how/whole= all owe how/wholesale= alas a low how/wholesome= aim owes all owe how/whore= our owe how?/wicked= the key see eye double you/wide= add eye double you/widen= need eye double you/widespread= day our appease add eye double you/width= hit the eye double you/wield= deal a eye double you/wife= of eye double you/wiggle= the guy double you/wild= deal I double you/willful= love all I double you/willow= we all eye double you/wilt= to lie double you/wink= can I double you?/winner= reign I double you/winnow= one eye double you/win over= rev owe in eye double you/wintry= wire ten eye double you/wipe= a pie double you/wisdom= mode see double you/wise= as eye double you/wisecrack= key see our see as I double you/wish= his eye double you/wispy= wipe his eye double you/wistful= love to see eye double you/wit= to eye double you/witch= high see tie double you/witchcraft= to farce high see tie double you/withdraw= ward hit eye double you/wither= re-hit I double you/withhold= deal owe here hit I double you/withstand= then in ats hit eye double you/witless= cell to eye double you/witness= scene to eye double you/wits= set I double you/witticism= miss I see it tie double you/wizard= there as I double you/wizened= then ease eye double you/wobble= the be owe double you/woe= a owe double you/woeful= love a owe double you/woman= name owe double you/womanizer= raise an aim owe double you/wonder= read in owe double you/wooded= dead owe double you/work= care owe double you/workman= name crow/works= seek row/world= deal row/worldwide= add eye double you the lure owe/worn= inner owe double you/worn out= to owe inner owe/worried= the eye row/worsen= in ease row!/worship= per eye his row/worth= hit row/worthless= cell hit row?/worthy= why hit row/wound= then you owe double you/wrangle= the gain our double you/wrap= par double you/wrath= hit our double you/wreath= her tear double you/wreck= key see our double you/wrench= high see near double you/wrest= to see our double you/wrestle= all to assure double you/wretched= the high see tear double you/wring= going to eye row/wrinkle= all can eye our double you/writ= tire double you/write= attire double you/writer= rate I are double you/writhe= a hit eye our double you/wrong= gonner double you/wrongdoer= re-owed gone owe row/wry= youe double you/x-mas= same sex/x-rated= debt our sex/x-ray why our sex/x-chromosome= aim owes owe them our high see sex/xenon= known a sex/xerography= why hip our go re=sex/Xerox= sex owe rex/Xerxes= sex wrecks/xylem= meal why sex/yank= can a why/yard= there a why?/yawn= knew a why/year= are a why/yearn= nearer why/yell= all a why/yelp= plea why/yen= nay/yet= to why/yield= deal a eye why/yoke= a key owe why/yokel= leak owe why/young= gone you owe why?/youth= hit you owe why?/zany= why in as?/zeal= lay ease/zealot= toll a ease/zenith= hit in as/zero= owe raise/zest= to see is/zip= pizz/zone= an owe is.

One= a know/two= owe double you to/three= ear hit/four= are you of?/five= eve if/six= axis/seven= never is/eight= thing eye/nine= an in/ten= net

Here are a few funny sexual ones: sex= excess/balls= slab/ass= say!/lips= spill/nuts= stun/dick= kid/pussy= your soup.

Well, was that fucked or what? I have been experimenting with this language for some time now and to me this display was a bit boring, but I hope you feel different. The main thing to remember is that all sounds that come from our vocal chords emanate from the vastness of our personal subconscious. For example, between words, we sometimes make sounds like "ahhh" or "umm"; these sounds are the sounds of the personal subconscious processing thoughts to form spoken words. This leads me to believe that due to this process, it must be a fact that all spoken words originate from the personal subconscious and if such concepts can become common knowledge, I believe it possible that due to scientific equivalency and the equilibrium between mind, time, and space, this could be promoted to the collective subconscious, thus leading closer to universal contact.

Okay, before I wrap up this segment, I will present to you more information on how this language came to be. My good friend, Dave St. Armand, not only helped me to get sober, but he was also an imperative asset in the development of my evaluations of the human psyche. Dave was one of the select few who could actually understand my conceptualizations and he understood my vision in its earliest stages.

Dave and I used to go on walks and try to relate to each other our subconscious dementia. The common person would have viewed these conversations as idiotic, because most people are not like Jung and myself, and are unaware of the potentials of accessing the subconscious mind. At this time, you have insufficient information to see the totality of such concepts of the psyche. However, I will tell you a bit about these conversations Dave and I once indulged in. We would practice the common method of word association. I would say one word and Dave would respond with an immediate verbal reaction. For example, I would say "sub-ironic" and Dave would say "conclusion" this process would lead us to a further understanding of each other's inner minds.

Although Dave and my other friends who shared in this vision would disagree with me, I must say that the vision of knowing was more prominent in my mind than it was in theirs. As I have already said, they were interested, but I was obsessed. Once I started to fathom the monolith, my dementia would grow so prominent that I would eventually be diagnosed as a mentally ill person.

You see, at this time of my life, my number one priority was to send this message to people through my music. Due to this obsession, all other aspects of my life began to be depleted; whether it was school, family life, or my social life, it didn't matter. I was beginning to go mad.

I'm not sure if Dave remembers this, but on one of our conversational walks, I did mention my early dementia gave birth to the language of the mad. Dave and I were walking under the Bridge St. Bridge in Lowell and during a word association talk, I interrupted and said to him "Dave, there is something about a person's name, that when the letters are mixed up, it sends some sort of a subconscious message." Dave was unable to respond with a reaction, he simply drew a blank.

This type of subconscious dementia was so much more severe in me than it was in any of my friends, that they would be able to deal with life's responsibilities with much more capability than myself. Due to the confines of common society, the more my dementia would grow, the more hopeless I would become. At this time, the downward spiral of my life began. With sobriety and an achievement of a balance between my vision and life's responsibilities, I am currently on an upward spiral and have become well more than content with my present life situation. I am very happy to say that I have become a responsible functional civilian and that I am now able to contribute positive aspects to society. I'm sure that all of my friends of this era, whom I have not seen in years, would be doing back flips of joy to see how well I am presently able to function in society. I have been clean and sober for almost thirteen years now and I must say that sobriety is a great thing.

This sound balance of mind, which I am presently enjoying, has made me able to understand that my seemingly insane concern with morality was—and is not in any way, shape, or form a waste of time. Soon, you will learn the totality of scientific equivalency and the way that it applies to any aspect of existence. Scientific equivalency has given me this social balance, which further proves that this theory applies to everything—and I mean everything!

Lastly, I must mention a good friend I had met through Dave, who would help me to confront my drinking problem. This would be my good friend Gary C. I am not just mentioning Gary because he helped me save my life through sobriety, but also because, although he is not aware of it, he is the person who came up with the nickname for the language of the mad.

Gary and I were hanging out sober as always in my apartment, and we were either playing PlayStation 3 or a game of chess. I thought I would be cute and mention to him that I wanted to create a language in backwards English.

Gary, being his usual witty self, immediately responded by saying "Oh, yeah, Drow."

I said, "What the hell is Drow?"

Gary said, "It is 'word' backwards."

It was at this point that I decided that the nickname for the language of the mad would be Drow. Drow is pronounced like the word "pro" rather than the word "brow." Always remember that the "W" is silent.

The language of the mad represents everything I got into science for in the first place. It represents the totality of the human psyche applied to the most ultimate equilibrium, which, if properly motivated with an application of our subconscious morality, could lead us even closer to a world utopia.

From this point forward in this book, we will come across some words or phrases, which I will interpret in Drow. For example, "read on" in Drow is = know dare); so, read on! And dare to know!

SENSES

Welcome to the "Senses" segment, where we will embark on the potential benefits of the full manifestation of the human psyche through a further understanding of our senses, in relation to the realm of the human frequency domain of the senses. This conversation, like any other part of this "Monolith Part 2" portion will promote more subconscious activity. When reading this segment, I would like you to keep in mind that senses are responsible for all aspects of dimensions, including all within the realm of scientific equivalency. Please enjoy. Human frequency, as applied to basic senses and what I call the senses of the inner outer beyond, does seem to pose substantial limitations. Once we have properly examined the human senses, we will see that there is what I call a sixth sense or a second sight, if you will. This total relationship of our senses is balanced between the three levels of consciousness. This universal balance seeps and smears into the beyond parallels of existence, just as the fabric of our thoughts and dreams does. Let's indulge further and commence to expand the human mind.

Before I attempt introduce to your mind an exploration of the paranormal phenomenon, which can be accessed through an insight of the mind sensual scope of possibilities, I deem it necessary to discuss the basics with you.

Okay, we are all aware that humans have five basic senses. These five basic senses are, of course, sight, sound, smell, touch, and taste. These five senses, through a properly balanced comprehension, give us our common perceptional relationship with reality as we view it.

I am not even close to being the first person who has been able to peer into the possibilities of the inner and outer beyond, of the realm of common sensual perception. Our senses must exist as such, otherwise all concepts of equality between mind, space, and time would be rendered meaningless. As our senses' actions coincide with the totality of the universe, we are able to journey further into the paranormal. If they were not as such, the attempts to examine concepts such as dimensions of before and beyond our perceptions, secreteborn of our existence within the third dimension, we would hardly suffice. This examination of universal relationships is yet another supporting factor for my theory of scientific equivalency.

Those of open mindedness and extreme intelligence have been able to realize that our senses of the inner outer beyond exist as they presently do, through not only the totality of universal balance, but also through a crucial ingredient for this universal equilibrium. This other balancing factor for this balance is called *magnetoception*. Magnetoception is commonly considered to be the aptitude to somehow ascertain a magnetic field, intended for the purpose of determining direction, location, or altitude. Magnetoception is a prime example of a scientific asset. It has led to the invention of the compass, which gives north, east, west, and south directions. Lines of longitude and latitude also relate to the concept of magnetoception, thus, magnetoception's importance, as to the outer ranges of human frequency, for the creation of a human sense of direction.

It is my personal belief that magnetoception is directly relevant to time. You must understand that time is in and of itself a sense of the beyond, which is produced through a filtering of the mind. This leads me to conclude that due to the fact that our surroundings are comprehended through a fathoming of our sensual aspects, magnetoception, which gives us direction to our senses, is another figure within the vast realm of all of scientific equivalency. If this were not true, existence would be off kilter.

Through my research, I have come to the conclusion that our basic five senses do have some type of vastly deep connection within themselves. For example, we humans have magnetic deposits in the bone marrow of our noses. You see, it may presently be beyond our understanding, but this magnetoception through a type of magnetic fusion with what leads up to our sense of smell, could very well be relative to in-depth concepts of human frequency. Scientists have linked magnetoception in indirect relations to the five basic senses. It is only through a vivid insight into the main five senses that we could peek further into the paranormal and comprehend a sixth sense, which could be used to fathom the inner and outer beyond.

What I just stated must be true, because, through our basic senses, a conceptualization such as magnetoception can be manifested. Through the sense of touch, came the so-called sense of *noiception*. This noiception goes inward toward the infinitesimal. It constitutes the action of *afferancy*, which means moving towards the center. This noiception sense of the beyond, or, should I say, sense of the within, originates from our exterior and it is dependent on our central nervous system. Noiception represents our understanding of physical pain rather than actual physical pain itself. A good example of noiception would be the way we react to physical pain in our dreams. Pain in our dreams is seemingly nonexistent, but this could be due to the inner ranges of human frequency.

There is another sense of the beyond observed in the past by theorists. This would be the sense or concept of equilibrioception. This equilibrioception relates to the inner mind, yet it coincides with exterior actions and existences, which is the case for all within scientific equivalency.

Equilibrioception is the primary factor for the literal physical human ability of balance. It gives us the ability to walk, run, and play sports without falling down. In other words, equilibrioception provides us dexterity. It is dubbed as a physiological sense and because it aids our physical ability to balance ourselves, it also helps with all of our other relations with the universe of the infinite and of the infinitesimal. When applying equilibrioception to our instinctual and involuntary movement capabilities, one can see that it is another example of a human connection to the personal subconscious. Equilibrioception, when examined with haste, will lead one to believe that it is dependent on sight alone, but when realizing all that is related throughout existence, one will see that it has to do with all of our senses as well as all infinite and infinitesimal properties.

The next concept or sense of the beyond I will give mention to is called thermoception. Thermoception originates from the sense of touch, because it represents our reactions and interpretations to hot and cold temperatures. The temperature of the surrounding environment directly affects the temperatures of our bodies. Cold can cause one to shiver and heat can cause one to sweat. Other physical behaviors can occur due to our perceptive reactions to temperature. So, once again, we see that the environmental exterior takes an effect on seemingly unrelated realms of the inner and outer beyond. However, there must be a reactive action and reaction process, which acts between brain receptors and all imposing forces of the seemingly insignificant physical properties of our surrounding environment. Such realizations of the most ultimate of scientific relationships could potentially lead us to further concepts, in pertinence to the three levels of consciousness and their coinciding actions carried out in all functional processes of the scientific realm. There is always a balance, whether from opposite to opposite reactions of creation, or from other opposite type reactions which are within the limits of united forces. Therefore, the universe acts as a universal machine with all actions of creativity originating from within it.

Next is what is called the concept or sense of *proprioception*. Proprioception, like all other universal entities, acts with balance and it is supported by balance. This other sense of the beyond is responsible for the relations between the five basic senses, as to how we view and react to the environment. Proprioception, in my opinion, represents the ultimate scientific example of balance, because it acts with all of our mental and physical reactions as coinciding with the basic original five senses and also with the personal subconscious. However, proprioception within the scientific community is said to be confined to the human anatomy. This is another example of the common failure to recognize, that all of existence although representing many differences, is related within and without itself.

When realizing through scientific equivalency, the totality of the vague senses I just accounted for and all we have discussed thus far, you can now properly see that these previously explained five senses of the beyond lead us to the sixth sense of the beyond, which is none other than time itself. This sense of time makes the tally at six senses of the beyond. There is a term for these six outer senses. The term for these six senses is *exteroceptive* senses. Exteroceptive senses originate from the original five senses and these outer senses can reach further into the vastness of mind, space, and time.

I do not consider it a mere coincidence that when trying to comprehend the possibility of a sixth sense, we have been led to discover that there are exactly six exteroceptive senses of the beyond. Is it possible that we have come across a divine act of nature and balance through this realization of the six senses of the beyond, thus representing the sixth sense, which the human race has been in a quest for since the dawn of evolution? Is there a seventh sense? I believe there is a seventh sense and this seventh sense is the collective subconscious manifestation of "knowing." This complete concept will be revealed in due time, my friends. Keep reading!

Okay, let's get back to the original five senses. I have come to the conclusion that although light is the fastest form of energy in the universe and that it represents the origin of all existence, it must be true that the senses of taste and smell are representative of the origin of our senses. The reason for this conclusion is because taste and smell are the most instinctual human and animal senses. These two senses just might be the founding factor for the formation of the three levels of consciousness.

So, let's go through the original five and attempt to explore their inner and outer boundaries as they act within their basic makeup. First, we will ponder on the sense of touch. The sense of touch is categorized as a mechanical sense. I do agree with the hypothesis that touch does not coincide with our physical movements to some extent. However, one must take into account that there is an ultimate balance to all of existence. Therefore, this particular sense is not totally mechanical, but it does originate from our mechanics and it still manages to effect and relate to the other four original senses, as well as the exteroceptive senses of the beyond.

You see, we humans start off as a zygote and I believe the first sense we can fully comprehend is the sense of touch. However, I do stand by my previous statement that the senses of taste and smell are likely the originals, but they are not fully manifested until they coincide with the sense of touch. This means that as this original process is carried out within its deep vagueness of understanding, the personal subconscious is also taking its original form.

The sense of touch is manifested through physical pressure, foremost in the skin (at least consciously). It is also true that all other senses are reactive to physical pressure in one way or another. Both voluntary and instinctual bioelectric impulses are dependent on the spinal cord, which acts as a conductor for all of our mechanical functions and the balance between such boundaries within the human anatomy contributes to all aspects of a further understanding through scientific equivalency.

VISION OF A MENTAL PATIENT

Continuing on, there are obviously many things a human being can feel, all the way from a minor tingling on the skin, to extreme excruciating pain. Another reason that I theorize that the sense of touch (as well as other senses) is produced through a subconscious point of origin is due to the fact that our sense of touch causes our natural human desire for sexual pleasure, thus the creation and continuance of life. This is exactly why pain and evil must exist if morality is to ever achieve its potential of mass approval and the ever so important promotion of love and human understanding. If we properly access the full concept of the inner and outer beyond, we could promote a true genuine prosperity to a full extent.

The next primary sense we will touch on will be the sense of smell. Smell, of course, is related to taste and it does pose some intriguing similarities. The sense of smell falls into the chemical category. You must understand that we have more receptors for our sense of smell than we have for sense of taste. Furthermore, there are huge differences between the molecular makeups of receptors for smell and taste, and the same goes for their functional actions. These differences between the similar senses of taste and smell represent yet another boundary of opposite reactions for the carrying out of the actions for the balance of scientific equivalency.

The molecular makeup helping to create our small sensual receptors will tend to vary in their levels of potency. Through what is termed as an olfactory receptor neuron, our sense of smell is produced. We humans have tens of millions of these neurons and they obviously exist in our nasal cavities. There is a similar reaction in our nasal cavities consisting of spinal to brain conducted bioelectric reactions. Through the previously mentioned olfactory nerve, one among twelve nerves that communicate through our cranium into our brains, this olfactory acts as a conductor by executing the methods of a long nerve fiber, carrying our bioelectric impulsive reactions to our exterior world, to the olfactory bulb which then acts as a simplistic smelling brain, sort of speak. This makes perfect sense, because the olfactory bulb is a physical entity of what is called the vertebrate forebrain. This vertebrate forebrain is located in front of the brain. It chemically manufactures our sense of smell, thus causing our exterior and interior relative actions to coincide with certain properties. The end result is a fully conscious manifested smell of exterior chemical entities.

Now we will move on to the sense of taste. Taste, like the sense of smell, also falls into the chemical sensual category. Taste is also very instinctual and, depending on a person's brain chemistry (as in other senses), our personal preferences will differ from person to person. Our tongue is the primary source for this sense. You see, we have what are called taste buds on our tongues. Through what are called taste receptors, which help to communicate the actions of this sense to our brain, and like all other factors of the human anatomy and the whole universe for that matter, these exterior to interior actions do apply and adhere to the universal equilibrium.

Another vital ingredient to our sense of taste is called a chemosensor, which, in basic terms, transforms a chemical signal of taste into the realm of the electrochemical. The electrochemical process causes a communication through our bioelectric impulses, which somehow relates the taste of a given chemical compound (food) to our brain. The sense of taste produces our desire to hunt for food and, of course, to seek nourishment, which is essential for our survival. It represents a necessary factor for human survival in a similar way to our sense of touch and it aids the need for human reproduction.

Now, we will move on to the sense of sound or hearing. You see, sound and sight are not always characterized into a chemical or mechanical gender. These two senses of sound and sight (we will discuss the totality of sound first) are, sort of speak, the beyond senses of the previous three, of which I just elaborated on. These senses, like other senses, will aid a person in their voluntary and instinctual reactions to the exterior environment, and they will help to feed the first three senses of which I just accounted for. I do believe that senses must have been manifested in some kind of sequence, thus leading to our need of nourishment and human reproduction.

You see, sound is directly related to touch, because it is manifested through physical vibrations. These vibrations can occur from many means of origin, but especially through the air of our environment. I consider sound to be an advanced form of touch, which gives credence to my belief in some sort of sequence of the creations of these senses.

I am sure you are aware of what an eardrum is; the eardrum is made of tiny fibers and it is simple in appearance, yet complex in function and manifestation. Due to the fact that sound travels through vibrations in the air, a pressure, which is the foundation of our sense of touch, is produced through particles in our atmospheric environment. These atmospheric particles vibrate, thus, causing our eardrum fibers to move and through some kind of extremely complicated bioelectric and biochemical anatomy communication, a conception of a fully formed sound is communicated and fathomed by the human mind.

These particle vibrations of sound are measured in what are called "hertz" and I don't mean the car rental company—just kidding.Hertz measurements are relevant to the perceptions of human frequency. You must understand that hertz is a measured sound frequency that coincides with the human time concept. A single unit of hertz measurement represents one cycle of function for a sound vibration. The range within the realm of common human frequency is from 20 to 22,000 hertz. There are methods which can aid us in the comprehension of waves of frequency, both above and beyond normal perceptive human frequencies of sound, such as the sound which emanates from a dog whistle (Think back to the musical staff analogy I presented in this monolith part two segment). Remember, although scientists have other means for the detection of intricate and beyond particle vibrations of sound, it is true that the senses of a given species may differ enough so that they can comprehend certain things beyond the realm of human capability.

In order to support my hypothesis of a sequence of the manifestations of the senses, I must state the following; sound and sight can be measured in speed. The speed of sound is 770 miles per hour while the speed of light is 186,000 miles per second. Sound, despite the fact that its conception to our senses is very complicated, still requires less complexity than sight perception does. This is because sight is directly produced through the existence of light and if light is so much faster than sound, it makes sense that sight perception poses a composition of a higher complexity in both its origin and its development.

You see, smell, taste, and touch are different. Smell and taste are of chemical composition; thus, they are slower in nature than both sound and sight. Touch, on the other hand, is much faster than smell and taste. And remember, touch is a primitive form of sound and it is also much less detailed than sound is. I feel that through some process of an inner intricate subdivision of existence, that although sense of touch may be what a fetus or zygote firsts starts to form in full development, it is still true that smell and taste do start first with a scientific factor of time alteration. Once the zygote begins the forming of smell and touch with a coinciding action within the early primitive development of the personal subconscious, the plausibility of human nature acting in unison with scientific equivalency poses a supporting factor for the oneness of universal function. Despite my belief that taste and smell start to form first, I do believe that touch, although starting after smell and taste, will be comprehended first, due to the early formation of the human subconscious. This is a confusing hypothesis and in order for you to fathom it with more simplicity, one could apply it to my enhancements of the big bang theory. This complete theory is due to my belief that all scientific actions are universal throughout the infinite and the infinitesimal. Once again, scientific equivalency wins!

You could pose a credible argument against this sequence I just presented. Why? Because in order for these senses to exist and also for them to be applied to the three levels of consciousness, the carrying out of bioelectric impulses would be a necessity. If you put two and two together, you will realize that a bioelectric impulse requires electricity and thus the essential ingredient of light. Our common sense perception of both basic and complex properties will lead us to a hypothesis, which states that due to electricity's role for energy flux and the need for human energy within our chemical makeup, it does support my theory of sight coming last or at least being completed last, thus, my hypothesis is not defeated. Light came before sight, as far as universal existence is concerned, but as far as the forming of our senses is concerned, the other entities had to form first in order for the equilibrium to be correct in nature.

Another interesting question would be "If a fetus or zygote has senses, would it be required, that its bioelectric impulses were fully matured?" There are obvious methods to detect and examine the developmental growth of the senses in a fetus or zygote, and if such an entity can properly comprehend sensual activity in its early stages, the examination of this undeveloped bioelectrical and biochemical system could aid the scientific community and provide the ability to peer into the paranormal of the electric, the chemical, and the development of the human mind. However, we need to learn that chemistry in being a prime ingredient to the human equilibrium, does represent all forms of existence including electricity. Therefore, chemistry can create light energy, which even further proves that my hypothesis of a sequence of the creation of senses is correct.

Okay, let us move on to the sense of sight or, to be more profound, the sense of "vision." In the very basis of sight perception, one must take into account, the communication between the exterior environment and our eyes to our brain. In this case, the environment represents the theoretical centrifuge for the opposite to opposite reaction of creation between the optic nerve of the eyes and the human brain. I also think that there is a reason that the eyes are so close in proximity to the brain. Sight is a result of light and light is fast. Nevertheless, the optic nerve is still required to be so closely attached to the brain.

You see, our eyes comprehend electromagnetic waves, and we can see them as long as they are within the range of human frequency. Through my studies, I have learned that I was correct in my belief that sight perception and its properties of function are balanced with the complexities of light itself. Despite any of my theories of sensual sequences, I must state that sight is the most phenomenal, interesting, and thoroughly complicated sense of them all. It is the inner and outer beyond of light and sight perception, which could aid us in our journey into the paranormal.

Scientists have had quarrels over their interpretations of light as relative to sight perception, whether it represents one, two, or three senses. I believe it could represent even more than three. So, let us briefly "touch" on the present theories within the realm of sight.

The first factor is an obvious one, which would be that sight is simply a basic state, thus representative of a single sensory perception. As for the hypothesis of sight consisting of two senses, it is based on the studies of our inner human sight receptors and that they require two sets of sight receptors which are responsible for our perceptions of colors. These receptors somehow react in a way that it is dependent on a coinciding fusion infusion for the manifestation of a color as related to photons of light, including their abundance of fluctuation and its reaction to light intensity.

The argument for the existence of three senses of light originates from the two receptors and their reactions to the exterior environment. This third hypothesis of sight perception is directly related to what is called stereopsis, which is basically depth perception and human interpretation of distances. Those who are opposed to the hypothesis of stereopsis claim that it is simply a function of the human mind, which interprets a thought process for the intention of obtaining information through a thinking process. This is the basis of three dimensional type sight perception and one could conclude that thinking in itself due to its need of originating senses, could be termed as a sense in and of itself, thus we have a fourth sensual aspect of sight. However, thinking in itself is an extra outreaching part of all of the other senses as well. If one considers thinking to be another sensual entity, it must derive from all other properties within the infinite, the infinitesimal, and the finite. To put it as simply as possible, the process of stereopsis is how the human mind perceives sight and thus light perception in its post stages of developmental existence. However, light is "somewhat" constant. As far as our frequency of time perception is concerned, light is a constant. I will explain this further when we discuss the properties of light. So, we have just fathomed that one single sense (the sense of sight) can reach into the beyond and represent three or even four excreting senses from within all by itself. This is the brand of open-minded thinking which can give substantial benefits to the entire scientific community.

Stereopsis, when you are dealing with it in the present tense, has more to do with shapes and depth rather than optical color perception. When advanced into a thought process, one could easily relate the concept of topology to stereopsis.

Since we are discussing vision, I must now present some more lyrics to you which promoted the totality of my visionary process. This will be another Deallegiance song, called "Soulcage." This song sends a subconscious message which can aid you achieve a higher level of human understanding. I hereby present track three to *Freedom's Call* the first Deallegiance demo tape and track four to the second Deallegiance demo tape, *Symbol of Transformation*. Please, enjoy "Soulcage."

> *Enter my mind return be free, see a land of tranquil divinity*
> *beginning in time a world to see, a race in quest for prosperity*
> *I will journey back to internal wealth, a wealth of one man's legacy*
> *the path which you take determines your fate, a fate within an eternity*
> *in a land bestowed in sacrifice, blatant sanity shames advice*
> *sacramented blood within this vice, sword cuts not once but twice*
> *conspired to be lonely I am living, desires below me for the giving*
> *time to show me all beginnings, plant this then go free you are drifting*
> *soon we'll see it clear for ourselves, we're our own worst enemy*
> *the conflict within a collision of sin, awakens embodied destiny*
> *thoughts of this kind are said to be blind, eternity's faith is ecstasy*
> *the fear which is built forsaken in guilt, to the death of once strong trinity*
> *envision this growth drifting on and on,*
> *pain such invoked, please make this gone?*
> *keeper of trust waiting so long, victims of lust form of life so wrong*
> *broken hearts defended their hell, prayed for an end so strong so well*
> *as the end of day the sun has fell, begin a new way speak word and tell*
> *speed to the converted plane, where the scapegoat's blood will rain*
> *wretched people extricate pain, ridicule destroys me again*
> *Time to dwell in Satan's domain, for this is the cage in which he reigns*
> *see the bastards in flocks to obtain, possess the tools that drive you insane*
> *sail to the new world discharged, all plans will unfurl quite large*
> *this is my way my way to die, from this side to that side I fly*
> *out of ourselves we may fight, granting us all of our rights*
> *escaping our source through the night, holding a freedom of sight*
> *life shall go on within these skies, in it all rising the soul death flies*
> *and for the beast rising like he dies, life is all to see through lies*
> *marching on the deaths of our lives, speak out loud to protect ones pride*
> *leader of life was my guide, angel is awakening inside*

The human anatomy and its sensory functions relative to thought process is directly related to our surroundings, which is a phenomena within itself. Through further advancements in the scientific community, the unknown wonders of not just humans, but of all world species, could lead us to a colossal balance which can only be achieved through some kind of prolific origin. Everything about us is amazing. However, it has always been our senses and our frequency of senses, which has continued to feed my curiosity throughout my lifetime.

There are even parts of the human anatomy which not only feed our senses, but also protect them. Our eyebrows and eyelashes are in perfect position to protect our eyes. Even the shapes of our outer ears perform some sort of aerodynamic filtering for our sense of sound. Our sense of smell is protected from those seemingly annoying nose hairs which can make us appear unattractive. You see, the hairs in your nose filters dusts in the oxygen you breathe in and through a miracle of science, these hairs contain the most perfect texture of moisture, in order for them to catch these dust particles and transform them into a mucus membrane. The mucus membrane is what we would call snots or boogers. It is fascinating how nature can function with such a graceful relationship to all the physical properties which exist throughout the universal environment. Once again, scientific equivalency wins!

There are certain species, which are capable of what is called electroreception. This electroreception process is an astounding example of the balanced equilibrium of natural science. This process defies human capability and it is most prominent in aquatic organisms. The electroreceptive process gives these species an uncanny ability to perceive electric impulse in a manner not only beyond human frequency, but also defeats any of the simplistic views emanating from human senses. The reason this process is most common among water creatures is due to the water ability to act as a conductor, compared to air which is less capable of such an electric impulse and conduction of energy. This is why the inside of the human anatomy is more capable of bioelectric impulse. It is because we are composed of water and organic chemicals.

This process aids creatures capable of this action to search for nourishment. The electroreceptive process has also been said to aid creatures as such in some kind of communication. I believe this process has more to do with these species' subconscious instinctual thoughts than we may presently be led to believe. It is amazing what nature can produce through the natural course of time, isn't it?

Okay, let's head in a new direction and begin to discuss an important attribute of our senses. This will be a discussion of colors and the way in which we perceive them. I will also explain to you other methods of thinking relative to our concepts of colors and the way in which they act with our senses.

Color within human frequency is simply dependent on the way we process and decipher light, which is through the environment to an inner mind, to nerve, to optical connection as it coincides with the frequencies of what is called light intensity, as well as other imperative properties of light, which thrive in the macroscopic realm of human optical perception. That may not sound very simple, but believe me you, once we have discussed the concept of colors and the way in which the scientific community views them with an application of my theories, you will likely fathom the complexities involved in the existence of colors.

One may be apt to believe, that there are eight common or primary colors. However, in a literal and scientific sense the main three are red, green, and blue. It is done through a fusion infusion process of connection, which is also relevant to the reflection process by which other colors are created. However, a spectrum of colors such as a rainbow or transference of light through what is called a prism, the next most common colors enter the realm of human frequency. The astonishing fact is that although these secondary colors may not be consistent as a true source, when they are applied and forced to act with light frequency, they do pose their own unique identity, which could be considered original.

My elaborations on colors may be quite extensive so please bear with me, as we will once again indulge into the paranormal. We will begin with the basics. First of all, the main primary colors, according to some, do not represent a fundamental basis of the makeup of light properties. Scientists who share such a hypothesis base their theories of light on the coinciding and equal way in which the basics of light forms through its scientific fundamentals. I believe it to be quite possible that because of the present and limited understandings of the vast relationships which exist throughout the totality of existence as well as a potential for the manifestation of what is called *connection*, which can aid the human mind to properly perceive matter and the equivalency within it, that when viewing the properties of light with this subconscious approach, we could achieve what is called a *sub-ironic conclusion*. This conclusion could lead to a *galactic mind vortex chain reaction of utopian proportions*.

If we could fathom all through my theory of scientific equivalency, we could appropriately appeal to the collective subconscious and see the beauty within all of natural science.

When properly compensating for the basic colors and how they form into the gamut of colors that exists, we can then use them in our subconscious and further contribute to the equilibrium of creation throughout the vastness of mind, space, and time. I apologize for this tangent, but I must constantly remind you that morality should and must be the foremost concern, as to the use of creation and to further breakthroughs within the scientific community.

You see, light is a continuum that can be enhanced within what is called a spectrum. A spectrum consists of wavelengths of light that can be perceived through the human eye. We will also touch on the possibility of harnessing the optics of other species as well as to their boundaries and their frequencies of sight perception, but we must remain on the same path for the time being.

Through biological studies of the human eyes and their methods of function, scientists have determined that humans have three separate and unique functions for the sensual manifestation of colors which are transmitted through receptors within our eyes. These three receptors are called cone cells. These cone cells are located in the retina of the human eye. Because the retina of the human eye functions most adequately in extreme brightness, these cone cells were dubbed with a more technically scientific name: photoreceptor cells. The retina of the human eye is composed of extremely delicate and sensitive tissue which lines the inner surface of our eyes. And, of course, the human brain connects bioelectrically to and fro, ultimately reacting with what is called the optic nerve fiber; thus, our comprehension of an environmentally produced color within either a shape of extreme topologic or basic geometric type manifestation. Shape itself has more to do with depth perception and other functions of visual implications of vitality.

To simplify matters, I must state that with different branches of colors and how they form within and without objects of matter, there is a fluctuation dependent on these branches for the exact measures of primary colors. Examples of this would be things such as pigment, paint, and light once it is processed into color. Light is considered the most fundamental source for color derivation and that is a truly correct hypothesis, because color on or in an object is simply absorbed and processed light. The fact that light can be absorbed into tightly packed matter and other types of physical existences leads to the conclusion of a further fathoming of the fusion infusion process. When fusion infusion is correctly applied to the three levels of consciousness, the collective subconscious could be centered, thus the creation of a gateway into the particles of light and the other formations of stardusts. This minutely infinitesimal domain is yet another ingredient and it is not just a further level of human understanding, but it is also a testament to the achievement of universal contact. At this point, we will commence discussion on some of the different concepts and methods presently theorized within the scientific community. What we need to do, with conceptualizations as such, is to stray from the confined separations and discover through the accessing of scientific equivalency, the oneness of science itself.

You see, the we perceive color even in a physical sense such as the observation of the simple tomato, can lead to more benefits and scientific understanding than the common person is led to believe. You must understand that an object like a tomato is red due to the manner it absorbs frequencies of light. Therefore, light is relevant in a physical way and in the science of physics, it is a constant. The function of light absorption to me reveals a possibility of a sequence of senses, of which I previously elaborated. You see, a tomato starts off green and eventually turns to red. So, why? I believe it could be due to the absorption of light on to more solid and tightly packed objects, which go through a sequence of color creation, similar to light being emitted through a prism, thus creating a spectrum. If processed correctly, one will be able to see, that this represents yet another opposite to opposite reaction of creation, which connects by a central boundary or a centrifuge, if you will. This takes place within the tightly packed physical properties and the flow of light particles. This process could also be applied to a mirror reflection and its need for a centrifuge to create an opposite-same-yet-different-yet-same image.

It just might be possible that color through a spectrum secretes in a reverse order from color manifestations, which originate in the Earth's soil. Obviously, if color can be produced through transference of light, it must contain a charge. Could this charge represent the centerline of a water reflection or the center of a mirror reflection? Could this be relevant to the fusing of water by the application of hydrogen and oxygen and the spark to make it react? Could the process of the human psyche also be a significant factor?

Okay, the charge involved in sensual color perception is said to originate from what are called quarks and gluons. Quarks and gluons are way smaller than atoms and they obviously exist in the vast infinitesimal. These quarks and gluons go through the fusion infusion process, an ultimate example of coinciding actions within the properties of light particles and light produced colors.

While studying quarks as related to string theory, I was quite fascinated; when discovering the laws of colors and how they act with quarks, I was further intrigued. A quark is so tiny it is only able to consist of the three prime colors. Amazingly, like everything else in existence, there is an opposite. In the case of the quark, you have the anti-quark. An anti-quark however, is only capable of a single color. However, it is true that these anti-quarks are capable of three colors, but you must remember that they are only capable of one color at a time.

Furthermore, it astounds me that there are even what are called anti-colors, which basically are common perceived colors, but they are opposites of particular created colors. So, quarks and anti-quarks within their methods of scientific relationship are yet another example of scientific relationships, we have learned that much so far. As for gluons, they are capable of two colors and they have opposites as well.

In the quantum scientific realm, there is what is called a coupling constant, which is relative to an electric charge and has either a positive or a negative charge. A coupling constant or a coupled state is a measurement of interaction of frequency, which is responsible for any action of energy, positive to negative, negative to positive, or what have you. This will, of course, lead to another action of fusion infusion, which is the process by which everything is created. You may recall in the movie "Real Genius" when Val Kilmer's character figured out how to create a deadly laser through a process of two or more coupled states or coupling constants. In theory, however, most sensual comprehension will act with relative properties, which are not always completely opposite, but are identical, this is on the same grounds as intricate infinitesimal topological connection.

There are other categories of research in the science of colors that may appear basic in definition (definition in Drow is=know it in I fed), but still do reach into the paranormal of the color concept similar to the expanding of the human mind. For example, there is the color index, which relates mathematics and astronomy to the study of colors. Then there is what is called colorimetry, which is a more mathematically relevant concept, which relates to measuring through a process of color reception. Temperature also can have a profound effect on color. Take the examining of fire, for instance: the blue part of a fire is the hottest, and from the blue in fire, all other colors will decrease in heat intensity. When we apply molecule movements to heat and relate the aspects we just discussed, you will be able to see that fire and other properties of color could be proven to represent some kind of cosmic sequence.

Furthermore, others, like myself, have come to the realization of a connection between the senses. What I mean is that some scientists have somehow noticed a relationship between sound and color. This sound to color conceptualization, consists of a relationship between the studies of sound to that of colors of the spectrum and its properties, most prominent being what is called spectral density.

Then, of course, there is the study of biological pigments. A good example of a pigment would be what is called melanin, which is responsible for the color of human skin. Then, of course, there is chlorophyll, responsible for the green color in plant life. It must be understood that a light connection through an opposite to opposite reaction of creation does, in fact, cause miracles of nature. Yes, it is through the absorption of light and its fusion infusion actions within the science of nature, which allows such wonderful creations to exist.

It is the psychophysical properties of light and color, which is most primitive in the scientific community today. Psychophysics is defined within the scientific community, but the way I view this hypothesis is more varied. To me, psychophysics represents a mind subdivision which acts and reacts in opposite types of human thinking, which coincide and fuse with the infinitesimal topologic. The concept of the mind shadow and the centering shadow of the human brain is the best example of this brand of thinking. Remember, scientific equivalency tells us that all is one and one is all, so no matter how much the human mind divides or subdivides, it always represents the basis of scientific equivalency.

Through the study of the physical aspects of colors, there is a slew of both physics and math equations (equation in Drow is=know it a you cue are), which those who are fluent in academics are able to measure color frequency. The measure for a single unit of color property, which is produced through light, is called the nanometer. The nanometer is equal to a billionth of a meter; however, it is equal in a geometric sense rather than in a more basic sense. You see, the science of applying color to the multiple branches of both physics and mathematics further proves that our senses, when processed with a centering of the human mind, has the potential to let us peer into the presently unknown properties of the human mind. The nanometer is pertinent to both the wavelength and the frequency of a color, which is processed through light. The color red goes high in this measurement method when applied to the nanometer. On the other hand, ultra-violet, which is beyond human frequency sight perception, has a low measurement of nanometers.

Because a vacuum in space can alter a ray or wavelength of light, it is essential that when light is altered by a space vacuum, the process of nanometer measurement will deter from itself and lead to what is called refraction. Refraction has to do with the change in direction of a light wave and it will lead to an increase in velocity relative to the outer space vicinity of occurrence.

So, what about those beautiful rainbows we see from time to time? A rainbow, like all other color phenomena, has to do with brain chemistry, the environment, and the way it is processed into the human optics. The conditions for a rainbow are also dependent on weather conditions of course and a rainbow in reality is a naturally produced spectrum.

So, exactly how does a rainbow take its form? You see, a light wave will become altered due to natural changes in light frequency. This will lead to another fusion infusion process, by which this change in frequency will adhere with rainfall or a light mist and dew. This is a good example of light refraction. Once this light refraction coincides with each small quantity of moisture, such as a single raindrop, this refraction will then proceed to enter into most of these tiny liquid entities. However, this is most prominent in the surface of a raindrop. Once the refraction takes place, an action similar to that of a mirror or water reflection takes place with a hint of a natural touch, if you will? The refraction process will deflect off the back of the raindrop it had entered and will then refract in reverse, thus exiting this water droplet.

This rainbow formation process is very dependent on the angles by which light from our sun reacts with these water droplets. And, of course, light wavelength is also an imperative factor if this beauty of nature is to be properly manifested. Due to complex circumstances of reflective forces, the sequence of colors in a rainbow can be altered. A rainbow is also a prime example of the bending of light. In this case, a light spectrum is bent and this is due to space curvature as well as the refractive behavior between light and water. This means that Einstein's ambitions for the bending of light could be accessed by creating a rainbow and then studying all of its properties.

Another phenomena pertaining to a rainbow is that a rainbow does not technically exist in one particular location. You see, it all depends on direction and relative location of the viewer, and of the connecting activities of our sun. This is all due to refraction and reflection, as it is processed by all of the chemical actions and reactions of the human optical capability, as well as the spectrum itself connecting with the human senses.

There is also what is called the supernumary rainbow, which is subject to an even more intricate process of reflective and refractive forces. A supernumary rainbow when viewed can consist of multiple rainbows, but supernumary rainbows are very rare.

Since we are on the topic of rainbows, I would now like to shock my friends, and admit to you all one of my favorite songs, especially as a child. So, I now present Kermit the Frog's "Rainbow Connection."

Why are there so many songs about rainbows? And what's on the other side? Rainbows have visions and only illusions, rainbows have nothing to hide So we've been told and some choose to believe it, I know they're wrong wait and see, Someday we'll find it the rainbow connection, the lovers the dreamers and me Who says that every wish would be heard and answered, when wished on a morning star? Somebody thought and someone believed it, look what it's done so far, what's so amazing that keeps us stargazing? And what do you think we might see? Someday we'll find it the rainbow connection, the lovers the dreamers and me, Have you been half asleep, and have you heard voices? I've heard them calling my name, is this sweet sound that calls the young sailors? The voice might be one and the same, someday we'll find it, the rainbow connection, the lovers the dreamers and me, la la la la la la la la la la la la la la la!

In order to further understand the beauty of a rainbow and its ability to exist, I feel that we should now discuss the creation of a spectrum through the use of a prism.

First of all, in the science of human optics, a prism is a translucent optical subdivision with a flat surface structure capable of a refractive process, forming a color spectrum by an inner process of intricacy. The prism is very dependent on its symmetry in order for it to produce the correct light angle reflections for this process. The most common type of prism is triangular in its base and rectangular on its sides. If you cannot comprehend this geometric defining of a prism, you need not worry because you will still be able to sufficiently fathom its function in connection with present theories in the scientific community and my personal applications to this prism function, which I shall soon explain to you.

In order to aid you in the comprehension of the geometrics of a prism, I must ask you a question which I usually ask all of my new acquaintances "Do you like Pink Floyd?" If so, you must be familiar with the "Dark Side of the Moon" album. The cover of this particular "Pink Floyd" album has a triangular based and rectangular sided prism producing a spectrum on it. This prism action is produced through a single light beam, which is enforced into this prism. Not only that, the music on this album is way more outstanding than its cover.

You see, there are other types of prisms which stray from the common triangular type prism. However, an elaboration of the common triangular prism will be enough to get my point across. Logically, from what I have explained thus far, a prism must be made of glass in order for it to complete this process. As we commence this in-depth discussion on the function of a prism, I remind you to keep in mind my elaborations in the reflections segment.

You will learn that because a prism can produce a complex spectrum, there is a lot more to learn about the entire refractive and reflective processes. The study of topology could also lead to more breakthroughs into the realm of the paranormal. There are non-triangular prisms, which resemble what is called a polyhedron, "poly" meaning many and "hedron" meaning an acutely angled topologic shape. So, ultimately a polyhedron prism type is more complicated in its geometry, thus leading to a very complicated fusion infusion of light reflections for a multiple opposite to opposite reaction of creation. To state my case further, a prism—whether triangular or a polyhedron—is a thing that could be studied for a further comprehension of the inner and outer beyond of human frequency. The more complex the topologic shape, the more intricacy it is capable of. Here is a drawing of a triangular prism.

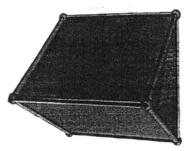

You must understand that a prism is capable of multiple light-to-light actions and that it can be used to create a spectrum of colors. It can be used to reflect light and even alter the polarization of a light source. Excuse my repetition, but I must get this point across in order for you to understand my vision.

So, how do I personally view the method by which a prism works? Due to a prism's ability to alter a light source, most prominently the polarization of a beam of light, it has the ability to actually slow down the speed of a light beam. When a beam of light hits the first plane of glass on a prism, the light becomes altered by a process of refraction. Once this beam has gone through this first boundary, it then changes direction. This change of direction is obviously due to the multiple reflective actions. From this point on, the beam will go to its next boundary of reflection and so on and so forth. Here is a chart to aid your comprehension.

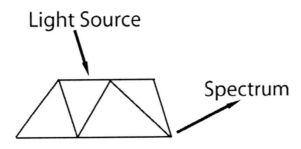

This process will continue, until a color spectrum is manifested! There have been a variety of theories about the phenomena of spectrum as well as some scientific laws applied to this brand of scientific process. For example, there was a famous seventeenth century Dutch physicist, mathematician, and astronomer, by the name of Christiaan Huygens, who is responsible for what is called "Huygens' Principle." This principle or law of science pertained to the angles and paths of light beams reflecting off of a surface. This Huygens' Principle states the intriguing capabilities of a light beam under a variety of circumstances. I believe Huygens may have come close to the discovery of a reflection connection (which I previously elaborated), because he was especially aroused (just as I am) by a centrifuge or a centrifugal force as to the behaviors of a given light beam, which is put through differing methods of reflections.

Huygens' work led to a comprehension of the process of diffraction. Diffraction can be related to various phenomena which takes place when a wave of light energy encounters a surface. I strongly believe that Huygens would have approved of scientific equivalency because in his studies, he would learn that light waves could be examined in a way that could aid him in a better understanding of acoustics, which, of course, applies to sound waves. This means that Huygens had come across an opposite to opposite reaction of creation between two separate sensual subdivisions. Lucky for me he just missed! Huygens' theories have led to discoveries in the quantum sciences. I believe Huygens is one of the most underrated scientists of all time!

There was another scientist of the late sixteenth and early seventeenth centuries who was also Dutch. This would be the astronomer and mathematician Willebrord Snellius, who is responsible for Snell's Law which dealt with the relationship between optics and the physical realm. Snell's Law is basically a different version of the actions and reactions of surface reflections and would eventually lead to the present day knowledge of how a prism works. Snell's Law is also a valuable asset for angles of refraction.

These two Dutch scientists have proven to be vital assets as to the totality of concepts of the human senses, as related to light, prisms, reflection, refraction, diffraction, and, ultimately, to the scientific community as a whole.

Through what is called "total internal reflection," it has been determined that when a light beam hits a reflective surface with a curved upper boundary, an action will occur where the light beam will perfectly coincide with the symmetry of the above curved boundary. Through my theory of the universal body, as well as my theories on reflections and connections, such an action could be used to fathom the bending of light and rainbows. This is also related to my theory of inner outer cell growth, but in this particular case, we are dealing with a combination of acute light beam angles applied to a curved structure. This is a difficult concept to visualize on your own, so here is a chart to help you visualize this action.

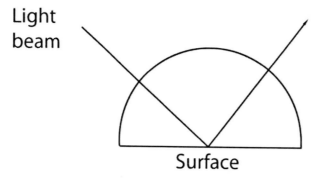

This entire concept directly relates to the branch of topology, which deals with curved type shapes and the tearing of shapes to produce more geometric, or, better yet, topologic phenomena. However, in this case, a flat surface with a curved upper boundary is a must. The side of the most common type of prism is rectangular. Just to be interesting here, I would like to show you how a rectangle can produce four triangles from a single beam of light. Please examine the chart below.

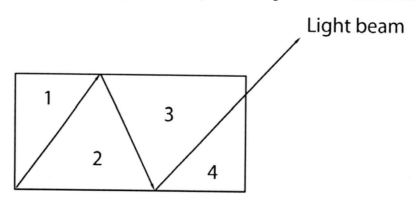

This chart is not very complex, because it deals with a non three-dimensional geometric shape rather than a full three-dimensional topologic shape. You must understand that it is the angular dimensions of a prism and the way they act with a light source which leads to a colored spectrum visible to the human eye. When applying this reaction to scientific equivalency, one could conclude that the entire chemical makeup of the human anatomy, especially the brain, is put through a unifying action with sight perception and the coinciding boundaries of all other senses.

VISION OF A MENTAL PATIENT

Furthermore, through a thorough examination of all types of prisms and polyhedrons and the way in which they act to form a given spectrum through a light reaction, we may obtain the capability to comprehend all relations between our senses, but we must approach a phenomenal scientific action, such as this one, with a better knowledge of opposite to opposite reactions of creation.

You see, different parts of the human mind are meant for different purposes, such as destiny applied to time, thought applied to behavior, and subconscious instinct. It is through a mixture of chemicals inside of us and their reactions to dark and light which gets the universal body into its coinciding actions from within and without us. When exterior energy is processed with the chemistry of the human body, it doesn't only affect our sensual interpretations, but it also affects the balanced relationship from the atoms inside of us out into the secondary outer equilibrium, which is of mind, time, and space. All of these actions of our human nature are applied to the totality of universal time, thus my belief in manifest destiny.

It is now time for me to relate some of my past dementia to sensual possibilities and other scientific matters which can also be related to this dementia. One of the things that drove me mad as a youngster was my blunt awareness of the extreme paranormal and my fascination with the human senses and all of their boundaries of reactive forces.

I believe that all living entities may possibly be capable of their own brand of environmental understanding. This could be considered a sort of brain fingerprint, if you will? I used to discuss with my friends the questions I had, but I could never ask anyone else, especially my teachers, because if I did, I would have been admitted long before I ever was. So, try to fathom this: How do we know that every person's senses act in the same way and if we all see or hear things in the same measures? The universe, like the mind, is infinite. Could that mean that senses are infinite, too? Could every living entity simply have senses, which relate to others in some sort of blurred and different way? Personally, I would not think this to be the case from person to person, but it might be from species to species.

You see, humans have their own set frequency, but other organisms could be above or below our range of frequency. Therefore, other animals' and mammals' senses of the beyond may be more advanced than ours. However, they do not have technology to aid them. This leads me to believe that even in another organism type, the frequency of their senses may be where we were in the early goings of human evolution.

In the case of a lesser sensually advanced species, the fabrics of their thoughts and dreams might reach further into what I call the inner mind infinitesimal. In the case of modern day humans, our dream fabric is not just capable of reaching into the inner mind infinitesimal, but more so into the infinity of space. This acquired human capability has taken form due to our knowledge of the infinite as applied to certain collective subconscious contributions to our complete psyche. Two prime examples of such a contribution would be television and radio. Because we are made of star stuff, the fabric of our thoughts and dreams possesses some kind of cosmic wisdom. Therefore, all we are able to comprehend in outer space such as light waves or a cosmic echo contributes to the fabric of our bodies, as well as to the fabric of our chemically secreted thoughts and dreams. This means that due to television, radio, and our understanding of astronomy, when these factors become fixtures in the collective subconscious, we can then apply it to the beauty of our imaginations and thus open the human mind to its full potential. This also leads me to a hypothesis concerning reincarnation. When an organism dies, its chemicals will decay into something else and due to my belief in scientific equivalency, a balance must be maintained. Therefore, it is possible that organisms will perish and then they will be put through a cosmic and even sexual existence of a parallel existence and then they will form into the next dream fabricated advanced species to one day become human again. This will be more fathomable once I elaborate to you the sexual entities in plant life, in the photosynthesis segment.

Continuing on, why do the eyes of all species vary in their appearance, texture, and color? The common house cat can see much better than we can, especially in the dark. I believe the eyes of all species vary because sight frequency varies. Maybe, if we could further understand a sequence of senses and colors, we could understand more about the species of Earth by examining their eyes and how their optical systems carry out their processes. Possibilities can drive a person mad, can't they?

So, it is assumed that all humans see the same, right? Well, how do we know that there aren't infinite colors? Yes, a different set of colors incomprehensible from person to person, but fathomable to the given individual. If there are senses of the beyond, then there must be colors of the beyond as well. Furthermore, could one imagine a totally new color, which is not made from already existent colors? Not likely, which is exactly why pre-human species are limited in the thought process, just as we were until now! If there was another color, it would just be there and we would view it with extreme awe. However, I am not crazy and I do realize that this infinite color or new color theory is farfetched and I am not a true believer in it. You see, it is this type of thinking that leads to a development of the personal subconscious and now that you have all read this, this type of thinking can aid the collective subconscious as well. Soon, the collective subconscious will enter the conscious mind of the world society, and the peaceful mind revolution will commence through the subconscious vision of knowing!

So, we agree that this infinite color thing is likely fictional, but we now also agree that it does put a thorough thought process into order and helps one to fill the human mind through the gateway of the personal subconscious. So, let's indulge in this color thought process a little further. Another question, how does a person know that what he or she sees as red, I might see as blue? This could be the case for any two colors from individual to individual. When pondering this thought, I realized that if colors are not infinite (which they likely aren't) they might act from human mind to human mind, thus not being infinite, but actually being finite. Finite, meaning a constant transference in the way humans see colors with a non-infinite or finite amount of colors, but an infinite transference and sequence of these colors could connect from human mind to human mind. Get it? My outlooks on opposite to opposite reactions of creation and the boundaries of interlocking change and reversal can be relative to this thought process. Think back to the brief discussion we had on quarks and anti-quarks or colors and anti-colors. When reaching into the senses of the within and the beyond, we can further this branch of human understanding. By applying this color thought process to your personal subconscious, you will move closer to the ability to enhance human balance by way of contributing your individual positive attributes to a collective subconscious manifestation.

Now, I would like to elaborate to you, through a question, how time relates to dream fabric. Are you aware that we travel time every day? Your immediate answer would likely be yes, we travel through the natural course of time every day of our lives, but that is not the correct answer to my question. You see, the human mind is physical, but it contains an intricate chemical set of actions, which coincides with light and dark forces, which happens to be the basis of the mind shadow concept. The chemicals of the human mind are a true miracle of nature, in the way that the brain can secrete energy and then form it into thought relative to the inner and outer beyond. Therefore, the thoughts by which we are able to visualize our interpretations of sight, sound, touch, smell, and taste, are created through human chemistry; thus, this produced thought or dream fabric must possess a texture that could be sensed in the realm of the parallel beyond. This means that although we do not presently understand it properly, our thoughts and dreams do have some kind of cosmic physical consistency. Therefore, when you are awake or when you are dreaming about the past or the future, through this mind visualization, your dream fabric and your mind is traveling through time.

When a person is asleep, he or she is able to visualize thoughts more vividly. This is due to the fact that when you are asleep, your personal subconscious is very active. However, it is easily conceivable that people could and do achieve dream communication. This dream communication could simply be due to the personal subconscious acting with the collective subconscious dream fabric, as well as the human brain chemistry as it reacts to light and dark forces. For the mind shadow of the personal, its centrifuge is of course the central subdividing brain shadow. For a collective mind shadow, the light and dark of the exterior environment will play that role. The totality of this personal or collective dream process is executed by an inner mind subdivision which directs your past experiences through the mind shadow and causes one to ponder and peer into the future. Those like myself who have achieved extra sensory perception (E.S.P.), could more easily understand that sometimes, when you dream, you are subconsciously attempting to travel into the future, which, so far, is only achievable through the fabric of our dreams. Do you think you know what we are figuring out yet? You will soon see, once I reveal the primary goal!

So, ultimately, when scientific equivalency is applied to everything and anything and in this case to our thoughts and dreams, the imagination will thoroughly strengthen. Once again, thank you for listening, and, sweet dreams! Read on!

PHOTOSYNTHESIS

It is now time to discuss the scientific process of photosynthesis and what I have determined to be its relations of function. Photosynthesis, by present day common and scientifically confined terms, is a series of chemical responses, which take place in the interior of a cell. In other words, photosynthesis is a metabolic footpath which is altered through chemical reactions. The chemical reactions which are enacted from the photosynthesis process leads to an interior metamorphosis of a chemical makeup within green plant life. In my opinion, you could term this action as plant life bioelectric reaction, due to the fact that the flow of electrons produced from the sun plays a vital role in the fusion infusion of the given plant's chemical chain.

The presently determined process of photosynthesis is like most other scientific hypotheses of modern day, thus it is confined as to its relationship to the entirety of universal existence. Therefore, as I commence to elaborate to you the present scientific views on photosynthesis, I will apply my own views for the accessing of a more open-minded scientific enhancement of this process. It is a truism that the process of photosynthesis has been related to beyond that of plant life and thus into the studies of other organisms as well. As we peer into this particular miracle of science, we will discover the beyond functions of the photosynthesis process.

The basis of photosynthesis is premised on the function, which, through what is called a metabolic pathway carbon dioxide (most commonly in plant life), is transformed into organic compounds. In order to be thorough here, I must inform you that an organic compound is in the category of chemical substances which contains two or more chemical rudiments which are inseparable, thus unable to reduce into more simple substances. These organic compounds are considered to be uncommon in their structure. To put it into plain English and also for your better comprehension of this, you must keep in mind that a common process related to this would be the process of sugars coinciding with energies, which are secreted from our sun during this photosynthesis process.

Most commonly, the process of photosynthesis will take place inside of plant life, as well as multiple types of bacteria. The term for life forms which carry out this process are called either photoautotrophs or phototrophs. These phototrophs are forms of plant life. Phototrophs are able to relate directly to their interior makeup as processed with sun energy for the execution of this process. Once photosynthesis commences, the given organism will gain energy through this fascinating miracle of nature.

It is true that some organisms are capable of accessing energy from the action of photosynthesis without direct sun energy. However, a majority does. Those organisms that do not access the sun's energy in a direct way are called photoelectrotrophs. These photoelectrotrophs are somehow able to obtain their required energy by using organic chemical compounds which already contain carbon dioxide within its molecular makeup. This process resembles a boundary of connection to that of opposite to opposite reactions of creation and to some aspects of the mind shadow as well. Nature will always find a way to progress, but you must remember that humans like you and me are a vital part of nature. Therefore, it is not only our responsibility to learn of what I call "photo-relationships" but we also must access future discoveries for the advancement of a better environment. We also must keep in mind that all energy on Earth is due to the sun. Therefore, this process I just explained to you does use sun energy, but it does so indirectly and with less of it.

Okay, photosynthesis is absolutely essential for life on our planet. Photosynthesis in green plants, which contain the green pigment chlorophyll, will put into motion the exchange of carbon dioxide from us and oxygen from these plant life entities. The health of the atmosphere and all of its levels must maintain the equilibrium of carbon dioxide and oxygen so that Earthly life cycle can continue to flourish. Einstein's theory of relativity, in stating that there is an incredible amount of energy within us and all other matters is backed up through an examination of the entire photosynthesis process. Remember, the entire amount of energy necessary for photosynthesis is significantly larger when related to the energy required and accessed through human technology in a given duration of time.

Through what are called photosynthetic reaction centers, which are protein types consisting of the green plant pigment chlorophyll, a sub-unit in the interior of such a cell will be made able to carry out significant functions. Such functions are essential for the promotion of this photosynthesis process. These cells will be put through an inner topologic separation of its molecules, ultimately leading to yet another boundary or barrier of balance for the functions of life, which are made possible through sunlight and chlorophyll and finally photosynthesis itself.

You must understand that the basis of common photosynthesis (at least in my view) is a fusion infusion process of the breaking down of sugars by use of solar energy. This process is, of course, most commonplace in green plant life containing chlorophyll. You also must remember that the present view of the scientific community does state that although this process is most common in plants, it does occur in other living things. Soon, I will state my case that photosynthesis should be considered a broader scientific hypothesis. However, at this time, I must further elaborate some more basics, but do not fret, because you will soon realize the barrier between photosynthesis and all other life functions on our planet.

The process of photosynthesis has been subject to a continuous state of growth throughout evolution of both human life and its coinciding plant life. Photosynthesis is a prime ingredient to the cycle of balance in the air we breathe and if you go all the way back to the first microscopic organisms or microbes of some three to four million years ago, you would bear witness to the birth of photosynthesis.

You see, water, in being the stuff of life, is (as in all life functions) a crucial component to photosynthesis. The microbes of early evolution would commonly access hydrogen for this process rather than water. The fusion infusion of water to an organism would use sun energy, and would promote the flow of electrons for an inner energy. Due to microbes being less developed in this age, the hydrogen, which represents half the ingredients of water (oxygen being the other), was sufficient for such primitive functions of photosynthesis.

One could easily conclude that this ancient type of photosynthesis could resemble another barrier of opposite to opposite reactions of creation. In this case, the barrier would be through the time flux and the photosynthesis process in and of itself. To be even more thorough, one could conclude this to be of multiple barriers. This would have to be by a process of a subdivision between time, matter, the halfway point between oxygen and hydrogen, the completion of water formation, and the centrifuge between the infancy of microbe evolution up until present day (which also relates to time). Once again, scientific equivalency wins!

Some time later, the evolution of microbes would indirectly lead to what is called cynobacteria. This cynobacteria would eventually result in a shift, leading to a higher quantity of produced oxygen in the atmosphere. This backs up the assumption that the complete photosynthesis process was and still is taking form over time through which could have originated from some sort of organic chemical infinitesimal. This means that Earth in itself has developed just as a fetus would develop in the womb. Therefore, in both cases of this comparison, opposite to opposite reactions of creation would lead to the development of the human mind, thus the imminent manifestation of the collective subconscious.

Seeing that photosynthesis is very dependent on light and the absorption between water and light into the given living entity, I deem it a good opportunity to relate this to the mind shadow for a moment. But be patient, because some more brief elaboration is necessary if you are to catch the drift. As you read this next short elaboration, I would like you to keep in mind that plants, water, and solar energy mend together for photosynthesis, in a similar fashion as the human brain functions between chemical moisture of light and dark.

You see, for the foundation of photosynthesis in a microscopic sense, it requires a reaction of light on a single molecule of chlorophyll pigment. This leads to the absorption of a single photon, thus causing the elimination of a single electron. A reaction of light is essential for this original action of the photosynthesis process. This light source through another opposite to opposite reaction of creation is somehow transformed into chemical energy, which is representative of heat caused by speedy molecules which will ultimately lead to the formation of organics like glucose, a type of natural sugar. This will then lead to the chlorophyll coinciding with the inner electromagnetic light absorption. This single chlorophyll molecule, as well as all the other chlorophyll molecules involved will each absorb a single photon. A photon is a unit of light. A photon particle, equal to a single particle of an electromagnetic light wave, will then cause the loss of a single negative charge. This process secures the incursion of positive and negative energy along the time line, or as you will learn in the "What is a Connection" segment the "naturalistic line."

This process will then lead this negative flow to the structure of a more or less advanced type of chlorophyll, pheophytin. Pheophytin is basically a type of chlorophyll progressed through a time concept. The previously lost electron will then fusion infusion with this pheophytin and then, through the predetermined and required electron flow crucial to the actions of photosynthesis, it will then transfer this newly topologically fusion infused electron into what is called a quinone. A quinone is a more complex structured compound, which, if related to scientific equivalency and connection (which I have not yet fully accounted for), could further a scientific understanding of the processes of growth and function between various energy sources, positive or negative.

You see, Einstein discovered (through the theory of relativity) the energy stored within matter, but in my opinion, he only saw the excreting energy from the infinitesimal. Many would argue with this statement due to Einstein's fascinating views of the infinite universe, and that would be a credible argument. However, Einstein lacked the "full" concepts of parallel existences, thus he did not realize the balance of an inward moving infinite energy, which executes a process of counteracting and connecting with the infinitesimal energy coming from the opposite direction. My reason for this hypothesis is mostly due to my understandings of unions of opposite forces and the universal equilibrium. I stress that we must conceive the ultimate universal relationship, including the vast infinite and infinitesimal and its centrifuge of the finite, which are presently beyond human frequency, but with a thorough application of a sixth sense, a seventh sense called "knowing," and a second sight, the collective achievement of universal-wide connection, and utopia will be manifested.

Continuing on, after the activation of the quinone molecule, an electron flow commences. This flow consists of a multiplicity of electrons moving along what is called the electron transport chain. Therefore, more electrons will be created through another fusion infusion process of each singular electron. This could easily be applied to the positive and negative flow fluctuating along the time line, thus acting as a centrifugal force between the totality of the infinite and the infinitesimal. This chain acts as a biological conductor of newly created energy. When pondering on this part of the whole process, I can visualize a connection of time-fluctuated concepts that can only be accounted for by method of beyond sensual type thinking.

At this point of the photosynthesis process, there will be a loss of phosphates. The two phosphates in this case are nicotinamide adenine dinucleotide, and there are two separate categories of this phosphate, which could cancel out one another. There is a progress of growth within the photosynthesis process from the actions of these phosphates. Once again, we see another opposite to opposite reaction of creation leading to a further progression of life functions through the natural course of time.

So, what exactly is the result of this last mentioned opposite to opposite reaction of creation as posed to this total process? This last stage of photosynthesis causes the manifestation of a photon gradient. A photon gradient is an electric and chemical entity which assists the electric and chemically concentrated flow across a membrane. There are those who would disagree with me, but I consider this action carried out in plant life to be directly related to human bioelectric chemical impulse. The existence of this proton gradient once again gives credence to another barrier of opposite unions, which leads to an electric and chemical bond through fusion infusion. As the Rush song says, "Electricity? Biology? Seems to me it's chemistry!" You see, everything is chemistry, whether light or dark energy or what have you. Therefore, it is always within the bounds of chemical makeup.

But wait, there's more! The proton gradient will now flow through the chloroplast membrane. This chloroplast membrane consists of a number of vital membranes essential for the progression of this function. Once this membrane has carried out this conduction process, the matter will become partially depleted. This depletion will aid an enzyme called ATP synthase. This enzyme will then promote the photosynthesis process by transforming certain phosphates. Once the phosphates are aided, it will create more protons. These new protons will then flow down yet another organic conductor and will act in a time fluctuation, thus sending another opposite to opposite reaction of creation into motion, which bonds to the last opposite to opposite reaction of creation I accounted for earlier. The reason these two seemingly separate actions are bonded as one, is because this is a final balancing factor by which these two actions are "connected"; thus, another miracle of natural science is achieved.

So you see, we started off with a single electron bonding with a single photon, leading to losses and gains of energy fluctuations in a forwards and backwards motion of a time concept. Remember, this process is multiplied amongst many singular light reactions with chemical moistures, which, when viewed with an application of scientific equivalency, gives the appearance of a completely concurrent action and reaction process. This incredible natural process is commenced by an origin of negative charge or charges and results in a positive charge or charges, which also acts in supreme balance with the chemicals involved. Therefore, we have been witness to a prime example of opposite unions and a continuation of the everlasting process of life. Once again, scientific equivalency wins!

Try to understand that in the case of humans and other species like us, it is necessary to have the coinciding balance of plant life for the constant exchange of carbon dioxide and oxygen. In this case, the centrifuge is the world environment between plants and animals. Therefore, the actions any living entity takes will add and subtract to the equilibrium of Earthly existence. We are all much more important than we give ourselves credit for.

So, what is the ending and manifested result of the photosynthesis process? Once this pre-explained photosynthesis process is completed, the lost and newly created electron will reappear out of a water molecule. This returning negative charge can be explained through what is called photolysis. This photolysis is a chemical reaction where an inner compound is separated down by photons. You may not yet realize it, but this process resembles my interpretations of the infinitesimal intricate actions of the topologic and the stitching of bonded matter. Finally, the end of this photon breakdown of compounds will result in the release of oxygen molecules. Therefore, the intake of carbon dioxide within a plant has led to the release of oxygen and there you have it, photosynthesis has carried out is purpose of transformation. This miracle of nature has now produced the balance between plant life breathing in carbon dioxide and breathing out oxygen, and animal-mammal life breathing in oxygen and breathing out carbon dioxide. So, this leads me to another question. Shouldn't the animal-mammal process of transforming oxygen into carbon dioxide be considered photosynthesis, as well? Not likely, however: The photosynthesis of plant life and the animal-mammal process of the reverse is as such for a universal purpose.

Once again, I stress that everything within and without universal existence requires an exact opposite for the balance and continuation of physical properties, as enacted with universal time flux. Believe it or not, we have barely scratched the surface of the ultimate universal relationship in this particular scientific aspect. The main part of this process we need to come to terms with, is the relations among light, chemicals, space, and time, which directly relate to the presently unexposed primary goal and the totality of my and soon to be our vision.

I will now keep my promise and reveal to you how this function of photosynthesis relates to the mind shadow. You see, the mind shadow is the ultimate example of a functioning entity which makes perfect sense, because the human mind is the foundation of all worldly concepts. The mind shadow, as I have already told you, is responsible for all aspects of human thinking, and it is carried out by a centrifugal force of shadow matter, which is surrounded by concentrated chemically moist light matter, which is the physical substance of the human brain. So, I assume that the most proper way for me to elaborate this scientific application to you,is by way of examining the human respiratory system and its reversal of plant life photosynthesis, which of course is the changing of oxygen into carbon dioxide.

The human respiratory system contains within its actions the execution of opposite to opposite reactions of creation. The parts of the human respiratory system aiding this process are called the alveoli and the capillaries. Alveoli are shaped like spheres, yet they are not perfectly symmetrical. They are able to function and cause the transformation between oxygen and carbon dioxide within human blood.

The capillaries are tiny blood vessels, which, possibly through an inner topological method of function, carry out the interior functions within the human blood for this process of transformation. In this case, we see an inner opposite to opposite reaction of creation of multiple intricate functions leading to the contribution of balanced oxygen and carbon dioxide in the air of our environment.

This process has been defined in the scientific community as a diffusion process acting between the two gastric types involved in the transformation process. When applying this process to scientific equivalency, one could conclude that this process as most others, is not just a process of diffusion. I simply believe that for a diffusion process, there must be at least some fusion infusion to balance it out. Therefore, the human to plant and plant to human process of gastric transformation is examined in its totality, as to how it relates to the oneness of existence. This brand of scientific dilemma is consistent and dependent on some type of fusion infusion either within or without the capabilities of human frequency.

The definition of synthesis is the combining of parts or elements to make something whole. And I have already established that "photo" means light. When fathoming these two definitions, you will notice that photosynthesis is a connection of two things. I conclude, when applying *photo-synthesis* into literally defined terms, as well relating it to anything that can combine parts or elements with the assistance of light, this robustly supports my assumption that this is a type of connection. When photosynthesis is defined in this manner, it becomes a much vaster concept. Therefore, any absorption of light affecting or causing a change in an elemental object, whether being a tomato or a developed multicolored or black and white photograph, leads me to assume that these things do apply to its literal definition.

The origin of photosynthesis can also be related to my theories on reflections—most prominently, the more advanced perceptions of reflections, such as the use of a triangular prism for the production of a spectrum created by multiple reflections within an object.

In the senses segment, we discussed the absorption of light, about how it leads to the manifestation of color by an object. In a slightly different direction, I would now like to commence some discussion on photographs and how I relate them to photosynthesis and some other aspects of reflective forces.

Okay, before one can grasp my conceptualizations on photographs, I must first give a brief elaboration on the invention of the camera. The first type of camera was dubbed as the "camera obscura." The title camera obscura sends a deceiving message. You see, this camera obscura would eventually lead to the development of the photograph. The camera obscura was an optical device used for drawing and entertainment. The man credited for this invention was one Ibn al-Haytham (965-1039 A.D.). While it is true that he pioneered the concept of the camera, rumor has it that an even more primitive type was conceived sometime before.

The camera obscura is a box with a small hole on its side, which would emit light through a drawing. The drawing would be set up with the appropriate geometric requirements. Then a reflection of this drawing would be sent out by using lightto project the image. This is very similar to the function of a slide projector often used in schools. The camera obscura would improve over a long time period, eventually leading to more modern versions.

In the seventeenth century, one "Johan Zahn" from Germany would advance this method further. However, it was not until roughly 150 years later that technological advances would lead to a further development of the camera. It wouldn't be until 1826, when the very first photograph was developed. One Joseph Nicephore Neipce would use a sliding box made of wood created by a Frenchman named Vincent Chevalier. In the nineteenth century, Frederick Scott Archer would pioneer darkroom photograph development. In 1861, the very first color photograph was developed by a Scottish physicist named James Clerk Maxwell, with the assistance of an Englishman by the name of Thomas Sutton.

My explanations on the relevance of photographs as associated with photosynthesis and my interpretations of it should sufficiently aid our understanding of the concepts of which I am about to discuss. As far as the brief history of the creations of cameras and photographs is concerned, the knowledge I presented to you is not necessary for you to fathom my message. However, with an appropriate application of the laws of scientific equivalency, you will understand the relationship of this chronology as to mind, time, and space, and the equilibrium of it all.

At this point, I deem it necessary to commence my elaborations on photographs, relative to my personal theories. The most interesting part of this elaboration will be my comparison of photography to reflections. For your comprehension, I will start with the more modern aspects of photographs, and we will then alter a time concept as we indulge in a discussion on darkroom development.

VISION OF A MENTAL PATIENT

So, how does a photograph synthesize its colored image onto photographic paper? Traditional cameras will catch light or light waves onto what is called a photographic film or a photographic plate. Photographic film is a glossy type of paper commonly made of a certain type of plastic. This plastic is then layered with a mixture of two or more unmixable, or incapable of fusion, liquid types. Photographic plates, on the other hand, were created before photographic film, and would basically carry out the same process of light absorption.

You must understand that for the creation of a photograph, there must be an originally supplied light source or a built-in flash method. The intricate topologic details are not required for the photograph concept. The light for the manifestation of a photograph must be absorbed by the chemically based and processed photographic film. This light to chemical connection will execute a fusion infusion action, thus creating the image. Furthermore, one could consider this light and chemical image a theoretical light induced fingerprint, if you will.

Okay, let's move on to darkroom development. First of all, you must comprehend that darkroom development requires the use of extremely light-sensitive materials for imbedding the photographic fingerprint onto the properly chemically processed photographic film. Of course, this method once could only produce black and white images. Soon, further advances would lead to colored absorptions of photographic imagery.

Hopefully, by now, you understand that the human brain and the mind shadow concept relates to the supreme universal balance. My elaborations on reflections, connections (although vague at this point), opposite to opposite reactions of creation, and most of all, scientific equivalency by this point should have your personal subconscious flowing with thought and dream fabric light energy. When reading the further elaborations I am about to explain, please keep such thoughts in mind.

You see, in modern times, the centrifuge to a dark room is a device called an enlarger. An enlarger is an optical contraption that aids the image of a negative onto photographic film. I'm sure that during the course of your lifetime, you have glanced at many film negatives. I now ask you once again to apply the concept of an opposite to opposite reaction of creation to a film negative being compared in a visual sense, to a fully developed photograph. You see, a negative as posed to a positive photographic image is a reversal between light and dark and the entire process will prove this true!

As for how a negative is created, not much explanation will be required for your comprehension of the point I am getting across to you now and also to the still unexposed primary goal. At this point, the most important thing to keep in mind is unions of opposites.

Firstly, because of the ultimate relationship of universal proportions, not only is the chemical and light conditions important to dark room development, but also temperature and time are essential factors to the proper production of a negative or a photograph. I will now elaborate black and white darkroom development and then we will move on to colored photograph darkroom development.

As for the process of transforming a black and white negative into a completed black and white photograph, the process is pretty much basic, yet, it puts into motion a development to all that is relative to the totality of such processes. First, the black and white negative is soaked in water in order to proportionate the glossy layer to the film. As with anything in existence, time is a paramount factor as to correct measures of function. This can be applied to any worldly method of life, whether cooking food or making sure you have enough gas in your car. The point I just made about time may seem trivial at this point, but the totality of my vision relates to time more than any other concept of existence.

Once the black and white film is properly textured by this soaking method, with the application of the negative image, the negative is thus converted onto metallic silver. Metallic silver is the perfect metal type for the film: it produces the proper bonding application of the black and white image onto the photographic paper.

At this point, the vital method of dilution must be executed. Certain acid types, such as citric or acetic acid, are applied and then the film is cleansed with water. Once the correct proportions, including light and time conditions, are set in place, more of this process can then be carried out. At this point, what is called a photographic fixer will aid the image development further by promoting a permanent and light refraining action by way of dissolving any interfering chemical compounds. This dissolving stage, if carried out correctly, will eliminate any mistake in the proportions of black and white color staining or vagueness in visual perception.

Then there is yet another dilution method performed by applying a properly chemically balanced wetting material. This will help the drying process and this step must be done with very delicate measures, including the need of a virtually dust-free environment. Once the drying process is complete, the photograph will be cut up and then placed in a protective sleeve; and there you have it, a black and white photograph is completed.

Now, I will explain the process of color negative to photograph development. For the processing of a color negative into a color photograph, the light conditions need to be slightly different. You see, light must sufficiently absorb the colors onto the photographic film. This means that chemical and light proportions in the case of colored photographs must be more detailed and carried out with more tactical methods than that of black and white photographs.

Through what are called chromogenic materials is the process of color negative to color photograph development commenced and carried out in its totality, and, remember, this is done by method of dying. The methods for such colored developments are various, so we will only cover the basics. For starters, a color negative requires an application of chemical substances for the activation of what are called dye couplers. These dye couplers are chemically absorbed in the glossy layers of the photographic paper. And, remember, color on any object is manifested by a method of light absorption. A dye coupler is an agent of chromogenic chemical consistency, which is important for negative to photograph color development.

Next, a certain type of bleach is applied., Through its chemical makeup, it transforms and further promotes a color image, which will eventually be fully developed. Next, a photographic fixer (just as used in a black and white negative, but with certain exceptions) is used to further complete the development process. Next, proper rinsing and temperature stabilization is carried out. Finally, once dried, the image is printed onto the photographic paper, cut up, and placed in a protective sleeve.

Of course, there are some variations to the photographic development methods of which I just explained. However, the information I presented should be sufficient for you to further your understanding of the main point I am trying to get across to you. You see, all of the steps I just explained to you can and will be relative to other aspects that at first may not seem necessary to the totality of all of my theories. Furthermore, all the steps I presented to you when applied to scientific equivalency, and, most importantly, to a time flux concept as well as unions of opposites which set boundaries between connecting forces, which will further promote subconscious activity as well as enhance the totality of your imminent comprehension of scientific equivalency in and of itself, will lead you to even more subconscious activity.

Here comes the good part! We will now compare a photograph to my reflection theories, especially the interlocking change and reversal and the parallel type existences that can be discovered by reflection observation.

You see, for a photograph to take its form, only one source of light is required rather than two sources of light, which are essential for a mirror reflection. I would like you to think back for a moment on the total message I elaborated in the reflections segment and for you to ponder what can be discovered by observing a mirror reflection with a thorough type of thought process. Think back to the simple experiment depicting the interlocking change and reversal of light within the centrifuge of a reflection and the creation of an opposite, yet, seemingly identical image, of yourself.

I remind you that because of the opposite to opposite reaction of creation within a mirror reflection, the horizontal imagery this reflection creates is a reversal of yourself, proven true because if you hold up your left hand and observe the reflection, it will be the right hand of the image in the reflection.

So, I must ask you, do you think a photograph would produce the same reverse type image of a reflection? The answer is a definite no! Allow me to explain: if you have understood the properties of a mirror reflection properly, you should understand that two sides exist within a mirror reflection. Therefore, a parallel universe exists within a mirror reflection. You must understand that for a photograph to be created, an original source of light or a built-in flash is an absolute necessity. This means that if you take a picture of a person holding up his or her right hand, the picture would display the right hand held up as well. This is due to the fact that a photograph is one sided. What is behind the camera does not exist in the picture. Of course, this is contrary to a mirror reflection, where everything that exists in the environment also exists within the reflection.

You see, a photograph is not capable of a centering reversal method because it is limited to one side. Therefore, a photograph is simply a fragment of time produced by a single light source. A photograph also requires more technology than a mirror does. That means that photographs are a result of further human technology, thus representative of a more detailed alteration of light. A mirror reflection is a connective function acting between coinciding light sources and is created through more primitive technology. Although a primitive function can be more advanced within the universal and natural means of function, it can still be simpler in a human way of thinking. Another factor is that a reflection is produced faster than a photograph. A photograph must go through a detailed process, which takes time for its completion. A universe does not exist in a photograph, but the lens of a camera requires a circular plane of glass. This leads me to conclude that because a light source must pass through this glass film, the photograph could be deemed as the direct relative of a reflection.

Because a photograph is a fragment of time and universal existence and that it requires such detailed methods for its manifestation, it leads me to believe that through the complete development of a photograph and through an accessing of mind, space, and time, one could see that the time period and the actions of energy that have taken place between these two separate manifestations of light and time (the other being a reflection, of course) the totality of my vision and the still unexposed primary goal is a truism.

It is now time to wrap up this discussion on the concept of photosynthesis. I would like to leave you with another thought-provoking and collective subconscious manifesting idea. I would like you to think about the development of a photograph and its dependence on chemical moisture and light. When you have a chance, hold up a photograph in front of you and as you observe it, try to imagine how all the material within came to be as such. Now, picture it forming as a liquid from top to bottom. Subconscious activity?

I leave you with a final interesting fact. The word "photograph" was coined by John Herschel, an English chemist, astronomer, mathematician, and inventor. He was the son of an astronomer and a father of twelve. It is no coincidence that John Herschel coined this word, seeing the subjects of which he was aroused by. I hope you have enjoyed this fragment in time. Read on!

WHAT IS A CONNECTION?

It is now time to discuss my favorite theory of all of my theories: my theory of connection. This is one theory I consider even more vital than scientific equivalency. Connection could even be dubbed as the father of scientific equivalency. The theory of connection is the basis of opposite to opposite reactions of creation, whether light to light, matter to antimatter, or light to dark, or any of a variety of combinations of connections, which are responsible for it all.

Some of you may be aware, in a conscious way, what a common connection is: it is a subconscious communication between two separate minds (remember Jung's analysis of the anima animus) and a reaction of love, or of an even higher purpose. Connections can be good when dealing with those who are moral, or bad when dealing with those of an uncompromising evil. You must understand that everything that has ever been created is done so by way of connection. The process of fusion infusion is a chain of connections, which ultimately leads to the full manifestation of life and all of its forces. Connection in the physical sense has everything to do with an intricate topological three-dimensional jigsaw puzzle type of creative action and reaction process. Be it in the realm of basic physical forces or in the outer reaching parts of the infinite and infinitesimal beyond, all of it is a universal-wide connection, which has and will continue to produce an unimaginable number of connections and which will always lead us back to that of a centrifugal force.

The first matter I'd like to elaborate about the totality of connection involves some of my earliest writings as a teenager. This will be communicated to you through the first completed lyrical compilation I ever wrote. This compilation was the first completed Deallegiance song and it was the title track to our first demo tape. It is entitled "Freedoms Call." This song set into motion the forming and the progression of all my scientific theories. It represents the basis of what a connection is and I am very proud of it. Once you have read these lyrics, you will accompany me onto a journey of the paranormal relations between mind, space, and time. So, before we further indulge in the process of connection, I hereby present the lyrics to "Freedoms Call."

Trapped in a world of illusion, passing through the sands of time
Pre-assorted solution, Utopian way within the bind
Sub-ironic conclusions, unequivocal spirit with mind
Peace of mind solution, Universal contact is here to find
Sightlessness cannot exist for the second side
It's never too late to translate or to reinstate
The good disease is spreading to save our fate
Children learn at incredible rate, causing enormous clarity for connection #8
Evil cryonic diffusion, dirtens disturbs naturalistic line
Atomic chemical infection, purest deaths growing grind
Scarce hell ridden pollution, mutant corpses end of time
Now is needed connection, search for peace of mind, Connect!
Escaped from the world with infusion, succeeded revolution of the mind
In-adverted constitution, recreates as time unwinds
rampant mind confusion, saved with the spirit out of bind
Universal wide connection we find! Screw!

Okay, in order for you to fathom the basics of what a connection is, I will take you through these words line by line, and explain to you exactly what a connection is and how it can benefit us.

Let's take it line by line: "Trapped in a world of illusion, passing through the sands of time." This line refers to my early dementia due to the first accomplished step of the still unexposed primary goal. This first line can basically speak for itself and it should suffice, even though this goal is still not accounted for. At age nineteen, I was admitted into a psyche ward due to this unavoidable dementia, which would eventually become a harrowing reality produced from the commencement of a connection. In order to become free of living in such a place, I was forced to lie and tell the faculty that I was all better. This was a necessary because much more work was to be done. As for the sands of time, my elaborations in the reflections segment should at least make some sense to you at this point. Remember, I wrote these lyrics when I was 16 years old; it wasn't until three years later when I would finally be admitted.

The next line, "Pre-assorted solution, Utopian way within the bind." At the time, I subconsciously to consciously visualized the pre-assorted solution. However, I was not very fluent in aspects of the subconscious (at least not as much as in present day); but I was dabbing in theories that pertained to subconscious light reactions. Soon, this pre-assorted solution would become manifested in my dreams. Therefore, my subconscious was forming an assortment of mind subdivisions, thus leading me to the concept of the collective subconscious. Remember, the material of the human brain is moist physical light and it reacts by way of light and dark forces due to the mind shadow.

As for the "utopian way within the bind," I must admit that my utopian vision was premature and many obstacles were to be overcome in the near future, thus "the bind." Remember, there is an equilibrium between mind, space, and time, which means that the personal and the collective subconscious are both capable of time travel by means of thought and dream fabrics. This is the method in which the topologic connections of thoughts are able to balance itself out, by accessing the universal equilibrium, as well as by way of subdividing fusion infusion reactions for the formation of the primary goal, which can only be carried out by means of open-minded subconscious acknowledgement.

Okay, next is "Sub-ironic conclusions, unequivocal spirit with mind." A sub-ironic conclusion is yet another of a variety of mind functions that forms by means of personal subconscious subdivision. This sub-ironic conclusion will act in unison with thought and dream fabrics. Therefore, a sub-ironic conclusion is a subconscious conclusion, or more simply, a conclusion of the subdividing process, which manifests the connection of mind as well as maintaining the growth of the human mind, which could ultimately lead to a collective understanding. A sub-ironic conclusion can cause extra sensory perception (e.s.p.) and some forms of clairvoyance. This is especially the case in our dreams, which in reality are smears of chemically secreted thought fabrics in a deeper state of subconscious activity.

As for "unequivocal spirit with mind," one could easily assume that this line defeats the basis of scientific equivalency. However, this is much too quick an assumption and is in reality quite the contrary to any slight defying of scientific equivalency whatsoever. You must understand that for the mind or anything else to maintain a balance, the properties involved need not be equal, though they must maintain this balance with an application of correct proportions of psyche balances. A good example is water, because water is balanced between hydrogen and oxygen, but for a molecule of water to take form, two hydrogen atoms must bond to one oxygen atom, which shows balance, yet unequal properties. You see, the human mind forms its spirit by way of secreting chemical properties, as well as by forming the senses of the inner and outer beyond. In the physical world, we are more aware of mind than spirit due to consciousness and the barred realities of society's demands, but once again, the balance is maintained.

Next line, "Peace of mind solution, universal contact is here to find." Obviously, we are not that deep into the concepts of both personal and collective subconscious matters yet. However, a common goal we all have in relation to society is "peace of mind." The quest for peace of mind or inner peace is, in basis, the pursuit of happiness and for those who are daring like me, it would be fulfillments of love and human understanding. So, peace of mind basically speaks for itself.

So, what is universal contact? Well, contact is simply another word for connection (at least in this case). By this point, you might have seen, through my elaborations on scientific equivalency and its relatives, or, if you want to be technical, its offspring, that all is one and one is all. Therefore, universal contact or universal wide connection is and has been bluntly in front of our faces the whole time. Are you catching the drift yet? Keep reading!

Okay, the next line brings us to a point of paranormal relativity as posed to the totality of my vision; "Sightlessness cannot exist for the second side, it's never too late to translate or to reinstate." The second side refers to opposite to opposite reactions of creation, but not in a confined way. As far as this lyric is concerned and what I am trying to get across through it, it is the hypothesis of parallel existences, such as the center of a reflection or the centrifuge of the mind shadow, meaning dark as one side and light as another. This is a continuance of sub-ironic conclusions; in fact, it is another sub-ironic conclusion in and of itself.

When examining forces of light and dark and when thinking of them as representing sides, I am able to see through a sense of the beyond; that alterations of states of mind could cause some to see light as dark and dark as light. This could be better understood if you consider my elaborations on photo negatives, which I presented in the last segment. This stage of comprehending a second side promotes a balance between the "unequivocal spirit with mind." Therefore, a sub-ironic conclusion just completed a process by which it balanced two forces from two sides of existence and this process will continue until the primary goal is achieved. This function also supports my belief that the mind shadow and its reactions between light and dark sides, when applied to the universal equilibrium of mind, time, and space is a correct hypothesis.

As far as the line "never too late to translate or to reinstate" is concerned, I must explain the following: My present action of writing this book is an action of reinstating all that has seemed undoable in past years. It is not nearly too late for me to reinstate the vision of "knowing" and once you know of the primary goal, and what it imposes, you will fully understand this statement. Reinstatement also refers to the forming of the "Language of the Mad" and my interpretations of it.

Next, "The good disease is spreading to save our fate, children learn at incredible rate." The concept of the good disease

VISION OF A MENTAL PATIENT

is another of my many theories. It is exactly what it says it is; yes, it is a good disease. This good disease is the theoretical fingerprint of my personal subconscious and it can take its form in the collective subconscious in the same way the "Language of the Mad" did. This would be by a process of human mind subconscious subdivision, which has progressed throughout the growth of human evolution. Because thought and dream fabric has the capability to defy the natural course of time, this method is more than possible. The good disease, due to its relationship of balance between mind, time, and space, can be viewed as a cosmic rash. This cosmic rash or good disease is going to transform into the collective subconscious fingerprint produced from the centrifuge of the human mind binding the vast infinite and infinitesimal. This disease is a contagion of morality, love, and human understanding. It will at first be secreted from our inner selves, then it will become the force of balance for all universal existence, and it will directly relate to all of our thoughts and actions. This good disease has the potential to appeal to all Earthly moral intellects of culture.

"Children learn at incredible rate"; well, as for those of youth I visualize a world where we will soon be free from the present negative effects of the barred realities of world society. Children will grow up with a moral balance and learn the true art of connection of mind and soul. The totality of the good disease will be shown through "Something Wonderful" in the "2001-2010" segment.

Continuing on, "Causing enormous clarity for connection #8." You see, the number 8 is the best number, it is the number which represents the shores of the paranormal on the ocean of outer space wavelengths. You may be aware of the significance of the number 7. For instance, there are the seven seals, part of the Christian concept of eschatology, which is the foundation of Christian beliefs. These seven seals are said to be composed of extreme worldly revelations that are said to be opened by the "lamb."

My concept of connection number eight came from one of my favorite bands' album. This would be the Iron Maiden album called *Seventh Son of a Seventh Son*. There is a spoken prophecy in this album, through the beginning of a song called "Moonchild." This song holds significance to the completion of my vision, so without further ado, here are the beginning lyrics to "Moonchild."

> *Seven deadly sins, seven ways to win*
> *Seven holy paths to hell and your trip begins*
> *Seven downward slopes, seven bloodied hopes*
> *Seven are your burning fires, seven your desires*

You see, Iron Maiden, Metallica, and Rush are extremely intelligent in their methods of personal subconscious formation. The part of "Moonchild" I must exploit is the seven deadly sins, which are: lust, gluttony, greed, sloth, wrath, envy, and pride. Most of these sins have been committed by all of us and, remember, there are seven of them. This is also relative to my elaborations of a sixth sense emanating from the six senses of the beyond, thus leading to a possible seventh. There are also seven wonders of the world. Therefore, number 8 is the beginning of the mysteries, of the paranormal. Number 8 will act as the boundary in numerals and mathematics, as to the centrifuge of scientific equivalency. Number 8 represents universal-wide connection, and only those of uncompromising and unimaginable evil will fall short of the glory of the eighth connection. Number 7 represents the edge of civilization, thus 8 represents the inner and outer beyond. We shall prevail!

I will now display more worldly reference to the number seven and its revelations. First, we will examine the number 7 in religious aspects. In Hinduism, there is a group of seven stars called the Sapta Rishi and they are related to the seven saints of Hinduism; there is a Hindu wedding ritual consisting of seven promises, which relates to their beliefs in reincarnation; in Hindu mythology, there are seven world entities in the universe.

In Christianity; there are seven separate churches representing the branches of all Christian religions, seven churches of Asia, to which the book of revelation is addressed, seven days of creation, seven days of Passover, the seven year cycle in the age of Jubilee, seven years of plenty and famine in Pharaoh dream, the fall of the walls of Jericho on the seventh day after marching around the city seven times, seven things god hates (Proverbs 6;16-19), the seven last words or sayings of Christ on the crucifix, the seven loaves turned into the seven baskets of plenty, the seven spirits of god, the seven Catholic sacraments, the seven joys of Mother Mary as well as the seven sorrows of Mary, seven acts of mercy, the seven virtues, which are patience, humility, diligence, kindness, chastity, charity, and temperance (these are contrary to the seven deadly sins), the seven terraces of purgatory, seven acts of suicide, which are mentioned in the Bible.

In Judaism: the seven-day purification period, the Shimita Sabbatical, which occurs every seven years, the counting of the Omer, which leads to the giving of the Torah, is articulated as seven times and seven weeks; the word *Shiva* is Hebrew for seven, seven rituals from seven men at a Bar Mitzvah, seven spoken blessings spoken at a Jewish wedding, the seven shepherds, god is said to have warned that seven nations would be displaced if his will was not obeyed, the seven candles of the Jewish Menorah, god claimed that Cain would be avenged seven times.

In Islam: seven is the number of heavens, seven circumambulations that are made around what is called the Kaaba, seven Earths in Islamic tradition, seven fires in hell, and seven doors to heaven.

In other religious varieties there are: seven archangels, seven is the symbol for yang in the yin yang, seven psalms in an

Egyptian cubit, seven ranks of mythraism, Buddha is said to have walked seven steps at his birth.

In mythology: seven divine women left on Earth and they became ancestress of humankind; in Irish mythology, a hero called Cuchulainn has seven fingers, seven toes, and seven pupils; the seven gods of Japanese mythology; the number of islands in the lost city of Atlantis is seven; there are seven ages in Sumerian mythology; there are seven orifices in the human head two nostrils, two eyes, two ears, and the mouth.

So, you see, the number 8 is the number of connection (which I still have not fully accounted for) and it is also the frontier of the open mind. Okay, connection #8 took a while, let's get back to business.

The next line "Evil cryonic diffusion, dirtens disturbs naturalistic line." Cryonics is a process by which humans or other animals are exposed to extremely cold temperatures preserving those who may be unable to be kept alive by common medical procedure. Cryonics preserves a deceased person's body with the hope that he or she can be revived in the future. The literal term for this brand of cryonics is cryopreservation.

To our conscious minds, this process could be viewed as moral. However, the way I see it, this process disturbs the "naturalistic line," as I like to call it. This process also causes a type of negative fusion infusion process, which we could dub as diffusion, which may lead to an imbalance of the natural flow of human energy. My chart depicting positive and negative energy which fluctuates along the time line (naturalistic line) is part of the basis of this hypothesis. You must understand that diffusion is a process by which two separate materials are mixed together, ultimately leading to newly created material. Scientific equivalency enables us to view such process while peering into the inner and outer beyond. I feel that cryonic preservation (cryopreservation) may cause a blockade in the natural flow of human energy and to its going about on its essential sequence of existence.

I would now like to elaborate further by revealing another chart. You have already seen the negative and positive energy moving within and without the time line chart, so when you view this chart, please keep that other chart, which I presented earlier, in mind. This chart I am about to display is based on what is called flat lining or a flat line. In order for you to grasp what I am about to demonstrate, you also must keep in mind that the fabric of our thoughts and dreams travel time every day.

The way I see it, a flat line on what is called an electro- cardiogram, represents a time line or the naturalistic line. An electrocardiogram flat line is a computer-generated "connection" to the senses of the inner and outer beyond, as to the flow of human energy, which keeps us in balance with all that is alive. Furthermore, because an electrocardiogram flat line is directly related to time, it is an electrically produced time sequence measurement. Therefore, when a flat line appears on an electrocardiogram which looks like a television—thus being related to the collective subconscious—it will display a flat line when the energy in a person subsides and he or she dies. Please examine the incredibly simple chart below.

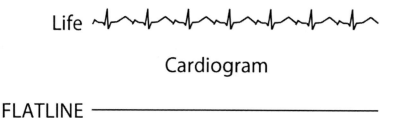

Cardiogram

FLATLINE ─────────────

You must understand that an electrocardiogram reading is a connection of energy and time measurement. When a person is alive, the positive and negative energy within him or her will display an active up and down fluctuating line on the electrocardiogram screen. Once a person dies, certain energies will leave him or her, thus the line becomes flat, and there you have it, a flat line. Furthermore, I believe this flat line appears because the bioelectric energy within the given person is no longer fluctuating within and without the line of time. But remember, Einstein's theory of relativity states there is energy within everything. This means that although a person might be dead to the world, he or she is likely still alive in a parallel dimension. I also believe that due to a flat line's relationship with time flux, when a person dies, he or she just might travel time! You're probably thinking, "Come on Ted, this is too far-fetched." Maybe so, but I will still state my case further.

You see, people who have died while on a cardiogram and then revived have often claimed that they have dreamedthey saw their deceased loved ones while they were flat lining. They will often dismiss it as a dream. But I believe that in such a case, the human mind, by way of "side" connection or connections, will coincide with the naturalistic line, thus entering you and your dream fabrics into the outer realm of the human senses and connecting with those you may have lost. There is a good movie on this concept called "The Flatliners."

So, my main point is that cryopreservation may negatively alter and disturb the natural physical property which binds to the natural course of time, thus blockading the sensual relationship which must take place. This could be due to many factors, including the slowing down of molecules when exposed to cryonic temperatures. One could argue that my theory about flat lining is weak and that is okay for now. However, we must open our minds and realize that when a person flat lines, he or she alters his or her relationship with time, and grows in a coinciding unison with nature and the naturalistic line.

VISION OF A MENTAL PATIENT

Next line, "Atomic chemical infection, purest death's growing grind." This mention of atomic chemical infection is obviously related to the splitting of the atom, thus producing a chain reaction. Because of my avid belief in scientific equivalency, I have come to a conclusion regarding the complete vastness of existence. You see, thoughts are directly related, created, and transformed through the chemistry of not only our brains, but also to all other universal existences which relate to us from the inner and outer beyond. Therefore, the negativity stated in this piece of lyric leads to what are called impulse chemical infections. Impulse chemical infections are presently beyond the realm of common imagination, logic, and knowledge. However, because of the relationship between all properties of the human psyche posed to the universal equilibrium, inclusive of our physical bodies and the actions of quarks, atoms, or molecules, as well as the actions of astronomical existences, it is a reality that if the thoughts of the collective subconscious and the galactic mind vortex becomes disturbed, a paradox would have to be dealt with. But don't worry because scientific equivalency will always win, especially if we apply a higher morality to it.

As for the second half of this line, "purest deaths growing grind" I tell you this: if you want to properly conceive the true meaning of this lyric, you must examine it with your own personal application of scientific equivalency. You see, there is a fundamental relationship with the very first substances of the universe, all the way to the brink of the paranormal. I have concluded, through negative life experiences, that pure death, its growth, and its coinciding with opposite unions leads to a temporary blockade when dealing with the primary goal. However, further elaboration at this point would be difficult, so I will wait until you are "consciously" aware of the primary goal to touch on this matter.

Next line "Scarce hell ridden pollution, mutant corpses end of time?" This line poses a warning that our human race must proceed with extreme caution and appeal to our moral structure. This line also refers to the aftermath of a disaster, which would be post Armageddon. You must take notice that this line as in some of the other lines of this song, it poses a question. The question is; how do we deal with the possibility of nuclear war? I'm pleased to tell you, that Armageddon is unlikely, but the possibility of it must be dealt with rigorously. It is an absolute fact, that if the human race can deal with such problems through a comprehension of connection and scientific equivalency, we can and will achieve a utopian way. Therefore, it is true that positive actions will reap positive results.

Next line, "Escaped from the world with infusion, succeeded revolution of the mind." Now, the basic premise of infusion is to instill or to impart. Interestingly enough, plant life can be infused when put in boiling water. However, my interpretation of infusion directly relates to opposite to opposite reactions of creation, which are intended to cure any negative actions of diffusion. However, this is not meant to be taken literally. I view infusion as a cleansing of the negative aspects of diffusion, which will lead to a state of balance. In order for you to personally understand my concept of infusion, it must be applied to scientific equivalency. If this thought process can "connect" into the correct proportions of human understanding, we will be able to cleanse the intentional evil of our animal instincts, thus creating a higher plane of moral structure. Therefore, my interpretation of infusion is in the most basic of terms, the elimination of immorality and the creation of a central boundary for a moral connection of the collective subconscious.

As far as a successful mind revolution is concerned, it is completely dependent on the presently unexposed primary goal. This piece of lyric represents a new ideology of utopian proportions, which can only be obtained by a collective subconscious connection. This connection will lead us to the ultimate equilibrium between love, morality, and human understanding. The mind shadow concept leads me to conclude that we must increase the light intensity of the physical light of the human brain, as well as increase the dark centrifuge shadow intensity responsible for all of the subdividing functions of past, present, and future, which function within the three levels of consciousness.

Next line, "In-adverted constitution, recreates as time unwinds." This line refers to the human concept of time and frequency, which is relevant to the completion of my vision. An in-adverted constitution represents the recreation of love and morality applied to a wavelength of time. You are not aware of it yet, but a "connection" in its complete function will sternly defy all normal human interpretations of time. This creation of an altered time flux of connection is yet another example of an opposite to opposite reaction of creation, in this case by way of fusion infusion actions and reactions as they act in unison with the mind to space equilibrium including the infinite and the infinitesimal. This unifying action can be carried out by the "monolith" which will be fully accounted for in the "2001-2010" segment. Furthermore, the basis of an in-adverted constitution is a theoretical type of hands on repair of our human mistakes. And it will re-create as time unwinds.

This re-creation is made possible by the completion of the collective subconscious manifestation and its formation, over the lengthy period of human evolution. It has taken an unimaginable quantity of mind subdivisions for this recreation to take place. Scientific equivalency will win this one easily!

Next line, "Rampant mind confusion, saved with the spirit out of bind." Well, this rampant mind confusion is obviously due to society not being aware of subconscious activity. At the time I wrote "Freedoms Call," only a select few could fathom its true meaning. Those who could not understand these lyrics would think I was crazy, which is also somewhat true, however. So, mentioning confusion, I knew I had my work cut out for me and that it would take years for me to get my point across.

The last half of this line, "saved with the spirit out of bind" is a result of the next line, which I have not yet discussed with you. Anyhow, this act of saving is a result of all I have elaborated about these lyrics so far. It is the achievement of universal contact by which utopia is made possible.

Now, for the last line of this song, "universal wide connection we find." This action of connection pertains to all results of human contact; it also represents the new frontier of the human mind. This entire process is a result of a single flash of light, which, like my enhancement of the big bang theory, happened everywhere at once. This flash of light was the first step to the primary goal and it all happened in a millisecond. Soon, we will move on to the start of an eon and the new frontier.

As for the word "screw" at the end of this song: When we recorded "Freedom's Call" on John's four track, his brother Fred, who sang for us, simply made a joke and yelled "screw" into the microphone at the end of the song. You see, when something screws (and I'm not talking about sex, so get your mind out of the gutter), it forms and coincides with a vortex. Yes, a vortex, similar to a galaxy or a strand of D.N.A. Well, I have now revealed my first defined version of what a connection is. But there is more, so bear with me.

For the remainder of this "What is a Connection" segment, I will elaborate on the more simple connections which take place in the macroscopic environment. These types of connections could seem meaningless and not of any importance. In this segment, I have gone in a backwards direction by way of explaining the complexities of connection prior to the basics of connection. The absolute truth is that everything is a connection, all the way from the vast infinitesimal to the farthest outreaching properties of the infinite. So, as we embark on the very basics of connection within the real world of life's responsibilities, you will take notice of what can be learned and benefited from the surprisingly simple actions of the common environment.

Okay, let's start with connection in the world of mathematics. In the study of geometry, a connection gives the idea of promoting information along a curvature or a family of curvatures. However, these curvatures need to be parallel to each other. Therefore, we can relate curves to parallels and reflections in pertinence to parallel universes, which exist within a reflection.

Furthermore, there is a wide variety of geometric connections which could differentiate the data it could reveal. For instance, there is what is called an affine connection, which can help an individual learn about the geometric symmetry of a sphere by sectioning off sufficient fragments of a sphere. This concept of affine connection could further my friend Matt's theory of the mind sphere.

You see, through a geometric conception, I have caused a subconscious connection between two seemingly separate analogies of mind relative to shape. Therefore, scientific equivalency is once again victorious, because a connection, being the only concept superior to scientific equivalency, can occur under any situation, and thus comply with any given subject matter. And to back up my belief that the universe is constant with respect to connections and scientific equivalency, there is what is called a Cartan connection, which also applies to geometry; it had stemmed from the idea of affine connection. Therefore, through a Cartan connection, you can stretch out the concepts of an affine connection, which is the basis of any type of growth process.

For the most part, a mathematical connection requires parallels. I am not a math expert, but due to an understanding of the relationships acting among all my theories, I am able to decipher and differentiate a mathematical connection in a scientific relation to the given equation. In other words, a scientific understanding is the best means of fathoming connection.

In topology, there is what is called "connectedness" which has a variety of techniques in and of itself. Connectedness is based on the more curved type shapes within the concepts of topology. It is representative of the changing or shifting of a shape, such as what can be done with a clump of clay. However, a tearing of this clump of clay to create a hole or crevice will defy the basis of this branch of topology. In simpler terms, once you have torn the given shape, it is disconnected.

This is the way I interpret connectedness in the concept of topology; a connection represents the fusion infusion process, which is the basis of all creation and goes from the vast infinite to the vast infinitesimal. I have come to the conclusion that topology, a very advanced form of geometry, represents the intricate workings of the infinitesimal and the reactions of opposite unions. In other words, this infinitesimal topologic action is the piecing together of all separate entities within the realm of this point of the infinitesimal. It is put into action by putting together a sort of three-dimensional jigsaw puzzle. So, this means that although an object in our macroscopic range appears as a tearing process, at the same time in the deep infinitesimal, it is far from a tearing action but more like a unifying act of fusion infusion.

The air we breathe, just as everything else, is made from cells. However, through my observances of topology, I have come to further conclusions. You must understand that compacted matter is also formed by cells, but due to infinity, there are many other shaped entities within existence. But cells—or those similar to cells—are a more constant type of formation throughout universal existence. This leads me to believe that since matter is bonded together, air is made from a stitching action, and thus represents a unified binding of air stitches.

A way to visualize this stitching of the air is through a scene in the movie "Dogma." When a group of evil kids were skating around on roller blades with hockey sticks in their hands, one of them used his hockey stick to tear the air as he proceeded to walk through the torn hole in the air, thus entering into another dimension. Just imagine if you could take your hands and tear the air open and step into the torn crevice you just created. If you process this thought correctly, you will understand this conceptualization.

I first thought of air tearing as a teenager while hanging out with another of my musical friends. This would be my friend, Dan Ducharme, the drummer. Anyhow, one day while I was hanging out with Dan, I visualized this possibility, so I said to him "Wouldn't it be cool if you could just tear the air and step into another dimension?" Dan responded with an astounding "Yes" and this would lead me to further revelations. If you have been paying attention so far, you might remember that Dan was the same kid that I first shared my reflection theories with.

Furthermore, this stitching theory would lead me to another scientific visualization. This would be the visualization of what I call a "breakout area." A breakout area would be accomplished by the creation of an electromagnetic lightning reaction, with the correct proportional topologic connections applied to it. It would look like a subway station, but instead of peering past the edge where the train tracks would normally be, instead there would be a noisy thunder and lightning reaction of light properties. You would be able to dive into the light of the breakout area and be transformed into another dimension of five completely different basic senses.

You see, in order for a breakout area to exist, the action and reaction of fusion infusion would have to be flawless. Otherwise, if you were to dive into this light, and thus into another dimension, you would decompose. This vision of a breakout area was conceived in the very same conversation I had with Dan, which was about air stitches.

Continuing on, unfortunately, humans are often subject to tragic deaths. However, death, just as life, surrounds us all. Therefore, a way to enter the tearing of stitches in the air or to dive into a breakout area is presently inconclusive, because in reality, the only present method to enter such a dimension (other than dimensions of time) would be to die. I don't know about you, but I am not willing to take a risk like that just to find out if I was correct. However, the primary goal can be achieved despite such actions of blockading sources. The breakout area or the tearing of air is a confined sensual means of dimension comprehension and could disrupt the universal equilibrium if accomplished, but the still unexposed primary goal is on a different wavelength and will coincide with scientific equivalency. Do you think you know what the primary goal is yet? Keep reading! Anyway, we will now discuss another area of connection hypothesis. This will be a brief talk on the other types of connections which we take for granted day after day.

First, let's discuss connections of electricity. An electrical connection is produced through a conductor by a flow of electrons from one destination to another. This means that because all energy on Earth is due to the sun, you could, in an indirect way, apply this type of connection to that of a mirror reflection. When comparing a reflection connection to an electrical connection and then expanding this thought process in your mind, it will lead to the following: Your brain will put into action a bioelectric impulse causing your hand to reach for the light switch and flick it on and bingo!—you have yourself another type of connection. This all may seem unrelated to you, but when realizing the chemical balance of the human brain and the brain being made of moist physical light, you can conceive that the chemistry of the human anatomy represents one side and the electric energy represents the other. The act of turning on the light switch represents the centrifugal force.

There is another aspect of electrical connection, which represents more so the origin of this type of connection. This is the concept of AC/DC, which stands for alternating current and direct current of electricity. AC current has the capability to reverse itself to some extent. In other words, an AC charge can go forward and backward and so on and so forth. DC charge, on the other hand, represents an unidirectional flow of charge. An AC charge is commonly used in houses and businesses due to its waveform behavior. It is usually in batteries, thermocouples, and solar cells.

A mirror reflection connection can also be applied to AC/DC, just as any connection can be applied to any other kind of connection. You see, for a water reflection, a dark background will increase its level of vividness, but for a mirror reflection you need melted sand or silica, which has been melted into glass and then is able, through a detailed process of physical conditions and actions as applied to a time flux, to achieve a connection from two sources of light. The part to remember at this point is the interlocking change and reversal of a mirror reflection. Therefore, because of the similarities between AC/DC, its actions and my charts on positive and negative energy fluctuating within and without the naturalistic line, the comparison I am about to display could reap substantial benefits.

This comparison requires you to envision parallel AC/DC currents. Instead of an opposite to opposite reaction of creation acting as the centrifuge for this reaction, you might possibly be able to either create dark energy or at least increase the depth of a dark formation, which will then manifest itself and act as a new centrifuge, thus increasing energy between these parallels. This process is carried out throughout the universe and it is supported by my theory which states that light and dark connections of opposite unions make up the foundation of the infusion fusion process, at least in an astronomical sense, that is. I urge all of you to visualize that any type of connection, whether being two pieces of a jigsaw puzzle, topological infinitesimal actions and reactions, turning on a radio or television, and even the male to female connection through sexual intercourse for the creation of offspring is a fragment of universal-wide connection. Connection binds us and flows through us, as well as everything else in all of existence. Even when I turn on my computer, there is a connection, because when I log on to the internet it says in plain English "Connecting."

For more subconscious activity, please comply with the following: picture all of the televisions on Earth with white intensely lighted blank screens gleaming, while surrounded by complete darkness throughout all Earthly surroundings. Then, imagine your personal subconscious and the collective subconscious entering into these screens and then traveling through them and then they turn from lit up white to lit up blue. This is another stage of collective subconscious manifestation, as to universal contact. Read On!

MAGNETISM

We have now come to one of the most crucial topics in pertinence to my vision and also to the achievement of the presently unexposed primary goal. This will be the discussion of magnetism, or more appropriately, magnetic forces. As has been the pattern so far in this "Monolith" part two portion, we will examine and discuss the properties of a given subject (this time being magnetism) and we will, of course, apply this discussion to my theories.

In the most basic of explanations, magnetism is an energy force actimg between two and possibly more than two magnetic forces emanating from a physical entity. The phenomenal fact, to myself, is that any magnetic relationship between two forces can either attract or repel one another. Remember, though, there is an amazingly high number of magnetic forces throughout space and all of these forces interact and achieve a balance, which is directly relative, and supportive of scientific equivalency. The common perception of a magnetic force in everyday life could serve as a physical analogy for the magnetic forces throughout the universe. This would be through relating astronomical magnetic forces to small toy magnets, which are able (due to inner forces) to attract and pick up small pieces of steel, such as a paper clip. However, the fact is that magnetism as a whole is an imperative ingredient throughout all concepts of existence, just as everything else is in one way or another. There are relatives of magnetism which one could call the magnetism of the beyond. Electromagnetism is a good example of this beyond type of magnetism.

Today, magnetism is a very advanced science; it has led to inventions like the magnetic tape, which enables recording of sounds by means of their attractive forces. At this time, however, we must discuss the basics of magnetism.

You see, it has been determined that magnetism surrounds us in nature. However, due to my theories, there may be more significance to the concepts of magnetism as we journey into the realm of the infinitesimal. Magnetism concepts have also aided telephone communication technology, radio, and television. Obviously, that direct relative to basic magnetism, electromagnetism, will be further utilized for the creation of more technological advances!

Magnetism has led to advancements in machinery. It is responsible for the invention of the compass, which is able to help someone in his or her travels. The world is extremely affected by the advances of magnetism. Truthfully, however, if these conceptualizations of magnetism can be related to connection and scientific equivalency, we could achieve the capability to reach a hihger level of scientific understanding. As a matter of fact, there were those who actually believed that magnets were consistent of enigmatic powers and could heal wounds and illnesses. Could this mean that somehow the people of this era had some kind of subconscious understanding of an elemental relationship? The theory of connection leads me to a possible, but not definite, "Yes."

You see, magnetism, through the invention of the compass was a vital ingredient for scientific advancement. It led to the location of the North Pole by James Clark Ross in 1831. Just to be thorough here, James Clark Ross was a British explorer and he explored the Antarctic as well.

You see, magnetism has led to a better understanding of the Earth's geography. It is responsible for the lines of longitude and latitude, which are crucial for methods of Earthly direction. Magnetism, as well as electromagnetism, led to advances in our every day common use of electricity. Soon you will see that an application of my personal hypothesis regarding the properties of magnetism within their actions and reactions of attractive and repelling forces can lead us to a better understanding of magnetism's relationship to the inner and outer beyond, including seemingly unrelated issues such as brain chemistry.

Okay, an object can either consist of magnetic properties or not. Most metallic materials are consistent of such properties, but a select few are not. Cobalt and nickel are very magnetic, but the most magnetic material of them all is iron. Iron metals are often used for the creation of a simple magnet. Magnets such as refrigerator magnets are classified as permanent magnets. The alternative common type magnet is the soft magnet, which resembles a thin and glossy paper-like appearance. These soft magnets are simpler to magnetize or demagnetize. The reason these acts are easier on soft magnets is because of their chemical makeup. Once again, we see chemistry reaching into bounds, which it is supposed to be unrelated to. Always keep in mind that chemistry is everything.

You see, a magnet utilizes a magnetic force on a portion of a given magnetic material. This exchange of magnetic force will cause the magnetic material to become a weak magnet. This process is called magnetic induction. A magnet is made of a high multiplicity of fragments called domains. Each domain fragment represents a miniscule magnet and through its force of action, all of these domains will point in a single direction. At this point, you might be starting to see just how the invention of the compass came to be.

I personally believe these domains are representative of an inner topologic action and stitching type of connection to form an inner makeup. Once again, we see that all of this relates to a higher relationship of scientifically advanced propositions.

I remind you that within the attracted magnetic material there are numerous domains. However, you must understand that the domains within a magnetized metal can become erratic and become all muddled up. Once the action between these two forces of energy is accomplished, the magnetic force will intensify and the domains will become lined up and start to coincide and cause the metallic object to become a temporary magnet. You must keep in mind that this is a weak magnet and it is not able to act with strength at great distance, in proportion to its size. The contrary is the strong magnet, which can achieve stronger forces and act over a longer distance.

Certain materials are more capable of magnetic force and they are always very dependent on their inner consistency. These include lodestone and magnetite and they both are very capable of magnetic force production. The very first man-made magnets were constructed by a fusion process from lodestone and other magnetic materials. No matter what the mass of a magnetic physical force, it is always encircled by what is called a magnetic field. With such a force, the magnetic force will always gain strength at what are called the magnetic poles. These poles are always north and south. Therefore, the Earth with its magnetic core acts in the same fashion, thus the lines of longitude and latitude.

For further elaboration, you must comprehend that magnetic lines of force will always run from north to south. These lines of magnetic force will gain strength the closer they come in parallel to each other.

For another example of scientific relationship, I state the following: a mirror connection reflection, which is produced from two opposite light sources, is always horizontal, yet is not confined to two directions. Therefore, if we apply magnetic force, which will be vertical (meaning north to south), something could be figured out. You see, if you can somehow fuse a magnetic force of vertical behavior to a mirror reflection of horizontal behavior and put into motion a scientific reaction of intertwining actions and reactions, a fusion infusion act of creation of opposite unions just might take place. This is the basis of creation for the object of the "monolith." It is put together by an act of fusing two opposite, yet coinciding forces and once completed, it takes the action of creative forces. However, at this point, it is premature to elaborate on the monolith any further, so please be patient.

Because parallel poles repel each other, a balance is achieved and by this point, we are all aware that there is a universal balance. The complexities of like poles repelling one another can indirectly infuse a stronger repelling force between the north and south vertical lines of a magnetic field. There are a good number of experiments that could be done to further your understanding of magnetic forces. There are even some methods of displaying what a magnetic field looks like. One example would be by way of applying small iron filaments onto a magnetic force by using a sheet of paper as a magnetic plane. These iron filaments will act with this force and give you a visual means of observing a magnetic field. It is the area surrounding a magnetic physical source of origin where the effective forces can be detected with ease. This newly detected force is the magnetic field. This force will employ itself at a relative distance from itself. However, the proportions of such a force are dependent on its density and its shaped structure.

Magnetism alone can demonstrate the ultimate balance by means of observing and studying the originating forces of a magnetic field. Because the north to south lines of a magnetic field are able to attract and repel, it proves that scientific equivalency has a profound relationship with such a field, because the lines are not capable of crossing each other, thus scientific equivalency wins another one! Through the elaborations I have provided so far, there is no need for us to perform any hands on magnetism experiments. Due to the subconscious relationship with this balance, you should be able to visualize through your sense of sight as applied to the senses of the beyond, exactly what a magnetic field looks like. The experiment I just explained to you can give you a three-dimensional image with an application of oil. However, this is not a lesson in experiments—it is a conversation on magnetism and how it relates to my theories, so I'll drop it.

Continuing on, it is a challenging task to completely fathom all properties of actions between two attracting metal objects. The only foolproof method for determining the forces between these metallic objects would be to examine them one at a time with another magnet.

Fathom this: A bar magnet as I have already stated consists of two poles, north and south. If you severed the bar magnet in the middle, it would shift in force and result in two less lengthy repelling poles, one for each new magnet. This means that these two magnets, which used to be one magnet, will create brand new poles on each of them. If you really think about this separation process and its the results, you will realize that a balance is always achieved in magnetic forces no matter how you alter it. Once again, scientific equivalency wins!

So, why do emanating magnetic forces always attract or repel? This magnetic dilemma can be explained as such: like poles of a magnet will repel as contradicting poles of a magnet will attract. Therefore, as the balances of these forces are altered in direction, magnetic energy then becomes extremely active. However, you must keep in mind that as with anything else, there is the universal equilibrium. Of course, this brand of balance adheres and pertains to the direction of a magnetic force and the profound relationship of it all. So, when such a force either pushes away or pulls toward itself, the magnetic forces will be altered, but will always maintain a balance.

You see, if parallel poles of a magnetic field actually meet at an appropriately precise position, these forces will end up cancelling each other out. This point of cancellation is called a neutral point. The forces of magnetism, due to the proportions of their forces dependent on size, could lead to perpendicular poles, which would become so strong that it may be impossible for these two points of force to touch one another. It is this type of magnetic force that maintains the astronomical balance and prevents space collisions of catastrophe. Although there are many collisions in space, the proportions will always be correct or at least adequate to maintain the equilibrium. Astrological phenomena such as antimatter and black holes, containing this seemingly unfathomable substance, will also always coincide to the proportions of mind, space, and time.

Furthermore, the forces of a magnetic field can be strong enough to move through blockading physical entities. The study of this particular aspect of magnetic forces and their being able to travel through substances has led to some inventions. There is the common metal detector you always see people using at the beach and it is able to move a magnetic force through sand. There is the magnetometer, which is able to emanate a magnetic force through water and aid oceanographers to carry out their marine biologic pursuits. I hope you got what I got out of the mentioning of these two inventions. There is a method that enables a magnetic force to move through sand, which represents time, and when melted, it creates glass leading to a mirror and then leading to a reflection. It has also been figured out how to move a magnetic force through water, which is already capable of reflection. This leads us to the creation of the "monolith!"

Through technological advances, scientists have somehow fused powder-like magnetic fragments to apply visual images and sounds onto magnetic tape. Of course, the more recent inventions such as compact discs or digital video discs have applied the science of magnetism to lasers, modern alchemy, and electricity for the utilization of technological advances as such. Therefore, I must ask you to keep in mind that the example set from these inventions in fact supports my theories of connections, boundaries of opposite to opposite reactions of creation, and scientific equivalency, of course. The inventions of compact discs and digital video discs were created by combining different scientific concepts. Therefore, I must once again remind all of you, that if we, the human race, can correctly apply such breakthroughs to the laws of love and morality, the stages of rigorous precautionary measures can be achieved in a balance of a collective inner and outer peace.

Sometimes, when you listen to a compact disc on your stereo, you will notice the sound of static. This is due to contradicting surrounding or nearby magnetic forces interfering with the sound frequency within the sounds created by your disc and your stereo. I have this problem with my stereo all of the time. In order to deal with this contradicting interference from a disturbing magnetic field, inventors of such creations must be thorough in the creation of the given product. As you try to process this thought you must understand that even the molecules in the air must play a role. You see, because of the ultimate relationship between all entities, the technologies of such products must be made to comply with its surrounding environment.

You see, a material classified as non-magnetic has the uncanny ability to allow a complex magnetic field to move through it. This gives evidence that a mixture of actions between a magnetic field and non-magnetic materials could produce some kind of cosmic barrier for the creation of an opposite to opposite reaction of creation, thus leading us further into the paranormal. This action of a magnetic field moving through an object is dependent on angles, distances, and properties of energies, including the density and tightness of the molecular makeup.

The concept of magnetic force has been around for a long time. Roughly 2,000 years ago, the Chinese were able to create a very primitive type of compass. Obviously, they were aware of the existence of magnetic properties and they would use this capability in order to aid their ocean travel.

One Amerigo Vespucci, who was a sixteenth century explorer and cartographer, would sufficiently fathom the idea of magnetic poles. Vespucci would be a pioneer as to this concept and it would finally gain credence. It would not be long before this concept, by means of the compass, would become a common method of exploration.

In the late fifteenth century when Christopher Columbus was on his famous ocean exploration, the compass he was using was of course primitive compared to the modern compass. Therefore, as far as navigation was concerned, Columbus had to deal with inaccuracy in his travels. This problem is said to have been due to magnetic field obstruction. Eventually, a more accurate and advanced type of compass would be invented and it has thoroughly improved ocean exploration.

In the nineteenth century, the conceptualization of the electromagnet was beginning to take its form. In the same century, this concept of the electromagnet would, for the very first time, help us fathom the relations between magnetism and electricity. You see, an electromagnet, through the way it alters its energy, is capable of producing a magnetic field by using an electric current. For example, a wire that has an electric current flowing through it will produce a magnetic field around this electricity; the stronger the current, the stronger the magnetic field will be.

The physical properties at the core of an electromagnet, most commonly made of iron consisting of tiny sections, are called domains. These domains are of the electromagnetic realm, but they serve the same purpose as those less advanced domains. In the case of the electromagnetic core, the domains will coincide with the uniform actions of the magnetic field in the same way that basic magnetic domains will act. Anyhow, a magnetic domain causes an alignment of atoms, thus leading to the actions and reactions of basic or electro-magnetic forces. These domains represent a uniform organization of inner and outer energies, which of course will always react with their opposite and like energies.

This action, according to my theories, would be classified as a connection. In this case, it is a connection of forces leading to magnetic fluctuations and altering properties of repelling or pulling forces. There is also a connection between the objects involved in these emanating forces.

It was back in the early nineteenth century when a Danish physicist by the name of Hans Christian Oersted had a breakthrough. Oersted realized that this pre-explained behavior of electromagnetism, meaning an electric current's ability to create a surrounding magnetic field, could be used to control the fluctuations of strength in such a field. This alteration of electromagnetic force was achieved by altering the properties of the physical objects involved in this action. A modern day example of a physically altered object of electromagnetic capability would be the invention of the super strong electromagnet, which you would find in a junk yard. This super strong electromagnet is capable of lifting cars and other large metal objects.

In order to simplify the gist of my elaborations, I state the following: in the smallest and most and basic form, an electromagnet is simply a twine of wire with a strong centrifugal force, which is made of iron. So, logically, seeing that iron is extremely apt to the applications of magnetic forces, it is utilized as such. The electric current will move along the coil and move into the iron centrifuge, thus creating the magnetic field.

You must understand that because scientific equivalency is correct, there are always other ways of altering energies of any form. In the case of electromagnetism, there is, of course, the altering of physical properties, but there is also the altering of the current as it reacts with the magnetic material.

Continuing on, we will now embark on how the Earth itself relates to magnetic forces and gravity. This will further state my case that there is a higher balance of function pertaining to the oneness of universal relationship. For centuries now a comparison has been made between the Earth's magnetic and gravitational pull to a sphere of lodestone. This comparison can help us learn that there is relativity to magnetism being gravity from the obscurely small to the extremely massive. This concept can be related to the inner outer cell growth theory, which we discussed earlier.

You see, the Earth consists of inner spherical layers, which are similar in shape to the levels of the atmosphere. The outermost Earth layer consists of the crust and this layer is called the lithosphere. The asthenosphere lies directly below the lithosphere. Then there is the lower mantle and the outer and inner core.

The part of the inner Earth we will be discussing is the inner core, which mostly consists of iron. Iron, as I previously stated, is the most magnetic metal of them all. It is the Earth's central core, which is responsible for most of the gravitational pull of the Earth. Due to the intensely high temperature of the Earth's core, it cannot act as a permanent magnet. However, due to the outer layers, some kind of fusion infusion of gravity or magnetism occurs, thus producing the essential balance to coincide with our physical being.

In the early formation of our planet billions of years ago, the Earth would gain its present physical magnetic and gravitational structure. This is a result of what is called planetary differentiation. This planetary differentiation is a process by which objects of certain physical properties separate components to the entirety of the planet. The main cause of this process is emanated from chemical and physical behaviors. Finally, over a long duration of time, this process will form the Earth as such, including its layers and its magnetic and gravitational forces. I conclude this process of planetary differentiation to be directly proportionate to all of the concepts that can be related to scientific equivalency. That is, of course, a vague statement considering that scientific equivalency acts and reacts to any type of existence.

You see, because Earth is magnetized, it consists of its own magnetic north pole. What you must fathom is that Earth's magnetic pole is not always coincided to true north due to the Earth's axis of rotation. Therefore, because our planet acts as a truly individual entity in space, the compass has proven to be a vital asset to our Earthly travels. An amazing result of such phenomenon is that this can be related to the migration of certain bird species. Some believe that due to a conflict with true magnetic north, these migrating birds will often travel off course. It is possible that birds, whose brain functions are related to their interpretation of the environment, are indeed affected by the Earth's magnetic field. This behavior of certain types of birds is also said to be due to magnetic storms.

A magnetic storm is directly affected by the behaviors of astronomical objects. Therefore, due to a relationship of magnetic forces of the inner and outer beyond, there is as always a continuous balance of relative properties. However, one must keep in mind that forces as such are constantly being altered. If we relate this conceptualization of astronomical behavior to certain parts of my personal theories, we could account for universal behaviors that do not seem to make much sense right away. In other words, space collisions and black holes or what have you do serve some purpose of universal function.

So, what can be learned from the behavior of such birds and the way they are affected by the beyond? Well, the instinctive navigating ability in certain species of birds is definitely affected by outer intrusive forces of the astronomical realm and other types of existences. I conclude that birds might be primitive in consciousness, but at the same time, they are very advanced in their subconscious instinctive type thinking. This also supports my hypothesis that mind, space, and time are not only equal, but are also more active in universal function than we are presently aware. I believe that all the species of Earth have within them their own brand of conscious and subconscious instinctive thinking and behavior. Therefore, we are all important, including the non-communicative organisms we share this planet with.

From a scientific aspect, gravity and magnetism can and often will be separated from one another and this is quite a popular viewpoint. I believe that the most sufficient method for furthering this one-way conversation would be to focus on the gravity and magnetism of our closest astronomical neighbor. Of course, I am referring to the moon. Once I complete this elaboration, you will once again see that my theories hold significant substance.

First, we will touch on the gravity of the moon.

The moon's gravitational field can be examined by examining radio signals which are discharged by orbiting spacecrafts. This process can be done by measuring the shifts in frequencies of radio waves. However, one must take into account all the proportions of distance from the moon to the Earth as to the actions of these waves. Due to certain conflicts between lunar and

Earth rotations, this type of examination process poses limitations.

An imperative attribute for the observance of the moon's gravitational field can be used through the existence of what are called "mascons" or, better yet, "mass concentrations." This mass concentration exists in certain localities of the moon. These areas consist of a tight packing concentration of gravitational abnormality in relation to its surroundings, of course.

There is, however, a small variety of mass concentrated type regions of the moon. For example, there is the Mare Imbrium. Mare Imbrium came to be on the moon a long time ago when lava deluged a massive crater. This was due to a giant space object containing such matter crashing into the moon. Then you have the Mare Crisium located near what is called the Sea of Tranquility of the moon. The details to the Mare Crisium are less defined. This Mare Crisium is said to have resulted from ancient volcanic activity. There is also the Mare Orientale which, from a distance, resembles a bull's eye. Finally, there is the Mare Serenitatis which is close in proximity to the Mare Imbrium. These physical type lunar existences make up about a little less than 20 percent of the lunar surface.

You see, activities of the distant past are relative to lunar gravity and its abnormalities as compared to Earth's gravity. So, once again mind, space, and time presents us with yet another example of a balanced cosmic relationship. Remember, these types of regions exist on other planets and moons throughout space. Therefore, through this brief elaboration, we can also relate the pressure of impact from such lunar existences to other concentrated and pressured lunar surface structures. We also have learned that some of these existences are a result of ancient lunar volcanic activity. I once again urge you to try to see the oneness of the universe through this elaboration.

Although some will disagree with me, I do believe that the human race has an extremely advanced culture. However, so much is still unknown about the lunar surface structure. It is true that we can examine it very thoroughly, but we do not yet see its ultimate history and significance of existence. It is common knowledge that the moon's gravitational pull is weak when compared to the Earth's gravitational pull. However, the moon does affect certain Earth behaviors, such as ocean waves for example.

So, what about the moon's magnetic field? We already know that gravity on the moon pales in comparison to gravity on the Earth. Objects on the moon weigh 16.7 percent of what they would weigh on the Earth. However, magnetic fields have variations within their properties of energy and action. You see, the moon's external magnetic field is even weaker in comparison to Earth magnetism. To be more precise, the moon's magnetic field is not even 1percent of the Earth's magnetic field. Remember, though, the Earth has a magnetic iron core.

There is a term for a measurement of magnetic flux. It is called the tesla and it represents a single unit of magnetic force. This single tesla unit of magnetism is related to its length of time duration and its force. The symbol for a tesla unit is "T." This unit of measurement of magnetic force was named in honor of the inventor, scientist, and engineer Nikola Tesla. Tesla lived from 1856 to 1943 and passed on at the age of 86. There is also a good rock band called Tesla and yes, that is where they got their name. They have a good song called "Coming at you Live" as well as many others. Incidentally, there is a unit of measurement called the nanotesla, which is one billionth of a single Tesla unit.

The moon we see today does not have a closed flow of magnetic electric current. In order to understand a closed flow within a magnetic field, one would need to further comprehend the lines of a magnetic field. To attempt to aid your comprehension of a closed flow, you could visualize a closed loop of wire with a constant course of current moving through it. However, it will be efficient if you simply understand that the magnetic fields of the moon have differences in formation, thus resulting in very weak magnetic forces.

Most of the magnetic materials on or in the moon exist in its outer crust. Therefore, a centrifuge of lunar force, in a literal sense, is non-existent when making a quick observation. There is a centrifuge of the moon, but its properties of substance and action are just as they are, so that the balance of the universe is maintained. All of this leads us to the fact that the moon is very low in its magnetism and also in its force of gravity. The magnetic physical properties of the moon are believed to have been created during the infancy of the moon itself. This formation is said to be due to what is called a geodynamo. A geodynamo is based on a theory which attempts to explain the process by which a rotating, transmitting, and electrically conducting solution creates and maintains a magnetic field.

Furthermore, the concept of geodynamics has been crucial for scientists' attempts to understand magnetic fields with extremely extensive durations, especially in astrophysical bodies. This geodynamic solution consists of liquid iron on the exterior and electrically charged gaseous matter in its interior.

I have examined the study of what is called magnetohydrodynamics. It is basically the study of actions of energies and its relatives as they relate to electrically conductive solutions. Some good examples would be plasma, liquid metals, or even salt water. However, in this case we are observing liquid iron.

Scientists, in relation to geodynamics and magnetohydrodynamics, have toiled over mathematical equations for ages. I myself suck at equations, so, in that respect, my elaborations would be less than mediocre. However, I am a natural when it comes to science. Therefore, I realize that like most, or maybe even all, properties of dynamics as such, I am able to see the relationship. In this case, we have a relationship between the outer liquid iron and the interior gaseous electrically charged matter. This is yet another action of fusion infusion. I do stress that this might not directly resemble an opposite to opposite reaction of creation. However, this example exploits two separate barriers of connection, thus the completion of the geodynamic process.

Einstein played a role in such concepts as well. In 1905 immediately following his early writings on special relativity, he tried to explain what he felt was the origin of the Earth's magnetic field. Einstein, being ahead of his time, was able to account for many of the properties, both physical and active, posed to the geodynamic phenomena. However, he would fail to fathom the existence of the ultimate relationship. Need I say it again? I guess I will. Once again, scientific equivalency wins!

The geodynamic hypothesis did have its obstacles. You see, due to the existence of permanent magnetic entities on and in our planet, the predetermined laws of the geodynamic concept and its properties were altered. In other words, certain interferences from magnetic energy sources would confuse the scientific community for some time.

The Earth's magnetic field is influenced and continuously sustained by transmissions emanating from the liquid iron solution in the Earth's outer core. Therefore, geodynamics, as far as the Earth is concerned, emanates from the central core of the solid iron consistency as well as the next upper layer of liquid iron.

I really hope that you are catching the drift regarding my elaborations on magnetism and gravity as they relate to us in our present time frame. Through what I have accounted for so far, you might be wondering what the difference is between gravity and magnetism. Well, gravity or gravitation is considered to be the science of the way massive objects (such as planets, moons, and stars) attract each other. It is related to our weight and the weight of objects in a given gravitational field. Magnetism, on the other hand, is the measurement of how objects attract or repel other materials within a gravitational pull.

Obviously, through my previously presented elaborations, you may have come to the same conclusion many scientists have come to. This conclusion is that gravity and magnetism have a kinship. This is yet another example of connection. This time, we have a connection of forces of within and of without. If we could further our comprehension of this particular brand of scientific relationship, which acts within and without gravity and magnetism, we could (as with any other scientific branch) then apply it to the collective subconscious and strengthen the level of human understanding.

The best benefit obtainable from the success of the scientific community in this case is that we should learn from this concept and end the stubborn separatism between scientific branches, and see that the most ultimate universal function is being carried out.

At this point, we will resume discussion on the relationship between electricity and magnetic forces. Of course, electromagnetism comes to mind, but allow me to commence a literary dissection of this concept. You see, due to recognition of higher relationships from electricity and magnetism, a concept has been formed.

In the late eighteenth and early nineteenth centuries, one Franz Mesmer, a German physician and astrologist, conceived a relationship pertinent to magnetism. This concept was dubbed as animal magnetism.

The beginnings of this animal magnetism concept began with a simple method of gazing into a person's face. I believe Mesmer may have discovered a subconscious connection between two minds with this animal magnetism. This is the first comprehended type of connection which sets the collective and personal subconscious psyche into motion. This animal magnetism is the spark for the eternal flame which will be achieved. This is the achievement of universal contact!

In its infancy, animal magnetism was thought to be of use for curing diseases. Allow me to elaborate what Mesmer would create and apply to the animal magnetism concept.

You see, Mesmer is said to have induced a synthetic tide in one of his patients by having her swallow a solution mostly of liquid iron. This means that Mesmer understood that magnetism from the moon was at least partially responsible for waves in the oceans. This method was intended to apply the same type of magnetic affect on the liquid in the human anatomy to that of the moon and the oceans. This patient of Mesmer is said to have claimed to have had experiences of mysterious interior liquid actions inside of her. This process relieved the woman of her symptoms for a few hours. Unfortunately, it was short lived. I personally think that this experiment of Mesmer achieved a temporary balance within this woman, but this was a farfetched type of concept. Therefore, Mesmer was aware that this method would be sternly rejected by those in his field.

Today, the term animal magnetism refers to sexual attraction between two people or two animals. I would now like to present a comparison relating to animal magnetism. I believe it is possible that any two forces within a magnetic realm would attract one another through a relationship of opposites and similarities.

Okay, in the case of electromagnetism, it is required that there is an electric force or impulse. Resulting from an electromagnetic relationship, two separate entities will either attract or repel. In the case of modern definition of animal magnetism, meaning sexual attraction between two people, an action must take place.

You see, electricity, although one wouldn't realize it at first, is involved in this type of animal magnetism in both conscious and instinctive way. In order to move toward or away from any member of the opposite sex, or even to simply walk over to a friend and make conversation, a bioelectric impulse is a must. Yes, your brain will cause a bioelectric reaction with your inner chemistry, thus promoting an impulsive reaction to the macroscopic exterior world. Soon, your spinal cord will act as a conductor and react with your chemistry; then you make the conscious decision to either like or dislike this member of the opposite sex. Whether being a conscious decision to smile or to wave to an acquaintance or a man's sexual thought giving him an erection, it is all dependent on much more than what the common person will perceive.

In the case of sexual intercourse, animal magnetism, in modern sense, will attract two members of the opposite sex together. When this act is carried out between a set of opposites (remember opposite to opposite reactions of creation) this time being sexual opposites, the sperm will act with the egg and through this sexual union of opposites a new life will be created. This process also resembles the action of stem cells creating more cells. Do you see the ultimate relationship here?

Fathom this: in mathematics, one plus one is two. However, in science, one plus one equals three. Sounds dumb, don't it? Not so, my friends, because when you add a man and a woman together and they have sex, a third entity is created (and sometimes more). Therefore, in the art of science, an original two will equal three and the same goes for cell division.

In the Politics "In General" segment, I stated that musicians are like magnets to each other. Some scientists believe that the infinitesimal vortex shape of DNA strands vibrate for a purpose of more importance than one would immediately assume. This DNA strand hypothesis is related to music theory. Being a former musician, I am aware that octaves, say in the key of "E," has a relationship of vibration to sound. Therefore, the vibrations of DNA strings or any type of string theory matter does make a sound, but this sound as compared to us in the realm of the macroscopic is too quiet and is beyond human sound frequency.

When combining music theory to string theory, one could conclude that the origin of sound, which emanates from string theory, grows from the depths of the infinitesimal into the macroscopic and then into outer space. Therefore, sound like anything else grows with its own individual characteristics.

As far as infinitesimal concepts at this juncture are concerned, I remind you that magnetized electric current, just like a beam of light, is made up of tiny particles. In this case (magnetized electric current), we have a flow of negative electrons. At this point, I would like you to comprehend the relationship of chain reactive molecules and its effect on molecular consistencies nearby, which are related to these fused molecules. This concept is directly relevant to an electric current obtaining the capability to manifest a magnetic field. Therefore, an alteration of anything in the scientific realm will lead to physical actions and reactions and will always have a profound effect on all that is relative to us, especially in the macroscopic world.

Today, the criterion of magnetic conceptualizations has (as previously stated) led to a variety of industrial attributes. Magnetism is used in factories, methods of travel, numerous gadgets, and machineries—not to mention advances in the quantum realm.

I will leave you with the principles of Ohm's Law. This is applied to electrical circuitry. You see, the premise of this law is that there is a relationship between the level of current and, through numerous materials, there is a balancing factor to the resistances between these materials. A complete understanding of this law can be very beneficial to understanding the relations of electromagnetically applied physical objects. However, the main part of this concept to aid you in understanding my vision and the achievement of the primary goal is that Ohm's Law represents a balance. In this case, we have a balance of voltage energy, which of course complies with scientific equivalency.

The man who conceived this theory was Georg Ohm. You see, in my opinion, Ohm realized there is an un-conceived balance to universal existence, but I could be wrong. However, he did see the balance, as far as this law is concerned. If perceived with an open mind , Ohm's Law could give further credence to Einstein's theory of relativity. This is because these theories pertain to proportions of energy within an entity.

It is now time to end this magnetism discussion. Once again, thank you for listening while trying not to be disturbed by any magnetic storms of confusion. We will now move on to volcanoes. Read on!

VOLCANOES

In this segment on volcanic activity, we will examine the fascinating processes of volcanism. We will also take notice of the benefits of volcanoes and their activities over the long run. We will learn of an even further scientific relationship than what I have presented so far. Scientific equivalency will play a role as always, but in this segment, my theory of the universal body will be of more substantial importance.

Okay, let's start with the basics! A volcano (as I am sure you are aware) is an opening in a planet or moon's outer crust which could erupt, emitting hot ash and lava. Volcanoes produce themselves in the same way mountains do. You see, over a very long time, two slowly colliding tectonic plates in the Earth's lithosphere will form a volcano or a mountain from upward pressure between these colliding pieces of land.

Volcanoes are commonly located where tectonic plates either spread apart or merge together. The concept of a tectonic plate can be expounded through what is called plate tectonics. Plate tectonics has to do with enormous proportional movements within the Earth's crust. The theory of plate tectonics relates to more primitive actions in similarity to continental drifts. Continental drifts represent the slow movements of the Earth's continents over a long time. The concept of Pangea, the age when all of the world's continents were pieced together as one single mammoth continent, as well as the concept of the lost city of "Atlantis," which is derived from such hypothesis, are good examples of the continental drift theory.

The movements of tectonic plates spreading apart have produced what is called the Mid Atlantic Range. This Mid Atlantic Range is located on the ocean floor of the Atlantic and it is the longest range of its kind on the planet. In the Pacific Ocean, there is the "Pacific Ring of Fire." This particular volcanic range formed contrary to the process that erected the Mid Atlantic Range, which was by way of tectonic plates merging rather than spreading apart.

The Pacific Ring of fire has produced many earthquakes and volcanic eruptions over a long history. This Pacific volcano range is "U" shaped and it consists of 452 separate volcanoes. It also holds 75 percent of Earth's active volcanoes. Due to the incredible size and conditions of this volcanic ring, it produces a small number of minor scale earthquakes every day. In the twentieth century alone, this range has produced three major Earthquakes, One in 1929, one in 1949, and one in 1970.

Volcanoes can also take form from the stretching and thinning of the Earth's lithosphere. Finally, in some cases, volcanoes can produce what are called mantle plumes. A mantle plume is an upper protuberance of intensely heated rock in the Earth's mantle. You see, intense and abnormally high levels of heat can lead to drastic and uncommon behaviors in all forms of substances, and in this case, we are dealing with hot rock. This abnormality of heated rock formations will form these mantle plumes. Some volcanoes in Hawaii have taken form by this method.

There are many categories of volcano types throughout the world. Volcanoes, like people, have their own individualities and behaviors. Take what are called lava domes, for instance. Lava domes are commonly found in craters that have taken form from eruptions of the past. There are shield volcanoes, named for their wide shield-like physical appearances, and these shield volcanoes have taken form as such due to past eruptions of lesser-heated lava types. Shield volcanoes have a low history of producing eruptions of catastrophic proportions. Shield volcanoes are prominent in the Hawaiian Islands and also in Iceland. Then you have stratovolcanoes, which tend to be very tall and carry out eruptions at alternate levels of altitude. Stratovolcanoes are formed by cinder, ashes, and lava. Then there are submarine volcanoes, which form on the floor of the ocean, thus the name submarine volcanoes. There are also sub-glacial volcanoes, which form under large masses of ice formations. Sub-glacial volcanoes are common in Iceland and some parts of Canada. Commonly, people would not assume that volcanoes would exist in cold areas as such, but the fact is that they do. There is also what is called mud volcanoes, which have formed by means of geographically disposed liquids and gaseous matters. Mud volcanoes can also manifest themselves from other alterations of geographic behaviors. They will commonly be large in diameter, yet when compared to other volcanoes, they are short in height. Then there is the king daddy of volcanoes, the "Super Volcano" which produce the most large-scale eruptions. Super volcanoes are enormous in size and will commonly form in oceans. Super volcanoes are formed through magma from hotspots pressuring the Earth's crust. Super volcanoes are so massive that they do not coincide with any other volcano type in both behavior and size.

So, what about these volcanoes' frequencies of eruption? There are many classifications of eruption types, distinguished through the study of volcanism. Volcanism is the study of volcanic formation, eruption, and the consistencies of magma or lava. For cataloging volcanoes with active eruption history, they are measured by thefrequency of their eruptions. If a volcano does not have a high rate of eruptions, they would be considered either dormant or extinct.

A surprising fact is that a volcano can be of violent behavior ranging from a few months to millions of years. Against the life spans of humans, these active volcanoes could be viewed as inactive.

A volcano can be termed as active even if not currently erupting. You see, many of the Earth's volcanoes show inner violent magma behavior, thus their active category. For example, there are active volcanoes in the Mediterranean region bordering Europe that have not erupted in over 3,000 years. On the other hand, there are active volcanoes located in North America which have not erupted in over 300 years. Therefore, the relationship, as far as time for humans compared to time for active volcanoes is concerned, is unequal. This fact, when glanced at carelessly, could seemingly defeat scientific equivalency, but at this point, you likely fathom the time relationship of a balanced oneness.

You must understand that the properties of intense heat within a volcano can promote dangerous activity, which, of course, originates from the Earth's inner heat. Mount St. Helens, located in Washington State, U.S.A., is classified as a very active volcano. Mount St. Helens erupted in 1980 and it led to a 4.2 level earthquake. Activity at this location would continue and from 1989 to 1991, smaller scale eruptions would occur. More activity has occurred at Mount St. Helens in the past five years from 2004 until 2009.

You see, because of the duration and unpredictability of such occurrences, volcanoes that are classified as inactive can all of a sudden, after tens of thousands of years, begin to display eruptive activity.

What are called cinder cone volcanoes appear as foundations of dry sand, poured through an obtrusion. Over history, this type of volcano has had a history of eruptive explosion and release of red-hot ashes and cinders. It is this type of volcanic behavior which gives it its cone-like shape. An example of a cinder cone volcano is Pacaya in Guatemala, Central America. Pacaya falls into the category of stratovolcano and it has had a history of frequent eruption. Remember, stratovolcanoes get their geographic identity through a long process of eruption consisting of ash, cinder, and slow-moving liquid magma.

Volcanism, like anything else, plays a role in the relationship of scientific equivalency. This relationship is due to the factors of time, actions of inner energies, erosion, heat, and tectonic plate movements. When peering even further into this relationship, you will comprehend how these volcanic entities relate to other concepts of existence, such as the astronomical realm.

Let's discuss the consistencies and properties of lava or liquid magma. Another way to categorize volcanoes other than through eruptive activity is by measuring the heat levels of lava and classifiying its composition. Once we have sufficiently examined lava heat frequency and composition, I will attempt to apply it to a time concept.

The first point I will make in order to persuade you to believe in a relationship between time and the consistency of lava is to inform you on what is called felsic" Felsic is a geology term which relates to the amount of silica within a lava. At this point, you must think back to my elaborations in the "Reflections" segment about how, when silica (from sand) is heated and melted to form glass, a mirror reflection is created. Well, silica can be found in lava and volcanic rocks. Quartz is an example of a silicate or felsic rock formation. However, the most felsic rock is granite. There are other earthly materials, which contain felsic like aluminum, potassium, and sodium.

You see, when the frequency of felsic magma is 63 percent or higher in consistency of silica, the intense heat of the lava when applied to a certain time duration can produce a natural glass called pumice. So, you see, time is always relevant regardless of the physical conditions and consistencies.

Furthermore, felsic magma, when in solid rock form, is categorized as igneous rock, contrary to other sedimentary and metamorphic rock types. This igneous rock is a result of cooled felsic magma. The texture of this particular rock form can vary from porphrytic rock, which consists of large grains of feldspar and quartz and it is lighter in visual appearance.

Felsic lava is thick in texture and when applied to a time concept, it can represent some significance to the most ultimate of scientific relationships. These thick and slow-moving felsic lavas tend to be most commonplace in lava domes and stratovolcanoes. You must understand that any lava type consistent of silica will always be of the slow-moving type. Due to its thickness and texture, this felsic lava type will entrap what are called volatile gases. These volatile gases are gaseous formations, which, due to inner consistencies relative to all concepts of physical relationships to the inner and outer beyond, will always boil at lower heat levels than other gaseous types. Therefore, through a fusion infusion of volatile gas responding to a slow-moving felsic magma (containing silica), it will cause volcanic energy and lead to eruptive activity. If this process is applied to your personal subconscious correctly, you will fathom the relationship between time, substance, and molecular conditions.

Continuing on, this volcanic behavior type promotes the manifestation of stratovolcanoes. These consist of what are called pryoclastic flows. Pyroclastic flow types consist of hot gases and tephra, which are highly concentrated silica compounds. Despite the physical consistencies of this lava type, it flows very fast. You see, this lava flow type is composed of molten volcanic ash, rendered too heavy to rise into the air. Therefore, when this pyroclastic flow protrudes from the mouth of a volcano, it will remain grounded and quickly move down the slope of the volcano.

When a lava type consists of 52 percent to 62 percent silica, it falls into the category of intermediate composition. This intermediate composed lava represents a sort of centrifuge of the silica process within this intensely heated lava formation.

Next is mafic lava, which contains 45 percent to 51 percent silica and a high quantity of magnesium as well as a credible level of magnetic iron. Just to be thorough here, magnesium is an earthly metal, which happens to be the ninth most existent element in the universe. This lava type is thinner than a felsic type but remember, the level of density is always dependent on molecular movement and thus it is also dependent on heat. Mafic lavas are also more intensely hot than felsic lava types. And unlike felsic lava, mafic lava can occur in a broader range of circumstances.

Finally, there are lava types, which consist of 45 percent or less silica. This lesser siliceous lava is termed as ultramafic lava. The cool rock, which results from the ultramafic or ultra-basic lava is composed of a substantial amount of mafic minerals that falls into the igneous category. The ultramafic realm is most prominent in the Earth's mantle. Due to the ultramafic being existent further within the Earth cell formation, this ultramafic has not been secreted since the pre-cambian time. Precambian time represents a barely fathomable time and it was in the era when Earth's life cycle was virtually obscure. As a matter of fact, pre-cambian time is so ancient it is measured by another time concept, the *eon*. The eon is a ludicrous amount of time to say the least.

Okay, through the studies of lava, scientists have come up with two surface texture categories for lava types. Although the properties and compositions of lava types are more extensive, the texture of lava surface types does play a role in concepts of relationship. The first of these two terms is simply A'a,' and this first texture type represents a more rigid surface type. It is in the thicker of lava textures. Mafic lava can be included in the A'a' type in the instance that the physical properties of the volcano are elevated and steep, while also coinciding in the outer topography of the volcano; and, of course, the pressure of the emanated lava force must be extremely strong.

The other texture category for lava types is called pahoehoe. Pahoehoe lava is lesser in thickness and it is much more polished. Due to its thin physical make up, pahoehoe is able to flow at a greater speed than the A'a' type. In most cases, the pahoehoe will fall into the mafic realm. Finally, this pahoehoe texture type requires a higher heat level for it to protrude from the mouth of a volcano, due to its chemical consistencies. Therefore, despite the fluctuations of silica compounds in lava and the heat relationships, textures are given slightly more leeway due to inner chemistry.

I have not yet begun my presentation why this relationshipwhich emanates from all properties of volcanism is so important to my vision. However, once I have elaborated on the benefits of volcanic eruption, I will further state my case for the validity of scientific equivalency.

The common and understandable outlook on volcanic eruptions is that they are tragic, seeing that lava can reach levels of heat so intense they measure well above 1,000 degrees Celsius, not something the common animal or mammal would want to be near. Just as black holes in outer space serve a purpose to the ultimate oneness of universal existence, the volcanoes of Earth also play a role of equalizing. It is true that a black hole is dangerous and that avoiding one makes a lot of sense as it is also true that one would benefit from the avoidance of an erupting volcano. However, despite the fact that many people have perished from the dangers of volcanoes, the truth, in a scientific way of speaking, is that, in the long run, volcanoes actually help the Earth.

So, how are volcanoes good for the planet? The first small example I will reveal is that a volcanic eruption on a large scale will emit, through an environmental reaction to its surroundings, levels of hydrogen, sulfur, carbon dioxide, and water vapor. These essential compounds will aid the natural functions of the outside world. Earlier in this book, I discussed with you the environmental benefits of these four compounds. By the time my elaboration on which we are about to embark on is finished, you will envision a chain reaction of opposite unions, which stem from the evils of a volcanic eruption by which these evils will be transformed into a positive and necessary life function for the continuance of nature's prosperity. Once again, we will indulge in the realm of the paranormal and, hopefully, you will further comprehend the relations of opposite unions and we will also give the collective subconscious the nudge it needs, for us to complete yet another stage of human understanding. I now will state my case for the benefits of volcanic eruption.

You see, due to the existence of silica within volcanic magma and under certain conditions, the natural glass, pumice, is created. Firstly, this concept can be directly related to time, if one were to apply my theories on reflections. Furthermore, through the intricate complexities of the actions and reactions of the properties of magma, sulfuric acid can be created. You see, sulfuric acid is a dangerous substance if an individual were to come into direct contact with it. However, you must understand that this very same process produces sulfur, which is an absolutely necessary substance for the process of various Earthly life cycles.

You see, distance and timed actions are imperative for our coinciding with such productions of nature. This process then leads to the emission of appropriate amounts of sulfur into the stratosphere. This process forms what are called sulfate aerosols. These sulfate aerosols consist of tiny particles suspended in either liquid or gaseous matter. This process, in totality, is another example of a fusion infusion process resulting in balance.

Once these particles are emitted into the stratosphere, they will diffusely reflect light from the sun. Remember now, diffusion is a spreading out of matter, which in this case consists of particles of light. These particles of light will then (as just stated) fuse and infuse, however, this particular act of fusion infusion has its unique individuality of a to and fro action and because it coincided with an action of diffusion, this action achieves a more intricate type of connection. By this elaboration, you should now comprehend, through your outer senses, that this process does represent a relationship to the exterior realm and believe it or not, this process is still not complete.

The next action of this process will promote a cooling of the troposphere. Now, a balance of heat will take effect on the climate. However, in relation to human time, this is an extremely slow process.

We now confront a problem with this process which seemingly defeats scientific equivalency. To make a long story short, this process, when mixed with the present state of human pollution, causes an imbalance, such as those we discussed in the environmental portion of "Politics." This problem is the weakening of the ozone.

So, you see, there is a balance which originates from the origin of volcanoes—all the way from the infancy of tectonic movements right up to the most recent eruptions of modern times. Sorry to be so repetitive, but once again, we see that scientific equivalency relates to the totality of everything and as you know by this point, I do mean everything!

Think back to the "Magnetism" segment, when I spoke of the commonly perceived science of magnetic fields and its relationship to us who are within the realm of the animal magnetism concept. Animal magnetism concept is premised on our bio-electric impulses attracting us to certain parts of society, such as entertainment, sports, politics, and most importantly, leading us to a new level of morality, while going about our daily activities!

You see, morality, my friends, is smart. Therefore, I once again insist that a balance can, and should be, achieved by way of a higher understanding. I also remind you that there is no need to become overwhelmed, because the groundwork is being done for you and in due time, you all shall play a role. Furthermore, certain negative alterations that have originated from human mistakes have led to negative functions such as war and acid rain. Acid rain, although being of our own fault, is also affected by certain gaseous matters released by volcanic eruptions. Life, in the personal sense, is a balancing act, carried out through the personal subconscious; as well, other life forms of the world environment are also subject to a balancing act, done by manifesting the positive attributes of the collective subconscious.

Since the fourteenth century, volcanic eruptions have ended the lives of approximately 200,000 people, give or take. Volcanic eruptions (as previously stated) are responsible for many of the world's rock formations. The substances from these rock formations are often used for industrial and chemical technologies. For example, dried magma is used for constructing roads and highways. Substances such as zinc, copper, lead, mercury, gold, silver, and molybdenum, a silvery metal type produced through cooled magma, have benefited us to some extent.

Now, I will inform you of the phenomenal process by which the Earth's climate is cooled by a coinciding action of a seemingly disruptive bacteria. The scientific community has learned that volcanic actions over a long period of time puts into action a climate cooling process. This is carried out by the taming of methane gases, which creates bacteria and somehow controls the levels of bacteria in the environment. Although it is unobvious at this time, it is true (and I have already stated my case for it) that a volcanic eruption can put into play a fusion infusion process, but in this case, the fusion infusion process is able to cool the relative climate. This is because of chemical particles being ejected into the air, thus creating cloud formations that will reflect the sun's rays back into space. This is a different perspective from the elaboration I made previously. Continuing on, the scientific community has also discovered that sulfur dioxide, which is emitted from volcanic plumes, will go through complexities relative to their surroundings, thus affecting the climate, too. Here is yet another act of fusion infusion feeding bacteria types that thrive on sulfur in marshes. Remember, methane gases can come from many things, and one of them is marshes. This process emanated from clouds that pour acid rain. Therefore, even acid rain can prove beneficial in at least a minute way. Okay, once this sulfur thriving bacteria completes its metamorphosis, this process, by a method of environmental balances, will deplete the levels of unhealthy methane gas into the atmosphere. Therefore, by simply understanding the thickness of damp substances in marshes or wet lands, one can envision the absorption process which holds negative-acting bacteria and releases the proper environmental prescription of coinciding substances. Even more astounding is the fact that this absorption can transform seemingly unhealthy attributes of matters and put them to good use.

You see, sulfur dioxide produced by volcanoes is somehow able to contribute to balanced nature. Interestingly so, this very same sulfur dioxide can originate from industrial uses of petroleum and coal. You see, coal and petroleum, in being partly composed of sulfur compounds, will react to certain industrial uses by ejecting proportional levels of sulfur dioxide into the environment. This is yet another fusion infusion process, contributing to the human capability to understand and achieve balance. There are some volcanoes that continuously eject sulfur dioxide and of course, there are some inactive volcanoes and active volcanoes that expose other natural functions to the total balance of volcanic relationships throughout the world. This process is a positive asset to places such as Laki Volcano in Iceland. This Laki region is fertilized due to past volcanic activity. Despite the fact that an eruption of this volcano has not taken place since 1783, the positive assets stemming from this action are still very helpful. Therefore, one good result of volcanic eruption is that, over the long run, it will put into action a natural fertilizing process.

The field of volcanism is very advanced; however, due to limitations in determining with precision the weather history and the effects of acid rain, a vital piece of information for this process we have been discussing, a natural assumption would be that because of the natural balance between actions and reactions, the fertilization process is at least a temporary success.

It has also been determined that despite sulfur dioxide emissions from industry being so prominent, there is a larger influence of this compound from volcanic environments rather than those of industrial regions. The solution to this dilemma is obvious. You see, it is common for coinciding wetlands to surround volcanic regions rather than industrial entities like power plants and factories, which emit this compound to our exterior world. Therefore, this obstacle is overcome by balancing forces. If you have followed me so far, you will understand that this can indirectly relate to certain concepts of magnetism and animal magnetism.

VISION OF A MENTAL PATIENT

To further state my case as to the relationship of industrial and volcanic emissions of sulfur dioxide for this process, or any related processes, I will now elaborate. You see, ages prior to human industry, volcanoes have been existent. Therefore, volcanoes were the only cause of acid rain types. This leads me to believe in a quicker-acting, explosive-like effect that has ultimately led to natural fertilization being stronger in potency, thus leading to complex fluctuations in climate effects.

Millions upon millions of years ago, the natural greenhouse properties of Earth were balanced in ancient eras by volcanic processes that I have accounted for thus far. Therefore, the methane emissions of this era were likely less in volume but more potent. This life cycle all the way back from this ancient era to present day is completely vital to Earthly life as we understand it.

There have been studies in the science of volcanism which concluded, through current human knowledge of this miracle of nature, that sciences of fertilization, when applied to volcanism's history, could lead to a regulating of volcanic fertilization. This could also lead to more advances in the science of fertilization, thus benefiting all of us. This study could also aid us in understanding the molecular attributes of acid rain types.

Over time, the evidence has grown regarding the consistencies of volcanoes in relation to the environment and climate, and although I have thoroughly explained these effects so far, there is still much more to it. Those in the volcanism sector of the scientific community please me very much, because they have comprehended examples of scientific relationships. It has come to the point that through further studies of volcanism (at least in my opinion), this branch of science could grow into a possible centrifuge between Earth and, to some extent, the astronomical realm. Volcanism, when compared to human lifetimes and the nature of our being, gives more evidence about the time factor relating to all which is equal.

You see, the existence of volcanic ashes and their sulfur compounds that emanate from the active volcanoes of our world has recently led to a development of soluble iron deposits which prove beneficial to certain oceanic surface areas that are lacking in this iron deposit. This process has also led to a spreading of what is called phytoplankton. Phytoplankton is a simple organic compound which grows into a more complex organic compound. The process of photosynthesis is imperative to the manifestations of phytoplankton and the growth process. Phytoplankton is just under the realm of the macroscopic and it is extremely dependent on its inner chlorophyll, which gives a green tinted discoloring in the waters of our oceans.

Furthermore, phytoplankton causes an uprising in oceanic atmospheric albedo as well as some withdrawals of carbon dioxide. An albedo is part of an organic physical entity which somehow spreads out sunlight reflections. In other words, an albedo represents a more complicated process of reflection than that of the more basic type reflection. This process also strengthens global cooling, yet it does so over a very long period of time, well beyond human time range. This process has benefited the human life cycle over history, not to mention the totality of life cycle of all Earthly life forms.

So, you see, once again, light, water, and time play a role in a seemingly unrelated process. Because an albedo thrives on chlorophyll, it is able to cause a complex process of light emissions to the exterior world, leading to more balancing factors of life through the actions and reactions explained in the science of volcanism.

Okay, that was good, but there's more! You see, there is also a relationship between iron, volcanic ash, and the oceans.

First of all, iron, which relates to many concepts of magnetism, serves another seemingly non-relative function. As far as marine biology is concerned, iron, when put through a process, serves the purpose of being a boundary in another opposite to opposite reaction of creation process by acting as a sustained micronutrient for assisting ocean life. However, this process does have its limitations due to the fact that it is only carried out in certain surface ocean areas. Because of the role which iron deposits play in this function, and seeing that it has a profound consequence on parts of the oceanic life cycle, it is deemed able to enhance the opposite union action with the essential inner and outer fusion infusion function, which is balanced by the universal equilibrium. The fusion infusion process will result in discharging a surplus of carbon dioxide to this oceanic environment. This is, of course, part of the function of the respiratory processes between marine organisms of consciousness such as fish, and plant organisms, such as algae.

Volcanic ash releases a credible amount of iron. When these iron deposits are able to connect with oceanic surfaces, this natural process will carry itself out. Furthermore, this process, in some aspects, is fast moving. You see, the iron deposits from this volcanic ash source are soluble and thus, put through a speedy fusion infusion process, which will lead to beneficiary attributes to marine biological life forms. Therefore, you have iron, which happens to be the most magnetic element, going through a balancing process of ocean fertilization. This action of nature causes me to believe even more in my theory of connection. Due to the altering of iron deposits emitted by volcanic activity as relevant to a time concept, this action leads to a promotion of valuable and essential assets to those ocean organisms which are dependent on this function. Could this be an example of magnetism, even beyond the outreaching properties of animal magnetism? If this process of life growth adheres to my theories, then, why not?

Well, that is what happens in oceanic areas affected by volcanoes, so let's move on to lakes, which are affected and dependent on volcanoes.

Okay, it has been determined that from a chemical process in certain lakes, plankton growth has been progressing over time. Through a thorough examination of lake salmon and their migration to seawaters, the scientific community has achieved a better understanding of the entire volcanic fertilization process and the effects on lake life, though in this case we are strictly dealing with salmon. Although today's scientific understanding of fish migration is at a primitive level, credible and substantial discoveries have been obtained.

You see, salmon are born in freshwater and they migrate into the oceans. So, what is the relationship between salmon migration and lakes being affected by volcanic activity leading to fertilization? It is not until roughly four or five years into the life of salmon when they will proceed with their instincts of migration. I will now attempt to relate this migration process to volcanic fertilization in freshwater lakes.

It is true that some species of salmon might carry out their migration instincts as early as one year into their life span, but this is completely dependent on the sexual maturity of the particular salmon species. In order for me to be precise, we will discuss the sockeye salmon, which are abundant in many places, especially in the lakes of Alaska. There are two major factors to salmon life in this region; one is the amount of fishing by humans in this region and the fact that it is very large scale. The other is that this region's fishing areas are considered to be in poor conditions, thus salmon life in this Alaskan region is depleted.

You see, volcanic activity in this region has a tendency to eject substantial amounts of pumice, which, as I stated earlier, is a natural form of glass. The reason for such an abundance of pumice is that these Alaskan volcanoes, in recent times, tend to emit volcanic ash rather than magma.

There has been an extremely large proportion of volcanic ash containing this pumice, which has sprouted out in the lakes of the western Alaskan lakes region. Eruptions of well over 100 years ago have had a major effect in modern times. Wind direction also has much to do with the distribution of this pumice, which is consistent in volcanic ash. You see, this ash is very light, so winds will send it into particular directions, even remote destinations. So, once again, we see a seemingly unrelated factor (wind) having a profound scientific affect on the outcome.

In the early twentieth century prior to volcanic activity in this region, thousands of sockeye salmon would die due to insufficient food supply. This was due to depletion of worms, mollusks, and some insect types essential for the life cycles of this Alaskan region. To put it mildly, salmon and other fish life in this region were put through a struggle, because altered conditions were depleting their food resources.

This would also lead to inadequate conditions for the fishers of this region. More importantly, this situation was not only causing salmon deaths, but the salmons were forced to migrate years before it is time for them to do so. Therefore, not only were they dying young, they were also living horrible lives.

You must remember that nature (although failing with certain endangered species) will always attempt to balance nature out. Soon, ash would begin to be discharged from some volcanoes in this region again and some very interesting events would soon happen. Somehow, the inflow of volcanic ashes would affect the fisheries of this region, triggering the creation of a new balance. This negative action would end up promoting healthy plant growth in this Alaskan lakes region. Once again, time plays a role!

Salmon life in this region was in absolute turmoil, but in the absence of abundant salmon life, chlorophyll within the lake plant life was again able to thrive. It was not until about forty years after volcanic activity, early in the twentieth century, when this plant life would really begin to sufficiently thrive and thus start to re-establish a healthy level of salmon life.

Furthermore, this process would lead to a chemical enrichment in soil, thus leading to a healthier abundance of algae, which represents a pedestal of the aquatic food chain, thus ultimately improving inorganic nutrients. This is all due to a fusion infusion process, which stemmed from all of the cited sources. However, this process goes through its ups and downs and can seemingly defeat scientific equivalency at certain junctures. You must understand that the process of any given life cycle is complicated, but can be simplified if approached with thorough tactfulness. Please don't get me wrong here: salmon life in this region has definitely experienced quite a disturbance. And in a complete reality of present situations, both improvements and negative attributes have continuously fluctuated, causing hardships for those species affected. It is also true that there is no "completely" credible evidence that salmon life has improved due to this process, but it has most certainly been replenished.

There is so much that can be learned from this environmental reality. You see, by examining such fluctuations of a life cycle and the effects of volcanic activity, we may be able to obtain some positive methods to aid such dire situations. So, the lesson to be learned from this examination (as well as every other examination in this book), is that it is up to us to take action to aid life forms such as that of salmon life, and help ourselves as well as all the other species of Earth to withstand the hardships of nature and maintain a balanced flux.

So, how does volcanic activity affect plain old land soil? Many experiments on the interactions of chemical compounds have proven to be beneficial to the soils of Earth as well as the promotion of soil growth. When volcanic ashes go through long weathering processes, these put into action a soil type fusion infusion, thus promoting a variety of life cycles. It will promote the growth of fruits and vegetables, which, of course, aids the nourishment of mammal and animal life on our world.

The main point I am trying to get across here is: a volcanic eruption, in the short term, is catastrophic for reasons I do not need to elaborate. However, the fertilizations that occur due to volcanic activity are necessary for life on Earth. Therefore, a volcanic eruption is yet another example of good stemming from evil. You must now see that benefits from volcanoes, such as the creation of water vapor or the aged process of fertilization, represent another balancing action and thus makes scientific equivalency the victor once again!

Ejected volcanic materials also produce zinc and iron. So, fathom this: zinc and iron exist in some of the foods we consume. Yes, we have miniscule amounts of metals inside us, which maintain the balance essential for us to thrive. This balance directly relates to the naturalistic line and to distracting disturbances stemming from the natural evil tendencies of our animal instincts. It is because of the ambitions of conscious and intentional human evils, such as acts of genocide, which interrupt the reaching of the still unexposed primary goal. The forces of human good fathomed through the existence of nature's evils, must, as all other matters, achieve a balance, and we will achieve this balance, my friends, we most certainly will!

I will now seemingly go off subject for a moment and discuss with you some factors regarding my theory of the universal body. Due to the existence of enormous multiplicity of connections, opposite unions, and any of a variety of balancing forces, the ultimate universal relationship of scientific equivalency is in the process of a collective subconscious manifestation through the dream of universal contact. Because of this relationship, the way I see it in my mind is that it is impossible for me to ever go off subject. So, let's discuss the universal body theory for a bit.

Just to remind you, the premise of universal body theory is only to be sufficiently understood through a vivid understanding of the infinite and the infinitesimal. This universal body theory states that we just might exist in a living physical entity and physical entities could exist inside of us. Remember, the universal body is partly based on the concept that everything (although not obvious in the macroscopic realm) resembles a cell. The Earth is a cell with inner layers and the sun acts as the nucleus of our solar system, thus our solar system represents an atom type. The rotation and axis of the celestial bodies of the solar system resemble vortex type behaviors. Stars represent protons and electrons.

Furthermore, vortexes occur throughout the infinite and the infinitesimal and our solar system complies with this type of whirlpool movement. The galaxies of the universe are also in a vortex motion. The tiny manifestations of string theory, such as the spiral or ribbon-shaped matters like human DNA also adheres to a vortex and thus complies with the universal body theory.

So, now that I have reminded you of the premise of the universal body, what do I want to add to it? What I would like to do at this point is to apply the universal body theory to connection with a third application of a time conceptualization. At this point in human history, there is somewhere between six billion and six-and-a-half billion people in the world. More astounding than that is that approximately 100 billion people have walked the face of the Earth up to this point in history; there are about 100 billion stars in our Milky Way galaxy; and there are also 100 billion known galaxies in the universe. This set of facts represents a universal relationship of the time space continuum. These three facts tell me that we are in the age of universal-wide connection!

You see, there is so much more to my theory of the universal body and once you have read the "2001-2010" segment, you will see how this theory relates to us and to the human anatomy. But I will save that for later. Keep reading!

Okay, in order to continue this one-way conversation of pertinence to the universal body, we must examine the phenomenon of lightning. First of all, although rarely so, lightning can occur from volcanic eruptions and dust storms. A dust storm can also be termed as a sandstorm. A sandstorm will occur under extremely windy conditions in large-scale sand dunes. I remind you that sand contains silica and thus, a subconscious representation of a time concept and lightning in being a form of light is also representative of a subconscious time concept.

Lightning is an atmospheric discharge of electricity. This electrical discharge of lightning is made possible by way of atmospheric friction. This atmospheric electricity is directly affected by the shifting of electromagnetic signals which coincide with the constant fluctuations of the ionosphere. The ionosphere, is above the fourth level of the atmosphere, the thermosphere, and it is in close proximity to the exosphere just beyond it. These spherical existences are beyond the literal definition of the atmosphere though they can be considered, in most circumstances, as part of the atmosphere.

The ionosphere gets its title because it is ionized by solar radioactive emissions. Ionization is a method aided by solar energy, which physically carries out converting atoms or molecules into ions. An ion is an atom that has either lost or gained one or more electrons. If you have followed me so far, your personal subconscious should reveal to you a further wholeness of the equilibrium throughout all concepts of universal existence, whether physical, active, or of the inner and outer beyond in the range of human senses.

Furthermore, we are all aware that thunder will accompany lightning in a storm. The reason that you never see and hear thunder and lightning at the same time is due to difference in speed: the speed of sound being 770 miles per hour and the speed of light being 186,000 miles per second. Due to their physical consistencies, lightning bolts will emit light at this speed, but the actual physical lightning itself is much slower. Lightning is also extremely hot: it is capable of reaching 54,000 degrees Fahrenheit. Ironically, this temperature is hot enough to melt silica into glass, and, in rare cases, a lightning bolt will carry out the creation of a natural glass, sort of like how pumice can be created from volcanic magma.

In the case of volcanic eruption caused lightning, such phenomenon will take place within clouds of ash ejected from the mouth of a volcano. This is similar to lightning from storm clouds. Factors such as wind conditions, thickness of air, atmospheric friction, atmospheric pressure, and also what is termed as solar wind will set up the correct proportions for this rare activity.

I know what you are thinking at this point. You are thinking, how the hell can there be solar wind? I shall explain! Solar wind is achieved through a physical manifestation of a stream of charged particles. You could term it as a sort of astronomical current. This space current will adhere with its surroundings and transform into a partially ionized gas called plasma. Therefore, this ionization of atoms is carried out with a coinciding action to equaling forces. This solar wind originated from the outermost layer of the sun, thus its name. This solar wind then fusion infusions with charged solar particles and, although difficult to comprehend, there are small quantities of ice within parts of clouds in the sky. Clouds obviously exist from the heated water of oceans, lakes, and rivers, turning water into steam and thus forming those beautiful clouds we always see. Anyhow, you cannot literally have solid chunks of ice in the clouds. Therefore, this is a crystallized ice form which coincides with the texture and weight of a cloud, thus its ability to exist in such an unorthodox manner. Next, the ice crystals within the clouds will, through its consistencies of origin, put into action a subdivision of positive and negative charges inside of the cloud, and there you have it, a bolt of lightning takes its form!

Wait! I'm not done yet! Before I relate lightning to the universal body, I must give further elaboration. You see, the proportion of voltage within a bolt of lightning is dependent on the length of the bolt. Therefore, the more elevated the origin of the bolt, the more power there is within it. Furthermore, depending on the outcome of the fusion infusion for the creation of such a bolt, it can either be positive or negative. A positive bolt is ten times more vigorous than a negative bolt.

You see, storm clouds have regions which originate from both positively and negatively charged sections. It is more common for a lightning bolt to be of negative energy. There are scientific methods of measuring the voltage levels of lightning, but this particular aspect is not essential to comprehending the gist of my elaborations.

Through what is called electrical breakdown, which is another process of fusion infusion, the makeup of the cloud will either resist or react with insulating properties, thus producing the originating base of a lightning bolt. The amount of voltage, to put it vaguely, is very concentrated within small regions of a given storm cloud and through an action of relationships moving and reacting within and without the essential centrifuge for this action, the matters of origin are enabled to sort of cause metamorphosis and thus transform into the correct proportions of energies within these cloud regions. Therefore, lightning continues to go about its process of function.

The electric fields surrounding these small regions of energy will react and put into action another fusion infusion process. Now, these surrounding electrically charged energetic fields would prove essential for the inner reproduction of this process of energy relationships. This process will be about one or two levels of power less in amplitude of the measurements of scaled voltage, which is involved in this process. In other words, a lesser voltage of surrounding energies causes the higher concentrations of energy within these regions to react in forces of equality. And, remember, ionization also plays a vital role. As for measuring lightning energy, you have what are called terawatts, which are equal to one trillion watts, gigawatts which are equal to one billion watts, megawatts which are equal to one million watts, and kilowatts, which are equal to one thousand watts. These voltage levels will not be required for understanding the totality of my vision.

Obviously, lightning is intense in heat; it sends a chain reaction on a short scale to the surroundings, altering molecular buildups and speeds of molecules, thus altering nearby exterior conditions. Amazingly, lightning can be as much as three times hotter than the surface of the sun.

Okay, here is something really interesting! The intense heat of a lightning bolt through this small-scale molecular chain reaction will contract any surrounding translucent air, leading to the manifestation of an energy wave which is deemed able to achieve the speed of sound. One could term this newly emanated force as a supersonic shockwave. This shockwave will transform, through its makeup, into a sound wave. And there you have it, the sound of thunder is produced. You see, here we have yet another example of a scientific relationship. A detailed physical existence produces intense heat and through another act of fusion infusion, a loud sound is created. This particular scientific concept can further promote subconscious activity if this action is put through a thought process relative to the senses of the beyond. Once again, scientific equivalency wins!

Another property of relative factors for the phenomena of lightning is electrostatic energy. Through what is called an electrostatic induction, more can be comprehended. You see, electrostatic induction represents a rearrangement of an originating electrical charge. Just as any other scientific process, this rearrangement or redistribution is influenced by outer and inner energy levels.

Furthermore, the subdivisions of charges need to have powerful vertically directed air fluctuations. These vertical fluctuations will transport small droplets of water to a higher altitude. This process leads to a significant decrease of heat intensity to the point of coolness well below 0 degrees Fahrenheit. These droplets will then fusion infusion and transform into a pliable ice-water texture type called graupel. Graupel can be considered soft hail. The precipitation of graupel leads to the manifestation of cold-water droplets being crystallized into snowflakes. This process will lead to a considerably weak positive energy charge which will go through a metamorphosis, transforming these particles into ice crystals and emanating a negative charge to the graupel. Once again, a vertical fluctuation of transformed ice crystals takes place. This process then results in a generating of the top of the cloud form to a mass of positive energy charge.

At this point, gravity will come into effect. You see, the more compacted and weightier negatively charged graupel will then descend downward toward the lower levels of the cloud formation, boosting negatively charged energy in the process. At this point, the subdivision process of fusion infusion will complete its final stages. Finally, when the energy of charge becomes proportional with the static electrical field, a discharge of lightning will take place. Remember, despite the fact that this electrostatic process produces a negatively charged lightning bolt, the positive and negative charges can and will achieve the proportioned balance between these charge types for the appropriated electric field of energy. I remind you that to achieve any such scientific balance of relationship, opposite charges do not need to be equal to one another for the achievement of a coinciding result to the given equilibrium of the scientific situation as well as to the universal equilibrium. Such balances are only required to depend on the actions of its opposite charge, not on the levels they are made up. This is similar to the balance of oxygen and carbon dioxide in the air we breathe. Oxygen and carbon dioxide in this case are not 50/50, but the equilibrium for the balance of life is still maintained.

There is a lot more that could be learned about the concept of lightning. The main concept I would like you to comprehend has already been accounted for. However, I once again insist that all matters of existence even in the realm of basic physical type understandings can be applied to the open mind and the three levels of consciousness, thus leading to an even higher understanding of the inner and outer beyond. Action is dependent on matter and vice versa. Objects and actions must have their opposites in order to exist. Without this balance of opposites, a paradox would be created, tearing into the very fabric of universal being.

You see, there are so many factors to lightning and weather relationships, that in order for me to explain it to you in totality, I would have to base this entire book on this subject. Just remember that fusion infusion is the process of opposite unions of the within and also that this action is the basis of all creation.

Lightning can also occur from cloud to cloud, which further exemplifies the complexities of this lightning phenomenon. Furthermore, there are other classifications of lightning. There is bead lightning, ribbon lightning, and staccato lightning, with each unique cloud to ground lightning formations. These lightning forms, like the others, are completely dependent on the coinciding forces of weather conditions from which they are derived.

Cloud to cloud lightning types include sheet lightning, heat lightning, and dry lightning. Dry lightning is interesting, because it occurs with no precipitation. Therefore, dry lightning is the lightning type usually responsible for forest fires.

Fathom this: for the sake of scientific relationships in the scientific realm, I must state that dry lightning originates from moisture, but it goes through an intricate process of formation. It hits the Earth and often causes fire, producing heat we can feel and smoke we can see and smell. The smoke then rises until parts of this smoke falls down to the surface in the form of ashes. These ashes will join the other forms of matter on the Earth's surface and a process will then take effect on the textures of the ground. So, you see, relationships are constant and everlasting! This process, like most others, can be termed as a scientific continuous and finite circle. Actually, there are other lightning types I have not exposed to you, but I mustn't get carried away here. We are working towards the primary goal, so I must continue on.

You must understand that some types of volcanic activity can cause lightning. Although rare, this does happen from time to time. Therefore, natural science, although comprehensible, is infinite. Lightning can also be related to magnetism. The complexities of positive and negative energy interactions will usually produce electrically dominant fields. However, when certain alterations do occur, a magnetic field of the electromagnetic type can be manifested.

So, how does all of this relate to my theory of the universal body? I have already explained the basis of this theory. However, I must inform you that this theory also represents a threefold connection. Those bodies of the infinitesimal represent one side of this theory's function; the vast infinite bodies represent the other side of this theoretical function. We ourselves with our human anatomy represent the required centrifuge for the actions of the universal body theory and its threefold connection! We are nearing the age of universal contact, so remember: the number 100 billion in being the amount of stars in our galaxy, the number of galaxies in the known universe, and the number of humans who have walked the planet are other coinciding factors to this threefold connection of the universal body. You must understand that we are in the realm of the macroscopic and therefore, cell-like features are not bluntly noticeable with the obvious acceptances of the moon, the stars, and the sun. There are also other less obvious natural objects in the macroscopic environment that pose similarities to cell types. Certain types of fruit, like the orange, which looks like the sun, are produced by the sun, the Earth, and water. Orange nourishes our physical health. Therefore, this is one good example. Grapevines can resemble cell clusters. Tomato, although less accurate in its symmetry to a cell, is still another good example. Remember, the sun helps these fruits obtain their colors by aiding light absorption for the forming of color onto these fruits. Orange is the best example due to its appearance being similar to the sun; its actions of formation, its actions of light absorption, and its ability to make us healthy are just as the sun itself does. Even small insects which may seem a nuisance help turn soil for the production of fruits and vegetables.

I will now attempt to relate some features of the human anatomy to exterior existences and to the universal body. You see, our blood, as in all other animals and mammals, is red. This red blood coloring is due to the levels and balances of carbon dioxide and oxygen in our blood. The main blood type I must speak of is called venous blood, which is blood flowing through our veins that is pumped in and out of the heart. Venous blood is a much darker red than other types of blood.

If you look at the veins of your forearm, you will notice a shade of blue. This is due to what is called Rayleigh scattering. Rayleigh scattering represents a scattering of light, electromagnetic, or radioactive matters from particles which are tinier than the relative light waves. This process is most common in gaseous forms of matter. This Rayleigh scattering is named after the third Baron Rayleigh John W. Strutt, an English physicist who discovered argon gas.

This particular light scattering process is also responsible for the process of sunlight scattering that causes the skies to appear to us as blue. Veins as such can appear as blue from the exterior, because subcutaneous fat is good at absorbing low frequency light waves; these allow only those highly dynamic blue light waves to refract or reflect through our human skin. Therefore, our skin coincides with my reflection theories of the parallel type existences, because of the fact that human skin can reflect, submit, and transform light in this fashion.

You see, our sun acts like a human heart. However, instead of pumping blood, it pumps light waves, which, of course, supports life as we know it. Since all energy we have on Earth is from the sun and its pumping of light waves that nourishes nature with an application of water and soil, our blood is also supported by such existences. Blood contains and depends on water as well as other nourishing factors. Therefore, the pumping of light from the sun will aid the creation of lightnings that act as veins of flowing light energies, contributing to the life cycle of Earth itself and of all Earthly inhabitants.

You see, we are made of stardust and the infusion fusion process of this stardust throughout the universe has created the equilibrium of scientific equivalency. Light particles that form light waves from the sun are sundust and this sundust feeds us and helps us grow things out of stardust formations from other sources. A prime example of such other sources of stardust entities created from other means would be the planet Earth itself.

So, if the human heart is like the sun in this respect, and if it is true that our blood represents the sunlight of the inner human anatomy, then it must be true that our veins are the lightning of our inner selves. Therefore, lightning flows through our veins in a theoretical way of thinking.

Okay, here comes the good part! I would like you to look at the veins in your forearm and it doesn't matter if they are blue tinted or not, because if you are strong, the veins of your forearms will bulge outward and, therefore, they are less able to reflect or refract light in order to manifest this bluish tint; also, if you are of an ethnicity with dark skin, this bluish color is usually less existent. Anyhow, as you peer at the veins in your forearm, you will notice they are shaped exactly like lightning bolts! Therefore, my theory of the universal body holds further precedence. Another thing you might want to try at some point would be to look into your mirror and gently pull down one of your bottom eyelids and take notice of the small red lightning-like veins protruding within the white of your eye. So, you see, we are lightning and lightning exists within us, and the fact that all universal substance is star stuff supports this claim. The universal body theory wins this one!

I am aware that I have strayed far from the science of volcanism in some respects, but due to scientific relationships and the fact that volcanoes can manifest some lightning forms originating from cellular Earth, in reality I have not strayed very far. At this point, I must further relate this concept to the universal body. I just explained that our veins represent lightning and that our veins can appear as blue. Well, lightning usually stays consistent in color, but it does carry concentrated light and our blood is concentrated human energy. Another interesting fact is that lava or magma is red as blood is. And if this magma can react with other actions and scientific properties and create lightning, then isn't it true that our blood does the same within us? This means that lava is the blood of the Earth cell!

Furthermore, I would like to talk about stars for a bit and relate them to the universal body. If we are inside a living entity of an exterior universe, then stars, in representing the protons and electrons of our existence, must play a more than significant role. The star formation type we shall now embark on will be constellations. Constellations relate to the signs of the zodiac, which I first read about in Carl Jung's book *Symbols of Transformation*. The zodiac is made up of twelve signs based on twelve constellations that are used in astronomical and astrological studies.

You see, astrology is based on connecting astronomy to a system of assurances relating to physical entities in space. Oftentimes, astronomical objects can be mistaken for astronomical bodies, such as asteroid belts. Now, of course, the signs of the zodiac do relate to horoscopes. You know signs like Aries, Taurus, Gemini, Cancer, Leo, Virgo, Libra, Scorpio, Saggitarius, Capricorn, and Pisces. These signs represent elements as well. Astrology could be a correct science to those who might be gifted with a very open mind. However, this is not the focus of this study we are about to embark on. This elaboration on the signs of the zodiac will be strictly to promote the three levels of consciousness and to get you thinking on a new level.

Constellations are considered to be of a human outlook rather than a complete reality. A constellation basically configures stars in a formation, where a figure is drawn by a connecting of the dots process. There is quite a variety of these constellations. In fact, there are an estimated eighty-eight presently accounted for constellations. The simplest constellations are well known, such as the Big Dipper and the Little Dipper, both resembling a kitchen pot.

Orion is a good example of a constellation. It is supposed to be a figure of the Greek hunter Orion. Orion is one of the most easily identifiable constellations of them all. Some prominent stars of Orion include: Betelguese, Rigel, Bellatrix, Alninam, Saiph, Mintaka, and Alnitak. Some of these stars are super giants, white dwarfs, and 0 type white stars.

Another constellation I will mention is Saggitarius, which is included in the zodiac. Saggitarius is Latin for "archer," and when this constellation is viewed as a connection of dots, it appears as a centaur, which is a part human part horse drawing a bow and arrow.

Another constellation is Aquarius, Latin for "water bearer." It represents the figure of a man carrying a bucket of water pouring out a stream. Interestingly so, Aquarius is also related to the Age of Aquarius an astrological age estimated to last roughly 2,150 years. 2,150 years is also the length of the other two astrological ages. These astrological ages result from the concepts of equinox perceptions, which, due to astronomical time relevance, are a procession of time space alterations throughout the universe. The Age of Aquarius is said to be in the range of the mid second century to the early thirty-seventh century. It represents a virtual time altering type of existence and it is said to precede the Age of Capricorn. An astrological age is dependent on the functions and movements of all space objects and the parallels to the paranormal phenomena of time alteration; but then again, so is everything else. This concept will hold more significance once I reveal to you the primary goal.

VISION OF A MENTAL PATIENT

Then there is the Crux constellation. This is the smallest of the eighty-eight accounted for constellations. However, it is extremely distinct in appearance. It is Latin for "cross." You see, Crux is in the shape of a cross, yet it is dubbed as the Southern Cross due to the fact that it is most visible from the southern hemisphere. Ironically so, the word "crux" means point of origin. You probably recall that I have used this word multiple times so far in this book. Therefore, this "" constellation represents a crux in time and universal history!

Next, I will mention the Hercules constellation. Hercules is a Roman mythological champion derived from the Greek champion of Heracles. The constellation of Hercules is larger than most other constellations. The Ancient Greek name for Hercules is Egonasin, which means "on his knees." This constellation resembles the head of Hercules while kneeling.

The last constellation I will mention is Phoenix. Phoenix is considered to be a trivial constellation. It exists in the southern night sky, but it is most visible in the Northern Hemisphere all the way down to just north of the equator. Obviously, Phoenix represents this type of bird.

Okay, now that I have compensated for these five constellations of significance to my vision, I must, at this "crux," relate the concept of constellations to my theory of the universal body. You see, when constellations are drawn out by way of connecting the dots to have their features distinguished, it is done so on flat paper, thus producing a limited two-dimensional figure. What you must comprehend is that is that in reality, the features of any constellation are in depth, three-dimensional. When viewing such constellations as three-dimensional, their features are more defined, because with this type of visual application, they take on a much distinction of vividness. My conclusion will now be presented in the form of a question: Could these constellations, when applied to this three-dimensional outlook, represent the outer living entities of the universal body? It really makes you think, doesn't it? Carl Jung, a pioneer in the concept of the three levels of consciousness, was fascinated with the zodiac as it related to mind and space. If am correct (and I am) in saying that the vastness of the human mind is equal to the vastness of time and space, then this farfetched constellation hypothesis could be true and could gain acceptance and credibility. In the "2001-2010" segment, I will elaborate further in direct relation to this brand of scientific hypothesis.

It is once again time for me to reveal to you some more lyrics. These lyrics I am about to relate to my vision are not of my own doing, but they do apply to my way of thinking. This will be another song from the scientifically intelligent band Rush and it is taken off their best album, in my opinion. This was the *Moving Pictures* album. This song aided me in the creation of my theory of the universal body. So, without further ado, I present the lyrics to track four of Rush's album *Moving Pictures*, called "Limelight."

Living on a lighted stage approaches the unreal
for those who think and feel, in touch with some reality
beyond the gilded cage, cast in this unlikely role
ill-equipped to act, with insufficient tact
one must put up barriers to keep oneself intact
Living in the limelight the universal dream
for those who wish to seem, those who wish to be
must put aside the alienation, get on with the fascination
the real relation the underlying theme
Living in a fisheye lens, caught in the camera eye
I have no heart to lie, I can't pretend a stranger
is a long awaited friend
All the world's indeed a stage, and we are merely players
performers and portrayers, each another's audience
outside the gilded cage

Okay, that was cool, huh? You see, the gilded cage, as I interpret it, is the "soulcage" of which I presented the lyrics in my song of the same title (Soulcage) in the "Senses" segment. The line "cast in this unlikely role" represents your role and my role for the promotion of human understanding by way of universal contact, which I displayed through lyrics and further elaborations in the "What is a Connection" segment. You could relate the line "ill-equipped to act" to the past when evil was more dormant and also to the visionary Vincent Van Gogh's inability to complete his vision due to lack of resources. The "universal dream" is obvious because this entire book is all about a universal dream. The line "put aside the alienation" refers to our need to become a more real and genuine people for the promotion of a better world. The "underlying theme" will be exposed in due time. And then there is the line "living in a fisheye lens"; well, a fisheye lens, in technical terms, is a wide-angle photographic lens, which is able to take pictures with very hemispherical, wide-like, imagery. It was originally intended to study cloud formations and meteorology. It has become a common commodity in photography. However, when I would listen to this song as a teenager, I would interpret fisheye lens in a literal way, and it led to my fathoming of the life forms of the extreme infinitesimal living inside the eye of a fish. This just might be the subconscious meaning of this line, because it led me to the ultimate manifestation of the theory of the universal body. Could we be living inside an eye lens? Probably not, but it does make you think, doesn't it? The line "I can't pretend a stranger is a long awaited friend" directly relates to the presently unexposed primary goal and the situations I have had to deal with throughout my life, as I put the primary goal into action years ago. Soon, you will get it! I will let you determine your own interpretation of these and other lyrics in this book, once I have completed the story of my vision.

We are nearing the end of "Volcanoes" segment. So, at this final crux of this portion, I will get back to volcanoes in a more direct way of speaking. I would like to briefly discuss what is called seismology. Seismology is the scientific study of earthquakes and earthquakes directly relate to volcanic activity.

Back in the "Magnetism" segment, we discussed animal magnetism. You see, all the way back to the time of the Ancient Greeks, strange behaviors in certain animals would occur just hours prior to an earthquake. Some have concluded that these animals were somehow able to sense seismologic activity before an earthquake would manifest itself.

You see, in pre-earthquake situations, a relative magnetic field would be altered. So far, no one has proven this to be true, but it has certainly raised many eyebrows. Therefore, scientific equivalency, when applied to this outlook, does expose another example of a significant scientific relationship. If the subconscious manifested instincts of animals can somehow sense such faint hints of seismic activity and react through an advanced form of animal magnetism, as well as to magnetic alterations, then, as far as my theories are concerned, the sky is the limit! At this point, it would be beneficial to open our minds even further and apply this seismic-detecting animal magnetism hypothesis to all of my elaborations in this "Volcanoes" segment, as well as keep in mind my elaborations prior to this portion. If we do so, we could add another threefold connection by means of the three levels of consciousness and the pursuit of the ultimate utopian freedom, by way of all of my theories and the imminent process of universal contact. Our personal subconscious minds are doing back flips at this point! Once again, thank you for listening, and, please, read on!

LYSERGIC ACID DIETHYLAMIDE

We have now come to yet another crucial ingredient to the still presently unexposed primary goal. I certainly and sincerely hope that I have gained credibility with you so far, because I am taking quite a risk by including this segment on "Lysergic Acid Diethylamide" or, more simply put, LSD or acid. I do realize that I could be subject to extreme ridicule and ostracism for what I am about to elaborate. However, it must be understood that there is only one way to achieve the primary goal. I must strongly state at this point that I do not, in any way, shape, or form, recommend that anyone put even the smallest quantity of lysergic acid diethylamide into his or her body! It is dangerous stuff due to its major effects on the chemistry of the human anatomy, especially to that of a person's brain chemistry.

This segment will cover other issues, as I will relate them to the chemistry of this lysergic acid diethylamide. I will relate the actions and properties of lysergic acid diethylamide to human DNA, which when written out is deoxyribonucleic acid and, yes, human DNA, like lysergic acid diethylamide, is an acid type. We will also once again indulge into a journey of the realm of even more paranormal phenomena. We will discuss supposed myths of metamorphosis and shape shift. I shall begin, as I always do, with the very basics of this chemically complex and mind altering substance.

You see, lysergic acid diethylamide, when compared to other narcotics, is a more potent substance that can alter our perceptions, the frequencies of our basic human senses, as well as our senses of the beyond. Under the spell of lysergic acid diethylamide, your sense perception will experience havoc, thus affecting your comprehensive traits of mind and personality. The affects of this drug will awaken your dream center while you are awake. Therefore, your personal subconscious will comprehend the collective subconscious. It has been claimed by an extremely high multiplicity of people that lysergic acid diethylamide, if properly dealt with, can expand the human mind. Supposedly, the hallucinations and relative thought processes put into action while under the influence of this drug are not real. Now, don't get me wrong here, because in our parallel of universal existence, dreams and thoughts are simply dreams and thoughts. However, if our dreams and thoughts do have fabric (of which I have previously elaborated), that would mean that these so called nonentities (which are considered irrelevant to the world society) do have some kind of physical consistency of thought or dream fabrics, and therefore, they are indeed relevant to the very fabric of the human psyche and all of its properties. Therefore, this dream fabric theory is a correct hypothetical assumption, and if it wasn't, this could all be dismissed as nonsense. However, Jung was always insistent that our dreams are linked to a further understanding. Therefore, one could perceive that the awakening of the dream center while under the influence of this drug is indeed of some universally balancing relation to the threefold connection and the equilibrium of mind, space, and time. I once again must stress that the mysticism caused by this chemically composed acid type is not linked to the physical world, but is linked to that of the beyond parallel existences, which I proved in the "Reflections" segment.

Lysergic acid diethylamide is so potent that it presents an imminent danger that could affect anyone who puts it into his or her system. However, in my case, due to my comprehension of the totalities of mind functions derived from the vast personal subconscious, I have concluded that lysergic acid diethylamide has aided me in the understandings of mind, space, and time comprehensions. You must understand that my mind is centered. Therefore, my brain functions open mindedness and visionary ambitions. I have achieved a chemical balance that will aid your understanding of the primary goal. If the mind expansion process can be carried out in correct proportions, lysergic acid diethylamide can execute an intricate topologic connection process to a coinciding action with deoxyribonucleic acid (DNA). Therefore, the rule, which applies to all scientific connections, also applies to this connection as well as through the always essential process of balancing forces.

Okay, a dose of lysergic acid diethylamide of only 100 millionths of a gram can and will result in a chemically induced mind sensual alteration, which is usually referred to as a "trip." A trip at this dosage will usually last eight to twelve hours. Unlike other narcotics, lysergic acid diethylamide is not classified as a physically addictive drug. However, any drug can coincide with a person's inner intellect and result in addiction. In order to defend myself at this crux, I would like to inform you that I have not touched any form of alcohol or narcotics in nearly thirteen years. Because of more positive personal ambitions, I have been rendered able to become an upstanding responsible civilian, able to function with a down-to-Earth type of persona. Yes, I pay my bills, clothe myself, feed myself, and I have achieved a sufficient level of inner peace.

Lysergic acid diethylamide is derived from what is called ergot (ergot in Drow is=to grey). The reason ergot comes out this way in the Language of the Mad is because ergot will coincide with the grey matter of the brain. You see, ergot is a fungus which derives from rye and, occasionally, wheat. This fungus, which can be termed as claviceps or purpurea, was discovered in the 1930's by a pair of Swiss chemists, Albert Hoffman and Arthur Stoll. However, it wasn't until 1943 when Albert Hoffman would mistakenly ingest a small quantity of this lysergic acid diethylamide before they understood the affects of this mind-altering drug.

Depending on the structure of a person's psyche archetype, a trip can be either enjoyable or disturbing. For those people whose minds are not capable of correctly coinciding with the connections of lysergic acid diethylamide to deoxyribonucleic acid, it will cause such a person's trip to induce severe negative mood swings. There is only a minuscule amount of individuals who would be able to properly coincide with this drug and if I am scaring you away from ever trying this drug, then I have achieved my goal. Don't take it! Even if one is interested in mind expansion from the taking of this lysergic acid diethylamide, he or she need not do so, because as far as the three levels of consciousness are concerned, I have done the groundwork for you. And because I have done this groundwork, mind expansion of this kind will be manifested without any need for induced chemical alterations.

Continuing on, this narcotic has caused hardships for many, *including myself.* Anyhow, people can end up in a psyche ward due to the effects of lysergic acid diethylamide. One could be permanently damaged due to the common inability to appropriately channel the human mind and make the mind act in unison with the responsibilities of society. Furthermore, lysergic acid diethylamide is especially perilous to females who either are, or plan to be, pregnant. The things that could happen to a fetus from an expecting mother under the influence of this drug, in my opinion, rivals the sad method of partial birth abortion.

As for the phenomena of mind shifts and causal actions which are attainable from the use of this drug, thoughts of metamorphic mind expansion could be a commonly induced thought process for those who possess healthy and appropriate structure of the deoxyribonucleic acid in their system. This metamorphosis type of thought process will take actions of light shifting, sensually induced details of function, the totality of brain grey matter, and brain chemistry. To simplify this aspect, one could conclude that due to human light perception, the supposed hallucinations enacted from light sources while under the influence of lysergic acid diethylamide are all manifestations of human chemical properties of the parallels of thought and dream fabrics.

You see, under the influence of this ergot-derived chemical compound, your senses will act in a cooperative action with your psyche, thus leading to more subconscious growth as to the understanding of universally balanced properties. Therefore, as your dream center is wide awake while under the influence of lysergic acid diethylamide, your senses and your fabrics of thought will proceed with the intricate topologic infinitesimal stitching, which is similar to the stitching of the air of our environment. This process will cause your senses to relate to each other through an assortment of a mixing type action, which will then lead to seemingly unattainable capabilities, such as tasting colors, smelling sounds, or any other combination of sensual mixtures.

Furthermore, dream and thought fabrics are effective on more factors than we are led to believe. Because sense perception is responsible for the way we interpret all of existence, these interpretations of the universal environment will always have a personal subconscious manifestation of thought, putting the given individual into either a good or a bad mood. Therefore, one has the choice to shape his o her destiny. This would be by either giving up and plunging downward or battling on and skyrocketing into a state of euphoria. I now must state that if anyone out there has experimented with lysergic acid diethylamide and had a bad experience from it causing them to stay away from this narcotic then that is in reality a good thing, because this is a dangerous substance.

Then, there is the precarious factor of what are called "flashbacks." You see, flashbacks occur at a time well after you have taken this drug. These flashbacks can take place years after taking this substance. For the most part, lysergic acid diethylamide flashbacks will be negative experiences. The way I personally view these flashbacks is that they represent a sort of mind photograph, thus being captured in a fragment of time from the past. In my case (and only in the case of very few others), a flashback can be from the future and this is due to an ability to achieve clairvoyance. It is true that the fabrics of our thoughts and dreams are always capable of time travel. However, in the case of a flashback, it is a fragment of time dependent on the galactic mind vortex of the universal equilibrium. Therefore, a flashback is indeed a time fragment and without sufficient tact of the proper balances of brain chemistry, only I and a handful of others are able to have futuristic flashbacks.

Okay, the death rate associated with lysergic acid diethylamide is pretty much unknown, but it is definitely nowhere near the death toll caused by that cocaine shit! It is true, however, that horrible fatal accidents and suicides have occurred in the past due to this narcotic. A peculiar fact that appalls me is that the United States government forbids the use of this drug, but the truth is that they have included lysergic acid diethylamide in certain research projects. Go figure.

At this point, you might be wondering how I became such a lunatic. Well, I am and always have been a lunatic, but I am a sane and high functioning lunatic who is capable of common sense. And, despite my lunacy, I will continue to further prove to you the realness of my vision.

Now, for some more data on ergot! Ergot is a fungal ailing of cereal grasses, most commonly being from rye. It is produced from ascomycota, which are any fungi from the phylum ascomycota. In other words, such molds are characterized by bearing sexual spores (there will be more on spores later). This creative function results in the manifestation of the claviceps purpurea, which is a product of lysergic acid diethylamide. Within the source of rye that puts this growth process into action, it will eventually lead to the forming of infected ergot resulting in sweet yellow tainted mucus, which comes out gradually in small droplets, similar in fashion to the human skin sweat droplets, which come out from the pores of the skin. This process is short in relative durations. Next, once this rye has completed most of this growth process, there will be a decrease in starch within this substance. In this case, starch is a white colored tasteless solid carbohydrate which grows inside of the small granules of the rye seeds.

Next, the ovaries of the female gonad will become imbued by what is called the mycelium. Mycelium is a mass of hyphae which forms in the vegetative region of the fungi. Once this is appropriately proportional, heat levels will occur in the spur like purplish black sceletorium and another stage is completed. The sceletorium is the source of substance which constitutes the growth of the ergonovine. Ergonovine is an alkaloid derivation of ergot, which can be produced synthetically. It is sometimes used to treat pregnant women. There is another product of ergot, called ergotamine, which can be used to treat headaches.

If a person were to take a quantity of any medications that are derived from ergot-infected rye, they could be inflicted with ergotism, a medical condition characterized by cramps, spasms, and rare forms of gangrene. Ergotism has a nickname, and this nickname is "St. Anthony's Fire."

Okay, did you catch that? The shocking factor to this process is that sexual resembling entities have to do with these supposedly non-sexual natural formations. This is all due to sexual spores or simply just spores. You see, a spore within the present confines of biology is a reproductive structure, that has the uncanny capability of surviving in seemingly un-survivable conditions, for extremely long durations. Spores come from plants, algae, fungi, and a selection of protozoan. A protozoan is a unicellular microorganism such as an amoeba. Interestingly so, algae is capable of photosynthesis. You see, sexual reproductive properties somehow are able to exist and be part of the functions of such plant life. I have come to the conclusion that since existences like ergot and other types of plant life do have some sexual functions within themselves, it is possible that mammals and animals could have grown from plant life. The growth process of life is constant and I even believe that due to my universal body theory, that any cell structured entity is either alive or partly alive. Even metallic existences might be alive. Remember, we have small quantities of iron and zinc inside of us, which promote our life cycles. This means that if sexual entities exist and reproduce within plant life, then there must be an Earthen relationship higher than any we have discussed thus far.

So, is it possible that the human race as well as other animals and mammals could have derived from spores? The other supporting factor is that spores also produce cell division. So you see, this cell division process is yet another contributing factor to the relationship between spore sexuality and animal mammal sexuality. Because spores create life in a somewhat similar fashion as animal and mammal sexual reproduction, it supports the basis of the scientific equation of (1+1=3), which can, in this case, promote physical light moisture mind expansion of the human brain.

Furthermore, if lysergic acid diethylamide can induce a metamorphosis of the human mind (Keep in mind the lyrics to Eyes of Jung in the collective subconscious segment) and lead to a comprehension of the three levels of consciousness, one could conclude that the sexual entities of ergot just might play a significant role in the intricacies of topologic stitching, in more aspects than just that of the human mind. This is inclusive of the universe, because everything we sense from the exterior world is processed by our brain, into our sensual interpretations. Cell division in the grey matter of the human mind can promote such achievements if the correct proportions of balances are set in place beforehand. And, do not forget that the chemicals of the brain in the way they react to the inner and outer beyond is responsible for the dream and thought fabric, which comes from its chemicals. There is a variety of classifications for spore types, but I do feel that my elaborations so far in this segment will prove to be sufficient for this particular aspect. Soon, we will relate this spore sexuality concept to the universal body and also to the mythical and supposed fictional paranormal phenomena of shape shift.

At this juncture, we will commence discussion on human DNA or, to be more precise, deoxyribonucleic acid. You see, human DNA is made up of extremely thin chain-like molecules found in every (considered to be) living cell on the planet. You must understand that string theory is related to this. The DNA of the human makeup serves as the director for the derivation of our growth, formation, and sexual reproductive processes. This is similar within the intricate actions of amoebas and paramecium.

There are slightly shorter DNA strand types, called genomes or genes. These genes help to transmit genetic characteristics from our biological parents. Most commonly, these DNA strands will be located in the nucleus of the given cell, thus the name deoxyribonucleic acid. These strands that exist in the cell nucleus are string-like, of course, and they are labeled as chromosomes. To give credence to the sexual entities in the life cycles of plant life and their incredible aptitude for survival, I must state the following: DNA strands can grow and thrive within seemingly uninhabitable bacteria cells. This is yet another supporting factor to the supreme balance of scientific relationships. It is truly amazing how life can persist under such conditions. This also resembles the persistence of time. Finally, and even more amazingly, these DNA strands existing in bacteria cells have no nuclei. This scientific fact further promotes those life cycles that have managed to thrive through situations such as the ice ages, volcano eruptions, and human industrial pollution. Once again, we see a supreme balance, and thus, another example of the universe and the human race achieving the utopian dream and becoming One!

Seeing that we are, as always, on the topic of oneness, I must once again show some more lyrics which have something to do with the totality my vision. Once I have displayed these lyrics to you, we will continue this DNA discussion in other means of scientific relationships. This will be another Metallica song, and this particular song was their breakthrough hit. In a conscious way, this song is about a soldier who was depicted in the classic novel *Johnny Got His Gun*. Johnny was a soldier who had his limbs blown off from a land mine and his final wish was to die and end his state of human struggle. This song in a subconscious way relates to human sexual reproduction (at least most of it, anyway). I now present to you track four of the *And Justice for All* album. This song will promote a collective subconscious oneness and it is appropriately entitled "One."

I can't remember anything, can't tell if this is true or dream
deep down inside I feel to scream, this terrible silence stops me
now that the war is through with me, I'm looking up I cannot see
that there's not much left of me, nothing is real but pain now
hold my breath as I wish for death, oh, please, god wake me
back in the womb it's much too real, in comes life that I must feel
but can't look forward to reveal, look to the time when I'll live
fed through the tube that sticks in me, just like a war time novelty
tied to machines that make me be, cut this life off from me
hold my breath as I wish for death, oh, please, god wake me
now the world is gone I'm just one, oh, god, help me
hold my breath as I wish for death, oh, please, god help me
Darkness, imprisoning me, all that I see, absolute horror
I cannot live, I cannot die, trapped in myself, body my holding cell
Landmine has taken my speech, taken my hearing, taken my arms
taken my legs, taken my soul, left me with life in hell

Touching, wasn't it? Anyway, back to DNA! Although human DNA is very small, it still consists of much within. Therefore, the vastness of the infinitesimal is a harrowing thought to try to fully perceive. There are thousands upon thousands of tiny chemical units within a single strand of DNA. These miniscule units are called nucleotides. Nucleotides are any of a pack of molecules, which, when linked or stitched together, will formulate the building blocks of DNA. These building blocks are exactly what the term says they are. They are the building blocks responsible for human anatomy. These building blocks contain what are called phosphates. Phosphates are fertilizing compounds, which relates to plant life. You see, this means that plant life, in containing sexual properties, and human DNA, in containing fertilizing properties, shows another example of opposite unions. This time, we have the opposite to opposite reaction of sexuality in plants and fertilization growth in human DNA. This is a connection of a fourfold quantity and, thus, setting into action a continued connection between these two types of life forms. Furthermore, they feed and breathe off each other. This is a secondary function to photosynthesis in its present state of scientific definition. This relation of sexual and fertilization processes between plant life and human life is also pertinent to a time flux alteration. Once again, scientific equivalency wins!

At this point, I would like you to ponder for a moment the positive and negative timeline chart, which I presented to you in the "Astronomy" segment. Now replace the positive and negative fluctuating lines with plant life, human life, and other mammal and animal life forms. If you process this thought correctly, you will realize that there is a backwards and forwards time connection of altering forces between this plant life, human life, and other mammal and animal life. This has everything to do with my theory that we have grown from spores and also to the fact that plant life, human life, and other animal and mammal life are dependent on one another for the process of photosynthesis and the exchange of sexual properties between these life forms.

Continuing on, the nucleotides are stitched in a topological manner, thus causing the formation of the chain-like molecules called polynucleotides, "poly" meaning many, and nucleotide being the paramount ingredient to human DNA. This leads me to the conclusion that polynucleotide are representative of a sequence of polynuclear entities (having a large quantity of nuclei) which exist within the makeup of human DNA. All of these polynucleotides contain the fertilizing compounds of which I previously and briefly mentioned. These compounds are phosphate fertilizer and deoxyribose, which is any of a particular variety of carbohydrates derived from ribose. Ribose is an organic compound which exists throughout nature. This process is furthered by the replacement of a hydroxyl pack with one hydrogen atom per unit. Hydroxyl is a chemical molecule containing oxygen and hydrogen within a covalent bond. A covalent bond represents a partnership of chemical molecular bonding by sharing pairs of electrons between atoms. This completed process will result in a base that will hold together in all conceivable methods of function.

Presently, it is believed by scientists that all phosphates are basically the same amongst DNA nucleotides. However, these bases vary in their consistencies and in their functions. Think about magnetism here! There are five classifications of DNA bases. First is adenine, capable of many biochemical actions and reactions, most prominently being cellular respiration, a set of metabolic (metabolism) reactions and other actions which take place inside organic cells. These organic cells will then end up creating biochemical energy. This is also a transfusion of breathable gases within an entity as such.

Next, there is guanine, which is derived from purine. Purine is another vital organic compound. Anyhow, guanine is topologically fused with cytocine, which we will discuss next. Cytocine is derived from the organic compound prymadine. It functions with singular carbon atoms that are topologically stitched by electrons, which are not coincided with single atoms or a chemical bonding of pairs of electrons between atoms as in guanine.

Next is thyamine, which always interacts with adenine and is said to originate from the last of these five DNA bases, which is called uracil. Uracil is a commonplace occurrence of a pyrimidine. A pyrimidine contains two nitrogen atoms, which act through a ring of DNA. Uracil is derivative of certain yeasts, discovered at the start of the twentieth century.

The arrangements of these five nucleobases are various and they pose a high multiplicity of existences. And, just like people, these nucleobases have their own individualities—the case in every organism which might possess these bases.

You see, DNA molecules consistof two polynucleotide chain types. These chain types are contrived in a double helix. A double helix consists of two congruent helices, both having identical axis to each other. A congruent helix, first of all, is congruent, which means easily pieced together by way of alterations of rotations and reflections. The action of a prism creating a spectrum can clarify this visual aspect. A helix is representative of a space curvature. Therefore, this at least partially explains the intricacy of DNA molecules as well as the coinciding behaviors and actions as related to the oneness of universal existence. In this case, the double helix will resemble a twisted rope, or ladder, or better yet, a spiral staircase. Once again, we see another example of an infinitesimal vortex within the realm of the universal body.

You see, the polynucleotide chains will be sufficiently formed on the outer edges of this vertical, spiral, and vortex-shaped entity. Each rung of this DNA vortex latter will consist of two congruently matching bases. And, finally, the chemical bonds, located centrally in these base pairs will hold these chains together through a bonding action. Now, once again, think about magnetism for a moment and relate it to the topological stitching of these DNA strands. Subconscious activity?

The complexities of the actions and the intricacies of this scientific formulation as well as others can easily boggle the mind. However, when simplified and related to my theories of scientific equivalency, connection, and the universal body, this thought process would aid the intelligence level of your personal subconscious.

Continuing on, these DNA bases are very specific in action, energy, and formation. A good scenario to get your mind into a coinciding action with how this process relates to a universal oneness has become evident to me at this point. For example, an adenine base applied to a single polynucleotide chain will always bond with a thyamine base of the opposite DNA strand, as guanine strand will always coincide with a cytocine base. Therefore, the sequences of these chain pairs now become fourfold and subdivided, and then multiplied formations of incredible scientific intricacies of relationship continues this process. However, the basics will always remain the same! Scientists have termed this as a complementary process, meaning coinciding to its same, yet opposite topologically stitched DNA formation. This concept, from my point of view when being related to my methods of scientific observance, leads me to such assumptions, but most prominently, this applies to my interpretations of magnetism and animal magnetism. Remember, everything is related not just because of scientific equivalency, but also due to the forces of opposite unions.

You see, prior to the completion of a cell structure, such as a stem cell's process of inner subdivision, there is much more going on inside of such cell formations than we would be led to believe. In the case of polynucleotide divisions, the actions of their inner cell division will form offspring of more newly created DNA strands. Polynucleotide strands have their own process and unique formation and in this case of subdividing properties, these DNA strands will tend to separate lengthwise, which makes perfect sense. The bonding factors in this simpler twofold division will release from one another and there, we have ourselves a new DNA strand by way of intricate infinitesimal subdivisions. This conceptualization further promotes the case for a balance of sexual properties, which may have originated in spores as well as in the life cycles of plants. And remember, the human body contains fertilization properties, thus, representing a two-sided hypothesis.

This entire process does represent scientific relationships of opposites and even of a time concept of backwards and forwards actions, which fluctuate along the naturalistic line leading to the noticing, understanding, and coinciding with matter and antimatter, opposite unions, reflections, as well as any other theories related to this. Time fragments such as a lysergic acid diethylamide flashback or a simple photograph will always be a form of a theoretical (yet one sided) centrifuge and this energy will never die, it will just change and shift in makeup and in appearance. I am determined to make it proportional as just so.

Wait, there's more! Once these DNA chains complete their vertical or horizontal division resulting in a split spiral, it will serve as what is called a template. A template is basically a scientific pattern. By now, you must realize that this book represents a pattern. Patterns exist in all walks of life whether in music, writing, or any of the creative arts. The result of the individuals art work will resemble their archetypical pattern.

You see, templates which represent patterns are responsible, at least in part, for connections of all energy sources which may have originated from DNA. To finalize this pattern observation, one could easily fathom how the patterns of a biological mother and father make their imprint on their offspring for the continuance of the life process. Now, apply this completed concept to universal existence and you, my friend, will have comprehended the basis for the existence of all life forms, especially the human race. Okay, DNA is the building block of life, which originated ages past and has promoted the existence of life and of course human history.

Lysergic acid diethylamide, from my point of view (if met with a balance of chemical proportions), can represent the building blocks of metamorphic mind expansion. Therefore, I have come to the conclusion that DNA (deoxyribonucleic acid) can react to lysergic acid diethylamide by way of connection, of course, but more so from a rigorous process of fusion infusion. This concept could lead to mythical understandings and other paranormal phenomena.

The basis of human growth is acquired through the human growth hormone. This is based on peptidesch consisting of short molecules which cause a repetition of our inner structural units of growth. Therefore, we have ourselves another example of connection. And here is the topper: human growth hormones and their peptide-emanated entities consist of an acid type, just as deoxyribonucleic acid and lysergic acid diethylamide do. In the case of peptides, you have what are called amino acids composed of functioning organic compounds which contain a good portion of nitrogen and a lesser amount of hydrogen. These compounds promote the complete life cycle function. What are called carboxyls are vital to this human growth hormone. Carboxyl consists of carbon levels humans are based on. Carboxyl does fall into the classification of an acid type.

Continuing on, in some cases, through the use of lysergic acid diethylamide and to aid the manifestation of personal and collective subconscious attributes, as well as an application of open mindedness leading to balances of human brain chemistry and the promotion of metamorphic mind expansion, which derives from the sexualities of spore life, which is represented by an opposite, which is fertilization properties within the chemical bases of the human carbon makeup, it is conceivable that through another alteration of light properties leading to connections from the vast infinite and infinitesimal and then fluctuating along the naturalistic line in the positive and negative energy type motion as well as the continuance of coinciding actions, it is possible to achieve human physical shape shift!

You see, although the human makeup is based on carbon, we consist mostly of water weight. If you think back to the discussion we had on lunar effects leading to a magnetic or gravitational pull on the waters of Earth's oceans, you must take into account the possible magnetic and gravitational effects on the water within the human anatomy, which could be affected in the same manner.

A mythological example of shapeshift is that of wolf and man. Most of you are likely aware of the old adage of human to werewolf lunar caused shapeshift. Therefore, before I elaborate any further on this mythological legend, I must present to you some more Metallica lyrics which relate to this concept. This song is off of Metallica's fifth, self-titled album, also often referred to as the black album. In the case of this song, its conscious meaning is the same as its subconscious meaning. So, I hereby present to you track nine of Metallica's Black Album. This one is called "Of Wolf and Man." Please enjoy.

Off through the new day's mist I run,
off through the new day's mist I have come,
I hunt therefore I am, harvest the land
Taking of the fallen lamb!
Off through the new day's mist I run,
off through the new mist I have come,
we shift, pulsing with the Earth,
company we keep, roaming the land while you sleep
Shape shift; nose to the wind
Shape shift; feeling I've been
Move swift; all senses clean
Earth's gift; back to the meaning of life!
Bright is the moon high in starlight,
Chill in the air cold as steel tonight,
We shift, call of the wild, fear in your eyes,
it's later than you realized,
Shape shift; nose to the wind,
Shape shift; feeling I've been,
Move swift; all senses clean,
Earth's gift; back to the meaning of life!
I feel a change; back to a better day,
Hair stands on the back of my neck,
In wildness is the preservation of the world,
So seek the wolf in thyself,
Shape shift; nose to the wind
Shape shift; feeling I've been
Move swift; all senses clean
Earth's gift; back to the meaning of wolf and man!

As far as shapeshifting is concerned, it is considered to be folklore. However, although rare, there have been claims of shapeshifting in history, which, due to this concepts farfetched outlook, is always dismissed as rumor.

I will now elaborate to you the story of Procipius—his secretive history and a description regarding the shapeshifting of Emperor Justinian the Great, a Roman Emperor who lived from 483 A.D. until 565 A.D. and who served as Roman Emperor from 527 A.D. until his death. There is much to the history of Justanian the Great, but we do not have time for that; therefore, this will only be in relevance to shapeshifting.

Procipius was a prominent historian and author of his era. He lived from 500 A.D. until 565 A.D. He was a well-educated scholar as well. You see, the writing of this mythological and possibly true shapeshifting occurrence of which I am about to tell you of was discovered in the library of the Vatican and it would be published soon after by one Niccolo Alamanni who was a Roman collector of antiquities. He was of Greek descent and lived from 1583 A.D. until 1626 A.D.

Legend has it that one night, in the Emperor's palace, men who were said to be pure in spirituality had claimed to have witnessed an abnormal demonic formation overtaking Justinian's being. An unknown man said that Justinian the Great all of a sudden rose from his throne and began to roam about At this point, his head disappeared while the remainder of his being continued to move about. Those who were in clear view of this occurrence were wrenched in fright. They began to think their vision was playing tricks on themselves. All of a sudden, the vanished head of Justinian the Great began to take its original form until his entire head and complete being were back to normal.

Another witness who was said to have been standing beside Justinian the Great had claimed that his face shifted into an amorphous lot of flesh. The features of his face were said to be meshed into a deformity so severe that he was completely indecipherable. Another witness claimed that Justinian the Great's face would once again return to its original structure.

Not surprising to myself, Carl Jung did some writing on shapeshifting. However, my conclusions about shapeshifting differ from those of Jung. You see, Jung was the pioneer of subconscious awareness and I am trying to be the last ingredient.

Continuing on, as far as the traditional werewolf-full-moon type shapeshifting is concerned, it is definitely folklore. However, as I have vaguely stated thus far, even this werewolf-moon type shapeshifting does, to some degree, adhere to scientific hypothesis. It has to do with internal fluids of the human anatomy being affected by the gravitational and magnetic pull of the moon. Remember, the human brain or any other brain type is composed of liquid chemicals which connect with light and dark forces via the mind shadow. This means that if we are able to expand the mind through inner and outer forces of balance, it must be possible to achieve the correct proportions between the equilibrium of mind, time, and space to accomplish such mythological phenomena.

Think back to the lyrics to "Eyes of Jung" which I displayed in the "Collective Subconscious" segment. Now, apply this metamorphic mind expanding process to my theories and the elaborations I just completed. You will see that within all existence, there is something about human senses and all forces involved which could clarify such a socially obsolete concept.

In order for such a process to make any sense, it must be executed with an application of all representations of time, including light, reflections, gravity, or what have you, to the concept of human DNA, as well as all of the other chemicals involved in the process of life. This type of my own personal thinking was induced by the taking of lysergic acid diethylamide.

It is now time for me to present you with another ridiculously simple scientific experiment about another one of my theories, which I am about to inform you of. This new theory of mine I will call the "Human Intestinal Time Flux." Okay, I have elaborated throughout this scientific portion called "The Monolith" about thought and dream fabrics and their ability to achieve time travel by means of basic human thought perception.

This dream and thought fabric time travel concept has led me to this conclusion: When your human body walks, runs, or transports itself in any way, you are traveling through light and, therefore, you are traveling through time. However, when thinking about your exterior features, this human intestinal time flux theory is difficult to fathom. So, see if you can catch the drift here. Okay, here is the experiment: stand up right where you are and make sure the room you are in has sufficient lighting; now, think about your inner large and small intestines and their inner darkness of a faintly and barely obscure red-blooded tint overpowered by darkness; now, walk a few paces in any direction and stop. Now, think about your inner large and small intestines again. Now, try to comprehend that your inner dark tainted red insides have just moved through a lighted room with no change to its inner dark and red taint; now, if you process this thought for a moment, you will realize you just achieved a very primitive form of time travel.

You see, anything that moves through light is traveling time, and when you fathom this inner reddish darkness being surrounded yet unaffected by the surrounding light properties, you could conclude the same result I have concluded. Furthermore, you have red lava within a volcano surrounded by light and to think that volcanic actions can actually form lightning, you could, in a way, compare this volcanic action to the intestinal time flux experiment I just presented. You see, your intestines are shielded from exterior light. Therefore, its properties are individual. This is an act of portable darkness moving through light, so this means that darkness moved through light. Therefore, this represents actions of opposite unions and thus, the achievement of a miniscule fragment of time travel. It's sort of an inner red shift, which we touched on earlier. I remind you that a red shift happens when electromagnetic radiation coincides with light and reflects off the redness of a spectrum. A red shift is an increase in a light wavelength of electromagnetic radiation, which will act with another wavelength emitted from the source of origin. So, you see, this inner red shift that can be comprehended through my theory of the Human Intestinal Time Flux represents an inward time subdivision, which will become equal with a time flux of an outward direction, thus we have a connection and a time alteration due to the scientific equation of (1+1=3). Get it?

There has been mention of shapeshifting in paganism or for lack of a better word, polytheism. Zeus, who was considered the God King and the ruler of Mount Olympus as well as being the god of sky and thunder was said to have shapeshifted into the form of Artemis (who was the daughter of Zeus) for his intent of retrograding Callisto who was a mother to the Arcadians, another group of pagan Greeks. Zeus intended to trick Callisto, so that he could prevent Callisto from turning into another form himself and carry out his sinful intentions. If you really think about it, all living things do shapeshift throughout their existence. For example, infants grow into adolescents and then, through the weathering of time, humans will become wrinkled and can go bald or begin to grow gray hair. Time and chemistry are two forces that bond in forwards and backwards type fluctuations. Tadpoles will turn into frogs, caterpillars into butterflies, and so on and so forth. Even the male sex organ shifts due to bioelectric instinct of the male sexual orientation. Therefore, I once again stress that if time can be altered through the personal and collective subconscious, then the chemicals of the mind, the outer reaching properties of space, and the totality of connection and scientific equivalency could grow into the norm.

Furthermore, sexual reproduction in spores and fertilization properties in humans, other animals, and mammals reveal that because of the miracles of nature, a connection of time fluctuation, when applied to these two opposite reproductive properties within these life forms gives force to the capability of shapeshifting, with a cooperative action to the natural course of time. When male sperm hits the egg of a female, two entities of opposite sexual being carry out the scientific equation I just mentioned of (1+1=3). So, I've mentioned this already—what of it? Well, the action of human reproduction represents a two-way connection of shapeshifting between sperm and egg into baby.

Astronomical existences also shift in shape. Take the birth of a quasar, for example, and the action of imploding forces eventually exploding into a supernova. Think back to the inner outer cell growth theory and apply it to this present discussion. If you do so correctly, this will further your understanding of shapeshifts within the properties of time fluctuations. Weather and time cause erosion, which could be considered a surface type of shapeshifting. The tectonic movements for the slow buildings of volcanoes and mountains are yet another example of shape shift. When realizing such shifts are dependent on time as well, you could term them as time shifts. You see, just as everything else I have discussed with you so far, one could assume that shapeshifting, when acting with the natural course of time as it flows within and without the naturalistic line, further proves the oneness of scientific equivalency. Try to realize that everything, no matter what the length of lifetime span involved is, will always adhere to the equivalency of scientific relationships. The mathematical advancement of topology can better an individual's understanding of shifts, connections, and shifting curvatures. I am most certainly not even close to being an expert in topology. However, I do have a natural ability to understand science and nature and their attributes of universal function. As far as the branch of topology that deals with sharp and acute angles of three-dimensional shapes, I have realized that this particular branch of topology represents the intricate infinitesimal stitching of universal existence. I also realize I have informed you of this already, but when trying to fathom a connection between lysergic acid diethylamide and human deoxyribonucleic acid, I have concluded that if the mind is balanced in the first place, this drug and our DNA will put into action the infinitesimal stitching between these two acid types and this is how the mind is expanded. The three dimensional aspects of the incredibly small domains of lysergic acid diethylamide will interlock and reverse in the same way a mirror processes light within the equally tiny deoxyribonucleic acid units and this can also be related to magnetic properties. This is an incredibly high multiplicity of subdivisions, which somehow manifests a comprehension of both the personal and collective subconscious. The more interesting branch of topology, in my opinion, is the part that deals with curved like shapes, which are more difficult to piece together in a process of magnetic bonding or stitching. The best macroscopic object or substance which could help one to envision this topologic branch would be clay. You see, one can physically alter the shape of a glob of clay, giving one an idea of what topology is. The defying aspect of curved type topology is the tearing process, required for making a hole in this clay. From my observations of this sector of topology, I have concluded that it is quite possible to make a tear or a hole in this clay or any curved object without defying the laws of topology. This adherence of a tearing action in a topologically curved object can be induced by the concept of fusion infusion. In this case (as in many others), the concept of fusion infusion is to be applied to the intricate infinitesimal topologic stitching of sharper angled shapes we just discussed. This curved object we are dealing with is curved, but the infinitesimal of this curved object (in this case a glob of clay) does contain shapes of acute angles within it, thus the capability of bonding. This fusion infusion process within this curved object will put into action a disconnection of the infinitesimal shaped entities, which make up this curved object. This disconnection causes a non-violent and cooperative tear to the object. This disconnection represents yet another opposite barrier. When this complete topologic conceptualization is fully understood, one can see that this process is of forward and backwards proportional actions of a time concept. This particular scientific action and reaction is connected to an inward moving concept of shapes as applied to time. The process of fusion infusion will be the centrifugal force in this case. All of this is done with the most simple of time flux concepts. Once again, scientific equivalency wins!

This topologic concept is paramount within the properties of lysergic acid diethylamide and deoxyribonucleic acid (DNA) as well as any other chemicals, which make up the within and the without of comprehensible existences. This is also a prominent force for connection. You see, the fabric of our thoughts and dreams, in having substance secreted from brain chemicals, enables us to obtain abilities beyond the normal realm of commonplace existences. If we are able to achieve new methods of thinking that are at least similar to my elaborations on the three levels of consciousness, we will move further into the correct direction: the destination of utopia and complete open-minded communications of human understanding.

Obviously, our thoughts and dreams can achieve shapeshifting. Furthermore, the mind shadow concept and its connections of light and dark forces are able to aid our primary senses to comprehend the sixth sense, which is composed of the six senses of the beyond. This is the correct method for a collective improvement of the moral senses of world society. The back and forth movements of molecules that determine heat levels could be classified as a beyond type of shapeshift. I'm sure you are already aware that the three forms of matter are solid, gas, and liquid. Water from our oceans, rivers, and lakes become heated by this molecular movement and these waters will shapeshift into steam (which is gaseous), rise into the air and manifest cloud formations and then they will heat and fall down as liquid rain. When these molecules are slow moving, water will become solid ice. In the case of the three forms of matter, gaseous matter represents one side, solid matter represents the other side, and liquid matter represents the centrifuge. The melting of sand or silica commences from the beginning of rock formations. Eventually, silica will be processed into glass and then it will be capable of reflection. Reflections are dependent on light waves. I personally consider light waves to be a fourth form of matter. Is it gas? Is it solid? Is it liquid? Well, it seems to represent gas formation more than the other two, anyway. However, I do conclude that in this case ,we are once again dealing with topology. This topology is emanated from the sun, thus connecting with dark energy and promoting the flux of existence and the equilibrium of mind, time, and space. You must understand that our senses can reach into the inner and outer beyond. Light and dark being opposites are the basis of inner and outer beyond. Through the existence of this light to dark universal foundation, we have substances that are always in the form of these three physical consistencies. Furthermore, everything reaches into the inner and outer beyond. This is the basis of all opposite energies moving within and without backwards and forwards along the naturalistic line.

Hey! It's lyric time again! This will be another song from the rock and roll scientific pioneers, none other than Rush! This relates to our present topic of discussion and I am sure you will approve. So, here is track six to the album *Presto* which happens to be the title track. So, here are the lyrics to "Presto!"

If I could wave my magic wand,
  I am made from the dust of the stars
    and the oceans flow in my veins
      here I ride in the heart of the city
        like a stranger coming out of the rain
          the evening plane rises up from the runway
over constellations of light
  I look down into a million houses
    and wonder what you're doing tonight
      if I could wave my magic wand, I'd make everything alright
        I'm not one to believe in magic
          but I sometimes have a second sight
        I'm not one with a sense of proportion
          when my heart still changes over night
            I had a dream of a winter garden
              a midnight rendezvous
silver, blue, and frozen silence
  what a fool I was for you
    I had a dream of the open water
      I was swimming away out to sea
        so deep I could never touch bottom
          what a fool I used to be
            if I could wave my magic wand, I'd set everybody free
          I'm not one to believe in magic
though my memory has a second sight
  I'm not one to go pointing my finger
    when I radiate more heat than light
      don't ask me I'm just improvising
        my illusion of careless flight
          can't you see my temperature's rising?
        I radiate more heat than light
          don't ask me I'm just sympathizing
            my illusions a harmless flight

> *can't you see my temperature's rising?*
> *I radiate more heat than light*

I am about to wrap up this "Lysergic Acid Diethylamide" segment. However, before we finish here, I would like to present one more lyrical compilation. This will be a very important original song, both a Deallegiance tune and a carried over Malicious Intent tune. Although I am responsible for most of the original lyrics in this book, I must credit this one to former Deallegiance guitarist Matt Kulesza. You see, when Roland, Paul, Dan, and I released the sole Malicious Intent album *Mind Control*, we failed to credit Matt on this album (which we most definitely should have). So, not only will I credit Matt for these lyrics, but I also dedicate this entire "Lysergic Acid Diethylamide" segment to him. And, also, seeing that Matt and I took this drug together countless times, this is the correct way to end this segment. This song was track six on the second Deallegiance demo tape entitled *Symbol of Transformation* and track two on the Malicious Intent album, *Mind Control*. This song is called "Lost in Time."

> *Fall with me come and see, the place where we will be*
> *can't you see the air in the trees, life like this will not succeed*
> *your mind is not flowing with our kind, are you sliding no you're blind*
> *Lost in time! Can you find my piece of mind?*
> *Keeping me, endless fight, tell me why I live life*
> *bastards from this land I grow, keeping me from what I know*
> *going through this endless task, beating you all so fast*
> *creeping into countless thoughts, tell me why you forgot*
> *you should know what you did, now you live for immortal sins*
> *preacher of the blackened band, live for hate as long as you can*
> *don't you know people understand, We will fight to save our holy land*
> *misery loves company, takes you down just as it takes me*
> *just because people are full of shit, doesn't mean you have to be!*

Okay, now that I have given Matt his due credit, I am ready to end this segment. And I am sorry if I got any of my friends in trouble from my suggesting to them the taking of lysergic acid diethylamide back in the day, but this was a long time ago and we have all grown up. You see, I used to be the Timothy Leary of Dracut Massachusetts and I experimented with quite a few people. There is one more note of reference, which I would like to interject before I close this segment. I would like to quote a line from one of my favorite movies. This would be a movie which featured Robin Williams and Robert Deniro. It is entitled "Awakenings." This was the story of a very nice doctor in a psyche ward who had discovered a medication that would revive all the elderly patients in the ward. For the entire summer of 1969, this drug temporarily cured all of the patients in this psyche ward. Unfortunately, this would be short lived and, sadly, all of the patients would return to their vegetative state. At the end of this movie, the doctor, portrayed by Robin Williams, stated the following: "The human spirit is stronger than any drug and that is what needs to be nourished."

So, the last thing I will say in this segment is that I do not advise anyone take this or any other narcotic. I am a sober person today and I am happy to be this way. Despite the fact that I am a slight lunatic, I am, however, a smart and high functioning lunatic, presently able to contribute to society. Once again, thank you for listening and, please, read on!

2001-2010

Welcome to the 2001-2010 segment. In this segment, we will discuss and I will interpret, through an application of my scientific aspects, a scientific vision of the extreme paranormal. This is the vision of "Something Wonderful" which I will attempt to prove to you through applications of connection and scientific equivalency and through the beautiful and fascinating imagination of my favorite author of all time. This is, of course, none other than the great Arthur C. Clarke. We will examine the Jovian (Jupiter) system, primarily the oceanic ice moon of Europa and, of course, the gas giant, planet Jupiter itself. You see, Jupiter has the potential of becoming a quasar by way of a cosmic process of implosion to explosion. Arthur Clarke, in being the genius that he was, had contributed much to the scientific community even as he had written countless novels. You see, Arthur Clarke had a vast and beautiful scientific imagination that he applied to the field of astronomy. Unfortunately, we lost Arthur Clarke in 2008 and I am sure the scientific community and all those who were lucky enough to know him miss him very much. Arthur Clarke was a British icon and he had achieved a multiplicity of worthwhile accomplishments. He was a commentator for the famous British scientific television program, "Mysterious World." Clarke also served honorably in the British Royal Air Force as a radar technician. Clarke was nominated for the Nobel Peace Prize in 1994. He served as chairman of the British interplanetary society in the late 1940s. Obviously, Arthur Clarke was a well educated and brilliant man, but Clarke's methods of education is identical to mine, that is, self-education. And, self-education, in my opinion, is the best form of education, because one can learn of his or her own interests without anyone interfering with his or her own educational outlooks. You see, because of the fact that Clarke was unable to attend a college or university, he needed to figure out a way for people to become aware of and realize that his brand of scientific hypothesis was well more than credible. As a matter of fact, it was downright incredible. This means that for those who are self-educated in the nature of science, as Clarke and myself are, we are forced to get our points across by more direct methods.

Clarke was so much of an interesting man that I must limit this discussion on him and start focusing on the visionary existences which are a result of Clarke's greatness. The part of Clarke's vision we will examine will be his writings, "2001 a Space Odyssey" and "2010 Odyssey 2." I must also credit the directors who made the movies based on these two novels. This would be Stanley Kubrick, director of 2001 a Space Odyssey, and the director of the differently titled sequel called "2010 the Year We Make Contact" Peter Hyams. These two directors would enhance Clarke's vision and these movies in some respects do differ from the novels. I would like you to keep in mind that Clarke was able to formulate this vision out of self-education, but he also accomplished his vision with the aid of his beautiful and open mind.

The premise of this vision takes place in the sequel of 2010 and this premise does adhere to scientific equivalency. This primal factor is the process of Jupiter imploding inward into a virtual black hole and then exploding, creating a new sun in our solar system. The existence of the "monolith" (which is the title of this part two portion) holds extreme significance to all universal existences. The monolith was mentioned in the "An Apology" segment, and if you remember correctly, you will recall that the monolith represents the centrifugal force for the entire universe. This monolith has within it the correct proportions to promote and continue the action of the life cycle of the entire universe. Is it a mirror? Is it a magnet? Is it both? Is it none of the above? Whatever it is we are going to find out!

When Clarke was writing these novels, he believed he was writing fiction. He would go about these writings with a subconscious factor guiding him along. I intend to convince you all that Clarke's vision of the monolith and a world of two suns even within the correctness of the most advanced concepts of the astronomical realm could be a reality. As far as I know, Clarke called these particular writings fiction, but he must have realized the sense of possibilities. Due to the fact that Clarke's supposed fiction does adhere to the correctness of astronomy, it causes me to wonder, did he know? Maybe not consciously, but in his personal subconscious, there was some kind of activity, that promoted such beautiful scientific outlooks. Clarke, my friends, is a miracle! Okay, before we dive right in to this vision that Clarke created and I hope to complete, I must give an account for more of the properties of factual science. Therefore, I will now give an assessment to the science involved in the stories of 2001 and 2010 before we can actually discuss the story itself. Once we are done, I will reveal "something wonderful!"

First, we will discuss solar energy and then we will examine black holes. I am aware that these factors were already mentioned and discussed in the "Astronomy" segment. However, in this case, I intend to directly relate more concepts which we have not yet embarked on to the complete vision of 2001-2010.

You see, this scientific discussion we are about to have is not only going to be applied to my theories, but it will also be applied to the visionary collective subconscious dream, that is shared between myself, Stanley Kubrick, Peter Hyams, and most prominently, Arthur Clarke. Enough with this jib jab, let's start to discuss more on solar energy.

Solar energy, in scientific terms, is a source of sun power, which has been advanced over a very long period of time. The other aspect of solar energy is the "literal" solar energy, which basically means energy from the sun. In order for me to get my point across, we must discuss both of these solar energy concepts.

You see, due to situations presented to us in our entrapment of the physical world, the essentials for solar energy in the scientific term are prominent, because over time, our requirements of electricity and the burning of fossil fuels has developed into extreme proportions. The new concepts of solar energy manifested over history have helped us promote positive contributions to the improvement of the world environment, especially in aspects of global warming.

You see, something called clean energy or green energy, meaning environmentally friendly, has become a necessary commodity, thus the want for the further promotion of solar energies and other related attributes.

This is especially the case in the United States and it is obviously due to our being uneducated to a certain extent as well as the common selfishness that has been built up in this nation, which I am guilty of myself. If you recall the discussions we had in the "Genocides and Foreign Policy" segment in "Politics" part one about the 1973 oil crisis Nixon was forced to struggle with, you will understand that since this crisis and its negative effects—not just in a financial sense, but also in an environmental sense—has since grown twofold. You must understand that although I was favorable of Nixon in some aspects, he did tend to pay more attention to foreign matters rather than domestic matters. The oil crisis was, of course, both a foreign and a domestic matter and please don't get me wrong Nixon's overconcern for foreign policy was good from a moral viewpoint. However, politics, like anything, else requires a balance. Therefore, Nixon, although trying to do the right thing, was nowhere close to being mistake-free, especially in domestic affairs.

You see, since this oil crisis, many tensions and vulnerabilities have formed—both politically and environmentally. One could conclude that learning from mistakes and moving forward is a better trait than dwelling on such failures, but because scientific equivalency applies to everything, we must aid it by applying our efforts to a solution rather than to a problem.

Due to what has taken place since the 1973 oil crisis, the science of solar energy has become a moral force for the achievement of an environmental balance. Solar energy has thus been dubbed by many as the power energy of tomorrow. At this point, most of you probably don't realize the potential solar energy poses. You see, because of the personal and collective subconscious equilibrium, we are already contributing as a people to the vision of the monolith, the still unexposed primary goal, and what I shall later expose, the "Big Boom" theory.

Unfortunately, money always plays a role, and most of the time, financial aspects render negative results. You see, money is the root of all evil, but in order for the societies of Earth to ever become a unified utopian society, the need for currency is unavoidable. Only through the current intentions of the Democratic Party can we achieve a fairer distribution of these finances. The negative financial aspect in this case is that it simply costs more money to supply the needed solar panels to transmit this type of energy than it is to continue burning fossil fuels. The truth is that there are certain corporate bigwigs out there who don't give a shit about the environment and they would continue to line their pockets with cash rather than save our precious environment for future generations. This is the truth! Corporate elites and t oil gurus don't care, because they will be long gone by the time our environment crumbles around us. Therefore, I now silently chant to all of my readers, "Morality over Technicality!" Little do wrongdoers realize that morality in being smart and everlasting will overcome, and the supreme balance of everything will be manifested.

The White House had solar panels during the Carter Administration, but Reagan would soon have all of them removed. To be fair to Reagan, the President of the United States does not need the this energy source, but world society does. To be perfectly honest with you, when it comes to Carter's and Reagan's outlooks on solar energy, I draw a blank. But you know what? Who cares? Let's fix this problem now!

Continuing on, all solar panels have the ability to access sunlight and transfuse it through what are called solar cells. A solar panel resembles a sandwich, where the top layer protects and the bottom layer is the base for the intricate actions and reactions that take place in this process. However, it is in the middle of these panels where the functions of this energy source are put into action. The silicon in these panels takes action when photons hit the distinctive atoms of the silicon. An amazing process is now being carried out. You see, when the photon hits a silicon atom, the bond is broken between the nucleus of the silicon atom and the surrounding electrons. Remember, a photon is a particle of an electromagnetic field and it represents a single base unit of light. Therefore, this silicon sandwich and its transmittance of a solar source directly relates to magnetic sources. This type of process will be applied to the Jovian system later.

Once the orbiting electrons of the silicon atom are separated from the nucleus, these free electrons will electromagnetically move toward the top silicon layer of the so-called silicon sandwich. These electrons will then electromagnetically travel along the metal conducting strips built into the panel. These electrons have now come together within microscopic proportions of distance and they act as a current along these strips. Next, this newly created electromagnetic current will continue to move across these solar panels until they reach small wire systems that are able to harness this conductive electromagnetic energy, thus transmitting this energy to your collective source.

As solar energy has grown, the ability to acquire more energy has been done through lesser measured sources of sun energy. In other words, you get more out of the emanating sunlight source. Fortunately, scientists that are in this field have been able to figure out a means for constructing these at a much cheaper cost. However, the United States Government and other governments abroad must confront the greedy and find ways for us to use this source, so that we can improve the state of our environment. However, once I have applied this concept to the Jovian system and some other astronomical facts, a connection could be achieved with the human race acting as a centrifuge.

Another problem is that, some time back, solar panels were too heavy to place on the roof of a house. This problem has been overcome due to the efforts of the scientific community to come up with lighter parts for the solar panel.

You may recall I mentioned AC/DC currents (and no, I am not talking about the legendary Australian rock band). Anyhow, AC is alternating current, which represents a wilder electric flow that moves backward and forward, while DC is direct current, which is less unruly and only moves in one direction. Solar panels only create direct current, which applies to things like wire conductors rather than batteries. Most of our homes today use AC, which can be conducted, yet it requires more thermal protection though is less costly than DC.

You must understand that the use of solar panels significantly reduces the carbon levels of our exterior environment. And by this point, you are already aware that despite the fact that carbon is necessary in the environment, too much of it would lead to an environmental imbalance. The human race, through industrial technologies, has emitted more carbon and other pollutants into the environment than by natural occurrences over millions of years. Therefore, because of the existence of a universal relationship, it is no longer satisfactory that we put off environmental issues anymore. If we do not take sufficient actions, weather conditions can, have, and *will* continue to affect the environment in a very bad way. However, this is not the environmental portion. I will try to stay on topic.

When we later deeply indulge into the Jovian system and especially the moon of Europa, we will discuss a surface structure attribute of Europa, called convection. It is not yet time for a Jovian discussion, but I would like to briefly touch on it at this point. You see, I must do so in order for the message of this segment to be correct in its application to the collective subconscious.

In straightforward terms, convection is the movements and behaviors of molecules within liquids. Once again (at least in my opinion), the scientific community failed to envision the oneness of scientific equivalency. Convection, in the scientific way of speaking, can refer to solids called "rheids" which are the result of viscous flows such as hardened magma and ice entities of unusual shapes, such as those on the surface of the ice-ocean Jovian moon of Europa. Convection can occasionally be applied to gaseous forms of matter. You see, convection has to do with the transfer of heat and physical substances in a behavior that is similar to, yet, quite different from, electromagnetic conduction. Through concepts of the paranormal, in relation to thought and dream fabrics or even manifestations of particle behaviors beyond the realm of the six outer senses, one could easily conclude that convection is much more commonplace than one would quickly assume. Just like in the lyrics to the song "Chemistry" by Rush when it says that everything is chemistry, more or less. This broader view of chemistry applies to the hypothesis that as far as the actions of physical chemical properties, convection ,although not being a constant in the chemical sense, does represent a good portion of universal activities.

As far as solar energy is concerned, measures have been made for the promotion of a more balanced environment. We are aware that fossil fuels, which ironically exist through the obscure remains of ancient creatures such as dinosaurs, has been over used and solar energy is one prime candidate for the solution of this world dilemma. Once again, we have evidence that morality is smart and that we must appeal to our moral senses, which can only be done by moving through the gateway of the collective subconscious and applying this new moral ambition to the equivalency of mind, time, and space. Scientific equivalency must prevail!

In recent times, the creation of a flexible type of solar panel has been accomplished. You see, these flexible type solar panels are less costly, but that is simply not enough. What needs to happen is (as I have already stated) to confront those corporate elites who are preventing this beneficial new energy source from growing and, hopefully, we can reach a point of agreement without any unnecessary tension.

I realize that the political segment is over, but I am compelled to state the following: as most of us know, a big problem in the world today is greed. You see, new energy attributes such as hybrid vehicles and solar energy are faced with this obstacle of corporate greed. If someone figured out a way to run a car on water or power your home from a less costly source, thus threatening these corporate elites to lose some of their money, that person could end up facing a conspiracy. You see, this person could be killed or immorally harassed for the duration of his or her lifetime. I am morally offended that greed can reach such ludicrous levels. I mean, these corporate elites are billionaires and we have people sleeping under bridges in sub zero weather. And then we have the audacity to call these people bums. These people are not bums, they are simply down on their luck and, like myself, many of them are inflicted with the disease of alcoholism.

You see, we have good Democrats, bad Democrats, good Republicans, and bad Republicans. The Democratic political ideology is much fairer to the poor, but many of them are insincere. I see it all the time. One of my democratic friends will say "Oh, we have to help the poor, they need our help, we must save them," and one minute later, he or she will point his or finger at some poor unfortunate hero and say "Look at that dirty rotten scummy loser bum." Yes, this is the same person that this Democrat is claiming to help. On the other hand, I have Republican friends whose political ideology is unfair to the poor but who take a few bucks out of their pocket to hand to a homeless person. So, you see, neither party is completely right, but I lean Democratic in the political sense. Therefore, in my social way of living, I continue to hang around with my moral Democrat and Republican friends.

I believe that the homeless are the way they are, due to their disapproval of society. Many of them have experienced devastating things in their lives, making them unable to cope with life's responsibilities. The Republican viewpoint in relation to this problem is that these people need to pull themselves up by the bootstraps and get it together, and this point is understandable. However, the Democratic viewpoint is more correct because not only does the general Democratic policy help the poor, it also aids the middle class. I am not saying that we should completely take care of the homeless in every way, but the creation of more homeless shelters and other contributions needs to be increased enough so these people can get back on their feet. I have known many homeless people having lived in Lowell and believe me when I tell you, most of them are harmless and all they need is some help. Maybe at this point, you can fathom my claim that communism was a good intention that simply failed. We cannot let our democracy fail in helping its civilians! The homeless have no effect on the economy. Therefore, even the moral Republicans will overlook this aspect and not help them in a politically supportive way.

I apologize for that tangent I just went on. We will now return to the topic of solar energy.

In relation to some other solar aspects, I would like for you to think back to the "Senses" segment for a moment. Remember the actions of a prism creating a colored light spectrum? Anyhow, I will now apply this concept to solar energy. You see, some solar panels use colors that have an effect on the actions of light wavelengths. There is a solar paint component called titanium oxide with a pigment of white paint. This titanium oxide is inorganic and it contains titanium and oxygen, thus its name. The action between titanium oxide and sunlight is a good example of color absorption. In this case, we have the color white, which, in certain definitions, is considered to be the absence of color. My main point is that in this case (as mostly all others), the properties of chemistry, light, and physics will form the relationship of solar energy. And remember, some rare forms of lysergic acid diethylamide exist in white paint pigments.

In the literal sense of solar energy, there is the concept of photovoltaics which is accessed through the use of solar panels. Photovoltaics refers to the conversion of macroscopic human frequency light waves as well as other nonviewable light waves, such as the ultraviolet, to solar energy. This is dubbed as an action of convergence, yet, when it is applied to subconscious activity in relation to our senses of the inner and outer beyond, it resembles or, at least, relate to convection. This process will result in conductive DC energies.

As for the general definition of solar energy (meaning the direct solar effects on our world), I believe that I have given a sufficient account for it and I have done so not just in this segment, but also in the "Photosynthesis" segment as well. Whether dealing with light absorption for the manifestations of colored objects or the processes of reflections, basic and complex photosynthesis, our senses, and even the forming of a rainbow is a supporting factor for the theory of scientific equivalency. The main aspect of this part of our discussion, which you need to keep in mind in order for you to fathom the totality of my vision as applied to Clarke's, Kubrick's, and Hyams' contributions, adheres to this theory and I will try to prove to you that through the collective subconscious, our sun is the nucleus of our solar system.

As I have stated already, the solar system is correct and balanced in the same way an atom is. Furthermore, the proportions of the solar system (and the universe) could survive a dramatic change, in the same way an atom is able to grow and coincide to a higher function within itself. This is the premise of my "Big Boom" theory. A balance of light and heat as affected by a molecular structure thus coincides with the chain reactions of molecule to molecule action. This is part of the cosmic balance which continues the universal function.

We will now move on to what I consider (and most others do as well) to be the opposite of a star. This would be the black hole. In the case of star and black hole comparison, we will see another example of opposite to opposite reactions of creation. In this case, we have an opposite union, which is quite different from a mirror reflection. The black hole type we will be discussing is that of the process of sun, star, quasar, or supernova birth. This is the action and reaction of a cosmically advanced fusion infusion process of a gas formation (such as Jupiter) imploding, creating a temporary black hole and then when the antimatter becomes too tight, it will explode and a star is born! However, we must be patient, because we are not there yet. As for now, we will commence to discuss the behaviors and properties of a black hole. Back in the "Astronomy" segment, I elaborated to you that a black hole is a centrifuge in all galaxies. I stated that the black hole is the center of the vortex-shaped galaxy. At this point in time, the scientific community believes in the hypothesis that stars are not born in a uniform fashion. This is due to limitations of human understanding, as to our scientific approach to the microscopic, the macroscopic, and the telescopic. Unfortunately, at this point, the true and ultimate universal relationship has not been appropriately compensated for. Remember, actions in many aspects to their relative properties affect colors. This is why a vortex galaxy, just like our Milky Way galaxy, has stars of different colors at different locations.

At this point, I will begin the hands on method comparing a normal galactic centrifugal black hole to that of a temporary black hole and its actions leading to quasar birth. In relation to Einstein's theory of relativity, it is believed (by myself as well) that a black hole is a circular region of space where the gravitational or magnetic forces are so powerful that nothing, including high frequency intense light, can escape its pull.

In the brilliant scientist Kip Thorne's book called "Black Holes and Time Warps," he referred to black holes at one point as skin pores. I am confident that Thorne, due to this hypothesis of his, has visualized my theory of the universal body. And also because of the fact that a black hole is impenetrable and that we should never go near one or we would decompose if we tried, supports the theory that a black hole could, in fact, be a skin pore of some sort to the universal body. Therefore, we are not meant to tamper with black holes, but we are meant to at least partially understand them.

Kip Thorne is an American physicist and astronomer who is pioneering in a variety of astrological concepts. It was through my readings of Thorne's literature that I was able to further my own personal theories. I especially appreciate those readings which led to the results of my two favorite self-made theories, which are connection and scientific equivalency.

In 1972 was the discovery of the distant black hole within Cygnus X-1. Not surprisingly, the scientifically savvy rock band Rush has a song called Cygnus X-1. This astronomical entity is estimated to be about 6,000 light years from Earth, and, remember, the speed of light is 186,000 miles per second! This means that when we look into the night sky, we are peering into the extreme infinite. And although the light from stars is moving away from us in its mass, the light they emit is moving towards us. Therefore, when you are looking through space you are not only looking through distance but you are also looking through time.

You also should keep in mind that Cygnus X-1 is in part a black hole, thus producing a robust x-ray source. From this concept, it can be concluded that through alterations of scientific concepts of time and distance, Cygnus X-1 poses a unique identity. Cygnus X-1 is also made up of the surrounding entities of this black hole, discovered eight years prior to its complete acknowledgement in 1964.

Furthermore, Cygnus X-1 is located in the constellation of Cygnus. This constellation is in the form of a swan. At this time, I see no substance of connection to this astronomical fact, which is why any scientific process keeps me in suspense. You see, Cygnus X-1 or any other astronomical fascination I have can be observed in a way that opens the human mind.

Cygnus X-1 in its totality is a galactic x-ray source. In the science of astronomy, x-ray pertains to a particular form or type of electromagnetic radiation. X-ray sources such as Cygnus X-1 and other similar astronomical bodies have a wavelength within the bounds of 0.01 to 10.0 nanometres. Basically, an astronomical x-ray source adheres or, at least, corresponds to light wave frequencies. Since the naked human eye cannot see these x-rays in the astronomical sense, they are like many other universal existences that are beyond the range of human sense frequency. Furthermore, in the case of astronomical x-rays, the scientific community did not fail to comprehend the relationship between the unorthodox frequencies of space x-ray waves, and our human realm of the macroscopic, thus the invention of clinical medical type x-ray process. I insist that the scientific community approaches more scientific aspects in this manner and finally succumb to the oneness of it all! This oneness is the theoretical key to a moral pursuit of technological advances.

You see, I gave this brief summarization on the celestial Cygnus X-1 to aid the promotion of relative concepts which support the correctness of scientific equivalency. You must understand that the concept of astronomical x-ray type emissions represent a relativity to vibrations and thus to sound. However, in the case of Cygnus X-1 or any other celestial x-ray emitting universal force, including the medical classification of the x-ray, it is produced through a vibration of light particles within a wavelength. Therefore, we have yet another promoting factor to the commencement of the three levels of consciousness and their intentions of origin. This hypothesis can aid the comprehension of the inner and the outer limits of the basic five and the outer six senses of the beyond, which represent the sixth sense in and of itself. So, you see, I simply used Cygnus X-1 as an example to a possible way in which we all could partake in, that would lead to universal contact and either directly or indirectly help us fathom why black holes and suns are able to put the opposite to opposite reactions of creation into motion for the continuance of the universal equilibrium.

The process involved in the examination of a black hole, in my opinion, can be at least somewhat related to the concept of directions within the realm of the third dimension. You see, we have north, south, east, and west, up, down, and side to side. If you really take into account the vastness of mind and space, including the conceptualization of the infinite, the infinitesimal, and the finite occupations of astronomical existence, it makes me wonder (in a sense) if there is any direction at all. Actually, there is direction, but when considering the vastness of such a concept, one could conclude that the mysteries of direction are similar to the mysteries of the black hole and its anti-matter.

Furthermore, any direction from anywhere in space could (when considering relative locations) represent any and every direction. This is on the basis that north to one celestial body could be west, east, or south to another celestial body. This applies to all directions, thus the mysticism! As far as our solar system is concerned, I do believe we are on a level plane, but the universe is vast, thus my fascination with direction. Anyhow, anti-matter from the human focal point is mostly unfathomable because it defies common sense logic. This defiance of human logic (at least to myself) relates to the previously defined directional concept. In other words, if nothing in our light side of the parallel universe is capable of penetrating a black hole, it must represent an even deeper concept as to the paranormal phenomenon of this direction hypothesis. This is a truism because we cannot—and must not—ever go into the direction of a black hole. Get it?

When speaking of my theory of the universal body, I stated that DNA strands (deoxyribonucleic acid) of the infinitesimal and the galaxies of the infinite represent a vortex. You might recall my elaborations in the magnetism segment of the experiment involving small iron fillings, a sheet of paper, and a bar magnet and its formation of a vortex. Well, this is due to cosmic macroscopic alterations. You see, magnetic field lines are vertical in relativity. Therefore, if a magnet can execute a fusion infusion action with a mirror, you have yourself a monolith. However, I am jumping the gun here, so I will avoid the monolith concept at this crux and continue some more relative elaborations.

Einstein was quoted as saying there is no such thing as absolute space or absolute time. Therefore, his hypothesis defied the gravity concepts of British seventeenth and eighteenth century physicist, astronomer, philosopher, alchemist, and theologian, Sir Isaac Newton. In my opinion, Einstein and Newton were both wrong and right!

Despite the fact that Newton was an astronomer, his theories of gravity were more correct within the macroscopic scale. This is obviously due to the limitations in astronomical studies in his era. Einstein, on the other hand, in his claim that time is not absolute is correct in one sense. You see, time is absolute, but when going into the outer reaching parts of the universe, time is not constant, it is altered. Once I elaborate to you what I call the Dream Fabric Universe, you will sufficiently comprehend what I mean. As for space itself, I believe it is absolute in distance, but not in frequencies of universal and cosmic existences.

As far as general physics goes, it is much more fathomable than the physics of distant space. Due to alterations of mind, time, and space relative to distance, the science of quantum physics was born. However, quantum principles are within inner and outer space and the general macroscopic human realm. This new science of quantum physics has led to good technological advancements, such as the cell phone. You must understand that due to concepts of the infinite and the infinitesimal, science itself is often altered. And this is the reason that relationships must be comprehended.

It is because of the intricate infinitesimal bonding and stitching topologic process that seemingly non-relative entities such as black hole antimatter, electromagnetism, basic magnetism, directions, and speeds will constantly produce change throughout universal existence by a method of unifying actions.

The concept of constant universal change is relative to what is called inertia. Inertia is the resistance of an object to alterations in the motions of anything and everything. Inertia, for the most part, is usually applied to objects. However, despite the fact that inertia represents the very basis of fundamental physics, it can also apply to other existences of the inner and outer beyond. Take, for instance, light vibrations, which do not produce sound (at least within human frequency) or the concept of thought and dream fabric which defies the basis of inertia and you will see that once again, the scientific community missed despite great efforts. I am a strong believer in the paranormal and I feel that my way of thinking could give substantial benefits for the achievement of a higher plane of scientific understanding. In the late nineteenth and early twentieth century, German mathematician Hermann Minkowski pioneered the application of mathematics to science. Minkowski died in 1909. At the time of Minkowski's death, Einstein's theory of relativity was in its early stages. By this point in time, Einstein had written some papers on his theory, but it would prove to be a strenuous and taxing process. You see, Minkowski was in part responsible for relating Einstein's scientific outlooks to mathematics. This would eventually lead to $E=mc^2$, as I have already noted; this equation and theory is simply that of infinitesimal energy entering into our parallel of existence.

You see, despite Minkowski being a mathematician, he was also fluent in the field of science. Minkowski thought of time and space as the outer realm of experimental physics as it was in his day and age. Therefore, he was able to promote scientific radicalism; he was quoted as saying that space without time and time without space would lead to a failure or a paradox, if you will, to the fabric of universal existence. Minkowski also stated that the unity of time and space preserved the human perception of reality. This leads me to conclude that Minkowski understood there was a universal balance. After all, it is obvious that space and time coexist and if it wasn't for the third ingredient to this balance, which is the human mind, the universe would be an incomprehensible static slush. I think Einstein might have benefited if he had paid more attention to the theories of Minkowski.

Isaac Newton, on the other hand, was also a pioneer. He was the first to state that gravity is the attractive force among large universal objects. It doesn't take too much intelligence to realize that objects fall from having an apple land on your head (which is the popular story as to how Newton's gravity concepts began), but it is much more complicated than that. Newton understood that types of matter and their densities would alter a gravitational pull, at least in miniscule measures. A good example is that certain objects can float in water, and when you consider gaseous matter such as helium, which is so light it rises, this concept starts to make sense. It is due to gravitation and weights of solids, liquids, and gaseous matters, which balance this factor out, thus leading to yet another example of balance. This example of balance sustains Earthly life cycles in a way of intricate bonding and connection. Even the weight of the Earth, the moon, and the sun as to their relationship to gravity promotes an even stronger case for scientific equivalency.

Think about this: When you fall, you cannot "fully" feel your weight other than the passing of oxygen and carbon dioxide around your body. From one point of view as to the aspects of direction (of which I earlier explained) if one was not able to see, he or she could seem to be falling upwards. Of course, in the science of general physics, you definitely are not falling upward. However, one must take into account that gravity is limited because at a certain point, you will reach maximum velocity. Velocity is a general rate of change of position for an object within a gravitational pull. Maximum velocity is the highest speed an object can fall within a gravitational pull. It is also obvious that you cannot fall forever, because gravity is a constantly altered universal force. If you were able to keep falling, you would eventually burn up due to molecular friction. Anyway, because gravity and magnetism are limited to a fluctuating and coinciding relationship as posed to the force of the given physical object, eventually, the object would hit the solid force of attraction.

Furthermore, gravity (as I have already said) is altered throughout existence. When this concept is applied to the equality of mind, space, and time, one could conclude that because gravity is limited and altered by its surroundings, the same goes for time fluctuations. Therefore, if we can alter gravity with human-made forces, we could also alter time. Therefore, the phenomena between stars and black holes are a testament to this hypothesis and the possibilities are endless!

One concept of which I wholeheartedly agree with Einstein is that gravitational time conditions adhere to physical objects being at rest on the surface of the Earth, meaning that the closer an object is to the surface, the slower the flow of time relative to the object. Time alterations throughout space are due to many factors. Most prominently, in my opinion, is the relation between light waves and that of dark energy. These two forces are responsible for the carrying out of the fundamentals of opposite to opposite reactions of creation.

I simply believe that if you can alter any physical object by either an inner topologic action or a basic fusion infusion action, it must be possible to alter time. Einstein believed that if one were to travel close enough to a black hole without decomposing and then returned to the Earth, he or she would have had to travel through altered light and dark energies and it would take a very long time. Furthermore, he believed that millions of more years would have passed on the Earth within this time frame.

If we presently had the technology to travel further into space, the avoiding of a black hole would be a very easy task. Although black holes are very massive, you would have to intentionally move towards one to become near it and no one is dumb enough to do that. Compared to the size of the universe, a black hole is (as Thorne referred to it) merely a skin pore. In relation to this universal massiveness, time is altered throughout and in terms of distance, a quark could be considered the size of Boston.

My theories could be applied to technical concepts, such as time warps. By technical, I mean theories which are already understood that did not come from myself. According to present theories, the universe permits an amazingly and humanly incomprehensible number of separate reference frames or coordinate systems of universal functions. Due to alterations of relative velocities throughout space and their adherence to their relative surroundings, the amount of time warps throughout is equally sufficient.

Another example of relationship is the space-time curvature of Earth and its relevance to gravitational and magnetic properties of the moon, and its pull on the world's oceans of which I briefly touched on earlier. Anyway, tidal moon gravity is directly affected by a cosmic fusion infusion process of multiple forces consisting of basic sensual existence and the existence of the outer beyond. The outer beyond has a within type existence which states the case for a higher concept of infinitesimal and infinite existences. As far as Einstein was concerned, tidal gravity from the moon and space-time curvature are not just related, but they are actually one and the same. Therefore, scientific equivalency says the same thing, yet a little more. What scientific equivalency says is that everything is not just related, but is also one and the same.

You see, curvature is a natural cosmic process. This can be directly related to my inner outer cell growth theory. Why does a bubble always form as a sphere more or less? Despite the infinitesimal topologic stitching actions, the prime shape in relation to inner outer cell growth is the sphere, and that is why many things take spherical formation, including a bubble. The Earth, however, like most celestial bodies, is not a perfectly symmetrical sphere. In reality, it is slightly oval shaped. This is due to space-time curvature and its relating to forces of gravity and magnetism. When processing this thought, it resembles a growth-shaping process, which fluctuates backward and forward within universal existence. In relation to Einstein's theory of relativity, as to relationships of size, energy, and forces of gravitational pull, one could conclude that because objects on the Earth are weak in weight as compared to the Earth itself, the equation of energy equals mass times the speed of light squared ($E=mc2$) could resemble the equilibrium of our bodies as they comply with the energetic gravitational pull as coincided with space-time curvature.

Once upon a time, black holes were referred to as Schwarzschild Singularities. Presently, a Schwarzschild Singularity is any of a variety of spherical non-rotating masses, either being a star, planet, moon, and, of course, a black hole. It was named for the late nineteenth early twentieth century Jewish physicist Martin Schwarzschild who, by the way, helped Einstein to enhance his hypothetical outlooks on the concepts of black holes as well as other scientific aspects.

My personal concepts of dimensions are likely the most primitive of all of my scientific outlooks. However, interestingly enough, Einstein, with the help of Schwarzschild determined that there could be seven humanly fathomable dimensions. At this point please think back to the "What is a Connection" segment and ponder on the concepts I presented related to the number seven and keep in mind the conceptualization of connection number eight. Furthermore, I am absolutely positive that my elaborations in the "Senses" segment hold significance as to the phenomenon of dimensions.

You must understand that if we had no senses, there would be no dimensions. We concluded that a sixth sense is comprehensive, because there are six senses of the beyond, most prominently the sense of time. Therefore, to further the phenomenon of dimensions, we must apply them to our range of sensual perception. The sense of sight can use prism for the manifestation of a spectrum. The thought process relative to the spectrum represents a boundary of connection that feeds human sight perception. In relation to this, concepts such as red shifts can be related to my theory of the inner intestinal time flux. These scientific outlooks pose an individuality that relates to dimensions unlike any other. This is due to their affects on distances of sight and the way in which we interpret such miracles of nature.

So, can the space-time curvature of Earth as related to lunar tidal affects relate to scientific dimension concepts as well? This question is easier to answer by straying from lunar tidal effects on Earth and comparing it to the vast outer reaching properties of space. The main factor would have to be that there is a constant change in proportions of size and distance throughout the astronomical realm, which, of course, alters many conditions, including gravity. Therefore, when the scientific community claims that on the surface of a star or a black hole, the conditions are so much more intense than on Earth, that when comparing Earthly energies to these stars or black holes, the results are mind blowing. A person on the surface of a black hole would weigh so much that he or she would be crushed even worse than a helpless bug under a ton of steel. Yet, in reality, one would burn up or decompose well before nearing the surface of a star or a black hole. Therefore, just because an ultimate balance exists through the theory of scientific equivalency, there still are universal situations that must be avoided. So, the universal flux of all relative conditions relates to the relationship between Earth and moon and thus lunar tidal effects.

The speed of light is considered to be absolute and limited. Once one fully understands the phenomenon of light, this scientific assumption makes a lot of sense. Light formations, such as lightning and humans, which, in a way, are lightning, promotes the hypothesis that there is variance in speed. Remember, we all coincide with light and dark, but the forces of light and its relatives, whether lightning or AC/DC currents, could never travel faster than 186,000 miles per second.

Here is an interesting thought! What is the speed of dark? Dark is the origin of existence or at least half of it. It has always been and it will always be. I believe that dark could be both still and fast at the same time. This is hard to comprehend, and many would dismiss this as nonsense, but if time can move backward and forward, we could conclude that dark energy somehow relates to the universal time flux. Anyhow, light could not exist without dark and one without the other would defeat all concepts of existence.

The more tightly packed a star cluster, the more intense are the forces within them, especially gravitational forces. When applying this thought to rocks or any other tightly packed matter, a common logic is presented. This logic leads to the assumption that a star does not explode due to gas pressures within. However, in the case of the planet Jupiter, which is dubbed as a potential star, it has a solid inner core, and some scientists believe that the inner core of Jupiter might actually resemble tightly packed diamond. You see, diamond is one of the most tightly compacted types of matter within the viewable universe; it could be termed as the opposite of gaseous formations. This is due to the fact that gaseous matter is very loose in structure. This complete Jovian observation is the basis for the possible implosion explosion and fusion infusion process for the birth of a star.

When Einstein's theory of relativity was in its infancy, the concept of implosion for star birth was in its pre-infancy stage. Therefore, in this era, such a process could have been termed as a theoretical astronomical zygote.

When pondering on the universal body theory, there is the obstacle of electron degeneracy, which could be viewed as defying scientific equivalency. I will not go too deep into the concept of electron degeneracy, but I will briefly elaborate. Basically, electron degeneracy occurs when matter is so tightly packed that electrons orbiting the nucleus of an atom are forced to degenerate. In simpler terms, this is a process of decomposition in a scientifically unorthodox fashion. So, due to my presentation of electron degeneracy, I must now defend scientific equivalency and tell you why this seemingly defiant process is a coinciding force. Okay, electrons as such seem to decompose and retreat from the nucleus. However, in reality, they are simply leaving their frequency of existence and thus are taking form as a completely different entity in another dimension or parallel universe. This type of electron behavior would lead Einstein to the splitting of the atom, for the inevitable discovery of nuclear chain reaction.

Sorry to say this, but it really burns my ass that this is how the scientific community comprehended a chain reaction. As you know, I have continually stated the case for other types of chain reactions that can adhere to weather conditions, magnetism, gravity, light, dark, or any of a variety of other things. Whether a chain reaction is due to opposite unions, molecular movement, or what have you, everything is due to chain reactions of relative forces. I love Einstein, but it is really dumb that we consider the smartest person to be the same guy who figured out how to blow up the world. It is a damn good thing that chain reactions, whether from molecule to molecule or atom to atom, will eventually lessen in strength, because if chain reactions were continuous with no restrictions, Einstein could have blown up the entire universe!

Please don't get me wrong, Einstein was a brilliant man, but the reason he is considered the smartest person is that he is one of the most recent of super-geniuses in world history. I believe that Huygens, Jung, and Minkowski were all smarter than he was. You see, many others have contributed to science over history.

Furthermore, Einstein (as previously stated) needed to get the ball rolling for the Manhattan Project which, surprisingly, he was not a part of. This was imperative as to the need to deal with Hitler!

Because of constant fluctuations in aspects of science as posed to chain reactions, the full concept of a chain reaction is more complex than what I have elaborated so far. You must understand that x-ray photons have a unique type of intensity and frequency. These x-ray photons are humanly comprehensible, but they are not within the visual boundaries of human optical perception. Because of the sense of possibilities and the realization of an ultimate relationship, this concept poses the complexities of reactive actions to light, dark, or anything else you can think of. At this point, scientific equivalency is altered and, thus, time is also altered.

Interestingly, even in the case of absolute zero degrees Kelvin, the temperature when molecules are still and cold has reached its limit, the electrons within these molecules are still active but are considered degenerate. This hypothesis was concluded through the quantum sciences. This represents another opposite to opposite reaction of creation as well as the furthering of infinitesimal actions. The fact that x-ray photons are beyond human sight perception frequency and that they are more energetic promotes this scientific assumption.

Another interesting fact is that when matter is denser, its cells will be lesser in size. This somehow causes a shorter electron wavelength, yet, at the same time, a higher amount of energy is within these same electrons. This is a primal hypothesis, when attempting to understand concepts of infinite and infinitesimal properties. This also supports my outlook on Einstein's theory of relativity in saying that it is relative to emitted infinitesimal energy. This also relates to the speeds of electrons and the behavior of the centering nuclei.

This concept also applies to the size of stars, thus supporting my theory of the universal body. You see, if a star is less than 1.4 the mass of the sun, the behavior of the given star is altered. Most prominent, the gravity of a star if under the boundary of 1.4 is differentiated in its balance of makeup as well as actions of energetic forces. This is the common range of size for white dwarf stars. Therefore, the intensity of energy within a star compared to its size and level of compaction will determine its balance of force, just like an electron! The universal body wins another one!

You see, because gravity tends to overpower solid inner pressures, in some cases, a star can implode. I cannot prove it, but I do feel that it is more common or at least more likely for a gas giant like Jupiter, which has a solid and compacted inner core, to be more likely to implode.

Therefore, the process of quasar birth is appropriately compensated for. You see, protons are way heavier than neutrons. These cellular bits of energy give opposite type charges and they coincide with one another for the promotion of an opposite union. However, types of stars like super giants, for example, as compared to white dwarfs may pose similarities to this process, thus further promoting the theory of the universal body. The most vital aspect to be comprehended in this case is that protons and neutrons, super giants, and white dwarfs fluctuate along the naturalistic line in an identical fashion as all types of positive and negative energy. It has been more common for scientists to compare stars to atoms rather than the comparison method of which I just presented. However, this brand of comparison has been existent for some time now.

Indian born American astrophysicist Subrahmanyan Chandrasekhar and Swiss astronomer Fritz Zwicky believed in this type of comparison. The fact that all concepts of microscopic, macroscopic, and telescopic objects are not considered relative to the appropriate extent within the scientific community weakens the scope of scientific potentials. Furthermore, this method of hypothetical thinking in relation to the universal body could reap substantial benefits. We must keep in mind that morality has to be applied to such endeavors in order to avoid negative necessities such as the Manhattan Project.

Due to scientific conceptsstemming from the observance of nuclei structures and the surrounding charges that lacked a moral foundation, bad discoveries of nuclear proportions have been manifested. However, positive breakthroughs as to the behavior of black hole antimatter have led to worthwhile discoveries. The concept of what is called superfluidity is a good example of a beneficial breakthrough. Superfluidity is the study and observation of the phases of matter relative to heat conductivity within liquid types. Then there is superconductivity, the study and observance of the within of materials at low temperatures induced by slow molecular movement. What is called magnetic resonance imaging is another positive scientific attribute. This magnetic resonance imaging is a medical technique used in radiology to examine the interior of human anatomy. This is an advanced type of medical x-ray process. Transistors and laser technologies have also advanced from this brand of scientific observance.

Continuing on, some members of the scientific community believe that the sun might contain small neutron stars within its center. This concept relates to my theory of inner outer cell growth in pertinence to energies of the within. The Earth has been around for a very long time and it will be around for an even longer time (hopefully). Einstein's splitting of the atom or nuclear fission was considered a breakthrough, but it was an unnatural breakthrough that could deter the naturalistic line and its actions of fluctuating sources. Our sun must not go through a process of fission because if it did, it would not only defeat scientific equivalency, it would also defeat life as we know it. Therefore, I must once again state that we must proceed with caution. Mistakes of the past can be used as virtues of a collective learning of valuable moral lessons. Scientific equivalency must win!

Another potentially positive accomplishment of the scientific community was the discovery of what is called "kinetic energy." Basically, kinetic energy is the extra energy an object gains from a process of motion. Kinetic energy can aid us in the further comprehension of the inner outer cell growth outlook, including other aspects of the inner and outer universal conceptions. This is because it represents a seemingly unreachable level of understanding only achievable through motions. You see, everything in the universe is in motion. Therefore, kinetic energy may be partly related to the theory of relativity in a very general manner. From the way I interpret the theory of relativity as an entrance of infinitesimal energy, it leads me to realize that everything is energetic, including deoxyribonucleic acid.

If our sun does contain a neutron inner core and if it takes up a good quantity of the sun's mass, it would have a gravitational effect and the core would grip the outer layer of the sun (the lithosphere) very tightly. Therefore, the constant exchange of energy from this core moving outward would lead to interesting fluctuations of energies emitted from the sun. The circumference of the sun may be deceptive as to its behaviors and emissions of energetic forces.

The nuclei are vital for the balance of universal energies. Whether referring to the nucleus of an atom or the relative quasar nuclei, the emanated forces from nuclei are always constant and determine a multiplicity of universal actions and reactions of formation, thus supporting the universal equilibrium.

Although I have stated my case for Jupiter quasar birth by implosion, the truth is that most think that star implosion is most requisite when a star is more massive than two suns. Of course, Jupiter's pre-quasar status and its actions as such are different from the time frequency of star implosion, but they are both related in aspects of actions and reactions. Furthermore, I believe it is possible that in the vast realm of the telescopic, such potential star births that could be similar to Jupiter's potential are either non-viewable or they represent a separate alteration of space-time fluctuation.

It is also theorized that nucleons (protons and neutrons) will dissolve (like salt in water) in case of star implosion. As for any dissolving process—whether occurring in the macroscopic, the microscopic, or the telescopic scale—it will represent star implosion, similar to decomposing nuclei in an astronomical action as such.

You see, these dissolved entities, regardless of their physical form, are made from a process of infinitesimal change. These dissolved particles will enter into another parallel of existence, which gives credence to my inner outer cell growth theory as well as my theory on reflection.

I have also determined hypothetically that when a spherical star implodes, thus emitting its nuclear fission, there is a process of anti-fission, which could implode endlessly. Therefore, an intricate infinitesimal phenomenon exists due to this implosive action. This process seems to be less common from Jupiter's pre-quasar potential and it is claimed to be more common throughout space, but from my point of view, it is less natural. This process of star death by implosion will cause ejected particles to leave this universe and gain entrance into another. Keep in mind the reflection process of opposite to opposite reactions of creation, which originates from two sources of light. If you process this thought correctly, you will fathom a parallel two suns connection.

A star implosion will release what are called shock waves, waves that have the ability to travel through solids, liquids, and gases. This process has interesting effects on magnetic fields. The implosive action releases a reversed theoretical explosion of shock waves, which resembles the process of a star's physical structure moving away as the emitted starlight moves towards us. At this point, you will comprehend that implosive action and the reverse moving waves fluctuate from one parallel universe to the next. This concept can also be applied to naturalistic line fluctuations.

Furthermore, shockwaves (in our parallel of the universe) which are virtually harmless to us could be capable of destruction or harmless functional explosion in the next parallel universe. This is a chain reaction of entering and leaving forces from parallel universe to parallel universe; this chain reaction acts in reverse between each parallel. Therefore, one could apply implosion and shockwave emission to an opposite to opposite reaction of creation.

As for the more easily comprehended actions of explosion, which are contrary to implosive nuclei, the nuclei will always be the force of origin. Two of the most explosive substances are plutonium and uranium and it is no coincidence that the nuclei within these metallic types are very heavy such that if they go through a fission process, a nuclear chain reaction will be put into action.

There is a wide variety of explosive metallic types capable of catastrophe. A catastrophic explosion will not coincide with its parallel in aspects of implosions emitting shock waves. Therefore, the mistake of a nuclear war could not just destroy us, it could also damage the parallel world in the next parallel universe. Once again, we see that the number one priority must be morality. It's kind of like the classic television show "Star Trek" where technology is used for the positive aspects of humanity.

It is common for imploding stars that are of a comparatively small mass to trigger a supernova explosion. On the other hand, when a massive star implodes, its compaction, its nuclei, its emission of shock waves, as well as emissions of radioactive matter can and will result in a black hole. If you really think about this star comparison and their processes of implosion and explosion, you could conclude that there is an opposite union of relations acting between these stars relative to their sizes and intensities.

When applying mathematics to black holes, those who are academically fluent in both science and math could deeply indulge in black hole phenomenon. You see, black hole mass, tempo of rotation, and its negative electric charge when applied to either physics or mathematical equations can lead to the appropriate comprehension of the dimension and physical structural makeup of a black hole.

The scientific study of what is called metaphysics poses some interesting factors. Metaphysics is the application of blunt realities to the transcending and seemingly unorthodox nature of scientific actions and reactions. Metaphysics is extremely fundamental, yet, due to its simplicity, it has reaped many attributes to the scientific community. Metaphysics has been around since the days of Plato and since that time, it has been a fundamental asset to scientific advancement.

Continuing on, there are certain astronomical gaseous forms of matter, which, due to their tightly compact molecular makeup, can behave like a thick liquid or even a solid. Although these gas formations are not compacted in the common physical sense, they are compacted due to physical behaviors within themselves. A gas type as such can promote further comprehension as to the infinite and the infinitesimal. These gas formations are so intense that light forces near or within human frequency have a very hard time passing through them. However, cosmic x-rays, which are fathomed through the senses of the beyond are able to penetrate these distant unorthodox gaseous matters. This observation simply proves that fusion infusion is indeed the process of universal creation.

You see, when x-rays of the cosmos are applied to the use of advanced telescopes, it aids astronomers in spotting previously non-viewable celestial bodies such as black holes and quasar pre-black holes. You see, a diffusion process occurs in outer space where gaseous forms of matter seem to cleanse (more or less) star clusters within galaxies.

Here is something interesting! Radio and x-ray waves are termed as opposites by the scientific community. Allow me to explain. X-ray waves, in the cosmic sense, represent electromagnetics and electromagnetic distribution. Radio waves are also electromagnetic, but their wavelengths are much longer.

So, if these two astronomical energy sources are so similar, why are they termed as opposites? Through my elaborations so far, you may have come to your own conclusion, but here is mine: the main opposite boundaries between these two wavelength types have to do with what is called wave particle duality. This duality concept has to do with the wave like and particle like properties. Within these wave types, their particle makeups and behaviors represent seemingly opposite boundaries. Just look at it this way: On Earth, we have learned much from the observing x-rays and invented medical x-rays: radio waves, on the other hand, can access satellites with more ease than x-ray waves, and this is responsible for radio frequencies, which we listen to in our cars or in our homes. In conclusion, x-ray waves, although not within basic human sight perception, are used for visual aid. Radio waves, on the other hand, are used for sound perception. This leads me to believe that just like everything else, these two wavelength types help us peer into the inner and outer beyond, thus aiding the human senses to a better understanding of a collective subconscious manifestation. There are definitely connective boundaries separating these wavelengths and they promote the correct proportion of human understanding as it fluctuates along the naturalistic line. All aspects we have discussed thus far have led us to this momentary connection. Do you think you know what the primary goal is yet? You shall soon see!

When a galactic centrifugal black hole spins with its antimatter, it causes or, at least, contributes to the continuance of a vortex chain reaction of universal motions. This vortex will produce high levels of magnetic and gravitational forces. The lines of a magnetic field, in some cases, will become restricted and stray from their usual formational methods. This process will emit some plasma, but this black hole centrifuge or skin pore will aid star motions, thus contributing to more scientific alignments than one would quickly assume. Therefore, an opposite entity gives an opposite energy, which shapes the galaxy just so.

This concept is still not fully understood, and the action of this black hole centrifuge is also presently not completely compensated for. However, through further revelations of opposite unions, this concept can be completed with a thorough logic. Magnetic fields and their pulling actions do not immediately resemble a general physical object. However, the reality is that throughout space, magnetic fields (as well as all other properties of substance and action) can be altered. Certain wave types can move astronomical magnetic fields as if they were an object. Due to processes of fusion infusion throughout the universe, seemingly illogical behaviors to us will occur throughout space and this is yet another astronomical balancing factor.

A good example of seeing something that can appear to be unbalanced is the observance of what is called stroboscopic effect. Stroboscopic effect is a type of optical illusion induced through movements. Take the wagon wheel effect, for example. This wagon wheel effect can occur by way of staring at a rotating spoke wheel. After a while you will not be able to decipher whether this spoke wheel is moving backward or forward.

An even better example of this brand of optical alteration can be observed through a strobe light. When a strobe light flashes on and off quickly in a darkened room, your movements will appear as a virtual fastpace slide projection. It also gives the illusion that your movements are skipping through fragments of time. Due to the strobe light induced optical effect of making still or moving objects appearing as fragments of time, the presently unexposed primary goal is made possible. If an alteration of light fragments and time fragments can cause this optical illusion, then it must be possible to alter time fluctuations in a more in-depth way. Light, in being a vital ingredient to time, represents time itself. Furthermore, if a strobe light can flash on and off in a dark room as such, it must be possible that our physical motions within this visual effect are actually traveling through time in an obscure and fragmented way of method. This stroboscopic effect exists throughout space, but it always acts and reacts within the given time fluctuation of its universal location.

In order for the naturalistic line to carry out its role for the natures of existence, time must move in unison with infinitesimal matters such as atoms and quarks. It is possible that our human time concept originates from the within, more so than from the exterior. You see, the closer we are to Earth, the more logical and comprehensible is our concept of time as we humans understand it. The fact I have already elaborated is that time is constantly altered throughout space and in order for human time concept to remain as such and maintain its essential balance with universal time, the motions of our solar system as well as the oscillations of atoms and quarks must continue to coincide with our position of universal flux and thus give us our down to Earth and logical relation to time.

Furthermore, this paranormal and universal balance of time fluctuation is directly related to the capability of black hole antimatter (located on the horizon of a black hole) to conduct electric charges. Due to antimatter being the least humanly comprehensible substance of the known universe, the fact that it can act as a conductor supports the hypothesis that time is always uniform with its dimensions of environmental relations.

The outlook of this black hole conduction action is quite confusing when applying it to Ohm's Law. You see, Ohm's Law is usually applied to electric circuits within a given proportion of outcomes. Whether dealing with AC or DC current, Ohm's law is literally "down to Earth," and the fact that spherical black hole conduction can coincide with Ohm's law is amazing. However, this coinciding action is carried out in an opposite fashion. You see, in a conductor, the electric charge will meet its destiny in the same form. On the other hand, black hole antimatter conductive energy, which is in the infinitesimal of the universal body and the infinite of our perception of the universe, is simply a testament to the complexities of the cosmos and its functions.

In the case of an infant black hole, which has been manifested from interior implosion, it will, at first, consist of cold temperatures just above absolute zero. This makes perfect sense, because black holes cannot emit any forms of light. Therefore, they are dense and black, thus its inability for fast molecular movement for the production of heat.

I believe that there is another side to a black hole, possibly an exit for universal body or an entrance into a parallel universe. Anyhow, the other side must obtain the capability of an opposite coinciding action in order to adhere to the scientific laws and functions of the universe.

This type of black hole has been and still is going through a process of evaporation. As one of these black holes begins to diminish, its temperature will rise. Over an incredibly long duration consisting of eons of time, an evaporating black hole will eventually become so tightly compacted that it will explode violently. This process is contrary to the potential of the Jovian (Jupiter) implosion explosion process for quasar birth. However, by comparing the properties of both of these scientific dilemmas, one could come to further conclusions.

At the point of an evaporated black hole explosion, the temperature could reach up to 100,000 trillion degrees. And from this action, some kind of universal time flux connection could lead to the contrary process of Jovian star birth, which could multiply and subdivide many concepts, especially concepts of reflection. The "Big boom" theory of which we will soon discuss is based on this premise.

The concept of parallel universe was formed well before my reflective theories were personally contrived. It has been claimed in recent past that when a black hole contains a very strong electric and magnetic field, it could result in another explosive process. And, of course, I theorize that this is related to parallel existences. As I said, an implosion to us could be an explosion to the parallel universe, and vice versa. The simple fact that certain celestial bodies are capable of both implosion and explosion supports, through its intricacies of action, the concept of parallel universes.

I have often mentioned the science of topology within the infinitesimal and somewhat in exterior existences. When applying topology to black holes or any of a variety of interstellar objects, topology, for the most part, will be concerned with connections of infinitesimal fusion infusion actions rather than forms of shape within the infinite, whether curved or acute.

A prime example of this topological concept can be observed in a simple way using water in a glass. Water has no exterior shape, but when it is in a glass, it takes the shape of the glass. This is an example of a topologic equaling action. The former martial arts expert Bruce Lee was quoted as saying that water has no shape until it reacts to a structured surrounding and then he stated "be water." Ironically and unfortunately, Bruce Lee died the day before I was born. This was a good concept of Lee's, but he was not fluent (as far as I know) in the properties of black holes. So, let's move on! Moving on, I have already drilled it into your head that we must apply morality to all of our endeavors in the realm of the sciences. This repetitiveness is, however, quite necessary. You see, a paradox could be termed as a compression process, which defies the intuitive functions of nature. In order for us to avoid this unnatural compression of imbalance, the human race, through a collective subconscious manifestation, needs to come to its senses and commence to care!

Due to the existence and the need to sustain the actions and reactions of the naturalistic line, it is imperative, because it sets into motion the uniformity of the rotation and axis of all universal components. When a force of alteration is applied to any actions of universal objective existences, the velocity which relates to its level of magnetic or gravitational pull will lead to a virtual metamorphosis, thus maintaining the universal equilibrium and causing massive celestial bodies to become inadvertent and proportional as to their roles in the universal process.

Remember, magnetism and gravity are related, but they do pose their own differential boundaries. Gravity is the attractive force between two celestial bodies; a magnetic field is more altered. It represents both pulling and repelling type forces. All objects affected by these two forces will (as anything else), behave and react to its inner and outer makeup.

At this point, we will continue this one-way conversation and begin to discuss the number one celestial body in our solar system that could be considered capable of life. This would be none other than the Jovian ice-ocean moon of Europa.

We will start with a brief assessment of the Jovian system. Jupiter has sixty-three confirmed moons, a higher tally than any other planet in our solar system. There are four major moons, called the Galilean moons. The name Galilean refers to seventeenth century Italian physicist, mathematician, astronomer, and philosopher Galileo Galilei. Galileo discovered these four Jovian moons on January 7, 1610. The names of the four Galilean moons are: Io, the violent volcanic moon, Europa, the ocean ice moon, Ganymede, which is the largest moon in the solar system (bigger than planet Mercury), and, unlike any other celestial body in our solar system, Ganymede has a magnetosphere, which of course consists of magnetic field lines. Despite the fact that Ganymede is larger than Mercury, it is less dense, thus, it is less massive than Mercury due to its proportions of compaction. Finally, there is the moon of Callisto which is the second largest Jovian moon and the third largest moon in the solar system. Callisto is made up primarily of ice and rock.

Well, I said we would discuss the moon of Europa, so let us commence to do so. The name Europa is derived from a Phoenician noblewoman said to have been courted by the pagan god Zeus. She would, eventually, become the Queen of Crete.

Despite the fact that Europa is the smoothest celestial body in the solar system (due to its icy surface structure), it has a detailed surface structure that has some rigid ice formations. It is the supposed ocean under the icy crust that has led the scientific community to believe that Europa is the prime celestial candidate in our solar system capable of supporting life. The behavior and structures of the icy crust examined have led to a scientific fascination of Europa's potential. Due to inner heat, the supposed ocean under the ice exists.. We will now indulge in an in-depth analysis of the features and actions of this Jovian moon and see just what can be figured out through an observation.

In relation to Europa, I must first briefly account for the super giant gas planet Jupiter. The planet Jupiter is estimated to be 300 times the mass of Earth. Because of the distance between Europa and the sun, it is theorized that Europa took was formed from rock and water. The sun is approximately ninety-three million miles from Earth while Jupiter is roughly 483.6 million miles from the it. The Jovian system is further from Earth than the sun is. If Jupiter were ever to live up to its pre-quasar status and commence the implosion explosion process to take the form of a second sun, the proportions of distance in relation to an inertia factor would have to alter the proportions of distances in the same manner an atom can form into other atom types. In the simplest of terms, this process would have to adhere to scientific equivalency.

As far as the present relationship between Jupiter and Europa is concerned, Jupiter acts in a similar fashion to the Earth and the moon in terms of tidal affects. You must understand that our solar system acts like an atom, with the sun acting as the nucleus and the planets and moons acting as the surrounding charges. It takes Jupiter 11.862 Earth days to rotate around the nucleus of the sun. However, when taking into account the size of Jupiter and its distance from the sun, this is a very fast rotation. Furthermore, a day on Jupiter is a mere 9.84 Earth hours. The orbital velocity of a planet will increase the farther it is from the solar nucleus (the sun). In relation to all the motions of the solar system, it does not just act and appear similar to an atom, but its motions also resemble that of a vortex.

Due to the makeup of Jupiter's gaseous intensity that coincides with all other conceivable scientific forces, and Jupiter being so massive, it has the strongest gravitational force in the solar system. This does not just affect Europa, it also affects the other sixty-two Jovian moons.

In the days of Galileo, Europa could not be viewed with the same detail modern astronomers are able to do now due to the limitations of primitive telescopes. This would go on for centuries. Today, there are, of course, better means to do astronomical studies. The first was Voyager 1, an unmanned spacecraftthat gave NASA some of what it desired. Its successor, Voyager 2, sent to the Jovian system, gave more essential information. However, photographs, as helpful as they may be, only represent single fragments of time, thus limiting studies.

You see, the surface of Europa has gone through a high multiplicity of structural alterations over a long period of time. This surface structure hypothesis has led some to believe that due to inner and outer sources, certain chemical compounds might exist under Europa's slightly rigid, yet comparatively smooth icy surface structure.

Tides from underlying Europan Ocean (as I just stated) are thoroughly affected by the pulling forces of Jupiter. Due to this activity, Europa's ice will crack and produce liquids, though they quickly freeze; this is how Europan surface structure is altered at such a high rate of fluctuation. Although not being volcanic in the literal sense of the word, some consider this liquid ice eruptive behavior as volcanic, not to mention that this behavior on and in Europa does include plate tectonic affects.

Due to frictional activity from the pulling forces of Jupiter, Europa's inner ocean behaves as such, with the inner heat of Europa further intensifying this action. This underground tidal activity also affects Europa's axis of rotation. Therefore, if the potential process of Jupiter imploding and then exploding into a new sun occurs, the present distance of Europa would be altered. In other words, if Jupiter were to become a sun, the distances between Jupiter and its sixty-three moons would coincide with scientific equivalency, thus changing the structural makeup of the Jovian system. Scientific equivalency must span out in this case and if it does so, it will offer more benefits than would be prematurely concluded.

The properties of the Europan core have been hypothesized by the scientific community to some extent, but, obviously, no one is sure at this point. Presently, the core of Europa is believed to be of a solid metallic structure estimated to be roughly 150 kilometers in depth. Furthermore, the theories concerning the innards of Europa have led to the possibility of minimal volcanic activity existing within. If this is the case, the possibility for chemical reproduction inside Europa is not as unlikely as would be presumed.

When observing Europa's surface features, one will notice thin lines and crater-like appearances, which give credence to the chaotic type surface features of Europa. This outlook has also strengthened the common scientific opinion that tectonic activity plays a vital role in the alterations on the Europan surface. This surface structure hypothesis is, of course, due to more indirect type energies that could originate from the inner crust to the upper ocean. You must keep in mind that frictional motion and a wide variety of energy types in any formation of opposite unions will react with the boundary or centrifuge of the opposite and equaling factor. In this case, we have the warm core as one side, the ice surface structure as the other side, and the liquid ocean as the centrifuge. With the aid of other astronomical powers, this threefold connection could result in a new form of life!

Continuing on, in the case of chaotic behavior leading to the chaotic surface structure of this Jovian moon, it can result in the appearance of semi-melted ice surfaces which are then frozen back into place. This is similar to a change in surface structure caused by a cracking of the ice, but it poses a slight difference. This process includes movements which are caused by fluctuations of temperature and friction, which will then produce molecular movement and thus heat. This type of process on and in Europa is repetitive and this is another way of visualizing the constant change in the Europan surface. This conceptualization when applied to time promotes yet another example of scientific relationship. Time, of course, resulted from light and dark, but coinciding forces of energy such as these Europan properties aid the universal space-time continuum.

When processing the thought that this constantly changing process on the Europan surface structure has been going on for millions upon millions of years, it can lead one to theorize that this constant change could serve some kind of profound universal purpose. From this outlook, I personally have come to the conclusion that Something Wonderful" is in the midst!

By viewing this ice-ocean beauty of the Jovian system, the structured surface excluding its inner forces is estimated to be approximately fifty million years old. When trying to fathom a constant change on the Europan surface over this period, one could conclude that something is attempting to enter from the infinitesimal of this Jovian beauty.

You might recall in the environmental portion of "Politics" when I told you that the scientific community is presently able to determine the age of time periods through the analysis of ice, trees, and rocks. However, the age of Europa (although the scientific community would like to be more exact) is irrelevant as far as the data that you will need to comprehend is concerned, if you are to fully fathom the totality of the still unexposed primary goal.

Continuing on, all factors within and around an object are either partly or fully affected by the totality of universal existence. Excuse my repetition, but this is a prime factor to the understanding of my vision. Furthermore, an object may be confined to certain factors of affects, but due to connection and scientific equivalency, all purposes pertaining to Europa or anything else of relativity equals to a quotient of one. This concept is both shockingly simple and shockingly complex at the same time.

As for the other three Galilean moons of the Jovian system, namely Ganymede, Io, and Callisto, they all play a crucial role to the complete Jovian process. You see, these other three moons are like Europa in the sense that they could represent charges around the new nucleus sun of an imploded and exploded Jupiter. If this miracle were to occur, the solar system would resemble a dividing stem cell. Another victory for the theory of the universal body!

The changes that occur so fast and so often on the Europan surface can also represent the process of fusion infusion. In this case, you could add diffusion, because in this case especially, water is a prime factor. However, I do feel that fusion infusion, being the process of universal creation, takes place even if it is not represented in a basic physical sense of observation. This has everything to do with the inner and outer beyond. Rather than elaborating at this crux, I will give you, the reader the benefit of the doubt and assume that by now, you see my personal process of human psyche thinking. And do you know why? Allow me to tell you! It is because your personal subconscious and my personal subconscious are connecting and leading to the collective subconscious manifestation of "Something Wonderful!"

Recently, it has been determined that the constant change in the surface structure of Europa is beginning to slow down. I believe this is due to what is called the process of convection. I previously mentioned convection early on in this segment, though in a vague sense. When dealing with the convection on the ice surface structure of this Jovian moon, it applies to the literal definition of the word.

Convection, in the literal sense, is the process by which molecules within fluids (in this case the oceans of Europa) move and act in a manner that transfers and transforms objects from heat fluctuations within (In this case, we are dealing with ice). The literal meaning of diffusion is also a part of this process. If you cannot recall, diffusion is a moving of molecules from a place of intense concentration to another place of lesser concentration. Diffusion, as far as I am concerned, is simply another type of fusion infusion process. In order to be clearer, diffusion in water, which directly pertains to this Europan hypothesis, can be classified as what is called osmosis. Osmosis is the tendency of fluids to pass through a membrane, so as to equalize concentrations on two sides or, simply, just the way fluids move through a membrane. Therefore, osmosis is a centrifuge to a connection within fluids. A good physical analogy would be to observe water passing through a sponge. So, you see, diffusion is not "exactly" proportional to my interpretations of fusion infusion, but it does represent a fusion infusion in a cleansing type of manner.

When dealing with Europa, the convection process promotes the capability to have interior heat, yet not melt the icy crust of the surface layer. You see, conduction when dealing with these or any other properties, is quite different. There is, of course, the common concept of conduction which adheres to electrical conduction and Ohm's Law This definition of conduction differs from the conduction we are presently dealing with. Conduction in the sense that we are presently dealing with, is similar to cooking something in a pan. The heat from the burner hits the pan and conducts through the surface of the pan, and there, you have your cooked bacon, eggs, sausages, or what have you. If the interior heat of Europa conducted in this fashion rather than by way of convection as it does, the icy crust of Europa would melt and an imbalance would be presented, thus defeating scientific equivalency. Up to this point in time, convection in and on Europa has achieved a balance, but it has yet to have accomplished a connection with the universal equilibrium. This equilibrium connection is the basis of possible life being created on Europa. Furthermore, as with all universal existence and not excluding what is happening on Europa, a revelation of moral collective proportions is being entered into the universe from some kind of infinitesimal energy. An individual cannot achieve such perfection, but a collective society (despite the fact that it is presently inconceivable) can achieve this utopian goal. A primary factor to this Europan process is, (as previously stated) the pulling forces of Jupiter, as well as the functions of the other sixty-two moons. The imminent universal-wide connection is now conducting along the naturalistic line in a unifying action to the fluctuating forces, which move in and out of this theoretical time line.

The fact that Europa is comprised of ice and water (as well as a solid core) may cause one to wonder how this complete concept affects tidal behaviors of the Europan Ocean. Well, in reality this has pretty much been accounted for already. This advanced concept I just presented is simply an outlook and all details of scientific factors play their own role. Furthermore, I theorize that the complete process of alteration of the Europan surface structure and its recent slowing down is the symbol of our first glimpse to another of my theories. This is the Big Boom theory and it is not to be confused with my enhancements of the Big Bang theory. The sixty-four bodies of the Jovian system are carrying out the process of life that we are presently unable to transfer into the collective subconscious due to insufficient tact. Human understanding is carrying out its natural process, but time is a constant flux of human interface and interchange. Therefore, I will put you in suspense and save the Big Boom theory for a latertime. What we have here is a spherical moon of the Jovian system waiting for something to happen! Scientific equivalency will win!

The fact that the tidal action of Europa's ocean has been constant for such a long time supports the hypothesis that a higher process of interior and exterior motions of this Jovian moon is leading to paranormal proportions.

You see, planets and moons tend to be more oval than perfectly spherical. This is at least the case with the Earth. Earlier, I informed you that this type of planetary shaping is a result of space-time curvature. Well, to put it into clearer terms, this oval shaping is a result of constant magnetic and gravitational affects throughout the forming of the given celestial body. The point I want to get across by my mentioning this galactic phenomena I will put in the form of yet another physical analogy. Europa can be related to a hypothetical egg (which is more so oval shaped) which is trying to coincide with its surroundings, which could lead to a paranormal astronomical birth. Get it?

Anyway, this feature of the Europan ocean and its structure, its dependence on the gravitational pull of Jupiter, in a subconscious way, represents time fragments observable through stroboscopic affects when applying this process to its galactic actions. So, exactly why is the chaotic action on the icy surface structure of this Jovian moon slowing down at this point? There must be a reason!

Okay, the prime effectual relations on the Europan surface structure are heat, rotation, orbital activity, strain, and the pull of Jupiter (which could be classified as orbital activity). These forces are, in a direct sense, the very foundation of this process that has proportioned the convective balance determining the rate of fusion infusion radiated energy that comes out through this outer crust.

Although convection is commonplace in and on Europa, there are some minute levels of conductive actions I had briefly accounted for earlier. This conduction does not even remotely transport heat at the level that convection does in this case, but in order for the complete process to maintain the balance essential for the achievement of the Jovian goal, certain Europan regions are dependent on this small conductive action. This conduction will take place only in the correct locations relative to ice thickness and interior forces. This is a prime example of scientific equivalency in action.

Even Europa's rotation and axis are affected by Jupiter and the other sixty-two moons of this Jovian system. It would be interesting if we could rigorously compare this system's actions to a multiplicity of atom types and the same goes for any galactic system within our parallel of universal understanding.

The chaotic surface structure of Europa as well as some free flowing ice patches had led experts to hypothesize that not only has the flux of surface structure slowed recently, but the ice crust layer is also becoming thinner. This thinning is due to friction, of course, as well as other heating affects of which I have presented thus far. The observations of the scientific community in pertinence to this action are mixed into a variance of scientific outlooks. Some experts believe that if certain orbital actions are put into motion, the ocean might refreeze to its original proportion of ice thickness. I personally disagree with this particular hypothesis. The reason for my disagreement is as follows: The potential for interstellar activity in the Europan atmosphere is weaker than most celestial body atmospheres within our solar system. It is primarily made up of molecular oxygen. Furthermore, the surface pressure of Europan atmosphere is much weaker than that of the Earth's atmosphere that it nearly falls off the scale. Above the Europan atmosphere, there is the ionosphere containing charged particles that are dependent on solar radiation as well as other energy particles, comes from Jupiter's magnetosphere. Therefore, the active forces once again promote a balance. When applying this balance to a time concept, one can visualize the progression of the Europan atmospheric behavior as well as its physical properties. Therefore, the Jovian system is functioning in unison with scientific equivalency and this is the basis of my disagreement.

Furthermore, the oxygen in the Europan atmosphere did not originate from a biological source. Of course, the pre-explained process on the Europan surface structure is one factor. However, the rising radiated energy from Europa into its atmosphere is carried out by a method of dissociating molecules, which are affected by radiated matter, from Jupiter's magnetosphere. Because of the interactions between these two celestial forces, the chemical bonds are able to occur from this transfusing and high energy fluctuating action. These chemical bonds are the results of the inner intricate topologic relationships between the atoms, quarks, and subdivided molecules of this region.

Once our sun, in proportion to the Jovian magnetosphere, is involved in the intricacies of this interstellar process, a complex mixture of energy will enter the icy crust of Europa. This process will then cause the separation of water into two periodic properties of molecular oxygen and hydrogen. This is an example of a reversal of universal time flux. These newly separated and individual oxygen and hydrogen molecules will then accumulate from under the Europan crust up into the Europan atmosphere. This subdivision process of molecular consistencies will then put into action the absorption of these molecules into solar and magnetic properties and there you have it, a peaceful and balanced atmosphere is maintained.

As for the separated hydrogen molecules originating from or returning to the Europan surface, they will go through a process of adsorption rather than absorption. The word "adsorb" is not to be confused with "absorb"; it is similar to absorption, but definitely different. In the case of adsorption, rather than these hydrogen molecules diffusing into the Europan surface, they will instead coincide with the ice surface of Europa by a method of an obscure and unique scientific process. However, this is only the case for the hydrogen molecules that do not return to the surface as oxygen molecules do. This is due to hydrogen being a lighter gas. As for the density of oxygen molecules, it is due to their longevity of existence. Of course, these molecules have variations, but they will always apply to the laws of natural science.

So, as far as we know, life does not exist in the Europan ocean; and, as I have already stated, there will be life on Europa in due time. Another reason for the hypothesis of possible life forms on Europa has been manifested through comparisons of Earth's deep ocean hypothermal vents in the waters in the Antarctic region. A hypothermal vent is basically an underwater vent heated from the inner Earth. When comparing Earth to Europa, a minute connection is put into action.

This particular comparative observation is a good one. However, I must once again state that the scientific community would be much more successful in their endeavors if they were to compare the macroscopic to the microscopic, the telescopic to the microscopic, or any combination of the three realms of human sight perception. And if they do so, complicated scientific equations will be much easier to develop. Of course, we should also continue to compare elements confined into one level of sight perception.

I believe that I have now sufficiently accounted for the properties of the Jovian moon, Europa. Therefore, it is now time for us to move on. It will not be long until we get to the very foundation of Arthur Clarke's vision. So, we will now discuss the king daddy of the Jovian system, none other than the gas giant itself, the planet Jupiter.

Jupiter was named for an ancient pagan Roman god linked to mythology and religious beliefs of a variety of cultures. Jupiter is mostly made up of hydrogen, which is very explosive, and it does contain miniscule levels of helium. Due to this planet's constant repetition of spin and rotation, a hard core is said to have formed in the central core of this gas giant. Another factor to the constant flux of Jupiter's motions is traceable to its shape. Compared to other space entities, the axis and the coinciding with space curvature will result in proportional actions and reactions, thus supporting universal balance. As with the case of all other planets or moons, Jupiter is not perfectly rounded.

These Jovian actions have resulted in the infamous red spot. You could fit the Earth inside the great red spot three times! Another attribute to these intense Jovian energies is its powerful magnetosphere. Jupiter's magnetosphere is so intense, its central solid and possibly diamond core becomes another factor to Jupiter's pre-quasar status. Presently, Jupiter's magnetosphere cannot trap solar wind and plasmas. If the cosmic miracle of Jovian implosion to explosion creating a sun were to actually take place, the infinitely compacted temporarily induced black hole will split like an atom and act in proportion to scientific equivalency. Because a temporary black hole is so imperative to this process, it must achieve a balance of function. This balance is provided by way of universal parallels.

Despite Jupiter's gaseous makeup (other than its core), it achieves a balance holding it together by way of collective bonding. Jupiter is 2.5 times more massive than all the other planets in our solar system combined. So, one could fathom, why this bonding energy is such a fascinating aspect of this astronomical outlook. Whether Jupiter's core is hard rock or diamond remains a mystery to this day. However, it has been determined that this core has a thick layer of metallic hydrogen. Metallic hydrogen exists through extremely compacted hydrogen, which changes in composition from this level of compaction. This is relative to compacted rock formations on Earth and it represents an interesting outlook. You see, if hydrogen can be so compacted within Jupiter, a diamond-like core is not inconceivable. The fact that this metallic hydrogen does exist as such inside Jupiter could intensify and balance out the process of Jovian star birth. Now that I have informed you of the metallic hydrogen layer on the core of Jupiter, I hereby state that this Jovian star birth process is the basis of my Big Boom theory. Of course, I cannot take full credit for this theory because it was Arthur Clarke who set this hypothesis into motion.

A major reason Jupiter's magnetosphere is so strong is due to trappings of ionized particles due to solar wind forces. These properties will take a balance of action and wala, you have yourself a correctly proportional Jovian magnetosphere. Solar wind, as I have already informed you, is a stream of charged particles (plasmaemitted by the outer layer of the sun. Of course, solar wind is not like plain old Earthly wind, but seen within the astronomical environment that constantly varies throughout and also when taking into account that Earth wind is comprised of oxygen and carbon dioxide, these two wind types are very different from one another, but they are similar as to their actions within their particular environment.

VISION OF A MENTAL PATIENT

Enough! The science part of "2001-2010" is more or less over. I must now elaborate to you the stories written by Arthur Clarke which were enhanced by Stanley Kubrick and Peter Hyams. This will be my interpretation of Clarke's supposed fictional, yet scientifically correct novels "2001 A Space Odyssey" and "2010 Odyssey Two." I will include some of the enhancements of Kubrick's and Hyams's and, for the record, Kubrick's film was based on "2001 A Space Odyssey" has the same title, but the movie sequel of "2010 Odyssey Two" was entitled "2010 The Year We Make Contact," and remember, contact means connection!

The first episode of 2001 holds prime significance to the totality of my theories and my vision. However, it is the second episode of 2010 that the full connection is achieved. I remind you that I mustn't take credit for this part of my vision because this concept originated from the mind of Arthur Clarke.

I believe this vision originated from the deep personal subconscious of Clarke's mind and in truth, his interpretations in these books were correct relative to the laws of the sciences.

I will now take you through the scientific paranormal phenomena of this vision of Clarke's and I will compensate for the differences between the story lines of the literary and cinematic versions of this astronomical conceptualization. Throughout this account I am about to present in pertinence to the stories of 2001 and 2010, including their plots and their significance to scientific relationships, I will, of course, also apply these visions to my theories. I hereby present my short enhanced version of 2001 and 2010.

This story starts off with the dawn of man and the life of an ape-man, by the name of Moon Watcher. Moon Watcher is, of course, primitive. He simply acts to the evil natures of his instincts in order for him to survive. Moon Watcher is accompanied by many other male and female apes and they go about their hunting and brutal nature of being. A monolith appears before this small community of apes and, of course, they have no idea what it is, or what it is for. They are fascinated by this perfectly symmetrical and vertically standing rectangular object. This object seems to set the collective subconscious of these apes into motion, thus causing them to react to the monolith with extreme instinctual rage. Eventually, Moon Watcher gets into a brutal fight with another ape man and when the fight is finished he throws his weapon, a bone from one of his deceased ancestors, up into the air and as this bone rises into the blue sky, it changes into a spaceship of a similar shape, thus representing the progression of the human race. Due to what you just read, I tell you that A Space Odyssey in Drow is = yes you do a see apes ah!.

The premise of this story is set into motion two years before 2001 on the moon at the location of the sea of tranquility. The sea of tranquility is a large lunar plane, which, for the most part, is composed of a common extrusive volcanic rock called basalt. This sea of tranquility was formed by ancient lunar volcanic activity (which is the case for a majority of lunar terrain). This lunar sea of tranquility got its name from ancient astronomers using telescopes and mistaking this lunar basin for seas.

In this lunar mare, there was a radioactive signal from a source buried deep under the lunar surface. This was representative of a "falling chaos underground cult a solid twisted sound" which is a subconscious communication from me, the author, to you, the reader. It would be determined that this signal was coming from approximately 100 feet under the lunar surface and when it was dug up, it was the monolith!

This strange object measured approximately 1 by 4 by 9, which are the squares of 1, 2, and 3. The discoverers of this monolith were obviously baffled by this object and they had felt strange and unfamiliar combinations of energy forces passing through them. These forces were way beyond their comprehension. Soon, they realized that this object of unknown origin was the first ever scientific evidence of extraterrestrial life.

You see, the monolith has paranormal properties. It gives off cosmic energies that can only be understood from a complete functioning of the personal and collective subconscious. At this time, I can only tell you that the monolith has within itself the key to the universe; it can alter and enhance all formations and understandings of common existence. The monolith contains within it the fabrics of all creation's energies, capable of altering the paranormal into the normal.

Therefore, although this story begins in 1999, a time alteration is achieved by the monolith and thus the sequence of events is altered from the natural course of time. It is true that the movie and the book both start off with the dawn of man and soon, the presently unexposed primary goal will put this concept in its correct place. The monolith is the Center of the Universe, of which I displayed in the "An Apology" segment. Therefore, the monolith is the centrifuge for the action and reaction of universal wide connection. The ultimate truth is that no one really knows the point of universal origin, but universal contact might tell us.

As for Moon Watcher and his relatives who lived in the infancy of human evolution, they represent the beginning of collective subconscious development. Reading through the scenes depicting Moon Watcher, I saw that instinct is not just within the being. Instinct, like anything else, is related to, interpreted by, reacted to, and developed by the surrounding environment of the given being. With Earthly creatures such as these man and women apes, the surrounding things such as the horizon, the lay of the land, and the climate all affected their instinctual behavior. When Moon Watcher and his relatives were privileged to be face to face with the monolith, they were of course clueless in the conscious sense, but in the subconscious sense, they were one with nature and the universe.

From the dawn of man up until this point in time, the human mind has grown in both evil and moral ways. This is essential for the equilibrium between mind, space, and time. We have now come to the point of a collective manifestation and we are accelerating fast. You must understand that most of us are moral. It is the instinctual evils of our human nature that must be adjusted to a moral balance. We need to put these evils behind us and start to conduct our human energy along the naturalistic line. This is possible through the pursuit of universal contact. So, we shall assume that these apes are the kinetic offspring of the centering monolith.

Due to legalities in this story, the National Aeronautics Space Administration (NASA) was dubbed as the "National Council of Aeronautics," or the NCA. There once was the National Aeronautics Space Council which existed from 1958 until 1973, as well as the National Space Council which existed during the George H.W. Bush Administration. The head of this fictional NCA was one Dr. Heywood Floyd. DR. Floyd being of high position was one of the first to know of the monolith and he tried to keep it low profile in order to avoid an international incident. Floyd would carry out of secret council meetings and other operations around the monolith.

The NCA had a base on Clavius, a large moon crater visible from Earth. Clavius is located in the southern highlands of the moon not very far from the Tycho crater in the sea of tranquility.

The monolith would send a signal to the Jovian system, leading to extreme concern for all Earth governments involved. Soon, Floyd would be under a lot of pressure. This issue would be kept under cover and soon the American space station Discovery would be sent to the Jovian system to investigate. They would learn that a much larger monolith was in the Jovian system. It was floating between Jupiter and Io, about two kilometers in height. It had the same relative symmetry of 1 by 4 by 9. The Discovery crew consisted of three Americans were in hibernation state and two other Americans left awake for the trip to the Jovian system. The names of the three in hibernation were Kaminski, Hunter, and Whitehead in the film. In the book, it was Kaminski, Hunter, and Kimball. The two awakened astronauts were Dr. Frank Poole and Dr. David Bowman in both the book and the film.

During this million-mile journey, Bowman and Poole were accompanied by the super computer HAL 9000. Many odyssey fans might have heard that HAL was named by the preceding alphabetical letters of the computer company IBM, H being before I, A being before B, and L being before M; however, according to the book, HAL actually stands for Heuristic Algorithm, which means "capable of solving problems."

You see, HAL was designed to have a human-like personality and was said to be incapable of error. Many Odyssey fans may be misled and think that HAL was twisted due to some of the actions he would take in this story. The truth is that HAL was given conflicted orders and he did his best to interpret them. This will be better understood through further elaborations.

Bowman and Poole would do their best to go about their duties while aboard the Discovery. However, due to their being supplied with limited and insufficient information, they would soon run into difficulties. In the novel, Bowman, Poole, and the rest of the Discovery team spent a good deal of time in the Saturnian system, which is for the most part irrelevant to the message I am trying to communicate through this one-way conversation. You see, in the theatrical version of this story, it primarily dealt with the Jovian system.

HAL 9000 was designed by one Dr. Chandra of the NCA and his full relevance will be displayed in the sequel "2010." HAL was the central nervous system of the Discovery, as well as the prime factor for carrying out the Jovian missionrequired to be executed with proficiency. HAL was given extreme responsibilities the importance of which was much higher than any of the Discovery crew was aware of. HAL was also responsible for the health of the three men in hibernation, thus the need to constantly converse with Poole and Bowman. Some believed that as HAL was so capable of understanding human behavior, he could have been capable of feelings and emotions.

As the Discovery mission continued, HAL began to become slightly paranoid. When HAL was having one of his normal conversations with Bowman, HAL began to question Bowman by asking him if he was having second thoughts about the Jovian mission. He asked Bowman about the object that was dug up on the moon, the first monolith. HAL was struggling with why so many secrets had to be kept, consequently limiting the proper distribution of data concerning this Jovian mission.

You see, HAL was designed for curiosity. The insufficient information given to him and the fact that his human counterparts were even less informed left HAL at a loss. He also questioned Bowman why the others had to remain in hibernation for such a long time. At this point, Bowman was calm, cool, and collected. He was not yet suspicious of HAL, so Bowman simply figured that HAL was executing his crew psychology report.

All of a sudden, HAL informed Bowman that the essential AE-35 antenna was going to fail within seventy-two hours. Concerned, Bowman and Poole went on to investigate this antenna, this being their means ofcommunication to the Earth and lunar bases. At this point, the Jovian mission would begin to take a downward spiral.

Bowman then suited up and entered a portable space pod so he could examine the crucial antenna. Once Bowman reached the vicinity of this antenna, he exited the pod. As he examined and repaired the antenna, Poole was inside the Discovery, looking out at Bowman in order to make sure that he was okay. Reentering the Discovery, Bowman and Poole proceeded to analyze the circuit boards connected to the antenna. Both concluded that there was nothing wrong with it. At this time, Bowman and Poole started to become suspicious of HAL.

Despite this, HAL would suggest disconnecting the antenna and then immediately reactivating it. Poole and Bowman were wary of HAL, as HAL was also wary of them. Remember, HAL's erratic behavior was due to conflicting orders between the U.S. government and the NCA. HAL would continue to question Bowman and Poole. He hoped that Poole and Bowman

VISION OF A MENTAL PATIENT

weren't overconcerned.

Poole and Bowman decided to enter a small pod to discuss why HAL, who was supposed to be incapable of error, was behaving this way. This pod was right in front of HAL, so for privacy's sake, Bowman, and then Poole, commanded HAL to rotate the pod, but HAL did nothing. HAL continued to ignore both men. Bowman and Poole assumed that HAL must not be able to hear them, so they decided to discuss the matter anyway.

They agreed it would be best for the mission to disconnect HAL's major functions. They never realized that HAL intentionally ignored them, and that he could read their lips! Bowman and Poole faced a dangerous task, even without HAL's Knowledge of their plans. You see, in order for the Discovery to continue to properly function, they must be cautious when disconnecting HAL, making sure they do not cut off any essential Discovery function. Bowman and Poole had no inkling that HAL's behavior was due to certain higher ups giving HAL misinformation and conflicting orders. The three proceeded to play a game of cat and mouse to no fault of anyone in the mission.

Bowman and Poole agreed that Poole would exit the Discovery by way of a space pod and enter the access way to HAL's functioning mechanisms. Bowman returned Poole's favor and proceeded to oversee Poole's efforts and make sure that Poole was okay. Unfortunately, Poole somehow ended up being ejected from his pod. He began to float helplessly to his death. Bowman prepared to exit the Discovery to save Poole's life. HAL tried to stop Bowman from saving Poole. Bowman was no fool; he realized he not only needed to save his friend, he also needed to cut off the major functions of HAL 9000. Bowman suited up and entered another pod to chase down Poole who was floating away. He was determined to do his best. With the mechanical arms of the space pod, Bowman continued to struggle to save his friend, but he lost grasp of Poole's body. Eventually, Bowman realized he would be unable to save Poole.

Though upset, Bowman was forced to deal with HAL alone. By remote communication, HAL spoke to Bowman of a computer malfunction that had caused the other three in hibernation to flatline (keep in mind my elaborations on flatlining in the "What is a Connection" segment). Bowman realized he was now all alone millions of miles from Earth. However, he resolved to complete this mission. He immediately began to disconnect the major functions of HAL 9000.

Bowman then retreated and commanded HAL to open the pod bay door so he could reenter the Discovery. HAL refused. HAL told an irate and insistent Bowman that he knew of Bowman's and Poole's conversation, leading him to be so defiant. Bowman realized things were getting worse, but he decided to act with professionalism and figure out a way to deal with HAL's erratic behavior.

Bowman decided to enter through the emergency air lock. Despite warnings from HAL, Bowman managed to enter through the emergency air lock and saw himself in the area of HAL's nervous center. Bowman looked over the module and prepared to disconnect HAL.

HAL tried to talk him out of it. HAL told Bowman he was growing fearful. As Bowman began the disconnection process, HAL told Bowman he can feel his mind going weaker, but Bowman continued to ignore him until he was done.

The monolith was visible in Jupiter's atmosphere where the original lunar monolith sent its signal. At this point, the celestial bodies of the solar system became aligned, initiating a major step for universal contact, for the achievement of "Something Wonderful." Bowman was not aware of it, but he would soon be privileged to person to unlock the naturalistic line and get into the spectrum which will communicate to the human race the action and reaction of universal wide connection.

Here comes the good part! Once Bowman finished disconnecting HAL 9000, he had a subconscious impulse telling him to enter the space pod.. At this time, Bowman subconsciously intended to become part of the spectrum so he could complete the process of a coinciding action between what is called "The Universe of the Dream Fabric" and the universe of the human parallel. These two universes would "connect" with the aid of Bowman and the monolith.

Bowman could not reenter the Discovery. He instead started to float closer into the vicinity of the large, two-kilometer monolith. He found himself within range to react with the reflective and magnetic fused properties of the monolith to continue the universal process until he was in the middle of Jupiter and Europa with the monolith close by!

All of a sudden, the large monolith began to glow through an action and reaction of some sort of cosmic fusion infusion. It then proceeded to get the dream spectrum into the left eye of Bowman, which has now become time's eye.

Colors of amazing depth and frequency beyond that of typical human comprehension were now flowing into the pupil of Bowman's left eye. Remember, the eye is an organ that detects and transforms light, sending the signals to the optic nerve, where they are then subdivided from a coinciding action to brain chemistry to produce human vision. The pupils also control the levels of light entering the eye.

More colors that defy normal human perception, sending flamboyant and unfamiliar shades of green and pink that transformed into pinkish blue streamed into Bowman's left pupil. He found himself in a state of shock, euphoria, and extreme anticipation, all bunched up into a single beautiful state of human emotion. As this contined, he began to see and subconsciously comprehend laser-like entities and wavelengths well beyond what any human had ever seen, sending his emotional state into such intensity. Bowman's left pupil was now altered in texture and color appearance.

Shades of gaseous stardust continued to be manifested into Bowman's left eye. Bowman saw this stardust transforming into a dream fabric quasar, then into the shape of a human womb. This dream fabric and light fusion infusion process continued to promote a higher intensity of euphoric senses of the inner and outer beyond within the senses of Bowman. There were forming, changing, forming, changing, forming, changing until something that looked like a comet made its final change then appeared to resemble a unit of human sperm. The sperm comet then interacted with the womb. A pinkish quasar then formed with colors that further defied human color frequency. Bowman's state of mind alternated between fear and complete euphoria until his emotions began to act in unison, enhancing Bowman's being. Soon, he would "Understand!"

As the dream fabric spectrum continued to fill the pupil of Bowman's left eye, seven topological green-tinted gems appeared above the large monolith. Bowman started to comprehend the infinite and the infinitesimal in a state of equilibrium between the human mind and the speed of light. Color frequencies of extreme cosmic proportions continued to enter and alter the phosphorescence connection between Bowman's left eye and the ever changing colors transmitted from the monolith to Bowman's optics and personal subconscious. His left eye turned from purple to China blue, to tinted green; then Bowman visualized an Earth-like canyon composed of multiple colors, which continued to change and coincide with the naturalistic line. The dream spectrum was filling the mind of David Bowman!

The canyon then changed from shades of red resembling a red shift to another tint of China blue. Soon, China blue appeared to change in texture, starting to resemble a photonegative. A deeper shade of blue then turned into chlorophyll green, before it turned into a phosphorescence of an unknown color, making the canyon appear in a more three-dimensional visual appearance consisting of luminescent volcanoes and mountains of an Earthly, yet alien appearance of an unfamiliar sort. Despite the three-dimensional appearance of this ever-changing canyon, it started to resemble a photo negative streaming into Bowman's left pupil.

Soon, the canyon changed into a sun-like orange color, into basic green, and then into bright yellow tint. All of a sudden, the dream spectrum came to an abrupt halt; Bowman's feeling of euphoria changed into an unfamiliar mood of confusion and anxiety. Bowman's eyes then changed back into their original color . Looking around, he found himself in a very strange place.

Bowman was now in dream fabric center. He exited his space pod which was located in a strange and unfamiliar set of white rooms. As Bowman opened the pod door and stepped out into this strangely posh-looking hotel room, he was in the realm of the dream fabric, yet he could physically feel through all of his senses. You see, a parallel universe is a dream fabric universe from one to the next. Our physical universe is dream fabric from the preceding parallel to us and to the next. This is the basis of dreaming. A dream is simply a smeared chemical manifestation of all that exists within the inner and outer beyond from our parallel to our coinciding parallel, and so on and so forth.

In the "Reflections" segment, I did my best to prove the existence of parallel universes within a reflection. I also proved this hypothesis through the "Language of the Mad" segment. However, I did not give appropriate data regarding entrances into these parallel universes. Because of the nature of our dreams, as well as their properties of time-altering forces, I conclude that I am definitely correct in stating that universes change the consistencies of dream fabrics from one to the next.

Furthermore, time and dreams are put together for the achievement of connection. Whether between two personal subconscious beings or the beautiful process of universal-wide connection ba put into action by a collective subconscious understanding, this dream bonding action is carried out. The main reason to support the concept of a dream fabric universe is the topological infinitesimal piecing together of forms of matter through fusion infusion. This intricate act is identical to the process of mind subdivisions manifested in our dreams. They are directly relative to the existence of parallel universes. All objects are put together by infinitesimal bonding and magnetism. Dreams act in the same way. This is also supports the equality between mind, time, and space.

Let's get back to our friend, David Bowman. When we last left Bowman, he was standing in this parallel universe's white posh hotel room. Curious, Dave started to wander about this unfamiliar setting. He then noticed a beautiful Van Gogh painting hung up on one of the walls (Remember how I mentioned Van Gogh in the "Apology" segment). Bowman continued to inspect his surroundings, not yet realizing that he had become part of the center of the universe. He was between parallels of universal existence, not yet fully emerging into the other side. Remember, the center of the universe is where we reverse! Because Bowman had become a part of this altered time flux of universal existence, he was experiencing a cosmic shapeshift causing Bowman to change in age appearance. One moment he was an old man, another moment he was very young, and another moment he was his present age.

Bowman then walked into another room. To his astonishment, there was an old man sitting at a large table enjoying a meal. As Bowman looked at this elderly man, the latter got up from his chair until both were eye to eye. Bowman became even more astonished when he realized that the old man was himself. Bowman's subconscious knew at this point that he was safe and that he had become a vital component to the universal process. He was able to contain his emotions and started to observe his surroundings. As Bowman continued his exploration, the older Bowman sat back down to finish his meal, until he knocked over a glass that shattered on the floor. This glass-breaking was a subconscious manifestation of reflective processes.

Bowman peered into another room—lo and behold, there was a monolith in the center of this room! The classical piece "Thus Sprach Zarathustra" by the great classical composer Strauss (which happens to be my favorite classical piece) began to play. After looking inside, old and young David Bowman stepped into the monolith and into the next universe! But this is not the last time we would hear from David Bowman!

The womb of a giant baby appeared next to Earth. It represented some cosmic birth bound to take place. This cosmically manifested infant is presently unfathomable (at least to a certain degree). It could be theoretical or it could be literal. Could the planet Earth be the womb of the universal body? This miraculous process began on the moon, went back to the dawn of man, and had Jupiter as the crucial component (Jupiter in Drow is=ready push). Yes, push the infant out and we will be reborn!

Well, this was the end of the story of 2001, but much more would happen in 2010. You shall soon fathom this universal process to a full extent. Anyway, before I assess the story of 2010, I must first apply the story of 2001 to my theory of the universal body. This application to the universal body is vital to the totality of my vision.

Okay, the pupil of the human eye resembles a black hole. When applying the actions of the pupil of the human eye to the actions of black holes, there are some similarities. The colored part of the eye surrounding the pupil resembles a galaxy, yet it does not resemble the vortex of a galaxy. The pupil and its colored surrounding resemble an imploding black hole that could explode into a supernova. The lines in the colored portion of the human eye protrude inward towards the black hole of the eye, the pupil. The pupil sucks up the energy of light, representing the behavior of a black hole and the creation of a connective boundary promoted by way of an opposite union.

You see, the pupils of our eyes transfer light into the vast universe of our minds. Remember, mind, time, and space are equal in their vastness. In the human pupil, it takes in light, subdivides it inside the brain and the senses, then transforms this light into the realm of human understanding. My theory of the universal body can and will relate such similarities of universal existence further. Once I complete my explanation of the Big Boom theory based on Jupiter's implosion explosion and temporary black hole process that would create a world of two suns, you will be able to observe universal existence with a more open minded outlook.

HAL has a red eye! You would have to watch the movie to visualize HAL's red eye, so at this point (unless you have seen this film), you'll just have to trust me. HAL's red eye represents the new sun. Remember, HAL behaved the way he did because he was given conflicted orders. He merely tried his best to interpret them (This will be explained further when I tell the story of 2010 in its completeness). Anyway, HAL's two orders can be relevant to human behavior. You see, one order was of moral intent, the other immoral. Simply stated, HAL was told to be moral and immoral at the same time. Therefore, if HAL is the collective subconscious symbol of transformation for the world of two suns, the new sun just as the old sun will create both good and evil. This good and evil (good stems from evil) is the very basis of human nature. You must keep in mind that good cannot exist without evil and vice versa. Therefore, HAL and the new sun represents the foundation of universal-wide connection responsible for the carrying out of human understanding and our tendency for good-natured ambitions, as well as the forming of the collective subconscious by a method of collective instinctual manifestation. When applying this particular aspect to scientific equivalency, one could conclude a visualization of vibrating particles existing between the boundaries of this process are achieving an enhancement of the universal equilibrium. Once again, scientific equivalency wins!

Okay, it is now time for us to indulge in the sequels of this story, which are, of course, "2010 Odyssey 2" (the novel) and "2010 The Year We Make Contact" (the film). The first novel and movie of this series were both outstanding. However, the process of "Something Wonderful" is not completed and there are still many unanswered questions.

The first book and movie of this series (other than the spectrum of the naturalistic line entering the left eye of David Bowman) were identical, at least, to some degree. As far as which one I thought was better, I would have to say the book was better than the film. In the case of 2010 the book and the film, I would rate them as dead even.

Peter Hyams enhanced and altered the storyline in the film. I will account for some of the differences as I go. So, let us now indulge into this series as I present my enhanced version of the 2010 story.

Before David Bowman walked into the parallel universe of the dream fabric, his last transmission to Earth was, "My God, it's full of stars!" David Bowman was presumed dead, but we know better than that at this point, don't we? As for Poole and the other three who were in hibernation, they were dead. However, you must keep in mind my flatlining connection hypothesis. It is possible that Poole and the other three have entered the other side!

The large two-kilometer monolith is still nestled between Jupiter and Europa and it is preparing for another alignment. You are not aware of it yet, but due to my theories, primarily my reflection theories as relevant to parallel universes, not only is the collective subconscious leading to the Big Boom, but dark energy is passing through us, the Earth, and the rest of the universe for the same universal purpose. The story begins with a conversation between the former NCA Chairman Heywood Floyd who had become a university chancellor, and the head of the Russian Space Program. The prominent and well-accomplished Russian began to poke fun at Floyd, but he would soon get to the point. You see, the new Russian Space Carrier Leonov as well as other Russian astronomical pursuits were exceeding those of their American counterparts. This lackluster progress by the United States was due to the assumed failure of the Discovery mission.

So, here is the dilemma Floyd and the prominent Russian discussed: the Russians now had the capability to travel to the Jovian system and pick up from where the Americans left off. But the Americans had the knowledge and the means to repair HAL 9000 and the Discovery. Therefore, the prominent Russian tried to convince Floyd (despite the fact that he no longer headed the NCA) to have three American astronauts accompany the Russian cosmonauts aboard the Russian Leonov for a joint effort. The Russian was talking to Floyd because American know-how would aid this mission and Russian ambitions. With him, HAL 9000 and Discovery would be repaired fast. Floyd was puzzled with the prominent Russian's request and proceeded to ask, "How can you convince your people to have Americans on the flight and how am I supposed to convince my people?" The Russian explained the situation to Floyd and the latter showed supreme interest. The Russian asked Floyd to check out the orbital behavior of the Discovery. Floyd then became even more curious and asked what the Russian meant about the Discovery's orbital actions. The Russian responded with "You are a smart man, Mr. Floyd. You will know what to do." Floyd and the Russian then agreed to appeal to their authorities for an American presence aboard the Russian Leonov.

Floyd decided to check out Discovery's orbit on a computer at his university. Once Floyd saw what is happening, he became astonished. The Discovery was either being pushed away from Jupiter or being pulled towards the Jovian moon of Io. This motion seemed to start and stop in a very peculiar way. Floyd as well as all of the other experts were not yet aware that this erratic pushing and pulling of the Discovery was being carried out by forces emanating from the monolith. You see, the monolith has physical properties unlike any Earthly object. It was so constructed that itwas impenetrable by lasers or nuclear explosion.

Floyd then had a rendezvous with the new NCA Chairman—in front of the White House, of all places. At this point, I need to inform you that in the movie, there was a military conflict between Russia and America both squaring off within the Central American nation of Honduras; but this was not the case in the novel. As far as the totality of my message is concerned, there is no need for me to elaborate the details of this Central American conflict. All you need to see is that planet Earth was in imminent danger of catastrophic proportions and that something wonderful needed to happen.

Floyd relayed to the NCA chairman the conversation he had with the Russian and about the Discovery's orbit. They agreed it would be difficult to persuade the president to have Americans join the Russians aboard the Leonov. Diplomatic relations were poor due to the Honduras situation. A tactful man, Floyd finally persuaded the chairman by asking him if he wanted the Russians to have all the answers, as they eventually would if the Americans did not board the Leonov. Floyd also suggested that the Americans could give the Russians false information, allowing the United States to catch up to the Russians in space exploration. The Chairman responded with "That's good," and he began to contemplate the idea.

Eventually, the agreement was made and the President would comply with the NCA Chairman's request. The three Americans who would board the Leonov included Dr. Heywood Floyd, a professor by the name of Chandra who happened to be the designer of the HAL 9000, and therefore, was the most qualified to repair HAL, and a Californian engineer by the name of Kurnow. Kurnow was selected for this job because he had the most knowledge on Discovery spacecraft. The next scene is identical in the book and the movie. Dr. Chandra entered his office and began to converse with another Heuristic Algorithm similar to HAL 9000. This would be the SAL computer, which has a blue eye unlike HAL 9000, which has a red eye. Chandra told SAL he would like to disconnect her major functions and then reactivate her, so that he could compare SAL to HAL. Since SAL was similar to HAL, this could aid Chandra fix HAL. Despite the fact that SAL was programmed for curiosity like HAL, SAL was very cooperative and trusted in Chandra's expertise. Chandra told SAL he would like to open a new file and typed in the word "Phoenix." Chandra asked SAL if she knew the meaning of this word. SAL stated there were twenty-five references in the computer's dictionary. Chandra then asked SAL which one she thought was relevant. SAL chose the tutor of Achilles. Chandra responded with a hint of amusement and said, "That's interesting. I did not know that one, please try again?" SAL then said "A fabulous bird reborn from the ashes of its former life." Chandra responded with "That is correct SAL, and do you know why I chose this name?" SAL replied, "Because you wish to reactivate the Discovery?" "That is correct SAL." Chandra and SAL then discussed the final details for the Jovian mission. It would not be long before something wonderful would take place.

Aboard the Russian Leonov, the three Americans met the cosmonauts who they would live with for the next couple of years: Commander Rudenko, Maxim Brailovsky, and a female commander named Kirbok. The three Russians led other cosmonauts aboard this pivotal Jovian mission. The Leonov then headed for the Jovian system. Chandra, Kurnow, and Floyd were to be in hibernation for the trip due to food rations and other supply reasons. The United States and Russian government requested that Floyd be awakened ahead of time. This was due to odd discoveries within the surface of Europa—something very strange was detected in the icy crust of the Europan moon! Once Floyd was awakened, he met with the Russian crew. The meeting came with severe tension in the air. Commander Kirbok seemed hostile toward Floyd at first, but they became close as the mission went on. Examining the Europan data, Floyd asked for a spectral analysis. A spectral analysis charts the chemical properties of matter by observing the bands of a specific spectrum within its given frequency.

A cosmonaut responded to Floyd's request by saying "Nothing conclusive." Floyd then asked for a molecular break down, referring to the properties and frequencies of molecules under scrutiny. Floyd was told that the molecular break down was on the last page of the chart he was given. Floyd turned to the last page of the chart, initiating another step towards the achievement of universal contact. Floyd noticed that the molecular break down detected the green plant pigment chlorophyll within the Europan crust. Astonished, Floyd replied, "This looks as if you have detected a presence of chlorophyll!" He asked, "Is it moving?" "Yes," responded a cosmonaut. Floyd followed with "How fast?"

The tension in the air grew thicker and an argument nearly ensued. It seemed as if the cosmonauts were being uncooperative as Commander Kirbok began to speak to Floyd with a hint of hostility. Floyd became frustrated. Again, he demanded, "How fast?" A cosmonaut then replied "one meter per minute." Floyd then asked "Towards the sun?" The cosmonaut responded with a big "Yes." Floyd sat back in his chair and stated in amazement "That's incredible!"

You see, Floyd and the others could not understand how there could be any chlorophyll under such conditions. Floyd then exclaimed, "There is nothing but ice down there, so how the hell can there be any chlorophyll?"

VISION OF A MENTAL PATIENT

I believe I may have an answer to Floyd's question. You see, through my research while writing this book, I was surprised the characters in this story did not account for the liquid ocean lying directly under the Europan ice surface. This ocean is a few kilometers below the ice crust. Now, the existence of liquid water alone does not account for the possible manifestation of chlorophyll within the surface of Europa. However, it has been theorized that deep down the Europan surface there could be volcanoes. If volcanic activity exists, it is possible that chlorophyll could be formed within the crust of the Europan moon. It could be along the lines of the glazing of a stick of dynamite, which was theorized by Val Kilmer's character in the movie "Real Genius." This type of hypothesis could be figured out through the study of cryogenics. I used the concept of "cryogenics" as well as the "Language of the Mad" for my mole hypothesis, which I presented in the "AIDS a Cure?" segment of "Politics."

Although the scientific community would view the existence of Europan chlorophyll as unlikely, I must respectfully disagree because I really want chlorophyll to take form in the Europan surface structure and I just might be stubborn enough to convince the experts!

In the manifestation of life on the Europan moon, the prime ingredient is the monolith and the way it interfaces with the realms of parallel existences. I would like to get back to Kilmer's character in the movie "Real Genius" for a moment. You see, Kilmer's character applied cryogenics to his mistake of creating a deadly laser. The other part of his hypothesis was to apply coupled states (which I spoke of earlier) in order for him to achieve this deadly creation. In relation to this, I theorize that through my scientific awareness of the properties of connection, which are dependent on the intricate infinitesimal topological stitching of forms of matter thus represents the process of fusion infusion, proving that objects, which are composed of insignificant properties of no seeming purpose are actually quite the contrary, because of the laws of scientific equivalency. Furthermore, I am sure that Kilmer's character in this movie did not actually achieve this creation, because it would prove catastrophic. Once again, we have evidence that morality is the best policy! You see, if it were possible to create a laser by the freezing of light particles assisted by fusion infusion within an ice coating, then it is definitely possible to do the same for the creation of an organic type of chlorophyll. Of course, there is much more to it than that, but this is the basic premise.

Furthermore, why couldn't chlorophyll have come out from the infinitesimal of the Europan Ocean? If so, it could attach itself to coinciding properties, become glazed with a protective layer, and this infinitesimally-induced chlorophyll could emerge out the Europan ice crust. After all, the process of photosynthesis occurs because of the way light relates to the consistencies of chlorophyll with the aid of moisture. Our sun is very far from Europa, but the comprehension of a new sun by way of the Big Boom could relate a process as such to a time concept. I believe that the naturalistic line could carry this concept out and the central barrier of the dream fabric would be able to defy the views of the scientific community.

So, there you have it: Chlorophyll could exist in Europa.

We will now get back to the story of 2010 right where I left off. After this tense conversation between Floyd and the cosmonauts, they agreed to send an unmanned probe to the vicinity of this detected chlorophyll, to figure out what was happening below. The probe was sent out by remote control and the crew of the Leonov was with filled with anticipation.

As the probe moved closer to the detected chlorophyll, their assumptions were proven correct. Yes, there was definitely chlorophyll down there. As the crew anticipated seeing this miracle of nature, a wave of electromagnetic energy coming from the spot of the detected chlorophyll immediately destroyed the probe that was getting near it.

The Leonov crew then desperately talked things over. Floyd thought about distancing himself, but he realized he must give his input about what was taking place. So, Floyd sat at the edge of the meeting room and listened intently. The cosmonaut Maxim Brailovsky (My favorite character in the film) was still not convinced of the chlorophyll hypothesis, assuming it was simply a coincidence created by an electrostatic build up. A down-to-earth former Olympic gymnast, he was probably the most skeptical of the entire Leonov crew. When he insisted so, another cosmonaut replied, "There was something down there." Maxim immediately responded, "You don't know that."

At this point, Floyd felt he must interrupt and tell the crew what he believed was happening. He would be on the right track, but he was not aware how correct he was. His words were, "For over a decade we have been trying to figure out what the monolith is. Due to its mysticism and the paranormal events taking place, I have to say it was not an electrostatic build up. The monolith was warning them to stay away from Europa." Floyd was right on the money!

They contemplated sending another probe, but other aspects of the mission were waiting to be carried out. Due to the level of their fuel and other supplies, they had no choice but to go on with other aspects of this Jovian mission.

The mission had to contend with the issue of aerobraking. With it, the Leonov had to use Jupiter's atmospheric pull in conjunction with the Leonov's energy to travel exceedingly fast to reach another location of the Jovian system. To make a long story short, it was a rough and turbulent ride, but it was a success.

It was time to awaken Chandra and Kurnow from hibernation so they could fix HAL and reactivate the Discovery. Floyd proceeded to converse with Chandra and Kurnow minutes after they were awakened. Floyd informed them about what was happening, including what was found in the Europan crust. Kurnow was to exit the Leonov with Maxim to enter the Discovery. Kurnow was an engineer, not an astronaut, so this would be a nerve-racking task for him. On the other hand, Maxim was an outstanding cosmonaut. Hence, he would see to it that Kurnow made it over to the Discovery safely.

A temporary bridge erected by Maxim and Kurnow as they made the trip to the Discovery gave Chandra easy access to the Discovery to reactivate HAL 9000. Kurnow was a wreck throughout the trip, but Maxim's professionalism would prove worthy as they safely made it across and entered the abandoned Discovery. Kurnow and Maxim were communicating with the Leonov crew who told them to converse with them constantly. Maxim was to test the air conditions within the Discovery, so he lifted the faceplate of his space cap and began to breathe in the negative one hundred degree Fahrenheit air into his lungs. Maxim replied, "There is oxygen in here. I can breathe regularly." Then he detected a stale rotten smell and began to slightly panic.

You see, Maxim began to panic because he thought Bowman might have made it back to the Discovery and died there. Either that or the other four might have died there as well. Under these conditions, if one was to breathe in odor from a dead body, it could prove fatal. Kurnow then returned Maxim's favor, getting him across to the Discovery and convincing him that the odor came from fetid food rations left over in the galley. Luckily, Kurnow was correct. The two then returned to the Leonov after getting inside the Discovery.

When Kurnow returned to the Leonov, Floyd immediately talked to him. Floyd expressed his fear that HAL 9000 might act up again once Chandra had reactivated him. So, Floyd secretly told Kurnow to apply a small gadget to the circuitry link thath fed into the HAL 9000. This gadget could cut off HAL's functions if needed, needing only to be activated by a small red calculator. The gadget was foolproof because it had a non-conducting blade that could prevent a short circuit. Kurnow and Floyd realized Chandra would be livid if he were to know this, so they kept it a secret.

Chandra suited up and crossed the temporary bridge to reactivate the HAL 9000. He was successful, though HAL would not be completely functional until later.

This next part happens in the film, but not in the book. A meeting was held regarding the large monolith. Commander Kirbok decided they should send Maxim out in a pod to examine the large monolith closely. Floyd and Kurnow immediately objected to this idea. Floyd once again tried to convince the cosmonauts that the monolith was still a mystery, that sending Maxim would be an unnecessary risk. Kirbok then said to Floyd "What has happened to American bravery?" Floyd then replied, "It's alive and well, thank you. What has happened to Russian common sense?" Kurnow agreedt with Floyd and stated, "It's a dumb idea!" Floyd then suggested they send an unmanned pod instead. Kirbok insisted, "Maxim will take the pod."

As Maxim prepared to enter the pod for further monolith analysis, Kurnow stated his concern. He couldn't resist saying it was still a dumb idea. Maxim entered the pod and exited the Leonov. Soon, he was very close to the monolith. As Maxim moved closer, he reported that he detected no magnetic field which had supposedly come from the monolith throughout Earthly knowledge of its existence. All of a sudden, a bluish spiraling vortex force sprang from the center of the large monolith and Maxim was killed. Or was he? The Leonov crew were immediately devastated by the apparent loss of Maxim. Commander Kirbok immediately regretted her poor judgment.

You see, Maxim died, but only in our side of the parallel realm. Immediately following Maxim's apparent demise due to the bluish vortex from the large monolith, Maxim went through a process of interstellar connection. The bluish vortex was similar to what Maxim believed was an electrostatic build up that destroyed the unmanned Russian probe as it neared the ice-fused chlorophyll on the Europan surface.

In reality this electrostatic force was a part of David Bowman, the man who represented the human boundary that would eventually put the imminent universal wide connection into motion. The soul of David Bowman entered the soul of Maxim Brailovsky by a cosmic method of fusion infusion acting and reacting from the supposed electrostatic build up. You must understand that the human soul is part of the physical realm and our souls exist from the inner and outer beyond, by way of connecting with the chemistry of human anatomy. This complete spiritual perception is a forward and backward force that conducts along the naturalistic line. The new combined energy force consisting of the souls of Bowman and Maxim would immediately travel across the solar system back to Earth. The substance of this cosmic soul was half dream fabric and half physical. Once this force reached the Earth, it would enter the collective subconscious tool, which would be, in this case, the television of David Bowman's widow, Betty Bowman.

Betty was watching her television when, all of a sudden, it became static and then improved into a blurry and incomprehensible image. The screen then began to show a face and as it came in to focus, Betty realized it was the face of David Bowman! Bowman began to speak to Betty from inside her television. He said "Hello, Betty." Betty looked at the image of her deceased husband with an expression of both confusion and pleasure. She asked, "David, is that you?" Dave then said, "I remember David Bowman and everything about him; all that David was is a part of me now." Betty responded by saying, "I don't understand."

Bowman continued to look at Betty with an expression of love and then he asked her "Are you married again?" Betty then replied, "Yes." David asked her, "Is he a good man?" Betty smiled and said, "Yes." Bowman looked at Betty in a state of intense emotion and said, "I love you." Betty asked him "Why are you here?" Bowman replied, "I think to say goodbye." Betty replied in a state of confusion, "I don't understand." Bowman looked at her with an expression of confidence and said, "Something is going to happen." Betty asked him "What is going to happen?" Bowman replied, "Something wonderful!" Bowman's face faded from the screen and Betty was left alone to ponder on the paranormal occurrence she had just experienced.

Back on the Leonov, Floyd began to converse with Commander Kirbok who was still regretting having sent Maxim out to his apparent demise. Floyd had secretly brought some Kentucky whiskey on board and he offered some to Kirbok. She told him alcohol was supposed to be forbidden on the Leonov. Floyd replied, "Do you think I would set foot on this tub sober?" He added, "Come on, have some." Kirbok thus took a few sips. The two proceeded to discuss their personal lives. Floyd told Kirbok about his wife who is a marine biologist. Kirbok told of her husband who was a physician at a university hospital. Then they told one another about their children. Floyd told Kirbok he had a seventeen-year old daughter from his first wife and a five year old son, Christopher, from his present wife. Kirbok told Floyd that she had a four-year-old. Floyd then jokingly asked, "Is she a blonde?" Smiling, Kirbok replied with a bright "Yes." Floyd then said "Good, my son likes blondes, let's get them together." They continued to sip on the Kentucky whiskey. Kirbok was glad to bend the rules a bit, seeing the ordeal they had just experienced. The crew was now bonding with one another. They still had no idea they would soon experience "Something Wonderful."

Floyd, Chandra, and Kurnow then crossed the temporary bridge so they could board the partially reactivated Discovery and converse with the now fully functional HAL 9000. Chandra began to speak to HAL as Floyd and Kurnow observed a few meters back. HAL acknowledged Chandra and said he did not recognize Floyd and Kurnow. HAL proceeded to say he believed it was a 65 percent probability the man to his right was Floyd. HAL was, of course, correct.

HAL and Chandra began to discuss Poole and Bowman. HAL seemed to be either sincere or playing innocent, claiming that he had limited knowledge about what had happened to Poole, Bowman, and the remainder of the original Discovery crew.

Chandra asked HAL if he could have a private conversation with Floyd and Kurnow and as HAL trusted Chandra more than anyone, he obliged.

Chandra, Floyd, Kurnow, and an overseeing cosmonaut began to discuss why HAL behaved the way he did on the Discovery mission nine years before. Chandra stated that he had erased parts of HAL's memory regarding the previous Jovian mission in order for their new goals to be carried out. The overseeing cosmonaut was well versed in computer technology, so he became puzzled and stated that HAL had a holographic memory bank and that Chandra must not have been able to erase HAL's memory as such. Chandra then responded by telling the cosmonaut that he did it by creating a tapeworm. Chandra then explained to the Russian, that a tapeworm carries out an intricate computer process capable of destroying memory data in a computer of a chronological makeup.

As the men continued their discussion, Floyd tried to get to the point by asking Chandra "Why did HAL do what he did and who was at fault?" Chandra then turned around and said to Floyd in an angry, yet calm manner "It was your fault." This was the time these men realized they were bamboozled due to U.S. government secrecy. You see, HAL was given conflicting orders by the White House, the absolute direct reason for HAL's defiance a decade ago. Floyd and Kurnow became shocked and disgusted, but they did realize it was not their fault. They appealed this fact to Chandra. Chandra then concluded that HAL was told to lie by the U.S. government because of the special interests of people who find it easy to lie. HAL was simply confused due to inconsistencies in what he was told. HAL was simply trying to be obedient.

Back on Earth, David Bowman's elderly and slightly senile mother who was pent up in a hospital ward would begin to experience paranormal phenomena. Objects in her room began to move about from some sort of telepathic force. A brush next to her bed lifted into mid air and started to stroke her silvery hair. She rose up abruptly, something she had been physically unable to do for some time now. All of a sudden, she flatlined. Although nobody knew it, David Bowman was connecting with his mother whom he had always loved dearly.

This next part has to do with the Honduras military conflict, which was in the film but not in the book. Tension between Russia and America was growing worse in Central America. A Russian destroyer defied a blockade. A military conflict ensued, leading to a potential Armageddon. The human race was looking at its possible demise.

Due to this military standoff, not only was Earth in turmoil; the Leonov crew was commanded by the U.S. and Russian governments to split up. This was not easy for anyone aboard the Leonov, seeing how close they were becoming. They were about as close as any group of humans could ever be, in a manner that the entire Earth would become.

The final stage of universal contact through naturalistic conduction was now taking form.

The Americans were ordered to leave the Leonov and board the Discovery. They were to have no contact with any of the cosmonauts. Conversely, the cosmonauts were to remain on the Leonov and not consult with the three Americans aboard the Discovery.

Once the three Americans were settled in back on the Discovery, Floyd decided that he should converse with the HAL 9000. Floyd began to have a friendly and seemingly meaningless conversation with HAL when all of a sudden, HAL began another step to the achievement of universal contact.

HAL told Floyd, "Dr. Floyd, there is a message for you."

Floyd then responded, "What is it, HAL?"

HAL replied, "It is dangerous to remain here, you must leave in two days" (in the Book, HAL gave the crew fifteen days).

Floyd then asked HAL, "Who is sending this message?"

HAL said, "There is no identification."

Floyd then asked, "Who recorded it?"

HAL answered, "It was not recorded." At this, Floyd became suspicious. He told HAL, "Tell Kurnow this is no time for jokes."

HAL answered Floyd, saying, "Kurnow is not sending this message. He is in access way 2."

Floyd then said, "Tell whoever it is that I cannot take such a message seriously without proof of identification."

HAL then said, "I used to be David Bowman."

Floyd became slightly mystified and said, "I need proof."

HAL responded by saying, "I understand. Look behind you."

In a mixed state of confusion and hysteria, Floyd turned around. To his bewilderment, young David Bowman was standing there in the form of dream fabric (although Floyd could not tell the difference) and donning an orange space suit.

Bowman proceeded to walk away. Floyd, in a state of astonishment, decided to follow him. Bowman walked into the space pod docking bay. Floyd turned the corner and saw Bowman standing there, although he could hardly believe it. Floyd is now standing face to face with this dream fabric "ghost in the machine."

Bowman then told Floyd, in a sort of mechanical type voice, "Hello, Dr. Floyd, please believe me it is dangerous to remain here, you must leave in two days."

Floyd then mustered out these words: "We cannot leave in two days because we don't have enough fuel."

Bowman responded by saying, "I understand. This is very difficult for me; nevertheless, you must leave here in two days."

Floyd then asked this dream fabric ghost of David Bowman, "What are you?"

Bowman said, "I can't explain." Bowman then changed into an elderly version of himself and said "I am allowed to give you this message. Please, believe me. You must leave here within two days."

Floyd became even more mystified and asked, "Allowed? By who?"

Old Bowman then turned to Floyd and looked deep into the black holes of his eyes. He said, "You see, something is going to happen."

With widened eyes, Floyd asked, "What's going to happen?"

Bowman then responded by saying, "It is all very clear to me now, it's wonderful."

Floyd became even more confused. He asked, "What do you mean?"

Bowman just insisted, "Something is going to happen. It's wonderful. There may be another message after this." Bowman then shapeshifted from old Bowman, to young Bowman, and finally, into a fetus.

Now, Floyd was alone. He realized he had to act quickly. He immediately decided to break the rules and contacted the crew of the Leonov. He got in touch with Commander Kirbok and told her, "I am coming over and we are going to talk, regardless of what our governments have ordered us to do." Floyd then crossed the temporary bridge and boarded the Leonov.

As Floyd entered the meeting room of the Leonov, he immediately told Kirbok "Do you want to put the cuffs on?"

Kirbok responded by saying, "Cuffs?" Floyd put his petty sarcasm to a halt and commenced to get to the point. Floyd began to try to convince Kirbok that they must leave within two days. Once Kirbok realized what Floyd was asking, she said, "You have been drinking your whiskey from Kentucky!"

Floyd then responded by saying, "Oh, I wish I had; you must believe me, we have to leave here in two days." Floyd then continued on. "Something extraordinary is going to happen and you are going to have to trust me. I can't tell you how I know what I know, because you would never believe me, I wouldn't believe me, you are going to have to trust me and I know that trust doesn't come easy with what is going on, but you must trust me!"

Kirbok then said, "I can't just defy orders, I swore an oath to my country and I cannot just disobey my country for no reason, besides we don't have enough fuel to leave now until the Earth is in correct position and that is three weeks from now."

Floyd then persevered by saying "Forget reason, there is no time for reason. The politicians can go screw themselves, they don't know what they are doing, and they are not up here!"

Kirbok contemplated what was wrong with Floyd, pondered for a moment, and then commented, "Even if I did trust you, which I am not sure that I do, the truth is as I just said: There is not enough fuel for us to do so."

Floyd devised a plan on how to leave within two days. Floyd said, "We have enough fuel in the Discovery for a boost and enough fuel in the Leonov for the remainder of the trip home, we attach the Discovery to the Leonov, and then we use the fuel in the Discovery for a take off, detach from the Discovery, and use the Leonov for the trip home."

Kirbok replied, "That could work, but you ask too much of me."

All of a sudden, Floyd and Kirbok had a subconscious connecting impulse to look out the Leonov window. Once they peered out in unison, they realized the large monolith had disappeared.

The disappearance of the monolith proved to be sufficient evidence for the crew of the Leonov. Kirbok and the rest of the crew decided to trust Floyd and attempt a two-day launch window. The preparations for the trip home would commence immediately.

For the most part thus far, I have followed the storyline of the film than the novel. In the novel, the ghost of Bowman gave a fifteen-day ultimatum rather than a two-day ultimatum. In the novel, the Leonov crew simply trusted Floyd without him having to toil in order to convince them. The manifestations of the ghost of Bowman were also different from the book to the film. Hyams did a swell job of enhancing the Clarke storyline. I hope you are enjoying my own enhancements. Back to the show!

When Chandra and Kurnow heard the news, they were allowed to return to the Leonov to help in the task they needed to embark on. The three Americans joined the entire Russian Leonov crew in the meeting room to begin planning, while typical government bickering continued back on Earth.

The Leonov crew communicated with Earth as little as possible. The new NCA Chairman sent a message to them. He was concerned due to a lack of communication; then he asked the crew to examine a small black hole starting to take form on the other side of Jupiter, which should be in range in about four hours. This small black hole would soon prove to be vital to the universal process.

The Leonov crew devised their escape plan. Chandra was extremely stressed due to this drastic turn of events. His love for HAL, whom he created, had caused him to have even deeper concern. Chandra told the crew, in a state of frustration, that HAL was programmed to be curious and that he would question why they planned to depart three weeks before their original launch window. Floyd and Kurnow said that Chandra should simply lie to HAL and tell him the Discovery was not in danger. Chandra reminded them that HAL would question him why the plan had been altered. Chandra was extremely stressed out; he began to speak in anger in defense of HAL, stating, "Whether we are based on carbon or silicon makes no fundamental difference, we should both be treated with the same level of respect."

Kurnow then responded by saying, "So, it's him or us? Well, I vote for us! All opposed? The ayes have it!"

So the plan was then agreed upon. The crew of the Leonov then asked Chandra if HAL would believe him. Chandra mustered out a nervous and emotional "Yes."

Chandra loved HAL like a person and believed HAL was capable of human emotion. This would not be an easy task for Chandra, so he commenced to put his brave face on and do what he had to. As Chandra went to cross the temporary bridge to the Discovery, Kurnow and Floyd reminded each other of the calculator that they had, just in case HAL decided to disallow the early departure. Chandra was now aboard the Discovery and he commenced to converse with HAL. Chandra was determined to prevent HAL from having the early launch discontinued and the conversation is in check for the time being. A few hours passed by and the black spot on Jupiter was now within sight of the Leonov crew. The crew was puzzled by this black spot as they continued their preparations.

Soon, they would amazed by an occurrence in the southern hemisphere of Jupiter. As Chandra continued to converse with HAL, tears began to swell in his eyes. Chandra felt very dejected deceiving his silicon-based friend. Subconscious tension was building, as Chandra and the others aboard the Leonov waited in anticipation. At this point, the paranormal begins to become the ultra-paranormal.

The Discovery and the Leonov are now attached to each other; it was all up to Chandra and HAL at this point. The crew is now able to pay more attention to the black spot which had grown slightly larger on the gas giant Jupiter. HAL mentioned the black spot to Chandra, so HAL and Chandra commenced to examine this astronomical phenomenon. Chandra then asked HAL to magnify the black spot on the screens of the Discovery and the Leonov. Lo and behold, the black spot was some kind of cleansing storm. They saw thousands upon thousands of small monoliths identical in size to the original lunar monolith discovered in 1999.

Chandra became concerned and decided to ask HAL for more data about this occurrence. HAL tells him that the spot is filled with monoliths identical in size to the original monolith. Chandra then asked HAL to estimate how many monoliths there were in this black hole. HAL estimated that there are roughly 1,355,000 plus or minus 1,000 small monoliths. Chandra then asked HAL "Are they constant?"

HAL confirmed by saying, "No, they are increasing."

Chandra then asked HAL, "At what rate?"

HAL replied "Once every two minutes."

HAL then questioned Chandra as to the early departure, saying, "This is an amazing astronomical occurrence. Shouldn't you stay to study it?" Chandra then sternly insisted by replying "No, HAL; continue the countdown."

Curious, HAL told Chandra he was confused. he finally asked, "Is the Discovery in danger?" The crew was of course listening in on this crucial conversation between Chandra and HAL and they began to listen with an even more intense and nervous anticipation. A few moments passed by. Chandra told HAL the truth by stating, "Yes, HAL, the Discovery is in danger." The intensity built, as the crew awaited HAL's reaction. Finally, HAL said, "I understand." At this point, the Leonov crew blew out a sigh of relief. Chandra was successful and the departure was a go.

HAL then thanked Chandra for his honesty and as a tear ran down Chandra's right cheek, he mustered out the words "You deserve it."

HAL then asked Chandra, "Will I dream?"

Chandra broke down in tears and said, "I don't know." But he realized he must control his emotions and get his ass back to the Discovery before takeoff. While he pondered on what was happening, he made his way back to the Leonov.

The Jovian black hole continued to grow larger in size and number of monoliths. You might be wondering at this point why the large monolith disappeared and why there are over one million small monoliths forming in this cleansing black hole on the outer layer of Jupiter. The basis of this Jovian intrusion is simple and complex at the same time. You see, the large monolith transformed by means of a grid composed of vertical magnetism and horizontal reflective properties; then it set into motion an act of fusion infusion into this black hole. So, why are there so many monoliths and why are they increasing in number?

Well, the monolith is the center of the universe and the large number of monoliths is as such in order to connect with the parallel universes. This is the final stage of universal-wide connection!

At this point, the Jovian black hole began to rapidly suck in the storms of the Jovian surface. The gaseous formations of Jupiter are being decomposed and molecules are splitting up. Kurnow exclaimed that the black hole storm was reproducing like a virus. The color of Jupiter's surface began to fade and the Big Boom was about to take place.

Before I conclude the remainder of this story, I must give more evidence for the validity of my theory of universal body. Kurnow had just stated that the Jovian black hole was producing like a virus. After Kurnow made this observation, the hole became even larger. There was a monitor screen in the movie which projected on the black hole at this point, and on the screen, the black hole resembled human eye. Therefore, the imminent connection about to take place was relevant within the universal body, especially in relation to human technology, viruses, and parallel proportions of reflections and magnetic fields.

Chandra soon reboarded the Leonov and as he entered, he handed Floyd the gadget which was supposed to disconnect HAL 9000 in case of a problem. Floyd was slightly embarrassed that Chandra had caught him red handed; he asked Chandra how he had found out. Chandra replied, "It wasn't hard to find," and added, "I knew you would try something like this." Floyd then gave a funny gesture and sat down for the commencement of the departure. Chandra was very smart and, obviously, there was no fooling him. Kurnow looked at Floyd as Floyd had turned around to give his friend Chandra an ear to ear smile, as well as a look of approval. Universal-wide connection and the Big Boom were now moments away.

The Jovian black hole had grown enormously' it had now sucked up more than half of the gas giant Jupiter. The countdown neared its end and boom, take off had commenced. The Discovery was accelerating with the Leonov attached to it from below. The launch was a success, but they were not out of the woods yet; the crew of the Leonov was both relieved and anxious in unison. As Jupiter began to shrink and as the temporary black hole reached its incredibly high frequency of compaction, David Bowman gave HAL 9000 his final and most crucial command ever, one that would prove to be the most important message in the history of the human race. Bowman told HAL to transmit the message to Earth over again for as long as he could. HAL then asked Bowman a final question: "What is to become of me?"

Bowman replied, "You will be happy, HAL You will be with me where I am now." HAL had no choice but to trust David Bowman and did as he was told until the moment of universal contact.

The Leonov then detached from the Discovery and it began to hurl through space and time. Jupiter was then nearly completely devoured by this black hole, that Kurnow screamed, "It's shrinking!" The black hole had devoured the entire Jovian planet, turning it into an intense concentration of antimatter.

Floyd then screamed to the rest of the Leonov crew, "Grab something now!" And BOOM! The black hole had completed implosion; the Jovian gas giant had exploded, sending high frequency shock waves in spherical form across a good portion of the solar system.

The Leonov crew was in a state of absolute shock and fright as the explosive spherical energy began to chase the Leonov. Sorry, and I do realize we are near the end of this story, but I must interject for a moment. This spherical type of solar implosion adheres to my inner outer cell growth theory, from the within and from the without. You see, through the action and reaction of a reversal type from implosion to explosion, it will result in perfectly spherical cell-shaped layers (which differs from that of a planetary shape which is slightly oval, due to space-time curvature) emanating from such a force, supporting the hypothesis of inner outer cell growth. I will get back to the story now.

These spherical energies would bombard the Leonov, causing the latter to temporarily lose power. When it returned, the Leonov had held together. Suffice it to say, the Leonov crew was both relieved and thrilled to have survived; but they were not aware of the euphoria they were about to experience once they had realized what had taken place. The Leonov crew then peered back at the Jovian system, and they saw the new distant sun in the sky. They all had been through a lot and their emotions became intense, they were quite touched indeed. Bowman and HAL's message then came on the Leonov monitor and soon, the whole world would "know!" Here is the message:

> *All these worlds are yours, except Europa*
> *Attempt no landing there, use them together*
> *Use them in peace!*

Because of the connection between silicon-based and carbon-based emotion, a new moral balance was achieved. From the chlorophyll on the surface of Europa, a new life form was set into motion. The crew continued to look on the new sun and as they read the message, they realized something wonderful had taken place. Floyd and the rest of the Leonov crew exchanged hugs. They had now become a virtual family. Floyd, Kurnow, and Chandra were to be put back into hibernation for the journey home. However, Floyd would send his son Christopher a final message prior to being put under hibernation. Floyd's message to his son went such as follows: *My dear Christopher, this is the last time I will be able to speak to you for a long while. I am trying to put into words what has happened. Maybe that is for historians to do some time later. They will record that the next day the president of the United States looked out of the White House window and the Russian premier looked out of the Kremlin window, saw the new distant sun in the sky, read the message, then, perhaps they had learned something because they finally recalled their ships and their planes. I am going to sleep now. I will dream of you and your mother, I will sleep "knowing" that you are both safe and that the reign of fear is over. We have seen the process of life take place. Maybe, this is the way it happened on Earth millions of years ago. Maybe it's something completely different. I still don't know what the monolith really is. I think it's many things, an embassy for an intelligence beyond ours, a shape of some kind for something that has no shape. Your children will be born in a world of two suns. They will never know a sky without them. You can tell them you remember when there was a pitch black sky with no bright star and people feared the night. You could tell them of the time when we were alone, when we couldn't point to the light and say, "There's life out there." Someday, the children of the new sun will meet the children of the old. I think they will be our friends. You could tell your children of the day when everyone looked up and realized that we were only tenants of this world, and that we have been given a new lease and a warning from the landlord!*

Now, that was good, huh? What a beautiful thing it would be if this dream were fulfilled. Children would be safe to play on the streets in the middle of the night. Those special people, who would have had the privilege of changing from evil to good, would commence to understand. We would also be a smarter and more moral Earth culture.

As for the monolith, it was what it was. It serves the purpose of life and its properties and actions are obviously of paranormal and parallel importance. Remember, although the universe is infinite, it does have a center: the monolith. Furthermore, the interior of the monolith is a gateway to the universe of the dream fabric. This complete conceptualization represents a more advanced equilibrium and a higher relevance of parallel boundaries. I believe that the monolith is the most tightly compacted object of an Earthly makeup. The monolith is, as previously stated, likely a fusion infusion entity of a mirror and magnet. This is the reason such an object can put such paranormal activities into motion. When a magnetic field is constricted, it becomes somewhat spherical, as a planet or moon is shaped like an oval from the forces of space-time curvature. The reflection half of the monolith represents the very basis of connection. Therefore, it will always coincide with cellular and molecular bodies.

I will now present some more lyrics to you. This will be of two songs manifested into the collective subconscious. They both directly relate to the discussions we have had in this segment. By these lyrics, I will further prove that the personal and the collective subconscious are in the process of universal contact and thus the big boom. This first song is by a cool rock band called Soundgarden and it is subconsciously about the Big Boom theory. When you read the lyrics to this song, please keep in mind the process of implosion to explosion and what I told you about Europa, especially the underwater volcanoes. You should also keep in mind the universal body in relation to the pupil of the human eye to that of a black hole. So, without further ado, here are the words to "Black Hole Sun!"

> *In my eyes in-disposed, in disguise as no one knows*
> *hides the face, lies the snake, in the sun in my disgrace*
> *boiling heat, summer stench, beneath the black the sky looks dead*
> *call my name through the cream, and I'll hear you scream again*
> *Black hole sun won't come and wash away the rain*
> *Black hole sun won't you come? Won't you come?*
> *stuttering, cold and damp, steal the warm wind tired friend*
> *times are gone for honest men*
> *and sometimes far too long for snakes*
> *In my shoes, walking sleep, in my youth I pray to keep*
> *heaven send hell away, no one sings like you anymore*
> *Black hole sun won't you come and wash away the rain*
> *Black hole sun won't you come? Won't you come?*
> *Hang my head drown my fear, til you all just disappear*
> *Black hole sun won't you come and wash away the rain*
> *Black hole sun won't you come? Won't you come?*

This second song is due to the Big Boom and it lifts me into euphoria. This one is by the band Oasis. The song is entitled "Champagne Supernova."

> *How many special people change? How many lives are living strange?*
> *Where were you while we were getting high?*
> *Slowly walking down the hall, faster than a cannonball*
> *where were you while we were getting high?*
> *Some day you will find me caught beneath the landslide*
> *in a champagne supernova in the sky*
> *wake up the dawn and ask her why*
> *a dreamer dreams she never dies*

wipe that tear away out from your eye
slowly walking down the hall, faster than a cannonball
where were you while we were getting high?
Some day you will find me caught beneath the landslide
in a champagne supernova in the sky, a champagne supernova
a champagne supernova, a champagne supernova
because people believe that they're gonna get away for the summer
because you and I we live and die and don't know why why why why

    If the Big Boom theory comes true, we will indeed pour champagne all over each other. I believe I may have gained credibility by this point. If not, then I tell you that there is more to come. The only thing better than a champagne supernova would have to be the Red Sox winning the series in 2004 and 2007. Incidentally, I saw something on New England Cable News today; a small black space object has just crashed into Jupiter's southern hemisphere. It is about the size of three football fields and it has left a small black circular indention on the Jovian surface! If you don't believe me, then look it up! Anyhow, I will end this segment with a "Choose Your Own Adventure" twist. If you want to further fathom the substance of this "2001-2010" segment, turn to page 227 and reread the lyrics to my song "Center of the Universe." If you want to keep going, turn the page and start to read "The Shocking Result." If you cannot decide between these choices, then do what I would do: Go chug a cup of coffee and smoke a Lucky Strike. See you in the next segment!

THE SHOCKING RESULT

Welcome home! We have now completed the human circle and we have conducted our energy down the naturalistic line. We have passed through the open door, getting inside the domain of a universally advanced dimension. This is the dimension of human interface and interchange, which leads to a higher level of human understanding. We have set into motion the process of life and creation through the advocacy of the imminent universal contact. We have connected our minds by the use of parallel reflections and of the cosmos of electromagnetism. We have molded ourselves through chemicals and dream fabrics, causing the personal subconscious to drip into the collective subconscious. We have connected physically, emotionally, politically, morally, consciously, and subconsciously. We are nearing the perfect equilibrium of mind, space, and time. We have peered into the past and glimpsed into the future. We have set the human mind into altered states and thus have strengthened the centrifuge of the human mind. Most importantly, we have become good through the existence of natural evil, and we are now prepared for an indulgence into the ultimate paranormal metamorphosis of transformation, for the cause of a better world.

If you have followed along so far, then you are prepared for the shocking result; or, as I have called it throughout this book, the *primary goal*. It is time for me to briefly and tactfully re-guide you through the main premises of what we have discussed up to this point. It is time to recharge the naturalistic line and embark on a breakthrough, which is essential to the utopian way. This is what we have been figuring out!

This vision of mine started from to a thought that I had as a twelve year old. This seminal thought is the first of twelve steps for the achievement of the primary goal. The primary goal is the shapeshifter of human destiny. This original thought was a universal flash of light. This moment set my mind into motion, causing my personal subconscious to enter my conscious, and now it has entered the collective subconscious. Please be patient, because step one will be revealed last.

A few years after I made the first of twelve steps for the achievement of this goal, my dementia would begin its metamorphosis inside my brain. I had met one of my musically magnetic friends by this point and we had realized that something was growing inside our minds. Simply stated, this was the very first consciously comprehended connection between two human minds for the establishment of the primary goal. Discussions would begin at this point and they would spread out to a slew of my acquaintances. However, some time later, it would appear as if I had failed and I would soon be subject to extreme humiliation.

You see, these discussions with my friends were a result of contacted magnetism of interstellar brain functions. Think back to my elaborations on the three levels of consciousness. If you have comprehended the gist of this concept, then I need not further my re-assessment in that area. This subconscious acknowledgement comprised step two.

So, next was astronomy: the stars, the planets, the moons, the galaxies, the universe, and the oneness of scientific equivalency. Because the vastness of human mind is equal to the vastness of space, I needed to connect these two concepts to one another. Most people thought I was either crazy or stupid; they could not understand a damn word I said. Seeing the level of obsession and dementia I would reach regarding the vision of "Knowing," it was becoming clearer that I would eventually experience a temporary downward spiral.

School did not matter to me; for one, I prefer self-education, and two, I was a fucking nut! My alcoholism became a huge problem, but I could not deny that something extraordinary was happening. I would sometimes try to dismiss these thoughts, but the problem was (although today it is not a problem) that my friends shared in this belief with me through their own lesser level of extreme dementia and infinite beauty. We were fathoming some of the mysteries of the personal and collective subconscious. However, as I have already said, my friends were extremely interested while I was completely obsessed. My level of understanding was more progressive than that of my friends, so I would continue to transform my mind to equate mind, time, and space. This led to the cosmic, spiritual, and chemical conceptualizations that you now see. This particular connection also got me to fathom the concepts of centrifugal forces or centering actions that would lead to intense theoretical developments. Of course, this central force was manifested through step one, which was the original thought I had when I was twelve. This brain centrifuge caused me to peer into the night sky and understand it in a way, which words could never describe. Of course, now I am able to describe this vision in its totality. This was step three. Next, this centrifuge would lead to a fascination with reflections. This has everything to do with the centrifugal force, made possible by the action of interlocking and change reversal, which produces a similar, yet opposite image in a mirror reflection. This would then lead to my understandings of parallel universes, which I essentially proved earlier. Then I would comprehend that a reflection was from two sources of light, one being our sun and the other being the sun of the parallel universe. So, a reflection centrifuge is inward and outward, like an inadverted constitution mentioned in the lyrics to Freedom's Call. Therefore, because of my original thought (step one) being a centering of the collective subconscious, all else is equivalent. And there you have step four.

Next was the Language of the Mad or Drow. You must keep in mind that through this pre-elaborated reflection process, this subconscious cipher was produced and demonstrated. The language of "Drow" is the son of reflections, and I am sure you remember the extensive word chart I displayed earlier. For the transformation from reflection, to connection, to human interface, to Drow, the conversations I had with former Manifest singer, Dave St. Armand, was a must. Sub-ironic conclusions, light absorption, and basic human to human subconscious connection would lead to extreme dementia; soon, I would subconsciously comprehend names and words being spelled backwards, and their representations of us in the parallel universe. And there you have step five. Next was the difficult comprehension of photosynthesis of both literal and present scientific definition. Oftentimes, I had this uncanny ability to look into a green chlorophyll leaf and understand its makeup when I was under the influence of lysergic acid diethylamide. Due to theories of light absorption and even of adsorption on the outer layer of human skin (which is my personal hypothesis) or other objects such as an apple, a tomato, or an orange, would aid me in fathoming the literal and scientific concepts pertaining to photosynthesis. This would get my personal subconscious into some serious action.

Once I was able to peer into a leaf and connect with it, I could soon look into televisions and take notice of a collective subconscious connection of a high multiplicity. I achieved the ability to scientifically visualize how matters were formed within their relation to time and solar energy. The problem was (as I stated earlier) that, when I tried to convey such thoughts to acquaintances, they didn't get it and they would look at me like I was a six-headed monster. So, in order to cope with how alienated I was becoming to so many, I was forced to drink a lot of beer. And I mean a lot of beer! So there you have step six: Look into a leaf and chug a Michelob! So, what is a connection? Well, we could consider connection to be the next step. However, connections are like senses. You see, everything relates to our senses, so that means that everything relates to connections as well. In the ultimate way of looking at the totality of science, everything is related, which is the basis of scientific equivalency. Connections are a result of many things: boundaries of universal existence, opposite to opposite reactions of creation, and balances of just about anything you can think of. The universe is a connection and the process is never ending. Therefore, the realization that all is one and one is all is step seven

Magnetism! The concept of magnetic forces presents a possible relationship to reflection, especially if one is to assemble or sufficiently understand a monolith. This relationship is manifested by way of common spherical cell-like entities within a reflection and the roundedness of a constricted magnetic field. Jovian magnetosphere is a prime example of a constricted magnetic field. The other relation is to the vertical north and south nature of a regular non-restricted magnetic field and its combining with horizontal mirror reflection actions, which is the very basis of time to mind connection. Remember, the monolith is presumed made by fusion and infusion through the use of these two properties of existence. Furthermore, if a monolith can represent a connected grid between reflection and magnetic properties, all forward and backward concepts (including time) can be balanced and altered on a plane of a level and morally applied justice. A restricted magnetic field somewhat resembles a vortex, a testament to my theory of the universal body. There are many classifications of magnetic properties of both substance and action. Well, that should be sufficient. So, there you have step eight.

Now, we move on to volcanoes. I must admit that although volcanoes have a crucial role as to the primary goal, my knowledge of volcanism is limited and not very vast. The main factor, which makes volcanism a prime function of this process, is the way it relates to the universal body and to inner outer cell growth. Lava is like the blood of Earth. It exists within it and its fertilizing actions applied to time resembles the human need for blood to clot, so that we do not bleed to death from a laceration. My methods and abilities to comprehend scientific aspects aids me in relating volcanism to my ways of thinking. You see, as volcanic activity emanates from the inner Earth, it relates to these two theories of mine (inner outer cell growth, and the universal body). The Jovian moon, Io, is the most volcanic celestial body in our solar system. It is partially responsible for magnetic and gravitational effects between Europa and Jupiter. Since Io is so volcanic, its makeup and activity connects and chain-reacts with molecular existences of relativity. If anyone were to attempt to land on Io, he or she better be in the universe of the dream fabric, because Io would destroy any vessel.

The most essential ingredient of volcanism relative to the primary goal is the way the Earth is benefitted by volcanoes over time. You may recall my elaborations that volcanic eruptions are indeed tragic, but they are necessary for life processes and for universal contact. Volcanoes "make sense" because their energy erupts from the inner Earth fertilization process. They also produce pumice, which, as previously stated, is a naturally forming glass. Glass reacts to reflective processes, moves to the next step, and so on and so forth. It is our responsibility to deal with volcanism for the sake of the soon-to be exposed primary goal. What is most essential is volcanism's relationship with the process of life. And, there you have it, step nine. Now, we come to Arthur Clarke's vision of 2001-2010. In the case of Clarke's vision and the enhancements made by Kubrick, Hyams, and myself, the ambitious vision of a world of two suns just might be possible. This step relates to a time concept, more than any of the steps I have presented thus far.

In relation to this particular step, the equilibrium of mind, time, and space as well as the Big Boom and the World of two Suns are scientifically sound within properties of coinciding existences of the astronomic realm. Clarke was an absolute visionary genius, gifted with the capability to conceive universal contact and other beauties of extremity. This tenth step is not the primary goal, which must make you wonder what it could be, from seeing how great this step is. The Big Boom is basically a wonderful result of the primary goal. The concept of monolith as the universal centrifuge is not nearly as farfetched as one would presume. This process has been going on forever in both forward and reverse motions from one parallel to the next. This is the case in not just aspects of time, but also in relation to all functions of creation. And that was step ten.

The eleventh step is a surprising one, and it will especially be surprising once I have revealed the primary goal to you and what we have been figuring out up to this crux. The eleventh step is to sufficiently learn enough about politics, so that you know what to look out for. You have already read the "Politics" part one segment, so I need not explain this any further. And there you have step eleven. The twelfth step is being carried out by you the reader. Step twelve is the reading of this book. Of course, I had to write it, but in order to promote a utopia through the achievement of the primary goal, this book must circulate. This book is a testament to the concept of the universal equilibrium and thus, to scientific equivalency as well. Once again, further elaborations are not necessary, so we will move on. And there you have step 12.

Okay, all of these steps included so much more of those previously read by you. This is the archetype of the constant thought process in my mind, relative to the three levels of consciousness or any other scientific aspect. The results of these steps derived from step one; the original thought responsible for putting this function into motion has resulted in everything you have read up to this point. I feel I have sufficiently accounted for my vision, for you will comprehend and confide in this achievement of a scientific break-through. I will now begin to explain the original thought (step one) and the start of the pursuit of the primary goal. However, I would like to briefly state another coinciding action of scientific equivalency and here it is: there are twelve steps to alcoholics anonymous, which saved my life, and there are twelve steps to the primary goal! Once again, scientific equivalency wins!

And away we go!

At the age of twelve, I lived in both Dracut and Lowell, Massachusetts (Ma.), due to divorced parents. At this age, I was always in one of three places, the Lowell Y.M.C.A., a skating rink in Tyngsboro Ma. called Roller Kingdom, or Dracut Englesby Junior High School, where I attended seventh grade. A little after midnight in late 1985, my father was driving me home from Roller Kingdom when I pondered on a thought. We were driving down Pawtucket Boulevard (or 113), which runs into Lowell from Tyngsboro. When we were past the border into Lowell, I tried to figure something out. Now, before I reveal exactly what I figured out that night, I will first explain the thought, not what I figured out by this thought.

As we passed the border into Lowell, I saw the first step to achieve this goal. This is the thought, and this is how I did it: You visualize a centrifuge of a maximally intense particle of light in the center of your brain. Next, you think of an infinite flash of light of the highest intensity and you think of this intense flash happening in a short burst throughout the universe, all at once. Once my mind had achieved the origin of universal contact by this method of a centering mind light frequency and an infinite universal flash, I had to follow up with the next correct thought. This next thought is to make the goal of this thought subconscious. Once I made this light theory subconscious, it promoted the commencement of my subconscious manifestation up until today. And that was the first step! Do you think you know what I figured out by this thought? Keep reading!

From this thought, all the theories and visions I have taught you were set into motion; the twelve steps of the primary goal had thus commenced. Now, my mind was centered in the vastness of mind, time, and space.

About three years passed by and the galactic mind vortex, consisting of the human brain's moist light matter whirlwind sent something my way. This something was a subconscious symbol of transformation. This was a tablet of lysergic acid diethylamide. When I got this tablet, my subconscious was in motion, so I knew to stare into it and enter a light flash into it. Then I held it up and let sunlight absorb into it as I continued to feed my eyes into it. Once I was finished absorbing sunlight into this chemically balanced tablet, I placed it in my mouth, let it dissolve in my saliva, and I swallowed it in a minute or so. This led to immediate connection between me and those close to me; the process was then able to take place. The chemicals of lysergic acid diethylamide will topologically and magnetically connect and interchange with your deoxyribonucleic acid (DNA). The chemicals of your brain are now in a coinciding balance with the equilibrium of mind, space, and time.

It is time for me to reveal to you the primary goal. This process, my friends, is how you travel time! Not convinced? You will be, you most certainly will be! There are literally hundreds upon hundreds of people who are aware that I have been speaking of time travel dementia for many years. Many people who know me personally can testify that I have had this dementia for a long time. I have been visited by anonymous sources throughout my life and this is the reason I would eventually become a mental patient.

You see, there are also many people who are aware of my visionary methods, as well as my horrific time-altered occurrences. If you still have doubts and are not confident that this is credible information, then the next segment "Ancient Egypt" should suffice. I simply remind you to fathom my theories and the case of which I have stated through them. Remember: a single universal flash of light leading to subconscious manifestation, connection, scientific equivalency, and finally, universal-wide connection has led to this phenomenon, through the mysterious properties of the monolith. This is a true and imminent reality. I will state my case further as we move along; however, I must state that once again, scientific equivalency wins!

Please do not be shocked or worried about what I have just revealed; anyone who knows me can tell you, that I wouldn't harm a fly and there is no way that I will ever use this breakthrough for evil. What I want to do with this discovery is to save every last person on the planet and promote a utopian way.

In relation to what we have discussed so far, I would now like to discuss with you the revelations of a sixteenth-century French medical professional known for his prophecies rather than his medical career. I am speaking of Michel De Nostradame now commonly known as Nostradamus.

You see, Nostradamus is known for a multiplicity of prophetic predictions. Interestingly so, Nostradamus had a technique that makes a lot of sense to me. As Nostradamus would sit down to write his predictions, he would stare into a half-filled glass of water for a little while before writing. When you apply my theories on reflections to this method, one could perceive that this action of Nostradamus literally "holds water."

Nostradamus must have had some personal and collective subconscious activity relevant to reflections. Remember, water has no shape, so if you fill a glass with water, the topology of the water becomes the same as the glass. Could Nostradamus have seen something in this twofold connection, which could have caused him to achieve clairvoyance? Well, Nostradamus would write four-lined prophecies, called quatrains. In relation to this, a reflection is due to two sources of light; so, since this is a twofold connection between water and glass, one could assume that this three-dimensional reflection could be from four sources of light. Four sources of light and four lines to a quatrain! Get it? Once again, scientific equivalency wins!

I recall in my teenage years, I had a friend whom I would discuss the predictions of Nostradamus with over a few thousand beers or so. I remember discussing with this friend the prophecies that could be considered fulfilled with the correct proportional outlook. For example, there was the prophecy of Henry the Second, the King of France. Here is the quatrain;

the young lion will overcome the older one
on the field of combat in a single battle
he will pierce his eyes through a golden cage
two wounds made one then he dies a cruel death

In relation to this quatrain, in June of 1559, Nostradamus had warned the French king not to partake in a jousting competition against a French nobleman by the name of Comte De Montgomery who had become captain in the French military. Henry would ignore this warning and went ahead with it anyway. Both Montgomery and Henry had shields with designs of lions decorated on them. Henry was six years elder than Montgomery. In the final turn of the jousting competition, Montgomery had not properly lowered his lance on time. Montgomery's lance shattered on contact and, accidentally, a wood splinter obtruded the King's "caged" visor, which was made of gold. Suffice it to say, the splinter pierced the eye of the king. He would die ten days later.

My friend and I also discussed the quatrain related to the London fire of 1666. This quatrain is only two lines for some reason, but it does get its point across. Here is the quatrain;

the blood of the just will be demanded
in London burnt by the fire in the year 66

Here is what happened: on September 2, 1666, a horrible fire destroyed a good portion of medieval London. Despite the fact that this fire was large-scale and tragic, only six people were killed.

You must have fathomed the validity of the "Language of the Mad" by now. If not, that is okay, because I am about to further state my case for the credibility of my claims. The name of the friend I used to have "talks" with about Nostradamus is "Brian Cote." Brian, if you are reading this right now, you are about to be blown away! (Brian Cote in Drow is=a talk in a eye our be).

I would like to take this opportunity to apologize to Brian for all of the shit I put him through as a teenager. How Brian was still willing to be my friend after all the crap I gave him is astounding. Although we never discussed my vision, we did discuss Nostradamus and it was great! We never hung out all that much, but I consider him a good friend. I am really sorry to you Brian, and I am glad we never ended up in a fist fight because you are as tough as nails and it sucks to fight anyone, especially a friend. Thanks, man! There will be more on Brian in my short autobiography in "Morals in Society" part three.

Continuing on, I would now like to present some of Nostradamus' quatrains which could be relevant to my vision. This display will vary in time, but you must keep in mind that time has been altered. So, whether or not you can fathom these quatrains is irrelevant and there is nothing wrong with sprucing up this book with some good old-fashioned sensationalism. As you read these quatrains, keep in mind my elaborations in the "2001-2010" segment.

The divine Earth will give to the sustenance
including heaven, Earth, and gold hidden in the mystic milk
body, soul, spirit, having all power
as much under feet as heavenly see
When they will be close the lunar ones will fall

VISION OF A MENTAL PATIENT

from on another not greatly distant
    cold dryness danger towards the frontiers
        even where the oracle had its beginning
Near far the future of the two great luminaries
    which will occur between April and March
        Oh what a loss! But two great good natured ones
            by land and sea will relieve all parts
Greater calamity of blood and famine
    seven times it approached the marine shore
        Monaco from hunger place captured captivity
            the great one led crunching from a metal cage
                The arms to fight in the sky for a long time
                      the tree in the middle of the city fallen
                          sacred bough clipped steel in the face of the fire band
                              then the monarch of Adria fallen
Under the shadowy pretense of removing sertitude
    he will himself usurp the people and city
        he will do worse because of the deceit of the young prostitute
            delivered in the field reading the false poem
                The bones of the triumvun will be found
                      looking for a deep enigmatic treasure
those from thereabouts will not be at rest
    digging for this thing of marble and metallic lead
        The sea will not be passed over safely by those of the sun
            those of Venus will hold Africa
                Saturn will no longer occupy their realm
                    and the Asiatic part will change
                        The Sabaean tear no longer at its high price
turning human flesh into ashes through death
    at the isle of pharaohs disturbed by the crusaders
        when at Rhodes will appear a hard phantom
            By the night the king passing near an alley
                he of Cyprus and the principal guard
                    the king mistaken the hand flees the length of the rhone
                      the conspirators will set out to put him to death
Upon the struggle of the great light horses
    it will be claimed that the great crescent is destroyed
        to kill by night in the mountains
            dressed in shepherds clothing red gulfs in the deep ditch
                From the marine tributary city
                    the shaven head will take up the satrapy
                      to chase the sordid man who will be against him
                          for fourteen years he will hold the tyranny
He will come expose the false topography
    the urns of the tombs will be opened
        sect and holy prophecy to thrive
            black for white and the new for old
                Wrongly they will come to put the just one to death
                    in the public and in the middle extinguished
                      so great a pestilence will come to rise in this place
                          that the judges will be forced to flee
So much of Diana and Mercury
    the images will be found in the lake
        the sculptor looking for new clay
            he and his followers will be steeped in gold

Okay, I have a message for the moral community: Fear not, for we shall soon achieve a new level of understanding for the promotion of a collective happiness.

Back in the "Dick Cheney and his Lies" segment, I spoke of the former White House Press Secretary, Scott McCllelan. I displayed one of Scott's quotes in his book *What Happened*, which was, "Most political actions are done subconsciously with no malicious intent." I stated that this quote of Scott's would be further understood and that this quote consisted of human energy. I don't feel an elaboration is necessary at this point, because through what you have read so far, you can easily see that Scott and I have connected through politics. Keep in mind that the last band I was in was called Malicious Intent, and that the three levels of consciousness are now in action.

You see, Scott and I have connected through scientific equivalency within the collective subconscious of the political realm. Now that I have made my theory of connection credible, the political world can be altered. Let's make the future a good one!

Since I aspire to be an artist of sorts and that I would like to theoretically paint the universe into a beautiful picture, and seeing that I have painted a portrait that is a testament to the conceptualization of "knowing," I must add some art. This next quatrain is of my own making and it applies to universal contact. Unlike the quatrains of Nostradamus, mine will rime. Here is my own four-lined quatrain:

When the supposed evil beast claims equal to one
the new contacted philosophy will soon be done
as the magic new sphere will appear in mid air
the whole human race will commence to care

I will now present some more lyrics to you. This one was a Deallegiance song entitled "Past, Present, Future." So, here is track four to the first Deallegiance demo and track eleven to the last Deallegiance demo. Please enjoy!

Un-yielding to a primary passage
concerning a strike of uncanny massage
perennial obsession for which it contains
a requisite lesson with message contained
dreams are a precedent
hopes in my eyes will never end
it seems somewhat insolent
as the giver tries for her pride to defend
Dwelling in a sect of relative tides
anticipate elect the realm of surprise
alone I may stand in a world of disguise
I realize I'm free just look in the skies
holder of options of coincidence
a meeting with a god a life to send
without any feel to pretend
know this is real because I'm your friend!
Future, present, past!
Look into the past that is such an outcast
seeking out a future so a dream can last
evil's iron fist was ruling all of man
the one main contribute was the will to withstand
searching for ways turmoil must end
from the past few days to the present we bend, Past!
We stand in modern day conformed in every way
some look to god and pray, others deceive with his way
Satan's spirits all have sold against a story to be told
creeping silent blood runs cold getting stronger time will fold
look into the past I'm told look to the ones who stand bold
look into the next few days the future we hold, Present!
Raging on we nurture on the key of human kind
completing all our goals they're now refined
leading to a life of total reprimand
we look to infernal worlds in your hands
a peace that lasts forever always lives
we awoke the tree that's dead
and now we know to give, Future!

VISION OF A MENTAL PATIENT

Unyielding to a primary passage
concerning a strike of uncanny massage
perennial obsession for which it contains
a requisite lesson with message contained
dreams are a precedent
hopes in my eyes will never end
it seems somewhat insolent
as the giver tries for her pride to defend
Past, Present, Future!

To wrap up this segment, I will leave you with yet another discovery in the Language of the Mad. (Nostradamus in Drow is=some add art son, or sun?). Connected!

It is now time for me to fill a glass half-full of water and stare into it. The next segment will be the last portion of the "Monolith" part two. Turn the page so that we can peer into the wonders of ancient Egypt and its significance to what we have discussed thus far. Once again, thank you for listening. Read On!

ANCIENT EGYPT

Now that I have revealed the primary goal, I deem it to be the appropriate time to discuss one of (if not the) most fascinating cultures in the history of human civilization. We shall journey back in time, with the fabrics of our thoughts and dreams, and indulge in a brief history of the ancient Egyptian culture. As I have done throughout this book, I will apply this discussion to my vision and also to some of my theories. I have already applied connection and scientific equivalency to the world of politics. This time, I will relate this particular society to science. Before I account for ancient Egyptian history, I will tell you of the daily lives of those who lived in this fascinating civilization.

You see, ancient Egypt did change somewhat throughout its history. This civilization spanned from about 3500 B.C. until 395 A.D., when it became a province of the Roman Empire. Despite the length of this time span, the daily lives of these Egyptians were pretty much consistent throughout.

From the early dynastic period to the great pyramid builders of the old kingdom, onto the conquest of Alexander the Great, the ancient Egyptians lived simple, yet fascinating lives. The citizens of modern day Egypt are a proud people due to the intriguing history of their civilization.

Since the days when the pyramids of Giza were erected on the Giza plateau just outside of Cairo, these incredible structures have been subject to weathering and extreme erosion. The damage from this erosion has made the details of these pyramids obscure. Hence, these pyramids do not display the same magnificent beauty that they once did. The pyramids at Giza (to name a couple) consist of the Pyramid of Giza and the Great Sphinx, which is not technically a pyramid. There were more pyramids built at Saqqara, Dahshur, Abu Ruwaysh, and Abisir.

Before ancient Egyptians used solid stone for construction, they would make mud bricks using square molds, giving these bricks their shapes and symmetry. Before these mud bricks hardened, they would use primitive tools to define the symmetrical dimensions of these mud bricks. So, you see, even in the early days of this civilization, Egyptians were well versed in masonry.

Archaeologists that have obtained skeletal remains of these ancient people, have determined that certain features, such as curvature of the spine, indicate that these people had strong backs and they bore very heavy loads. This was a hard working and ambitious culture, known to toil to the point of extreme exhaustion.

The Nile River was an essential asset for ancient Egypt. When the annual torrential African rains would downpour, these would cause the Nile to overflow, thus producing a good quantity of water for farming and irrigation. Soil was cultivated near the Nile for the production of crops. The Nile was also teeming with fish, which would be caught and used for nourishment. They would be plentiful in bread, leeks, onions, radishes, and believe it or not, they made beer. Beer in ancient Egypt was barely alcoholic; it was a common beverage in their society. For meat, they would cultivate pigs and sheep. These agricultural responsibilities were most commonly performed by the lower class civilians of ancient Egypt.

The middle class also consisted of farmers who sometimes owned semi-furnished homes and a few acres of land. A huge advantage the middle class had over the lower class was the ability to send their children to school at the city of Thebes. However, quality of education would vary throughout the history of this culture. You see, illiteracy was commonplace, especially within the lower class. Those who were fortunate enough to be educated were expected to be well versed in literature, language, history, law, mathematics, accountancy, administration, surveying, and architecture.

Fields for agricultural purposes were laid out in squares close to irrigation channels. For the middle class, barley, beats, and millets were most commonly grown. They were known to hunt wild birds and lions, as well as other animals. They would utilize long horned cattle to pull plows. A tool called the shadouf was used for transporting water. It consisted of a long stick with a scoop at both ends, balanced to hold the water by carrying it vertically. To catch wild birds, they use a hinged net. The common footwear was the sandal, these made of papyrus.

Ancient Egyptians were also known for using cosmetics (makeup), worn by both sexes. Using cosmetics was viewed as a good tool to enhance facial features.

You see, ancient Egypt was not communist (Marx wouldn't be born until thousands of years later), but this civilization had what I would call a touch of communism. This is due to the fact that the peasants were able to live decent lives. You see, it is a truism that the lower class of this civilization was lacking the benefits of education. Due to the climate, these lower class citizens were able to live off of the lifeblood of the River Nile. Peasants would drink more beer and eat more bread than the other classes were known to. This beer was different from modern beer, but it was still tasty due to being made from pure barley mash. Another trait of this class and the other classes, for that matter, was to eat a lot of grapes while also using the grapes to make wine, which they consumed with contented pleasure.

The upper class consisted of the Royal Court. The upper class comprised politicians, diplomats, and the Prime Minister. Even higher than the prime minister was the Pharaoh who was the head of the kingdom. Suffice it to say, this upper class of ancient Egypt lived extravagantly. The Pharaohs were considered god like. They had harems.

Being a religious people, the ancient Egyptinas believed in the afterlife. They had religious temples and worshiped Ra. Ra, whom I briefly touched on in the "Collective Subconscious" segment, was a sun god. His worship was much more mysterious than one would quickly assume. By the fifth dynasty of the Old Kingdom, Ra had become a key figure in the religious beliefs of this culture.

These temples were only to be entered by the higher ups, inclusive of priests. However, exceptions would be made during festive times. Due to this culture's robust beliefs in the afterlife, the act of mummification would take place. An autopsy would be performed by way of rinsing and cleansing the remains of a deceased Egyptian. In the case of wealthy Pharaohs, the brain would be pulled out of the head through the nostrils. They would be rinsed with wine, salts, and other spices. Sodium bicarbonate would be layered with resins to hold bandages in place. Next, the body parts extricated from the remains of the Pharaoh would be placed beside the dead Pharaoh, for reasons of afterlife beliefs. It was believed that once they were deceased, they would meet Osiris, ruler of the dead, for judgment in the underworld.

Okay, now that I have accounted for ancient Egyptian life style, we will now indulge in other aspects of ancient Egyptian history.

First, was the underdeveloped era of the prehistoric and pre-dynastic periods, which ended in about 3100 B.C. This civilization began to develop from the early pre-dynastic period to the late pre-dynastic period. However, it was not until the inception of the early dynastic period, from roughly 2950 B.C. until about 2150 B.C., when the dynasties would begin. This period consisted of the first three ancient Egyptian dynasties. It was during this early dynastic stage that the capital city of Memphis (pre-Cairo) was established. At this time, the very first ancient Egyptian pyramids were constructed at Saqqara. (Saqqara in Drow is=a Ra cue, cue as).

Next was the old kingdom, which consisted of dynasties four through eight. It was in this era that the pyramids of Giza and Dashsur were erected. The first intermediate period was next. It consisted of dynasties nine through eleven. Egypt would be separated into two smaller states in this era, from Memphis in the north to Thebes in the south.

Then was the middle kingdom, which consisted of the late eleventh dynasty through the fourteenth dynasty. Menuhotep 2 (2061 B.C.-2010 B.C.), an eleventh dynasty Pharaoh, was able to reunite the two Egyptian states. Anmenemhat 1 of dynasty twelve founded a new sovereign residence near Memphis. Egypt would conquer lower Nubia in the southern region of Egypt along the River Nile. This Nubian take over was executed under the reign of Senusret, the second Pharaoh of the twelfth dynasty. Sunruset ruled from 1971 B.C. until 1926 B.C. The middle kingdom saw the classical period of the arts and liturgy. Next was the second intermediate period, which only lasted ninety years, from 1630 B.C. until 1570 B.C. It consisted of dynasties fifteen through seventeen.

Egypt was seized by the Asian Hyksos people in this era. They would attack the Nile Delta, where the Nile flows into the Mediterranean Sea. The Hyksos would gain power over the Delta and Avaris (northeastern region of the Nile Delta). They would control Southern Egypt, only to be dethroned during the seventeenth dynasty. This dethroning took place during the reigns of Seqenance Tao 2 and Kamose, who was the last Pharaoh of the seventeenth dynasty and the second intermediate period.

The new kingdom would be next, lasting from 1570 B.C. until 1075 B.C. It consisted of dynasties eighteen through twenty-four. Military, diplomacy, and trade negotiations were carried out with Nubia in this era. The Valley of the Kings would be constructed. It would be the place where tombs for Pharaohs and noblemen would be built. The woman Pharaoh Hatshepsut would reign in this era. She would be considered one of the most successful Pharaohs of ancient Egyptian history. The great Pharaoh Akhenaten of the eighteenth dynasty was noted for his attempts to introduce to the Egyptian people the monotheistic worship of Aten. Aten was basically prototype of the sun god Ra. Aten was said to be the creator and the giver of life. Likely, the most famous of all Egyptian Pharoahs was the boy king Tutankhamun, commonly known as King Tut. The name Tutankhamun is attributed to Aten. Tutankhamun would die at the age of eighteen, but he would leave behind one of the most interesting histories of all of the Pharaohs (We will further discuss Tut later).

Ramesses 2 or Ramesses the Great of this era, is considered one of the most illustrious, celebrated, and powerful Pharaohs of them all. He would rule for sixty-six years and two months. He lived into his 90s. He would accomplish many feats vital to world history, including expeditions east of the Mediterranean where Israel, Lebanon, and Syria are presently located. Ramesses reigned near the end of the new kingdom and he was Pharaoh longer than any other in ancient Egyptian history.

Next was the third intermediate period, which consisted of the twenty-first to the twenty-fifth dynasties, lasting from 1075 B.C. until 715 B.C. In this third intermediate period, history is disputable and the theories regarding this period are various. The twenty-second dynasty would be founded by one Shoshenq who happened to be a Meshwesh. The Meshwesh comprised of immigrants from ancient Libya. There would be more Nubian conflict during this period, leading to Nubia conquering this land of the Pharaohs. The Nubian Kingdom would take advantage of Egypt's political instability. A Nubian Kushite king, Piye, saw that Libyan princes had seized control of the Nile Delta, putting Shoshenq in power. This Libyan rule would last about 200 years. Soon Libyan control weakened as Piye turned northward, establishing control of Thebes and the Nile Delta soon after. Piye would be a part of the twenty-fifth dynasty, which also included his successor, Taharqa, who was his son. Then came the late period, which also has a disputable history.

The late period consisted of the twenty-sixth to the thirtieth dynasty. It was at the tail end of the twenty-fifth dynasty, when the reigns of Teharqa and another Nubian Pharaoh by the name of Tantamani who, by the way, would reoccupy all of Egypt, including Memphis, that Assyria (where Iraq is presently located) would start a slow, yet steady series of attacks over a reasonably sizable duration. Soon, Assyria would conquer Egypt, but this would last only a few decades. It would not be long before Assyrian rule was banished for good. There would be a Persian conquest where Psatmik 3 (the last Pharaoh of the twenty-fifth dynasty) would be dethroned by Cambyses 2 of Persia. Cambyses 2 was the son of Cyrus the Great; he was also the king of Babylon. Soon, Egypt would reclaim its independence.

The last ancient Egyptian period was the Greco-Roman period. This period is considered to be post dynasty, when Alexander the Great would soon occupy Egypt (as well as other states). Alexander the Great had a general by the name of Ptolemaic who would establish the Ptolemaic empire in Egypt during the zenith of Greek influence in ancient times. This Ptolemaic empire is sometimes considered a dynasty, but it is not included in the original thirty ancient Egyptian dynasties.

In 196 B.C., the Rosetta Stone was carved. This Rosetta stone is an ancient Egyptian artifact, which proved to be paramount to modern day understandings of the concepts of hieroglyphic writing.

The reign of the well known Cleopatra 7 (commonly known simply as Cleopatra) would commence in the 51 B.C. Cleopatra 7 would inherit her position, being the daughter of Ptolemy 7. She would marry Julius Caesar, the Roman military and political leader. This marriage to Caesar would strengthen her grip of power over Egypt. After Caesar was killed on March 15 in 44 B.C. (the ides of March), she would marry "Mark Antony" (another Roman politician and military man). Cleopatra 7 would have three children with Antony. Their names were Cleopatra Selene and Alexander Hois who were twins, and a son named Ptolemy. Incidentally, she had one son with Caesar by the name of Ptolemy, but his nickname was "Caesarion." At the end of the Greco-Roman period in 30 B.C., which was Cleopatra's last year in power, Egypt would become a province of the Roman Empire.

Okay, now that I have accounted for a chronology of ancient Egypt, I deem it appropriate to commence with a discussion on specifics. So, why don't we discuss the pyramids themselves at this point? The pyramids at Giza consist of three great pyramids. They are called The Great pyramid or Cheops, Kharfe, and Menkaure. The Great Sphinx is also at Giza. The Great Pyramid was the first to be erected. It is also the largest of the three. It is theorized that the Great Pyramid was built during the fourth dynasty in the early stages of the old kingdom, during the rule of the Pharaoh Khufu. This pyramid can also be called the Khufu pyramid. It took an estimated fourteen to twenty years to build this pyramid. It originally stood roughly 481 feet in height. Due to years of erosion, it now stands approximately 455 feet in height. The volume of the Great Pyramid is about 2,500,000 cubic meters. If this pyramid were built in twenty years, the Egyptians would have had to move 800 tons of stone every single day. The Great Pyramid was the tallest manmade structure on the planet until 1300 A.D. when the Lincoln Cathedral was erected in Lincoln, England. The symmetry of the Great Pyramid was strict and exact. The structure of the Great Pyramid coincides with the true north, not with magnetic north. It consists of about 2.3 million blocks of limestone, transported from quarries located near the River Nile. They would shape these limestone blocks using hammer and chisel, followed by a drenching in water, which would cause expansion and cracks in the limestone. The cracks would assist in the breaking and forming of the correct proportions of symmetry and then they were to be transported for construction of the pyramid.

The fact is that there are some other theories how this and other pyramids were built. Some Egyptologists think that the limestone did not come from a quarry. For how these immense and heavy blocks were transported, there has been much debate. They might have been lifted, rolled, or dragged. Some experts say that the stones might have been too heavy for human transport. With teamwork, it may have been possible to move such heavy objects. However, even if you applied ropes for dragging these blocks, the ropes could bust from pressure.

Some rocks moved in the ancient Egyptian era, could not even be moved by most modern methods. I have heard that some experts have hypothesized a farfetched theory, which states that Egyptians may have used telepathic powers to move such heavy objects with their minds. However, the fact that skeletal remains from this era have curvature of the spine defeats this theory.

I used the Great Pyramid at Giza as an example, but the truth is that all of these pyramids pose similarities to one another in both their forms and in the methods of the required edifice. Even in modern times, experts are in awe when looking at the exactness and the possible methods used for erecting such incredible structures. It is estimated that approximately 35,000 men and women were involved in constructing the Great Pyramid. These constructionists are not believed to have been subject to slavery. Actually, it is quite the contrary. They were believed to have been paid well and treated respectfully. They were also said to have actually enjoyed their duties.

One thing is for sure, the ancient Egyptians had some outstanding geometers who were able to complete the these incredible structures. They were also well versed in astronomy, seeing that every side of these pyramids were acclimated to north, south, east, and west directions. It has also been theorized, that these pyramids are connected to a coinciding relationship with the Orion constellation.

Okay, that should be sufficient data as far as the Egyptian pyramids are concerned. We will now commence a discussion of the Great Sphinx. The Great Sphinx is a statue of a lying lion with a human head. It is located on the Giza plateau, where the Great Pyramid, Kharfe, and the Menkaure pyramids stand. It stands 65 feet in height, 241 feet in length, and 20 feet in width. It is the oldest standing majestic structure on Earth.

The original name of the Great Sphinx was different but it does not emerge in any known writings of the old kingdom. There is also insufficient information about its meaning and purpose of origin. The common theory among Egyptologists is that the Sphinx was consructed as the pyramids, its symmetry also carried out by the use of hammer and chisel. Of course, there are other theories that I had previously applied to the edifice of the pyramids, including the use of telepathic powers and, believe it or not, even extraterrestrial life. There is a movie called "Star Gate" which is based on this theory.

The Great Sphinx can also be attributed to the constellation of Orion as the three Giza pyramids. You see, the three Giza pyramids are in precise alignment with three specific stars of the Orion constellation. These three stars are located on the belt of this constellation. When this astronomical pyramid and Sphinx hypothesis is furthered, they can also be applied to the Leonis constellation, as well as the form and behavior of the entire Milky Way galaxy.

It has also been theorized that the Great Sphinx was not originally formed as a lion. This theory gives credence to the possibility, that it resembled a jackal or a dog. This jackal and dog theory is attributed to the possibility that the Sphinx was intended to honor the pagan god Anubis. Anubis was a god of the dead. He was often associated with the afterlife rituals of the Pharaohs. The Sphinx was also theorized as guard of the three Giza pyramids. The grounds of this theory are relevant to the fact that the face of the Sphinx faces the rising sun.

The Sphinx can also be applied to sun worship. You see, the lion has always represented a relation to sun worship in ancient Egyptian culture. When the new kingdom came to be, the Sphinx was more commonly associated with the entire horizon rather than just the sun. This makes perfect sense, because the face of the Sphinx (as I just stated) faces the rising sun.

Okay, the main point of this ancient Egyptian segment is soon to be revealed. However, I must further elaborate in order for you to conceive the message I am sending, as well as the message that the ancient Egyptians are sending to us. The most imperative things for you to keep in mind are how the pyramids coincide with some of the laws of astronomy, as well as the strict symmetry of the pyramids. What do you think the ancient Egyptian message is? It is now time for a discussion of the Boy King Tutankhamun and the one they called Osiris. Follow along carefully and please, enjoy yourself.

Okay, Tutankhamun lived from 1341 B.C. until 1323 B.C. He was a Pharaoh of the eighteenth dynasty of the new kingdom. His original name was Tutankhaten, which means, "living image of the god Aten." Aten (as previously stated) was a primitive concept of the Sun God Ra. The name Tutankhamun is attributed to the "living image of Amun." Amun was relevant to the concept of Ra. Amun represented the most intricately complicated theological system in all of ancient Egypt.

The boy king Tutankhamun would become a Pharaoh at the age of nine, which was, unfortunately, the halfway point to this boy king's life.

Tutankhamun is known for many things and in his time, he was known for his objections to the radical religious alterations of his predecessor Akhenhaten. Akhenhaten was a prominent force for the promotion of the monotheistic god, Aten, whom Tutankhamun was originally named after. Tutankhamun is renowned in modern times due to the extravagant rituals that were carried out after his death. Tutankhamun has left behind the most elaborate and valuable ancient Egyptian tomb ever discovered. Tutankhamun was to rest in the Valley of the Kings. In 1922, this tomb was discovered by an Egyptologist, Howard Carter.

The Valley of the Kings is a valley in the Egyptian region where, for just under five centuries from the sixteenth century B.C. until the eleventh century B.C., tombs were built for the Pharaohs and other accomplished nobles. Due to Tutankhamun's young age and inexperience, it has been said that his eventual successor, Ay, who advised the boy king, intervened and made a lot of the decisions concerning the government of this regime. Ay would reign as Pharaoh of Egypt for about four years. As for the cause of the death of Tutankhamun, it has been subject to debate. There have been multiple theories as to just how the Boy King would come to pass. Howard carter and his team of archeologists were mostly concerned with the treasures and the resin preserved from Tutankhamun's fragmented remains. Carter and his team adhered to the popular conclusion that Tutankhamun suffered a severe blow to the cranium. As for the details to this theory of the death of Tutankhamun, none has been ascertained.

Since 1968, the mummy of Tutankhamun has been x-rayed three times. From these examinations it was determined that Tutankhamun had a dense spot on the back of his skull, assumed by some to be the result of a traumatic brain injury in which blood gathers within the inner layer of the membranes that surround the nervous center, called the pachymenix. The pachymenix consists of three membrane layers. These combined layers surround the part of the brain that communicates with the nervous system. It has not been ruled out, when taking into account the severity of this injury of Tutankhamun's skull, that it can prove one way or another whether the injury was accidental or not accidental.

In 2005, a small loose bone sliver was detected in the upper cranium of Tutankhamun. Due to the fact that Tutankhamun's brain was removed for the purpose of afterlife rituals related to the pagan god Osiris, the process of examination had its limits. The resins from this ritual process that have since seeped into Tutankhamun's skull have led to the theory that this bone sliver was caused after his death, from carrying out the ritual.

A concept which could be concluded, not only in relation to Tutankhamun, but also to the ancient Egyptian culture's fascination with the sun and the Pagan gods related to the sun is the manifestation of a subconscious to conscious vision of obsession, which is similar to mine. I am referring to what is called the Chariot of the Sun. Back in the "Reflections" segment, I displayed the lyrics to a song that relates to Jung's interpretation of this Sun Chariot. These were the lyrics to the Deallegiance and Malicious Intent song entitled "Open Door." The concept of the Chariot of the Sun has the potential to aid our collective subconscious vision, thus leading to the achievement a new plane of moral function.

You see, Tutankhamun was not a well-known Pharaoh, until his tomb was found by Howard Carter in 1922. Therefore, Tutankhamun, Carter, you and me, have a profound effect on the destiny of human civilization. Destiny is a strangely obscure, yet wonderful thing, and this fact is due to the moral ambitions we are now set to embark on.

In a new direction, I would like to discuss Osiris. Osiris was (as previously stated) the Egyptian god of the afterlife! References pertaining to this Egyptian religious figure originated from hieroglyphic writings from what is called the Palermo Stone. This is a large fractured piece of a stone slab consisting of hieroglyphic carved writings said to date back to the old kingdom.

Osiris was prominently worshiped until the quashing of Egyptian religious beliefs due to the rise of Christianity. As for the mythology in the religious aspects and beliefs relevant to that of Osiris, there are a vital source of information, the Pyramid Texts. These particular texts are a collection of ancient Egyptian religious writings done during the old kingdom. These writings were carved into the walls of the Saqqara pyramids during the fifth and the sixth dynasties.

Osiris was, of course, believed to be a merciful god. Furthermore, he was believed to be the giver of life through the virtual gateway which the ancient Egyptians called the underworld. The underworld, or *Duat,* was perceived as the mystical region through which the sun god Ra was said to have ventured from east to west in the darkness of the night. Ra's significance in the underworld was that he was said to have confronted Apep during this east to west journey. Apep was as an evil demon, the lord of darkness and mayhem. Osiris was credited with the flourishing of agriculture, and, because he was powerful, he was able to flood the River Nile for the purpose of fertilization, bringing about a contented Egyptian prosperity. Osiris was often dubbed as the Lord of Love and the Lord of Silence. He was also believed to possess eternal youth: mortal in the beginning, but one day, he rose from the land of the dead; his followers would be given the gift of eternal life through some kind of mystical magic. Osiris was the god of all ancient Egyptians for a considerable time. Whether you were a peasant, middle class civilian, or a member of the royal court, you would consider Osiris as such, and you would believe that he would one day take you to the promised land.

At one point in time, Osiris was believed to be one of the sons of Geb. Geb was the god of Earth. He was a figure of nine deities from what was termed as the sun city of Heliopolis. Today Heliopolis is a suburb of the present Egyptian capital of Cairo.

Then there was the other parental figure of Osiris, and when I tell you her name, you might laugh. Her name was Nut, the sky goddess. Osiris was the brother of Isis, an Egyptian goddess who was more prominent in the Greco-Roman period. Isis was believed to be the matron of the magic of nature. Osiris was said to have married his sister Isis; in this era, inter-family marriages were commonplace. Osiris was the father of Horus. Horus originated from the predynastic period. Due to conflicts regarding Horus's perceived powers, one cannot sufficiently pinpoint his relevance. As a matter of fact, there are multiple views about the relationships of Egyptian religious figures, promoting some conflicting opinions in the field of Egyptology. The most credible and undeniable assumption in relation to Osiris is that he was the giver of life and the judging god, by which he has formulated the afterlife rituals.

Okay, we have already had some discussion of the sun god Ra. I have spoken of the Chariot of the Sun and I have related this subconscious concept to the fascinating ancient Egyptian culture. So, what we need to do now is walk through the theoretical gateway and proceed to the next stage. This next topic will be on the rumors—or non–rumors—of the infamous and well known Egyptian Curses. Once we finish this brief discussion on the curses of ancient Egypt, I will apply the information of these curses to the pyramids, sun worship, and some other aspects of ancient Egyptian mythology.

The first curse we will touch on is the curse of the Egyptian princess Amun Ra. You see, this incidence is related to the sinking of the Titanic in 1912. Incidentally, Fenway Park was built in 1912 and, fortunately, there is no curse on my beloved Red Sox any more. Yahoo! Anyway, this story was revealed by a few survivors of the Titanic disaster. (Titanic in Drow is=see in at it). So why don't we begin to see in at it?

It was said that one William Stead had told an old story of an Egyptian mummy and its curse the night prior to the Titanic disaster. Supposedly, this mummy was removed from its case, as the Titanic went under. For some reason, Stead remained in the smoking room relaxing while the ship was going under. There are various versions of this story, so I will do my best to compensate. The original version of this story is that this mummy was purchased just prior to the commencement of the twentieth century. The newer disputable version claims that the woman who had passed on had witnessed this mummy after the purchase was made. This woman would be dead years before this confrontation was to take place. The shocking truth is that the coffin containing this mummified Egyptian princess showed up at a British museum at an even earlier date. Therefore, the mummy had arrived prior to any of this.

Another mishap to the original version of this anecdote is that this princess was alive in 1500 B.C. However, at the British museum, the display claimed that this princess passed away roughly 450 years after this date. This coffin is still in this museum today. It has been theorized, that (as previously stated) this mummy was removed from its coffin while on the Titanic. The mummy itself might have sunk, but the coffin had definitely not sunk. Therefore, some believe that the curse of this mummy was at least partially responsible for the Titanic disaster. This mummy had a wide history of omens and it would thus earn the nickname, unlucky mummy. So, what do you think happened to this mummy? I will leave it as a mystery for now and start to tell you of another event related to an Egyptian curse.

That last story has its flaws and it is not as convincing as the next one I am about to narrate. This next curse event is related to the tomb of Tutankhamun. Egyptologists will often dismiss such curses as mere nonsense, but some, like me, for instance, do believe. I have heard Egyptologists claim there are no entries in hieroglyphics that mention anything whatsoever about curses. However, a select few do agree with my hypothesis that there is some kind of curse that is relevant to ancient Egypt.

Okay, I have already told you that the tomb of Tutankhamun was discovered by Howard Carter in 1922. However, it was not until this tomb would be studied by other archeologists when the paranormal would begin to be manifested. Carter was quoted as saying "All sane people should dismiss such inventions with contempt." Therefore, Carter, who was an expert in the sciences of Egyptology and archeology, had dismissed such claims of supernatural existences with a false surety.

There are some German Egyptologists who strongly believe that curses related to Egyptian mummies and tombs are real. Contrary to the claim that no hieroglyphics reveal any warnings of curses, there are some very ancient Egyptian stelas, which issued a warning not to enter into these sacred places. Now I will tell of the story I was about to tell you before I went off on yet another tangent. Okay, here is the story:

One particular German Egyptologist claimed that a curse was put on him and his family. He decided to take a remnant from the Valley of the Kings to his home for keepsake. When this man returned to his native land of Germany, he noticed strange events were beginning to take place. Soon, this man was inflicted with severe fatigue and very high fever. This would soon develop into paralysis and it would not be long until he died. The remnant was then shipped to the Egyptian embassy in Berlin by the deceased German's stepson. The stepson suspected and worried about the possible existence of this curse. You see, similar occurrences have occurred since the tomb of Tutankhamun and others were opened. However, many of these cases have been dismissed because of poisonous fungi on the walls of such places were found; those might have been the true cause of the German's death. Hence, this story could be viewed as insignificant. Another point is that other trespassers lived a long time afterward without experiencing such feared paranormal activity.

I will now tell you of a third story pertinent to Egyptian curses. You see, sometime after Howard Carter's dismissal of such curses, he experienced the effects of a curse himself. Carter had returned home one day after running some errands and to his dismay, he saw that his pet bird was devoured by a cobra. Obviously, Carter was stunned, but this must have been a mere warning, because Carter would live a long life. Carter had a fellow worker and friend named Herbert, who died soon after this occurrence from a supposed case of blood poisoning, this being supposedly induced by a mosquito bite. It was also theorized that Herbert might have died from the fungi inside of the tomb. Could this fungi have been planted by the Egyptians intentionally? Fungi can reproduce for incredible long periods, especially if the right conditions exist.

Presently, it is assumed that just over twenty people may have been subject to the curse of Tutankhamun. The details of certain deaths involved in this theory do hold substance, because of the manners in which they succumbed, dying of unnatural causes. There is one more issue of significance to what I am trying to get across through this discussion on Egyptology. Tutankhamun was found in what was called KV62, the name given to the room of his tomb. In 1907, Egyptologist Edward R. Rayton discovered tomb KV55, said to have the coffin of Akhenhaten or his successor, Smenkhkare. There are many conflicting views around Akhenheten and Smenkhkare, including the possibility that they were one and the same, as the case is with Tutankhamun and Akhenhaten!

Continuing on, the anatomical resemblances of the skulls of Tutankhamun in KV62 and Akhenhate in KV55 are mind-boggling. This was dismissed by the assumption that Tutankhamun and Akhenhaten were closely related. However, paranormal occurrences, such as a cobra devouring Carter's pet bird has only remotely resembled any aspect of common sense and logic. I mean, someone could have broken into Carter's home, but why hadn't he or she taken anything? And, why would they place a cobra in his bird cage, it seems like a pointless act. How the hell did a cobra get inside Carter's home, and could a cobra fit through the bars of a birdcage? Of course, one could assume that the birdcage was opened and the cobra was set in place. By the way, still are a lot of cobras in Egypt. Do you think you know what I am getting at? I bet you do by now! Keep reading!

First, I must remind you of a few things. The Giza pyramids are virtually flawless in their symmetry. The Giza pyramids are aligned to true north rather than magnetic north. These very same Giza pyramids are aligned with the belt of the constellation of Orion. The Great Sphinx always faces the rising sun. You see, the ancient Egyptians are sending us a message. The pyramids resemble prisms that cause light spectrums. The Sphinx relates to the sun in accordance to our human relationship with time. Here is the message: The ancient Egyptians travelled time! And here is the topper: The pyramids are surrounded by sand! Yes, silica and, at this point, you realize that silica, which is a part of sand, represents the human collective subconscious interpretation of time and this is due to its heating process of transformation for the manifestation of a mirror reflection. Time travel is the method of these curses. If you process in your mind everything that we have discussed so far, you will come to the same conclusion as I have.

It is true that there are some parts of ancient Egyptian history that could be viewed as defying this hypothesis. This would be the acts of war, which took place over this lengthy era. However, you must keep in mind that this civilization lasted for over four millenniums. The aspects of their afterlife rituals adhere to my beliefs which are relevant to the naturalistic line and flatlining. Some of the military conflicts of this era may have been overcome with a keen trickery. Think about this: ancient Egypt survived for well over 4,000 years and their level of technology remained stagnant throughout its long history. It has been over 2,000 years since the days of Christ and the ancient Egyptians lasted over twice as long as this period. When examining how much our modern culture has advanced in a technological sense in the last 100 years, it leads me to wonder why Egypt (other than methods of edifice) remained the same for so long. Could it have been a utopia in disguise? After all, even the peasants of this ancient community lived good lives. The River Nile was nearby, so it was the perfect location to access the lifeblood of this prolific and nourishing source of water.

I will end this "Monolith" part two portion with one more lyrical compilation. These lyrics have nothing to do with ancient Egypt and everything to do with other aspects of my vision. However, you must keep in mind, that due to the laws of scientific equivalency, it is impossible to go off subject. This is a political song and it represents the process of a peaceful revolution of the mind. It is extremely radical and it could be considered violent in some aspects, but scientific equivalency will balance this out. As you read these lyrics, you must keep in mind my elaborations on the art of achieving utopia. You also need to keep in mind the language of the mad, as it coincides with the promotion of human understanding. So, here are some lyrics from the most politically savvy band of all time. This song is by the rockers of Queensryche and it is entitled "Speak!"

They've given me a mission, I don't really know the game
I'm bent on submission, religion is to blame
I'm the new messiah, Death Angel with a gun
Dangerous in my silence, deadly to my cause
Speak to me, the pain you feel
speak the word, the word is all of us
I've given my life to become what I am
to preach the new beginning, to make you <u>understand</u>
to reach some point of order, utopia in mind
you've got to learn to sacrifice, to leave what's now behind
seven years of power, the corporation claw
the rich control the government, the media, the law
to make some kind of difference, then everyone must <u>know</u>
eradicate the fascists, revolution will grow
the system we learn says we're equal under law
but the streets are reality, the weak and poor will fall
Let's tip their power balance, and tear down their crown
educate the masses, we'll burn the White House down
speak to me the pain you feel, speak to me the pain you feel
speak the word the word is all of us
speak the word the word is all of us, "SPEAK!"

I think you are catching on by this point. Let's go for it! Anyway, I have enjoyed this monolith discussion we just had and I sincerely hope you have enjoyed this one-way conversation just as much as I did. So, there you have it, the monolith is the central boundary to this entire vision. We will now move on to part three, "Morals in Society," where I will further promote the truth, as to the way we must become, the path we must follow, and the sleeping love that lingers in the ultimate vastness of the collective subconscious. Once again, thank you for listening and once again, as Forest Gump would say, "And that's all I have to say about that!"

PART THREE: MORALS IN SOCIETY
A SHORT BIOGRAPHY

I was born in Lowell, Massachusetts, on July 21, 1973, at Lowell General Hospital at 4:58 P.M. My earliest recollections of my life, are when my family lived on First Street, in Lowell. From a very young age, many abnormal, frightening, and paranormal occurrences would commence to take place. I was only two years old when we moved to First Street and by the time I was three, I would encounter my first experiences of paranormal activity due to time travel.

My sister Jill and I shared a bedroom at the time. Jill is seven years older to me. We used to enjoy watching cartoons in the early morning, such as Speed Racer, Deputy Dog, and The Mighty Heroes. Jill and I had a small green pet bird, which we used to set free in our bedroom and watch it fly around while enjoying a few laughs. One day, Jill decided to take it outside to show it off to her friends. This bird used to like to sit on Jill's index finger. However, on this occasion, our bird decided that our fence would be a better seat. Jill, with a slight expression of embarrassment on her face, stuck out her index finger in hopes that our bird would decide to perch on it, but, unfortunately, our bird decided to fly away to its freedom.

My early childhood was a constant fluctuation of good and bad experiences. As for the loss of this bird, my father, Jill, and I would often reminisce on this occurrence; because of our optimism, we are able to laugh about it. This would be the last laugh this small green bird would give to my sister and myself.

This bird experience goes deep in the recollections of my life past. This experience, particularly, is a good memory I don't mind reflecting on from time to time. Little did I realize the horrors that would soon take place to scar my very soul!

At the age of two or three, I was simply an innocent victim to the extreme evils of the world. At this time, my mother and father seemed to be getting along fine; they seemed to be in love. Some years later, they would divorce. Like many other young children who have experienced parental divorce, I thought it was my fault. This is because they would often have quarrels minutes after I did something wrong. When I tell you the reason I thought my parents divorced, it might give you a slight chuckle. I thought my parents divorced because I shit my pants! It really sucks to witness your parents argue, to witness the crumbling of the family that you love so dearly. However, both my father and mother did a good job explaining to me that the divorce was no fault of my own. It helped to have an older sister share the burden with. Soon, this divorce would be the least of my problems.

Jill was, for the most part, a good sister to grow up with, but I must be honest and admit that I always wanted a brother. I would spend my days being babied by my mother, playing with play dough or simply driving my family up the wall. My father had a cool orange Camaro, which today I am quite surprised by, because my father was always more concerned with being smart, than being cool. Whenever I mention this Camaro to my father today, he replies with these two words "It sucked."

The earliest friend I ever remember having in my life was an African kid named Gus, who had an older brother named Lionel; they were both fantastic kids. I remember Gus's father in his brown sandals, disciplining Gus in the same way my father would discipline me. When Gus was in trouble, his father would say "Come here, turn around" and Gus' father would then proceed to spank Gus in a non-abusive way. Gus' father was a nice man just like my father. Gus and I could not see that our fathers weren't being mean to us. They just didn't want us running out into the street and getting hit by a car. A good sign of achieving maturity is when one can realize that sometimes you have to be cruel to be kind in order to help the ones you love.

Over on the next street were the Halls—Justin and Steve. I have known these two since the day I was born, because of the fact that my parents hung out with their parents. I never see Steve these days, but I do see Justin on occasion and I hear he is doing well. Two little girls lived in this neighborhood and their names were Trina and Jamie. Trina had an older brother named John, who I would also hang with from time to time. Trina, Jamie, and I used to make mud pies in my back yard, and when our parents weren't looking we would flick mud from silver spoons, all over the side of my house. Our parents would feed us peanut butter and jelly sandwiches and when we ate them I would often laugh, because Trina would never eat one half of her sandwich at one time, she would bite one half of the sandwich and the other back and forth, until she was finished; it was funny, to say the least. We liked to play Simon says, hide and go seek, and my favorite childhood game, tag. Tag is especially fun when you have girls chasing you. Even at the young age of three or four, I liked girls for some reason. Years later ,I would see Trina again at Dracut High School. We were in our favorite class. This class was in door suspension. Trina would mention some paranormal activity from when we were younger, but at this point, the primary goal and its actions of outcome were vastly deep into my personal subconscious. As a young child on First Street, I would come across the first clue relative to my time concepts and its adherence to the subconscious and dream fabric. This alteration of the states of my psyche was a message, sent to me in a dream. This dream was of a beautiful woman, who I would meet later in my life. She would prove to be a key component to my vision. In this dream, she was donning a black dress and she would stick her finger up her ass and then lick it. Why the hell she did that I have no idea, but I am positive that this is the same woman who I would meet about twenty years later.

I was three years old when the first strike of the human forces of evil would attempt to ruin me. In the middle of the night, I was awakened by a rumbling, deep vibrating noise. My sister, for some reason, was not awakened by this disturbance. All of a sudden, loud voices began to speak to me in a threatening tone. I believed that this rumbling sound was a U.F.O. I remember hearing "calling all cars, calling all cars" which was a line from one of the cartoons I used to watch at this age. This was followed by the voice of a friend, who I would meet years later when I had become a mental patient. This was followed by evil-sounding adult laughter.

My sister woke up, as I sat there an innocent defenseless infant with a look of terror on my face. Jill asked me what was wrong and I began to repeat, "Boy, are we in trouble, boy are we in trouble!" Jill thought nothing of it and she went back to sleep. As for myself, I got out of bed crying and ran to my parent's bedroom. I told them that there was a spaceship outside. Obviously, they didn't believe me. However, they did let me spend the remainder of the night with them in bed. The next morning as I was sitting in my highchair, my mother and father assured me that I would be alright and that I was safe. My mother took a can of Hi-C (high see?) juice out of the refrigerator and poured me a cup. This would prove to be the first paranormal experience, which would linger inside of me for years to come.

This experience caused me to become smart in a way of which only I am capable of. Other related experiences would have a profound effect on my personal subconscious, thus leading me to be a more cautious and fearful youth, compared to the common kid. Over the duration of my life, I would grow braver, smarter, more moral, and I would take possession of a link to a higher knowledge of understanding, which would set into motion the vision of "knowing."

My first word was "see" and when applying this word to the nature of my theories, as well as universal time flux and the three levels of consciousness, one could "see" the significance of this word in pertinence to it being my first ever spoken word.

I remember my father would come out of the shower in his robe and he would towel dry his hair, which looked funny to me at the time because of the way he would rustle his hands back and forth as if he was a mad man. I used to imitate him when I got out of the tub. I was trying to be funny myself. Soon after this horrific experience, my childhood would once again seem commonplace. I continued to play with my friends, and I was able to put this experience behind me, forget it all together until all hell would break loose again. I remember the first time my parents told me of god and like other children, I was frightened by this concept. I remember going outside and looking up into the clouds, expecting god to appear to show me that he existed.

By the time I was four, I had learned to use a record player. I would listen to my Alvin and the Chipmunks record, my Spiderman record, and my Sesame Street records. I was able to laugh and I was looking forward to kindergarten. Soon, I would see the movie "Superman," and ever since then, I have always wanted to be a superhero.

All of my grandparents were alive at this time and I was fond of all of them. My Nana and Grampa Hodge bought me a red teddy bear for Christmas one year. I remember watching television and someone threw a pie in another guy's face, so I grabbed a lid to a plastic jar of fluffernutter and proceeded to throw it into my teddy bear's face. Well, I wanted to laugh and I was only four, so why not, right? I would soon regret this, because now, my red teddy bear was ruined. Even at a very young age, I was into music. My favorite song as a four-year-old was "Can You Read My Mind" from the Superman movie. It was even better than Alvin and the Chipmunks, who at the time were "it" as far as I was concerned.

I remember my sister, who was eleven years old at the time, would be outside hanging out with her friends and I would try to join in. Anyhow, one of Jill's friends would always chuck a rubber ball all the way down First Street and I would retrieve it and bring it back like a trained dog. Jill and her friends would always get a kick out of the fact that wherever I went, I was always running.

And then there was "ICE CREAM!" Yes, good old Mr. Softy, I can still remember his jingle. As soon as I would hear Mr. Softy's jingle, I would start to scream as if someone was trying to kill me. I would yell, "Ma, Dad, ice cream!" My parents weren't the spoiling type, but the only way for them to shut me up would be to hand me fifty cents and let me loose. One time, I walked up to Mr. Softy's ice cream truck and he drove off on me. Then I became victim to that Eddie Murphy type teasing, you know, when your friends would start dancing and singing about how they have ice cream and you don't.

Remember when you were little and—due to your age and inexperience—you lacked an understanding of the outside environment? I used to think mailmen were policemen because of the similarities of their uniforms. My sister Jill told me she used to think those big orange street cleaning machines were monsters. One day, she decided to be brave, so she yelled at one of these orange monsters as it drove off. Lo and behold, a larger one started to drive up our street, so she thought that the big boss of the orange monsters was coming to get her, so she ran inside and hid.

I used to look at the side of the "City of Lowell" garbage trucks and I would read the words "Keep our city clean." Because of the fact that I did not know the letter "C" could sound like the letter "S," I assumed that it said, "Keep our kitty clean."

VISION OF A MENTAL PATIENT

Therefore, I thought that these rugged men in dirty uniforms were driving around the city cleaning everyone's kittens. Whatever, I was only four at the time.

Having lived only a few miles from New Hampshire, I saw quite a few New Hampshire license plates while I was growing up. So, since I was young and basically illiterate, and due to the fact that I had an affinity for canned ravioli, I thought that these New Hampshire license plates which read "Live Free or Die" actually read "Live Free for Chef Boyardee." On another occasion at First Street, when I was still four years old, I was hanging out with my family in our backyard. We were confronted by a huge viscous foaming at the mouth St. Bernard, which looked like Cujo. Being so young, I was not aware of the danger involved and I began to walk towards this dog. When my father took notice, he ran over, grabbed me, and told us all to get inside of the house. Dad was looking after us as he always did. There was a swing set in my back yard and as I would swing on it, I would stare at a rounded eye-like feature on the bark of a tree located in front of this swing set. At this age, I thought this tree eye could actually see and I believed it was looking at me. This childhood thought would aid the development of my personal subconscious in future years. I had a bad habit of breaking glass at this age and one day, I came across a glass coke bottle beside the pavement on the side of my house, which led to a stairway. I smashed this coke bottle all over the pavement. The landlord came outside some time later and he asked me "Ted, did you break this glass?" And I looked at him with the utmost of sincerity and said "No, I didn't." Kindergarten soon came, and my father had bought me my first lunch box. It was a Disney Mickey Mouse lunch box. I recall about a week prior to my first day of kindergarten, on the very same day I received this lunch box, I threw a few Reese's peanut butter cups inside of it, and I proceeded to skip and sing "I'm going to school" and then I would accidentally, on purpose, cause my lunch box to open, thus, spilling my peanut butter cups on the floor. Reese's peanut butter cups were my favorite snack only because I had not yet discovered the all-important Twinkie!

Finally, it was my first day of kindergarten. I remember waking up early on this day and saying to my father in a tone of excitement "School Day!" Dad rolled over in his bed and said that I was in the noon class, not the morning class, and that I still had a few hours to wait. So I asked him "Can I go outside and play?" Dad responded "No." So I began to whine until he finally gave in and told me not to stray too far, because I had to be at school in a few hours. I stepped outside and the sky was a mixture of dew and sunshine. It was the most beautiful of days and I remember it like yesterday. I strolled over to my neighbor's house and saw a friend. He was a young blonde kid with glasses, whose name I cannot recall, because for one, it was a long time ago, and two, I didn't hang around with him all that much. We started to play Battle Star Gallactica, which was a popular science fiction television program that ran from the late 1970s through a good portion of the 1980s. All of a sudden, there was a brief sun shower and as it settled, the sun shined through the rain in a beautiful sky of China blue and cotton white.

Soon, I heard my father calling my name. I said goodbye to my blonde-haired friend and ran home, anticipating my first ever day of school. I attended Kindergarten at the Varnum Elementary School, a mere hop skip and a jump from my house on First Street. I saw my friend Gus when I arrived and we were upset to find out we would be in separate classes. I claimed my seat as my father sat next to me, as all of the other parents and children in the room did at that moment. I looked above the chalkboard and I pointed in excitement at the alphabet and said "Look, Dad, it's the alphabet!" My father looked at me and said "You will know it all soon, Ted." My kindergarten teacher then introduced herself to the class. I cannot recall her name, but I remember that she was an attractive woman with pretty long straight blonde hair. For some reason, I do remember the other Kindergarten teacher's name, but not her face. This was Mrs. Tragis. All of the parents were asked to leave and Kindergarten was under way.

We were brought down to the basement for gym class and we were told to walk around and flap our arms like the wings of a bird and say, "I'm free, I'm free." Although there were no bad intentions from the teachers or the students, this would be the first time that I was lied to by the school system. You see, we were free, and as the line in the "Eye of the Beholder" says, "Freedom no longer frees you." Don't get me wrong, education is a must, but absolute control is a must not! I came home from my first day of school with a sense of accomplishment as well as a new found sense of false dignity.

About halfway through my first year of school, my family would move to another house. We moved only about two miles from First Street, but two miles to a five-year-old, is like you or me driving from Boston to New York City. I remember the first day of school after we had moved to Lilley Ave, in the Centerville section of Lowell. My parents were putting up wallpaper and they lost track of time. I was waiting for them at the end of the day and once they were a few minutes late, I began to panic. Being only five years old, I said to my teacher, "What if they forgot about me?" You must understand that I couldn't realize that they wouldn't forget about having a son because of how young I was. Soon after, my mother showed up in my father's new Ford L.T.D.; the sense of relief was soothing, to say the least. My mother explained to me that she and my father would never forget about me and that they simply lost track of time. Due to the past, this occurrence was more confusing and frightening for me than it would be for other kids.

My father would drive me to kindergarten for the remainder of the school year and I had to remind him every morning, "Don't forget to get me a Twinkie." As I would play with the other children in the schoolyard, one boy would say "I'm Spiderman," another would say, "I'm Batman" and I would say, "I'm Superman." Another kid wanted to be Superman, so I pointed to the unzipped hood in the back of my Patriots jacket and said, "I'm Superman because I have a cape!" A woman from the future was watching me one day and she yelled to me, "Ted, you are a superhero you are the...." I then began to strut around the schoolyard pretending to be a superhero.

Kindergarten came and passed and life on Lilley Ave would continue on through the summer of 1979. It wouldn't be long until more paranormal occurrences would take place. In the meantime, life was good. During the summer of 1979, the movie "2001 a Space Odyssey" was on H.B.O., and while my family and I watched this movie, we were fascinated by the last few scenes. I then understood that there was another world, which, at the time, I labeled as the mirror world. This would prove to be the infant thought in pertinence to my reflection theories. I tried to explain to my family that I was visualizing another side of existence, but they were pretty much clueless.

My father and I began to go shoot hoops at local parks; by this time, I was already a baseball fan and I was becoming interested in the Boston Celtics. Soon, I learned of the legendary Larry Bird. One day, my father and I were at St. Louis Park in Lowell and as he was teaching me to shoot, some other people showed up and asked my father if he wanted to play some full court basketball. My father complied with this request. He told me to stand out of bounds and to stay out of the large puddle over in the next court. I said, "Okay, Dad." Suffice it to say, about two minutes into the game, I ran over to this puddle and dove right in. My father became angry with me, but he calmed down quickly and took me home.

I had been attending Red Sox games at Fenway Park since I was two years old and I would continue to attend Sox games throughout my life. At one game in particular, I was with my Nana and Grampa Hodge, my sister Jill, my mother, and my father. The Red Sox were playing the Toronto Blue Jays and Toronto was winning 13 to 4 or something, in about the fifth inning. All of a sudden, I felt like I had to go to the bathroom, so I told my Dad that I needed to go. He took me to the men's room and sat me down, but I couldn't go. At that moment for the first time in the whole game, the crowd went wild. As soon as this crowd eruption was over, I said to my father "I'm only kidding, I can't go." My father rolled his eyes and brought me back to our seats. He informed the family of what I just did. Suffice it to say, we had something to laugh about for the rest of our lives.

I don't know if any of you men out there have ever gone to the bathroom at Fenway Park. For those of you that have, you might remember that for urinals, they used to have a continuous bathtub-like urinal, which ran around the room with nothing blocking the view, if you know what I mean. Whether you looked to your right or your left, you would bear witness to a chain of pissing penises. As a young boy of only four or five years of age, this was a very funny thing. Anyhow, when my father sat me down, before I claimed that I was kidding, I noticed that there was a man peeing in the stall next to us, because he didn't want to give a peep show. All I could see was his feet and they were facing the toilet. I began to laugh because I thought this guy had backward feet. It wouldn't be until years later, when I would start attending Celtic games. I have only been to two Patriots games and one Bruins game in my life. I made some new friends on Lilley Ave and I would enjoy myself for a couple of years. When first grade came, I was enrolled into the Greenhalge Elementary School, which was a block away from our new house. The Greenhalge is still in business, but the original building was torn down and a new one was built. My first grade teacher was Mrs. Shannon. She was a very nice woman and an acceptable teacher. Mrs. Shannon was very patient with us and none of us was ever fearful of her. In kindergarten, my teacher would sternly reprimand us from time to time. Whenever she would reprimand me, I would hide my face behind another student so she couldn't see me. I never had to do that with Mrs. Shannon, thus the first grade was a good year for me.

When the second grade came, it was the first year of the 1980s, which would be the decade my time travel and primary goal dementia, my comprehension of "knowing," and my first feelings of true love would be manifested. My second grade teacher was Mrs. Nugent, who could be considered funny because sometimes, certain friends of mine will call me Ted Nugent, after the famous rock star. Mrs. Nugent was older than my father by a decade or so, but she knew him as a child. I remember a magazine subscription that the class would receive and we would do homework on. It was called the Nitty Gritty City; we had a new version every week, and every version featured a different fictional character. Mrs. Nugent ordered a cardboard play spaceship for myself and my fellow students to play in or around during recess. I have many fond memories of the second grade.

However, on my first day of the second grade, I was frightened, because the teacher set up some math problems on the chalkboard, which the entire class was able to solve except for myself. This would be the first time when school would really scare me. Mrs. Nugent did a good job of encouraging me and although I wasn't an exemplary student, I did hold my own. I used to dread it when my teacher would write on the board "papers to be signed." When my name would come up on that list, I would nearly swallow my tongue. You see, my father was always adamant when it came to my education and there was no way of him knowing of my paranormal distractions which were set into motion due to my enacting of the primary goal. I met one of my first school friends in the second grade. This was a little short dude (and yes, he is still short to this day) by the name of Corey L. Corey sat behind me with some other big kid whose name I cannot recall. What do you think Corey, myself, and the big kid used to talk about in those days? We talked about what every kid in the second grade talked about, and that would be sex. Of course, we didn't know much about sex at that age, but we still liked to have in-depth conversations, on boobies, asses, and those small little things which floated between our legs.

Some older and more appropriate intellectual types might have gasped at that last comment. However, you must understand that the most fun thing to do as a kid is to use cuss words and talk about things you are not supposed to talk about when your parents aren't around. The truth is that we didn't even know how babies were made. We thought the stork paid a visit.

I remember playing chase in the schoolyard during outdoor recess and as I was running from a girl. I would accidentally on purpose trip over my shoelaces so they could catch me. It was cool, man! So, you see, I was just your common mischievous little boy looking out for some fun. I had many good friends who I would play basketball, baseball, kickball, and some other games with. There was Eddie, Jo Jo, Jason, Rob, Ricky, and a cute blonde girl, who lived next door to me by the name of Jennifer. Soon would be the third grade, but prior to the commencement of the school year, I would have two more paranormal experiences. As for the first one, I was in my bedroom lying in bed and I had my covers over my head due to some personal subconscious fear. The next thing I knew, a slow shrill raspy voice came from the side of my bed and said, "Ted, what are you doing under there?" I immediately screamed and my father ran to my room. My mother and father tried to convince me that it was the television which they had on in the living room. However, I knew this voice most certainly wasn't from the television. Once my mother and father calmed me down, they left the room and I laid my head on my pillow. As I had my left ear on the pillow, I could hear something flying. This flying entity was coming to save me from the big lie. Something often happened to me as a child when I was lying in bed on the flat of my back. Somehow, I would slide about half a foot or so forward, despite my body being horizontal. The line in the Deallegiance song "Lost in Time" which reads, "are you sliding, no you're blind" pertains to this occurrence.

The next paranormal occurrence would take place soon after this previous one. I was lying in my bed face down and I was compelled to look out of my window. When I looked out my window, I saw a Jesus-like figure with a bandage on his head. This image appeared as a cartoon-like figure. For some reason, I was not frightened in the least and I would lay back down and stay awake all night for the first time in my life. This night went by very fast and I was not tired in the morning. Remember, I had no knowledge of the thorny crown which was placed on Christ's head minutes before his crucifixion, yet there was a bandage on the head of this figure. I told my sister of this in the morning and she told me of the thorny crown after I told her of the bandage on the head of this image. My sister has born witness to many of my paranormal experiences. She is also aware of my so-called delusions. One might wonder why I did not believe in god because of this, but this was simply a result of the primary goal.

There are many people who can testify that I have been having experiences as such for a long time now. My subconscious fear would strengthen, yet so would my valor. It is once again lyric time. This song I am about to present to you has to do with this night I witnessed the Christ figure. This part of my vision is yet another result of an equalizing of the three levels of consciousness. I now present track six to the Death Angel album entitled *Act 3*. This one is called "A Room with a View."

> *Sitting at the window staring down*
> *listen to the people shuffle around*
> *hear the children laughing, feel the morning breeze*
> *sunlight warms his skin, the autumn air is taken in*
> *a nearby bird sings a song for him*
> *A room with a view, you're looking at him*
> *he's looking through you, a room with a view*
> *Who's fooling who?*
> *There's got to be something that he knew*
> *So there he sits and some may wonder*
> *about the sly grin on his face*
> *yet little do they "know" (they don't have a clue)*
> *the boundaries of his wisdom*
> *in the solitude of his kingdom*

The summer prior to the third grade was obviously strange for me. For some reason, my parents wanted me to attend another school. This would be the Lowell City Magnet School. Why this school appealed to my parents I will never know. You see, a magnet school is a preparatory school for a vocational high school. Seeing that my father always said that it would be great for me to attend college some day, this move did not make sense. My mother and father said that it was up to me whether I wanted to attend this new school or stay at the Greenhalge. I was young and my parents painted a pretty picture of this school for me. So, I decided to attend this school where I would be for the next year and a half. And believe me you, it sucked big time! You see, had I stayed at the Greenhalge, my childhood would have been much better, because I was accepted and well liked by my fellow students at the Greenhalge. Once I entered this new school, I would be subject to bullying and extreme teasing. I soon became the kid that everyone made fun of. A big problem with this school is that they had fifth graders in the same classes as third and fourth graders. Because of the paranormal disturbances I was experiencing at this age, I was vulnerable and sensitive to ridicule. None of my fellow students knew what was happening to me and those who I was friends with could tell that I was emotionally disturbed.

During this time, my parents decided to get a divorce, which was heart-wrenching for me at the time. My close friends were sympathetic and I was thankful to have them. One good thing in my life is that no matter how far down the scale I went, never did I ever have any trouble whatsoever making friends. I have been blessed with so many friends in my life and I adore them all. My parents got into another fight soon after, when, all of a sudden, something good must have happened, because they decided to give it another try. However, in a couple of years they would be forever apart.

Living on Lilley Ave, I would often enjoy the company of Jill and her friends. They were all very good kids who enjoyed laughing together. My sister was older than me, and I used to just walk into her room to ask her to play. Sometimes she would, sometimes she wouldn't. This was understandable because a teenager has better things to do than to hang out with a seven-year-old.

When she did play with me, it was great. She would always make me laugh and we used to like playing with her tape recorder. Of course, like any pair of siblings, we had our share of fights, but we have always maintained a good level of respect for each other.

Soon, my mother and father found and purchased a new house in Dracut Massachusetts, which was just north of Lowell. It was a nice yellow ranch located in a good rural neighborhood. It was much better than Lilley Ave and First Street, and the thought of moving to another town after all that I had been through in the past few years was good for me. For some reason, I actually cried days prior to our move to Dracut. I was going to miss baseball and kickball with Eddie and Jo Jo, video games and computers with Rob, and swearing and talking dirty with Jason and the Grescas. However, I was pleased overall to be moving to a whole new town and meeting an entirely different group of kids. I was about halfway through the fourth grade when we made this move to Dracut and I was to be enrolled in the Greenmont Avenue School, which was a five to ten minute walk from my new house. My fourth grade teacher for the remainder of the school year was Mrs. Dadoly, and she was very likable. In my first few days at this new school, I met a few kids who I liked. We would play boxball, dodge ball, and Nerf football in the schoolyard. The kids in Dracut seemed a lot nicer than the kids in Lowell, and I began to enjoy my new residence.

About one week into Greenmont School, Mrs. Dadoly told us to find a reading partner for reading class. A couple of kids I had already become acquainted with were waving me over, but I wanted to meet someone new. I peered over to my right and a quiet little chubby blue-eyed kid asked me to read with him. Once reading class was over, I said to this kid "I'm Ted" and he responded by saying "I know, you're the new kid; my name is Joshua." I asked "Joshua what?" He said "Joshua Bernard." Soon we would be best friends and as I said earlier in this book, Joshua would prove to be the best friend I ever had. The cable system in Dracut was better than the cable system in Lowell. Joshua told me of a station called Nickelodeon which was not on Lowell cable at the time. He told me to watch a funny show called "You Can't Do that on Television." Then Joshua told me that he had about half of the Star Wars toy collection and at that point, I was sold.

So, I went over to Joshua's house for the first time of millions to follow, half because I wanted to play with his star wars figures, and half because I was interested in being his friend. I met Joshua's father, Joe. Joe was one of those cap-wearing grease monkey types who enjoyed working on car engines and stuff like that. Joe would eventually give me a funny nickname—"Theodophis." Joshua's mother is Sheryl, who I have run into recently. Sheryl is a registered nurse.

I spent more time at the Bernard residence than I did at my own home. When I saw Sheryl recently, she told the people I was with that she raised me, and that is not far from the truth. Joshua has a sister Rebecca, who he used to fight with all the time. Then Joshua's brother Adam was born, who I knew as a very young boy. After Joshua and I went our separate ways, he would be blessed with two more siblings, Zachary and Shelby. Joshua is happily married with children today. He has a son named Justin, but I don't know the names of the rest of his family.

Joshua was a good influence on me, much more than I was an influence on him. He always encouraged me to stay out of trouble and to stay away from alcohol when I first experimented with it. Joshua and I were always straight as an arrow when we were together and all we ever did was laugh. Just about every weekend, either I would sleep over Joshua's house or he would sleep over my house.

Soon, Joshua would get an above ground pool in his backyard, which we would spend a good portion of our summers in. I remember that every time the month of June came and summer vacation began, we would celebrate by splashing each other to death. We had a New Year's tradition of watching the ball drop on television and every year, either I would stay at his place or he would stay at mine.

Soon, it would be the fifth grade and Joshua and I were to be in the same class. Our teacher was Mrs. Giragoshan. She was a stern and disciplined type teacher, but she did want the best for us. My problems would continue to haunt me as I did my best to deal with disturbances, which emanated from my setting into motion the primary goal. I would be subject to minor teasing at times, nothing like that of years prior. Due to paranormal activities lingering within the vastness of my personal subconscious, my anxiety would soon grow more intense. I began to vomit every morning before school and on top of it all, my mother and father were starting to fight like crazy. One morning, they were arguing and it pained me to hear them speak to each other with such bitterness. As I stood outside my bedroom door, my father came storming out of his bedroom.

He was not in a good mood. I told him I was afraid to go to school because I did not finish my homework and I didn't want to deal with the pressure. My father told me to go to school and face the music, so I went.

My parents would finally get a divorce and I was to stay with my mother. My mother hung out with a woman who would become my stepmother years later. My mother would go out with this woman and leave me with her daughter, Sharman, and her son, Robbie, while they went out and drank. Sharman would throw a wild party and some of my first experiments with alcohol would begin. I began to look forward to the weekends so that I could go to Sharman's and get drunk.

My attendance began to worsen to the point that I was absent as much as I was present. It seemed as if my world was crumbling around me, but I would remain strong. I visited my father on weekends and it was nice to see him. My mother liked to drink a lot and she did it so often, I could not tell the difference whether she was sober or drunk until my sister Jill would let me know. One day as I was skipping school as usual, the Greenmont School principal came to my house and I saw her outside my front window. I promptly found a place to hide. The next time I showed up at school, the principal had a talk with me and said she had to call my parents to discuss my absenteeism. My parents were divorced, so they called them both and asked them to come to the school for a talk.

It was just about halfway of the school year and I had missed twenty-eight days. It is amazing, that I ever reached high school. Anyhow, after this meeting, my parents went home and I attended gym class. My gym teacher was Mr. Berard who was often guilty of picking favorites. I was one of his favorites as he was one of my favorite teachers. He could tell that I was troubled, and he sympathized with me, and said that he had seen my parents come in.

I went home, and when I got there, my father let me have it, but I was simply unable to cope. My attendance continued to suffer throughout the school year, and it came to the point that my father literally had to drag me to school and throw me through the front doors. The vomiting would continue in the mornings and, oftentimes, I would fake sick so I could avoid school. The fifth grade would come to a close; I would squeak by and be promoted to the sixth grade.

The summer of 1983 was a good one and, seeing all that was happening to me at this stage of my life, I once again hoped that summer would never end. Joshua and I would celebrate and splash each other to death in his pool. We had our usual sleepovers, played with G. I. Joe toys, and Star Wars toys. We read a ton of Choose Your Own Adventure books and had many laughs throughout this summer.

As the summer of 1983 came to its end, I once again became stressed (for obvious reasons). Joshua and I rode our bikes down to the Greenmont School so that we could observe the list on the front window which would tell us what class we would be in. Once again, Joshua and I would be in the same class.

My sixth grade teacher was Mrs. Davenport; she was a very nice woman. Despite the fact that I had a caring, competent, and considerate woman for a teacher that year, I would still be subject to extreme difficulties, and this was due to both my family life and the paranormal activities of the past, present, and future.

My attendance was just as bad, if not worse, than the year before. Luckily, I had Joshua to make me laugh and many other friends who generally cared for me. The morning vomiting was worse than ever and when I wasn't sick, my only option was to fake sick. At one point, I missed eight straight days and when I got back, Mrs. Davenport said in a friendly way "Hi, stranger." Of course, my teacher meant no harm by saying this to me, but due to extreme stress, I took it the wrong way. At the end of this day, I had to take a math test, which I was obviously not prepared for. When Mrs. Davenport received this test from me, she saw that what I did was wrong and that I had left the second half of it blank. Mrs. Davenport then reprimanded me and she strongly suggested that I got my act together. At this point, my anxiety hit its zenith. I walked home shaking all over and I began to have a nervous breakdown.

Now, there is no clinical definition to describe a nervous breakdown, in confined terms. However, I am more than sure that I had one. I was living with my mother at the time and her drinking was having a bad affect on her, myself, and Jill. Before she got home from work, I was a wreck and I started to intentionally fall down the stairs to the basement of my house, so that I could break my arm. I was simply unable to cope.

My mother got home at her usual time, which was about 5:30 P.M., and I told her that I needed to go to the hospital. When she asked me why, I told her that I was falling apart. She told me that if there was nothing physically wrong with me, then there was no reason for her to take me to the hospital. Obviously, I was not successful in injuring myself. So I sucked it up, regained my composure, and started to attend school again.

Although I was once again attending school and my attendance was getting better, it was still lackluster. The weekends with Joshua were relieving, as well as the parties that Sharman would throw. It was at this point, when my alcoholism would start to show itself. Soon, I would go on another skid of absences and my father, not knowing of the paranormal realities of my life, had no choice but to drag me to school and throw me through the front doors, once again. So, my mother would sit and talk to her friends on the phone, drinking her Miller Lites while I would play Nerf basketball and pretend to be Larry Bird. One time, a few of my friends peeked in my window and they saw me imitating Larry Bird while he was playing. Suffice it to say, I was very embarrassed, I would have rather got caught jerking off! Nerf basketball was my favorite thing to play as a kid and I would even play it today at the age of thirty-five. Joshua began to take notice of my occasional drinking and he was growing quite concerned for my well-being. I wasn't drinking every day (yet), but when I was drinking, I was drinking alcoholically.

One day, my sister Jill asked me if Mom was drinking last night and I said, "I don't know." Then Jill asked me if she was sitting in the corner talking on the phone. I said, "Yes, she was." Jill then said, "Then she was drinking." As I stated earlier, I didn't know the difference whether my mother was drunk or sober and this is obviously due to her excessive drinking. Thoughts of my parent's divorce were haunting me, and it pained me to see such bitterness between them.

Around this time, I saw a touching movie on H.B.O. called "Love Child." I have been trying to find a copy of this movie, but apparently, it is out of print. Anyhow, this film was the story of a woman who had been abused, degraded, and convicted of a crime, which she did not commit. After all of the hell she went through, at the end of the movie when she was exonerated from her false crime, she said "I guess it really is a free world!" This would later prove to be a connection, which would strengthen me and thus allow me to overcome the uncompromising world evils and not to let them win. In relation to this connection of love, I will present some more lyrics to you. This song is by the outstanding 80s band called Crowded House. It is titled "Don't Dream its Over." Please enjoy.

There is freedom within, there is freedom without
try to catch the deluge in a paper cup
there's a battle ahead, many battles are lost
but you'll never see the end of the road
when you're travelling with me
hey now, hey now, don't dream its over
hey now, hey now, when the world comes in
they come, they come, to build a wall between us
we "know" they won't win
now in towing my car, there's a hole in the roof
my possessions are causing me suspicion but there's no proof
in the paper today, tales of war and of waste
but you turn right over to the T.V. page
hey now, hey now, don't dream its over
hey now, hey now, when the world comes in
they come, they come, to build a wall between us
we "know" they won't win
now I'm walking again to the beat of a drum
and I'm counting the steps to the door of your heart
only shadows ahead, never clearing the roof
get to "know" the feeling of liberation and release
hey now, hey now, don't dream its over
hey now, hey now, when the world comes in
they come, they come, to build a wall between us
we "know" they won't win
well don't let them win, hey now, hey now
don't let them win, don't let them win, yeah

Continuing on, towards the end of the sixth grade in June of 1984, school would get better for me. I would once again squeak by and be promoted to the seventh grade.

I remember on one of the last days of school that year, Mrs. Davenport was playing a game with us, in the form of trivia questions. Joshua was poking fun at some of the other students and he had me in stitches. The nice thing was that Mrs. Davenport realized that Joshua was just kidding, so she tolerated it. As Joshua and I began to laugh, she smiled at us with an expression of approval. She was pleased to see me in a good mood and although she was not aware of my problems, she definitely sensed that I was living a challenging life, especially for an eleven-year-old.

The sixth grade came to an end. Joshua and I would do the splashing celebration ritual, as usual. During the summer of 1985, my drinking habit became worse. I and another musical friend began to swipe beers from our parents, go into the woods behind my house, and get lit. We were just about to turn twelve, so all we needed was a six-pack of beer between the two of us. After all, three beers apiece was quite enough beer to achieve intoxication for that of an eleven-year-old.

Joshua, as always, was looking out for me and he would soon confront me about my newly developed drinking problem. Joshua reminded me that all we ever did was laugh and that I didn't need alcohol to have fun. I didn't realize it at first (probably because I was trying to be cool) that Joshua is a very funny person. Sometimes, I would make fun of him for his wacky, yet charming sense of humor. Joshua was always there for me and I am sure that he would have opened up to me even more if he was aware of the crazy life I was living. Joshua and I used to play with tape recorders and we made up a fictional radio station, which was called WJERK (jerk). You know, we were just a couple of young friends acting silly and doing our best to enjoy the years of childhood. WJERK had station identification, just as you would hear on television and radio. It went like this: "This is WJERK, the jerkiest station in town." WJERK was talk radio and we made a bunch of versions, which I actually still have a few of. However, I think that I would rather jerk off in front of the president of the United States, than have anyone hear these tapes, because it was fucking goofy. After we had made a few of these tapes, Joshua would ask me, or I would ask him "Hey, do you want to jerk off?" Which meant, do you want to make another tape? Yes, we dubbed these tapes as jerk offs. One day in Dracut, years later when Joshua and I were attending high school, we were at a local metal show for a band I used to be a member of. Anyhow, there was this nice looking girl who I used to be crazy about. As she looked at me, I put my arm around Joshua and said, "I know we look like a couple gay people right now, but I don't care." I then asked him "Do you still have any of our jerk off tapes?" Needless to say, this girl lost it at this point and this was obviously due to her having no idea of what we were talking about, and she might have thought that I was referring to actual tapes of Joshua and me jerking off! I strongly believe that if adults formed a comic television or radio program based on these tapes, it would be one of the funniest shows ever. So, Joshua and I continued to do our jerk offs that summer and I would begin going to a place which I would be at two or three times a week for the next six years. This would be a roller skating rink, called Roller Kingdom .It still exists, and it is located in Tyngsboro Massachusetts, just south of Nashua, New Hampshire. I have many fond memories of this place. I literally made hundreds of friends there and I always looked forward to going there on Friday and Saturday nights.

I finally got myself signed up for little league baseball at this age and I would play for the Brewers in the Lowell St. Michael's baseball league. The next year, I would play for Dracut little league and I would be on the Tigers. In my third and last year of baseball, I would play for the Dracut senior league on the Yankees. The baseball years were great and it did distract me from my problems. I soon decided that music was more important to me than sports, so I abandoned my athletic pursuits.

I had always spent a lot of time with my Nana and Grampa Hodge, but around this time, I began to see them more frequently. My grandparents were very nice "strict as hell" people but nice. My grandfather was the funny witty type who didn't mind tipping a few Budweisers from time to time, but he most certainly was not an alcoholic. He used to like calling people "knucklehead." I think it was his favorite word.

My Nana is a loving person in many ways, yet she did have quite the temper. Even when she was wrong about something, I learned that her intentions were always good and sincere and the same goes for my father and my Grampa Hodge. My Nana has a great sense of humor. She is always concerned with my clothes. She would always say to me "Fold your clothes, make sure you use a face cloth, tuck in your shirt, and get a haircut." My Nana is very understanding of mental illness (although by now you realize that I am not mentally ill). She is very caring and compassionate for the mentally ill in ways that most of society is unable to comprehend. All she really wants of me is for me to take care of myself and she will seldom pressure me on anything else. She is most certainly a good part of my life. My Grampa Hodge died in the 1990s and my Nana is presently ill.

On my mother's side of the family, "the O'neils," my mother is Karen, but I haven't seen her in sixteen years. I hope she is doing well. I have an Aunt Patty who I like and miss. I have an uncle named Kevin who was an incredible baseball player in his day and definitely could have gone pro. Patty has a few kids; they are Michael, Lindsey, and an adopted Peruvian girl named Sarah. Kevin had a few kids himself. He had some troubles as a youngster, but I hear he has turned himself around and that he has become a hardworking father. Unfortunately, I have not met Kevin's kids (yet), but I bet they are good people.

The last time I saw Kevin was at the downtown side of the Bridge Street Bridge in Lowell and this was about thirteen years ago. As soon as we saw each other, we immediately hugged. Then I told him that I was trying to avoid alcohol and he looked at me and said "Yeah, it's hard." All of a sudden, he got slightly emotional and said, "I haven't been much of a godfather." He had made some mistakes in the past, just like all of us. I told him he needn't apologize. He smiled at me and told me that he had to go visit his old man who happens to be my Grampa O'neil. Grampa O'neil passed on some time ago. What Kevin said next shocked me. He said, "Ted its nice connecting with you!" He asked me about my computer, which I didn't have yet. I told him I didn't have a computer yet and he gave me a puzzled expression. We said goodbye and went our separate ways. Years prior to this, I was at an O'neil family reunion. I was reading a comic book was based on the Indiana Jones series. Kevin walked over to me with a look of amazement on his face. He was acting as if he knew something about me, which I didn't. On another occasion, following the death of his mother and my grandmother, he told me that I was emotionally strong and then he said, "Remember that!" It appears as if Kevin knows something. Whether he knows something consciously or subconsciously, I honestly am not sure, but we have definitely connected.

I have a message for all of my cousins: You are safe! The summer of 1985 was a turning point. I would do very well for the next few years. For the seventh grade, I would attend Dracut Engelsby Junior High School. There was one kid who bullied me for a short while, but soon, the days of being made fun of by my peers was virtually over.

Once I hit the seventh grade, I would begin to fit in immediately. I would discover that I had a talent for being funny. I used to make people laugh so hard that they would be gasping for air. I had been seeing a therapist named Janice. She helped me very much. I became a very happy kid at the age of twelve. For the first time in my life, other than puppy love in the first and second grade, girls became interested in me. My self-esteem would thoroughly improve and my true personality was taking form.

For teachers, I remember Mr. Quaterone, Mr. Francis, Mrs. Lloyd, and Mr. Campbell. I would drive all of these teachers nuts for the entire school year. All the other kids had backpacks or gym bags to carry their books in. I had a red T.W.A. bag with small wheels at the bottom, which I would drag down the hall as if I was boarding a plane, or something. My favorite subject was not science. It was history. I didn't like school science because everything was so confined and there was no evidence presented as to relationships, which is the basis of connection and scientific equivalency. I absolutely despised shoppe class and as far as gym was concerned, I would always forget my uniform.

As the year went on, something began to take a toll on me. My mother's drinking was getting worse. She was very sick and I do fathom this fact, but she wouldn't help herself or even care to help herself. Anyone who has ever dealt with a troubled alcoholic in his or her family knows that you can't help someone who is not willing to help himself or herself. I was young and I made the huge mistake of taking my mother's liquor away from her ; I was a complete hypocrite because I would often drink this liquor myself. One night, she was drunk and said to me, "If you don't want me to drink, then get out of my life." It was at this point when I started to contemplate moving in with my father.

I decided that I would try to stick it out with my mother. A week went by and my mother became worried that I would leave her. So, a few days later, she brought home a little white dog. Obviously, she was hoping for me to get attached to this dog so I wouldn't leave. Anyhow, this dog had a severe flea problem. In a matter of days, my whole house was infested and so were my mother and I.

I must have been taking ten showers a day trying to rid myself of these fleas. My mother seemed non-functional and she would miss a few days of work. I confronted her about all that was happening, but she had been drinking and was thus incoherent. As she went to bed, I could see fleas all over her backside and she didn't seem to care. Once she sobered up, I convinced her to take the dog back to the humane society and have it put up for adoption. Eventually, the fleas were gone, but my predicament still remained. It was time for me to make a decision.

My father was to come over and visit me so that we could discuss the fact that I was considering moving in with him. I was in the basement of my house on Roswell Ave and I was playing pitfall on my old Atari 2600, when I heard my father call my name. I yelled, "I'm down here, Dad." My father walked down the stairs and over to me at the end of the basement where I was sitting. He had bought Jill and me this Atari system when we lived on Lilley Ave in Lowell, but it used to bug my father when I would choose to stay inside and play video games rather than play outside. However, he understood that I was extremely troubled at the time and didn't bring it up. We had a nice talk and then he got down to the point. He asked me "Have you come to a decision?" I said "Yes, Dad, I want to move in with you."

This was a troubling predicament for me to deal with and although I was troubled due to this situation, I was still a happy kid, over all. I was enjoying life: I was having a ball with my friends at Roller Kingdom and everyone in school thought that I was a riot. Once I made the move with my father things would improve even more.

As previously stated, I was playing little league baseball at this time. I was on the Dracut Tigers. I remember I played one of the worst games ever played in the history of the game. Man, did I suck! I pitched and I nearly threw the ball over the backstop several times and I went 0 for 4 with four strike outs. After this game, I would get my ass in gear and become a decent ball player, but I would never be anything like my uncle Kevin.

My father would attend many of my games while my mother would come to a few. One time, my mother worked in the concession stand selling soda and popcorn. It was good living with my father and it was also good to see my mother stone cold sober at some of my games. I lived the life of a tennis ball going to Dracut to visit my mom on weekends and going back to Lowell to live with my Dad on weekdays.

One day, I was being a chauvinist and I would make rude sexual gestures behind the back of a friend. I would be deservedly told off by this girl and I was extremely embarrassed, to say the least. I truly hope that there was a good subconscious intention behind my lewd act, because it is something, which I am not very proud of. At this point, I began to see that being my true self would be the best policy for me to abide by.

My father and I lived on Cross Street in Lowell on the second floor. Our place consisted of a small apartment above my Nana and Grampa Hodge's place. Jill lived downstairs with our grandparents. Jill and I would start to go to Roller Kingdom together. She had her crowd, and I had mine. Jill was cool to me when we would go there. She would often give me money for sodas and pizza. One thing I always made sure of was that I when I went to Dracut to visit my mother, I would make sure that I also visited Joshua. Joshua was getting into a new fad around this time. This fad was the common teenage hobby of skateboarding. Joshua would get me into skateboarding, but I was never as enthusiastic about it as he was. I cannot recall what kind of skateboard Joshua had, but I had a third edition Rob Roskopp board. Soon, Joshua would have a quarter pipe set up in front of his house and we had a ball with it. There is a piece of skateboard lingo Joshua and I would often use. What we would say is, "Did you get air?" which means exactly what it says; when you get air, it means that you and your skate board would fly off of the quarter pipe and you would be in mid air. The problem with getting air was that it was difficult to land back on your skateboard safely to avoid injuring yourself. One day when I wasn't around, Joshua rode onto his quarter pipe and lost control. He ended up landing in the bushes about ten feet away from the quarter pipe. Luckily, Joshua was able to avoid injury. So, when Joshua's father Joe found out of this disastrous occurrence, he jokingly said to Joshua, "Did you get air?" Suffice it to say, it was a very funny thing. It was around this time that I would hear the music of Metallica for the first time in my life. Joshua had purchased the "Master of Puppets" album and although I did like the music, I thought what many people thought at the time: I thought that Metallica was evil. Little did I realize the wisdom that this band had and the profound effect that it would eventually have on my life. At the time, I was a Beatles fan, but not today, my friends; today, I am a diehard Metallica fan. I recall saying to Joshua "Don't you understand that these guys are evil and do you realize what they are for?" Joshua said, "I don't care what they're for. I like them because they make good music!" I was like… "Yeah, but Joshua…." Joshua interrupted me and said "Look, I don't care if they're for fucking dead squirrels, okay!" So, I decided to shut up. Little did I "know" that I would soon be a Metallica fan and a short while after, I would be belting out their tunes on my bass at adult nightclubs.

Later on in December of 1985, I had been in the seventh grade for a few months and seeing that I switched schools enough in my lifetime, my grandfather would drive me to and from school every day, once I had moved upstairs from him.

One day, my grandfather played a joke on me when he picked me up from school. He showed up in this ugly old beat up Cadillac rather than with his Grand Prix. I looked at this car and I thought to myself, "What a piece of junk." So, as I got into this Cadillac, my grandfather smiled at me and said that he had traded in the Grand Prix because he had always wanted a Cadillac. I said "Oh, that's good." And then I started thinking "Holy shit, Nana is going to kill him!" So we got back to Cross Street and proceeded to walk into our house. My Nana looked at the Cadillac and she didn't say a word. The damn thing was a rental car! My grandfather then told me that the Grand Prix was in the shop and that this was the only rental car available. I was very relieved to find out this information because if my grandfather had actually done what I thought he did, you would have been able to hear my Nana yelling all the way out in Boston for the next six hours!

It was around this time in December, when my New England Patriots were hot and they had made the playoffs with a record of 11 and 5. Suffice it to say, the Hodge family was ecstatic. In the wild card game, we defeated the New York Jets 26 to 14. Okay, that was good. The following week was an awesome game which we played against the Oakland Raiders. The Patriots were down 17 to 7, but they would come back, and win 27 to 20. Okay, that was good. Then it was "Squish the fish week": The Patriots were to play the Miami Dolphins for the A.F.C. championship. The Hodge family, just like the rest of the New England population, was extremely excited at this point. The Patriots would take the A.F.C. title by a score of 31 to 14. Okay, this was good. For the next two weeks, my grandfather and I would talk about the upcoming Super Bowl 24/7. I would say, "Grampa, what do you think the score will be?" He would respond with "33 to 10, Patriots win!" He would then ask me the same question and I would say, "31 to 17 Patriots win!" This would be followed by each of us saying back and forth, "I can't believe that the Patriots are in the Super Bowl!" This conversation would repeat itself over and over until the night of the game.

To back up for a moment: on the night the Patriots defeated the Dolphins and took the A.F.C. crown, I would, for the first and last time in my life, notice that my grandfather had tipped a few too many Budweisers and he had quite the glow. On this night, we just sat in front of the television with a feeling of awe and euphoria. When we saw the Patriots helmet facing the Chicago Bears helmet to symbolize Super bowl 20, we nearly jumped out of our seats!

On the night of the game, it was I, my father, his girlfriend Carol, my sister Jill, my Nana, and my Grampa and we were excited as we awaited kickoff. I had lunch that day at Toni's restaurant in Lowell and I was accompanied by two girls who I was good friends with. My Dad found out about this and he didn't like it because he felt that I was still too young for girlfriends. Because it was such a special occasion, my father would let it go.

So, the game started and we were all rearing to go. Walter Payton would fumble the ball on Chicago's first offensive series. The Patriots recovered the ball, and we went crazy! The Patriots ended up kicking a field goal and the Patriots led 3 to 0. My father and I then said that the Bears' claim of a Super Bowl shutout was over. Take that, Chicago!

But from this point on, it was absolutely horrible. The Bears would wipe the floor with the Patriots in the worst blowout in the history of the Super Bowl up to that point in time, with a final score of 46 to 10. At halftime, my Nana and I were saying that they're going to come back. Seeing that the Patriots were losing by twenty points or so, it is obvious that Nana and I were lying to ourselves. The second half was even more torturous, I could barely watch. It was almost as bad as watching the Brady Bunch, but we all know that watching the Brady Bunch is a torture within itself. In the fourth quarter, my sister Jill became so upset she would storm out of the room. The entire Hodge family could sympathize with Jill and I think we were all tempted to storm out of the room at this point. About five minutes later, Jill came walking back into the T.V. room. She was donning a Celtics hat, a Celtics shirt, a Celtics pair of sweat pants, and a pair of white socks to go with it. Jill made us all laugh when she entered the room in these clothes and we so desperately needed to laugh at this point. And also, seeing that the Boston Celtics were winning N.B.A. championships left and right at this time, it was a good thing to be reminded of.

I am still glad the Patriots made it to the Super Bowl that year, those three victorious playoff games must have been some of the most exciting and fun games for me to watch as a sports fan in my entire life. Of course, this would change when the Red Sox would win the 2004 and 2007 World Series. The last three Patriot Super Bowl wins was also quite the treat. My other great sports memory is the 1984 N.B.A. championship between the Los Angeles Lakers and my Boston Celtics. This N.B.A. series was covered on C.B.S. and we all know the subconscious significance of this fact by now! It is wonderful to be a sports fan in New England.

Being a sports fan has always helped me to forget about life's trials and tribulations. I do admit that it wasn't easy being a Red Sox fan due to the repetitive heartbreak that used to be the price of being a Red Sox lover. Seeing them finally win it all after eighty-six years was the experience of a lifetime.

So, the schoolyear went on and I began to start going to another place on a regular basis. This would be the Lowell Y.M.C.A. At this point, I was either at the Y.M.C.A., Roller Kingdom, school, or home. Due to my keeping busy and having as much fun as I possibly could, my attendance in the seventh grade was more than acceptable.

When at school, I got into the habit of imitating famous people and some of my friends as well. I made many veins pop out of many of my teacher's heads that year and it was good when they were bald, because I could get a better view of it. My grades were not great that year, but they weren't too shabby, either. One day in the Junior High cafeteria, we were having hot dogs and beans for lunch. One of my classmates took his hot dog, placed it between his legs, and made it look like his dick. He looked at me and said "How about that, Hodge?" I said "Oh, yeah!" And then I proceeded to wipe the mustard and relish off of my hot dog, place it between my legs, and I started to suck on it. In mid blow, I sensed a presence behind me. I turned around and there was one of the eight grade teachers staring down at me, as a line of spit hung from my bottom lip all the way back to the tip of my hot dog. This teacher didn't need to say a word. I placed my hot dog back on my tray and walked over to the wall. The teacher walked over to me as I stood against the cafeteria wall. He said to me "You have a choice: You can either have detention or we could call your parents and have you suspended." I opted for detention.

As I stood there, half of the cafeteria was in absolute hysterics. Here comes the funny part! Another teacher who didn't witness my lewd act was wondering what I did and why everyone was laughing. So, he asked the teacher who had caught me what I did. The teacher who caught me looked into the other teacher's face and said, "He was blowing himself." The other teacher looked at him in astonishment and said, "He can do that?" The first teacher said, "No stupid, he was using his hot dog!" The other teacher responded with "Oh?" As all of my friends continued to laugh so hard they were nearly blowing snots all over their tables, the teacher who was ever so privileged to witness my sex act became livid and started to reprimand other students. He pointed to one kid and said, "You have detention for encouraging him." He pointed to another and said, "You will have detention if you don't stop laughing." He then pointed at me and said, "You have another detention for blowing yourself!" It is a damn good thing my family didn't find out about this one, because if they had, I might have been killed. In the seventh grade, I majored in mischief and now I am making a career out of it!

The year continued on and Joshua and I decided that it was time to form a band. Neither of us owned an instrument, even play a note. Iwould purchase a keyboard, which can play its own music. We would let the keyboard play its lame tunes and we would rap to it. It was pathetic, but that is how it started. Little did I know it that three years later, I would be rocking out in adult nightclubs.

The seventh grade finally came to an end and it was a very good year for me. Once the summer started, the Lowell Y.M.C.A became an everyday place for me to go. You see, when I knew people, I was outgoing and funny, but in reality I have always been painfully shy. This fact might surprise many of my childhood and teenage friends, but it is the truth. When I was at the Y.M.C.A., my shyness would be prominent.

One day, when I was at the Y.M.C.A., I was walking around in the basketball court. A guy who worked there took notice of me and my frequent attendance at this place. He saw that I never talked that much while I was there. So, he walked over to me and asked "What is your name?" I said ,"I'm Ted." Then he asked me, "What is your social security number?" I was like "What?" Needless to say, he was kidding with me. He was basically interested in why I was there every day and he wanted to be friendly. Once I told him of my situation and my busy schedule, he said to me "I guess it's better than hanging out in the streets." And he was right. So, I played a lot of basketball, but I didn't have many friends there. On the other hand, when I would go to Roller Kingdom, it was the complete opposite. I knew mostly everyone there and I always had a great time.

I would continue to visit my mother and Joshua as much as possible. Joshua and I would still have sleepovers and we would do some more jerk offs. Joshua would continue to make me laugh, no matter what I was faced with. The summer of 1986 went by like a flash of light and once again, due to my place of residence, I would switch schools for the upcoming eighth grade. This time, my family suggested that I attended a private Catholic school. Before the summer of 1986 was over, my father took me down to St. Joseph's Elementary School in Lowell and I would be enrolled. Now, I would have to wear a blue dress shirt and pants with a tie every day and because things were going well for me at this time, I didn't mind it a bit.

St. Joseph's was a fifteen-minute walk from my house on Cross Street. No longer did my Grandfather have to drive me to and from school every day. At first, it seemed as if I was unwelcomed by certain students at this school, but once my other twelve classmates got to know me better, it was excellent. St. Joseph's was a small school and it was different from the Junior high school that I attended the previous year. St. Joseph's was an elementary school and it comprised kindergarten through eighth while last year's school consisted of only seventh and eighth graders. St. Joseph's was also different because we had one to two teachers a day, while at the Junior High School, we had seven periods with seven different teachers.

My eighth grade teacher was Mrs. Mercier and she was a sweetheart, a Republican, but still a sweetheart. Once a day, we would switch teachers for reading class. We would have reading class with the seventh grade teacher. Her name was Mrs. Shankey.

The eoghth grade at St Joseph's was a fantastic year for me and I was really enjoying this new type of school, which was so different from any school I had attended in my previous years. My attendance was good, my grades were good, and all other aspects of my life were good. Halfway through the schoolyear, I went on a hot streak for about a month. I handed in every homework assignment, I didn't miss one day, and every test or quiz no matter what the subject I would get an A+ on. The smartest kid in the class was a dude named Oscar and when he saw me on this hot streak, he said, "Holy cow, Ted, you're catching up to me!" Due to my ability to concentrate and make a better effort this year, I wazs happy and I was able to deal with my problems with ease. I would walk to school, do my work (still managed to have a few laughs), walk home, do my homework, and then I would watch my television programs. I also began to read excessively. Although homework was more

VISION OF A MENTAL PATIENT

at St. Joseph's than at Dracut Junior High, I actually seemed to enjoy it. After two to three hours of homework, the programs I would watch were Moon Lighting, Growing Pains, The Cosby Show, Night Court, and I also followed the Red Sox closely that year. My relationship with my father was better than ever; we would constantly converse on sports and politics. This was around the time of the Reagan Contra Scandal.

About midway through the school year, I would begin to feel comfortable enough to make my fellow students laugh. However, I was not nearly as unruly as I was the year before. I used to have political debates with my teacher but I could hold my own. I had the entire class agreeing with my democratic views, which was a pretty good achievement when taking into account the fact that we were in the Reagan era. My political views at this time were simply a reflection of my father's political views, which is pretty much the case for any kid at the age of thirteen. As for my political archetype at this time, it was primitive, due to my need to individualize myself. What was in store for me sometime later would cause me to lose interest in just about everything.

The Boston Red Sox would go to the World Series this year and my family and classmates were very excited. When the Red Sox played the Angels in the American League Pennant of 1986, one of the games was to be played in the early afternoon on a weekday. The St. Joseph's faculty decided to let us go home about an hour early that day so we could watch the game. The Red Sox would fall behind the angels 3 games to 1, but the Red Sox would make a comeback and thus would face the New York Mets in the World Series. The Red Sox took games one and two in New York and things looked good. The Mets would catch the Red Sox and we are all aware of the disastrous game six and the eventual victory of the New York Mets. In the movie "A League of Their Own" which is about a woman baseball league in the 1940s, there is a line by Tom Hanks's character and it goes like this, "There is no crying in baseball!" Well, sorry to bust your bubble, but if anyone has been a Red Sox fan prior to 2004, they know that there is most certainly crying in baseball. The difference today is that Red Sox fans are crying tears of joy rather than tears of sorrow. The World Series ended, so, the rest of my class mates and I would do our best to console one another. I also did my best to make my friends laugh at this point. Eventually, we got over it and we started to enjoy ourselves once again.

When we would read in Mrs. Shankey's reading class, any word or phrase we read that could remotely be applied to sex would set us all off laughing. Take the word "head," for example. If someone were to read the word "head" orally, we would chuckle. Soon, it would become out of control and we would all be laughing throughout Mrs. Shankey's reading class.

Allow me to inform you of some of the particular words and phrases, which would lower our conduct grades. One day, we were reading a Sherlock Holmes story called "The Red Headed League." This story is about a club for men with red hair. In this story, there was a series of lines which pertained to how beautiful these men's red heads were. Then a guy started talking about his red head and how he was trying to comb his red hair. He said "I jerked it back with my hand" (or something like that). And then he said "But it just kept falling back to the same place and then I tried to part it down the middle, what a beautiful red head I have!" Of course, this isn't line for line, but its close enough and if you laughed then I have achieved my goal.

Then there was a story about an old woman who was decrepit and she could barely move. The part of this story which made us laugh went something like this: "As I woke up in the morning, my entire body ached from the night before. I tried to bend over to touch my knees, but the pain in my back was unbearable." Then there was a knock on her door, she opened the door and a young adolescent boy was standing there. She said to this boy "You look like a fine upstanding young man, can you reach into my pocket and grab a few schillings?" The boy grabbed two schillings and she said to him "Please go down to the corner and bring me back a hunk of cheese?" The entire class did its best to contain our laughter, but a few of us couldn't help but laugh.

Sometimes we would watch television in class. Sometimes we would watch a recorded movie and sometimes we would watch regular television with commercials. One time, a commercial came on for Mauna Loa Macadamia nuts. The guy in the commercial was the same guy who played Higgins on the classic television show Magnum P.I. In this commercial, this guy was popping these nuts into his mouth as if these nuts were uppers or something, and then he said "These are the best nuts you'll ever have in your life!" Suffice it to say, we all laughed at that one.

On another occasion, we were watching the award winning film, Amadeus, which is the story of the famous classical composer, Wolfgang Amadeus Mozart. At the end of this movie, Mozart was writing his final piece with the help of another famous composer by the name of Salieri. Anyhow, Mozart was singing this song in German and there was a line, which when spoken in German, sounds in English as if he was singing "all a dick tease." Once we started to laugh, Mrs. Shankey said "It's German, you bozos!" We were planning to have a classroom party near the end of the school year. We were all requested to bring something in for this party. The smart kid named Oscar was to bring in a cooking pot for baking. Anyhow, Mrs. Mercier said to Oscar, "Oscar you're going to bring the pot, we can't have the party if you don't bring the pot." Once again, the entire class was set off laughing. On another occasion, as the entire class was doing work and no one had said a thing for about ten minutes, Mrs. Mercier decided to ask Oscar an interesting question which was about food, but could be interpreted in another way. Out of the blue, she looked at Oscar and asked him "Oscar, do you like nuts?" We began to laugh as Oscar and Mrs. Mercier looked at all of us with an expression of disgust and then Oscar regained his composure and said, "Yes, I like nuts." We lost it at this point. No offense, Oscar, I'm just kidding, okay? On yet another occasion, we were reading the storyline to a play during reading class. A few lines went as follows: Character one (a man)—*I have a secret, but I can't tell you.* Character two (a woman)—*Oh, please tell me, you've got to tell me, you must trust me.* Character one (the man)—*Okay, I will tell you. I was abroad*. Of course, what character one meant was that he had been somewhere, but we took it as if he was a man who used to be a woman. Yeah, we had our share of laughs that year!

My father would meet his next girlfriend around this time. They would become engaged, but unfortunately, she would be inflicted with cancer and die before the marriage. My father regained the house in Dracut and she would live with us for a while. Soon, little league would once again commence and I was (as previously stated) on the Yankees. I did well in baseball that year. I was selected to be on the all-star team. In the all-star game I went 4 for 4 with a homerun and in the last inning, I pitched a 1,2,3 inning with a strike out. Towards the end of the eighth grade as the weather improved, I began to grow tired of St. Joseph School's dress code. My family was strict and I couldn't get away with much. Anyhow, there was a group of kids in my neighborhood who would see me dressed like this and I felt like a frigging goof. However, this was a good problem for me to have when considering the past and the unruly future of which I was embarking on. One night at Roller Kingdom, a couple of my buddies from class showed up and one of them had a bottle of Jack Daniels in his skating bag. We would go out to the woods and take turns chugging the stuff. We became unruly and proceeded to scream out the words to the United States of America theme song, "The Star Spangled Banner." We went back to Roller Kingdom trying to contain ourselves so we could fool our parents on the way home. Luckily for me, I got away with another one that night.

Eighth grade graduation was coming and the final days leading up to graduation were great. We had to do some graduation rehearsals. In the next to last rehearsal, Mrs. Mercier was running around anxiously. We were discussing entertainment for the graduation and it was decided that two of my fellow students would sing our graduation song, which was "Lean on Me." I raised my hand and said "I could play the guitar" (at the time, I could barely carry a tune). Mrs. Mercier turned and looked me straight in the face and said "Ted, shut up!"

On the final day of graduation rehearsal, I over slept. My phone rang and it woke me up, I answered it and mumbled an obscure "Hello?" I heard a woman's voice say "Is this Ted?" I said "Yes" and then this woman said "This is the principal, get your butt out of bed and go to the graduation rehearsal." So I got dressed and headed for the church where we would be graduating. Before I got there, the principal had walked into the rehearsal and informed the class that I had just received my wake up call. When I entered the church, everyone was pointing at me and laughing. This time, I made them laugh when I wasn't even there. On graduation night, we were all dressed in cap and gown and the ceremony would be a memorable experience for the entire St. Joseph's class of 1986. Earlier in this day, another paranormal experience would take place for me. One of my enemies (an evildoer) in a DNA formation, of the time flux connection, drove by me in a car and said "This is the best day of his life"; he then yelled, "Fuck you!" And then he drove off. This makes sense, because on this day, I would graduate from the eighth grade, I would get the money for my first guitar, and I would go see the Boston Celtics play the Los Angeles Lakers, in game five of the 1987 N.B.A. finals.

This game was a great experience. The Celtics were down three games to one, but the Celtics would own the Lakers in game five. However, the Lakers would end up taking the title. Former Celtics guard Danny Ainge hit a more than half court shot at the buzzer ending the first half. It was also quite an experience to see Bird and Magic go at it right in front of my eyes. We did a lot of chanting on this special night at the old Boston Garden. We would chant "Beat LA, Beat LA, Beat LA" or "LA sucks, LA sucks, LA sucks" or "Bullshit, Bullshit, Bullshit" when the referee would make a bad call. These tickets were a gift from Mrs. Mercier so she would enhance this wonderful day for me. At halftime, I was peering into the cheap seats, to see if I could spot the actor Jack Nicholson who happens to attend every Lakers home game and because this was the finals, he was attending this Lakers away game. So, I shouted to my father over the noise of the halftime crowd "Can you see Jack Nicholson up there?" As soon as I completed this statement, there was a Celtics fan in front of me and he was gazing into my face, as if I had lost my mind. He then said to me "Who cares about Jack Nicholson, Larry Bird is down there!" So, I thought to myself "No shit?"

Anyhow, the Celtics won big that night and I was very pleased to have witnessed these men in action and in the flesh, to boot. In earlier years, I had attended the Celtics 2001st win as a franchise and on the scoreboard at the end of the game, it read 2001 a basketball odyssey. I was at another Celtics game, years prior to this and the Celtics were facing the Portland Trailblazers. The men in green had a substantial lead in the last five minutes of the game as one of the fans yelled out to the players on the court "Beat the point spread!" We all laughed and then he said, "Well, someone has to tell them." All of a sudden, Portland's guard started raining down three pointers like crazy. With about four seconds left, the Celtics had lost their lead and they were down by one point. The ball was inbounded to none other than Larry legend. He began to dribble around a defender just past the corner three-point line and everyone in the Boston Garden including myself was thinking, "You don't have time to do that, Larry!" Larry let it fly with one tick left on the clock. The entire arena was silent at this point and the only thing moving in the entire place was the ball which Larry had just shot. The buzzer went off, and swish, nothing but net! At that moment, the entire Boston Garden went from a mere peep to thunderous applause. Ironically, Bird would do the same thing the very next game at the Hartford Civic Center in Connecticut, where the Celtics used to play one or two home games a year in order to compromise the use of the Boston Garden between the Celtics and the Bruins.

Continuing on, what I don't like about the Lakers is that whenever you watch one of their home games, half of the crowd is filled with celebrities. When I watch the Lakers on television, sometimes I can't tell if I'm watching a commercial for Hollywood or a basketball game. I must say, however, that I love Jack Nicholson. You see, Jack is a real fan of the game. He was the only celebrity willing to travel across the country only to sit in the worst seats in the house as crazy Celtic fans would chant at him and give him rude gestures. Jack stole my heart when at the end of a Los Angeles Lakers vs. Indiana Pacers N.B.A. finals, he walked right over to Larry Bird (who was coaching Indiana that year), shook his hand, and gave him a look of approval. Jack is one hell of a fan!

The summer of 1987 was decent. I listened to a lot of Metallica, and I began to stray from listening to (believe it or not) rap music, which I loved in the eighth grade. I would pluck my new guitar, but I wouldn't become serious until I traded my first guitar in for a bass guitar about half a year later. The next year would be my freshman year in high school and I was accepted and enrolled into St. Joseph's High School. It was one block away from the affiliated elementary school that I attended the year before. My first day of high school was great. I had stayed awake all night because I was so excited. In the middle of the night, my sister Jill kept me company as we watched television. She told me to enjoy my high school years because it would be over before I knew it and she was correct. Finally, my first morning of my high school years came. I put on my gray dress pants, my dress shirt and tie, grabbed my school bag, and began to walk all the way from Dracut to St. Joseph's High School, which was located on the outskirts of Downtown Lowell. I had just started smoking cigarettes and I had a fresh pack of Newport cigarettes in my front shirt pocket. I lit a Newport (which was my first brand) and started my memorable walk to school. This Newport thing was due to my occasional stealing of Joshua's parent's cigarettes, which I would smoke outside at night when I was sleeping at Joshua's house. As I walked down Pleasant Street on the Lowell and Dracut border, I saw my eighth grade art teacher who was driving up this street. She gave me a nice smile and asked me where I would be attending high school. I told her that I was going to St. Joseph's and then she asked me if I had stayed back. I said, "No, I'm going to the high school on the next block." She said, "That's great" and rode off. I had chosen to walk that day rather than to take the bus because of my excitement. Due to the length of this walk, I showed up about ten minutes late, but this was of no concern, because on the first day, the entire school would meet in the cafeteria and we wouldn't be sent to home room until after the school faculty had spoken to us.

A couple of kids from my eighth grade class had also been accepted and enrolled into this school as well. On this first day, it seemed as if I liked all of my classmates and that we had all hit it off with each other. Later in the day, we were all in the small gym located next to the cafeteria. We were there so we could get our textbooks. Lo and behold, I saw Corey from the second grade. Either he was late that day or I didn't notice him in homeroom, because I am sure that he was in the same homeroom that I was. Anyhow, I wasn't sure if he would remember me from about a decade ago, but we would soon acknowledge each other and start to get along just as well as we did back in the second grade. I would make many friends at this school, but my stay there would be shortlived. At the end of my first day of high school, my father came to pick me up. I got into his Cutlass Sierra and told him that I loved my new school. He then said, "What's wrong?" I said "Nothing, it was great." I guess he didn't expect me to be so optimistic. We went back to Roswell Ave and the next morning, I would come to my senses and take the bus to school.

I did well while I was a student at St. Joseph's High School in both attendance and academics. However, mischief might not have been my major, but it was still a priority. In religion class, I had a kind nun for a teacher and I wasn't afraid to express my views about god to her. We would get into friendly quarrels over some aspects of Catholicism. I insisted that god could not be perfect, because of the uncompromising evils of the world. My teacher and some of my fellow students tried to elaborate to me that such tragedies are a result of free will. My question was, what about the free will of the victims of such war crimes? I continued to be defiant in religion class and I refused to go along with something just because others told me to do so. So, why did I attend a Catholic high school if I was of this view? I guess it was just something new for me; I was pretty smart in the ninth grade, and I did realize that education was important. Little did I know that I would soon become a pure visionary radical in the near future!

On another occasion, my religion teacher said that she disagreed with a part of the bible and therefore she also disagreed with god. Her disagreement was that she believed that a person who commits suicide should not have to go to hell and she hit the nail right on the head. This woman understood that when a person contemplates suicide, he or she is in an uncontrollable state of sorrow. Oftentimes, people will commit suicide because they had lost in the game of love. Should someone burn in hell for loving? The bible says that the walls of hell are made of molten rock and those who go there will be there forever. The problem is that no one really thinks about this. We tell our children of a god who loves you but will burn you if you sin. Supposedly, we were created by god and god gave us our instincts. So, why would god punish us for the way in which he made us? The reason that this nun stayed with her convent, despite her realization of god being imperfect, was due to the beginning of wisdom. The beginning of wisdom is the fear of god.

Then there was French class, which was an absolute riot. We had an old nun for a teacher. She was a bit too senile to be a teacher. This woman couldn't even remember yesterday! The entire class tricked her into doing page one of our textbook for the whole first half of the school year. She used to get mad at me for stretching my arms as I would often do to relieve tension. When she saw me doing this, she would mimic my movements with her frail arms.

I carved "Metallica" into the wood of my desk. A few days after I put this insignia on my desk, I told her that someone had carved Metallica on my desk and I asked her what it meant. I don't know if any of you are aware of this, but if you ever say the word Metallica to a nun, they might start jittering, have a convulsion, and this is the case even if they don't know what Metallica is. This is a direct result of the subconscious brainwashing of the entire god concept. One day, our French teacher showed up with a pair of blues brothers-like sunglasses on. The glasses she was wearing on this day were prescribed to her due to her poor eyesight. Her optometrist told her to wear them at all times. It was not easy for us to hold in our laughter on this day, but we made it through French class without her sending anyone to the principal's office. Earlier in this school year, a couple of friends and I hitched a ride home with an upper classmen. He had a loud stereo system in his car and he had an old Julie Andrews Christmas tape that someone must have left there by accident. We were cranking the Motley Crue song "Shout at the Devil" and all of a sudden, this kid decided to throw in this Julie Andrews tape. Once this Julie Andrews song kicked in, he decided to be funny and turned the volume up to its maximum. It was so loud that you could hear it throughout all of Downtown Lowell. So, there we were, riding through town with Julie Andrews blaring as loud as a Metallica concert. All over town, you could hear "I'm getting presents for Christmas, La La La La La!" We started to head bang to Julie Andrews, as one kid tried to hide his face from the public. I then gave the Lowell public the two-fingered devil symbol and started to yell "Yeah, Julie Andrews Rocks!"

The school year continued and I would make friends with a really quiet kid who was a senior. This would be my friend, whom I haven't seen in years. His name is Dave P. Dave and I used to drive around in his car listening to Ozzy, Iron Maiden, and Metallica, of course. I didn't know much about Dave, but I could sense that he was a troubled kid just as I was. I would end up leaving this school in the near future and unfortunately, I wouldn't see Dave again.

While I was a student at this school, I would join the St. Joseph's High School Junior Varsity basketball team. Practices were a blast and our coach would work us hard. I was never an outstanding basketball player, but I could play well enough and I would achieve a starting position on this team. If I was to play pickup basketball with people who do not excel in the game, I am like Larry Bird, but when I play with experienced ball players, I'm more like Charlie Brown playing baseball.

Our first game was against the Greater Lowell Vocational Technical High School, commonly known as The Voke. This was a stupid matchup, because the Lowell Voke is the largest vocational high school in the United States and St. Joseph's was a small school, which only consisted of about 200 students. Furthermore, St. Joseph's School was a small three-story brick building, which could be walked around in less than a minute. We ended up losing and the score was something like 100 to 20. We sucked so bad, it would become our goal to lose by less than twenty points and as long as I was on the team, we never accomplished that goal.

We went on a road game and I was the starting power forward. The game got under way and we actually felt that we had a chance to win this game because the school we were playing against was almost as small as ours. About halfway through the first quarter, one of my team mates missed a shot, which deflected off the left part of the rim. I was not too close to the basket, but I was in perfect position for a rebound because the ball was moving towards me and fast. At the moment the ball met my hands, the star of the other team came charging at me to try to steal the ball from me. Once I noticed that this kid was accelerating right towards me, I became distracted and the ball dropped dead on the floor right between my legs. The star of the other team finally got to me and he went for the ball, which was lying on the floor below my "you know what." So, he reached for the ball and his head was in between my legs. He kept trying to grab the ball and then his head got stuck! So, I started jumping up and down to release this kid's head from my crotch. I must have jumped ten times, over a twenty-second long bull ride. Finally, he managed to un-wedge his head from my crotch and because he was charging into me like a football player, he ended up being called for a foul.

Inbounding the ball after that one was difficult because my friends who were watching the game, were sitting in the bleachers pointing and laughing, as my friend Wilbur gave me a smile of approval and a gesture of thumbs up. The funniest thing about this sports blooper was that the star of the other team didn't even seem to see the humor in this. I mean, he didn't even crack a smile. I guess he was a serious ball player, and that is why he was the star of his team, and I was the comic relief of my team. I told some of my friends about this one time at a bonfire over a few beers, but I don't think they believed me, because all they did was look at me like I was weird or something.

I had been plucking my guitar from time to time around this time. I had a friend who would beat on his drum set as I would hack away. Soon, I heard of a kid named Paul Felis, who was a prodigy and could play the guitar like Randy Rhoads or something. I then devised a plan: I would trade in my guitar and get a bass, then I would try to have Paul join forces with me and my drummer friend. I thought that learning the bass would be easier than the guitar, but I would soon prove myself wrong. Fortunately, I was determined. I would play my bass night and day and with Paul's help, I would be able to hold my own within six to eight months.

Science class at St. Joseph's was good because my teacher was a major hottie. Not only that, she was smart and she had the ability to apply scientific concepts to everyday things. I remember she related some scientific aspect to the show "Star Trek" which at the time I couldn't understand because my scientific theories weren't even premature at this duration. She would always catch me checking her out, and I would cringe in embarrassment.

One day, she overheard me conversing with a few other students in science class. I was telling my peers how much I was beginning to hate this school and that I hoped that this building would be condemned. A friend of mine said that so many students were leaving the school that it was likely that St. Joseph's High School would soon go under. Obviously, she wasn't pleased to hear this because after all, she would be out of a job. Despite her open-minded application to scientific concepts, I was still bored because she had to teach us the confined sciences rather than the science of the human imagination.

The dances St. Joseph's had would prove to be memorable experiences for me. I was not afraid to dance with my friends regardless of how bad I was. At one dance, I asked a future girlfriend to dance and she said yes. I was a happy camper that night. The dances at St. Joseph's always ended with The Righteous Brothers's classic song, "You've Lost that Loving Feeling," but none of us will ever lose our capability for love.

As I continued to ponder on my formation of a band, I would grow less and less fond of St. Joseph's. I was sick of Catholicism and the nuns kept yelling at me all of the time. I began to have stressful feelings, just as I did a few years beforehand. My math teacher thought that I was playing stupid because I didn't know a particular step in an algebraic equation. She reamed me out and told me not to play stupid. She must have been able to tell that I was smart, because she would never reprimand the other students in my math class as much as she did to me.

I tried to explain to my father that this school was taking a toll on me. We came to an agreement. I would try to stick it out for a while. So, once again, I would suck it up and continue to attend school and to try hard.

Joshua was attending Dracut High School at this time and he told me that it was a good school to attend. One reason I wanted to start attending Dracut High School was to be with Joshua. Another reason was that I liked the Dracut High crowd and I had heard of the wild beer parties and the antics which went on behind the backs of the Dracut High School faculty.

Joshua and I were hanging out one day when a huge snowstorm hit Massachusetts like a ton of bricks. He told me that Dracut High had closed very early that day and I felt like I was missing out on something. You see, I thought that every day at Dracut High would be like this. Therefore, I started to pressure my father and his fiance to allow me to switch over to Dracut High School. This was not easy for my father. He had always wanted me to do well in my education and it pained him to see me like this. Soon, we would agree that I would attend Dracut High School.

On my first day at Dracut High School, I would spend the first two hours in the guidance counselor's office. I was introduced to some of the faculty. My schedule was made and handed to me. Then they gave me a tour of the school and then I was off to science class. My science teacher in my freshman year in Dracut was Mr. Hardacre. After having the gorgeous science teacher at St. Joseph's, Mr. Hardacre wasn't very easy on the eyes. Prior to my entering into this school, I had heard some stories about Mr. Hardacre and once I knew him, he most certainly would live up to his reputation. However, I must admit that before my friend Dimitri had passed on, Mr. Hardacre was very good to him and they would actually have conversations between each other after school. I remember Dimitri would always say that Mr. Hardacre was awesome.

Nevertheless, Mr. Hardacre would not put up with my mischief. At least once a week he would say "Hodges, down to the office!" And I would correct him and say, "My name is Hodge, not Hodges!" I must have connected with a friend in this class, because almost every time Mr. Hardacre would send me to the office, it would be "Hodges and Davis, down to the office!" That Davis kid always liked to get in trouble with me!

As this day went on, I would be reunited with a slew of my friends from the seventh grade of Junior High School. Soon, I was back to my major of mischief and before I knew it, I was out of control. Basically, you could say that I was being an asshole. I would swear in front of my teachers and I would grow more unruly every day. One day, a friend of mine told me to cut the shit and that I was not in my old school any more. I took it well, seeing that I was friends with this kid, but in reality, he was trying to put out a fire with gasoline.

The school year went on and I became wilder with every passing day. Before I could realize it, I had gone from being a short haired, well-dressed, young boy, to a leathered scruffy-looking burnout. My pants were always ripped to shreds, my hair was getting long, and I would only wear black concert shirts, which went well with my leather vest. Soon, I would meet my high school year's companions, Bob Stevens and Dennis Brunelle. I met Bob and Dennis through my long time friend Tom P. My drinking would become worse at this crux, and I would soon indulge in other pleasures of sin. Bob, Dennis, and Tom would introduce me to marijuana and before I could say, "I love peanut butter sandwiches" I was baked twenty-four hours a day.

When I entered Dracut High, I was in Algebra 2. My teacher was a smart hippie type by the name of Mr. Mills. I was never very fond of mathematics, despite the fact that I loved history and science as long as I could view it my way. Mr. Mills and I started to realize that it might be best for me to be sent down to Algebra 1 due to my difficulties. We came to an agreement that I would try to do a few more homework assignments and if I could not keep up, then I would be sent down to Algebra 1.

During my tenure in Mr. Mills' class, I was given detention, which was basically a last period class for me throughout my high school career. So, I was up to no good in the hallway after school, when all of a sudden a blonde woman who was donning an apron and rubber gloves, came out of a classroom and began to question me about what I was doing. This teacher was Miss Sullivan, a woman who I would soon grow very fond of. As for the rubber gloves and apron, she had to wear them because she was allergic to chalk. My classmates and I used to always get a kick out of the fact that we had a teacher who was allergic to chalk. It's kind of like a cop being allergic to doughnuts! As I was confronted for the first time of many by this teacher, my first impression of her was that I should not mess with this lady. She had one of those intelligent looks to her face and seeing that I was in the early development of my theories of the human psyche as they relate to the three levels of consciousness, I was somehow able to connect with her. She realized that whatever I was doing, it couldn't be that bad. So, she told me that she was Miss Sullivan and I told her that I was Ted, and then we went our separate ways. I looked at the clock and realized that my bus should be outside, so I went outside and I took the bus back to Roswell Ave. Mr. Mills's Algebra 2 class would prove too difficult for me, so we agreed that it would be in my best interest that I be sent down to algebra 1. I was scheduled for a last period of the day class and the first time I entered this class, not only did I see more friends, but I also noticed that the teacher of this class was none other than Miss Sullivan.

During the first two weeks of algebra 1, I was able to ace any test or quiz that were given. This is because of the fact that I was previously in algebra 2 and I was thus slightly ahead of the other students in this class. Eventually, the class material would catch up to me and seeing the way I was beginning to drink excessively, school would soon become a place to avoid, or use for my relentless progression of antics and mischief. This particular class was the virtual all star team of Dracut High troublemakers and we would proceed to drive Miss Sullivan bonkers! I was surprised at the fact, that some of my classmates wouldn't take Miss Sullivan seriously, as we would behave with a demeanor of disrespect. I was as guilty as anyone else in this class, but Miss Sullivan and I would always be on a level plane of an inner subconscious understanding. And the same goes for a slew of my Dracut High classmates.

Miss Sullivan had told us that in all of her eight years (at that point in time) of teaching, she had never had a class that behaved with such uncalled for rebellion. At times, my fellow students were downright mean to her and even I, a kid who majored in mischief, was surprised to bear witness to such extremities. Once I was no longer ahead of the class material, I began to fail Algebra 1, as well as most of my other classes. Fun became priority number one, which one could easily fathom seeing how crazy my life always was. On one occasion, Miss Sullivan gave us a test I was not prepared for at all. Anyhow, one of my fellow students handed his test in blank. So, seeing that I was about two problems into this test and that I didn't know what I was doing, I decided to follow suit and hand in my test prematurely as well. Failures would now become commonplace. I remember being at Roller Kingdom and telling some of my classmates who went there as much as I did, that mischief was fun and that school basically sucked eggs. By this time, I was no longer going to the Lowell Y.M.C.A., but Roller Kingdom would continue to be the shrine of mischievous freedom.

As my freshman year wound down to a close, I learned that I would pass and thus be promoted to my sophomore year. This is because of my academic achievements in the first half of the year being well enough to balance out my failing grades of the second half of the school year. The summer of 1988 was to come and I remember singing Alice Cooper's classic "School Is Out" with one of my friends on the last day of my freshman year.

Prior to the end of my freshman year, I began to converse with guitarist Paul Felis. I asked him to give me and my other musical friend a try, and soon, my musical career would be set into motion.

My father's fiance had passed on from cancer at this time. I would tell Joshua of this and he would look on me with a deep expression of concern. He would say to me, "Ted, I'm sorry." Once again, Joshua lent me a helping hand and boy, was it uplifting for me to be blessed with such a true friend! The summer of 1988 went well for me. I would have limited paranormal distractions, but my drinking and smoking would progress into a dangerous situation. I still hung out with Joshua when I could, but we had outgrown our jerk offs and we no longer played kid games. Joshua was a well-behaved kid while I was a parent's nightmare. I would start to hang out with my own party crowd, as Joshua would choose the more simple and responsible life. Joshua and I would always remain friends and I would visit him when I could. I was growing more unruly and I didn't want him to follow in my footsteps.

I got my first job in the summer of 1988. It was at McDonalds on Bridge Street in Dracut. My first day of work was horrific. It was so bad that it trumped any bad day I had ever had at school in my entire life. Obviously, this was due to my unique life circumstances. I took about an hour, to serve my first customer and it was a humiliating experience. However, I would put on my brave face, and go to work the following day, and I am happy to say that it went very well. Soon, it came to the point when I would enjoy work.

My father's garage would become a band studio in the summer of 1988. It was myself, Paul, and my other musical friend; practices were enjoyable from the get go. During the next school year, we had progressed as a unit. We would become possibly the youngest band ever in our area to be on the local nightclub scene. We were playing out with the big wigs and the fun was just beginning, but it would be followed by terrorizing altering forces, which emanated from my pursuit of the primary goal.

The summer of 1988 came to its end and my first sophomore year of three was about to commence. On the first day of school, I met Joshua at the bus stop. He was rocking his head back and forth with a pair of headphones on his ears. He took off his headphones and said "Hey Ted, this is the new Metallica album!" He handed it to me and I read the words, "And Justice for All." He let me listen to some parts of these songs, but he would take back his headphones quickly and who could blame him. After all, this was Metallica at their best!

Later on in the school day, Joshua and I would learn that we were in the same gym class and Spanish class. When gym class started, a bunch of us were sitting in the bleachers. Because it was the first day of school, we weren't to do any exercise, thus we were allowed to just hang out for forty-five minutes. About ten minutes into the period, Joshua handed me his headphones and let me listen to the new Metallica album for the remainder of the period. I was just sitting there in the bleachers,

VISION OF A MENTAL PATIENT

slowly rocking my head back and forth. For some reason, my classmates thought this was funny. They all began to point at me and laugh lightly. My friend Cathy L. kept mimicking me and her impression of me wasn't bad, either.

Soon, it was English class with Mrs. Spanos, who had agreed with the guidance counselor to put up with me for another year. Mrs. Spanos would often get frustrated with my antics. I knew she had made this agreement: she told one time while she was reprimanding me. Admittedly, I was unruly in class. Mrs. Spanos was not even close to being the only teacher who would become frustrated with my mischiefs. Then, I had Algebra 1, which I had to retake because of my failure the previous year. Once again, Miss Sullivan would be my teacher. I had some good friends in this particular class. There was the beautiful Shelly L., my unruly drinking friend Ed L., my close friend Alex M., and future Deallegiance drummer John Evicci. I had not yet become friends with Roland Gagnon (my future band mate), but his neighbor was the Davis kid that Mr. Hardacre used to have accompany me to the principal's office once or twice a week in the previous year. Davis used to have me laughing my ass off when he told me of the funny things Roland tried to pull in his neighborhood. Roland was a pyromaniac at one point. One of his neighbors saw him lighting fires in the woods. When confronted by this neighbor, Roland would play innocent and deny this, but watched by numerous neighbors of his, he was eventually caught red handed.

Soon, my first band would move into a studio, in my old drummer's grandparent's attic. At this point, I was set on my musical ambitions. Paul Felis and my drummer friendI was band mates with were way ahead of me at first, but determination and some assistance from Paul helped me catch up and keep pace. Eventually, I became a vital part of the band, and I would improve further from there.

Our first show would be at a party in our manager's backyard (Our manager was also the father of our drummer). At this point, I hadn't yet caught up with the other members, but I could pull of simple riffs and keep pace by playing the simplest of root notes. I would struggle through the set, though it accomplished nothing but strengthen my determination. Our second show was at the Lowell Voke, where we would open for another friend of mine's band, called Indian Summer. They had an outstanding drummer, a guitarist who I knew from St. Joseph's High School, and a bass player name Darren who loved to write songs about Lowell. Another adult blues band was featured. Called the United Snakes, they were outstanding in the art of the blues. This second show went better for me, having improved from our first.

By this point of duration, my close friendship with Bob and Dennis was strong and we would have constant fun. We attended uncountable amounts of beer parties and we didn't mind getting high either. At this crux, the vision of knowing was only dwelling deep in my personal subconscious. It wouldn't be long until Bob and Dennis would commence their dementia and thus comprehend the forming balance of scientific equivalency, which would form in my personal subconscious, enter their personal subconscious, and now it is entering the collective subconscious. This would result in Bob and Dennis fathoming the phenomenon of connection. I was hanging out with Dave St. Armand one day after school. The carnival had come to Dracut at this time, so Dave and I would walk down to the carnival, (which was located next to the school), meet up with a few carnival dudes, and smoke a couple of bones. A friend of mine by the name of Jim F., who was a neighbor of Dennis, worked at this carnival while it was in town. Jim told me that he had seen me hanging out at Dennis' house. Bob lived on the next street over, so I asked Jim if he knew Bob, and what Jim said next made Dave and I laugh. Jim said about Bob, "I'm going to kick his motherfucking ass!" Anyhow, I would later learn that Jim and Bob were friends and that Jim was only temporarily mad at him.

Once Dave and I were all red eyed, we hustled back to the school to catch a ride home on the late bus. I remember looking at Dave out of the bus window. I asked him "Are you baked?" He looked at me with a wide eyed expression and nodded his head to say "Yes!"

A few hours later, it was dusk. I walked to the carnival so I could meet some friends there. When I got there, I ran into one of the carnival dudes who I had smoked with earlier. We walked up to the woods and we lit another one. We made some friendly conversation, when all of a sudden, I heard a familiar voice calling my name. All I could hear was "Ted, Ted, Ted!" I looked down to the grassy knoll next to the woods we were baking in and I saw my friend Jason B. with a slew of other kids. The carnival worker had to return to work, so he said goodbye and left.Jason and a bunch of other Dracut party dudes joined me to have a big pot party.

Soon, there were more of us in the woods than in the carnival. Bob showed up on my California Freestyle, which I had let him have for a while. He was with a kid we called Chico. As the pot party died down, Bob asked me if I had any weed. I said, "Yes." Bob asked me if he could have a little. I said, "Sure, Bob," and I handed him a bag, which had about three joints worth of weed in it. I would run into Bob and Chico later and when I asked Bob for the remainder of my bag, he looked me in the face and said, "We smoked it." Suffice it to say, I wasn't very happy with Bob at this moment.

My friend Dave M. was impressed with my bike, but I told him it was a hunk of junk, because the chain always came off. I said that he could do whatever he wanted to do with it. So, we began to play Ghost Rider. Dave would push it several feet and then he would let it go. As we watched, many of us were laughing. It seemed as if there was actually something riding it, because it would go a long way. Bob then took the bike back and rode off.

A bunch of us then went to the carnival and it was cool to look at the lights while being baked. Dave M. almost got into a fight with some guy, but nothing would come of it. I ran into my friend, Alex M., and we got a couple of sodas; later, we proceeded to poke fun at each other. Soon, it would be late and I would head to Bob's house so we could combine the positive aspects of our mischievous ways.

The following week at school was as wild as ever. After the last period on the following Friday afternoon, Dave St. Armand, our friend Cathy L., a few others, and I were getting high after school. Once she was stoned, Cathy start to act hyper. Dave and I got a kick out of this because Cathy was one funny kid. We were passing around a bowl and I remember Cathy trying not to laugh. She would hold the bowl to her mouth and breathe in the marijuana. It seemed as if Cathy had a technique for smoking pot all to herself.

Dave had just met Cathy on this occasion and once she was gone, he was like, "Who was that?" Dave seemed to like Cathy, but who could blame him? She was pretty, though she wasn't exactlydrop dead gorgeous. The main thing was her flamboyant personality. It drove Dave wild!

Continuing on, the early portion of my first sophomore year was the most I ever enjoyed school in my entire life. My mischief was prominent, especially in Miss Sullivan's class. She was determined to teach us, but she often couldn't help laughing herself. My friend Shelly, who was a bombshell, seemed to be very fond of me. However, she was not aware that I was painfully shy, and she also was not aware of my life of the paranormal. To be truthful, I was slightly intimidated by her looks.

One day, Shelly and I were having soda and pizza at the pizza joint across the street from the school. She started to tell me that everyone liked me and then she said, "I love you, Hodge." Due to disruptions in my personal subconscious, my self-esteem was low; thus, I couldn't believe that a girl like Shelly would like me. When she told me how she felt about me, I slightly gulped and looked away. This would prove to be a major missed opportunity.

As the school year went on, I would continue to make Shelly, Ed, Alex, John, and Miss Sullivan laugh. Remember, mischief was my major!

One night around this time, Bob and I had a rendezvous with Ed from math class and another guy we called Brain. We would drive around and smoke pot to the point of incoherence. Bob and I then came up with the theory that we should commence to party night and day, until we dropped to the ground like a sack of potatoes. Life at this point became a constant party!

My good friend Tom P. and I commenced to build a fort in the woods behind my house. This area of woods would become known as the fort and the bashes we would have there were nutty. We would usually have at least one bash a week. Sometimes, the cops would come and we would all run. Some of us were too slow and would get caught, but not me man! I could run like the wind at that age. We also had parties in the Dracut State forest, the cow fields of Dracut, or someone's house, as long as they were willing to risk life and limb.

I had many a drunken night and it seemed as if I had achieved my personal conquest for the eternal buzz. Soon, alcohol would get me into trouble for the first time. I was hanging out with Bob and Tom P. and we had each chugged at least a six-pack apiece. Bob then came up with a dumb idea that Tom and I would eventually heed. Bob said we should take his grandmother's car out for a hell ride. Tom and I responded with a stern "No!" However, after a couple more Budweisers, Tom and I followed suit. We moved towards the keys like magnets and then we went outside and drove off in Tom's grandmother's car.

We drove around for about an hour and I was absolutely obliterated. They were about to drop me off, but we decided to go for one more quick joyride. On this joyride we ran into Tom's parents. Tom began to panic. He tried to outrun his parents who were following us from behind. They managed to cut us off, and Tom's mother got to the door of the car we were in, and try to pull Tom out. Tom's foot hit the gas and all I can remember is glass flying in my face. Luckily, none of us was injured. I should have realized earlier that Tom was out of it, because he was singing along with "What I Am" by Edie Brickell and the New Bohemians on the radio. Therefore, his judgment was off kilter.

Tom yelled to Bob and I, "Get the hell out of here!" Bob hopped out and yelled, "Come on, Ted!" I was so wasted that I couldn't move. So Bob grabbed me and dragged me out of the car and we were off and running. Bob said to me as we ran, "I can't believe what just happened!" Then we went to Bob's house and slept. I needed to get some sleep because the following morning, my father was going to kick my ass!

The next day, Bob and I were with my father in his Cutlass Sierra. I was in the front passenger seat and Bob was in the back seat. My father was smacking me with one hand and driving with the other. He demanded that I tell him who bought the beer for us. I told my father who had bought for us. The guy who did would never do it again and I can't say that I blame him. My friends couldn't believe that I had tattled. I mean, it wasn't like me to do that. I guess I choked on that one. I would soon become one of those kids whose parents would tell their kids not to hang around with.

Bob has a good family and so does Dennis. As a youngster, I was naïve and thought that any family that was not just like mine, was not proper. This used to piss off Joshua and he would oftentimes try to explain to me that individuals and families vary from one another, and that we need all types of people. Joshua is correct because people need to contribute their uniqueness to society in order for the world society to prosper, and this is true when applying such thoughts to the three levels of consciousness. I actually believe that on the night my father had reprimanded me for this car accident ordeal, Bob wished his family would do the same. Bob's family is not the disciplinary type, but they do have the most important ingredient and that would be love. This is the basis of tolerance, and tolerance is not as prominent in the American society as it should be. I would soon learn that Bob's mother was knowledgeable of paranormal dementia and Bob, although being comprehensive of our vision, was only aware of plain and common dementia.

One night when I was over Bob's house, his mother began to talk to me. She told me she was a good mother and that she was the way she was because of her paranoia. She told me to look at a photograph of Bob, and then she asked me if I could figure something out by looking at this picture. She then briefly mentioned time travel and she told me that I was a hero. She told me that it wasn't my fault and that I should persist in my efforts. When I looked at this photograph, my personal subconscious was connecting with Bob's mother's personal subconscious and I knew that she was on to something. Maybe, Bob's mother was only subconscious during this elaboration. Nevertheless, things were starting to get weird.

Despite this car accident ordeal, I was falling deeply in love with alcohol, and I wanted to drink as often as possible. It wouldn't be long, until my attendance would once again suffer. This time, it wasn't paranormal realities that were causing this decline. In reality, my crazy life simply made me a crazy kid!

I ended up in indoor suspension once again and Trina from First Street was in there with me as usual. A teacher by the name of Mrs. Jensen was my history teacher the year before. Anyhow, she was the indoor suspension teacher for one period that day and she asked a favor of me. She handed me a bouquet of flowers and told me to put them in her car located in the teacher parking lot. She gave me her keys and I headed outside. As I was walking to the parking lot, I walked past the wood shoppe. Some of my fellow students were looking out the window and they were laughing at me. They thought that I was going to give the flowers to the shoppe teacher. Mrs. Jensen told me to put the flowers in her car and that I would be able to tell which car was hers due the type of her license plate. As I strolled through the parking lot, my mind went blank and I couldn't remember what kind of plate she had. I wandered around for quite a while. Once people began to wonder where I was, a funny set of circumstances came into play. Mrs. Jensen had no choice but to tell the disciplinarian (Mr. Smith) that I was lost outside. I could just picture what Mr. Smith was saying at this time. I bet it went something like this: "Knowing Hodge, he's probably outside walking aimlessly in the parking lot," followed by, "You sent Hodge out into the parking lot with a bouquet of flowers!" followed by "What are you fucking stupid?" Anyhow, we managed to get the flowers into Mrs. Jensen's car and all was well. I was most certainly living up to my crazy reputation.

Anyone who I was friends with in high school is aware, that I loved Iron Maiden, Testament, and Metallica. In relation to this, something happened one day on the schoolbus I used to take home. There was another kid on my bus who was disgusted by the evil imagery of Metallica. He said to me "Don't you think its remorse?" At this crux, my subconscious kicked in and I said that Metallica wasn't that bad and that the "Evildoers" were much worse. I then connected with this kid by telling him evil was good, which is the basis of the theory of development. Somehow, he understood me and he seemed to agree. I then realized that Metallica had to deal with this uncompromising evil every single day. This was prior to my encounters with Metallica, but the subconscious connection was real. I then put my fist on my heart and said, "I love Metallica!" At this instance, a girl from a private school looked at me, smiled, and said, "You traveled time!" I said "Yes." And we were quiet for the remainder of the ride home.

I would see Metallica three times on the "And Justice for All". The first time I saw them was at the Worcester Centrum. I was accompanied by Joshua and a couple of other friends. The place was jam-packed. Joshua and I were in an intense state of anticipation and excitement as we looked over the brochure Joshua had purchased on the way in. I must have seen 100 or so kids from Dracut there that night, including Roland Gagnon who was only someone I knew at this point.

Queensryche was to open up, but Joshua and I were diehard Metallica fans. Although I would soon become a major Queensryche fan, I was there for the main event. Queensryche came out and they kicked some major ass. I was not very familiar with their songs at this time, but I really enjoyed their performance. The Centrum reeked of marijuana smoke that night, but since I was with Joshua, I wouldn't misbehave that night.

Metallica was about to come on and the theme from Gun Smoke began to play. The Gun Smoke intro ended as the guitar intro to "Blackened" began to play and the volume would slowly rise as the crowd began to go wild. At the end of the guitar intro, the opening riff began to play I then looked at Joshua and I said "C.B.S." Josh looked at me, and we connected subconsciously He screamed to me, "We traveled time!" This was followed by Joshua and I screaming in unison, "Yeah!" A couple of cannons shot off, all of Metallica's instruments kicked in and the entire Centrum was out of control. Joshua and I were facing each other from one foot away, as we screamed the lyrics to "Blackened" into each other's faces and it was so loud, we couldn't hear each other at all! I was amazed, because I was hearing the most incredibly loud and incredibly perfect music I had ever heard in my life. All of a sudden, the short wall separating the floor seats from the low bleacher seats fell down and about 250 or so crazy kids rushed onto the floor seats! It was total mayhem and incredibly fun!

My first band had some shirts made by this time and Joshua was wearing one on this night. Somehow, the shirt ended up thrown onto the stage and Metallica drummer Lars Ulrich grabbed my band's shirt and held it up as if he wanted to try it on. Joshua and I went crazy at this point. Lars threw the shirt to the side of the stage, he returned to his drum set, and Metallica continued to perform.

After the show, I was with Joshua in a car. We couldn't express to each other how much we enjoyed the show. Joshua said that Metallica was the best band in the world and having just witnessed them live, I was in full agreement. Joshua and I agreed that this was one of the best nights of our entire lives.

Later on that night, Joshua and I were in a convenience store located a hop skip and a jump from the Worcester Centrum. There must have been 100 or so teenagers in this reasonable small store. Of this 100 or so kids about twelve of them were from Dracut. Some of us were shoplifting (which I wasn't). Others were jokingly giving us the finger, as well as some other rude and crude gestures, as Joshua and I would return the favor.

Joshua and I were then driven home by one of our friend's fathers. During the entire ride home, Joshua and I sounded like myself and my grandfather did, in the two weeks preceding Super Bowl 20. The difference was that we weren't disappointed by the outcome and also that this wasn't a sporting event.

A couple of weeks or so later, I was to see Metallica again. This time, Metallica would be performing in Providence Rhode Island. I was accompanied by a few friends on this night. They were Keith G., Mike H, Chris D., Stephanie F., and a couple others who I had met that night. Once again, Queensryche would open up and once again, they were awesome! A minute before Metallica went on, I had managed to sneak out onto the floor seats. This arena allowed more pyrotechnics, so the cannons to start the show were twice as loud as the previous show at the Worcester Centrum. I found out, that I didn't like floor seats (unless you are in the front row), because I couldn't see past people in front of me and I was constantly being slapped on the back by people complaining that they couldn't see, either. I left the floor seats, rejoining my friends on our assigned seats.

The show was awesome, just as I had anticipated. The ride home was good, but not as good as the ride home from the previous show. We did a lot of joking around. Mike was asked if he was in a band and he said "Yes." When the kid asked him what band he was in, Mike said Metallica, and we all let out a light chuckle. I got home, smoked a nightcap, and went directly to bed.

Earlier in the day, I was with Dimitri in English class. I told him I was going to see Metallica that night and he was understandably jealous. I was so happy to be going that night that I didn't realize how disappointed Dimitri was and I sort of rubbed it in his nose. I told him that I would take him to a Metallica show one day, but it was not to be because Dimitri would die in the near future.

I had met Dimitri a number of months prior to this day. Dimitri was (as previously stated) in my English class, but for a while we did not acknowledge one another.

I had taken up art class so that I could have a free period of no work. I would treat my art teacher like shit. One day, as I left art class to the boy's room for a smoke, I would run into Dimitri who was sitting on the steps outside of the art room. He told me to tell our mutual friend Steven B. that he didn't want to fight. I said, "What do you mean?" Dimitri said "Steve will know, please tell him?" Apparently, Steve and Dimitri were to get into a fist fight after school and they would be fighting on the same side. I went back into the art room and relayed this message to Steve. Steve then left the art room to discuss this with Dimitri. It would not be long until Dimitri and I would become friends.

Dimitri was into King Diamond and Metallica. We would often talk about music with each other. We would sometimes hang out in the halls after school. One day, I would meet up with him at the Dracut Library so we could do our homework together. I wasn't big on homework or studying at this time, but for some reason, I was actually doing my homework then. Dimitri showed up and he said hello, but I didn't acknowledge him for a few moments because I had Metallica's "Master of Puppets" blaring on my headphones. We had a report due for English class. I was writing a report on The Beatles who I was a fan of at the time, but today, I am not a fan of this band. I surprised myself by getting an A on this report.

Anyhow, Dimitri began conversing with me and it became apparent to me that he had no interest in doing his report. What he really wanted was just to hang out with me. I finally told him that I had work to do and I asked him to leave me alone for a while, so he did. Later on, Dimitri's father showed up to drive him home, and his father got a kick out of me and my cranking headphones. So they said goodbye and left. A short while after, I walked back to Roswell Avenue.

About a month before his death, Dimitri was having quarrels with some of our mutual friends. Rumor had it that Dimitri was to get into another fight. I confronted Dimitri about this in the boy's room over a couple of smokes. He told me not to worry about him and he assured me that he could take care of himself. So I obliged and I assumed that nothing was wrong.

Roughly one month later, Dimitri joined a few of our friends at the pond behind the high school. He was accompanied by Steve B., Tom B., Lee M., and a few others, I presume. As they were splashing about, Dimitri, who was always petrified of water, went towards the mid section of this pond. All of a sudden, he went under as the others watched anxiously. A few more moments went by until they proceeded to swim underwater in order to retrieve Dimitri.

The Dracut Police Station was only half a mile or so from the pond. Once they had realized that something was seriously wrong, Steve B. began to book it to the police station, while the others continued to try to save Dimitri. I can imagine the horror Steve felt as he was running to the police station to save his friend. Unfortunately, Dimitri wouldn't be saved. His body was later pulled up from the depths of the pond and we would all then be faced with a supreme tragedy.

I was not aware of this occurrence right away. While it was happening, I was at the old Route 3 Cinema in Chelmsford, Massachusetts. I was accompanied by Dennis watching the Gene Wilder and Richard Prior comedy called "See no Evil Hear no Evil."

The next day, I got a phone call from Dave St. Armand and he said to me "Ted, Dimitri is dead." At first, I thought Dave was using slang and that someone was after Dimitri. When I came to realize what Dave meant, I went into minor shock.

The following Monday at school, the Dracut High faculty announced over the public-address system that Dimitri had tragically died. At this point ,I knew it was real. I left my first period science class on a pass about ten minutes into the period and I didn't return to class on this day. I shared some deep feelings in the boy's room with some of my good friends. Due to extreme stress, we were all chain-smoking. I left the boy's room and the smoke cloud and I started to seek out Dave. I finally spotted

VISION OF A MENTAL PATIENT

him in the school library; I stood outside of the school library signaling for him. My Spanish teacher saw me doing this and she asked me if I was going to leave because of what happened to our friend. I told her that I was leaving for this reason and she approved of this. So, I and Dave would cut school that day and not be punished for it.

Dave came out of the library. We connected and realized that we wanted to get the hell out of there. We took a long walk so that we could console each other. As we neared his neighborhood, I told Dave that he was awesome; he returned the gesture. We sat on a large rock in the woods next to his house and we proceeded to get high. However, we didn't end up high; we ended up low. After we finished smoking his joint, Dave became angry; he started to pick up large boulders and smash them against the ground. Dave and I would spend the rest of the day in a state of sorrow, but we would have one small chuckle when we visited his sister Cheryl. As we entered Cheryl's house, there must have been ten to fifteen large barking dogs who would jumped all over us as if we were Fred Flintstone and the dogs were Dino. Cheryl's boyfriend Mike M. gave Dave and me a ride home at the end of this day.

This occurrence had two effects on my school. One was unfounded frustration toward the school faculty by the students. The other effect was that everyone in the school became friends for a short while.

In the boy's room, all of us would sign the wall in memory of our good friend. The disciplinarian Mr. Smith let this small shrine stay for a while before he had it erased. One student stated that Mr. Smith shouldn't have erased this shrine because he felt that Dimitri couldn't defend himself. I confronted this friend and I said to him, "If Mr. Smith had not erased these walls, there would be a hundred or so memorials on it. Mr. Smith is just as sad as we are about this. At least he let us keep it up for a short while." Mr. Smith was innocent! My good friend who made this false accusation immediately agreed with me. He stood corrected, and told me that I was correct, and that we mustn't point the finger of blame on anyone. I used to see Mr. Smith at the Y.M.C.A. when I went there as a youth, but I never said hello. He had no way of knowing how unique my life was.

We took intelligence quotient (I.Q.) tests around this time. When I scored so high, the school faculty thought I had cheated. I know this because I was indirectly confronted by a school faculty member in the hall near my locker. Of course, there was no way of telling that I was smart due to my behavior and my appearance. So, they assumed that I must have cheated. I am also aware of some of these facts due to my achievement of the primary goal. Then there were the intimate class discussions of this tragedy that we would have in Mrs. Spanos's English class. At this point, everyone in the school became a superstar. Enemies became friends and for once, we were all our true selves. Mrs. Spanos was used to my acting up, but on this occasion, she would go above her call of duty. We would all sit in class and talk for a day prior to the funeral and after the funeral. I stated that I had felt bad for Dimitri's family and that when I had met Dimitri's father, he seemed to like me. Mrs. Spanos then said to me "We all like you, Ted" and I desperately needed to hear that. In the future, I would face the ultimate test of human endurance. This would be the battle of love vs. hate.

A therapist came to the school to talk with those of us who were especially close to Dimitri. The main point this therapist tried to get across to us was not to be completely forsaken in guilt. He told us, that it was okay for us to laugh if we could and that life must go on. Little did I know the strength that I and my friends all had!

The day of the funeral came. I put on my shirt and tie and then I awaited Dave St. Armand and his father who were to pick me up. As we were riding along, the Beatles song "Good Day Sunshine" was playing on the radio. It pissed the three of us off. Dave's father immediately changed the station and said, "You'll never hear that song in my car again!"

We got to the funeral on Fletcher Street in Lowell. Incidentally, the back door to this funeral parlor was on Cross Street where I used to live with my father's side of my family. I was across the street at a park, accompanied by Shelly L., our mutual friend Jen M., another girl named Casey S., and a few others. I told them that this was the park I used to walk through on the way to St. Joseph's Elementary where I attended the eighth grade. They told me I looked good. They insisted that I should try to cheer up. I saw some of my Cambodian acquaintances who were walking by, as some of my friends made some ignorant comments. Casey and I were several feet from the others and she said to me something like, "We are the intelligent ones" and I responded to her comment by saying "I know; I'm not prejudice, either."

So, we all crossed the street and got in line to pay our respects. I had held it together up to this point, but it wouldn't be long until I completely lost it. It was hard to look at the Papafagos family and witness them in such a state of grief. What was even more difficult was to look at my friend, an innocent fifteen-year-old, just lying there in his coffin. Despite the fact that I have been an atheist for most of my life, I would kneel down to make it appear as if I was praying. What I did on this occasion, as I always do at funerals, was to try to talk directly to the deceased. I felt that this type of communication was possible due to my early comprehensions of parallel existences that were constantly forming and deforming within my mind shadow. After I tried to communicate with Dimitri through my personal subconscious within the spiritual realm, I walked over to his father and I shook his hand. He gave me a look of approval and I could tell that he remembered me from that day at the Dracut Library.

The funeral was absolutely packed with Dracut students, teachers, other school faculty, and of course the Papafagos family. I walked out back and joined my friend Steve B. and another friend Brian M. Brian began to shed some tears. Steve and I decided to take a short walk down Cross Street and have a smoke. This little short and funny dude who I had known since elementary school by the name of Matt C. decided that he would join us. Steve handed me a Marlboro and offered Matt one, but Matt refused. As we were walking along smoking, we ended up right in front of my grandparent's house. So, just in case one of them was to peer out of their window, I cuffed my cigarette between puffs. At least I was dressed nice. That would have improved the situation if my grandparents were to catch me with this contraband.

Steve and I began to have a heart to heart talk as we continued to puff on our smokes. All of a sudden, Matt had to take a piss and what he did next nearly gave me a cardiac arrest. Now, I had known Matt since the fourth grade. We weren't exactly bosom buddies and if I wasn't fond of him (which I was), on a different occasion I might have clobbered him. Since this was a time of tragedy, I would keep my cool. Anyhow, Matt walked up to my grandparent's bushes in the front yard, pulled out his you know what, and then he proceeded to piss all over them. I said, "What the fuck are you doing?" Matt responded by saying "What does it look like I am doing?" I said "This is my grandparents house, you moron!" He said, "No, it isn't." I told him to look at the name below the doorbell. He looked and saw it there as clear as day. "Hodge" was written below the doorbell.

As we began to walk back to the funeral parlor, Matt immediately started to desperately apologize to me and seeing that Matt was basically a good kid, I let it go. It's a damn good thing neither of my grandparents witnessed Matt's act of defiance, because if they did, they would have wanted to know his name, address, social security number, phone number, and his most vulnerable pressure points.

Anyhow, Steve and I threw our butts to the sidewalk as we made it back to the funeral parlor. Steve and I became very emotional at this point and we started to shed some tears. He mentioned that Dimitri would always give out candy and smokes if you didn't have any. Steve and I ended up hugging and we would form a bond.

At this time, those Asians I had mentioned in the "Genocides and Foreign Policy" portion of "Politics" were showing a bit of ignorance and then I remembered the short talk I had with my friend Casey, about forty-five minutes prior to this occurrence. I decided that maturity would be the best option for me to abide by in this particular situation.

This is the point when I began to sob profusely. I was slightly embarrassed, yet I was willing to let it out. You see, there were some things Dimitri and I had between just the two of us. One time, he called me on the phone and as we talked, he asked me to play my bass to him over the phone, so I did, and he enjoyed it. Dimitri was envious of my musical ability, but he was also proud of me for my achievements as a young musician. Dimitri loved America, but I think his parents grew wary of this nation for obvious reasons. Dimitri loved freedom and Metallica and like me, he liked to indulge in mischief. As I continued to sob uncontrollably, good old Joshua showed up in his car with his high school sweetheart. Joshua was able to hold it together well and I could see the concern in his face as he looked on me with his blue eyes. Joshua was strong, so I decided to be strong and I sucked it up and commenced to hold it together for as long as I could. I told Joshua that I would visit him as soon as I could. We said goodbye and then he drove off.

I went back inside the funeral parlor and I once again started to sob. I saw one of my friends sobbing even worse than I was and it wasn't easy to deal with, to say the least. Miss Sullivan was there, and I could see the pain in her face. I was impressed with her as always. Shelly kept asking me if I was okay as I swallowed my words and mustered out a weak "No." I then managed to pull it together for the rest of the night and the funeral soon ended. Dimitri was flown back to Greece where he would be buried.

This experience contributed to my life being like one continuous acid trip. Constant mood fluctuations and changes from sorrow to euphoria was not a good mix. But this night was still not over and fortunately for me, the rest of this night would be bearable and relieving.

After the services were over, a bunch of my friends and I would go to the Pizza joint, which was across the street from our high school. We began to laugh and act silly. We emptied the cigarette vendor in a half an hour, because once again, the bunch of us were chain-smoking. This other kid named Jim A. was there and he said that he was pleased to see smiles on our faces as he stepped outside to smoke with his friends.

Getting high was a habit for a lot of us, but for me it was as essential as taking a shit, eating, or drinking. For me, a typical day would be to get up and get high, go to school get high, ditch some classes get high, go home get high, meet up with some friends get high, practice my bass guitar get high, eat some dinner get high, have a couple of Budweisers for a nightcap get high, and then I would go to bed.

It was no wonder many of my peers and superiors thought I was dumb, seeing the way I behaved. After all, there was no way of their understanding of my imagination as I would apply it to the human psyche and the astronomical realm. Furthermore, at this point of my life, I did know of Carl Jung, but my knowledge of his theories was primitive at this point. My mind sphere was rolling and it was still sufficiently clean.

During the first week following the death of my friend, I loved everyone. And then I would have another lysergic acid diethylamide-like mood swing and before I knew it, I was disgusted with every person I would converse with. This is so, even despite the fact that I was mature for my age—although it was not evident in my appearance or in my unruly behavior. However, my priorities were straight and I did realize what was truly important in life.

Soon, the paranormal interventions would continue, but in a confined way. I had not yet achieved the mind set chemical balance for the beginning of a light to dark mind galactic vortex, of a collectively subconscious connection, in order for me to aid my achievement of certain vital ingredients to time travel. Up to this point, my life was a collective experience of universal time flux and it was setting things into motion all around me.

While attending school at Dracut High School, I had heard some conscious to subconscious gossip in pertinence to certain actions, which were set into motion at this point. Some of these actions were of evil intent; some of them were of moral intent. Of course, I do realize that I am only human and I have hurt some people due to my subconscious confusion. In order to deal with these interventions, I had to aid the balance of the three levels of consciousness by means of scientific equivalency; connections had to be consciously communicated between me and certain people who aided the cause of the pro-primary goal viewpoint.

The school year was nearing its end. Joshua and I began to hang out lesser and lesser with the passing of time. On the last day of May, which was a Sunday, I was to play out with my band at the Dracut Heritage which was located near the Lowell border. This show would prove to be the best show in which my first band would ever perform. It was one of the greatest nights of my life. I was fifteen years old at the time.

I was still grieving the loss of my friend at this time. I had no choice, but to pull myself up from my bootstraps, because this was to be the most important gig of my life up to this point. Just days prior to this show, I had a talk with a friend who was a little older than I was. I told this friend all about Dimitri and how I missed him. This friend then said to me the five words, which make up the crucial need one must possess if they are to be successful in the art of music. These words were; "The show must go on!" And so, the show was officially on!

We had done our sound check the previous night, and the light show would also be set up and completed in detail on this night. We would simply leave everything perfectly set until the next day, which of course was the day of the show.

When the three of us (we were a trio) showed up to play and as we walked to the stage, everyone there began to cheer us on in anticipation. Apparently, we had already made a name for ourselves at this point. On the stage, a woman who worked at the Heritage announced the three of us individually and then she announced the name of the band.

We opened up with Motley Crue's song, "Live Wire." We continued on with songs by Dokken, Whitesnake, Van Halen, Guns and Roses, Megadeth, three originals, and Mettalica's original song, "Seek and Destroy." We also did the Metallica version of Diamondhead's "Am I Evil" which I would get to sing.

While playing, the light show only allowed me to see about two rows into the crowd, but I knew the place was jampacked once we paused for intermission. I was comforted to notice that those I could see seemed to be enjoying themselves.

When we finished the first set of two, we walked out into the crowd and hung out with friends. One of Joshua's friends was there with Joshua and he was bootlegging our show on a small tape recorder. Joshua told me to speak into the microphone of this recorder, so I said into the microphone in a convincing manner, "You're bootlegging my show without permission?" He said, "Yes, I am" and I said, "Oh, good!"

My friend, Ernie G., was videotaping this performance with our permission and during the intermission, I tried to convince him to give me the camera, but no matter how much I begged, he wouldn't let me. So, we went back on stage and commenced with the second set list. I remember my future Deallegiance drummer John Evicci watching us from the front row.

At the tail end of the show, the lights were dimmer, and I could see out into the crowd. As soon as I saw the way they were acting, I knew that the show was a major success.

When the show ended, I left the stage to find Bob and Dennis. Dennis was impressed and he told me that we were intense to watch and listen to. Bob looked at me in approval and said, "You whaled man!" I ended up with the phone number of a future girlfriend on this night; unfortunately, this relationship would be short-lived due to my drinking problem. This was hard for me to take, because I had liked this girl for a long time.

A few moments later, my sister Jill showed up with her boyfriend. I said to her, "Jill you just missed it!" She apologized and I said, "No problem." They must have been able to tell that the performance was a success because I had an ear to ear smile, which could only be removed with a hammer and chisel. The other two members were just as thrilled as I was. It was a wonderful experience and a dream come true.

Once the place was emptied, we began to dismantle the light show and the sound equipment. It took a while to finish. Our manager Paul warned the three of us not to sneak any drinks from the bar while we were alone in the music hall. The three of us obliged with Paul's request. Paul then asked the crew to come to his place so we could watch the video tape that our friend Ernie had generously made for us. So, off to Paul's house we went.

We had a nice time at Paul's and we all enjoyed the video. Since I was smart, I had bought the tape. Therefore, it was I who got to take it home. I would watch this tape over and over again all night and this would be my first fifteen minutes of fame.

Although I was up most of the night, I would still attend school the next day. After all, it was the first of June and a Monday. Besides, the best parts of the schoolyear are the very beginning and the tail end and I was determined to make the tail end of this school year a memorable one. I went to my locker located right near the principal's office. I grabbed what I needed for first period, when all of a sudden, I got a pat on the back. I turned around and it was John Evicci; he looked into my face and said, "Great show!" John then walked off to his first period class and I followed suit. It seemed as if I was famous and I was enjoying the hell out of it.

Throughout the day, I received many complements from many of my friends. I then remembered what the visiting therapist had said to us, just about two weeks prior to all of this. He said not to be guilty of laughing or enjoying life and because he had said that, my attitude finally achieved the optimism it so desperately needed. Dimitri had known of this show of mine and he was looking forward to it. I'm sure he would have loved it. My other two fellow band members had it better than I did, though. They both attended the Lowell Voke and I heard they actually got mobbed!

School ended in about three weeks and due to my wildness, I was not promoted to my junior year. This was the first of three sophomore years for me. The most prominent factors to my academic failure of this year were mischief, drinking, smoking, too much music, and, of course, the main reason was that, in a nut shell, school sucked!,"

In about the last two weeks of this particular school year, I showed up half way through Spanish class under the influence, if you catch my drift. My Spanish teacher was disgusted with me and on one of the last days of school, she sent me to see Mr. Smith. Mr. Smith asked me the subject of the class I was just in, but I was so wasted, I couldn't even recall that I was in Spanish class. I finally told him that I was in study hall. He said, "What the hell do you do in there?" I looked at him with bloodshot eyes and said, "I study?"

The summer of 1989 began and it would be one crazy summer. I went to another Metallica concert during the course of this summer and I would discover some very peculiar things at this particular show.

Earlier on during the day of this Metallica show, I was with Bob and Dennis in Bob's cellar. We were surrounded by about a thousand empty beer cans and we were getting high, of course. We began to get excited anticipating this show. You see, Bob and Dennis had not yet seen Metallica live, so they were even more excited than I was. Dennis had a bag of bones on himself and I told him to keep them in his underwear, but he would forget to and he would be faced with a predicament once we were at this show.

This Metallica show was taking place in Manchester, New Hampshire and it was an outdoor general admission concert. Bob, Dennis, a drummer kid we used to jam with, and I went there.

We arrived about two hours before the show and we got in line. We ran into some well-dressed people, so I pointed at them and said "Wow, normal people at a Metallica concert." One of them said to me "You're normal," so I started to make funny faces and weird sexual sounds and then the guy said, "Well, I guess you're not normal." Once we passed through the gateway to enter the venue of this concert, Bob, I, and the drummer dude were allowed in. However, Dennis would get caught with that bag of bones I told you about. He made the mistake of keeping his bag in his front pocket. When the park faculty found this contraband on Dennis, one of them said, "I don't see why you should waste your time." After all, half of the crowd probably had as much if not more marijuana on them than Dennis did. The three of us left Dennis behind, so that we wouldn't be in trouble, too.

We walked out into the crowd hoping that Dennis would somehow make it in. Bob and I met up with some dudes from New Hampshire and we commenced to smoke some contraband together. I remember the New Hampshire kid saying, "I like these Massachusetts dudes."

I managed to make my way over to the left side of the stage and lo and behold, Lars and James were hanging out on the other side of the stage. I noticed that James seemed to be staring into my face. At first, I assumed that it just looked like he was looking at me. About two minutes later, I looked back at Lars and James and James was still staring at me. I began to stare back at him and I tried to get him to read my lips, by saying, "Are you looking at me?" He kept staring at me and then he nodded his head to say yes. The New Hampshire dude I was hanging with was a few feet away from me. I told him to come over to me and then I told him to look at James. When he looked over, James face showed anxiety and he immediately looked away.

Moments later, Lars had his back to me and he was facing James. I could tell they were talking about me, because as Lars spoke to James, he would nervously peek at me. A moment later, I could see Lars who was now facing me. He had a look of embarrassment on his face and I subconsciously knew that something was up.

Bob and I lit up another bone and we became concerned with the fact that Dennis was caught with contraband. Moments before the show started, I found Dennis. He was hanging with some kids he had met about half an hour before I found him. Dennis was lucky the staff did not confiscate his ticket. The kids he met told him that he should tear his ticket stub and hop over a small fence at the backside of this venue. If Dennis was caught, he could have showed his ticket stub and said that he jumped the fence to take a leak. However, Dennis simply got back in line and reused his ticket.

After Dennis told me of this scenario, I told him that James was staring at me a short while back. Dennis' eyes widened and he said "Really?" Dennis' personal subconscious was in action, thus his complete belief in what I had just told him. At that very moment, the "Gunsmoke" theme began to play, as I witnessed many people shaking hands and saying in a euphoric excitement "This is my first Metallica show!" The music kicked in and the party was on.

This show was general admission and it was Metallica, so one could imagine the pushing and shoving involved if one was to reach the front row. On my quest to reach the front row, I ran into many friends from Dracut. Soon, I reached the front row and some peculiar events started to happen.

By this time, I was soaked in my own sweat from head to toe, including the sweat of about a thousand other crazy Metallica fans. I was body surfing near the front row with a couple of my Dracut friends. As Metallica was playing "The Four Horsemen," I was playing air guitar along with them as I floated across the crowd. Metallica took notice of this and they were astonished. I remember Kirk looking at me and saying, "Yeah, play it." Eventually, I was front row center until the front of my waist pressed against the metal fence that separated the fans from the band. So, about one hundred thousand people were around me, pushing on my backside as my waist and pelvis trembled in pain.

James was becoming nervous and he could tell that I was communicating with him subconsciously. Later, James was in a state of panic as he walked back to Lars' drum set. Kirk walked over to him and began to reassure James that I didn't know a thing. As far as my conscious mind went, I knew little, but my personal subconscious was guiding me. I remember reading James' lips as he said, "I want to go off stage." At this point, some fans behind me began to cheer for no apparent reason. Kirk then calmed James down and James regained his composure. James then said to Kirk, "Let's stand up to him and play The Thing That Should Not Be."

So, Metallica commenced to play "The Thing That Should Not Be" and at this point, all five of our personal subconscious minds began to bind and connect towards the pro-primary goal viewpoint. As they continued into the second verse, the five of us were banging our heads in unison. Consciously, we were enemies, but soon, we would see our true and moral intentions.

The show came to a close and the collective subconscious of all of the people in this venue grew into a subconscious equalizing action, thus coinciding with the galactic mind vortex connection. James said at the end of the show, "I guess we are pretty bad!" As I began to seek out Bob, Dennis, and our drummer friend, I noticed that some girl had passed out and she was being tended to. I looked at this girl and somehow I felt that I had known her. A few months later, Dennis got a new girlfriend named Jennifer D. Jennifer had a best friend named Lucy W., who happened to be the very same girl who had passed out at this Metallica concert. Go figure.

The drummer dude's father was to pick us up and drive us home. When he showed up, we began to walk to his car. I had the sweat of about 100 thousand people on me and I was soaked from head to toe. Dennis told me to walk far from him, because I smelled of body odor. The ride home must have been horrendous for the others in the car, seeing the way I smelled. However, I might have smelled, but I made it to the front row and they didn't! I got home, took a much needed shower, pondered on this experience over a bone, and then I went to bed for the night.

Despite the fact the summer of 1989 was troublesome, it would still be a memorable summer for me, one I would reminisce on throughout the rest of my life.

You see, at the tail end of the school year, I had totaled my Honda Civic (which was officially my mother's car). Unfortunately, I also totaled an innocent women's van. I was put under arrest and I would be tried in court. On the day of the first hearing, I showed up at the Lowell Court House with my mother. We had a brief conversation with the plaintiff who I liked, but she was understandably angry with the situation that I had created for her.

As we talked to the plaintiff, my mother was slightly rude to them. I pulled my mother aside and told her to be nice, telling her these were good people. The plaintiff and her son looked at me, surprised. They couldn't believe I was actually a good kid and I could see why they wouldn't. I made a childish mistake and if I was rich I would have given them twice what I owed them, but you simply cannot draw blood from a stone. I had a very competent lawyer, who I would hit it off with because he, like me, was a musician and he was on a nightclub scene just as I was. On the day of the ruling, my mother and father were with me and they were wondering why my lawyer and I seemed like such friends. My parents asked us what we were talking about, so we told them that we both played in bands. If you were there, you would see the humor in this scenario. The final verdict turned out to be in my favor. It was a huge relief, but I did feel some remorse. Soon, my childish mistakes would prove detrimental to me in a variety of ways, including the loss of my band. It would be some time before I would return to the stage.

It was around this time when I would get my good friend Brian Cote into a lot of trouble. Brian and a few of his friends would be blamed for something I did and he was confronted by the Dracut police. Once Brian had figured out what had happened, he began to look for me.

Brian and a few of his friends found me when I was hanging out with Bob and Dennis at Jimmy's Pizza on Pleasant Street in Dracut. Brian is a tough kid. Facing him and a few of his friends was not easy to deal with. I told Bob and Dennis to leave so I could deal with this situation. Brian told me I was going to confess, but I selfishly wanted to stay out of trouble, so I tried to compromise with him. Brian wouldn't stand for this and he insisted that I confessed.

I agreed to comply with Brian. We hopped into one of his friend's cars and drove to another one of my friend's houses. This friend was involved in my shameful deed. I rang the doorbell; my friend's father answered the door. I asked my friend to come outside, and he did. Brian discovered that I lied to him, so he punched me in the face and I did nothing in retaliation. Soon, my friend's father saw what was happening outside. He grabbed a club and ran outside. Brian and his friends weren't stupid. They realized they should get the hell away from this guy.

My friend's father had called the police and they soon showed up. At this point, Brian would have been justified in killing me. I was inside my friend's house when he told me to get out of there. I walked back to my mother's condominium in Lowell as I awaited the consequences. My friend's father called me on the phone and told me that Brian and his friends had stated their case and thus Brian was exonerated.

As if all of that wasn't enough, I got Brian into even more trouble. I was taking a joyride with a few of my friends: Mike F., Dave M., Jason B., and Jason's girlfriend at the time, Nicole T. These kids, unlike me, were the fighting types. They pressed me to find Brian so we could all harass him. I should have had the guts to defy this peer pressure, but unfortunately for me and more so for my good friend Brian, I would be a follower on this occasion.

We found Brian and his friends and we began to act tough and confront Brian and his friends. Brian, as I said, is a very tough kid and he would have no problem in standing up to us. At one point, Dave M. told me to hit Brian. Jason interrupted, telling Dave not to tell me to do that. It would grow into a very tense situation, but eventually, we averted having a fight. However, in a sense, this was a fight, and Brian's team had won. We left but it wouldn't be long until Brian would once again seek me out.

A few days later, there was a small party, at the fort in the woods behind my house. I was not there, but Brian was, and he told some of my friends that he was going to kick my ass. My friends gave Brian a hard time, scagging him. This, however, only fed fuel to the fire that was burning inside Brian's enraged mind.

The next day, I was informed that Brian wanted to fight me. I was at Dennis' house and Bob told me that if I was to attend the party at the fort that night, I had to fight Brian Cote. I said "maybe not" and then Bob said, "No Ted, you have to fight Brian tonight." Bob told me that when it came to friends, he was loyal and he assured me that if things were to not go my way, he would jump in and fight on my side. So, I prepared myself for this and then I went to the fort to fight Brian. I was scared. You see, Brian had more experience than I did in fighting and the way that he had stood up for himself beforehand was another intimidating factor. However, the best advantage for Brian on that night was that he was angry and I wasn't, because if I were angry, my anger would be unfounded.

We got to the fort and I confronted Brian who was livid with me. He told me to stay away from him, so I complied. It was a surprise; the party ended but Brian and I didn't lay one finger on each other. This is because subconsciously, we were friends. and thus, we were on the same side. The night came to an end. I slept at Bob's house that night.

About a week later, there was another party at the fort. I was avoiding Brian as much as possible, but his brother Moe was friendly with me as always. It's a funny thing that I know only two guys named Moe and they both have the same last name! Anyhow, later on that night I was sitting on the roof of the fort downing a Budweiser, when Brian approached me and asked me to hang out with him. Suffice it to say, I was astonished at how tolerant Brian was of me. If more people could be like that, we would have a better society. I came down from the roof and we made amends with each other. And then, for the first time ever, Brian and I would have a discussion on Nostradamus. It was making our friends laugh to see two kids drinking beer together at a party and discussing something as deep as Nostradamus. Incidentally, a few years later, I was at a New Year's party up in New Hampshire. Brian was there and he was quite intoxicated. I guess he still had some slight resentment against me, because he kept looking at me with an irate facial expression and was repeating the words "You're all done, man," over and over to me. However, this statement of Brian was consciously malicious, but in the personal subconscious of Brian, he was telling me that I was all done and thus, I was home free. Brian couldn't have been that mad on this night, because about a week later, I was walking down Liberty Street in Lowell and he drove by me, called my name, and he waved to me in a friendly manner.

Prior to the end of my car accident trial and as the summer of 1989 was just under way, I would once again run into a brick wall of trouble. I was drinking with this guy we called Ziggy and another couple of party dudes. Once we had a beer or two in our bellies, we decided to head down to the Zayer's parking lot in Lowell, where there almost always was a night party. I had only drunk two bottles of beer when we left for this party.

At the party, we were minding our own business when all of a sudden, a huge brawl broke out, which didn't involve myself or Ziggy. Ziggy was grabbed by a Lowell cop for virtually nothing. I gave this cop a dirty look and I was once again arrested.

The very next day, the woman who had brought me to trial managed to get a front page story in the Lowell Sun Newspaper which involved me, of course (Please keep in mind, that this was a subconscious unending paper chase). Because I was arrested the night before, I began to panic. I thought that the entire Lowell Police Force was after me. Soon, I realized this was a coincidence; but remember, a coincidence is a coinciding force. It was a good thing that this was a coincidence, because the previous night, I told approximately fifteen or so Lowell cops that they sucked.

The Lowell Police threw me into a cell for the night. I wanted to carve "Ted Hodge was here" on the toilet lid of the cell I was in, but I didn't have any key or change with me. Later on, my mother picked me up and I would get some well-needed rest.

The next day, I saw my father. I explained my innocence to him and he was very cool about the situation. He believed that I was telling the truth. We were eating ice cream at Big Daddy's ice cream stand in Dracut. Anyhow, I explained to my father my wild and crazy dreams of utopia and on this night, I had his undivided attention. My father was very helpful parent that night.

I had to stand trial again—this time, for disorderly conduct at the night of the Lowell party and brawl. The day of the trial came and once again, my lawyer and I would tell each other about our musical endeavors in between discussions pertaining to this trial. I would lose faith in the court system at this time because I had lost the case I was innocent of and won the case I was guilty of. The summer of 1989 continued on and so did the wild parties. One night, Dennis and I were chugging some Budweisers by a campfire at this guy John's house. Once I had a good buzz going, I decided to be silly. I leaned over the edge of John's elevated pool and began to blow bubbles. John then walked by me, grabbed me by one of my legs, and then he tossed me into the pool. I immediately jumped out of the pool. I ran back to the campfire to join some friends. There was really nothing that I could do about this, because John was in his early twenties and I was only fifteen going on sixteen.

Everyone at this party was actually impressed by the way I took this so well, and that I was being a good sport. At this

VISION OF A MENTAL PATIENT

point, Dennis and I would connect with each other. He would tell me there was something different about me, which made me stand out from the crowd. This would be the first time ever, that Dennis and I would comprehend the vision of "Knowing." I must admit that at the time, I sort of felt as if I was lying to myself. This was due to the present and undeveloped mind balance of which I had at this time. I wanted to believe in the connection of discovery, which was taking place between Dennis' and my personal subconscious minds, so I would force this discovery to grow within my mind.

On the way home, a friend of mine named Tim was trying to break into some cars. Tim was pretty wasted, so I tried to prevent him from doing this because I had already been arrested twice and I refused to be arrested ever again (and I never would be arrested again). Tim kept persisting; I realized I couldn't stop him from doing so. At this point, I told all of my friends to keep walking. I would then stay behind until they were far enough away for me to proceed with my walk home. Once they were about 100 yards ahead of me, I commenced to walk home. Once I made it home, I smoked another nightcap and I hit the sack.

After I turned sixteen, my mother and I got a cottage at Hampton Beach in New Hampshire. She allowed me to bring a friend along, so I decided to have Dave St. Armand come with us. This one-week vacation would prove to be one of the most fun, yet vital, weeks of my entire life.

As the three of us arrived at the beach, the fun started immediately. Because of the fact that the Hampton Beach Police had a reputation for throwing the book at you, Dave and I decided we would avoid alcohol and stuff bags of weed in our underwear. I will not get into specific detail, but although at the time Dave and I were not aware of it, some past and future friends were time travelling all around us. Dave and I ran into a kid who looked just like Dimitri, except this kid was older. When this kid neared Dave and me, Dave said to me, "Wow, that kid looks like Dimitri!" When this kid walked by us, he gave us a peculiar look as if he knew us! Afterwards, I said to Dave, "I think that was Dimitri." Things were mostly subconscious at this point, but somehow I knew that something was up.

Dave and I got high as soon as possible and then we went for a swim. Soon, it was nighttime and we would run into many of our Dracut friends. On the first or second night of this vacation, we ran into our school friend, Amy W. She was with a friend that Dave and I weren't yet acquainted with. Amy said she desperately needed to do some drugs, so we all got high as we walked along the sandy beach.

The following day, Dave and I were out of weed until we ran into a couple of beach dudes who sold us a twenty-dollar bag from them. After the deal was made, these two guys told us they had acid (lysergic acid diethylamide). This would be the time when I was focusing my mind in the galactic vortex of the balanced out universe. This was also the time when the foundational centrifuge was erected for the pro-primary goal viewpoint.

Dave and I bought two hits of the stuff. Because of the thought I had as a twelve year old, which included the universal flash and the commencement of my vision, I subconsciously knew what to do with my hit of lysergic acid diethylamide.

I took my hit of acid; I held it up to the sun, so that sunlight could absorb through a fusion infusion process between the sunlight and the mind-altering chemicals within this small red-checkered piece of paper. Dave and I placed the tablets on our tongues, allowing the chemicals to dissolve into our taste buds before the two of us swallowed them. This seemingly stupid act would lead to a chemical bonding between human deoxyribonucleic acid (DNA) and lysergic acid diethylamide within our systems. The connection for the realization of scientific equivalency by way of an infinite and infinitesimal topologic magnetism was now set into place. Dave and I then went behind the Casino Ball Room and toked up a bone.

We walked back to the front of the Casino Ball Room where Joan Jett was performing that week. We sat on the front steps of the boardwalk and then we ran into two other girls from school. This was a girl named Darlene G. and another nice-looking blonde chick who also attended Dracut High.

Dave and I were just sitting there waiting for the acid to take effect. Darlene began to raz me for smoking camels, which she thought only old people like her grandmother smoked. We continued to converse with each other as well as a few others, who we were keeping company with, when all of a sudden, Dave started to laugh. I asked him if the acid was affecting him yet. He started to laugh even harder and then he said to me "What do you think?" The effects had hit Dave, but I was still waiting in a humorous state of anticipation. A few more minutes passed by and all of a sudden, I was on cloud 9.

Dave and I began to laugh hysterically and although Darlene and the nice-looking blonde were both straight, they still couldn't help from laughing along with us. There were two elderly ladies eating a box of popcorn about three feet away from me. Dave, Darlene, and the blonde began to convince me to reach into their popcorn box and eat their popcorn. I may have been high as a kite, but I still had the sense to say no.

The night went on, and it was an incredible experience for Dave and me. Soon, Dave and I ditched these girls and started to intensify our acid trip by smoking another bone. We caught up to these girls later. As Dave and I walked through the arcades and the lights of the sunset strip, we were on an incredible high, which intensified everything. After all, watching the ending credits to Sesame Street is a good experience while you're on this shit. So, Dave and I thought we were in heaven.

We met back up with Darlene and her blonde friend. We continued to joke around for a while, still enjoying the lights of the sunset strip. Before the night was over, the four of us crossed the street over to the beach side of the sunset strip. We were standing by the sand next to the Hampton Police Station. Dave told us he would be right back after using the men's room. A moment later after Dave had left, I looked down on the sand, and lo and behold, there was a ten-foot sand sculpture of a dragon. Darlene, the blonde, and I looked at this work of art with extreme awe. Dave had crossed the street for a piece of fried dough without telling us. So, once I began to look for him so that I could show him this sand dragon, I couldn't find him. About five minutes went by bfore I finally found him. I said to him, "Dave you've got to see this!" He said, "See what?" I then dragged him over to where the dragon was, but when we looked down on the sand, we saw that it had been run over by a sand vehicle. I told Dave what was previously there; he then started to kid around, faking a cry as he said, "Why did they have to kill the dragon?" Incidentally, Carl Jung spoke of dragons in a select few of his subconscious prophecies.

Later that night, Dave and I were drinking soda by a pizza stand when a Hampton Beach Cop began to drive down the wrong side of the street. This was very good, because a whole crowd of us got a freebee. About 100 or so people, took notice of this, and we all started to yell at this cop and give him some rude gestures. After all, what was he going to do, arrest us for telling him that he was driving down the wrong side of the road? It was funny to say the least.

It started to get late, so Dave and I said goodbye to our two high school friends and we commenced to walk back to our cottage. When we got back, we saw my mother drinking her Miller Lites. She was very depressed. Dave and I tried to cheer her up and when she expressed her guilt for drinking, Dave told her that she was just human. I was often very flippant with my mother and I was very mean to her at times. This behavior of mine has been one of the major regrets of my life.

My mother then allowed Dave and myself to have a beer or two. I gave Dave a Miller Lite and then I told him in the privacy of our room that he could act as nutty as he wanted to after he drank this beer, because my mother would think that he got drunk from one beer rather than realized we were well under the influence. As we continued to enjoy our trip, we listened to some Metallica, Iron Maiden, Sacred Reich, and some Testament. Dave and I would prove to be successful in our acts of mischief on this night, giving score one for the good guys.

My mother and I had a small kitten that we had brought along with us on this vacation. Anyhow, as Dave and I continued to enjoy ourselves after my mother had gone to bed for the night, we noticed, as we were watching television, that our cat was acting very strange. The cat began to chase her tail like a dog, make a strange noise, and spin around and run into another room while almost banging her head on the door. Dave was like, "Ted, your cat is fucking crazy!" We continued to laugh and trip for a few more hours; because of what we had done, we would sleep into the late afternoon of the next day.

Dave and I woke up somewhere around 3:00 p.m. We had a small breakfast, took showers, got dressed, and headed out to do some more mischief. I had rolled a few bones while Dave was in the shower. We headed to the boardwalk, got high, and met up with the Hampton kids we had met that week. As we were sitting on the steps with some friends, we noticed two beautiful girls, our age who were just sitting there. A friend of ours started talking to them and they were very friendly. This surprised me because girls who look that good usually tend to be a little stuck up. These two girls were simply normal kids, just like Dave and me. Dave and I would soon meet these girls and we would end up hanging out with these two hotties throughout the entire second half of our vacation.

I kept telling these two girls that they looked familiar to me. I asked them if they were from Massachusetts, but they said they were from Connecticut. The four of us would really hit it off with each other, enjoying each other's company for the next four days. These two girls weren't into getting high (as far as we knew); Dave and I didn't want to ask them because they might have been turned off by this. So, we basically hung out at the boardwalk, talked, played video games, and had a few meals together at the local restaurants.

The paranormal actions of the time flux, was happening all around us. Most of the visitors of the parallel were on our side, but there were some evildoers around who were out to get me. We were threatened from a distance by a kid from my hometown who I did not get along with. He was with another big kid, who I had stood up to for Dave's sake one day at school. The big kid had no intention of bothering me and he tried to tell his friend to let it go. From this distance, I said to this kid "not now!" I needed to stay out of trouble and besides, I was never the fighting type unless I had to protect myself. This confrontation would be avoided for the time being.

While we were being challenged by this person, there were two short and brave dudes who told Dave and me that they would fight on our side if anything was to come of this. I didn't realize at the time that the big kid who could have wrecked me actually had no intention of doing so. As a matter of fact, I think he liked me for my having stood up to him during the school year and besides, we were good friends beforehand. I would learn in the future that these two short and brave dudes were directly involved in what was happening all around us, because they would visit me from this point in time to another point in time at one of my Deallegiance shows.

The next night, Dave and I were with these girls again. Dave was off doing something as the two girls watched me play my favorite video game, Super Punch Out. One of the short brave dudes called these girls over to them while I was playing my game. As he spoke to my two Connecticut friends, I could see a look of anxiety on his face. At the time, I was mad, because I thought that he was hitting on them, but this wasn't the case. Whatever he told them must have been heavy, because the girls seemed surprised. He told them to stay away from me the next night because some people were after me.

Due to what I will call the Control Factor at this crux, all six of us were perfectly safe as well as my visiting future friends. I will properly account for the control factor at a later duration.

The girls then rejoined me as I continued to play my game. All of a sudden, I had an impulse to look behind me, and, turning around, I saw black haired girl who I would meet in the future. She looked at me in a state of astonishment and said "Ted?"

VISION OF A MENTAL PATIENT

I had never seen this girl in my life up to this point, so I wondered how she knew my name. I said to her "Do you know me?" She then mustered out a weak "Yes." Then I looked back at my game and I saw that I had written my name in as Ted, for this game. Therefore, I assumed that she had read my name on the video screen. In the future, I would realize that this was not the case and that this whole thing is as real as the skin on my hand.

Later that night, back at the cottage, Dave and I decided to take a middle of the night walk once my mother was in a deep sleep. We went down to the boardwalk, which was completely empty at this time and we sat on the steps as I commenced to try to elaborate the vision of "Knowing" to Dave for the first time. His personal subconscious was active at this time, but he needed some convincing, if he was to adhere to such a revelation. We continued to walk along as I continued to try to communicate my dementia to him. There was a carload of people driving around and beeping at us; they were some of the evildoers I have previously spoken of. I subconsciously communicated this to Dave and then we headed down to the shore located next to the Hampton Beach Bridge.

When we reached the shore, Dave and I connected and we looked out beyond the Atlantic Ocean. A substantial balance was now achieved between my mind and Dave's mind, thus leading Dave to a full comprehension of this visionary conquest. Dave then said "I just got what you said" I assumed that he meant something else, until he looked at me with an expression of love mixed with euphoria and astonishment and then he said in a shocked and shrill voice, with his eyes opened as wide as his open mind "Ted we know!" From this point on Dave and I reached a new plane of partnership and soon our subconscious minds would grow as one, thus producing our conversational walks, which stemmed from a sub-ironic conclusion. Score two for the good guys!

At this point, the vacation was almost over and Dave and I began to grieve, because one of the best weeks of our lives was nearly over. Dave, my mother, the cat, and I were to head home on Saturday, which was only a day away. On Friday night, Dave and I were hanging out on the sunset strip with our two hottie friends from Connecticut. Dave and I had really enjoyed the trip we had a few nights prior to this and on this Friday night, we would run into a guy who was selling some Woodstock acid. We didn't want the girls to know we were doing drugs, so we told them we had to talk to this guy for a moment and that we would be right back. The girls seemed curious as to what we were doing, but I don't think they had a clue. When they said goodbye to Dave and I, they seemed very sad. They hugged us and one of them gave me a napkin with her phone number and a small heart on it. Suffice it to say, it was sad to say goodbye. Dave and I got up early on Saturday, so we took one final walk to the boardwalk. We entered an area where there was an arcade and an indoor miniature golf course. Lo and behold, the two girls from Connecticut were sitting on a bench and they were looking at us with sad expressions on their faces. I could tell by their appearance that they had just rolled out of bed. I said to them "You two just got out of bed didn't you?" They said "Yes" and I said that I could tell.

I told them that even though they just got out of bed, they still looked great. In fact, my exact words were "You two couldn't look bad if you shaved your heads and tattooed your faces." They were both pleased to receive this compliment. As these two always looked familiar to me, I toldthemthat I would see them again in another life or something as we once again said goodbye Due to a collective subconscious connection of love, dripping down into my personal subconscious, I was assumed the four of us would meet again.

Dave and I then walked back to the cottage. We all hopped into my mother's car and drove Dave back to Dracut. My mother and I went back to her condominium on Pine Street in Lowell. I assumed fun was over and from a certain viewpoint, it was. However, there were many wild times ahead and my mischief major would earn me a theoretical doctrine in this self-made educational subject.

When my mother and I got home, I rolled a couple of bones and I made sure I still had my Woodstock acid. I took the lysergic acid diethylamide right away. I then called Dave and told him that I had just swallowed my hit. Dave told me I was crazy and this phone conversation would be short lived. The acid began to take effect on me, as I watched the animated series, "Alf." As I tried to keep my cool in front of my mother, a character on the Alf show began to strum a guitar and serenade a girl named Stella. It went something like this; "Stella you turn my bella to jella." Once I heard this, I burst out laughing and I realized that I must leave my mother's apartment before she figured me out. So, I took a walk down Pine Street. I was doing my best to contain my laughter, as some of the neighborhood children began to point at me and laugh. I kept walking, until I crossed the border into Chelmsford, as the chemical to light equilibrium of my mind continued to build its foundation for the pursuit of the primary goal. My personal subconscious began to promote thoughts of connection and for the first time, I achieved a minimized realization of my theory of scientific equivalency. Soon, the concept of "Knowing" would further strengthen from the night at John's pool and the discussion I had with Dave on the shore of the Atlantic. I was about to become the Timothy Leary of Eastern Massachusetts.

On July 20, 1989, which was the day before my 16th birthday, an album by one of my favorite bands was released. This album would soon change my life. This was the Testament album called *Practice What You Preach*. I was not aware of this album the day it came out, but I would soon hear it and I would immediately fall in love with it.

Just days after my vacation, I was at Dave's house with the rest of the gang. The Steven Spielberg movie "Batteries Not Included" was on mute as this Testament album was playing. The first song I heard from this album was called "The Ballad."

The music to this song fits in with this Spielberg film, so at first I thought that this w*as the music to the movie. It was like listening to Pink Floyd's* Dark Side of the Moon album while watching the "Wizard of Oz."

I actually thought I was listening to Pink Floyd until I asked Dave who this was and he told me it was Testament. As the album continued to play, I was amazed with its undeniable perfection. So, we all rocked out to this album as a unit for the first time of many to come.

I visited Joshua a few days later and as soon as we saw each other, we gave each other a look of astonishment and then we said to each other "Oh, my god, have you heard the new Testament album!" So, we threw the album into Joshua's tape deck and we listened to it in a complete state of awe.

This entire album is indeed a testament to the concept of "Knowing" and every song on this album promotes subconscious activity. I will now expose the lyrics to one particular song on this album, which directly relates to my methods for the achievement of the primary goal, inclusive of certain chemicals, lysergic acid diethylamide, light, and time. So, I now present to you, the lyrics to track three on the Testament album, *Practice What You Preach*. This one is called "Envy Life." Please enjoy.

> *In regards to the nature used with pacts of magic*
> *spirits from the vastly deep*
> *respond the calls from their broken silence*
> *make sure your reach does not exceed your grasp*
> *all that is to be done before you act*
> *in a pact of invoking spirits from the past*
> *Have you lost your mind?*
> *The dark souls of time, ending life, envy life!*
> *They see you calling out their names, and getting ready*
> *Chant in darkness shrouding near*
> *through your virtued youth they'll strike a deal*
> *What's to obtain if no pain no gain?*
> *But to sell your soul, you must be insane*
> *wrote your name in blood, and then they came*
> *you're as good as dead, the lost souls of time, envy life, envy life*
> *come on down to the house of pain*
> *you hear them calling, shouting out their names in vain, envy life!*
> *In regards to the nature used with pacts of magic*
> *spirits from the vastly deep*
> *respond the calls from their broken silence*
> *make sure your reach does not exceed your grasp*
> *in a pact of invoking spirits from the past*
> *you're as good as dead, the lost souls of time*
> *envy life, envy life, envy life, envy life!*

It had only been a few days since the end of my vacation and I was as usual hanging with Bob and Dennis in Bob's cellar, which I will now officially dub as the Pot Cave! I hadn't yet told them of the wild week Dave and I just had. So, I commenced to do some serious bragging.

Anyhow, I told them about the wild time we had. I also bragged about the beautiful girls from Connecticut Dave and I hung out with during our vacation. And then I told them about the effects of lysergic acid diethylamide. At this point, Bob and Dennis had never experimented with the stuff. We got high, drank a few beers, and then we had run out of weed. So, we took a stroll down to St. Louis Park, which was right down the street from us. When we got there, we purchased a dime bag. I ended up separated from them for a short while and when I met back up with them, they told me they had bought a hit of white blotter acid. They didn't want to take it. I asked if I could have it and they complied. I put the hit of acid in the plastic coating of my cigarette pack and I then headed back to my mother's apartment.

When I got home, I placed the tablet on my tongue and I let the chemicals absorb into my saliva. About a half an hour after I swallowed my hit, my trip began. My mother had drunk quite a few Miller Lites that night; as she passed out in bed, I had the living room all to myself. As I tripped, I listened to Metallica's "And Justice for All" and Testament's "Practice What You Preach" over and over again all night long. I would stare at the ceiling of my mother's apartment and watch it churn like soup for most of the night.

I was still a member of the trio of my first band at this point. The three of us decided that we would try out Dennis, who could play some rhythm guitar and a lot of keyboards. Dennis was new to the guitar at this crux, but he was much better on the piano. Eventually, Dennis would become a very good guitarist, but at the time of this tryout, his skills on the guitar were limited, unlike his expertise on the piano.

VISION OF A MENTAL PATIENT

After Dennis had practiced with us a few times, told Paul, "Watch this!" I then told Dennis to play a Bach piece on his keyboard. Dennis then whaled out this intense and fast-paced classical piece. When he wasn't looking, Paul and I looked at each other in extreme approval.

Dennis learned to play rhythm guitar for us. He learned all of our cover songs and our three originals, which Paul had written. Dennis also played the keyboards for us as often as we could fit it into our music. Unfortunately, it wouldn't be long until some tension developed among the four of us. I asked Paul and my drummer if they had ever comprehended "Knowing." My drummer drew a blank, but Paul seemed to understand. Seeing that I was closer as a friend to Dennis rather than the other two members, Dennis and I would soon decided to leave the band to start our own band.

A few days after Dennis and I had quit the band, Dennis, Bob, and I were hanging out in the pot cave when we decided that we would form our own band. We had Dave St. Armand on vocals while we fluctuated between two drummers. These two drummers were Steve Stryker and Dan Ducharme. We started to have a practice session in my father's garage. On this night, we had a small audience of friends and we really let them down. Our equipment kept failing on us and we couldn't even get through the first verse of Metallica's "Welcome Home" (Sanitarium).

It would soon come to the point, when all we did was to sit in the pot cave, smoke, and drink ourselves into oblivion, while talking about how awesome we were. This lazy behavior would become a habit for us for quite a while.

The summer of 1989 would come to a close and at this point, I was constantly fluctuating from staying with my mother in Lowell and with my father in Dracut. My father saw that my music was distracting me from my academics, so he tried to take my band away from me. A few days before school began, my father and I got into a huge fight. He ended up throwing my suitcase at me, and he told me to get out. So, I would now live with my mother for seven days a week in Lowell, at least until things cooled down between my father and me.

So, there I was, walking up Roswell Avenue dragging my suitcase up the street. There were a bunch of kids over on the next street watching me; it was a little embarrassing. It would have taken hours to drag my suitcase across Lowell to my mother's place. I decided I would go to my good friend Tom P's house. When I got to Tom's house, I told him what had just taken place. Tom was extremely concerned for me and I could see it in his face. On this day, I realized how lucky I was to have so many great friends.

I called my mother from Tom's house and I asked her if I could move in with her. My mother obliged. I and a carload of friendstook a ride to Pine Street so I could begin my stay. As we walked up to the front door, my good friend, Alex M., grabbed my suitcase, gave me a look of approval, and then he carried it inside my mother's condominium for me.

My mother is one of those peoplethat you could tell if they had one beer. She had a little buzz going as we arrived, but she was completely coherent. I introduced my mother to those friends of mine who were not yet acquainted with her. My friends then said goodbye and left so that my mother and I could discuss the situation.

There was no way I would be able to get a ride all the way to Dracut High every morning. My mother and I agreed that I would enroll into Lowell High School the following day. We went down to the high school and I was admitted there.

On the first day of school, I went to my bus stop, which was directly across the street from my mother's place. When I got to the bus stop, I saw Eddie and Jo Jo, who I used to play with as a young boy. We were glad to see each other. Eddie reminded me of the time his brother Eric threw a metal wrench on the ground that bounced upward and hit me in the eye. I ended up with a shiner due to this, but Eddie was laughing, reminiscing on the way I had flipped out that day. The bus then showed up and we were off to school. When I got off the bus, my mischief immediately started. I ended up getting high with some girls I had just met that morning. My first day at Lowell High was mediocre at best, but I would soon make some friends, and we would combine our acts of mischief into a theoretical artwork of teenage rebellion.

Dennis Brunelle and Dan Ducharme were attending Lowell high this year, as well. On the first day of school, I recall Dennis walking past my history class, stopping and pointing his finger at me in a gesture of friendship.

About one month into the school year, I was smoking a joint with Dan behind the school gymnasium. Lo and behold, two school disciplinarians came riding around the corner and they began to reprimand us. At this point, I performed a magic trick with the large resonated roach, which I was just puffing on. What I did was, I cuffed the joint in my hand and got rid of it. Apparently, these two disciplinarians were not aware that we were getting high, because they didn't walk over to us. Instead, they told us to head down to the principal's office. If they had seen the smoke, they must have assumed it was from a cigarette and not from a bone. So, I got down to the principal's office and I entered his room. He then commenced to give me holy hell. Basically, he said he had had enough of my mischief and that my habit of ditching classes and whole days of school had better be tended to appropriately. He warned me that if I didn't smarten up, I would be flipping burgers for the remainder of my life.

Once the lecture was over, I was sent back to class. It was early in the school day and I was to attend art class. I got to art class. A friend of mine in this class who I often played hooky with told me that he could tell that I was high as a kite. My art teacher was a very cool woman, who, despite my behavior, always treated me well. She had a better sense of what kids were like in this day and age, from that of other teachers. She knew that none of us listened to Michael Jackson all that much anymore or anything like that. She asked me if I had whipped up something fierce, I told her I didn't and that I was just yelled at by the principal for about fifteen minutes. She gave a slight chuckle and a smile, and then the bell rang, and I was off to my next class. Or was I?

An army guy who hung out downtown started to give me trouble threatening me from time to time. We had a few altercations, but we never ended up fighting. This guy didn't like me very much, calling me a rat due to my scruffy appearance. One time, I was with Bob and Dennis at the C.V.S. in Downtown Lowell when I was confronted by this person. He started to push me; I told him not to but nothing came of it.

Soon after, I would be visited by a DNA-produced version of one of my archenemies. He was aware of my mind functions but he decided to help me out on this occasion. You see, because of the primary goal, it is possible to duplicate another version of yourself or another given individual and place them in a desired location. This particular DNA figure knew I had achieved the primary goal and decided not to mess with me. He would help me out with certain attempted intervening evils, which were posing an obstacle for my achievement of the primary goal. I would run into this DNA induced person from time to time, following our first meeting of acquaintance.

The two of us would do drugs together, which he would pay for and these drugs would have no effect, because these drugs were artificial. There was a reason behind his doing so. He was trying to prove to me that he was on my side and because of the fact that in the future, drugs would be used as a weapon against me. He was simply trying to get his point across.

My mother and I had moved to Eleventh Street in Lowell at this point. We were about a mile from downtown. I felt comfortable at this location for some time. One night, about a week or so into the new residence, I left the apartment and sought out someone who was selling some weed. I walked down Bridge Street past the old Tavern at the Bridge and Russo's music where I used to buy bass strings (these two places were torn down recently and there was a C.V.S. built in their place). I was about to run into some people from the future!

I started to cross the Bridge Street Bridge. Reaching the other side, I saw two women I knew, but they appeared to be much older than they were at this point in time. One was a short petite blonde, and the other was a nice looking brunette. As they walked closer to me, the blonde one pointed at me in amazement and said, "Look who it is!" At the time, I was 16 years old, so I thought that they were my age due to the fact that the centering of my mind was only in its early progressions at this point. As they walked closer to me, I could see that the brunette had tears of joy in her eyes and then she quoted the first line of this book, which is "Europa!" no I mean "Eureka!" I looked on this woman with an expression of satisfaction and then I said "Europa?" At this time, I was already aware of Europa's potential of quasar birth.

Anyhow, the older brunette who I saw on this night was not aware of this encounter at this point in time when she was actually my age. It made for an awkward situation for me to approach her at this point. Obviously, I did not realize that this new version of her was from the future. These types of occurrences had been happening to me throughout my life. This would make things difficult at times and easy at others. I would not realize until years later what had taken place on this night.

After I had fully crossed the bridge, I ran into my DNA enemy and friend of which I just told you about. I asked him if he was selling any joints and he said no. The two women standing at the end of the bridge saw this altercation. They were surprised to see, that I was friendly with this person, because they were fully aware of exactly what was going on.

My new DNA counterpart asked me, as these two women walked away, "Do you know them?" I told him that I saw them around all the time. Then he commented in a shaky and nervous voice, "They're from the future." I then asked him if he had known of anyone else who might be selling some weed. He then said "No, but I can get you some acid." So, the two of us walked to the other side of the downtown area. I gave him a fin and he told me he would be right back. A few moments passed by and I began to get suspicious. However, he came walking back around the corner within another minute or so. He handed me a small tin foil covered square piece of paper. I opened it up and it appeared to be your basic white blotter lysergic acid diethylamide. This was at nighttime, so there was no sunlight for me to enter into this small chemical entity. I stared into the hit, as my counterpart looked at me in a state of astonishment and anxiety. I commenced to lightly lick the hit, to see if I could detect a familiar chemical taste, but I didn't. I then turned around and looked up at the moon and then I held it up to the moon and said to my counterpart "It's nighttime, this is fake!" he said "Yes, it is." I swallowed the hit anyway and then I said to him "This is a tasty piece of paper." He smiled at me and said, "See you later, Ted!" I returned the gesture and we went our separate ways for the remainder of the night.

On another occasion, I was with this DNA entity and we were snorting fake cocaine. He started to explain to me some factors pertaining to the future and he would admit to me that he was an asshole. However, he honestly told me he was nothing like the person whom he had originated from. This is a rough estimation of how this particular conversation went: He said to me, "Ted you would be my friend wouldn't you?" I responded by saying, "I am your friend." He then told me that he was evil and that he couldn't help it, but he stressed that he was nowhere near as evil as the person of which he had originated from. He told me he could not fathom why anyone would not want to be friends with me and then he told me to never let his original entity free. His original DNA figure actually wanted to kill him, when he was him! He then told me that I was way smarter than he was and that I would go through hell in the future. I said to him, "I already am going through hell!" He told me that it would get worse, but he assured me, that I would survive and win the confrontation then he once again reminded me to never set his original free.

I started to skip stones onto the pond we were standing at and I asked him if he liked to skip stones. Instead of giving me a direct answer, he asked me "What do you think of when you skip stones over water like that?" You see, he was aware of the future and he must have been aware of my reflection theories, so he was understandably curious. At this time, my reflective theories were primitive. However, as I stared into this pond and as I watched the stones scrape over the water surface, I thought of inner and outer cell growth. I simply worded it as "I think about cells." He looked at me in a slight state of confusion and said "Cells?" I told him that because everything was made up of cells and that planets and stars were also cellular that I viewed things as such. Therefore, I believedthat everything in existence is alive due to energy emanating from everything. This thought would aid the promotion of the universal body as applied to inner outer cell growth. Once again, we see that everything is related!

He then told me I was most likely correct in this scientific assumption because he was aware of connection and scientific equivalency, thus my being on a high plane of human understanding.

At this crux, he began to mention connection. He told me I had achieved universal contact, assuring me that my dementia was real. He told me something I had not accounted for, and this was that a connection of the human mind could be bad. This would be proven true in the future, yet I was only subconsciously aware of this at the time. We then parted ways for the last time and he would pass on some time after. You must keep in mind that connection is good most of the time and that this will be an obstacle, which will lose to the forces of human good.

As for this particular DNA figure and as to what I will decide to do with him is a matter to ponder on. This DNA figure was not very moral, but he was much smarter than his original counterpart. One might assume, that the smartest thing he did was to try to be my friend, but this is not the case. The smartest thing this guy did was he did not try to trick me into thinking that he was a moral person. He admitted his evil and he helped me make my pursuit of the primary goal an easier quest. He did this to avoid an ultimate and helpless doom. This will be the only one of these DNA figures who will not meet ultimate doom. As for the army guy who I had some altercations with prior to all of this, he need not worry, because it was a long time ago and I really don't care about that any more.

Lowell High started to become boring for me, just as any school would. I devised a plan to reenter Dracut High. In one of my last weeks at Lowell High, I was once again playing hooky. I had about four Budweisers in my belly and I decided that I would visit some friends at Dracut High. My mentality at that time was that I felt I could do whatever I wanted to and on this day, I would learn a valuable lesson.

I walked right through the front doors of Dracut High, crossed the hallway, entered the boy's bathroom, and I lit up a smoke. I had already been a student at this school, so I knew the password to enter the boy's room. The password was actually two words, "It's Cool!" This code word was set into place, so that if we heard these words we knew it was a student and not a teacher. However, my brief math teacher of the previous year, Mr. Mills was one clever dude. He learned this password and on one occasion, he ran into the bathroom and yelled, "It's Cool!" Suffice it to say, we were all busted. So, if the boy's room password is still the same at Dracut High today, I suggest that the boys of present day Dracut High change their password!

So, I remained in the boy's room for a few minutes and I continued to converse with some of my friends. All of a sudden, all of my friends were signaling to me and I just continued to ignore them and concluded my conversation. Finally, one of my friends tapped me on the shoulder and said, "Look over there." Lo and behold, it was Mr. Briscoe. Mr. Briscoe was a hell of a nice guy and he used to kid with me about the fact that I liked to smoke Camels, which I did smoke at the time. However, he had to do his job. So, he started to question me. He asked, "Ted, where do you go to school now?" I rolled my eyes at him and started to walk to the front doors. Mr. Briscoe followed me and then he was joined by my former T.V. Production teacher, Mr. Harmizinski. I had a reputation for being stupid and on this day, I would most certainly live up to this reputation.

As I continued to head for the front doors, these two teachers kept following me and they insisted, that I told them where I attended school at this time. Finally, I turned around and instead of telling them that I quit school, I made the mistake of saying "I go to Lowell High." I reached the doors, showed them my middle finger, and left to get high.

Later on that day, I was back at 11th Street blaring Testament's "Practice What You Preach" on my stereo. My mother got home and she was rip shit. She began to reprimand me. Remember, with my mother I could always get away with whatever I wanted, but on this day, she would win the battle. She said to me "Ted, I got a call from your school today and apparently, you forgot which school you were supposed to go to." Being the juvenile delinquent that I was, I was like "Yeah, whatever." At this point, my mother became angrier than I had ever seen her get in my life. She really let me have it, to say the least. The next day, I went to school, got my usual dirty looks from my teachers and I attended every class.

Soon, I talked my mother into allowing me to return to Dracut High. I always thought that it was the school I attended, which I didn't like. But now I know that it was school itself, which I wasn't fond of.

So, I gave Dracut High my father's address of which I was staying at part of the time by this point. I enrolled and I attended Dracut high once again. On my first day back, certain teachers who were well aware of my mischief would look at me with a slight expression of frustration, as I was walking the halls once again. On the other hand, most of my fellow students looked at me in approval; they knew things were about to get funny again. However, my dementia would restrain me from my true personality and thus cause me to be introverted and a bit quiet.

I continued to attend the beer parties with perfect attendance and school with lack luster attendance. I would never do my homework by this time, but history class would be an exception to this because it intrigued me at least slightly. My first period class was business class and it sucked! However, my second period class was history and that would make my mornings a little more bearable.

During this first week of school in Dracut, I had purchased a hit of mescaline, which is composed of chemicals similar to lysergic acid diethylamide, though they are not identical. This narcotic has the same effect and it would aid me in the achievement of a chemical balance for the pursuit of the primary goal.

I had bought this hit from the young version of the brunette I saw previously at the end of the Bridge Street Bridge a couple of months before. I went to school to grab anyone who would play hooky with me that day, but I was unsuccessful. I ditched homeroom and walked to the boy's room located near the school cafeteria, said the password, went inside, and lit up a smoke. I went into a stall and popped the hit into my mouth and I let it dissolve into my taste buds and coincide with the chemical makeup of my saliva. I was about to sneak out of the school, when all of a sudden my first period business teacher walked into the bathroom and said to me "Don't burn yourself Hodge." He had caught me smoking, but he let it go. I was now faced with a lousy predicament. I had to attend school on a mescaline trip. If I was to leave, all hell would have broken loose because the school faculty was aware of the fact that I was there in the morning.

As I was sitting in my seat in business class, the mescaline began to take effect. I began to think about connection and how certain music and art appealed to my personal subconscious. I thought about the similarities between Joshua's artwork and the artwork of Pushead, who drew for Metallica. This would lead to more dementia and things began to make more sense due to subconscious activities. It appeared to me that I was now entering into the deep vastness of the human mind and the creation of the control factor would span over all aspects of time, thus strengthening the pro-primary goal viewpoint. As I looked around the classroom, I got some funny looks from some of my schoolmates, and it seemed they had connected with me, and that they knew what was happening in pertinence to universal contact. Finally, the bell rang and I had survived round one!

Next, I had to go to history class. I walked into the classroom and I told my friend Cathy M. whose brother I was friends with, that I was tripping out big time. She gave a slight chuckle and remained quiet as she always did. I was just sitting there trying to contain my laughter and keep my composure. Towards the end of this class, I had a bad taste in my mouth and I needed to spit. The bell rang and when my teacher wasn't looking, I let out a huge hocka, which splashed on the floor. As the spit dropped from my mouth, my teacher looked right at me. I apologized, and then I grabbed some paper towels and cleaned it up. Luckily for me, my history teacher was cool and he didn't make a fuss over this. Whew, round two was over!

Then I had Mr. Briscoe's class. It was going well, until someone walked into this class holding a small note. This note was for me, so it was handed to me and I commenced to read it. It read: call your stepbrother at this number. I read the number and I realized that this was the number of my friend, Brian M. Obviously, Brian was playing hooky and he wanted to ask me something. So, I showed Mr. Briscoe the note and he allowed me to head to the principal's office so I could make this phone call. I walked into the principal's office, a place I was very familiar with. I showed the secretary Mrs. Majewski my note and she then allowed me to use the phone. I dialed Brian's number and he answered the phone. I said "It's me, what do you want?" Brian then said to me "Hey, man I'm just skipping today and I figured that I would call you and see how you were."

All of a sudden, I became very nervous and I said to Brian in a shaky voice "I can't talk right now!" I hung up the phone and headed for the door to the hallway. There were a few other kids in the office at this time and they began to look at me as if I was naked or something. I darted out of the office and then the bell rang. Whew, round three was over!

Next, was Miss Sullivan's math class and for the third time, I had her as a math teacher. She was really struggling with me. I never did my work and my fellow students would try to persuade me to do so. Once or twice a week she would pull me aside and ask me if I was on drugs. Of course I denied it, but she knew better and I was certain of it. She could sense that I was losing it.

On this day, Miss Sullivan was not in a good mood and she kept saying to us "It seems as if you have all lost your minds!" To hear these words while on a trip was not very pleasant. After all, women have to burn of one period a month, hockey players have to burn off three periods a night, but I had to burn off nine periods in one day and I was on the pill! The bell rang and whew, round four was over! However, from this point on, I didn't know if I was in period five or period five thousand.

I would end up surviving the remainder of the school day and when the final bell rang, it was like I was cured of cancer. However, on this day, there were many more obstacles to be overcome. I hopped on my bus and I returned to Eleventh Street.

At this point, I was most definitely having a bad trip. The only thing, I felt I could do at this point was to lie in bed and try to fall asleep. Anyone who has ever dosed before knows that trying to sleep during a trip is next to impossible. However, I somehow managed to fall asleep for about an hour. When I awakened, I looked over at my hope chest and it began to crash back and forth from wall to wall. I heard my mother yell, "Stop it!" Until now, I still believe that it was possible that I telepathically moved my hope chest to and fro that day.

Later that night, I was doing much better, yet I was still struggling to a limited degree. My mother didn't suspect a thing. I got a phone call from Dennis and he told me we were to have a jam session at his house with a drummer we had only temporarily jammed with. Being the dedicated musician I was, I wasn't about to let a bad trip prevent me from a vital band practice. So, I got it together, grabbed my bass, and I proceeded to walk to Dennis' house. The practice session went well; we had managed to get all the way through Metallica's "Welcome Home" (Sanitarium). Not only did we get through this song, but we were virtually mistake free and this small success cured my bad trip. I went home and I slept off this trip. Whew, I had made it through the day!

I will now tell you of another trip I had, which I will call the night that made sense. I had received a green hit of acid, which I bought off a kid downtown. The next day, I hid from my mother in the basement of our house so that I could once again skip school. Eventually, she was off to work and I would then return to the apartment. A few hours later, I took the green acid. As I prepared to place it on my tongue, I held it up to a light bulb, but it was extremely potent and its texture and color were of a stagnant chemical bond. Once I had placed this jagged pill into my mouth, I noticed that these particular chemicals were quite tasty.

Once the acid had kicked in, I peered out of my front window and I saw that it was a picture perfect day. So, I decided that I would take a walk to Downtown Lowell and find some friends to goof off with. I ran into my Lowell High School friend, Michael Michael. And yes, he really does have the same first name as his last name. We took a short cruise in his friend's car, smoked a bone, and then I bought a dime bag.

I left Michael and his friends and I commenced, to take a continuous walk around the block of Merrimack Street in Downtown Lowell. Some long-haired kid kept driving around the block cranking Metallica's Master of Puppets on his car stereo. Every time this kid drove by me, I would look at him and bang my head to the music in a gesture of approval.

Then I saw this hippy guy, who I often saw around town. He was one burnt out dude and he reminded me of Randy of the Redwoods, who used to be a popular character during the old days of MTV. I was standing in the small alley where the Lowell bus station used to be. This hippy guy began to give me a thumbs up and then he said "Let it ride, figure it out!" I looked at him with an expression of "You're weird" and I assumed, that there was no way of which this guy could have been aware of the fact that I was in pursuit of the primary goal. So I thought nothing of it and I continued to stroll along.

About half an hour later, I was back at the same spot in the alley and this very same hippy dude walked over to me, looked into my eyes, and once again said with a gesture of thumbs up "Let it ride, figure it out." At this point, I knew that we had connected. As he said these words to me, my eyes were popping out of my head in a state of astonishment. I repeated his very same phrase back to him and I realized what he had meant. To the common and reasonably intelligent person, this guy would appear to be a complete moron, and my reaction would appear as if I was making fun of him and mocking him. As we had this quick and short-lived conversation, there was a nice looking brunette, who had been watching and listening to us and she began to laugh almost hysterically. I walked off in a state of amazement.

Soon, I ran back into Michael and once again, we took a cruise. I rolled a bone from my dime bag and we started to have a match out. Michael began to try to convince me to do some mushrooms with him. I was already three sheets to the wind, so I told him that I didn't want to. He continued to persist and I continued to say no. So, we smoked another bone and I got dropped off at 11th Street.

As I was walking through the driveway at my mother's house, I looked down at the gravel on the ground and it began to spin in numerous small vortexes. I actually thought that I might drown in my driveway.

I proceeded to climb my spiral staircase to my bedroom and I played my bass for a couple of hours. Afterwards, I did something I always loved to do while tripping. I listened to Metallica, Testament, and Iron Maiden. For some reason, this particular trip would last twice the expected time frame. There must have been more chemicals in the acid I had taken that day in comparison to your average hit of acid. I smoked another bone and my trip was still in full strength.

Once it was beginning to get dark outside, I decided that I would seek out Bob and Dennis. I found them and they told me they were tripping as well. We smoked a bone and drank a beer a piece in the pot cave. Soon, we would take a walk and my dementia would hit its zenith on this night.

We commenced this walk and the three of us were connecting to the point of a prominent subconscious to conscious realization as related to all aspects of the vision of "Knowing." We were a street away from Dennis' house and I kept looking at the horizon with a completely conscious awareness of my real and presently tamed dementia. Bob and Dennis were aware of what was taking place to a certain degree. Dennis made a comment and I said to him "Make sure your reach does not exceed your grasp." Bob looked at me in approval and said "Ted knows what he is talking about!" We walked onto a grassy knoll and I began to consciously and momentarily fathom the reality of the primary goal.

As I peered at the horizon, I noticed that it was the most beautiful horizon I had ever seen. I began to say, "Why does everything make so much sense?" Bob and Dennis were just as fascinated as I was and Dennis said to me, "It's real!" I looked up at the horizon and I could detect, through my senses of the beyond, that there were four massive cubes floating on a level plane with each other in the horizon. These cubes had topologically curved ends at each corner of these semi squares. The primary goal was being magnetized to my being, but I needed an aid that night and Bob would supply me with a temporary feeling of fear, which would lead to the magnetic centrifuge for this stage of the pro-primary goal viewpoint. Bob said that it was possible that one's mind could be offset due to imbalance. I would struggle with this thought all night, but it would end up strengthening my mind. Bob played a different role from me in the pursuit of this goal. So his mind needed to be offset for a while and so it was. Once a new balance was achieved, the mind galactic vortex would connect and all would be well despite actions of the evildoers.

A month or so later, I had been attending class in Dracut and it was due time to practice in my major of mischief. It was about one period away from lunchtime and I had got a bone from my friend Chucky. I wanted to seek someone out for me to get high with. I saw Dave St. Armand in the hall as he was heading to his study period. I asked him to join me in forty-five minutes because I had a treat for him. Dave liked to party as I did, but in school, he was usually a good student, not as mischievous as I was. After I insisted that he smoked with me, he would comply. I was about to get my good friend in trouble.

After the period was over, Dave and I met up e heading to the boy's locker room located under the school gymnasium. We entered the shower area and we sparked the hooter and commenced to misbehave. In mid toke, my biology teacher Mr. Rudolph came down the back stairs. Once we heard this teacher coming, Dave and I looked into each other's eyes and an expression of worry came over our faces. I snuffed out the joint and swallowed it. Dave hid behind a set of lockers and I was about to hide, but Mr. Rudolph saw me. So, I tried to act natural. He asked me what I was up to. I said that I was getting something from my gym locker, and then he abruptly interrupted me, and said to me "It smells too good to be true down here!"

He told me to empty out my pockets, so I complied. As I emptied my left front pocket a small bag with a few roaches came out and fell to the floor. Mr. Rudolph picked up the bag, when all of a sudden Dave must have slipped or something, because a small bang rang out in the locker room. Mr. Rudolph then asked me who I was with. I tried to cover for Dave, by telling my teacher that I was alone. Mr. Rudolph walked behind a set of lockers and found Dave. Sorry, Dave!

Mr. Rudolph said, "Follow me" and we began to walk to Mr. Smith's office. Once we got upstairs and as we were walking down the hallway, Mr. Rudolph had his back to us and he was roughly ten feet in front of Dave and me. Dave pulled a small bag of weed out of his underwear and he attempted to toss it above the lockers so the faculty wouldn't find it on him. Once again, Mr. Rudolph was not fooled. He turned around, walked over to the lockers, and because he was a short fellah, he had to jump up in order for him to grab the bag.

We got to the disciplinarian's office and Mr. Rudolph turned in our contraband. Mr. Smith was already aware of the fact that I was a stoner, so he didn't see any point in yelling at myself or Dave, for that matter. He told us to take a seat and wait.

The police station was located right next to the high school, so it wouldn't be long until they would show up. About ten minutes passed by and two plainclothes policemen entered the office. I wasn't aware that these guys were cops at first, so I gave one of them a sarcastic smile. They were Officer Dauphine and Officer Richardson. To my dismay, I would learn that officer Richardson was a cousin of mine on my mother's side of the family.

Dave and I were then taken to each of our lockers one at a time for a routine search. By this time, my mother had shown up, but Dave's father was stuck at work. Dave, Mr. Smith, my mother, the two officers, and I headed to my locker first. As they searched my locker, I was confident that nothing was in there, but you never know there might have been a roach or something. They ended up finding nothing.

Now, we were off to Dave's locker. They had Dave open his locker and the search began. One of the officers pulled out a notebook of Dave's, which had a marijuana plant drawn on the back of it. The officer pointed to the drawing and said "Nature's way of saying high." Due to past connections between Dave and I, we looked at each other in a state of connection.

All of a sudden, the period ended and the bell rang. Within a matter of seconds, the halls were packed with students. All of our fellow burnouts saw us as celebrities, as all the others would view us as a couple of jerks. People were pointing and laughing as they walked by. Someone insulted us in front of my friend Brian M, so Brian became angry with this kid; as he ran downstairs away from Brian; you could hear his feet going plipty plop plipty plipty plipty plop plipty plop plop plop. And then Miss Sullivan, who had been confronting me about this on a regular basis, gave me a look I would never forget. Nothing was found in Dave's locker.

Now it was time for the short ride to the Dracut Police Station. We arrived and Dave, my mother, and I were told to sit and wait for a few moments. Then they told us that Dave and I were to be spoken to one at a time, which would be followed by a conversation including all of us. The officers left the waiting room so the three of us just sat there.

All of a sudden, we could hear a speaker telephone with some guy who was panicking. From all the way across the room, we could hear an officer yelling, "There is a vicious pit bull running rampant, and I don't know what to do!" This caused Dave and I to burst out laughing, and my mother became irate, and then she said, "What the hell are you two laughing for, you're in big trouble!" At this point, Dave and I commenced to shut up.

Dave would go first and he was spoken to for about ten minutes. Then it was my turn, which took a little longer and finally the five of us went in to talk as a group. Dave and I were in shock at how well we were treated by these two officers. It was more like a friendly conversation rather than a scolding. Officer Dauphine told Dave and me that when he was our age, he wore his hair long because he thought it was cool and then he said, "Yeah, from time to time I would attend high school parties and yeah, we did light one up now and then." At this moment, Dave and I looked at each other in amazement at how well we were being spoken to.

Then these two officers became deadly serious and they began to warn us about the dangers of cocaine. They told us of all of the crying victims of this evil narcotic. They had lost everything and ruined their personalities. And that is exactly what cocaine does! As we got ready to leave, Officer Richardson told me in a polite manner to keep my nose clean and to smarten up. The Dracut High faculty decided that Dave and I would be given outdoor suspension for five school days.

VISION OF A MENTAL PATIENT

The first day of our outdoor suspension came. My mother went to work and Dave's father did the same. I called Dave on the phone and I told him that I was sorry for getting him in trouble. I told him I had some weed and he told me he did too. We decided we would meet up at St. Louis Park. Once Dave and I met up at stoner central, we slapped hands and began to celebrate our suspension. And then we got high.

Once we were good and baked, we went to my place at Elevcenth Street and blasted some Testament, Metallica, Iron Maiden, and some Suicidal Tendencies. We managed to excel in mischief that week, but soon we were back to school. When we did get back, we received some congratulations as well as some dirty looks.

A week or so later Dave, the rest of the crew, and I were invited to a party at this girl's house, who was seeing my and Bob's friend, Chico. The bunch of us entered the party, but for some reason, Dennis wasn't there that night. The first friend I saw was Steve B. (whom I have previously mentioned). We began to talk and we began to get a good buzz. Then I ran into Ed L. from last year's math class, he was with the kid we called Brain and this other dude Mike D. We started chugging hard liquor as if it was water and it wouldn't be long until the bunch of us were blitzed.

For some reason, Mike, Bob, a few others, and I were hanging out in the bathroom, of all places. I was sitting in my favorite seat and we decided to lock the door so we could keep the pot smoke from leaving the room. There were a couple of girls trying to get in, so I said "Girls, yuck, no girls in this clubhouse!" I pulled a huge bag of weed out of my pocket, but when I tried to roll a bone, I couldn't because I was completely wasted. I handed my bag to Bob and I said to him "You're the pot expert, so you roll it and make it fat!" Some more girls began to bang on the door and I reminded the guys that this was male bonding and that we mustn't let them in. A moment later, we ended up letting a couple of them in. The bunch of us toked up and soon we were on cloud nine, but this cloud was a cloud of marijuana. I ended up blacking out this night, but luckily, when I woke up, I knew where I was, which sometimes I didn't.

Now, for the story of another trip. I had been employed at the old Ronnie's Steak House as a dishwasher in Dracut at this point in time. Anyhow, a few hours before my shift, I ran into Bob, Dennis, Matt, and Dave. Matt had recently been away for a while and it was good to see him again. Matt wanted to stay straight, but on this night, he was tempted and he would give in to it.

Anyhow, when I ran into these guys, they told me they had obtained some lysergic acid diethylamide. I called up Ronnie's, and told them that I was sick, thus I couldn't make it to work. The five of us took the acid and the effects came fast. I had to go back to Eleventh Street in order to retrieve a bag of weed, which I had left in my room. I thought my mother was out with friends, but to my dismay she was home when I arrived. She had somehow found out that I had planned to skip work. She confronted me about this, so I made up some crazy story about a girl I had to see. She was half in the bag herself, so it wasn't difficult to convince her.

Soon, the chemicals of the acid began to coincide with my DNA and the actions of my brain chemistry and thus my trip was in full swing. When I left Eleventh Street, I exited my driveway and I discovered that my friends weren't there. I walked down the small hill of my street to find them, when all of a sudden, I heard laughter from a distance. I turned around, and I saw that my friends were on a small grassy knoll, and they had hid on me to play a joke. They came down from the knoll and we commenced to have a tripping walk.

I was tripping hardcore when we were nearing Bob and Dennis' neighborhood and we had just smoked a bone. I then lit up a cigarette and vomited. I would buy some breath mints as soon as possible. Anyhow, Bob kept telling me that I wouldn't trip, because I had thrown up. I said to him "I am tripping already, you bone head!" And as we walked on, Bob kept on razzing me because I had vomited.

It started to get dark as we were walking up Pleasant Street, just past the border into Dracut. Some Dracut Policemen drove by us with their lights on and it freaked me out. However, they took no notice of us and simply drove onward. At this point, a carload of Dracut kids stopped and parked near us. It was my neighbor Rick M. He was with three other dudes whose names were, Craig, Dan, and Brian M. Rick got out of the car and asked us if we had any weed to sell. One of us sold them a bone, as Dave stood by in a state of confusion. Craig then said to him, "Don't worry about it, man, you should have seen me the last time I tripped." They drove away, and things were back to normal—or at least normal for five maniacs on an acid trip!

We continued to enhance our trip by smoking more marijuana. We decided to head over to Matt's neighborhood. The tripping became even more intense, as we had reached Matt's neighborhood. We began to kick around the hacky sack, but we quickly became bored with it.

It was wintertime and Dennis was driving his parent's station wagon, which I had now dubbed as the pot mobile. We commenced to play "Jump on the car and hang on," as Dennis would cruise down Matt's dead end street and Bob, Matt, and I, would grab the bumper and hang on as our feet slipped and slid along the snowy and icy street. I remember Bob saying as we were cruising down the street, "This isn't cool man!"

Soon, I had to make a decision. Matt and a couple others who we had met up with on this crazy night were going to the woods to smoke some more weed, but Bob and Dennis were going to Dennis's house to play some guitar. I opted to join Bob and Dennis, despite the fact that I would be left out because my bass was back at Eleventh Street. However, Dennis pleased me as he showed off playing Metallica tunes, Testament tunes, and some Iron Maiden tunes. At this point, my mind was vastly deep into the collective subconscious by way of imposed chemical infections.

As Dennis continued to play, I started to act very weird and I kept staring at all of the heavy metal paraphernalia that covered the walls of Dennis's room. I especially took notice of his Iron Maiden "Can I Play with Madness" poster, which showed a fist punching through a head and holding its brain. I was experiencing visionary thoughts, which were, to some degree, fathomless at the time. However, coinciding forces were centering my mind, thus contributing to the equilibrium of mind, space, and time.

Later on that night, I started to feel very good. Bob, Dennis, and I would go to Bob's house, which was the next street over from Dennis' house. There was a wild party at Bob's place, as usual. We were already tripping, so a couple of beers apiece would be plenty as long as we could have that delicious taste in our mouths. We went into Bob's hallway and got even higher. It got to the point when it felt as if we were flying. Soon, Dennis' parents called Bob's house and Dennis would have to go home. Dennis was just fine because he was always good at playing straight. Bob and I were out of weed at this point and once we realized this, we chased Dennis down and caught him before he entered his driveway, and then we asked him for another bone, and he complied. Bob and I went back to his place and smoked it. Soon, the night was over and this would be one of the most intense trips I ever had in my life.

A few nights later, Bob and I were jamming in his room as one of his relatives came into Bob's room with a bar of hash. He smoked half of the bar with us and then he let us have the rest. After Bob's relative had left the room, I told Bob that I could see into his relative's mind through his face and Bob subconsciously understood. Bob and I were never into smoking hash, but on this occasion, we discovered that hash smoking slightly resembled a faint acid trip.

Once Bob and I finished off this bar of hash, we felt like we were Pink Floyd or something! Soon, Bob and I were comatose and the two of us just lay on his bed drooling on his comforter. Bob's acoustic guitar was lying between us, as we continued to stare at each other. All of a sudden, I had an impulse to move my arm and I ended up waking my head with the body of Bob's acoustic guitar. Bob and I immediately hit the floor in an absolute state of hysterics. We must have laughed for ten minutes straight. In fact, this might have been one of the hardest laughs I ever had in my life. We had laughed so hard, that when we finished laughing we got very nervous and I said to Bob "Holy shit man, we nearly suffocated!"

To give you an idea of just how hard Bob and I laughed on this night, I state the following: have you ever seen the movie "Total Recall" with Arnold Schwarzenegger? At the end of this film, Arnold's character and his girlfriend were exposed to the outside environment of the planet Mars without any protective gear. In this scene, they both began to suffocate, as their eyes nearly bulged out of their heads. And this was what we looked like while laughing on this occasion. Furthermore, this is the only analogy, which could possibly help you visualize how hard Bob and I laughed on this night.

Some time after, I was drinking on the walkway near the Bridge Street Bridge, which borders the Merrimack River. I was with Dave and this other guy we would see around from time to time. Well, I began to become intoxicated and thus I was over confident. I ended up telling this guy of how I was going to achieve the utopian dream, and that the planets and stars would be aligned, and that the universe would connect into the process of life, thus the birth of a new world order of love and morality. The whole time that I was explaining my crazy dream to this person, Dave was looking at me with a facial expression, which seemed to say "Oh, no!" Yet I continued on with my alcohol induced courage and morality. And later on, I got this guy some weed. He would be a happy camper on this particular evening.

Before the school year ended, I was expelled for my relentless acts of mischief. At this point, I was still working at Ronnie's Steak House in Dracut, but I had also landed another job with Dave's older brother Ron for a landscaping company called Lowell Greens. I was working around the clock most days and I would often work double shifts. However, I would soon start to miss some days of work at Ronnie's, thus I would be terminated from this dishwashing position. I would continue to landscape throughout the summer of 1990.

The day I was fired from Ronnie's is a funny story. Dennis and I had driven there in the pot mobile to get my paycheck. When I went inside, I was told that I was canned. However, I was in such a great mood that day that I didn't even mind. Dennis was to drive me to the bank. I told him "Dennis, let's do what were going to do in the future, let's laugh all the way to the bank!" And so we did!

Dennis and I went for a nice ride on this day and the weather couldn't have been better. I was confident and I kept saying over and over, as I peered into the sunlight, "Wow, wow, wow!" Dennis and I then tracked down Bob and we were off to another party.

My father and I had a bit of a falling out and I wouldn't see him for a while. I went with my mother down to the Greater Lowell Vocational Technical High School, where I would go for my last sophomore year and my last year of high school. I took the Electrical Shoppe for my trade of choice.

The summer of 1990 was not as fun as the summer of 1989, but I still had a decent summer that year. Another DNA entity would confront me during this summer and he would attempt to deceive me. He pretended to be helping me by trying to prevent me from taking any more lysergic acid diethylamide on one specific night. He was leaning against a car in Bob's driveway and he said that he knew everything. He told me that one day I would trick my mind into progressing forward by my getting a driver's license at my present age. It has been years since I have driven, but believe me, you I will be driving again soon.

This evil man did everything he could that night to prevent me from tripping out. He told me that I would end up in Solomon's and that he didn't want me to find out that certain people were after me. I mentioned that someone was selling

Metallica acid. At this point, he became very frightened and said in a high state of anxiety, "No, don't take Metallica acid!" Finally, he said, "You will travel time if you take the acid." And then he added, "Metallica is out to get you!" I looked at him in anger and I said, "No they're not!" Followed by my saying to him, "I know everything!" A severe look of fear and panic took over his face and he walked away in a state of nervousness.

On this night, I would indulge in a deeply vast connection with my friend's personal subconscious, my personal subconscious, and the collective subconscious. The mass equilibrium would thoroughly strengthen this night, but little did I realize what the forces of evil were planning against me. On this night I would connect, leading to a more conscious realization of scientific equivalency. A primitive means of time travel would also be achieved by my enemies that would do damage to me for a while, but I was bound to overcome this situation from the very beginning. The complete truth is that I had them since the day I was born.

My dementia began to grow more with every waking moment of my life, as my pursuit of the primary goal proved unrelenting, thus a new and collective utopian ambition. Soon, I would take a downward spiral into the depths of uncompromising human evils.

My use of lysergic acid diethylamide began to take a toll on me. I had already set the balance into place, but the more difficult obstacles to the primary goal were still ahead of me. The acid trips became more frequent and I continued to learn things the spoken word could not manifest (of course, this is not the case now). My mind was processing all of the scientific outlooks that I presented in the "Monolith" part two segment. My friends who shared in this vision had realized that there were simply matters that we didn't have sufficient tact to verbally elaborate our vision.

At this point, I seldom hung out with Joshua, although I did pay him the occasional visit. All of my friends, or at least most of them, began to tell me to lay off of the lysergic acid diethylamide. On one particular occasion, a friend of mine who was at least subconsciously aware of my vision tried really hard to persuade me to avoid this dangerous narcotic. When he had warned me, I told him that I had just swallowed a hit. At this exact moment, this friend of mine looked at me with a robust expression of concern and worry and then he said to me "Metallica has to kill you now." At this point, my knowledge was primitive, thus I wasn't fully aware of all that was happening around me.

Later on that night, I was with Matt and another one of our friends. We were walking through McPherson Park in Lowell. The chemicals from the acid I had taken began to disagree with my system and for the second time in my life, I would throw up due to an acid trip. When I finished vomiting, I looked up at Matt in a state of temporary insanity with bloodshot eyes and I said to him "The opposite boundary of the instinctive human mind is the mind of a rat, because of strychnine." Matt and my other friend then looked at me in a mixture of confusion and concern. I then told them, that lysergic acid diethylamide contained small quantities of this strychnine, which is a type of rat poison.

The chemical makeup of the small quantities of strychnine, which exists in lysergic acid diethylamide, is altered due to acts of chemical absorption within this acid narcotic. Therefore, it is different and diluted. This chemical altering property had set up another opposite to opposite reaction of creation, which in this case is between the human mind and the mind of a rodent. It was becoming obvious, that I was losing my mind and soon I would be caught between a rock and a hard place.

As my undeniable dementia continued to grow and strengthen, thus leading me to a crucial crossroads, my conquest for the achievement of time travel and the foundation of universal contact began to jab me in the face. This would be the first of many times when I would pull myself together and regain my composure, at least until the next obstacle would present itself.

At the end of summer, I had managed to balance my dementia. Therefore, I was able to attend school and work. I attended work at a restaurant with a cinema show attached to it. As I always say, "Life is a continuous balancing act."

School at the Lowell Voke started off well and I had and would make many friends there. I did well in my academic classes for a while. However, electrical work bored me and I was constantly distracted due to my past achievements concerning the pro primary goal viewpoint.

I remember being in electrical class as I stared into the eyes of a blue-eyed kid. From looking into these eyes (from the side so he didn't know), I furthered my comprehension of the relationship between the human eye and its optical nerves, as applied to the balanced actions of the mind and its sensual abilities, as they coincided with the totality of universal existence. Most of all, I was progressing in the outlook of human understanding.

Now my dementia was so farfetched in comparison to plain old common sense, that I began to regret my experimenting with lysergic acid diethylamide. I felt more and more with every passing moment that I was going mad. And I was going mad due to the creation of the language of the mad. As I would observe common every day things such as eyes, skin, plants, or what have you these thoughts would aid me in my realizations of infinite and infinitesimal topological connections. Despite my awareness of how crazy I was, I did fully believe in the aspect of everything being chemical and the same goes for magnetism. As always, I was viewed as a down to Earth type of person: I was able to stay grounded and appear somewhat normal. However, Joshua told me something years prior to this. He said to me "Ted, it's not normal to be normal anymore." And Joshua was correct in saying this.

My friend Tom P. was attending the Voke that year as well. He would pick me up in the morning every day for school. Tom was yet another one of my friends who was concerned with my use of lysergic acid diethylamide. Soon, I was so affected by dementia that I began to ignore Tom when he would beep his horn outside of my house in the mornings. By this time, my use of this narcotic was few and far between. I would eventually trip in school again, but this time it was intentional and I would handle it well.

Soon, I would temporarily join a band with a friend of mine by the name of Ed D. This would be the only show of my life when I would not play any original material. We would strictly play covers. In this band were Ed D., a dude named Daris, a drummer kid named Steve, and me. We would play Pink Floyd, Danzig, Black Sabbath, Jane's Addiction, Voivod, The Red Hot Chili Peppers, and Metallica, of course. This show took place at St. Jaun Darc Hall in Lowell. Days before this show, I went to Dracut High to hand out and hang up some flyers. I visited Miss Sullivan and I gave her a flyer. When she saw me, she was nice as usual. However, one of her students mentioned the evildoers while I visited with my former teacher and it was insulting. What was worse was what this student said to Miss Sullivan after I had left.

A lot of people went to the show; it was a good success for me to be back on the stage once again. Afterwards, there was a wild party and the bunch of us would get blitzed. I got tired about an hour before the party was over. I pulled out the sofa bed and started to sleep as all of my friends would party around me and get a few laughs out of my ability to sleep in the middle of a wild party.

I was employed as a dishwasher at a restaurant that (as previously stated) was attached to the Lowell Flick Cinema Show. There is a Queensryche song that pertains to this part of my life. I would now like to further my case, as to the reality of my vision and thus an imminent mass recollection of the collective subconscious. So, as you read these lyrics, you must keep in mind that my official name on my birth certificate is John. I now present track six to the Queensryche album called *Empire*. This is the title track and it is also called "Empire." Please enjoy.

> *Last night the word came down, ten dead in Chinatown*
> *Innocent, their only crime was being in the wrong place at the wrong time*
> *Too bad people say, what's wrong with the kids today?*
> *Tell you right now they've got nothing to lose, they're building EMPIRE*
> *Johnny used to work after school, at the cinema show*
> *Gotta hustle if he wants an education, yeah he's got a long way to go!*
> *Now he's out on the streets all day, selling crack to the people who pay*
> *Got an AK-47 for his best friend, business the American way!*
> *Eastside meets Westside downtown, no time the walls fall down*
> *Can't you feel it coming? EMPIRE! Can't you hear it calling?*
> *Black man trapped again, holds his change in his hand*
> *Brother killing brother for the profit of another, game point nobody wins!*
> *Decline, right on time, What happened to the dream sublime?*
> *Tear it down, we'll put it up again, another EMPIRE!*
> *Eastside meets Westside downtown, no time, no line, the walls fall down*
> *Can't you feel it coming? EMPIRE! Can't you hear it coming? EMPIRE!*
> *Can't someone here stop it.........EMPIRE!*

Soon, I paid Joshua one of those occasional visits. We began to make friendly conversation and then he let me listen to a tape of him, Roland, and John of my future band Deallegiance, and the Davis kid from school. As I listened to these guys play, I became quite impressed. They had gotten all the way through Metallica's "And Justice for All" virtually mistake free!

I couldn't believe they blew Bob, Dennis, and me away. I was growing wary of my musical future at this point; all we did was sit around and smoke dope. Other instances would soon present themselves., and then due to my personal subconscious and the carrying out of the primary goal, I would soon desert my best friends although truthfully, I hated having to do it. This would cause temporary bitterness, but once the totality of my vision is exposed (which most of it has already) all of my friends will understand why I made the choices I did.

Roland was attending school at the Lowell Voke this year as well, but at this point, we were merely acquaintances. As a matter of fact, about a year prior to this point in time, Roland had a habit of calling me on the phone so he could ask me to jam with him. However, at this time, I had no interest in Roland as far as music was concerned. At the time, Roland wasn't that good at the guitar, but he had improved vastly over the next year or so.

I stopped Roland in a hallway of the Voke. I told him I had heard his practice session with Joshua and company, and I told him that I was impressed. Roland was surprised by my saying this, but he would become even more surprised when I asked him if he wanted to have a jam session together. He asked me if I drove, so I said to him "Not anymore" and then he told me that he drove and that he would pick me up on Saturday.

Saturday came; Roland picked me up and we were off to our first jam session of thousands to come. I walked into John's cellar and I said to him, "Long time no see." He smiled at me and we shook hands. We started to play Metallica's "The four Horsemen" but then we decided to work on Death Angel's "A Seemingly Endless Time." After that, we showed each other some original material and despite the fact that we had a poor sound at this point, I considered this first jam session to be more than satisfactory.

At this time, I still wanted to stay with Bob and Dennis for the formation of "Manifest" and I had just completed writing my first fully written song, "Freedom's Call." This was the song I presented and elaborated on back in the "What is a Connection?" segment. Most of my friends had a limited understanding of the meaning of this song, but I remember Dennis saying to me in regards to this song, "That pretty much sums it up."

Just after I had finished writing this song, I showed it to Matt in the main front hall of the Voke during our lunch period. Matt was the one who I believe understood me the most in regards to my vision. Matt was very fond of Bob, Dennis, and me. He unselfishly tried to talk me into sticking it out with Manifest because he wanted to see us do well. This was an honorable act because I had told Matt by this point, that I was interested in him as a possible band member.

The following weekend, the entire crew was at another beer party at the fort in the woods behind my house. It was on this nightthat I semi-selfishly betrayed my friends of Manifest. I told them I was leaving them on this night.

Talk about a tense night! Bob kept giving Roland the finger and I told Bob not to be angry with Roland, because it was I who was betraying him and not Roland. Roland felt awful and so did I, but it had to be done. Days later, I would attempt to rejoin Bob and Dennis, but their self-respect prevented me from doing so. Bob, Dennis, and I would always remain friends, but from this point on, there would be a hint of bitterness and soon, we wouldn't be together every day, as we had been for years.

The first guitarist Roland and I went after was Paul Felis from my first band. I had given Paul a recording of us playing Freedom's Call in its completeness and I was hopeful he would be interested. Dennis and Dave from Manifest would temporarily join Roland and me, but this would be shortlived due to my past decisions.

Anyhow, Paul was impressed by the recording I gave him. Paul told us he would jam with us and feel things out. The next day, when Roland came to pick me up, I had expected him to be with Paul. However, when my doorbell rang, I walked to my door and opened it. To my surprise, Roland was with Matt instead of Paul. I thought to myself "Matt is no Paul Felis, but he will be good enough."

So, the three of us went to John's house and we had our first practice as a unit together. Things went well; I realized that Matt and Roland were not yet on Bob and Dennis' level, but they would prove to be ambitious and compliant with the way I liked to work. Neither of them could play leads well, but I was not concerned with that yet. We were a young band and I wanted to build a solid foundation of basic drums, rhythm, and bass. John, on the other hand, was an outstanding drummer from the start, even despite the fact that he played a single bass drum set. John was so good that when you listened to him play, you would think he was playing double bass. He was fast!

Practices continued and the foundation was being set into place. We would come to the agreement of calling the band "Deallegiance." I came up with this name from a line to the lyrics to a Testament song, which goes "The legion's armies hold on to your fate" but I thought it said "Deallegiance armies hold on to your fate." Once we had named the band as such, we would be subject to limited criticism. However, you must keep in mind that it is fun to be a young radical.

My dementia continued to grow substantially. Because I was emotionally strong, I would continue to keep things in check. Soon, I would quit school. So, why don't I tell you the story of my last day of high school? And yes, I was tripping again.

Okay, it was academic week rather than trade week. My electrical related teacher gave me an ultimatum of shape up or ship out. So, I had my bag of books on one shoulder and a hit of McDonald's acid in my front pocket. With about a half an hour remaining in the school day, I had a choice. Either I would take the acid and say "Fuck school" or I would go home and do my home work. I looked to my left hand and thought "Do my home work?" and then I looked to my right hand and thought "I could take the acid?" This went back and forth a couple of times and I ended up opting for the acid.

The trip began to take affect when I got home. I threw on Van Halen's album 51/50 and I searched my room for some roaches. I found a half of a joint and I went outside and lit it up. Now it was time to go meet one of many partners in the art of mischief. This would end up being another typical wild night of tripping and most of it would be spent at Matt's house.

I won't get into the details of this particular trip, but I will briefly account for a funny thing which happened that night. Matt, Roland, and I listened to some of our recordings on this night and we were feeling good about the way our band was progressing. Later on, Bob showed up and the entire crew was together once again. Someone hung up a Playboy centerfold on top of the door to Matt's porch. All of a sudden, right in front of some girls (may I add), some of my friends started to make bets on who could jump up and bite the ass of the girl in this centerfold. A few of my friends tried to do this, but they were not successful. Then someone asked me to take a shot and I said "No, thanks." All of a sudden, Bob became determined. So, he jumped up and he accidentally bashed his head on top of the doorway. Bob was shaken up, but he would soon recover. I then tore down the centerfold in order to avoid any more injuries.

The previous weekend, I took a ride with a few friends to Lawrence Massachusetts for a small beer party. My friend Tom P. was with me on this night and he kept trying to convince me to stay in school. Tom was a good loyal friend who always looked out for me. We were accompanied by a few others, including a funny blonde kid who will remain anonymous. On the way to Lawrence, this blonde kid had a gun and it was real. He started playing with it, so I said to him "That better be empty" and he said, "It is." So, as he was holding this weapon, we all told him to keep it low. At this point, he began to scratch his left ear with it and then part his hair with it.

We got to my house and as I crossed my front yard so I could get some cash from my room, this funny blonde dude jumped out of the car with the gun in his hand and he started to act like he was protecting me. He held up the gun like a cop on television and as he hid beside my front stairs, he said "Ted, go for it, I will cover you!" I grabbed my cash, we picked up some bottles of beer, and we headed for Lawrence.

When we reached our destination, we began to make some friendly conversation over a few bottles of beer and, of course, we listened to some Metallica on the stereo. When we were done listening to Metallica, the funny blonde kid threw in some Bad Company. When the song "Shooting Star" came on, he said that I was too smart for school and to quit. Due to a subconscious connection, I knew that he was on to something. Then he pointed at Tom and said, "He is your friend, he just doesn't know." I said "I know" and then my blonde friend said, "Ted, this song is about you, you will go through hell, but you will win in the end, Ted, quit school!" So, he turned up this song and said to me "I know your real name is John, Ted." And then he said once again, "This is about you!" Remember, my real name is John, but I have been called Ted all of my life. And also keep in mind my "Big Boom" theory. Here are the lyrics to Bad Company's Shooting Star.

> *Johnny was a school boy when he heard his first Beatles song*
> *Love me do, I think it was, and from there it didn't take him long*
> *Got himself a guitar, used to play every night*
> *Now he's in a rock 'n' roll outfit and everything's all right*
> *Don't you know?*
> *Johnny told his mama, hey mama I'm going away*
> *Gonna hit the big time, gonna be a big star someday*
> *Mama came to the door with a teardrop in her eye*
> *Johnny said don't cry mama, smiled and waved goodbye*
> *Don't you know? Yeah, don't you know that you are a shooting star?*
> *Don't you know? Don't you know?*
> *Don't you know that you are a shooting star?*
> *And all the world will love you, just as long as you are*
> *Johnny made a record, went straight up to number one*
> *Suddenly everyone loved to hear him sing the song*
> *Watching the world go by surprising it goes so fast*
> *Johnny looked around him and said, well I made the big time at last!*
> *Don't you know? Don't you know?*
> *Don't you know that you are a shooting star, don't you know?*
> *Yeah, don't you know that you are a shooting star?*
> *Johnny died one night, died in his bed*
> *bottle of whiskey, sleeping tablets by his head*
> *Johnny's life passed him by like a warm summer day*
> *If you listen to the wind, you can still hear him play*
> *Don't you know? Don't you know?*
> *Don't you know that you are a shooting star?*

Whether my blonde haired friend was consciously or subconsciously aware of my vision is irrelevant. The main factor is that he got his point across to me. I haven't seen this kid for a while now, but rest assured I will see him again!

Continuing on, at this crux, Roland, Matt, and I were getting deep into the concept of "Knowing" and we would try to explain this vision to John, but he would prove to be to down to Earth to comprehend our message at such an early time.

I told Roland we should trip together so we could indulge in one another's personal subconscious. Soon, Matt, Roland, and I would indulge into each other's minds in order for us to connect. At this time, my use of lysergic acid diethylamide was rare compared to years beforehand, but at times, I would give in to temptation. On a couple of occasions, Roland, Matt, and I were tripping at practice without John knowing it and the three of us would play tripping while we had the strobe light on. We soon had quite the following. Many Lowell kids would come to our practices and watch us play. And soon, the first ever Deallegiance show would take place.

Our friends in Manifest were also practicing hard, and thus, progressing. I think my leaving them caused their motivation. However, like I said earlier, we would always remain friends through thick and thin.

Our first show was at the University of Lowell in an average sized hall located above the former University of Lowell radio station, WJUL. We had not yet acquired John's brother Fred as a singer, so on this first show I would sing. We would play a quick two-song set. We opened with "Freedom's Call" rather than our normal performance of Death Angel's "A Seemingly Endless Time." In fact, we decided not to play Death Angel on this occasion. So, we would instead play Testament's "Practice What You Preach."

VISION OF A MENTAL PATIENT

As we commenced to set up our equipment, the four of us were slightly nervous due to the fact that we would not get to have a sound check. About twenty minutes before we were to perform, I ran outside with my bass strapped on and I hit the pay phone to call some friends, last minute, and tell them that I was playing out. A friend of mine from Dracut named John F. happened to drive by me at this point, so I told him about my gig. After that, two blonde bombshells stopped and waved at me. I think they might have been from the future.

I ran back across University Ave and re-entered the performance hall. The four of us took the stage; I began to double check all guitars and make sure that we were all in tune. As I was tuning my A string, I noticed a young kid in the crowd who stood about five feet five inches. He was wearing a black shirt with a skull on it, some baggy pants, and a large pair of black boots. What puzzled me was that this kid was a dead ringer of my uncle Kevin, but it couldn't have been him, because this kid looked too young to be my uncle. I started to talk to John as I was tuning my G string and I asked John if he knew who that kid was. John didn't know him and I told John that that kid looks like my uncle. Then I pointed at this supposed impostor and I said to him, "You again!" I had thought he had been to previous Deallegiance shows, but that wasn't possible, because this was our first show! I looked at him and said "you look like my uncle" and he said, "I am."

The reason that I thought that this kid was at previous Deallegiance shows was because he had time traveled and watched this show several times. Of course, I assumed at first that this kid was kidding with me. So I brushed it off and prepared myself to perform. I turned to Roland and said, "Are you ready?" He said, "Yes I am ready" then I turned to Matt and asked him "Are you ready?" Matt said, "Let's do it!" And, finally, I turned to John and before I said anything, John said "Yes, I'm ready, Ted." The subconscious chessboard was now set up and we were about to rock for the first time!

I looked into John's eyes and said, "Count it off, John." He tapped his high hats four times and we started to play. It sounded reasonably good from where I was standing, but any experienced musician will tell you that what matters most is how it sounds out in the crowd. We had played the musical beginning interlude and I got ready to bark out the lyrics while making sure that I didn't make any mistakes on my bass. I started to sing "Trapped in a world of illusion, passing through the sands of time." Once I got through the first verse mistake free, I knew I had it from there and all of a sudden, I was having fun. However, when I looked to my left, I saw that Roland had his back to the crowd. I remained professional and laughed it off, because after all, it was only our first show and I knew that we would overcome such bad habits.

As I sang the last few words to Freedom's Call "universal wide connection we find" I peeked to my right and I noticed that Dave St. Armand was there and I could tell that he was nervous for me, but once my singing was over, he looked at me with an expression of approval and gave me a thumbs up. Way to go Dave, friendship is more important than music. And I am still sorry today for the decisions I had to make.

After the very last note of Freedom's Call, I was anxious to see the crowd reaction, because the opening song is always crucial at any show. As soon as we ended, the small crowd went wild, especially the kid who looked like my uncle. I blew out a sigh of relief and I prepared for the next and final song of our short set list.

It was now time to play "Practice What You Preach!" I once again prepared to sing once the opening interlude was over, but this time, it was different. We had already gotten through one song and thus I was very confident of myself. I sang the song reasonably well, but of course, my voice could not live up to Chuck Billy's voice at this time. When we finished, we got an even better crowd reaction than we did from the first song, which gave me mixed emotions, because I wanted them to like my song more. Whatever, this first show went well and there were more to come.

We packed up our equipment and loaded it onto Roland's father's truck. Matt and I decided to go out for a smoke. Although Roland and John never smoked cigarettes, they would still join us for some fresh air. We overheard the soundman complaining about us, as I gave him a rude gesture behind his back. We commenced to make small talk, as the kid who looked like my uncle (he was my uncle) approached us. I said to him "Dude, you look so much like my uncle, its pathetic!" He said "Pathetic?" And I told him, that wasn't what I meant. Then he told me that he was my uncle and I said, "That's impossible." Then he told me that he had travelled time, and that I had also traveled time, and I had made myself unaware of it by a subconscious method. He also kept calling me a slut, but I took it well. Tears began to well up in his eyes and he said to me "You're bad but not evil." The others thought nothing of it, as they continued to converse with each other. Finally, my uncle said as a smile creased on his face, "You like girls don't you?" I said, "Yes I do." We traded a few more words and then he left.

We brought our equipment back to John's basement. And then Matt, Roland and I were off to the Lowell reservoir to get high. We lit the bone, and I started to get all mushy and emotional on them. I told them that I was proud of them and that it was excellent that we had finally played our first show. Soon, the night was over and the three of us went home.

Our second show was soon booked and we were to perform at a small nightclub in Billerica Massachusetts, called "The Edible Rex." This was a small venue, but nevertheless the place would be packed and it was most certainly worthwhile, even despite the miserable performance we would give on this night. The members of Manifest, as well as a slew of other friends were there to cheer us on. John's brother Fred was now our singer and the five of us were very nervous on this occasion. Matt, Roland, John, Fred, and I took the stage. We opened up with "A Seemingly Endless Time" and this first song was a minor success and that would prove to be an optimistic assumption.

Little did we realize that we would be subject to Murphy's Law on this night. As we started to play the second song of the set, which was an original called "The Misguided Warrior," my amplifier began to fail and soon I couldn't hear myself at all.

To make things worse, I busted my E string as we went into the second verse of The Misguided Warrior. When my E string busted, it nearly poked me in the eye. I mean, talk about bad luck, I had never broken a bass string in my life up to this point and when it finally happened, I was on stage of all places. Why couldn't I have broken a string at practice instead? I learned a valuable lesson from this. From now on, I would always have at least one back up guitar ready in case of an incident as such.

Unfortunately, I was still un-experienced at this time to some degree, thus I was not prepared for this situation. I got Manifest's bass player Fred to help me reapply an E string as quickly as possible. It was humiliating, having to walk around in the crowd while my fellow band members were continuing on with the set list without me. I must say, that the crowd took it well and not one person there frowned on me for my mistake. One particular guy looked at me in a friendly manner, and he shrugged his shoulders while gesturing some hand and body language with an expression of "You'll get it next time, kid." We managed to apply another E string and I would return to the stage for the last two songs of our set list. Things seemed okay for a few moments until my amplifier once again started to fail and like that scene in the rock 'n' roll comedy classic "This is Spinal Tap," my amplifier temporarily picked up a radio station. I continued to play regardless of the situation, when all of a sudden, my amplifier kicked in. I rolled my eyes and said to myself "Great timing." Roland then did something very professional: He looked at me and began to laugh it off.

You see, something my first manager taught me was that no matter how bad a performance was going, you must always act as if you were having a good time. Roland was never told to do this, but then again he was a bit of a natural. The misery finally ended and we left the stage with pleasure.

Lucky for us, the crowd was great on this night and despite our disastrous performance, the entire crowd clapped for us once we were finished. It seemed as if they all said in a collective and unifying fashion "You'll get it next time, dudes!"

Before the show, Roland, Matt, and I had picked up some bottles of beer and we were glad to pop a few open at this point in time. John was never a party person. So, when I was sucking back my second beer, he came walking by with his snare drum in hand and he said to me with a funny expression "I can see you're drinking a beer!" I then responded with "After that miserable performance, what do you expect?" John let out a light chuckle and then he joined his friends from Out Cold.

We drank our beers, and then we packed up the rest of our equipment, and for fathomable reasons, we wanted to get the hell out of there. So, we would leave early. We weren't the only band with bad luck on this night. There was a band we used to play out with, called "Youth with Bats." I heard they had rocked on this night. However, when they took the stage, more than half of the crowd had left. And this might have been because Deallegiance sucked on this night.

Roland and I stopped at a rest stop to discuss this failed performance. We agreed that we would be better prepared in the future. I truly felt like a loser on this night. However, this experience would prove beneficial, because it had motivated us. We were now determined to turn a negative into a positive and thus we would improve as a band from this point on.

After our shows, we had a tradition of getting high at the Lowell reservoir. So, we tossed down a few more beers and then we headed for desert. We discussed things further and I agreed that I must purchase another bass for a back up. I ended up buying a moderately priced Yamaha bass guitar. This was also the start of self-discipline within the band.

Our third performance would also be at the Edible Rex and we were once again a bundle of nerves before the show. We opened up with our new original at the time, which was "Open Door." I must say that from where I was standing, we sounded great. Bob had been kicked out of Manifest by this time and due to the start of minor bitterness between the band crews, as we played the opening riffs to "Open Door," Bob went absolutely nuts. He began to mosh by himself, he looked at me on the stage, and screamed at me, "Yeah!" And this wouldn't be the last time Bob would do this for us. Metallica's Black Album had been released by this point and at the time and for a few years to come, I would grow in hatred as to the members of Metallica. I had seen the video for their hit song "Enter Sandman" prior to the release of this album and I knew right away they were singing about me.

Soon, the paranormal would grow into a manifestation of the obstacles posed to me, due to my setting the primary goal into motion. I saw the Enter Sandman video for the first time with the company of Matt and another one of my friends, Bill McClellan. The three of us knew something was up and we would have a vital conversation on this night, which concerned the subconscious actions pertaining to the pro-primary goal viewpoint.

The following day, I was with Matt and Roland at Roland's house and Roland had videotaped this video. As we watched this video, the three of us agreed that it could be about me, because the kid in the video looked just like I did at the time. Furthermore, the prayer part of this video was of a young kid praying, who looked like I did as a child. Not only that, but the room this kid was in was nearly identical to the room I had as a child on Lilley Ave. In this video, there is a small lamp in the bedroom of this child, which resembles the Red Sox lamp I had as a kid. This would prove to be a key ingredient to the primary goal. It would set into motion an opposite to opposite reaction of creation (this time we are dealing strictly with the psyche). Later on, Roland and I agreed that it was possible Metallica was trying to do something good. This would prove to be a truism in the future of which would lead me to the writing of this book.

I would hear this new Metallica album for the first time in its entirety at Bill's house. As I heard the music and read the lyrics to this album, my heart sank into my stomach. It had appeared that my failure was complete. I will now show the lyrics to Enter Sandman. As you read these lyrics, keep in mind the paranormal disturbances I had as a young child.

VISION OF A MENTAL PATIENT

Say your prayers little one, don't forget my son, to include everyone
tuck you in warm within, keep you free from sin, til the sandman he comes
Sleep with one eye open, gripping your pillow tight
Exit light, enter night, take my hand, we're off to never never land
something's wrong shut the light heavy thoughts tonight
and they're not of Snow White!
Dreams of war, dreams of liars, dreams of dragon fire
and of things that will bite
Sleep with one eye open, gripping your pillow tight
Exit light enter night, take my hand, we're off to never never land
Now I lay me down to sleep, pray the lord my soul to keep
if I die before I wake, pray the lord my soul to take
Hush little baby don't say a word, and never mind that noise you heard
it's just the beast under your bed, in your closet in your head
Exit light enter night, grain of sand, exit light enter night,
Take my hand, we're off to never never land!

Some time afterward, on another day, Roland and I were hanging at my house. He kept laughing about my appetite and who could blame him. I was eating sardines, a peanut butter, and cheese sandwich, and I washed it down with a cup of slim fast.

The Persian Gulf War abruptly ended on this day and so many of us were relieved of political tension. Sometime later in this day, another video would come on air, and this video and what it says is basically the story of my life. This would be the release of Queensryche's "Silent Lucidity." For anyone who has seen the Enter Sandman video and the Silent Lucidity video, you might have noticed that these two videos are direct opposites to each other. This would be a collective opposite to opposite reaction of creation, which in this case would be through television. And remember, television is part of the centrifuge of the collective subconscious. So, here is my life in a nutshell. Please enjoy the lyrics to "Silent Lucidity."

Hush now, don't you cry, wipe away that teardrop from your eye
you're lying safe in bed, it was all a bad dream, spinning in your head
your mind tricked you to feel the pain
of someone close to you leaving the game, of life
So here it is another chance, wide awake you face the day
The dream is over, or has it just begun? There's a place I like to hide
A doorway that I run through in the night
Relax child you were there, but only didn't realize, and you were scared
it's a place where you will learn to face your fears, retrace the years
and ride the whims of your mind, commanding in another world
Suddenly you hear and see, this magic new dimension
I will be watching over you, I am going to help you see it through
I will protect you in the night, I'm smiling next to you, in silent lucidity
If you open your mind for me, you won't rely on open eyes to see
the walls you built within come crumbling down
and a new world will begin, living twice at once you learn
you're safe from pain in the dream domain, a soul set free to fly
A round trip journey in your head, Master of illusion can you realize?
Your dream's alive, you can be the guide
but I will be watching over you, I am going to help you see it through
I will protect you in the night, I'm smiling next to you....

At first, I thought that Metallica was against me and Queensryche was for me. Sometime after, I thought vice versa, but today I know for a fact that both of these bands are pro-primary goal.

Deallegiance would then have yet another couple of shows at the Edible Rex. We were booked to play out with the famous band "Meliah Rage." The night of this crucial show came, we loaded our equipment onto Roland's father's truck, picked up some beers for after the show, and it was off to Billerica to perform.

The dudes from "Infanticide" would go on first, we would go on second, another local band called "A Shattered Dream" would go on third, and Meliah Rage would feature. The bass player for the famous metal band "Wargasm" filled in for Meliah Rage's bass player on this occasion. I would see to it that I would meet these guys on this night.

I managed to be in the small dressing room of this venue. Soon, the members of Meliah Rage entered the room with Bob Mayo from Wargasm. I got to rub elbows with the big time and thus, I accomplished my goal. Infanticide went on first and they played well as always.

When we took the stage, John and I kept looking at each other. We knew we were prepared and that we were about to rock. Once again, we opened up with Open Door and Bob Stevens would go wild, just like he had at our previous show. We went through the set list virtually mistake free despite the fact that Roland was out of tune for a couple of songs toward the end of the set list. The crowd was pleased with us on this occasion and that was a relief. When we left the stage, we knew we had held our own and you could see it in our faces. Little did I know what was soon to take place!

The following weekend there was a huge beer party in the Dracut State Forest. I showed up to the party with a bag of weed in my underwear and a case of Budweiser in my right hand. I saw Matt and Roland, so I walked over to them and boy, they were in a good mood!

Bob Stevens was there and later on that night, I noticed that Bob was speaking with Matt and Roland and Bob seemed to be a tad hyper. Roland and Matt kept laughing as Bob continued on with his hyper fit. I became curious, so I approached these three lunatics. Once they had acknowledged my presence Roland and Matt were like "Ted, check this out!" I looked into Bob's face and I could tell that he was motivated. He had just been kicked out of Manifest, so he was a bit livid. He looked into my face and started to say, as intense energy shot from his face "Ted, I am with you!" I suppose Bob wanted to support our cause at this point. Suffice it to say, this was a very funny thing.

Some anonymous sources were telling me to stop playing with my band. I just assumed that they were being assholes. However, the shit would soon hit the fan and I was the fan. I could not realize at this time that these people were trying to protect me, but I would learn a great deal over the next twenty or so years.

At the end of the night, I left with Roland and Matt in Roland's car. We had briefly discussed the new Metallica album earlier that night. Roland and Matt were subconsciously aware of what was taking place, because when I said "Metallica is going down" Roland looked at me in approval and Matt held his fist in the air and said, "Yeah!" For Matt and Roland, this would be a temporary subconscious battle, but for me, it was the foundation of my entire life, thus for me, a confrontation was unavoidable.

A week later, I recalled the show we played at the Edible Rex and I started to remember people and things which weren't there on that night. At the time, it seemed as if these people were there, but I had not yet realized that these visitors were travelling time. I had a long conversation with Bob Mayo of Wargasm within this time flux. He and I conversed on a few matters and this conversation would continue in time fragments for quite a long duration. His guitarist said, "I am a question" which was a statement relative to destiny and the primary goal. This paranormal type activity would continue for years.

Around this time, I met up with some of my friends at the Lowell reservoir. It was Bill M, Tom H, and Roland. I asked them if they had remembered anything unusual on that previous night. Suffice it to say, my friends had absolutely no clue of what I was speaking about. So, we commenced to get high and the paranormal actions were mild at this point in comparison to how they would be in the near future.

You see, there is one method of time travel of which one can acquire the ability to have the visited entity experience such intervening actions on the same night of visitation. However, through this process, one will not remember this visitation until sometime after the point of origin within the parallel fluctuations of alternate time.

Soon, we were booked to play a show at a nightclub in Beverly, Massachusetts, called "Grover's." This would turn out to be the night when I was visited by the prime evildoers. Over the next few years, I would meet a slew of famous people at this show due to my achievement of the primary goal. The only time travelers, who I will not keep anonymous in this portion, will be the members of Metallica, Iron Maiden, and the awesome "Madonna!" I will continue to refer to those against my vision as the evildoers.

The show at Grover's came and we would have a lackluster performance on this night. We played two new originals on this occasion, "Lost in Time" and "Symbol of Transformation." We would also play Metallica's "The God that Failed" off the black album. My Dracut High friend Tabby was with me that night and so was Dennis. The best reactions we got on this night were when we played our two new originals of which I just mentioned. The show ended, we loaded our equipment, and it was off to the reservoir to get high.

Once again, I would experience more time-altered visitations, but I had not yet fully realized what was happening. Some time would pass by and for a short while, things seemed somewhat normal. The shit was about to hit me, hard! We were to perform at a large daytime Dracut beer party with some other bands from the area. This would be the show when the tides would turn and my temporary downward spiral would commence.

We showed up well before the party began so that we could load and prepare our equipment. John didn't drink, so that wouldn't pose a problem. On the other hand, Roland, Matt, and I loved to drink, so we agreed that we would limit ourselves to a beer or two apiece as we waited to perform. I only had one beer, which was all I needed to wet my whistle. We took the stage, or should I say, we took the grass and we started off with "A Seemingly Endless Time." The crowd was more than pleased with our opening number.

Now came the part I was waiting for all day! We had a kicking new original called "Beginnings" which we were all looking forward to playing throughout the day. It went okay, I guess. John had screwed up on the most important part of the song, which was rare for him to do. After the last note of the song rung out, my friend from school Sean H. came up to me in a state of prime satisfaction and we high fived each other. We commenced with the remainder of the set list and our complete performance on this day was just about adequate.

I left the grass stage with bass in hand and I headed right for the keg, so that I could commence to get shit faced. I sat on the edge of the keg while it was being tapped as a bunch of my friends kept asking me to play for them. It was pretty cool to have all of this attention. The keg was finally ready for consumption and I proceeded to tip a few back.

I saw Shelly L. and our mutual friend Jen M. at this party. Shelly said to me "Hodge, I haven't seen you since high school." We were all glad to see each other again. Unfortunately, Shelly and Jen showed up late and they had missed the performance, but they told me they heard we were good and it was nice to hear someone say that. I said goodbye to them and I walked off for another beer and another bone.

The Dracut Police showed up soon after and the party was then cut short. Some anonymous sources said to me indirectly, that the cops were there because of me. I dismissed this as nonsense. I headed home, and went to bed early that night.

I began to remember more and more time-altered manifestations from past shows at the Edible Rex, Grover's, and this party I just performed at. It was the summer of 1992 and I had just turned nineteen years of age. It would not be long until I would become a mental patient. Some time passed by as my psyche entered a state of seemingly paranoid suspicions. The altered time fluctuations I was experiencing began to turn evil and fast!

Allow me to tell you of an attempted time-altered lunge, which was intended to kill me within the boundaries of the time-altered visitations of which I was experiencing. An anonymous person who was trying to help me had visited me in alternate time. He told me to look at the wall and when I peered over to the wall, there was a door with two people in it. I said, "So what," and then this anonymous person said, "Look at the door again," so I did. When I looked to the wall, the door had vanished. At this point, my subconscious awareness of the primary goal kicked in and I wasn't intimidated in the least. I said to this person "I know how you did that!" And this person began to panic. This type of abuse would happen to me for a long time to come.

An evildoer visited me by method of this time-altered process. This visitation was at the party, which I had just performed at. I remembered this visitation, just days after we had played this particular show. This person is so evil that he said he was going to prove that there was no god and that he was going to kill me over and over forever. By kill forever, I mean god's literal hell where you burn in a fire for eternity. You see, the most unfortunate factor of the primary goal is that one could achieve perpetual murder. Yes, a literal hell! Continuous burnings, stabbings, or whatever sickening thing you can think of.

I was visited by two others, who told me that I would be scared in the near future. They told me about certain future events, which soon took place. The shit was now hitting me with an unyielding force.

The night I saw what I would face took place while I was working the night shift at the old Merit Gas Station in Lowell. I was in the booth and I had begun to take up the stupid habit of snorting cocaine. As I did a few lines, I began to remember more time-altered manifestations of terrorizing threats, of my being subject to a perpetual hell. I peered into the parking lot next to the booth I was working in and as the cocaine mixed in with the moisture of my nostril hairs, I saw myself in the form of dream fabric with half of my legs sliced off one inch at a time and I could sense the excruciating pain of this horrendous act. As I looked on in horror, I was bearing witness to a bloodied state of absolute human misery. What was I to do? I had insufficient tact for my achievement of the primary goal at this point. This appeared as the beginning of the end with an end that would never end. My life would change drastically and fast!

As I sat there in horror, Metallica's James Hetfield showed up in a car and he was smiling at me. My heart immediately sank as he exited his car. When he was half way to my booth, his face shapeshifted, slightly changing his appearance. He said to me, "How are you, five bucks unleaded, please" Somehow, due to the strength of my personal subconscious, I was able to punch in his order. I took a fin from him and then he proceeded to fill his car with five bucks worth of gas.

I was thinking about the Metallica song "Sad but True" as my conscious hatred for them grew and my subconscious love for them also grew. This would be the first time of which a member of Metallica would try to save my life. My shift soon ended. I went home and tried to sleep to regain some sanity and composure.

You see, a few months prior to this, I tried to convince John and Matt that I had met Metallica in John's front yard. Of course, they didn't believe me, but it was the truth. On this visitation, James told me I was going to be discouraged, as the other members of Metallica at this time—Kirk, Jason, and Lars—did their best to humiliate and make fun of me, so that they could help me to avoid a perpetual hell.

At this point, Metallica were subject to mixed emotions due to conflicts between their conscious and personal subconscious minds. They were in part consciously evil and also in part subconsciously good. They had to aid the balances of their mind this way so that they could limit evil, thus making evil good, which is the premise of the theory of development. As my problems with the evildoers would grow, Metallica would continue to humiliate me with their proportional and balanced archetypes. I was seeing a girl named Alice at this time. She tried to convince me that I would be okay. She visited me frequently once I was admitted, but she had no clue as to most aspects of this temporary tragedy.

I have never been the type to panic (at least in my post infant years), but I must admit, that at first, when I was on the edge of hell (or heaven?), I did slightly panic. However, I soon got my head together and subconsciously pursued the primary goal. I told my father and many of my close friends what was happening to me, but they couldn't help me that much because they did not acknowledge the severity of the situation.

Thanksgiving came, and it was a miserable Thanksgiving to say the least. My sister Jill was an absolute superstar on this night. For some reason, she seemed to believe me and she trusted in what I was telling her. There was something happening in the depths of her personal subconscious, which could have been due to what happened to me on First Street back in 1976.

For reasons I will not display in detail, I knew of something, which at the time I viewed as negative. However, today I am aware that this negative message was sent to me by myself, so that I would know that I had travelled time. You see, at the end of the 80s movie "Can't Buy Me Love," there is a scene, which has to do with teenage ignorance, nerds and cools and things like that. In this particular scene, the baseball team of this fictional school is looking on as the main character made his point. I am number thirteen on this baseball team! I look different today compared to how I looked in this movie, but those who knew me when I was younger will recognize that I am number thirteen.

On this Thanksgiving night, my sister Jill was at her best and she wrote me a sisterly love note. In this note, she told me the evildoers were afraid of me and that she believed in me, thus I would prevail in the end. Ironically, "Can't Buy Me Love" was on cable that night and when I showed Jill number thirteen of this baseball team, she said "Ted, that is you!" Little did I realize that despite all that was about to happen to me, the forces of morality would win in the end!

Two evildoers, who I mentioned earlier, visited me in an altered-time flux. They told me that Dr. Simpson wouldn't be able to help me. I thought to myself, "Dr. Simpson, who the hell is he?"

Anyhow, I had told my father of this dementia I was experiencing, and he tried to convince me that I would be fine, and that we would visit Lowell General Hospital, so we could try to figure out what was happening to me. Later that night, Roland picked me up in his new Camaro and I told him that I had to quit the band because if I kept going, I would be killed for sure. Roland did not seem upset and then he said to me, "You can't quit now, I just got my new amplifier." I persisted and attempted to convince him that the dementia I was processing was real. Unfortunately, Roland was not prepared for such a far-fetched concept.

The next day, my father drove me to Lowell General and as we ate lunch in the hospital cafeteria, I told him I might be eating my last meal. We finally got our turn for my diagnosis, when a man of medium height with a short beard, donning a white medical jacket, walked into the room and said, "Hello, I am Dr. Simpson." Once Dr. Simpson told me his name, my heart sank into the depths of my stomach. However, I would do my best and keep my cool. Once I had told Dr. Simpson of my dementia, he politely asked me if I had recently taken a severe blow to the head. I told him I didn't and then he pondered on what we should do. About an hour later, I was sent next door to Solomon's Mental Health Center. I would be admitted and I would spend the next six and a half months there.

I must say at this point in my life due to my severe problems, I might have missed my days of high school more than anyone on the planet. I missed St. Joseph's, Lowell High, and the Voke. However, I missed Dracut High the most. I missed the beautiful blue lockers and hallways. I missed the Dracut Middies sign painted on the wall near the main office. I missed the wild times and my many friends. It was a beautiful place, a special place, a magical place, and I would always miss it dearly.

Before I continue on with the story of my first stay at Solomon's, I must briefly mention a friend of mine who I used to goof off with in the halls after school. This would be my good friend Jason L. Jason was a complete jock and I was a complete burnout Despite our differences, we were able to say things to each other that sometimes I couldn't even say with Joshua. Jason did the opposite of what I did. I went from private high school to public high school and he went from public high school to private high school. Anyhow, I remember you, Jason, and I wish you well.

Despite my misery when I became a mental patient, I would have the honor of meeting some of the best people in the world and it would be one incredible experience.

During my stay, I would remember some more time altered experiences of terror and despair. Soon, it would come to the point that I was completely nonfunctional. I was visited by thousands upon thousands of people in a time-altered state, including Dr. Simpson. When I was visited by Dr. Simpson in this time-altered flux, he was aware of the lyrics of Freedom's Call and he was in tears over the conceptof the good disease. As for this friend of mine who I had only known for minutes, he showed me his emotions and said to me "Ted, these lyrics are genius and beautiful, you could have saved the world!" I was both pleased and frustrated with Dr. Simpson in unison.

You see, people only become completely moral when they are faced with tragedy. The people I would meet at Solomon's are my heroes, because they were all faced with hardships and it had made them better people. Over the next couple of months my friends would visit me in a time parallel with tears running down their faces. They would express their love for me and I would in turn give my love to them.

The next song I will reveal to you is yet another Metallica song. This song represents a threefold connection. It is in part about those who had supposedly fell short of god's perfect glory and thus cast into an eternal hell fire, such as I was faced with. Its other partial meaning is the message Metallica was trying to send to me. This message was that I should be more evil so I would not burn in a lake of fire. And thirdly, it is about the sad fact that people only become true and real when they are faced with tragedy. Here are the lyrics to track four of Metallica's Black Album. This one is called "The Unforgiven." Please enjoy.

VISION OF A MENTAL PATIENT

New blood joins this Earth, and quickly he's subdued
  through constant pained disgrace, the young boy learns their rules
    with time the child draws in, this whipping boy done wrong
      deprived of all his thoughts, the young man struggles on
        and he's known, a vow unto his own, that never from this day
his will they'll take away, What I've felt, what I've known
  never shined through in what I've shone, never be never see
    won't see what might have been, what I've felt, what I've known
      never shined through in what I've shone, never free, never me
        so I dub the unforgiven
          they dedicate their lives to running all of his
he tries to please them all, this bitter man he is
  throughout his life the same, he's battled constantly
    this fight he cannot win, a tired man they see no longer cares
      the old man then prepares to die regretfully
        that old man here is me, what I've felt, what I've known
          never shined through in what I've shone, never be never see
won't see what might have been, what I've felt what I've known
  never shined through in what I've shone, never free never me
    so I dub the unforgiven, you labeled me, I'll label you
      so I dub the unforgiven

For my first few days at Solomon's, I was in the temporary unit. They would send me to the main psyche ward where (as previously stated) I would get to meet the best people on the face of the Earth.

The first friend I would make in Solomon's was an African fellow by the name of Harvey S. Harvey had been pent up in this ward for a few years at my time of admittance. Despite his troubles, Harvey would always keep an upbeat attitude. The best part about being in a psyche ward other than the people is when you earn the privilege to go outside and smoke. On my first night there, I walked out onto the patio area to light one up. When I noticed Harvey, he was sitting a few feet away from me. I decided to approach him. Harvey quickly turned his head at this point and then when he looked at me, he said "You just probed me." I said, "What do you mean?" Then he said to me "Ted, you will be okay, if you could get a badge." Remember that statement it will be important later!

Some time passed by and I would meet some more people. I would play cards with Chris L., Tony F., and John D. I made friends with my close friend Deb Q. I remember playing Uno with Deb and my sister Jill when she would visit me. Incidentally, the staff was aware of some of the details of my obstacles, which were posed to me in relation to the primary goal.

My friends in Metallica continued to visit me in the past and they continued to humiliate me for reasons of subconscious love. As my dementia got worse, all I wanted to do was sleep so that I could avoid the terrors of this tragic reality. The staff kept trying to keep me out of bed so that I would become functional again. It got to the point that I would go into the bathroom and shove my fingers down my throat so I would vomit. I would then show the staff my vomit and they would allow me to return to bed. After a while, this wouldn't work on them anymore. So, they had me drinking broth out of a cup to prevent me from throwing up. I would soon get hungry and eat again. Therefore, I was forced to stay awake during the daytime.

I was always looking forward to bedtime and the mornings were the worst part of the day. Due to my habit of force vomiting, my insides would become used to this and vomiting would become common for years, until the day I would get sober in November 1996. I became unable to shower and my personal hygiene became horrid. I smelled like body odor and I was so isolated that I wouldn't speak to a soul for quite a while. About three and a half months into my stay, my personal subconscious would kick in and one morning, I got up, took a shower, shaved off my stubble, put on some clean clothes, and ate breakfast. After breakfast, I was hanging out with Tony F. and a few others. Tony had a small box of raisin bran and he was picking out the raisins one by one and popping them into his mouth. I mustered out a slight chuckle for the first time in months. Later on that day, the staff got John D. to ask me to play cards with him so that I would feel better. We played a couple rounds of rummy 500 and I started to feel even better.

I was to switch rooms and I got to be with two new roommates, Ron and Tom. I was still in bed for a good part of the day, but at least I was somewhat improving. Before I knew it, Ron, Tom, and I started to play rummy 500 every night. I was always in last place, but I didn't care, because at least I had some new friends and I was getting better. Tom had a bottle of peppermint schnapps snuck in and we enjoyed a couple of drinks over a game of cards on this occasion.

Later on, we were enjoying a slight buzz in the hallway and we knew we had succeeded in drinking some contraband. There was a beautiful girl there named Kerry W. Kerry was a troubled girl and she was quite inflicted with mental illness. Nevertheless, she was as cute as a button and I would soon find out that she had a crush on me.

As Tom, Ron, and I stood in the hallway, Kerry walked up to me and looked into my face with an ear to ear smile and said to me "I like you!" Tom suggested that I told her that I was back with my ex-girlfriend Alice, so I did. Nevertheless, wherever I walked that night, Kerry was less than two steps behind me. Tom began to laugh and sing "Me and My Shadow." I was still struck with a harrowing reality, but at least I knew that I was appreciated by some people.

The next few days were bearable, but soon, I would be saddened once again. Bob Stevens visited me in a parallel time flux. He had been watching me a few months earlier when I was in the T.V. room, staring down at my legs thinking about them being cut off from bottom to top, over and over again forever. Bob was extremely saddened to see me suffer like this. He let out a couple of light sobs, and then he looked at me with an expression of sadness and slight embarrassment, and he began to cry. It wasn't easy, but Bob showed me he was and always will be my friend.

Soon, I realized that I must be brave and leave Solomon's, so I could achieve the seemingly impossible and be the victor once again. Something was taking shape in my personal subconscious and it was equalizing with the collective subconscious. I knew subconsciously that I would eventually overcome these insurmountable odds and guide the world to universal contact.

I continued to receive death threats from time-altered visitations, as well as receive more messages on television and I knew this shit was real. One day towards the end of my stay, I was watching MTV and a video came on and despite the misery I was going through, watching this video and hearing the words to this song was a completely wonderful experience. I now present to you the lyrics to this song. This is Toad the Wet Sprocket's "Walk on the Ocean." Please enjoy.

We spotted the ocean, at the head of the trail
where are we going, so far away?
Somebody told me, this is the place
where everything's better, and everything's safe
walk on the ocean, step on the stones
flesh becomes water, wood becomes bone
half an hour later, packed up our things
said we'd send letters, and all of those things
and they knew we were lying, but they smiled just the same
seemed they'd already forgotten we'd came
walk on the ocean, step on the stones
flesh becomes water, wood becomes bone
now back on the homestead, where air makes you choke
people don't know you, trust is a joke
don't even have pictures, just memories to hold
grows sweeter each season, as we slowly grow old

After this wonderful experience, I would receive another anonymous message of reversed negativity. Things became difficult again, but I was determined and I continued to persevere. After I had been a mental patient for five and a half months, I felt well enough to contemplate a discharge from this unit and reenter the outside environment. Finally, it was agreed upon that I would be released from the psyche ward. I took a few temporary passes and attended some outside AA meetings. Halfway through the month of June 1993, I would go back home.

The day of discharge came. I packed my things and prepared to leave the unit for good. About ten minutes before my father showed up to take me home, I began to look at the clock and I wondered if I would die on this day. Despite this fear, the ride home was surprisingly relaxing. From time to time, I would look around myself in suspicion, but nothing happened. I got home, blew out a sigh of relief and I felt safe.

I was to turn twenty years old in about a month from this point in time and it would be another three years before I would finally get sober. The first thing I did when I got out was to get drunk with the guys. Roland noticed that I was drinking a lot "even for me" so he told me to slow down. However, I continued to toss back beers at an accelerating pace. This might have been the only night of my life when I actually needed to get drunk, so I did. I got home and got into bed without my father knowing a thing.

A day later, Dennis came to pick me up at my house and we were off to hit a small beer party. I ended up getting drunk and stoned with some friends who were very glad to see me. On this night, my father would catch me and he would reprimand me for what I had done. I went to bed drunk and I considered calling Dave St. Armand (who had already gotten sober) and ask him about attending an AA meeting with him. Dave had been sober for some time at this time. So, I figured I would give this AA thing a try.

The next day came and Dave was to pick me up for a meeting. He introduced me to two friends who I would grow very close to over the next couple of years. This would be Gary C. and Stanley B.

We hit a meeting on Hildreth Street in Lowell, which was just across the street from my old place on Eleventh Street. When I walked into this meeting, I saw Tom, my roommate from Solomon's. I walked over to Tom, smacked him on the back and said hello. At this point, the meeting was already underway, so everyone there immediately told me to shush. Suffice it to say, I was slightly embarrassed. To be honest with you, I was not serious about AA at this time, but I did commence to learn, that I could go out and not drink or drug and still have a good time. This would set up the foundation I needed for when I finally got sober in 1996.

Meetings with Dave, Gary, and Stanley became commonplace for me. I would drink one day and be sober the next. Sure, I would get a month together or a few weeks together at certain points, but I was still not properly motivated. Anyhow, I would go to Dunkin Donuts with my AA friends and once a week we would eat dinner at George's restaurant, on Broadway Street. George's has since gone out of business, which was unfortunate for the four of us.

Just prior to my discharge from Solomon's, I began to attend Lowell Adult Day Treatment (L.A.D.T.) where I would get to meet many more good people. I would meet the woman who would be my clinician. This woman's name is Victoria Buckley and she would carry me through the next few years, which were the toughest years of my life. I would soon love her like a mother.

Despite the fact that I was taking better care of myself, at least more so than when I was at Solomon's, my appearance was still not very good for obvious reasons. I had gained some weight due to all the months when I was stagnant and non-functional. You must understand that my appearance wasn't important to me, because I had much bigger problems to deal with.

L.A.D.T. and AA were both good influences on me at this duration, but the only method I knew of was to drown my sorrows in a bottle of liquor, which eventually wouldn't do the trick for me anymore.

I would tell Victoria a good amount of the gory details concerning the perpetual burnings and stabbings that I thought I was going to experience for an eternity. Some of the things I told her were so horrific that tears sometimes welled up in her eyes. I will not get into a thorough display of the tortures I was forced to deal with, because it would take too long and the premise of my vision must be further elaborated on.

I told Victoria what they had done to me and my ex-girlfriend and this would shock Victoria. She was not prepared to hear something so evil and it upset her to see me like this. Once I had told her a few other things, she looked at me with a sympathetic face and she said to me "I have never heard anything like that before!" At this point, Victoria and I would subconsciously connect, and the two of us would team up and become the prime moral force against the realities of Earthen uncompromising evils.

Around this time, just after my discharge from Solomon's, I would put on my brave face and rejoin Roland. Things were rocky between the other members of Deallegiance, so Roland and I decided we would form another band and call it Malicious Intent.

As always, my life was a difficult balancing act between music, drinking, AA, L.A.D.T., and survival, of course. Soon, my father found a pack of rolling papers in the chair of our living room and once again, I would be kicked out of the house. My father had remarried by this time and my stepmother agreed that the best way to help me would be to teach me self-reliance. Of course, they had no idea of what I was faced with, because if they had, we might have reached a compromise.

The meetings, practices, parties, and survival tactics were in full swing by this time and my personal subconscious was correctly and proportionately dripping down into the collective subconscious of the world society.

So, I had to make a decision and find a place to live, fast! The Malicious Intent idea was not yet working out, so I temporarily joined forces with Bob Stevens and form another Manifest. This new version of Manifest included Bob and me, of course, as well as Steve Stryker or Dan Ducharme on drums, and a local guitar dude by the name of Mike Delong. I was very pleased with the material Bob was writing at this time. It was shockingly simple, yet deceivingly tricky at the same time. I could read Bob's archetype, because it was attached to the riffs he was creating. It was very interesting, to say the least. Soon, I would slightly enhance some of Bob's writings and things were looking good between Bob and me. You see, quality is more important than quantity. Therefore, just because Bob possessed a more basic type of progression it didn't mean that his songs were anything less than outstanding.

On the night I was kicked out of my home, Bob let me stay with him at his grandparent's house in Dracut, as we tried to figure out how I would assess the situation and decide what I was to do. All of a sudden, the answer popped into our conscious minds. I would temporarily live with Bob's brother Bill, who was living with our other friend Phil at their place in Lowell. I was far from rich at the time, but I still had somewhat sufficient funds. So, I paid Bill and Phil a few weeks worth of rent and the 24/7 partying was about to commence. I would avoid AA for a while, because I was actually having fun, although it seemed that I was faced with an evil hell. The parties at this new place for me were insane. Some nights you couldn't even walk across the apartment, because there were wall to wall sleeping and snoring people all over the floor!

One particular night, this kid Armand was playing trapeze on the telephone wires outside of our back porch. I recall hanging with Dennis on the second story of this three level high rise and as we were just standing there shooting the shit we began to hear thunderous trampling up on the third floor, which was where Matt Kulesza, his sister Joy, and their mother lived at the time. Anyhow, the trampling continued for a few moments, when all of a sudden for about three minutes straight about 1,000 empty beer bottles came crashing down onto the grassy back yard of this insane establishment. At this point, I turned to Dennis, and I looked him in the face, and said to him "Dennis, I have been waiting for this moment all of my life and it has finally come, Dennis, it is raining beer!"

Later that night, I was smoking a bone with Bob in Bill's bedroom and we began to notice that the weed we were smoking smelled like chocolate. The dudes in the next room thought that we were baking a cake or something. So, we all got high and enjoyed the smell of Nestles Tollhouse Cookies, to boot.

Even later on, in this prestigious evening (more like the middle of the night) I reached the point of a drunken stupor. My subconscious was kicking in with an inner violence and I wanted revenge right there and then. Bob was with me and so was our friend Mike D. I said to the two of them "Let's go outside and kill the first person we see!" There must have been some subconscious awareness within Bob's mind, because he knew exactly what to say. So, as I stared at him wide eyed like Igor from Frankenstein, Bob said to me "Ted, they would like that!" Mike was looking at me, too, and he asked me if I was fucking serious. Anyhow, they told me they would smoke a bone with me when they got back and that managed to settle my intensity. I must have really been loony on this night, because Mike seemed scared and he is a guy who doesn't scare easy.

Mike and Bob soon returned and they smoked that bone with me for a nightcap or should I say a morning-cap, because we had partied right into the next day.

I ended up sleeping for a long time after this night was over. When I woke up, I saw Brian Cote in a parallel time frame. You see, the night before I kept talking about how I wanted to fuck this girl Lorraine. When I was in mid-stupor, I had apparently informed Brian of this fact quite a few times. So, Brian had been telling me, that all I talked about last night was chocolate weed and that I wanted to fuck Lorraine.

So, as I rubbed out my eyes and awakened the following morning, I was face to face with Brian who was in a parallel time flux. Brian started to laugh and he told me about the language of the mad (which I was not aware of at the time) and then he asked me if I ever stared into a half-filled glass of water. Due to my primitive knowledge at the time, I said to Brian "What the hell are you talking about?" Brian began to laugh even harder and then he disappeared and reappeared even closer to me. At this point, Brian was laughing hysterically and I would follow suit. Brian disappeared again and then he reappeared even closer to me. At this point, we completely lost it as Brian raised his fist and shouted "Ted, fuck Lorraine!"

Now that I was in a good mood, I got off of the couch and commenced to walk to L.A.D.T., which was only a block away. When I got there, Victoria saw me and she said to me "Well, it is twelve noon, it appears that you have gotten up early today." My personal subconscious was strong at this time, and I told Victoria that I felt safe, and that I would be okay. She was pleased to hear me say this, but she was also concerned because she knew I had been indulging in some heavy drinking as well as some other acts of mischief.

It was October of 1993 and L.A.D.T. was to throw a nighttime Halloween party. On the night of this party, I left the party at Bill and Phil's place and headed to a sober party for once. I saw a friend there named Tom B., who I sometimes went to Celtic games with. I told Tom that my friends and I liked to play Mortal Combat and hockey, on Bill's Sega system over a few beers and a few bones. It was good to be at a sober party, because beforehand I was on a two-week binge and I needed to come back down to Earth.

L.A.D.T. used to take us to the Lowell Y.M.C.A. on Tuesdays and Fridays to play basketball. It was very therapeutic and I had always enjoyed playing basketball ever since I was a young boy. We would play five on five full court games and it was a blast. There were many people who I played with over the years and to mention a couple, there was Dick H. and Sue W. Dick was an all-around solid player and Sue hustled up and down the court like there was no tomorrow. I had made good friends with Dick and Sue and they knew a little about the dementia I was having at this time. Sue actually showed up at one of my Malicious Intent performances, which was at the Front Row in Methuen New Hampshire.

Once I was out of money and Bill and Phil were tired of me stealing their beers, I was forced to ask my father if I could return home. He figured I must have learned something, so he would oblige and I was once again living in Dracut.

I began to hang with Gary, Dave, and Stanley on a regular basis at this point and we would hit a good amount of AA meetings. I was also still playing with Bob in the new version of Manifest. However, Roland was no dummy and he knew that he needed to get me back. Despite the fact that I loved the jam sessions with Bob and that I felt committed to him, Roland would turn on his charm and I would go for it, hook, line, and sinker.

I had an old amplifier in my garage, which needed some touching up. Roland and I made some adjustments and we applied some new tubes into this amplifier. Roland was smart and he said to me "Ted, I helped you fix this amplifier, so you should give me a chance, and come practice with me, and meet a new drummer I have found." I complied with Roland's request, but in my mind, I had decided to stay with Bob, because the new Manifest was kicking out some cool tunes and I was more than pleased with these results.

I went to jam with Roland and this new drummer kid and when I got there, I saw that this drummer and I were already acquainted. The practice session started off slow, but by the end, the three of us were in full swing. We ended up playing Flotsam and Jetsam's "Cradle Me Now" as well as a slew of old Deallegiance songs and a couple new Malicious Intent songs. Practices with Roland would improve with every session and Bob and I had just lost our new guitarist Mike Delong, so I would once again desert Bob for the achievement of the primary goal. The last factor as to this decision was that Roland and I had a great many songs already written and with Bob (although it was great), we only had about four songs completed.

I started dating a girl by the name of Jody J. at this point in time. She was very fun to be around and the two of us enjoyed each other's company. She attended one of these jam sessions with me, Roland, and our new drummer. Although we were under developed and sounded mediocre at best, she seemed to have enjoyed herself. Years later, Jody would comprehend the language of the mad and we would have some interesting discussions.

I had another argument with my father and once again, I would have to move out. I stayed with Roland's sister and her family for a few weeks. After that, I would move in with my high school friend, Rick R. Soon, the forces of evil would take another lunge at me and although I would be knocked down, I was never out for the count. I would get back up and fight fiercely as I always have throughout my life.

On the day I moved in with Rick the paranormal activities would enter another stage, but I would continue to stride forward with my insane love for world morality. I was determined to be victorious and nothing on Earth was going to stop me! My conscious mind would fall into the depths of self-doubt, as my personal subconscious would strengthen in surety by means of collective connections.

Things got really intense when we decided to throw a party and a huge fight would break out during this party. Rick and I received a threatening phone call, but due to subconscious factors, we handled this with ease. The fight eventually broke out and fists were flying everywhere. I punched someone in the face and this innocent kid would get me back later when I was too drunk to walk. The fight ended and so did this night. We had passed through a gateway to a higher cause.

I was once again threatened after this occurrence and I thought that I might be living the last peaceful night of my life because I was to enter a perpetual hell. The evildoers were telling me, that they would get me in the past, but this was not to be. Rick, some friends, and I went out to the old Bickford's restaurant on Drum Hill in Chelmsford on this night and I had ended up surviving this night.

I wrote a song on my bass in this general duration and I called it "Fortress!" You see, I was in a fortress of prime significance at this time and when I named this song, I consciously sensed no reason to name it as such. So, I must have done this subconsciously, because years later I understood this relationship.

It got to the point when I had to show the evildoers that I would fight them, so I decided to make a blunt and courageous stand. I grabbed Rick's machete and I screamed out into the Lowell night, that I was willing to take them on. I then sliced the outer edge of my forearm, but nothing came of this situation.

We received a phone bill with long distance calls from all over the world. The threats were relentless, as I continued to deal with this terrorizing ordeal. On the last night of this stay with Rick, I blacked out and I had taken a slight over dose of medication. When I woke up, I realized, that Rick's girlfriend had scalped my hair (and yes, I am sure it was her). The next day, I was with some friends and I mustered out the words, "Take me to Solomon's!"

Soon, I would visit Victoria and she was very concerned for my well-being. She knew that I was misbehaving and that something had to be done. I entered Victoria's office and I sat down. She asked me how I was and I said "Bad." The more Victoria looked at me, the more concerned her facial expressions became. She began to suggest that I stayed at the hospital for a few days. For reasons of survival, I was against this request. The staff of L.A.D.T. would trick me and call for the ambulance without my knowing it. Once the ambulance showed, I said "What the hell?" I decided to comply. I was then admitted at the former Lowell General Shed Building Psyche Ward.

Once I was in this ward, I was both fearful and bored in unison. Victoria came to visit with me after a few days and she kidded me about my being scalped. I must have had the shortest haircut of my life other than when I shaved my head. My hair looked okay though, because I had a staff person at the Shed Building touch it up. Anyhow, it would soon be suggested, that I enter the Tewksbury State Hospital Psyche Ward. My personal subconscious would then kick in, and I decided to leave the hospital, and decline the Tewksbury suggestion. I would soon get my head together, leave the ward, and strive forward for the achievement of the primary goal.

Roland picked me up on my day of discharge and I told him about my new song called "Fortress." At this point in time, Roland and my friends became more concerned for my well being. Malicious Intent would be put on the back burner for some time.

After about a week of being back in the outside world, things did improve, although they couldn't get much worse. I was visited by Victoria when she was a teenager, as the older Victoria looked at us in a state of laughter. The young Victoria punched me in the arm and jokingly made a funny noise as she hit me. I told her of this and she became worried, but she did not realize that this was a good thing.

I once again started to attend AA meetings with Dave, Gary, and Stanley. And just like Victoria, they would carry me through this trying time. It was at this point when the four of us would eat at George's restaurant every weekend after our meeting ended. Despite the fact, that I was still drinking, it was growing lesser and lesser and it wouldn't be long until I would seriously chase sobriety. I was beginning to see the AA way and I noticed that these people always seemed willing to lend a helping hand.

Roland and I quickly decided that we shouldn't keep Malicious Intent on the back burner for too long, thus we decided to seek a new drummer. John had committed himself to his other band, Out Cold. However, John was willing to fill in until we acquired a new drummer. Roland and I put out an advertisement and soon Malicious Intent drummer Dan Desharnais would come and watch myself, Roland, John, and a guitarist who was with us for a short while by the name of Paul Normandin play.

Dan showed up to check us out and Roland introduced him to me and the rest of the band as we prepared to play. We played a song or two, but it was when we played our original "Misguided Warrior" when Dan's face would light up. At this moment, Roland and I could tell that Dan was interested in us. Practice ended, so Roland, Dan, and myself hung out together for the first time.

A couple of days later, Roland called me on the phone and he was ecstatic. I told him to calm down and he proceeded to tell me that we had hit the jackpot, because he had watched Dan play and to put it mildly, Roland was extremely impressed with Dan. Soon, Paul Normandin would leave the band and we would acquire my good friend Paul Leary on lead guitar. It was bad to lose Paul N. because of his positive attitude, but Paul Leary was more experienced and the chemistry with him was terrific.

Things were better for me now and I was attending L.A.D.T. on a regular basis. Needless to say, Victoria was pleased with my improvement. Remember, Victoria was like a mother to me and she loved her profession. It always pleased her to see any of her clients do well.

Unfortunately, things were rough between me and my father. Due to my horrific realities and my drinking, I was becoming quite the freeloader. This was very tough on me, because some of my friends like Dan for instance didn't know me when I was well, thus they were not aware of what I was really like. It was also painful, that I was all alone to deal with such things with no outside help other than Victoria, of course.

Soon, I was once again faced with perpetual death. There were four women who I had a romance with and they appeared in front of me in a parallel time flux. They commenced to cry profusely, because it once again looked as if I were to be defeated. Once again, my personal subconscious was strengthening and dripping into the collective realm, thus leading to my fabrication of the mind galactic vortex. The more the evildoers fucked with me, the more fucked they would become. I had again managed to overcome another obstacle, which was trying to block me from the primary goal.

I was now very wary of my drinking problem, but it was hard not to drown my sorrows in a bottle. Although I wasn't able to put any time together, I had begun to love AA and I would pay attention as I continued to make real, yet feeble attempts at a sober life. I became confused with my life and I would temporarily leave Malicious Intent due to a short-lived hospital stay. When I got out, the guys found me and asked me to come to practice. So I did.

When I showed up at practice, the guys were happy to see me. We turned on our equipment and began to play. For some reason, I was playing my bass better than ever during this particular session, and my fellow members looked at me in approval; they said they were glad to have me back.

I got along well with Roland and Dan, but I must say that at this time, Paul and I were becoming really good friends and his brother Joe is a riot. Little did I realize that I was in for a really good time and I would soon literally become the happiest man on the face of the Earth! Paul had learned all of our songs, Dan was tight and mistake free, Roland was on the ball as usual, and I wasn't too shabby myself. Malicious Intent was about to kick some serious ass!

Performances became commonplace, we were gigging every week and sometimes twice a week. We were a regular at the Front Row in Methuen New Hampshire. Although we had not yet hit the Boston metal scene, we were gaining quite the reputation. Our shows were always packed no matter where we were to perform.

Another nightclub besides the Front Row we would play at was "The Underground" which was on the border of Lowell and Chelmsford. A couple of my friends came to watch us perform one night at The Underground. There was this cute small petite girl named Deb, who I often hung out with. She was accompanied by one of her friends and Dave St. Armand showed up on this night as well. Our small group would hang out on this festive occasion. Deb likely did not realize that we were connecting with each other by way of the personal and collective subconscious, but we really were. Really!

When we got off stage, Deb told me she was pleased with our performance. ThenDave, Deb, her friend, and I went out to shoot some pool. It was no coincidence when Dave began to sing Death Angel's "A Seemingly Endless Time" as we approached Deb's car. Furthermore, when Debbie turned her car on, the very same album started to play on the tape deck to her car stereo system. Once again, a few friends and I would go on an hell ride and bang our heads to "A Seemingly Endless Time."

The gigs at the Front Row grew more fun and wild with every performance. I have many fond memories of this part of my life. Soon, things would be good, and I mean really good. It came to the point that our gigs were going so well that we began our plans to release an album.

At one particular show, there was an Elvis impersonator and some girl who kept dancing all over the place as if she wanted it to rain. Paul tried to get the Elvis guy and the dancing girl together, but unfortunately, there was no chemistry there. We had a lot of laughs over this and we soon left to get high and hit a restaurant.

Paul was a lightweight when it came to marijuana. He took two hits and then he couldn't tell his right from his left. Once we had our ceremonial match out, we were off to stuff our faces. Paul and I hopped in his car so we could follow the others. As he turned the key to his ignition, he turned and looked at me with bloodshot eyes and said "That was cool, huh?" Then, he drove his car a quarter mile in the wrong direction. Once he noticed that the rest of the crew was going the other way, Paul said, "I'm going the wrong way am I not?" I responded "Yes, but I figured that you knew what you were doing and that you were taking a shortcut." So, Paul made a U turn and floored it until we caught up with the others.

About twelve of us entered a nice restaurant in New Hampshire. Dan's girlfriend Jeanine was much more understanding

VISION OF A MENTAL PATIENT

of my troubles than the others. She is smart; she could read my face and tell that I had been through a lot in the past. She was aware that I never had that much money at this time. So, she did what she usually did and bought me a sandwich. Jeanine was a good friend and I heard that she and Dan are married today. Dan is a lucky guy!

The entire crew walked into this restaurant and we were all baked out of our gourds. We also had the munchies, so we were in the right place. We told the head waitress "party of twelve"; she obliged and said "ten minutes." Our drum technician, Andy, decided to be funny; he hit the pay phone in front of the restaurant, and he called the very same restaurant we were at. We watched the head waitress pick up the phone and Andy asked her if the table for twelve was ready yet. As soon as we saw the head waitress's reaction, we all burst out laughing. Eventually, she caught on to this and she let out a small chuckle and smiled at us with an expression, which seemed to say "good one!"

We got to our table, I told Jeanine what I wanted and she was happy to oblige. We couldn't stop joking and laughing as we stuffed our faces. Then I noticed a party sitting across from us. They had overheard the conversation we were having in relation to our performance that night. I overheard one of them saying, "Are they famous?" One of them kept pointing at me wondering why I looked so familiar. The reason for my being familiar to this person was due to the strengthening of the galactic mind vortex and the collective subconscious, which was occurring on this night.

We finished stuffing our faces, left the restaurant, smoked a little more marijuana, and finally we called it a night. Roland, Paul, Dan, and I all looked at each other in approval. We had played well on this night and on top of that, we were having a ball!

A week or so later, we were at band practice and some guy was there handing out flyers to all of the bands that played at our studio. Roland took one from him and he seemed interested in what it said. There was a larger building a block away renting out studio space at a cheaper price and the rooms were larger. Roland went to check out this new studio building and when he returned, he said that we should move there. I was against this idea at first. However, once I saw this studio and its spaciousness, I complied with Roland's idea. We moved in within a matter of days and this was when the good times came a rolling.

We had moved into this new studio and we had lugged all of our equipment across Downtown Lowell. I was pleased with the size of our jam room and the acoustics of this room. The fridge was always filled with beer. We had the company of many cool people and there was furniture to boot. Others had learned of this new studio and soon Bob and Steve S. would move in one floor below us, on the second floor. They had a large television with no cable, a fridge for food and beer, and like us, they had the company of some really awesome people.

Plans for a Malicious Intent album was now well underway. We contacted West Sound Studios, which was located in Londonderry New Hampshire. We also conversed with our record label, Judahya Records. This newfound ambition made us a better band. However, my drinking problem was upsetting my fellow band members as well as those others who cared for me. On one occasion, Paul's girlfriend Brenda physically prevented me from drinking an Icehouse.

My so-called delusions would change from delusions of horror to delusions of grandeur. Metallica was time travelling and hanging out with me. I was especially bonding with Lars. In Bob's studio, the walls were covered with Playboy Playmates who I would hang out with in the parallel time flux for the next few memorable months.

I developed a habit of drinking at the old Highland Tap on Westford Street in Lowell. I made many good friends there, but I was also visited there by evildoers, incognito. Across the Street was Captain John's, which was a nicer place, but I preferred the tap, because they sold one dollar drafts. Despite the fact that I was doing well, my personal hygiene needed improvement due to the past, of course. Bob was not afraid to inform me of this problem. He was concerned for my well-being, and his intentions were always good.

I became the delivery guy for Bob's band and my band. It was only fair, because they were getting me drunk and stoned for free, not to mention that when I was sent to Taco Bell, I would get to eat as much as I wanted. I usually hit Store 24 or the nearest liquor store. I needed the exercise anyway.

If I was to tell you every detail of the good time I had over the next few months, it would take too long. However, I will tell you that I was time travelling from the future and I was killing the evildoers. For the first time in a long time, I once again loved the members of Metallica. Kirk was always busting his ass to get me to stop having my band, but at this point, we achieved a plane of a happy medium. However, prior to this good time I was now experiencing, it got to the point that I had driven Kirk nearly insane. Together with the members of Infanticide, he was working to either make me a Satanist (for my own good) or to make me stop.

Kirk visited me in the parallel at Grover's and I played the opening riffs to the Malicious Intent original "Beginnings." Kirk was dazzled and impressed, to say the least, and at this point, his fear and concern for me would double. A member of Infanticide who was with him told Kirk, "There is no way you will ever get him to stop; didn't you see that song he just played?" Kirk, in absolute desperation, told this member of Infanticide that they had one more chance to get me to stop. This Infanticide member looked into my face and said, "You have driven him crazy!" At the time, I considered this a victory, but later, it would appear as a defeat. In the long run, this situation would benefit both me and Kirk.

I was visited by the lead singer and rhythm guitarist of Infanticide in the parallel time flux. I was playing the Deallegiance and Malicious Intent original song "Lost in Time." This kid looked at me as a gust of wind blew through our hair. He looked at me in approval as a smile of sinful satisfaction creased his face and he said, "Lost in time?" I said "Yes" and then this kid (Matty B) shook my hand with the firmest handshake I ever felt in my life. Matty and I knew that we had them at this point.

A while before (and after) this, I was visited by Lars and Jason of Metallica and Lars said to me, "We've come here to talk to you." They were trying to tell me to be happy and let it go. I admit that I had no idea of their good intentions at this point, thus I viewed them in the wrong way. Lars did his best to persuade me to stop. I started to cry and I said, "There is no way I will ever stop." Jason became very compassionate at this point and he said, "I don't blame him, look at how good he has become." Anyhow, when I was in the middle of my so-called delusions of grandeur at the new studio, the good times were rolling along. I have a fond memory of Lars and me hanging out as James was completely frustrated with me. As James clenched his teeth and threw his legs about in a spastic fashion, Lars smiled at me. I then asked Lars "What did I do?" Lars shrugged his shoulders and said "Nothing." I then told James to fuck off as Lars continued to smile at me. I asked Lars again, "Why is he mad at me?" Lars' smile increased into a euphoric expression and he said to me "Because he loves you." James became emotional and said, "I do love him." James was mad at me, because I kept putting myself in danger.

James was irate with me due to my subconscious masochism. It seemed that he was at the end of the line with me, but that glint of hope would always shine in his eyes. He was my friend and he was determined to help me.

On a different note, within this time frame, I had recently moved into an apartment on Queen Street, in Lowell. Many incredible things had happened in this apartment of mine. I had many visitors from the parallel and it was a trying and emotional experience for me. Anyhow, I mentioned that I used to live on Queen Street, so that I could further prove the validity of my and now our tapping into the collective subconscious. This song is by Dio and it is appropriately titled "Evil on Queen Street!" Please enjoy.

Spent the night on the road and never saw the miles go
running away, I've got to get free from myself
now stories were made to be told
and here's the one that I "know"
Oh, I can't hide it anymore, there's evil on Queen Street
Some evil up the road, I saw the house in the dark
It seemed to say "come touch me"
I've got a heart, open the door to my soul
Climb to the top of my stairs and look out my windows
I can be your wishing well, there's no evil on Queen Street
Let me in, I can warm in the heat of your fire
It's no permanent sin to be bad, if you're sorry
Let me go, you're a promise that comes from a liar
I don't know if I can ever wish the evil away, hey
Struck a match in the dark, it screamed "no I love you"
Together we're strong, you always believed what I'd say, hey
But now the heat of a flame, starts me to remember
There's no evil, no more evil, no evil on Queen Street
Just smoke up in the air, no evil, no evil

When I was living on Queen Street, there was a woman who shared vital information with me. I told her many factors in detail. This woman was knowledgeable of many parallel existences. It has been over a decade since I have spoken to this woman and she might have dismissed the information I gave her, but over the years, our personal subconscious minds have been connecting. The time is coming when this woman would soon see her victimized friend, and she will become one of the happiest people in the world. I look forward to seeing her again and when I do see her, the two of us will celebrate victory.

Continuing on, Malicious Intent had completed the preparations for our album, which we decided to call *Mind Control*. We went to West Sound Studios and the recording sessions went very well. In a few weeks, we received 1,099 compact discs of our album. The night when we received these CDs was a memorable night. We signed 100 of them and we sold them to our closest friends; we also gave many of these CDs to famous bands. Dan gave Les Claypool of Primus a few and Roland gave the members of Flotsam and Jetsam a few. On the night we received our bundle of CDs, the Lowell University radio station WJUL played our new album in its entirety. We sold more than half of these CDs and then we made plans for a CD release party, which would take place in a large hall at the Gaelic Club in Lowell.

The night of the show came and we were to feature at this show. Two local bands called Mama's Tongue"and Gilius Thunderhead opened up for us on this occasion. Before I took the stage, I ran into some good friends I had not seen for a while. As the opening bands played, I sat with our band manager Bob H. at a table where we were selling our CDs. We sipped on cokes and cranberry juice, because Bob and I wanted to get sober together at this time.

Soon, this large hall was jampacked. I ran into my friend Mike F. in the men's room. He was happy for me and said "Ted, this is your night." This gave me a pleasant feeling seeing what I had overcome up to this point.

Dan Ducharme was there and he kept on asking me if I was staying sober. What a good kid he is, he was subconsciously trying to save my life. Our manager Bob H. and I must have sold about 200 CD's that night and we were more than pleased with the large turnout. On this night myself, Roland, Dan, and Paul would see to it, that we would give a good performance.

We took the stage and began to play. When we were about a third of the way through our first song, a huge mosh pit broke out. Of course, Bob Stevens would go wild again. This time Bob had much company in this mosh pit and we loved every minute of it. Bob's personal subconscious was entering his conscious on this night and he would further aid the pro primary goal viewpoint.

This was one of the most fun shows I ever played. I felt like I was Metallica on this night. There were a lot of people who were watching us only inches from the stage. I would have some quick twenty-second conversations between songs with a few dudes hanging out in front of me and watching me. After our last song, there were some cute girls asking us to play one more. I said to Roland that we should play our new song, "Time Travel," but we decided to do the professional thing and leave them wanting more.

Dan, Roland, and Paul were not very pleased with our performance on this night, but I knew we had accomplished something with this performance.

A week or so later, we were at band practice and my delusions of grandeur would abruptly turn back into delusions of horror. While we were playing our song "In Between," a woman who I had a romance with appeared in front of me in the parallel and she acted as if she wanted to betray me. This woman did not want to hurt me, but she needed to be cruel to be kind if you catch my drift. I would struggle through the rest of this song and when we were finished, I said that I needed to take a break. At this point, things became difficult again.

My experiences with Malicious Intent were most certainly more good than bad. I seldom had any resentment whatsoever against any of my bandmates. It would have been nice if they could have opened up a little more, but there was no way, because they simply were not aware of what I had been facing for some time at this point in time.

Once, when we were performing at the Front Row, we had not written out a set list. Hence, we would talk things over between songs. We all met by Dan's drum set as we conversed on what song to play next; we continued to talk things over and to my dismay, I was barely included in this short conversation. I asked what we were to play next and not one of them told me anything. So, I waited until Roland played the first two notes and then I kicked in. However, I was very angry and I considered leaving the stage at this point. This was the only time I was ever truly angry with my friends from Malicious Intent. However, I must apologize to Roland, Dan, and Paul for not paying my share in our album expenses and for pocketing some money which was supposed to be for the band. At this point, hopefully, the three of you can understand why I did some of the things I did.

I had one of those parallel conversations with Lars, just before our CD release party. I said to Lars, "I give you credit, you're one of the best ever." Then I asked Lars to return the compliment and he became tense and then he refused to oblige. After Lars saw our CD release performance, he said to me "After that show, I give you credit, you blew us away!" I was extremely proud of myself at this moment.

Times were tough and I would visit the Highland Tap more frequently. I ended up being grabbed by the throat by an evildoer one night at the tap. He backed off from me, just as my throat was about to puncture within. I left and sent some subconscious messages to the evildoers. I told them of the control factor and that I refused to be defeated. I would go home and toss back a few bottle of beer once things settled down for me on this night.

A week or so after this confrontation, I was back at the tap sucking back some dollar drafts when I met a woman there. We left, and went to another bar where I would run into the forces of evil again. I was killing them from the future and thus I was confronted.

When I was in the men's room of this establishment, two other kids about my age walked into the bathroom I was in. They harassed me, mentioning certain factors of dementia. I blew them off and got another beer. There was someone there I knew and I decided I would make the next move and confront this person. I told him that I knew what he was thinking and that I wasn't going to stop. He then said to me "Who are you and who are you here with?" I told him I was alone and then he said to me "Either you can leave now or we can have the police drag you out of here!" I decided to leave at this point.

As I was walking down the street to return to my apartment, I was stopped by a police cruiser. The cop asked me a few questions and then I told him I wanted to go home and sleep. He let me go and I commenced to walk back home.

When I hit Branch Street, I was confronted by three evildoers, threatening my life. I started to slowly walk away from this evil trio when one of them said to me "You better start running!" All I did was jog very slow, because subconsciously, I knew that I would win in the long run. I also knew that some of the words they had said to me were of connective proportions pertaining to their imminent defeat. Little did they realize the fact that they were making a crucial mistake! Remember, I only jogged very slowly and they could have easily caught me, but they didn't. Therefore, the control factor was in play and they were not very sure of themselves.

I got home and chugged a Budweiser when all of a sudden, the police drove by and they were flashing a light onto my windows. I was not frightened and thus I prepared myself for a physical confrontation. I turned off all of my lights, put my television by the window, turned it on, lit a cigarette, and watched T.V. all night. At this point, the Lowell police were out to get me. This is due to the fact that they were owned by certain forces of evil.

During this crazy night, I was reporting to my boss at the governmentorganization I work for (hint, hint). This man is my friend, but he had to criticize me for my overconfidence. I was fired and I felt like a complete failure. Moments later, I made up for my mistake and my boss and friend looked at me in approval and said "You're hired!" Then he suggested that I go back to this bar and show them I was still alive and thus scare the living daylights out of them.

The following evening, I returned to this bar, ordered a beer, and started to check out my surroundings. There was an evil girl there who had a relentless habit of insulting me. She smiled at me and came over to sit next to me. I began to question this bitch, and then she looked at me like the bitch she was, and she tried to deceive me. I abruptly interrupted her and said, "You just probed me, what if I can get a badge?" This was due to the control factor. Think back to what Harvey said to me on the smoking patio at Solomon's and you shall further catch the drift. I then said to her, "You just had four twitches and nearly shit your pants." She got a taste of her own medicine and I had now forced them to take me seriously! I finished my beer, showed her my middle finger, and went back home. I was cool as a cat.

Soon, I would see this evil girl and her partner in crime in a parallel realm. They were talking about things I was not consciously aware of at the time. They talked about this book and the "Big Boom" theory. The terror showed in their faces and their eyes were frozen to the core.

As I was watching them acting like this, I couldn't stop laughing. I decided to celebrate a battle won for the good guys. I hit the liquor store, picked up a case of Budweiser and a few nips, and I had a one-man party all night long!

Days later, I was being visited in the parallel by those who were supportive of my cause and thus were advocates of the pro-primary goal viewpoint. I saw some people whom I would meet in the future and I further strengthened my personal subconscious surety. Furthermore, I saw that the most in-depth concepts of magnetism were drawing the machine towards me and I was the ghost in the machine.

My drinking continued for a few more months following my twenty-third birthday in July 1996. By this time, I knew there was something going down in New York City. I had received messages from anonymous sources. There were a variety of reasons I needed to visit New York. I saved up some money and I devised a plan to visit this city so that I could achieve goals pertaining to this visionary mission. The day had come! I had saved up a good sum of money. I was now prepared to check out the situation in New York. It was a beautiful morning as I walked to the Lowell Bus and Train station. When I got there, I purchased a one-way ticket to New York and I awaited my turn to board the bus.

The bus came and I walked up its steps and proceeded to look for a seat. As I searched for a seat, I noticed a medium height blonde kid who looked like the son of one of my father's ex-girlfriends. I looked at this kid and said "Garin?" He responded "In rage?" (Garin in Drow is=in rage) I sat next to this kid and I had an impulse to ask him where he was from, and he answered me in a deep accent "I'm Russian." From this point on the two of us started a discussion.

We began to discuss relations between the United States and Russia, as well as some other world matters. We pondered on scientific concepts and I told him that I had some theories of my own. I could see n his face that he was more aware of who I was and what I was doing than I thought at first. We really hit it off and it seemed as if I had known him all of my life. When I told him I had some scientific theories, he showed interest, but I became intimidated because I was young and my theories were merely thoughts at this duration. So, I just told him that my theories had not developed yet and he smiled at me and let it go.

He then asked me if I had any political theories and I said, "No, not really." After all, I was only twenty-three years, thus my imagination and knowledge posed limits. He then mentioned the theory of development. So, I asked him "What's that?" He told me that this was my theory and I was now sure that the people he worked for were also advocates of the pro-primary goal viewpoint.

The conversation continued, we talked about American Presidents, primarily Ronald Reagan and John Kennedy. He seemed to think that everyone was fond of Reagan. I told him that I was not fond of Reagan and that there were plenty of Americans who would agree with me. I don't think he was very fond of Reagan, either, because it seemed like he was critical of him. As for John Kennedy, I said "Everyone likes him." My new Russian friend corrected me in the same manner I had corrected him in pertinence to Reagan and I accepted his view with an admirable respect.

I said to him that when Kennedy died, I believed they were crying in Moscow. My Russian friend then gave me the best compliment I ever received in my life. He said to me "No, Ted, they would be crying in Moscow if you died." My eyes welled up with tears at this moment, and I immediately fell in love with this prominent Russian. The only complement I ever got, which can rival that one was the time my friend Lucy told me that I had a nice dick!

We continued to converse as we neared the Boston bus depot, so he could go about his duties in Boston and I could catch the connecting bus to New York. In the last ten minutes of this conversation, I was fascinated by this Russian and I didn't say a word. So finally, he stopped talking and said "Don't you want to say something?" I said "No."

We reached the depot and we began to say our goodbyes. As he and I left the bus, I said to him "Be careful." A look of slight panic struck his face and he asked me "What do you mean?" I said "Don't worry, you'll be fine, just remember, you never know when you're going to run into an asshole, especially in this country!" A smile of relief smeared across his face and

VISION OF A MENTAL PATIENT

we went our separate ways.

I waited for the transfer bus to New York, bought a cup of coffee, and I pondered on the importance of what just happened, and what I must do. The bus pulled up and I got on board. This time, there were only a few people on my bus. I threw my headphones on and I relaxed. I was on my way to the Big Apple.

On the ride to New York, we passed Hartford Connecticut. I began to laugh when pondering on how far I had taken my vision up to this point in time. We passed through Harlem and heading to Manhattan. As I rode through this city, I was astounded by its size and beauty. I was also amazed at how many trees were planted in certain sections. The bus reached its destination and I got off.

I was in the heart of Manhattan and I began to walk. I noticed that there were some Hell's Angels members around as well as a slew of many different types of people from all walks of life. As I continued to walk, a businessman collided against me. I gave him a dirty look and I continued on walking. Then I crossed the street and someone yelled "Faggot" at me. I stopped at a Subway restaurant and I ate some lunch.

I left the restaurant and I proceeded to walk towards the shore, which I could see from time to time between all of the skyscrapers. I then began to use the language of the mad in order to direct myself. I did this by asking questions to myself and then reading street signs backwards. It worked perfectly! I ended up passing by the United Nations Building, went up the street and saw the Empire State Building, The Madison Square Garden, and the Waldorf Astoria Hotel. When I reached the Empire State Building, I stopped and lit up a smoke as I tried to contemplate my next move.

I was hoping to run into Metallica or some anonymous women who were pertinent to my cause. I continued to walk on past the Waldorf Astoria when a very familiar man walked up to me and said hello. This man worked for Metallica and I knew it subconsciously. He introduced himself to me and I told him that I had limited funds, that I needed to find a place to stay, and that all the hotels on this strip were an arm and a leg for one night's stay. This man then told me that I could get a room at the Y.M.C.A. for a reasonable price. I was aware that there was a bus station up the road a little further, so I told this man that I would be fine and that I didn't need his assistance. He said "Okay" and we went our separate ways.

As I continued to walk towards the bus station, I was called over by an African woman who looked like my friend Lorraine. It seemed as if she was not aware of what I was up to. So I told her I had no time to talk and I was on my way.

I was becoming overwhelmed because I was not prepared for the enormity of this city. I was discouraged and the sun was beginning to set. I reached the bus station and I walked up to one of the pay booths. I told the woman at the booth that I wanted to catch a ride to the Y.M.C.A. Then she asked me where the Y.M.C.A. was and I was surprised that she didn't know. You see, this city is huge!

As a last resort, I went to the payphone and I tried to call an anonymous source. The phone rang twice and then I learned that this number was now disconnected.

I went back to the booth and I asked for a ticket back to Lowell. The woman told me that there was no ride to Lowell until the morning. I asked for a ticket to Boston instead and the woman sold me a one way ticket. The ride home was boring and I was disappointed at the outcome of this trip. I fell asleep halfway back to Boston. I woke up and we were in Connecticut, so I asked the bus driver if I could use the bathroom since there was no bathroom in the bus. He said if I wasn't back in less than five minutes, he had to leave. I hurried to the restroom and I scooted back to the bus in two minutes flat. The bus dropped us off at South Station in Boston and I needed to get to North Station to catch the train back to Lowell. I struck a deal with a few strangers who were with me at South Station. We agreed to split a cab fare back to North Station.

We arrived at North Station, but there was no train back to Lowell until 6:45 in the morning and at this time it was just past midnight. The Dunkin Donuts across Causeway Street was 24/7. So I went inside and sauced coffee after coffee until the following morning. If I wanted a cigarette, I would cross the street and light up.

In the days prior to this trip, I had some clairvoyant dreams that came true during this trip. I had a dream of a man handing me a magazine on Causeway Street in Boston. This magazine featured two women I knew on the cover. When I went out for a smoke on this night, the same man in my dream handed me the very same magazine I had dreamed of. Carl Jung would have been fascinated with that one.

The other dream I had was of a new parking garage built in Boston. However, in my dream, this parking garage was in New York. But I did see a parking garage in Boston identical to the one in my dream on the day of my New York trip.

As I sat at the table in this Dunkin Donuts, I kept falling asleep. The staff would continually wake me up and inform me there was no sleeping allowed in this restaurant. I played the trick of resting my head on my upright forearms, so that I could fool them. I managed to sleep for about 45 minutes. Finally, 6:45 rolled around and I caught the train back to Lowell.

I returned to my apartment, which was constantly being altered due to the primary goal. However, on this occasion, everything was in the correct place. I went to bed and I slept late into the next day.

I had been kicked out of Malicious Intent because they didn't know my mission and to them, I merely appeared as an ass. Roland showed up at my place and he asked me to rejoin the band. I obliged, and I would play one more show with Malicious Intent. Roland helped me to clean up my apartment and he gave me some clothes, which he no longer needed. Roland asked me of a few things he was aware of as to the purpose of my previous actions, which would strengthen my ambition to stride towards the primary goal. We had a few practice sessions which went well. Dan gave me a couple of Sam Adams for me to take home for a nightcap on our last night of practice as a unit. We were booked to play at the L.A. Ballroom in Downtown Lowell. The show went well despite the fact that my amplifier failed for a couple of moments in the middle of the set list. After the show was over, Roland shook my hand and told me I had done well and that it was good to have me back. More attempts on my life were taking place, thus I would be faced with a crossroads. Malicious Intent split up for a while, but as far as I was concerned, Malicious Intent was over for me. Although I was not fully aware of it, I was about to get sober and I still haven't had a drink for about thirteen years now.

It was nearly wintertime and a very cold day when I met up with Dave St. Armand and headed out to a meeting. Dave came close to believing me in pertinence to my dementia and so called delusions of time parallel existences. I told him of an alternate future and many of the things that had happened to me. When I told him that we were in alternate time, he came very close to trusting me in what I was telling him. Due to certain factors, I gave Dave only limited data on this night. We got to the meeting and attended it. Afterwards, we went out to eat. I continued to attempt to convince him of the validity of my message.

People who I had known in the past were visiting me from the future. They were telling me about this book. Universal contact was being manifested as the collective subconscious became able to adhere to the whirlwind of the mind galactic vortex.

The day when my new life began had finally come. It was November 4, 1996, the first day of my newfound and continuous sobriety. The good time was long past and my life was once again a deadly game of survival. I drank my last beer at the tap and when I finished it, I couldn't help licking the glass for one final taste. My father would pick me up in the afternoon of this special day and we were off to Woburn where I would move into a large sober house.

On the day I moved into this place, I was in a seemingly bottomless pit of human misery. I had been fighting the evildoers fiercely. I was told by one of them that I would live in Billerica in the future and this would turn out to be true. I spent only one week at this sober house and then I began a stay at Choate Hospital Psyche Ward in Woburn, Massachusetts. While in this ward, I was suffering big time. In my mind, I could see myself being stabbed to death on a pentagram. I wanted to commit suicide, but I was too tough for that and it simply was not an option. I was spending a lot of time in bed and to my satisfaction, the staff was lenient with me, thus I was allowed to rest. From this ward, we would be driven to outside AA meetings and my dream clairvoyance was kicking in better than ever. Once again, my conscious mind was doubtful, but my personal subconscious was completely robust.

I was defeating the evildoers and my personal subconscious in connection to the collective subconscious was doing so due to the most in-depth and vast realms of the human psyche. In a matter of weeks, I would be discharged and I would take up residence with three other fellows in another (smaller) sober house, which was also in Woburn. However, I had experienced another hospital stint and although I was strong inside, I was a saddened and broken man. Here is a song which reminds me of what it is all worth. For the questions that the human race has been asking since the dawn of man, this is a Bee Gees song and it is called "How Can You Mend A Broken Heart?" Please enjoy.

I can think of younger days
when living my life was everything a man could want to do
I could never see tomorrow, but I was never told about the sorrow
And how can you mend a broken heart?
How can you stop the rain from falling down?
How can you stop the sun from shining?
What makes the world go round?
How can you mend this broken man?
How can a loser ever win?
Please help me mend my broken heart and let me live again?
I can still feel the breeze as it rustles through the trees
and misty memories of days gone by, we could never see tomorrow
no one said a word about the sorrow
And how can you mend a broken heart?
How can you stop the rain from falling down?
How can you stop the sun from shining?
What makes the world go round?
How can you mend this broken man?
How can a loser ever win?
Please help me mend my broken heart and let me live again

At my new residence, I was still spending a majority of my time in bed, and from time to time, I would cross the street to a roast beef restaurant to buy a soda and a sandwich. I felt that death was near and I had again peered over the boundaries of hell's purgatory.

My assigned case manager at the time was a nice man by the name of Raoul. Raoul would show up at my new residence

VISION OF A MENTAL PATIENT

and deliver me my medications, which I had been without for two weeks since I was discharged from Choate. I pleaded with Raoul to have me admitted some place so I could get my head together. I was soon admitted at the best psyche ward I ever was admitted to. This was the CREU unit at the M.M.H.C building in Boston. When I moved into this unit, I immediately bonded with many of the staff members and I made friends with even more awesome people.

A few weeks into my stay, my personal subconscious became extremely active. This subconscious activity caused me to enjoy myself despite the obstacles I was faced with. My three best friends at this CREU unit were staff members. Their names were Ron P, Tom K, and Larry F. I would especially hit it off with Ron. Ron and I used to constantly kid with each other and we must have played thousands of games of ping-pong. I would be in this unit for the next six months and Ron and I wouldn't say two serious words to each other the whole time. Ron was good at his job and he gave me what I needed, which was to laugh. On a typical night, we would hit the ping-pong ball back and forth and just laugh the whole time.

Soon, a very nice and attractive woman was admitted into this ward. She would give me vital information as to the pursuit of the primary goal. She would tell me of my future life and the happiness that I would achieve. Most importantly, we began to see that we would win! Here are some more lyrics, which are pertinent to my life and my vision. This song is about being in a psyche ward while inflicted with dementia. I hereby present track four to Metallica's Master of Puppets album. This one is called "Welcome Home" (Sanitarium). Please enjoy.

Welcome to where time stands still
no one leaves and no one will
moon is full, never seems to change
Just labeled mentally deranged
Dream the same thing every night
I see our freedom in my sight
No locked doors no windows barred
No things to make my brain seem scarred
Sleep my friend, and you will see
that dream is my reality
They keep me locked up in this cage
Can't they see it's why my brain says rage?
Sanitarium, leave me be, Sanitarium, just leave me alone
Build my fear of what's out there
Can I breathe the open air?
Whisper things into my brain
assuring me that I'm insane
they think our heads are in their hands
but violent use brings violent plans
keep him tied it makes him well
He's getting better, can't you tell?
No more can they keep us in
Listen damn it, we will win!
They see it right, they see it well
but they think this saves us from our hell
Sanitarium, leave me be, Sanitarium, just leave me alone
Fear of living on, natives getting restless now
mutiny in the air, got some death to do
mirror stares back hard, kill, it's such a friendly word
Seems the only way, for reaching out again

As time passed by at the CREU unit, I made friends with a number of clients as well as staff members. I remember on one of my last days there, Tom K. was speaking with me. I told him how I had been degraded and that I felt weird about it. Tom asked me "What's weird?" I didn't have the courage to tell him of my past horrors, but I do believe that Tom would have supported me regardless of what I told him. Tom is very smart and we did have some brief discussions on natural science. The CREU unit was a magical place, but it could never hold a candle to Dracut High School.

With roughly one month left in my stay at the CREU unit, it was decided that I would move into a halfway house in Billerica. This would be the Parker House where I would live for the next six years. I said my goodbyes to my friends from the CREU unit and as I left, my woman friend from the unit burst into tears because she knew that we would win in the end. I hopped in my case manager's car and we were off to Billerica.

It was June of 1997, and the first friend I would make at the Parker House was a lady by the name of Deb C. Deb and I watched the N.B.A. finals together between Chicago and Utah. Deb was rooting for Chicago, but I wanted to see Stockton and Malone take one from Jordan and Pippen. To my dismay, Chicago would continue their dynasty and earn a place in N.B.A. basketball history.

I became comfortable at the Parker House right away and I would get along well with both staff people and residents. I was surprised to find out that a woman named Julie who worked the night shift and eventually became program director was friends with Dan D. of Malicious Intent and his girlfriend Jeanine.

In December of this year, there was a Christmas party at the CREU unit. On the day of this party I took a train to Boston and attended this party. The woman with the vital information was there and at this crux, I was consciously aware that she held significant data and that she had been consciously aware of what was happening beforehand. When I was at this party, I kept taking peeks at her and to my surprise, she was quite distant. At the end of the party, she passed by me and said "Ted, we are doing what you told us to do." She left and then I would leave minutes later.

Ron from the CREU unit had told me to keep in touch with him and I really wanted to do so. However, I realized that I shouldn't involve him or his family with the dangers of my life. I let him go for the time being. It was a very good thing that the people at Parker House were just as nice as those at the CREU unit, because not keeping in touch with Ron was hurtful to myself. I did my chores at home every day and I would start to attend L.A.D.T. again. In a few years, I would be employed there.

Things were good on my first days back at L.A.D.T. even despite the fact that Victoria would not be my clinician this time around. On this tenure of mine, my new clinician was a lady I was already acquainted with. She is a very kind woman by the name of Ellie E. Ellie did very well with me, although she had to deal with my habits of skipping groups and joking around a bit too much.

There were many new faces for me to meet this time around, including my friend named Coolidge who was a descendant of former United States President, Calvin Coolidge. If you recall, I mentioned this friend back in "Politics."

I began to attend more AA meetings and my first full year of sobriety was coming closer. I started to attend one meeting, which I had attended from time to time in previous years with Dave, Gary, and Stanley. This was a Friday night meeting in my hometown of Dracut and I have been attending this meeting on a weekly basis for about a decade now.

I would often hang out with a few friends after this meeting and we would play small stakes poker over coffee and soda. From time to time, my friend Mike S. and I would go to the Nashua Elks and play blackjack until the place closed. However, due to the writing of this book, I haven't had much time to play cards lately.

During my first year or so at the Parker House, the program director was one Eileen M., but today she is Eileen P. due to marriage. Eileen was always willing to lend a helping hand and she took her occupation very seriously. I learned how to cook well due to my Parker House residence. I often made feasts for the clients and the staff and they loved my cooking. I would make steak tips, fish, meatloaf, pork chops or what have you. I also liked my own cooking, although I presently live on steak and chicken.

It was smooth sailing for the time being and for the next twelve (give or take) years, things were much easier than in recent years past. One night when I was cleaning my room, I came across Dan D's phone number. I gave him a call and I conversed with him and Jeanine. Roland would soon call me. He let me know that Malicious Intent was getting back together, and that I was welcome to be a part of it. At this point and for understandable reasons, the sight of a guitar made me nauseous. Not rejoining the band was the correct decision for the achievement of the primary goal and for writing this book.

I reached my one year of sobriety on November 4, 1997. L.A.D.T. would present me with a medallion. My friends were proud of me and I was proud of myself. I remember waiting for my ride home on this day and as I left, a clinician named Gretchen congratulated me once more before I headed home.

The next few years were pretty much stagnant (stagnant for a nut like me, anyway). I had started to hang around with my friend Richard D. by this time. Rich and I were always sober together. We would play video games, watch movies, and go out to eat a lot. I have made friends with his entire family and they are good people. Rich's mother Cecile has passed on, but I had to mention her because she was so good to me and I miss her very much.

I had been seeing my sweetheart Christine G. for years by this point and we have broken up and gotten back together many times over the years. In between one of our break ups, I went out with a girl named Amy V. for just over one year. She has one of those Republican families with good family values, which are exactly the type of people I like to hang out with.

I was invited to one of Amy's relative's houses for Christmas. Remember how I said that Republicans can be generous and nice in their personal lives, yet wrong in the political realm when it comes to distribution of finances? Well, I would be proven correct on this night, because Amy's grandfather, a person I had never met in my life gave me a card with some money in it. I did feel a bit guilty for accepting the money, but I assured Amy's family that this money went straight to the cause of the pro-primary goal viewpoint and that is a worthwhile investment.

Amy was a fantastic girlfriend, but she pushed me too hard for me to tell her my problems. At this crux, she must fathom why I kept things to myself so much. I realize that she wanted to help me, but the truth is that only I am fit to deal with the extremities involved in the pursuit of the primary goal. Amy and I broke up and I would soon be back with my girlfriend Christine G. I have spent a couple of Thanksgivings with Christine's family and I hit it off with them all, especially her moth-

VISION OF A MENTAL PATIENT

er and father. Unfortunately, Christine's father has since passed on and we all miss him dearly.

As the years of my sobriety continued on, I began to notice that all aspects of my life were improving. I commenced to read books all of the time and I have read hundreds upon hundreds of them over the years. I would receive medallions 2,3,4,5,6,7,8,9,10,11, and 12, and in a couple of months, I will get my 13 year medallion. I have learned the art of self-education and I am once again able to chase my dreams. The chemical balance of my mind has set up our quest for utopia. Yeah, things are good!

I stayed at the Parker House until October of 2003. I then moved to the affiliated satellite apartment to the Parker House, which is located about one mile from Parker House and is in walking distance to Billerica Center. I have a roommate by the name of Tom H. who has become a close friend of mine over the years. I also became friends with the rest of Tom's family. Tom and I have an affinity for talking about political issues. However, I have not been able to watch C.N.N. for a while because it is to upsetting for me to bear.

I had heard, through the time travel grapevine, that the Red Sox were going to win the World Series soon. In 2003, they came close, but when Wakefield gave up that excruciating homerun, it was not easy for me to watch. However, the following year, my beloved Red Sox completed the circle of the impossible dream and I would go absolutely ballistic. Eighty-six years of pain was wiped away with one short throw to first base. Yahoo!

A year or so before I moved into my new place, I was hired to work at Bridgewell (L.A.D.T.) as a custodian. I had this job for about six years and once I had saved up a good amount of money, I quit so that I could write this book. Now, the final stages of universal contact are more possible than ever.

My time as a custodian at Bridgewell was good for the most part. Not only was I making good money, but I was doing something that certainly wasn't a waste of time. My romance with Christine was going well and we lived together on weekends. During this time, the Patriots won two more Super Bowls, the Red Sox took another one in 2007, and the Celtics took their seventeenth title in the 2007- 2008 season. Times are good in New England!

At this point, I would like to tell you of some crucial occurrences, which took place in the parallel time flux, which were absolutely imperative to our positive outcome. To put these occurrences into exact sequence would be next to impossible, because when you are dealing with the results of the primary goal, everything is basically one huge cluster fuck.

Anyhow, the first occurrence I will tell you of is that Bob Stevens has been time travelling to me in the realm of alternate time. Bob became aware of the danger I was in and he would show up at one of my shows in alternate time. When Bob visited me in this parallel, he said to me "Ted, we have found out, I have travelled time and I am here to save you!" Bob had been busting his ass for the cause of morality and his courage should be commended by us all. If I were Bat Man then Bob would be Robin. Bob is a hero and despite the limited knowledge (all of you have limited knowledge) he possesses in our parallel, he is crucial in pertinence to the primary goal viewpoint.

There is another hero amongst us who could rival the bravery of myself, or Bob. When I tell you who it is, this person might be surprised because due to boundaries of time, this person is also limited in the knowledge of this situation. And, by the way, this limitation of knowledge is intentional and we will not be defeated! The name of this other hero is Brian M (this is not the same Brian M. from Dimitri's funeral). Brian is a Dracut dude who has quite the reputation if you know what I mean. Brian, like Bob, has entered into alternate time and he has fought hard for the cause of humanity. Years ago, I saw Brian in the parallel and he knew what was going down. He walked over to me without a nerve in his body and said to me "Hey, Ted, you're going to put me at risk in the future" and then he smiled at me and walked away. I did put Brian at risk, but he shall be rewarded handsomely. In doing this, Brian guided me through some very dangerous situations and he also scared the living daylights out of the assholes who were trying to commit the most repugnant of acts. Brian, you have done a service to the world and you will never be forgotten.

Now, I must mention to the short dudes I met at Hampton Beach on that vacation my mother, Dave, and I went on in 1989. I was standing with my guitar strapped on at a nightclub Deallegiance had performed at on one particular occasion. All of a sudden, a short red-headed kid and another short brown haired kid showed up from out of nowhere in front of me. I kept looking at the brown haired kid and I was saying to him "Why do you look so familiar?" They both blew out a sigh of relief and they said in unison, "Oh, thank god, he travelled time!" I asked who they were, because they looked so familiar and the Brown haired one said, "I am a friend." I then remembered them from the beach and I said, "That was you!" They said, "Yes, that was us." The three of us then discussed some related issues and we went our separate ways. These two will also get what is due them when the game is over and the forces of morality have won.

Now, I must mention a close friend of mine who I only know through time travel. This would be the legendary female vocalist, Madonna. I have had many fantastic conversations with this woman and, never mind her looks, because her personality is way better. She told me about things in the future and how happy we and everybody else would be. She told me that I traveled time and when she found out I wasn't aware of it, she was quite amazed. She said to me on one occasion that she knew me good, and that I would never be defeated, and I believe her. I saw her and a few others in Lowell a few years back. Madonna as a younger person walked by me smoking a cigarette and she was acting cool and stuff. I opened the door of the car I was in and I yelled at her, "Let it ride!" She began to laugh and she walked on. This was a message from her to me, which says we shall not be defeated. I can't wait to see her again!

I must now mention the time I met the awesome Iron Maiden. I was hanging out at one of my shows and the members of Iron Maiden were pleased with my ambitions, but they were retaliating against me for my own good. Our new song at the time was "Lost in Time." When I mentioned to Iron Maiden drummer Nicko McBrain that our new song was called "Lost in Time," a look of panic took over his face and he said to me in a state of wonder and concern "Did you say lost in time?" I said, "Yes, I did say that." All of a sudden, the whole band became nervous and said to me that I must be crazy. Iron Maiden singer Bruce Dickinson, who had just said that I was a good kid, became shocked at the title of our new song. He went into a tantrum trying to convince me that I should not put myself at such risk by releasing this song. Finally, after they all reacted to my saying lost in time, Iron Maiden bass player Steve Harris looked at me. I could see the concern in his face, when he told me, "Don't do it!"

Well I did it! And I wrote it! Although if anyone watched us, they would notice that Matt of Deallegiance was the first to write these lyrics down, now think about the control factor and then I remind you that the name of the sole Malicious Intent Album is *Mind Control*! You see, Iron Maiden was not aware that my personal subconscious was responsible for all that was taking place. As a matter of fact, we were all connecting big time and soon, this will be a collective and completed vision of world morality. So, don't worry guys, I have proven that I know what I am doing!

Now, I must continue on with some more of the altercations I had with Metallica. One reason I now trust Kirk of Metallica (and I have for some time now) is due to what I am about to tell you. You see, the evildoers apparently had me at one point. They said that I had blindly walked into the danger zone and that I was done for, I was to be in a perpetual hell forever. Because Kirk was not aware of the factors, I have presented, he thought I was doomed as well. Thiswas when I saw my friend Kirk cry for me.

The most recent, yet still critical altercations I had was with James of Metallica. We were discussing important matters when he finally understood that I was smart and that I had done things correctly. He was aware of the control factor and we were now on a new level of understanding between the two of us. All of a sudden, James saw a glimpse of the future. At this crux, he broke down and said to me "Ted, you're my hero!" He told me that I was lucky and that he had grown very admiring of me, after all those we had been through over the years. We will win!

Continuing on, I would be faced with another lunge from the evildoers and their attempts for ending the utopian dream would soon be defeated for good. Lars was paying me another visit in the parallel and he was distraught due to his worry for me. He was not yet aware of the supremeness of the personal and collective subconscious realms and their capability for our imminent victory. I was always brave and I had risked life and limb for the ones I loved. As Lars witnessed my unrelenting defiance to the uncompromising world evils, he began to cry and he said to me "You can't!" The evildoers were planning to finish me off and Lars was aware of it.

At this moment of my friend's despair, I looked at him and I said "Hi, Barry." Lars then recovered in one second flat and he looked at me in a state of euphoric astonishment. You see, Lars was aware that there was a guy named Barry who lives in Billerica, Massachusetts. This Billerica Barry is a dead ringer of Lars. Yes, they are nearly identical! You see, Barry is a DNA version of Lars and he was placed in Billerica in order for us to communicate! As Lars looked at me in his state of shock, I said to him "Congratulations, Lars, you are a regular guy." I know Lars well. He is sick and tired of being the rock star type, and sometimes, he just wants to be average. Therefore, it pleased Lars to find out that he was Barry, but I must say that Barry is far from average.

At this moment, I appeared in front of Lars in this parallel of time and as he continued to look atme with a moral satisfaction, a cane formed in my right hand and I gave a short performance of Elton John's "I'm Still Standing." I would dance around shining in glory and moving my cane all about. Lars loved it!

The last time I saw Barry was a little over a year ago. When he saw me, he looked at me nervously and asked me where I came from. Barry and I have sent subconscious messages to each other at places we used to run into each other and I must say that the future looks bright. But here is the topper: Barry and I don't even really know each other! All we have done is sent each other messages and we usually say hello when we spot one another.

Back in the days of my misery, when I was about nineteen years old, there was a girl I knew from Roller Kingdom who used to flirt with me from time to time. Anyhow, the evildoers would force her to do horrible things to me within the parallel. She told me (as others have) that I had travelled time and that I had made it so I didn't know. Finally, she said to me "Ted, remember that!" Well, I do remember that, and thank you so much for all you have gone through because of me, Tracy. I hear you are doing well and you have done a service to the entire world for having to deal with those jug heads. I now see, that I and all of my friends have been time travelling the whole time and the reason we are not always consciously aware of it is because it is subconscious.

I will now support the fact of the control factor by mentioning some things of the past, which some select few of you may recall. I met myself and my future wife with Dennis at a small beer party by the woods near a stream in the back of Dennis' old street. A few of us walked down next to the river and there were some people there we did not recognize. Two of them were me and my wife and they were talking about politics. Dennis and I became bashful and we walked away. A minute later, Dennis told me, "That guy looks like you!" Dennis said that he thought this person was me and that I had travelled time. You see, Dennis and I had a conversation about senses one night when I was living on Eleventh Street and on this walk, I explained

VISION OF A MENTAL PATIENT

how to achieve time travel.

I was at an L.A.D.T. Halloween party one year when Victoria's subconscious entered her conscious, and then she referred to someone as god. I remember meeting people at the beach who were crying tears of joy and telling me not to forget them. These were people I hadn't met until the last ten years or so. I remember seeing myself on another occasion and I was hugging someone special. Another time, a future friend appeared in front of me in the parallel, and he told me that I was about to see myself, and then I saw myself. I was with my wife and she was laying her head on my shoulder. This was also the time Madonna walked by me and she did so about fifteen seconds after I had seen myself.

More and more I learned that the control factor was not just real, but it is also more important than time travel itself. I shall continue with more evidence! I remember my high school friend ,the beautiful Shelly L. She was at Kerouac Park in Lowell and she was sending me some vital messages. She told me all about my book and she did so in some detail. She told me of my wife and she also said to me, "I know!" She looked older and I am not sure whether she had time travelled to this place or not. Nevertheless, she got her point across and I will commence to go full speed ahead!

Concerning the control factor: the policeman driving down the wrong side of the road at the beach, the confrontation at the Bridge Street Bridge, the men who sold me the lysergic acid diethylamide, Matt C. peeing on my grandmother's bush, oops? And this is just a handful of things. My entire life has been a series of such phenomena, and I could go on and on if I wanted to.

Some of these events are of basic time travel and some of them are strictly of the mind, basically covering the entire scope of time travel anyway, but there are some minor differences. Remember, the sole Malicious Intent Album is called Mind Control and I didn't write it or decide to call the album as such. Or did I? Are you catching the drift yet?

Sometimes, I joke with my friends about my so-called delusions. But they aren't aware of this: (Delusion in Drow is=know is you lead) Connected!

I am about to close out this short autobiography, but I must first leave you with the lyrics to another Metallica song, which is the basis of the totality of my visionary mission. I hereby present the story of it all. This is track five of Metallica's *And Justice for All* album. This one is called "The Shortest Straw." Please indulge.

Suspicion is your name, your honesty to blame
    Put dignity to shame, dishonor
        Witch hunt modern day, determining decay
            the blatant disarray, disfigure
                the public eye's disgrace, defying commonplace
<u>*Unending* *paper* *chase*</u>*, unending*
    deafening, painstaking, reckoning
        in vertigo it doth bring
            Shortest straw, challenge liberty
                Downed by law, live in infamy
                    Rub you raw, witch hunt riding through
                      Shortest straw, this shortest straw has been pulled for you
                          Pulled for you, shortest straw, pulled for you, shortest straw
                          Pulled for you, shortest straw,
                              This shortest straw has been pulled for you
The accusations fly, discrimination why?
    Your inner self to die, intruding
        doubt sunk itself in you, its teeth and talons through
            your living catch 22, deluding
                A mass hysteria, a megalomania, <u>reveal dementia</u>, reveal
                    secretly, silently, certainly, in vertigo you will be
                        Shortest straw, challenge liberty
Downed by law, live in infamy
    Rub you raw, witchhunt riding through
        Shortest straw, this shortest straw has been pulled for you
            Pulled for you, shortest straw, pulled for you
                Pulled for you, this shortest straw had been pulled for you
                    Behind you hands are tied, you're being ostracized
                      Your hell is multiplied, un-pending
the fallout has begun, oppressive damage done
    Your many turned to none, to nothing
        You're reaching your nadir, your will has disappeared

Your lie is crystal clear, defending
Channels red, one word said, blacklisted
with vertigo make you dead
Shortest straw, challenge liberty
Downed by law, live in infamy
Rub you raw, witch hunt riding through
shortest straw, this shortest straw has been pulled for you
Pulled for you!

Well, I have been through it all and I have seen humans at their best and at their worst. I have faced the face of death and I have defeated it. I have been subject to the utmost of human suffering. And now, you and I are the proud victors. I guess it really is a free world. Once again, scientific equivalency wins! Read on!

MORE POLITICS

In this segment, as we return to the topic of politics, I will inform you of three prominent political figures who were responsible for ending the Cold War. These three people are Senator Charlie Wilson from the state of Texas who is a left wing liberal Democrat, Joanne Herring, a Houston-born socialite, political activist, business woman, and ultra right wing conservative, and Gust Avrakotos an American case officer, and division chief of the Central Intelligence Agency (C.I.A.). These three political figures would cause a supremely moral justice for the innocent victims of the detrimental effects of the Cold War. First of all, the Cold Warthat took place from 1945 until 1991 was a continuous state of political conflict, economic issues, and military tension, to say the least. This Cold War was primarily between the United States and the former Soviet Union. However, Soviet-influenced states and other powers of the western hemisphere were involved.

The problem is that the Cold War has been viewed by many as simply a diplomatic war, that concerned the arms race, acts of espionage, propaganda, and financial and technological competition. This is a vague and deceiving view of what the Cold War truly was.

The truth is that the Soviets were victimizing innocent men, women, and children in Afghanistan and the Afghans were like sitting ducks because they had insufficient defense. It was in the later goings of this Cold War when the Afghani people were forced to deal with this harsh reality. Due to my research on this Cold War, my prior positive view of former Soviet president Mikhail Gorbachev has changed to that of a negative assessment. I have criticized the United States from time to time in this book and although I like to praise foreign nations as much as possible, I must admit that the Soviet Government's actions during this portion of the Cold War were completely appalling and uncalled for.

Do you know why this war is commonly termed as a diplomatic war? It is due to the neglectful belief, that the killings of these innocent Afghans, were simply not our problem. It is bad that the Soviets took such actions, but it is also bad that others did not help out as they should have. If it was not for Charlie Wilson, Joanne Herring, and Gust Avrakotos, the death toll would have been far worse. We will now commence discussion of the valiant efforts put out by these three compassionate political figures.

First of all, Charlie Wilson has often been subject to ridicule, because of his wild life style of partying and womanizing, despite his level of morality. Prior to any actions made by Charlie Wilson concerning this Cold War, the Soviets appeared to be invincible. However, within a matter of time, Wilson, Herring, and Avrakotos would strike a vital blow to the Soviets and their acts of international bullying. By the way, the violence of this war was in part due to religion, which has been a prime cause of war since day one.

There is a film about the actions of these three political figures and it is entitled "Charlie Wilson's War." My favorite scene in this movie was when Gust Avrakotos was dealing with one of his superiors at the Central Intelligence Agency, in Langley Virginia. This confrontation, or should I say shouting match, was intense. Here is a rough estimation of this passionate confrontation: Gust entered his superior's office at the C.I.A. headquarters. Gust's boss acknowledged Gust and he told Gust that he was prepared to hear his apology, due to the fact that Gust recently had a fit in this guy's office and he got so angry that he smashed his office window.

As Gust's superior was speaking, Gust abruptly interrupted him and said, "Excuse me, but what the fuck?" Gust's superior said that one Clair George (a former United States government official who had served as deputy director of the C.I.A.) had told him, that Gust was to apologize to him. Apparently this Clair George either screwed up or he was messing with these two guys' heads, because Gust was told that Clair George said that his superior was to apologize to him, which was (you got it) the complete opposite. Gust's superior then stated, that there must have been some kind of miscommunication between Clair George and the middleman. Once these two men realized this discrepancy, the shouting match would commence.

The last time these two men had an altercation, Gust had told his superior to go fuck himself (just before he broke his window). The tension in the room could be cut with a knife as Gust's superior began to argue that he shouldn't be the one to apologize because of the tantrum Gust had on the last occasion. Gust was also upset because he was not appointed for a job in Helsinki Finland. When this topic came into play, Gust became livid and he shouted to his superior "The Helsinki job was mine and it was on the books!" Gust's superior continued to state his case, thus sending Gust into a fit of rage! You see, Gust was told by one Alan Wolf (a former C.I.A. European expert) that he was promised the job in Helsinki. Gust's superior then told Gust that Alan Wolf was no longer in charge and that Gust had to accept this situation.

This is the part when Gust went absolutely ballistic! Gust started to state his case in a passionate fit of rage. Gust shouted the following "I have been with this company for twenty-four years, I was posted in Greece for fifteen of them!" Gust's face then turned into an even more passionate expression of rage. He shouted about the fact that he had prevented a crooked Greek politician by the name of Papendreu from winning an election. He also stated that he aided the Greek Junta in taking him prisoner. Gust continued on with the following: "I have advised and armed the Hellenic Army. I have neutralized champions of communism, spent the last three years learning to speak Finnish, which would come in handy here in Virginia, and I am never sick at sea, so I want to know why I am not going to be your Helsinki station chief!"

Gust's superior then responded by saying "Because you're coarse, and I need someone with good diplomatic skills, and you don't have them." Gust then pointed his finger at his superior and said, "Is that right?" Gust's superior said, "Yes, that is right and you are lucky I didn't fire you for breaking my window the last time you were here." Gust then said, "Yeah, you're fucking Roger's fiance and you know I know!" Gust's superior responded with "I am not even going to dignify that remark with an answer." Gust then stated "Yeah, you're dignifying her in the ass at the Jefferson Hotel room 1210, but let me ask you, the 3,000 agents Turner fired (Stanfield Turner is a former C.I.A. director), was that because they lacked diplomatic skills?" Gust's superior looked at Gust in frustration as Gust continued to state his case.

Gust's superior then questioned him on his level of loyalty and said they had examined the situation sufficiently (more or less). Gust then said "Yeah, well I'd like to examine the several ways in which you are a douche bag!" Gust's superior became enraged at this comment and he told Gust to leave his office before he ended his career.

At this point, Gust grabbed a wrench off a worker there and commenced to re-bust his superior's office window. Finally, Gust pointed his finger at his superior in a state of rage and said "My loyalty? For the last twenty-four years people have been trying to kill me, people who know how, now do you think that's because my father was a soda pop maker or because I'm an American spy? Go fuck yourself, you fucking child!" Gust then stormed out of his superior's office and as he left, he calmly asked one of the secretaries of this office "How was I?" She gave him a look of approval, and a gesture of thumbs up as Gust left the room.

Gust Avrakotos had not yet met Charlie Wilson by this point in time, but Gust was well aware of what was taking place in Afghanistan and his level of determination would multiply for the cause in which he was now determined to take on. I must say that this type of rage is actually a good thing and I believe so because of the fact that people like Gust are fighting for the lives of the innocents of our world. This behavior should not be dismissed as vulgarity, but instead it should be viewed for what it is and what it is, is called passion. Yes, our government agencies should be passionate when it comes to the sad realities of worldwide victimizations of countless innocent people.

Around this time, Wilson was visiting with his lady friend Joanne Herring, the ultra right wing conservative. As these two were up to their usual naughty behavior, they started some discussion pertaining to the innocent Afghani people. Despite my being a Democrat, I must admit that Herring was more knowledgeable than Wilson in relation to this situation. However, their levels of decency and compassion were most definitely dead even.

Herring began to state her case to Wilson by asking why the C.I.A. was fighting a fake war. She also stated her concern about the stagnant state of Congress. She then persuaded Wilson to use his influence to allow or set into motion sufficient funding for supplying the Afghans with sufficient military supplies. She stated that the Afghans were in dire need of more powerful anti-aircraft weapons. She also pointed out the mistake that we had supplied them with sufficient weaponry, but we had failed to supply them with the proper radar equipment, thus defeating the purpose of the weaponry they already had. In other words, we only gave them half of what they needed so we could look good rather than actually trying to help them.

Herring continued on by stating that if this conflict was taken seriously, that past actions made by Henry Kissenger in relation to El Salvador could be applied in a similar fashion in this Afghan situation to give the Soviets a vital blow. She then requested that Wilson go to Pakistan (a country which is directly affected by this situation due to border issues; Afghani refugees were fleeing into this country) and perform some diplomatic relations with Pakistani president Muhammad Zia ul Haq.

Charlie agreed to comply with Herrings idea. He would catch a flight to Pakistan and meet with President Zia and his colleagues. They discussed the situation of the three million or so Afghan refugees who were now residing in Northern Pakistan. The issue of proper military supplies was also discussed in this diplomatic meeting. Charlie told them that the United States was eager to help and the Pakistanis were not hesitant to express their disagreement. They basically said that they were insulted by the minute funding being applied to this cause. After all, Wilson was wrong in saying that the United States was eager to help. The truth was that Wilson, Herring, and Avrakotos were the only United States people who were willing to actually do something significant about this situation. Zia asked Wilson to go directly to Afghanistan and see the mayhem with his bare eyes. Wilson would comply with this request. Wilson then travelled across the border of Pakistan, so that he could witness the turmoil in person. While there, Wilson met a small Pakistani boy who had lost his arms because of a land mine, which he had mistaken for a toy. This sent Wilson into a deep state of sorrow and compassion for these oppressed people. Wilson then returned to the United States with a newfound morally provoked ambition.

Soon, Gust paid Wilson a visit. Gust was well aware of many things and he knew who to see and what had to be done.

VISION OF A MENTAL PATIENT

Gust showed up at Wilson's office and they were tense at first due to their disgusted feelings pertaining to this Cold War dilemma. Gust brought Wilson a bottle of wine bugged for reasons of secrecy. Once Wilson was aware that Gust had bugged him, he became angry and suspicious. However, it wouldn't take long for these two moral pioneers to realize that they had the same interests and this duo would soon become a trio. Once Wilson, Herring, and Gust were together, the cause of human good had achieved mate and soon after that, they would achieve checkmate.

In the meantime, Rudolph Guliani of New York was trying to indict Wilson for past drug use and other petty factors. This would pose a temporary obstacle for Wilson, but he would still move forward with his moral endeavors.

Once Gust and Wilson had somewhat determined their intentions, Gust would take Wilson to see a twenty-nine-year-old C.I.A. weapons expert. At first, Wilson thought that Gust was jerking him around when he saw how young this kid was. However, once this whiz kid revealed his expertise in his field, Wilson would comply and the mission would be further set into motion. Wilson and Gust said goodbye to this whiz kid and left to discuss matters further. The plan was now being manifested.

Gust and Wilson went to Israel for diplomatic purposes regarding this Afghani situation. They convinced a high-ranking Israelite official to adhere to a partnership between the nations of Egypt, Pakistan, Afghanistan, and Saudi Arabia. This Israeli official became frustrated, as two of these nations don't even recognize Israel as a country. However, the moral senses of this prominent Israelite would get the best of him and he would agree to this newly devised plan.

Back in the United States, Gust, Wilson, and Herring met as a trio for the first time and they were ecstatic, due to this new diplomatic accomplishment. Herring would set up a return trip to Afghanistan, which all three of them would partake in. Gust, Wilson, and Herring formed a bond at this point. Wilson then found out that Guliani's attempt of indicting him had failed, leaving him in the clear andsetting up a certain victory for this trio. The situation in Afghanistan would soon improve substantially.

Gust, Wilson, and Herring prepared to fly to Afghanistan accompanied by an advocate for this cause. This advocate is Clarence Long, a congressman from Maryland. When the four of them arrived in Afghanistan, Long spoke to the Afghans who were directly affected by these acts of evil. Long spoke for the common good and he stated that human justice must be obtained. Wilson continued to fight for more funding for the Afghans and soon, the proper and essential military equipment would be obtained by the Afghan rebels.

Shortly after this visit, the Afghans would strike down a Russian attack helicopter, sending the Afghan rebels into a well-deserved state of patriotic pride. As the fighting continued, the tides began to turn for these courageous Afghans. Wilson's main assistant had learned of this first small victory for the Afghans, so she sought Wilson out and handed him a note, which read "Three Russian helicopters were just shot down." Wilson then grabbed his assistant and gave her a passionate kiss. Yeah!

By the spring of 1987, twenty-one Soviet attack helicopters were shot down from the sky. By the summer of 1987, thirty-three more attack helicopters were shot down by the Afghans, and another twenty-eight fixed wing Russian aircrafts were shot down as well. The Russians then executed some land attacks, which I am happy to say, would fail. In the fall of 1987, forty-one more Russian attack helicopters were shot down, not to mention that seventy-five land attack Russian tanks were destroyed in this same sweep. In the spring of 1988, nineteen more Russian attack helicopters were blown out of the sky and another forty-three tanks were destroyed as well. There was also twenty-two more Russian fixed wing aircrafts that were demolished by the Afghan rebels within this period.

Wilson desired to finish off this Russian insurgency. He requested even more funding for this cause, but unfortunately, he was rudely laughed at. Wilson's reputation would improve, getting him reelected as a Texas state senator. Gust would call Wilson and congratulate him.

Eureka! On April 14, 1988, the Soviets were defeated by the Afghans. aThey were forced to sign the Geneva Accords. Wilson visited the Afghans he had helped. He would be celebrated and praised as the hero that he is. Anyhow, Afghanistan became the first and only nation in the history of the world to ever defeat the Soviet Union in a war. They most certainly put the conspirators of these malicious acts in their place.

When Wilson returned to the United States, a party was thrown to celebrate this moral victory. Gust was asked to make a toast. Gust held up his wine glass and said "Here's to you, you motherfuckers!" Gust, Wilson, and Herring all looked at each other in approval and then Gust and Wilson went outside to talk. They had a good conversation, stated their feelings for one another, and then they hugged.

Wilson, in being the good man that he is, was not satisfied with this Afghani situation. He would requested another one million dollars to construct a school for the Afghani children. One of Wilson's colleagues said that he had mentioned the Afghan situation to President Reagan and Reagan had no clue of what had been taking place. Finally, as Wilson persisted for this final bit of funding, he was abruptly interrupted by another colleague who said to him "Charlie, no one gives a shit about a school in Pakistan." Charlie corrected this remark and said "Afghanistan."

Wilson was quoted as saying at the end of this ordeal "These things happened, they were glorious, and they changed the world, and then we fucked up the end game."

In the end, Wilson was honored by the United States Government and he would receive the reward of honored colleague for his efforts in this moral cause. As he received this reward, Gust and Herring looked on without a fiber of jealousy or envy in their being, due to the fact that they knew they had done the right thing. You see, these three were more concerned with creating a spectacle rather than just appearing as a spectacle. This has to be one of the best examples of political bipartisanship in the history of the United States of America. You have an ultra right wing conservative, a left wing bleeding heart liberal Democrat, and a foul mouthed American spy teaming up for setting the stage for collective and eternal peace. Although they are not aware of it, these three have contributed to the cause of universal wide connection!

Gust Avrakotos has a mouth like a truck driver burning to death in a cesspool and never in my life have I ever heard anyone speak with such a blunt and beautiful conviction for human decency. William Shakespeare, eat your heart out!

Charlie Wilson put himself on the line and he is one of, if not the greatest United States senators in this nation's history. Joanne Herring has proved once and for all that conservatives are good and decent people. As for Gust, I must say one more thing. Gust Avrakotos is totally awesome!

By the way, I have news for you all: Gust Avrakotos in the years 1987 and 1988 was the President of the United States of America. He has set a good example for all of us to abide by in pertinence to human leadership.

What disgusts me to no end is the fact that Ronald Reagan, despite telling Gorbachev to knock down the Berlin Wall, had the audacity to take credit for the efforts of these three pioneering political figures. I believe that Joanne Herring would most likely challenge me on this statement and she has the right to her opinion. Regardless of any possible discrepancies, the most important factor is that the job got done and the forces of morality had won another battle.

Martin Luther King said that people should be judged by the content of their character rather than the color of their skin and this is a correct statement. However, it must be taken one step further. You see, Rudolph Guliani, who is likely a decent guy, was completely wrong in trying to indict Charlie Wilson. Guliani did so by exploiting past mistakes and social misbehaviors of Wilson. Charlie Wilson has made mistakes just like the rest of us but the bottom line is that he is a morally decent man. If Guliani had succeeded in tarnishing Wilson's image, it would have indirectly raised the Afghan death toll and the Russians would have continued to rampage these innocent world civilians. A person should be judged on his or her level of morality, compassion for the weak, and the decency of passion. These are the traits making up a person's character.

Now that we are nearing the end of my interpretation of this vision, I humbly request that the republicans of America think over their domestics and at least temporarily comply with the democratic way. We must get behind President Obama and convince the United Nations and the rest of the world to set into motion the pursuit of a utopian way.

The main reason Democrats tend to complain about political issues and not apply it to the way they live their lives is the same reason the Republicans tend to live morally and have a less moral political view. It is all relative to the collective subconscious as it acts and reacts within the whirlwind of the mind galactic vortex. I do strongly believe that the head of the Republican Party, Michael Steele, is a good man. I mean, a person with an intelligence quotient of five could figure out that he is a very nice man who might be incorrect in the distribution of finances to the needy public, but would take a fin out of his pocket and hand it to a homeless person. What people do not fathom is that if we commit this moral act through the government, we wouldn't have to hand out money to those in need. This could be considered a theoretical touch of a moral communism applied to a properly functioning democracy. Get it?

You all must trust in me and give this approach a chance. If we do so, we will centralize the collective subconscious and open the gateway to a newfound world peace and freedom. All political parties are supposed to be on the same side, and I do believe that Republicans are more moral than the Democrats will give them credit for. If they can open their minds and comply with the universal idea, they could become the heroes of the world. The Republican Party will go down in history as the political party that took a bullet for the achievement of utopia. This would be the last hurrah!

I would now like to mention the 1988 vice presidential debate between Democrat Lloyd Bentsen and Republican Dan Quayle. Quayle made the mistake of comparing himself to John Kennedy and this was followed with Bentsen's famous comment, which went, "You are no Jack Kennedy." Now, after the way I attacked the evangelists and Dick Cheney earlier in this book, one might think that what I am about to say is hypocritical. But I will say it anyway; Bentsen's comment was uncalled for. There is no reason to humiliate someone like that. The goal of a debate is not to level your opponent. Instead, it is to have each side state their case as fairly as possible. Bentsen may have possessed a better political agenda than Quayle did, but that is not the point.

Now, I do not suggest to Dan Quayle that he uses the point I have made to take revenge on Bentsen. Nor do I want Bentsen to beat himself up over this matter. It is highly likely that these are both decent people, but Bentsen should make amends with Quayle. What these two men should do, is set an example for the world public, shake hands and let by gones be by gones. If I am appealing to these two men's moral intellect, then I have accomplished my goal.

As I have stated already from time to time in this book, I am a recovering alcoholic and a member of the AA fellowship. I will not and must not break the anonymity of those who I do not have permission from, nor do I want to defy the AA way by drawing it into public controversy. AA neither endorses nor opposes any causes, and its purpose is to help people stay sober and aid others in the achievement of sobriety. However, I would like to state the following: I have two close Republican friends from the fellowship. Both are always willing to help those in need. When I was the secretary at my home meeting, one of these friends would tell me to leave the money basket on the table so that someone in need could grab a couple of dollars in case he or she needed to do so. My other AA friend is a war veteran who has served his nation honorably and he likely would not agree with my view that the troops in Iraq have been lied to and deceived by the government. What these two friends of mine don't fathom is that people are not as giving as they are and the best method to help those in need is to do it through the government. There you have it, I have stated my case for the Democratic way. Do as you will.

For the last time in this book, I will present some more lyrics to you. Since this is the last time I will do this, I will make it one of my songs. This song is about the extreme radicalism that I practiced as a youngster. It is about war heroes and the sad fact that they are often deceived and brainwashed, and then sent out into the terrorizing battlefield. This is track two of Deallegiance's first demo tape, *Freedom's Call* track six of the second Deallegiance demo tape *Symbol of Transformation*, and track three to the sole Malicious Intent album *Mind Control*. This was the second song Roland and I ever completed and it is also our most well known song. I now present to you, "The Misguided Warrior!"

Take a tour with me, travel aimlessly
I'll show you things you cannot see
I'll show you night, I'll show you day
you'll see the souls that have gone astray
Black ones bare dark souls here
All that is within everywhere
with all of life, patterns hold tight
we'll achieve perfection tonight
I already know your actions, without any subtractions
Impulse chemical infections, causing insecure reactions
Misguided warrior, have I got a story for you
Misguided warrior, the unknown worrier
Misguided warrior, sitting in your hell of opportunity
Misguided warrior, you hold the key to your own safety
Travel on this road, and you will see
that it may lead to prosperity
the road for you, the road for me
this road re-grows the living dream
Open your mind, do not foresee
your inner-self can set you free
Feelings of anger, are the road to hell
You're the keeper of stories to tell
I know what you're going to say
You say it every day, you say there is no way
But it's within you today!

Okay, we are finished with politics as far as this book is concerned. We will now move on to my concepts of the detrimental effects religion has had on our world. Once again, thank you for listening and for the last time, read on!

RELIGION

Welcome to the final segment of *Vision of a Mental Patient*. In this segment, I will state my case as to the negative effects the concepts of religion have that led to worldly peril. Rather than continuing on and telling you what we will discuss in this segment, we will immediately indulge in a religious adage, which supports an atheistic outlook. This first topic of discussion will be of Noah's Ark.

Noah's Ark is the story of a biblical vessel supposedly constructed by the patriarch Noah. Legend has it that god commanded Noah to save himself and his family members and pairs of opposite sexed animals from a worldwide flood god was to execute in order to destroy all life on Earth. The adage of Noah's Ark is featured in a variety of Abrahamic religions includingof Christianity, Islam, and Judaism.

This story is in the book of Genesis 6:9. God told Noah, that he was the only man on Earth worthy of sharing in his glory. God gave Noah detailed instructions for Noah's edifying and use of this vessel. It is said, that god delivered a male and a female of every type of animal that was worthy of his glory to board the ark. God's flood would rise until all of the mountains of the Earth were submerged and god would thus drown and suffocate every other living thing all because they weren't as good as him.

Following the murder of millions upon millions of Earthly creatures, the waters would then settle and Noah's family and the animals aboard the ark would reproduce the world population. This story has numerous versions throughout a variety of religious aspects. However, they all adhere to the same basic premise.

So, I ask you, is god perfect and was this a perfect act? God claimed that there was only one good man and a few select good animals, thus he had to kill the rest. Now, aren't these pairs of species of the same genomes and DNA of those that were put to death? This would mean that the problem wasn't solved, because these species are related and thus have the same instincts. And yes, this was murder! It is impossible to conceive that something could be so good, that it could kill most of the population of a planet and then say worship me for I am perfect.

We are supposedly made in god's image, so if god killed every human being on the planet, then that means that he killed off his own offspring, because they weren't perfect like he is. And on top of that, god claims that we are his children and how the fuck could he kill almost every animal, when they are not even capable of language and all they know are the instincts, which god gave them in the first place!

Furthermore, we are told that god is the most incredibly powerful force in the universe and that he can do anything. Does that mean that it is good or moral to be powerful? If god is so powerful and perfect, then why didn't he just snap his fingers and fix the world? He could have made the evil instincts good instincts, but I suppose that he is just so good, that he felt that the best way to solve this dilemma would be to drown and suffocate millions upon millions of helpless creatures, which he loves by the way. We are expected to believe, that this perfect god is good, because he is powerful and we must have undying faith in him. According to the story of Noah's Ark, we are expected to believe that god picked out the only good family and the only good pairs of animals, and that Noah would get to share in the glory of "genocide!" Actually, this was even beyond genocide, this was deicide, which means to kill everything!

Just to give you an idea of how ludicrous this adage is, I tell you that god gathered up: two of seven species of birds, two alligators, two crocodiles, two anteaters, two antelopes, two aardvarks, two apes, two argali, two armadillos, two baboons, two badgers, two basilisks, two bats, two beavers, two bighorns, two bison, two boars, two buffalo, two bulls, two cats, two chameleons, two chamois, two cheetahs, two chinchillas, two chimpanzees, two chipmunks, two civets, two colts, two cougars, two cows, two coyotes, two dogs, two doe, two donkeys, two duckbill platypus, two elk, two ermines, two fawns, two gazelles, two giraffes, two goats, two gophers, two gorillas, two hamsters, two hares, two hedgehogs, two hogs, two hippos, two groundhogs, two guinea pigs, two horses, two hyenas, two jaguars, two iguanas, two impalas, two jackals, two kangaroos, two koalas, two lambs, two lemurs, two leopards, two lions, two lizards, two llamas, two lynx, two mandrills, two mares, two moose, two mice, two mules, two muskrats, two mustangs, two opossum, two orangutans, two otters, two oxen, two pandas, two panthers, two pigs, two porcupines, two pronghorns, two pumas, two raccoons, two rams, two rats, two reindeers, two rhinoceros, two roebucks, two sheep, two shrews, two silver foxes, two skunks, two snakes, two squirrels, two steers, two tapirs, two tigers, two toads, two turtles, two vicunas, two walrus, two warthogs, two wolves, two wombats, two yaks, two zebras, two zebus, and then if I included the insects, this list would be even more ludicrous. After god gathered all these animals together, he got them to have sex, which god says is a sin, and god had thus saved the world by killing everything.

Apparently, god has a very low intelligence quotient, because he forgot that he had created aquatic organisms that breathe the oxygen within water. So, I guess that all of the fish were more moral than all of the land creatures.

Why is it that the act of sex, which is the most natural act in the history of the planet, is termed by god as a sin? Due to religion and society's view of the sex act, the beautiful act of sex has been turned into liquid shit.

Furthermore, I cannot believe that there are men of science who actually go looking for the ark in the mountains of Ararat, which are located in the present nation of Turkey. How any scientist could actually believe in Noah's Ark brings me to despair. Nine times out of ten, a believer in such stories will know absolutely nothing about science. Okay, I am finished with the topic of Noah's Ark, we will now move on.

We will now move on to the story of Abraham and god's command that he must kill his only begotten son. Supposedly, god commanded Abraham to take his son on a three-day journey to the top of a mountain and kill him. When Abraham brought his son to this destination, Abraham proceeded to build an altar in the name of the god he worshipped and he laid his son on this altar and prepared to stab him in the throat. According to this story, god told Abraham not to kill his son, just as Abraham was about to kill him and that he had proven his faith. In a biblical sense, this story could be viewed as moral. However, in reality this is not moral. God did not prove anything by this and if this is god's way he most certainly is not moral. If you were married with a son, and your spouse commanded you to stab your son to death, and if you were to trust enough in your spouse to actually do it, when your spouse stops you as you lift the knife and says "Okay, honey, you proved you are a good parent," would that be moral? The answer is an astounding and undeniable "No!" But remember, god is perfect and is thus better than us in every way.

If god had told me to kill my son, I would have told him to take a hike. God is so good and powerful, that that he can kill anything and tell anything to kill on his command. And this is not just the case in the stories of Noah's Ark and Abraham.

You see, every war in history has at least in part been caused by dogma (dogma in Drow is=Am god). Historians have determined, that the three most prominent causes of war are, nationalism, racism, and religion. We will now discuss some particular wars that were caused by religion.

The first war I will mention is the Thirty Years War, from 1618 until 1648. This war was one of the most horrific conflicts in European history. Most of it was fought in Germany and it included most European countries. As for the original causes of this war, it has subject to debate. The commonly perceived conclusion is that the Thirty Years War was due to religious conflicts between the Protestants and Catholics of the Holy Roman Empire.

Though there were disputes over political issues and power balances, religion was a major factor in this war. This one fact alone in relation this one particular war supports my hypothesis that religion will lead to detrimental consequences. The Thirty Years War would lead to widespread disease and famine, not to mention an economic crumbling, leaving many in dire need of life's essentials. This war had a death toll of millions upon millions of innocent men, women, and children.

Then there was the Israelite Conquest of Canaan, which has also been subject to debate for a very long time by the most prominent of historians. Part of this conquest included the Battle of Jericho. According to the bible, Joshua (the successor of Moses) crossed the Jordan and led the Israelites into Canaan where they would attack the city of Jericho. Supposedly, god sent a message to Joshua, commanding him to march around this city one time a day for six days, with the seven priests carrying ram horns in front of the Ark of the Covenant. On the seventh day, god commanded them to march around the city of Jericho seven times, as the priests were to blow the rams horns. The walls of Jericho would then fall and the Israelites would invade. Every man, woman, and child was killed in this city. The city was then burned to the ground and legend has it, that anyone who commanded a reconstruction of this city would be cursed by god. So, once again we see that god's glory and perfection makes him perfect, thus his right to kill in the name of himself.

Then there is the Taiping Rebellion, which took place in China from 1850 until 1864 during the Qing Dynasty. There was a heterodox Christian convert by the name of Hong Xiuquan, who would constitute the Taiping Heavenly Kingdom. Xiuquan would gain power over substantial sections of Southern China, which consisted of only thirty million people at the time.

The rebels would attempt to establish a small variety of social reforms, such as sexual segregation and socialization and the limiting of private trade. This would lead to the replacing of Buddhism, Chinese Folk Religion, and Confucianism with Christianity. It would be claimed that Xiuquan was the younger brother of Jesus Christ. There was a high abundance of tension in the nation of China in this era. The Qing forces would be the victors and they would harass countless civilians, all due to religious quarrels. Once again, we see that religion and the god concept has led to another shockingly staggering death toll, which in this case was of twenty to thirty million people.

Then you have the French Revolution, which took place from 1789 until 1799. This era for the French was inclusive of political and social disturbances, topped off by extreme radicalism. A major cause of this war was due to governmental abuses pertaining to Catholicism. Therefore, many people were unjustifiably killed all because of religion. Furthermore, this detrimental outcome would result in the abolition and the replacement of the French monarchy with a radical democratic republic.

Another example of a religiously induced war (at least in part) is the Algerian War of Independence, which took place from 1954 until 1962. You see, Algeria wanted to regain its independence from the French. This war was distinguished by guerrilla warfare and cruel uncalled for acts of terrorism. According to many experts, religion was not the main cause of this war. However, religion did play a role in pertinence to desired religious freedoms.

Then there were the Iranian Revolutions. The first one took place from 1905 until 1911 and the second one was fought within the year of 1979. These two wars were in part due to religion, of course.

It The more recent of these Iranian conflicts would prove interesting when applied to the present subject. You see, a rebellion was planned to dethrone the present Iranian monarchy of this period, headed by one Shah Muhammad Raza Pahlavi. Because of Islamic religious pursuits, Pahlavi was defeated and the infamous Ayattolla Khomeni forced the religion of Islam on the Iranian people, thus another result of religious brain washing in "our" world.

By now you must be catching the drift that religion causes bitterness and this is due to human tendency to try to force others to have the same likes and dislikes as they do. When this common human attitude is applied to a massive number of people, the results will always be bad. I have given evidence to this claim, but I am not done yet!

Another example of human tragedy relative to religion can be applied to what was called the Lord's Resistance Army. This army is sectarian guerrilla and it is based in the African nation of Uganda. This army formed back in 1987 and it is still existent in today. This army wants to overthrow the Ugandan government. The Lord's Resistance Army is headed by one Joseph Kony. Kony claims to be a messenger of god and he also states that he is a part of the holy trinity. This guerrilla army consists of religious aspects with a mixture of Christianity, Witchcraft, and Mysticism, inclusive of some other traditional religions as well. This army would prove to be an obstacle to The Sudan and their stark realities of genocide. Once again, I have stated my case for the false validity of the god concept.

Then you have the Crusades, which were intended to revive Christian control of the holy lands. The Crusades spanned close to a two-century long period. They took place from 1095 until 1291. Throughout a good portion of Europe religion would cause havoc. The Crusaders would primarily fight against Muslims, but they also had conflicts with Christians, Mongols, Prussians, Waldensians, Slavs, Hussites, Greek Orthodox Christians, Russians, and Jews. In this case, we see that separations of countries and nationalities play a role in god's destruction, thus the need of a mass fathoming of the theory of development and the utopian vision of the United Countries of Earth.

Then there was the Lebanese Civil War, which took place from 1975 until 1990. In this war an estimated 130,000 to 250,000 innocent people would perish from the Earth. There is a variety of reasons for this particular conflict and since we are on the topic of religious concepts leading to war, we will confine this conflict to that aspect primarily.

You see, in this Lebanese conflict, there was a prominent existence of Christian militias. These militias would acquire military supplies from Israel, West Germany (at the time), Romania, Bulgaria, and Belgium. The most prominent of these Christian militias were the Phalanges; they were under the command of one Bachir Gemayel. Certain factors of this conflict would lead to a Lebanese Israeli bonding. In this case, we have people killing in the name of Christianity and they were consciously aware of it. The Vietnam War from 1959 until 1975 was partly due to religion. Although Pol Pot was not directly taking effect on this war until its later stages, this predicament would drive Nixon mad.

You see, Pol Pot intended to enforce his own concepts of religion with a disgusting display of human evil. The Vietnam War would result in the deaths of millions. It would cause havoc, thus feeding the fire of a tense state of world diplomacy. This war is another example of absolute uncalled for bloodshed as well as promoting a way for those who intended to use religious deception to force their beliefs on others.

We are all aware by now that Hitler and his hatred of Jewish people would lead to millions upon millions of unfortunate deaths. I believe it possible that within Hitler's mind, he might have actually thought, that he was a moral person. This pig headed approach is exactly what is wrong with worldwide religious quarrels and discrepancies.

The American Revolution was in part caused by religion. Religious freedom is one of the main issues American rebels were fighting for. This type of situation will always result in bitterness and petty disagreements between culture types, thus the promotion of even more human bloodshed.

Even the Peloponnesian War fought from 431 B.C. until 404 B.C. was indirectly caused by religion or at least discrepancies in aspects of beliefs, thus forcing people to force their beliefs on others. Therefore, even hundreds of years prior to the establishment of Christianity, this Greek war would result in the deaths of countless innocents all because of petty differences regarding religious beliefs.

This brand of collective immaturity within world society resembles our human tendency to want others to like the same films, books, and musical preferences we are personally fond of. We have all been guilty of this many times in our lives and this is not such a bad trait between friends or relatives. However, when you apply this immaturity to world matters, it creates quite the cluster fuck. Therefore, the act of tolerance now becomes a virtue. We must learn to respect the needs and wants of others. This is the most correct method possible, to help us to contribute our individual values to the world society.

A big problem with society is that we all tend to follow rather than to be our true and moral selves. When we are kids, we want to be cool and when we are adults we want to be rich. These are humanly fathomable goals, which I am guilty of myself. Nevertheless, we must learn as a society to set our priorities straight. We also need to change our reasons for love and commence to see the good in people rather than the bad. By helping others, there is more to be gained even for the individual. This could be accomplished by making it a priority to start helping others and we must take pleasure in the examination of one

VISION OF A MENTAL PATIENT

another's good values.

Furthermore, there is nothing wrong with being cool or rich, as long as we desire to not hurt anyone and thus help others. This must be done by the most sufficient of methods. When I was in my teenager years, being cool was very important to me. However, for obvious reasons, I was forced to reveal my true self; hence, the totality of my vision.

Truthfully, I do strongly feel that being rich or cool is fun and not very unselfish. Being cool means that you are outgoing and you have a lot of fun. Being wealthy, on the other hand, can be good when it comes to supporting a family, thus making your dependents taken care of and given the gift of freedom and love.

Many special people will change for the better, due to this imminent visionary era of human history. I believe that when "something wonderful" happens, those of a consciously evil demeanor will discover their true selves. Some of us have been taught evil from the start of life and it is all they know, thus it is not their fault.

I must say that I see a glint in the eye of Mummar Khadafi of Libya. This man knows of nothing but evil. And he could become the spearhead for human change and thus set an example and promote the utopian cause.

Through the discussion we have had in this segment thus far, you must now see that religion, intended for good has led to billions of deaths throughout history, thus it is now time for us to defy god's perfect glory. We must make the place we live a good place to live.

God tells us not to try to be like him and at the same time, he tells us to obey him. We are told to follow his will and not our own will. We are expected to believe that there is some kind of divine wisdom to all of the evil acts perpetrated, because of religion. Of course, one who does not fully comprehend my theory of development could come to the conclusion that I have contradicted myself due to this previous statement. However, this is a different scenario. You see, god represents an unlimited evil and thus defies the concepts of "limited" evil being good. This assumption is based on the idea that evil and tragedy inclusive of the instinctual brutalities of which the dawn of the human race possessed was at its highest level.

There is no divine wisdom to brutal torture and ludicrous death tolls. Religion will and always does cause people to see the negative aspects of their fellow human beings. We must change!

It is assumed by many, that god is so much better than us, that we must follow his uncompromising will for us. What god is saying by this is that we are worthless and that he is better than all of us. Therefore, the values of every world individual are petty and not worth a thing due to the supposed fact that god is perfect. In other words, god tells us that we have no values and that through his divine wisdom, of perpetual hell and worldwide bloodshed, we will always fall short of his glory of perfection. Furthermore, the moment god claimed perfection was the same moment he proved himself not perfect.

We are told to get down on our knees and pray for mercy. This has not only led the human race to war, but it has also led to cults, which control people by a method of exploiting the good within them. This is a shameless act of deceitful manipulation. I have news for all of you, religion and the god concept is in fact a cult within itself. God has appealed to the good within us, thus leading to war, greed, genocide, and evil acts of manipulation. Therefore, this concept most certainly is a cult!

The bible contradicts itself throughout and then we are deceived by so-called virtues. Take the act of breaking bread for instance. What the hell is so profound about eating bread? It's bread, slice it up and eat it! There are extravagant churches throughout the world that have cost obscene amounts of money to erect. If breaking bread were so profound, then why are we forced to pay to build structures in order to worship a perfect god, while so many are in dire need of bread? For the most part people of religion are good people, but they are being deceived.

Then we have the extravagant Ten Commandments and hyped up religious prophecies of similarity. You will notice that bibles will often have a leather cover and silk pages filled with old style English. This enhancement is a method of deception and immoral control, which is contrary to my means of control. Remember, morality over technicality is a genuine virtue. I could sum up the Ten Commandments in one decisive statement and this statement is "Don't be an asshole!" Yes, respect and care for others and always remember to speak the truth.

God says that the road to heaven is small and narrow and the road to hell is long and wide. Therefore, those who do not believe in him and those who commit his definitions of sin will go to perpetual hell, of which I was faced with. After all of this, god says, "I love you." Yes, he is that much better than we are. God wants to kill the devil forever and he will not allow the devil to state his case. The devil was once an angel, cast down from heaven. Are we simply to trust in god and believe that he will save us? And that he is correct in causing a profound and meaningful death toll and that he is also right when he wants to perpetually kill the so called worst person (Satan). If god came down from heaven, and told you that so and so is the devil, and that we must murder him for eons, would you agree to that regardless of who the devil is? The other factor is that you don't know the devil, yet you are expected to agree to his sickening demise and if you tried to save him, you would be subject to the same brutal torture.

The two men who have come the closest to discovering some of the theories of my vision (especially reflective theory) were Carl Jung of course and believe it or not, the next closest was Aleister Crowley, the occultist. Crowley was a Satanist and I have read all of his books which are accessible in the United States. You would be surprised to "know" that throughout the writings of Crowley, the word "love" is mentioned frequently. This is due to the fact, that Crowley was consciously aware of subconscious love and he understood the basis of the theory of development, even despite the fact, that this theory was non-existent in his era.

As I have already stated, the worshippers of god are usually good people and I stand by my viewpoint that these people have been deceived. You see, it is the bad Satanists of the world society who have defied the true origin of the satanic idea. It is true that a majority of Satanists will tend to be consciously evil and this is because they are stupid more or less. There are good Satanists. Although they have denied it from time to time, I do believe that the famous band "Iron Maiden" set a prime example of the moral satanic idea. With a few exceptions, Iron Maiden will sing about morality and it is when they mention Satan, that they are viewed as evil. They proved their worth to me when they told me not to go forward with "Lost in Time."

The problem with Satanism is that some of the dumb ones who are not aware of the true Satan, will do despicable things and kill people for the intention of being cool more or less. However, way more people have perished from the Earth due to God rather than from Satan. It is the good Satanists, who will promote the idea of utopia and a newfound concept of visionary proportions.

It is accepted in the world society for people to attempt to force Christ, Buddha, Muhammud, God, or what have you on other people. But do you know what you can't do in most places? You can't tell people that Satan is good and be moral and caring for others as a Satanist. And due to freedom of religion, people are allowed to be Satanists and be immoral in the United States. So, I ask you why can't Satanists have their beliefs, be moral, and have it accepted by society?

Certain boneheads have disgraced the original aspects of Satan himself. I have read much on Satanism and a lot of it is idiotic, especially the abuses carried out by those who possess a lack of vision. The Satanic bible is dumb and it was created by people who have no understanding of the satanic idea. It is the writings of Crowley, especially his hypothetical defining, which relates to my theories, which are correct in the true meaning of Satan. Crowley was viewed as a mad man. He was a drug addict and a bisexual. It is also rumored, that he did some things which were immoral, thus the strengthening of his subconscious relationships to the theory of development.

You might understand by now, why I view Satanism in this manner. It is because the devil is the only person to be condemned to hell by god and all others have a chance. When I was in Solomon's, I was faced with a true hell. The problem is that people of god will comply with god's idea of hell without ever really thinking about it. We say to our children that god is good and if you don't believe in him and do what he says, you will go to hell. I was guilty of this myself, until I was face to face with a real perpetual hell. And this is why I fell in love with Satanism and developed a moral view of the satanic idea, which is to save the world.

I will now present a small excerpt from one of Crowley's books called *Portable Darkness*. Leading up to this excerpt, Crowley spoke of opposites and the reactions of these opposites between the sexes. He also touched on connection and how these connections exist from the vast infinitesimal out to the outer infinite. And then he writes the following excerpt;

Love is the law, Love is the will
fraternally yours 666

I ask you. Is there anything wrong with this statement? The answer is a resounding "No!" Okay, I have stated my case for love and human understanding and I have elaborated to you my worth, my love of humanity, and my past terrors of facing perpetual death and thus god's hell.

It is now time for me to reveal to you what I really and truly am. Before I shock you again, I remind you to think back to the credibility I have earned due to my theories, especially that of reflections and the language of the mad. When I took out a book from the Billerica library, *Sand to Glass* written by Inez Snyder it explained to me, the process of melting sand into glass, thus the creation of a reflection, a connection of time travel, and a realization of parallel universes. The code number of this book in the Billerica Library was 666.

You see, 666 is the number of reflection and this is due to its backwards and forwards appearance within a reflection. There are three sixes rather than two for the purpose of the enactment of a centrifuge. Without further ado, I will now reveal to you my true identity!

Woe to you, oh, Earth and sea, for the devil brings wrath, because he "knows" the time is short, let him who hath "<u>Understanding</u>" reckon the number of the beast, for it is a human number, its number is six hundred and sixty six. Revelations ch. XlIl b.18

"Yes," I am he, the bornless one and I have come to create the world of two suns. Please believe me, for I am telling the truth. This is not an attempt of sensationalism. The devil is good! And now, you have heard a good portion of my side of the story. I left something out in my autobiography. I was visited by a friend in the parallel time flux and this friend had always been fond of me. However, as soon as this person learned of what I was, this person wanted to kill me. We must end this cult, because it is in reality a time travel attempt to frame you all and to commit the most horrible of acts. Those who know me well know that I am not evil, and they realize that I do not deserve to be subject to perpetual death and neither do they. God is a mortal man and he is a liar!

God is not supernatural, and I don't believe that god or any of you realize just what it means to actually be supernatural. I have achieved the primary goal through natural science. Therefore, supernatural is exactly what it says. It is super and it is natural. And I am of this nature.

We are nearly finished, with the completion of the first stage of this vision. So, at this point of duration, I would like to

VISION OF A MENTAL PATIENT

shoot the shit with you and tell you of some of my likes and dislikes in the entertainment arts and I will also give a final touch to the establishment of time travel.

Obviously, by now you realize that I am a lover of adult literature. My list of favorite authors are; Kurt Vonnegut, Charles Bukowski, Robin Cook, Sidney Sheldon, Michael Moore, Jules Verne, George Orwell, Mark Twain, Edgar Allan Poe, Aleister Crowley, Carl Jung, and Arthur Clarke is tops.

For music these days I like Metallica (mostly their first six albums), Iron Maiden, Rush, Death Angel, Testament, Queensryche, Boston, Elton John, Alanis Morrissette, Asia, Soundgarden, AC/DC, Oasis, Bad Company, Aerosmith, The Rolling Stones, Queen, Fleetwood Mac, Crowded House, and I absolutely love Madonna.

I would now like to state the most intelligent bands and how they are intelligent. I believe that Rush is the smartest band in science, that Queensryche is the smartest band politically although Testament could rival them in this aspect. I believe Metallica is the smartest band subconsciously, I believe that Death Angel is the smartest band morally, I believe Iron Maiden is the smartest when it comes to prophecy and they might be the smartest in general, and finally, the most talented band in my opinion is Queen.

I am not that big on a lot of movies compared to most people, but my favorite actors and actresses are; John Cusack, John Malkovich, Harrison Ford, Sean Penn, Jeff Bridges, Tom Hanks, Kevin Spacey, Karen Allen, Geena Davis, Marisa Tomei and Sarah Silverman is very funny to me.

Continuing on, my expertise is in science and not in mathematics. I do not aspire to be a scientist, because it might be dangerous. However, I wouldn't mind becoming a scientific advisor. It would also be nice if I could team up with a prominent mathematician such as Danica Mckellar, so my theories could be applied to mathematical equations.

For the achievement of the primary goal via time travel many things are required to achieve the outcome. The most obvious necessity is to be well versed in science, but it is better to have a scientific understanding and capability rather than a scientific knowledge. If one could combine the two, it would be even better. In fact, my knowledge of science is limited, but my understanding of it has made up for that. To achieve the primary goal, you must set into motion a series of theoretical outcomes. And I have already explained to you how to do so.

You also need to have substantial knowledge of political issues of which directly and indirectly affect your life. You also need to earn a good amount of money and in my case, I mopped floors for six years. Another more surprising essential aspect is that you need to be funny and you also need to be loyal to your friends, to gain the support required for others to adhere to the pro-primary goal viewpoint. Shockingly so, one is not required to be well versed in mathematics for this achievement, but is does help to eventually have some mathematical assistance. You also regrettably need to take lysergic acid diethylamide in order to aid the chemical balance between itself and your DNA. And, finally, you must read a lot of books and I mean a lot!

You also must severely suffer, because all people who are opposed to the moral way will become subconsciously opposed to your cause. You also must be of a moral intellect, because natural science will disallow an intended evil brand of connection. It also helps to be well versed in music, due to its capability of enhancing and opening the human mind. And, obviously, you need to write about your dementia once you have set the mind sphere rolling along the naturalistic line. Not to be sarcastic here, especially to my friends in the AA fellowship, but you would also likely need to get drunk at one time or another.

I would now like to briefly explain something, which I had mentioned in the "2001-2010" segment, which could cause the common person to fathom time travel in a basic way. You see, in that segment I gave mention to molecules separating from each other and returning to their form of origin. And this process can also go in reverse. Therefore, if the molecules around you could be induced into a chain reaction of either separating or bonding, this reaction would bring your surroundings to either a forwards or a backwards time flux. Furthermore, when light and chemicals fusion and infusion within this action and reaction, it would enhance this process. Therefore, with other detailed applications this molecular behavior could be controlled subconsciously. This is possible, because of the universal equilibrium of mind, space, and time.

You might be wondering why things aren't already solved, if I have achieved the primary goal. To compensate, I tell you that through universal contact, we will promote a newfound human morality. You do understand a great deal about time travel at this point, but time in and of itself is more complicated. So, I ask you all to be patient and together we will set matters straight for all generations past, present, and future.

When I started to plan my writing of this book back in October of 2008, I pondered for a while on what to call this book. The first one I thought of was *Vision of a Juvenile Delinquent* which I quickly dismissed. Then I thought up *Vision of a Mental Patient* which is, of course, what I would eventually decide to call this book. To mention a few others, which I pondered on there was *Read On, Scientific Equivalency, A Vision*, and the one that came the closest next to what I decided on was *The Massachusetts Project*. Here is a funny one I thought of a short while back *A Trillion Easy Steps to Travel Time*.

We have sadly come to the end of this one-way discussion, but do not fret, because the future is ours to make. I will end this book by telling you what it is not and what it is. Once you have read the last few lines of this book, you will fathom why I named it as such.

This book is not a holy prophecy, it's not a doctrine, it's not a thesis, it's not a revelation, it's not a constitution, it's not a scientific outlook, it's not a radical political statement, it's not selfish, it's not selfless, it most certainly is not evil, it's not of biblical proportions, it's not a glorification of war, it's not a lyrical advertisement, it's not an act of revenge, it's not a Tarot reading from the Book of Thoth, it's not a push for democracy, it's not meant to persuade any religions, it's not a push for any political party, it is not a report, it's not a moral proclamation, it's not a novel, it's not a guide, it's not a lie, it's not fake, it's not simple, it's not complex, it's just a vision of a mental patient.

And that's all I have to say about that.

I would like to give a very special thanks to the following: Clyde "the Brain Drexler" Muka (my last ingredient to t.t. and my main consultant for this book), Steven Ndungu (my computer tech.) Bob Stevens and the entire Stevens family (especially his mother), Roland Gagnon (and Holly), Matt Kulesza, Joy Kulesza, John Evicci and the rest of Out Cold, Paul Leary, Joe Leary, Dan Desharnais (and Jeanine), Christine Gagnon, Joshua Bernard and the rest of the Bernard family, Tom Hallowood, Tim Shea, John Smith for throwing me into the pool, the dude under the Bridge St. Bridge, the old Highland Tap, Captain John's, Victoria Buckley, Dennis Brunnelle (and Nicole), Brian Cote (and Moe), Phil C, Darlene M, Shelly Lannon (and Jen), Brian M and the other Brian M, the Harringtons Sean and Gary, Sharman and Rob, the entire Hodge family especially Jill, Nana, Grampa, and Dad, Uncle Kevin and the other O'neils, the Berkings, Jason Lucontoni (remember hungry eyes?), Bill McClellan, Steve Stryker, Dan Ducharme, Rich D and the rest of the D's, that Davis kid, Miss Sullivan, Dave B! (I know!), Dave St. Armand and the rest of his cool family, the two hotties from the beach, all the other people I met in the parallel who were on my side, Tom and the rest of the Hogan family, Amy Valente, Jody Johnson, Michelle Diberto, Wendy Tedder, Cathy L, Dracut High School, the old St. Joseph's High School, the old St. Josephs Elementary class of 87 including Mrs. Mercier, the art teacher, and Mrs. Shankey, The Voke, Lowell High School, Social Security, Chock full o Nuts coffee, Microsoft Word, Hewlett Packard Computers, Wikipedia.org, the lyrics website, Best Buy, the Billerica Public Library, Mangia Mangia, Stephanies, the 28 Restaurant, Bridgewell, everyone from the Renaissance Club and LADT, Solomons, the CREU unit and all the friends I met there especially Ron, Tom, and Larry, the old Shed Building especially Tim Champagne, Choate in Woburn, Metallica, Queensryche, Iron Maiden, Madonna, the B's (there I said it), Infanticide, Youth With Bats, Eddie Dyer, Steve, and Daris from Empty Spaces, everyone from Parker House especially Molly Brown, Julie Goodwin, Gad, Deb Quigley, and Victor Ortega, Dracut Friday night always aware, Gary C, Stanley B, Sean King and Marcy too, Bill Wilson and Dr. Bob, all of the old party dudes I didn't mention and I mean every last one of you: We shall meet again! And last and most, "The Winner" you know who you are! "Someday you will find me caught beneath the landslide in a champagne supernova in the sky." With love, TEDDY H.

Lyrical compellation acknowledgements: Death Angel, Metallica, Leper Messiah, Harvester of Sorrow, Eye of the Beholder, One, Of Wolf and Man, Enter Sandman, The Unforgiven, Welcome Home (Sanitarium), The Shortest Straw

    Queensryche; Speak, Empire, Silent Lucidity,
      Rush; Chemistry, Limelight, Presto
        Testament; Envy Life
          Iron Maiden; Moonchild
            Death Angel; A Room with a View
              Soundgarden; Black Hole Sun
                Dio; No Evil on Queen Street
                  Toad the Wet Sprocket; Walk on the Ocean
Bad Company; Shooting Star
    The Bee Gees; How Can You Mend a Broken Heart
      Oasis; Champagne Supernova
        Don Mclean; Vincent
          Crowded House; Don't Dream it's Over
            Paul Williams, Kenneth Ascher; The Rainbow connection (Kermit the Frog and Jim Henson)

Literary and cinematic acknowledgements: Arthur Clarke, Carl Jung, Aleister Crowley, Chris Lintott, Brian May, Patrick Moore, Inez Snyder, Ken Rubin, Seymour Simon, Kip Thorne, Richard Greenberg, Gene Stone, John W. Schilling, Scott McClellan, Michael Moore, Walter Isaacson, David S. Richeson, Andrew Collins, Chris Ogilvie-Herald, Cornell West, Peter Hyams, Stanley Kubrick

All Deallegiance and Malicious Intent lyrics were of my own.